T0140355

Communications
in Computer and Information Science 1306

More information about this series at http://www.springer.com/series/7899

Tran Khanh Dang · Josef Küng ·
Makoto Takizawa · Tai M. Chung (Eds.)

Future Data and Security Engineering

Big Data, Security and Privacy, Smart City and Industry 4.0 Applications

7th International Conference, FDSE 2020
Quy Nhon, Vietnam, November 25–27, 2020
Proceedings

Springer

Editors
Tran Khanh Dang (iD)
Ho Chi Minh City University of Technology
Ho Chi Minh City, Vietnam

Josef Küng
Johannes Kepler University of Linz
Linz, Austria

Makoto Takizawa
Hosei University
Tokyo, Japan

Tai M. Chung
Sungkyunkwan University
Suwon, Korea (Republic of)

ISSN 1865-0929   ISSN 1865-0937 (electronic)
Communications in Computer and Information Science
ISBN 978-981-33-4369-6   ISBN 978-981-33-4370-2 (eBook)
https://doi.org/10.1007/978-981-33-4370-2

This Springer imprint is published by the registered company Springer Nature Singapore Pte Ltd.
The registered company address is: 152 Beach Road, #21-01/04 Gateway East, Singapore 189721, Singapore

Preface

In LNCS 12466 and CCIS 1306 volumes we present the accepted contributions for the 7th International Conference on Future Data and Security Engineering (FDSE 2020). The conference took place during November 25–27, 2020, in an entirely virtual mode (Quy Nhon University, Binh Dinh Province, Vietnam). The proceedings of FDSE are published in the LNCS series by Springer. Besides DBLP and other major indexing systems, the FDSE proceedings have also been indexed by Scopus and listed in Conference Proceeding Citation Index (CPCI) of Thomson Reuters.

The annual FDSE conference is a premier forum designed for researchers, scientists, and practitioners interested in state-of-the-art and state-of-the-practice activities in data, information, knowledge, and security engineering to explore cutting-edge ideas, to present and exchange their research results and advanced data-intensive applications, as well as to discuss emerging issues on data, information, knowledge, and security engineering. At the annual FDSE, the researchers and practitioners are not only able to share research solutions to problems of today's data and security engineering themes, but are also able to identify new issues and directions for future related research and development work.

The two-round call for papers resulted in the submission of 161 papers. A rigorous peer-review process was applied to all of them. This resulted in 24 accepted papers (acceptance rate: 14.9%) and 2 keynote speeches for LNCS 12466, and 37 accepted papers (including 8 short papers, acceptance rate: 23%) for CCIS 1306, which were presented online at the conference. Every paper was reviewed by at least three members of the International Program Committee, who were carefully chosen based on their knowledge and competence. This careful process resulted in the high quality of the contributions published in these two volumes. The accepted papers were grouped into the following sessions:

- Advances in Big Data Query Processing and Optimization (LNCS)
- Advanced Studies in Machine Learning for Security (LNCS)
- Big Data Analytics and Distributed Systems (LNCS and CCIS)
- Blockchain and Applications (LNCS)
- Security Issues in Big Data (LNCS)
- Data Analytics and Healthcare Systems (CCIS)
- Machine Learning based Big Data Processing (CCIS)
- Security and Privacy Engineering (CCIS)
- Industry 4.0 and Smart City: Data Analytics and Security (LNCS and CCIS)
- Emerging Data Management Systems and Applications (LNCS and CCIS)

In addition to the papers selected by the Program Committee, five internationally recognized scholars delivered keynote speeches:

- Prof. Johann Eder, Alpen-Adria-Universität Klagenfurt, Austria
- Prof. Dirk Draheim, Tallinn University of Technology, Estonia

- Prof. Tai M. Chung, Sungkyunkwan University, South Korea
- Prof. Sun Jun, Singapore Management University, Singapore
- Prof. Jian Yang, Macquarie University, Australia

The success of FDSE 2020 was the result of the efforts of many people, to whom we would like to express our gratitude. First, we would like to thank all authors who submitted papers to FDSE 2020, especially the invited speakers for the keynotes. We would also like to thank the members of the committees and external reviewers for their timely reviewing and lively participation in the subsequent discussion in order to select such high-quality papers published in these two volumes. Last but not least, we thank Prof. Do Ngoc My and the Organizing Committee members from Quy Nhon University, for their great hospitality and support of FDSE 2020.

November 2020

Tran Khanh Dang
Josef Küng
Makoto Takizawa
Tai M. Chung

Organization

Honorary Chair

Do Ngoc My — Quy Nhon University, Vietnam

Program Committee Chairs

Tran Khanh Dang — Ho Chi Minh City University of Technology, Vietnam
Josef Küng — Johannes Kepler University Linz, Austria
Makoto Takizawa — Hosei University, Japan
Tai M. Chung — Sungkyunkwan University, South Korea

Steering Committee

Dirk Draheim — Tallinn University of Technology, Estonia
Dinh Nho Hao — Institute of Mathematics, Vietnam Academy of Science and Technology, Vietnam
Dieter Kranzlmüller — Ludwig Maximilian University of Munich, Germany
Fabio Massacci — University of Trento, Italy
Erich Neuhold — University of Vienna, Austria
Silvio Ranise — Fondazione Bruno Kessler, Italy
A Min Tjoa — Technical University of Vienna, Austria
Fukuda Kensuke — National Institute of Informatics, Japan

Local Organizing Committee

Do Ngoc My (Co-chair) — Quy Nhon University, Vietnam
Tran Khanh Dang (Chair) — Ho Chi Minh City University of Technology, Vietnam
La Hue Anh — Ho Chi Minh City University of Technology, Vietnam
Josef Küng — Johannes Kepler University Linz, Austria
Nguyen Tien Trung — Quy Nhon University, Vietnam
Tran Tri Dang — RMIT University, Vietnam
Nguyen Le Hoang — Ho Chi Minh City University of Technology, Vietnam
Ta Manh Huy — Ho Chi Minh City University of Technology, Vietnam

Publicity Chairs

Tran Minh Quang — Ho Chi Minh City University of Technology, Vietnam
Nguyen Quoc Viet Hung — Griffith University, Australia
Le Hong Trang — Ho Chi Minh City University of Technology, Vietnam
Nam Ngo-Chan — University of Trento, Italy

Program Committee

Artur Andrzejak	Heidelberg University, Germany
Pham The Bao	Saigon University, Vietnam
Hyunseung Choo	Sungkyunkwan University, South Korea
H. K. Dai	Oklahoma State University, USA
Vitalian Danciu	Ludwig Maximilian University of Munich, Germany
Nguyen Tuan Dang	Saigon University, Vietnam
Tran Tri Dang	RMIT University, Vietnam
Thanh-Nghi Do	Can Tho University, Vietnam
Nguyen Van Doan	Japan Advanced Institute of Science and Technology, Japan
Johann Eder	Alpen-Adria-Universität Klagenfurt, Austria
Jungho Eom	Daejeon University, South Korea
Michael Felderer	University of Innsbruck, Austria
Fukuda Kensuke	National Institute of Informatics, Japan
Alban Gabillon	University of French Polynesia, France
Verena Geist	Software Competence Center Hagenberg, Austria
Osvaldo Gervasi	University of Perugia, Italy
Manuel Clavel	Vietnamese-German University, Vietnam
Raju Halder	Indian Institute of Technology Patna, India
Nguyen Huu Hoa	Can Tho University, Vietnam
Tran Van Hoai	Ho Chi Minh City University of Technology, Vietnam
Phan Duy Hung	FPT University Hanoi, Vietnam
Nguyen Viet Hung	University of Trento, Italy
Trung-Hieu Huynh	Industrial University of Ho Chi Minh City, Vietnam
Kien Huynh	Stony Brook University, USA
Kha-Tu Huynh	International University - VNU-HCM, Vietnam
Tomohiko Igasaki	Kumamoto University, Japan
Koichiro Ishibashi	The University of Electro-Communications, Japan
Eiji Kamioka	Shibaura Institute of Technology, Japan
M-Tahar Kechadi	University College Dublin, Ireland
Andrea Ko	Corvinus University of Budapest, Hungary
Duc-Anh Le	Center for Open Data in the Humanities, Tokyo, Japan
Lam-Son Le	Ho Chi Minh City University of Technology, Vietnam
Nhien-An Le-Khac	University College Dublin, Ireland
Truong Thi Dieu Linh	Hanoi University of Science and Technology, Vietnam
Cao Van Loi	Le Quy Don Technical University, Vietnam
Hoang Duc Minh	National Physical Laboratory, UK
Nguyen Thai-Nghe	Can Tho University, Vietnam
Nam Ngo-Chan	University of Trento, Italy
Thanh Binh Nguyen	Ho Chi Minh City University of Technology, Vietnam
Binh Thanh Nguyen	International Institute for Applied Systems Analysis, Austria
Anh-Tuan Nguyen	Ho Chi Minh City University of Foreign Languages and Information Technology, Vietnam

Benjamin Nguyen	Institut National des Sciences Appliqués Centre Val de Loire, France
An Khuong Nguyen	Ho Chi Minh City University of Technology, Vietnam
Khoa Nguyen	CSIRO, Australia
Vu Thanh Nguyen	Van Hien University, Vietnam
Truong Toan Nguyen	Curtin University, Australia
Luong The Nhan	Amadeus IT Group, France
Alex Norta	Tallinn University of Technology, Estonia
Duu - Sheng Ong	Multimedia University, Malaysia
Eric Pardede	La Trobe University, Australia
Cong Duc Pham	University of Pau, France
Vinh Pham	Sungkyunkwan University, South Korea
Nhat Hai Phan	New Jersey Institute of Technology, USA
Thanh An Phan	Institute of Mathematics, Vietnam Academy of Science and Technology, Vietnam
Phu H. Phung	University of Dayton, USA
Nguyen Van Sinh	International University - VNU-HCM, Vietnam
Erik Sonnleitner	Johannes Kepler University Linz, Austria
Huynh Quyct Thang	Hanoi University of Science and Technology, Vietnam
Nguyen Hoang Thuan	RMIT University, Vietnam
Michel Toulouse	Hanoi University of Science and Technology, Vietnam
Thien Khai Tran	Ho Chi Minh City University of Foreign Languages and Information Technology, Vietnam
Ha-Manh Tran	Hong Bang International University, Vietnam
Le Hong Trang	Ho Chi Minh City University of Technology, Vietnam
Tran Minh Triet	HCMC University of Natural Sciences, Vietnam
Takeshi Tsuchiya	Tokyo University of Science, Japan
Le Pham Tuyen	Kyunghee University, South Korea
Hoang Huu Viet	Vinh University, Vietnam
Edgar Weippl	SBA Research, Austria
Wolfram Woess	Johannes Kepler University Linz, Austria
Honguk Woo	Sungkyunkwan University, South Korea
Sadok Ben Yahia	Tallinn University of Technology, Estonia
Szabó Zoltán	Corvinus University of Budapest, Hungary

External Reviewers

Thu Le Thi Bao	National Institute of Informatics, Japan
Tran Manh Hung	Sungkyunkwan University, South Korea
Le Thi Kim Tuyen	Heidelberg University, Germany
Trung Ha	University of Information Technology, Vietnam
Dan Ho Duc	Ho Chi Minh City University of Technology, Vietnam
Hieu Le	Ho Chi Minh City University of Technology, Vietnam
Pham Nguyen Hoang Nam	Industrial University of Ho Chi Minh City, Vietnam
Manh-Tuan Nguyen	COFICO Company, Vietnam
Trung-Viet Nguyen	Can Tho University of Technology, Vietnam

Thai-Minh Truong   Ho Chi Minh City University of Technology, Vietnam
Chau D. M. Pham   Zalo, Vietnam
Tan Ha Mai   Ho Chi Minh City University of Technology, Vietnam
Pham Thi Vuong   Saigon University, Vietnam

Contents

Machine Learning-Based Big Data Processing

Emerging Data Management Systems and Applications

Short Papers: Security and Data Engineering

Big Data Analytics and Distributed Systems

On the Potential of Numerical Association Rule Mining

Minakshi Kaushik[1]([✉]) [iD], Rahul Sharma[1] [iD], Sijo Arakkal Peious[1] [iD],
Mahtab Shahin[1], Sadok Ben Yahia[2] [iD], and Dirk Draheim[1] [iD]

[1] Information Systems Group, Tallinn University of Technology, Akadeemia tee 15a,
12618 Tallinn, Estonia
{minakshi.kaushik,rahul.sharma,sijo.arakkal,mahtab.shahin,
dirk.draheim}@taltech.ee
[2] Software Science Department, Tallinn University of Technology, Akadeemia tee
15a, 12618 Tallinn, Estonia
sadok.ben@taltech.ee

Abstract. In association rule mining, both the classical algorithms and today's available tools either use binary data items or discretized data. However, in real-world scenarios, data are available in many different forms (numerical, text) and these types of data items are not supported in the classical association rule mining algorithms. There are some association rule mining algorithms that have been proposed for numerical data items but unfortunately, for working data scientists and decision makers, it is challenging to find concrete algorithms that fit their purposes best. Therefore, it is highly desired to have a study on the different existing numerical association rule mining algorithms (NARM). In this paper, we provide such a detailed study by thoroughly reviewing 24 NARM algorithms from different categories (optimization, discretization, distribution).

Keywords: Knowledge discovery in databases · Association rule mining · Numerical association rule mining

1 Introduction

Data mining is a widely used technique for extracting useful information from large repositories of data. To extract useful information from data, there are many well-known data mining techniques such as association rule mining, characterization, classification, clustering, evolution, generalization, regression, prediction, outlier detection, etc. that have been proposed in the literature. Out of all the data mining techniques, association rule mining (ARM) is one of the most established ones.

ARM was first introduced by Agrawal [2] to understand the relationship between different data items and since then has been widely used for market basket analysis, bio-informatics, medical diagnosis, etc. Agrawal [3] proposed the apriori algorithm to discover all significant association rules in large databases

© Springer Nature Singapore Pte Ltd. 2020
T. K. Dang et al. (Eds.): FDSE 2020, CCIS 1306, pp. 3–20, 2020.
https://doi.org/10.1007/978-981-33-4370-2_1

in 1994. The main aim of ARM is not just finding frequent itemsets but also finding interesting association rules.

In classical association rule mining, most of the algorithms work in two phases. In the first phase, all frequent itemsets are found, and in the second phase, rules are drawn. Apriori and FP-growth are the two most algorithms based on binary columns and are usually perceived as the classical association rule mining algorithms. The classical association rule mining algorithms work only with binary data items and do not support numerical data items, therefore, whenever data is in numerical form (height, weight, or age) the data items need to be changed from *numerical* to *categorical* using a discretization process. This process of finding association rules in numerical data items has been referred to as numerical association rule mining (NARM).

Research in the area of association rule mining generally considers binary data items as input for the proposed algorithms but excludes numerical data sets. A tool named Grand report has been proposed that reports mean values of a chosen numeric target column concerning all possible combinations of influencing factors [45]. There are some association rule mining algorithms available for numerical data items but it is still challenging to find the best algorithms, NARM algorithms have the potential to deal with different types of attributes, therefore, it's important to have a study on different numerical association rule mining algorithms.

In this paper, we discussed different solutions and problems in the 24 NARM algorithms proposed under the optimization, discretization and distribution methods. The paper is structured as follows. In Sect. 2, we describe preliminaries. In Sect. 3, we discuss all three methods to solve numerical association rule mining problems. In Sect. 4, the optimization method is discussed with all its sub-methods. In Sect. 5, the distribution method is introduced and discussed and in Sect. 6 Discretization method is discussed. We finish the paper with a conclusion in Sect. 7.

2 Preliminaries

In ARM, association rules have been developed based on the If-then relations which consist of antecedents (If) and consequents (Then) [2]. For example, (1) shows the following association rule: "If a customer buys bread and butter then he also buys milk and sugar". Here, *bread and butter* appear as antecedent and *milk and sugar* as consequent. Generally, an association rule may be represented as a production rule in an expert system, an *if statement* in a programming language or implication in a logical calculus.

$$\{Bread, Butter\} \Rightarrow \{Milk, Sugar\} \tag{1}$$

In a database, let I be a set of m binary attributes $\{i_1, i_2, i_3, \ldots, i_m\}$ called database items. Let T be a set of n transactions $\{t_1, t_2, t_3, \ldots, t_n\}$, where each transaction t_i has a unique ID and consists of a subset of the items in I, i.e., $t_i \subseteq I$. As in (1), an association rule is an implication of the form

$$X \Rightarrow Y \qquad (2)$$

where $X, Y \subseteq I$ (itemsets) and $X \cap Y = \emptyset$.

In association rule mining, frequent itemsets and association rules are discovered based on boolean data columns, therefore, it is known as boolean association rule mining. Different measures of interestingess are proposed in the literature to find out the interesting rules [53]. Boolean association rules are meaningful, but data are often available in different forms (categorical, quantitative, text) and in these cases, boolean association rule mining techniques do not fit. Thus, the term numeric association rule mining was introduced by [26] and the problem was first discussed by Srikant in 1996 [55]. A numerical association rule can easily be understood by the following example.

$$Age \in [40, 50] \wedge Gender = M \Rightarrow NumberOfCars = 2 \qquad (3)$$

Given a set of transactions T, let $Antecedent$ denote the set of transactions in T in which Age has a value between 40 and 50 and $Gender$ equals M. Similarly, let $Consequent$ denote the set of transactions in which $NumberOfCars = 2$. Now, the association rule (3) stands for the following fraction.

$$\frac{\text{number of transcations in } Antecedent \cap Consequent}{\text{number of transcations in } Antecedent} \qquad (4)$$

As an early solution, the problem of association rules for numerical data was solved using a discretization process where numeric attributes are divided into different intervals and, henceforth, these attributes are treated as categorical attributes [12]. For example, an attribute Age with values between 20 to 80 can be divided into six different age intervals (20–30, 30–40, 40–50, 50–60, 60–70, 70–80). The data discretization process is an obvious solution, however, it reveals a loss of valuable information which might cause poor results [16]. Thus, we review solutions from three different approaches (discretization, distribution and optimization) to solve issues with numerical association rule mining in Sect. 3.

3 Methods to Solve Numerical ARM Problems

To solve the issues in numerical association rule mining, three main approaches (discretization, distribution and optimization) have been discussed in the literature. Based on these three approaches, many different NARM algorithms have been proposed. The optimization method has several sub-methods as swarm intelligence and evolution based algorithms which cover most of the area to deal with NARM. The Distribution method does not contribute much in this area, however, the discretization method is a common method that transforms continuous attributes into discrete attributes. The discretization is further subdivided into three sub-methods. Figure 1 (compare also with Fig. 1 in [9]) is showing all three approaches and different algorithms proposed under each approach.

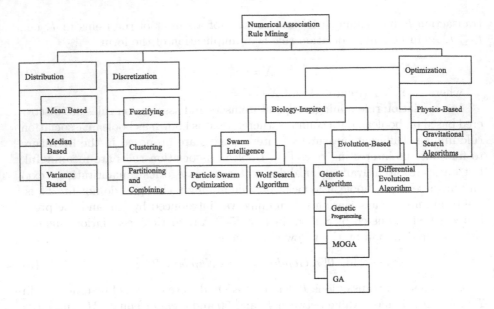

Fig. 1. Methods to solve numerical association rule mining problems.

4   The Optimization Method

To solve the numerical association rule mining problem, many researchers have moved towards optimization methods. Optimization methods provide a robust and efficient approach to explore a massive search space. In this method, researchers have invented a collection of heuristic optimization methods inspired by the movements of animals and insects. For finding association rules, optimization methods work in two phases. In the first phase, all the frequent itemsets are found and in the second phase, all relevant association rules are extracted. As shown in Fig. 1, optimization methods are divided into two parts, bio-inspired optimization methods and physics-based optimization methods. Table 1 shows an overview of all those algorithms that come under the optimization method.

4.1   The Bio-Inspired Optimization Method

Biology-based algorithms are generally divided into two parts: swarm-intelligence-based algorithms and evolution-based algorithms [14]. The origin of these algorithms is the biological behavior of natural objects [64].

Evolution-Based Algorithms. Evolution-based algorithms are inspired by Darwinian principles and were first applied in [42]. These algorithms mimic the capability of nature to develop living beings that are well-adapted to their environment [64]. Evolution-based algorithms exploit stochastic search methods that follow the idea of natural selection and genetics. The algorithms show strong

Table 1. An overview of optimization method algorithms for NARM.

Methods	Basic technique	Algorithms
GA	Genetic Algorithm	GENAR [41], GAR [42], EGAR [33], ARMGA, EARMGA [68], GAR-PLUS [10], QuantMiner [51], RelQM-J [52], RCGA [40]
MOGA	Genetic Algorithm	ARMMGA [47], QAR-CIP-NSGA-II [39], MOEA [20]
DE	Differential Evolution	MODENAR [7], ARM-DE [18]
PSO	Particle Swarm Optimization	RPSO [4], CENPSO [5], MOPAR [12], PPQAR [67], PARCD [61]
WSA	Swarm Intelligence	WSA [1]
GSA	Physics-based (Gravity)	GSA [13]

adaptability and self organization [14] and use biology-inspired operators such as crossover, mutation, and natural selection [64]. The *Genetic Algorithm* [25] and the *Differential Evolution Algorithm* [58] are two example of evolution-based algorithms. Table 2 shows an overview of the evolution-based algorithms for NARM, together with concepts.

Genetic Algorithms (GA). GA was first proposed by Holland [25] and they are one of the most popular algorithms in bio-inspired optimization methods at all. A basic genetic algorithm consists of five phases: initialization, evaluation, reproduction, crossover, and mutation. GAs for NARM can be divided into three fields, i.e., basic genetic algorithms, genetic programming and multiobjective genetic algorithms. A basic genetic algorithm has been proposed by Mata et al. [41] and together with the tool GENAR (GENetic Association Rules) to discover association rule with numeric attributes. Association rules in GENAR algorithms allow for intervals (maximum and minimum values) for each numeric attribute. Mata et al. [42] further extended the GENAR algorithms and proposed a technique named GAR (Genetic Association Rule) to discover association rules in numeric databases without discretization. In this paper, a genetic algorithm was used to find the suitable amplitude of the intervals that conform k-itemset and can have a high support value without too wide intervals. In [33], the GAR algorithm was further extended to EGAR (extended genetic association rule). This algorithm generates frequent patterns with continuous data [42].

A genetic-based strategy and two other algorithms ARMGA and EARMGA were proposed by Yan et al. [68] In this approach, an encoding method was developed with relative confidence as the fitness function. In these algorithms, there was no requirement of a minimum support threshold. The GAR-plus tool was presented by Alvarez [10]. This tool deals with categorical and numeric attributes in large databases without any need of a prior discretization of numeric attributes.

Based on the genetic algorithm, in 2013, Salleb et al. [51] proposed "Quant-Miner", a quantitative association rule mining system. This tool dynamically discovers meaningful intervals in association rules by optimizing both the confidence and the support values.

Seki and Nagao [52] worked on GA-based QuantMiner for multi-relational data mining and developed RelQM-J, a tool for relational quantitative association rules5 in Java programming language. In this tool, efficient computation of the support of the rules has been realized by using a hash-based data structure.

A real-coded [30] genetic algorithm was presented in [40] in 2010. The proposed algorithm RCGA follows the CHC binary-coded evolutionary algorithm [17]. RCGA algorithm has been applied to pollutant agent time series and helps to find all existing relations between atmospheric pollution and climatological conditions.

Genetic Programming for ARM. Genetic Programming [31] is a well-known type of GA. In GA, the genome is in string structure while in GP, the genome is in the form of tree structure [24]. Genetic Network Programming (GNP) is a graph-based evolutionary algorithm and find the association rules for continuous attributes. In this method, important rules are stored in a pool and these extracted rules are measured by the chi-squared test. This pool is updated in every generation by exchanging the association rule with higher chi-squared value for the same association rule with lower chi-squared value [59].

Multi-Objective Genetic Algorithm. The multi-objective genetic algorithm was proposed by Fonseca et al. in 1993 [19]. Generally, the resource consumption of an association rule mining computation is affected by two parameters, i.e., minimum support and minimum confidence. In classical ARM algorithms, only a single measure (support or confidence) has been used as a measure to evaluate the rule interestingness, therefore, if the values of minimum support and minimum confidence are not set properly then the number of association rules may be very less or it may be very large. This problem can be solved by using more objectives or measures as referred in multi-objective ARM.

Gosh and Nath [20] used a Pareto-based genetic algorithm to solve the multi-objective rule mining problem by using three measures: interestingness, comprehensibility and predictive accuracy. The single objective algorithm, ARMGA [68] had issues that were addressed by introducing the multi-objective genetic algorithm called ARMMGA by Qodmanan et al. in [47]. The ARMGA algorithm finds high confidence and low support rules, whereas ARMMGA finds high confidence and high support rules. ARMGA has a large set of rules in comparison to ARMMGA; this problem was solved using a new fitness function in ARM-MGA. To prevent invalid chromosomes in ARMGA, new crossover and mutation operators are presented in the literature.

To solve multi-objective optimization problems, Srinivasan and Deb [56] proposed a non dominated genetic sorting algorithm. In 2002, Deb et al. [15] extended NSGA to NSGA-II. In 2011, Martin et al. [39] extended NSGA-II with a trade-off between interpretability and accuracy. NSGA-II performs evolutionary learning of intervals of attributes. For each rule, condition selection is done for three objectives (interestingness, comprehensibility and performance). This method did not depend on minimum support and confidence thresholds. Martin et al. again extended their research on NSGA-II to a new approach called QAR-CIP-NSGA-II and compared the results of this algorithm with other MOEA algorithms.

Differential Evolutionary Algorithms. Differential evolutionary (DE) algorithms are evolution-based algorithms. These algorithms were proposed by Storn and Price in [57]. DE algorithms are simple and effective single-objective optimization algorithms that solve real-valued problems based on the principle of natural evolution. DE algorithms use Genetic-based operators such as crossover, mutation, and selection. Although the evolution process of DE is similar to the one of GA but it relies on a mutation operator instead of a crossover operator [65].

A pareto-based multi-objective DE algorithm for ARM was first proposed in [7] by Alatas et al. for searching accurate and comprehensible association rules. The problem of mining association rules was formulated with four objective optimization problems, i.e., support, confidence, comprehensibility and amplitude. Here, support, confidence and comprehensibility are maximization objectives and the amplitude of intervals is a minimization objective. In a single run, a pareto-based multi-objective DE algorithm search intervals of numeric attributes and association rules.

In 2018, [18] proposed a novel approach for mining association rules with numerical as well as categorical attributes based on DE. In this algorithm, a single objective optimization problem is considered in which support and confidence of association rules are combined into a fitness function. This new DE using ARM (ARM-DE) with mixed (i.e., numerical and categorical) attributes consist of three stages: 1. domain analysis, 2. representation of a solution, 3. definition of a fitness function.

Swarm Intelligence Based Algorithms are further divided into two sub-optimization methods, particle swarm optimization and the wolf search algorithm. Table 3 provides an overview of swarm intelligence algorithms for NARM.

Particle Swarm Optimization. Particle Swarm Optimization (PSO) is a population-based optimization algorithm for nonlinear function. This algorithm is oriented towards animal behavior such as birds flocking or fish schooling. It was developed in 1995 [27,46]. PSO was first used for NARM to find intervals of the numerical attributes in 2008 [4].

Rough PSOA, based on rough patterns was proposed in [4], in which rough values are defined with upper and lower intervals. This algorithm can complement the existing tools developed in rough computing. Rough values are useful in representing an interval for an attribute. In this work, each particle consists of a decision variable that has three parts. The first part of each decision variable

Table 2. An overview of evolution-based algorithms for NARM.

Algorithm	Proposer	Concept
GENAR [41]	J. Mata Vázquez et al. (2001)	Based on finding frequent itemsets in numerical databases and intervals of all attributes that conform to those frequent itemsets
GAR [42]	J. Mata Vázquez et al. (2002)	Extended version of GENAR
EGAR [33]	H. Kwaśnicka et al. (2006)	Uses medical databases where attributes are continuous and discrete; extended version of GAR
ARMGA [68]	A. Yan et al. (2009)	No requirement of minimum support threshold
EARMGA [68]	A. Yan et al. (2009)	
GARPLUS [10]	V. Álvarez et al. (2012)	Based on the finding intervals of numeric attribute
QUANTMINER [51]	A. Salleb-Aouissi et al. (2013)	Based on genetic algorithm to find good intervals by optimizing both support and confidence
RelQM-J [52]	H. Sekil (2017)	Based on mining numeric rules from relational databases, implemented in Java
RCGA [40]	M. Martinez-Ballesterosa (2010)	Based on CHC binary-coded evolutionary algorithm
ARMMGA [47]	H. Reza Qodmanan (2011)	Based on multi-objective genetic algorithm
QAR-CIP-NSGA-II	D. Martın et al. (2011)	Based on NSGA with three measures (comprehensibility, interestingness, performance)
MODENAR [7]	B. Alatas (2008)	Based on multi-objective differential evolutionary algorithm
ARM-DE [18]	I. Fister Jr. (2018)	Single objective optimization problem where features consist of numerical as well as categorical attributes

represents the antecedent or consequent of the rule and can take values between 0 and 1. The second part represents the lower bound, the third part represents the upper bound of the item interval. The second and third parts are combined as one rough value during the implementation phase of particle representation.

Table 3. An overview of swarm-intelligence-based algorithms for NARM.

Algorithm	Proposer	Concept
RPSO [4]	B. Alatas et al. (2008)	RPSOA is based on the notion of rough patterns that use rough values defined with upper and lower intervals.
CENPSO [5]	B. Alatas et al. (2009)	CENPSO is based on chaos numbers
MOPAR [12]	V. Beiranvand et al. (2014)	MOPAR is Based on Multi objectives (confidence, comprehensibility and interestingness)
Parallel PSO [67]	A. Yan et al. (2019)	Parallel PSO is based on two methods of parallel algorithm: particle-oriented and data-oriented parallelization
PARCD [61]	I. Tahyudin et al. (2017)	Combined PSO method with cauchy distribution
WSA [1]	I.E. Agbehadji et al. (2016)	Based on wolves hunting strategy

Alatas and Akin [5] proposed a novel PSO algorithm based on chaos numbers. The CENPSOA algorithm (chaotically encoded PSO) uses chaos decision variables and chaos particles. Chaos and PSO relation were first discovered by Liu et al. [36], CENPSOA algorithm performs encoding of particles given by chaos numbers. The Chaos numbers consist of the midpoint and radius part of values [5]. Alatas and Akin [6] also proposed a multi-objective chaotic particle swarm optimization algorithm for mining accurate and comprehensible classification rules.

Yan et al. [67] proposed a parallel PSO algorithm for numerical association rule mining. This parallel algorithm was designed with two strategies called particle-oriented and data-oriented parallelization. Particle-oriented parallelization is more efficient and data-oriented parallelization is more scalable to process large datasets.

To discover association rules in a single step without prior discretization of numerical attributes, Beiranvand et al. [12] proposed a multi-objective particle swarm optimization algorithm (MOPAR). The algorithm defines multiple objectives such as confidence, comprehensibility and interestingness. In the pareto method, a candidate solution is identified better than all other candidates. And in multi-objective optimization, a set of best solutions is identified in which the members are superior among all the candidates.

Kuo et al. [32] proposed a multi-objective particle swarm optimization algorithm using an adaptive archive grid for NARM. It is also based on Pareto optimal strategy. In this algorithm, minimum support and minimum confidence are not required before mining. MOPSO algorithm includes a discretization procedure to process numerical data. This algorithm is executed in three parts: 1. initialization, 2. adaptive archive grid, and 3. particle swarm optimization searching.

PSO for numerical association rule mining with cauchy distribution (PARCD) has been evaluated by [61] and it showed that the result of PARCD is better than the method of MOPAR.

Wolf Search Algorithm. The wolf search algorithm (WSA) is a bio-inspired heuristic optimization algorithm. It was proposed by [63] and imitates the way wolves search for food and survive by avoiding their enemies. WSA is tested and compared with other heuristic algorithms and investigated with respect to its memory requirements. The group of wolves has characteristics of commuting together as a nuclear family, that is why it is different from particle swarm optimization [66].

Agbehadji and Fong [1] proposed a new meta-heuristic algorithm that used the wolf search algorithm for NARM. The wolf has three different features of preying. These are prey initiatively, prey passively and escape. The *preying initiatively* feature allows the wolf to check its visual perimeter to detect prey. If the prey is found within visual distance, the wolf moves towards the prey with the highest fitness value, else, the wolves will maintain its direction. In *prey passively* mode, the wolf only stays alert from threats and tries to improve its position. In the *escape* mode, when a threat is detected, the wolf escapes quickly by relocating itself to a new position with an escape distance that is greater than its visual range.

4.2   Physics-Based Algorithm

The physics-based meta-heuristic optimization algorithm simulates the physical behavior and properties of the matter or follows the laws of physics [14]. For NARM, the gravitational search algorithm is a physics-based meta-heuristic optimization algorithm.

Gravitational Search Algorithm. Rashedi et al. proposed a new optimization algorithm based on the law of gravity and named it gravitational search algorithm (GSA) [48]. Newtonian gravity laws state that "Every particle in the universe attracts every other particle with a force that is directly proportional to the product of their masses and inversely proportional to the square of the distance between them". In GSA, agents act as objects and their performance is evaluated by their mass. Each mass presents a solution and it is expected that masses will be attracted by the heaviest mass. GSA is like a small artificial world of masses obeying the Newtonian laws of gravitation and motion. There are four ways for representing the agents or coding the problem variables. These are continuous (real-valued), binary-valued, discrete, and mixed, which are called GSA variants [49].

Can and Alatas [13] first used GSA for NARM. GSA eliminated the task of finding the minimum values of support and confidence. Automatically mined rules have high confidence and support values. In this work, GSA has been designed to find the numerical intervals of the attributes automatically, i.e., without any *a priori* data process at the time of rule mining. The problem of interactions within attributes has been eliminated with the designed GSA by not selecting one attribute at a time and not evaluating a partially-constructed candidate rule due to its global searching with a population.

5   The Distribution Method

In [11], Aumann and Lindell have introduced a new definition for numerical association rules based on statistical inference theory. In this study, they have implemented several distribution scales including mean, median, and variance. The following example shows the kind of generalization of ARM proposed by the authors.

$$Gender{=}F \Rightarrow Wage{:}mean{=}\$8.50 \quad (overall\ mean\ wage = \$12.60) \quad (5)$$

As the above example shows, the average wage for females was $ 8.50 p/hr. The rule displays that the wage of that group was far less than the average wage; therefore, this rule can be considered useful. They also used the algorithm which identifies repeated item-sets and then calculates the desired statistics for the purpose with respect to repeated itemset. This procedure is restricted by the requirement to store every repeated item-sets in memory throughout repeated itemset generation. Where the data is not sparse, the number of frequent item-sets will be huge and repeated itemset storage and access will dominate the calculation. Moreover, they concluded that the suggested algorithm is beneficial and may find rules between two given quantitative attributes.

6   The Discretization Method

Discretization is a process of quantizing numerical attributes into groups of intervals and it is one of the most popular methods to solve the problem of numerical association rule mining. There are numerous methods of discretization in literature. Due to different needs, discretization methods have been developed in different ways such as supervised vs. unsupervised, dynamic vs. static, global vs. local, splitting (top-down) vs. merging (bottom-up) and direct vs. incremental [37]. In classical ARM algorithms, numerical columns cannot be processed directly [38], i.e., all columns need to be categorical, which is a major limitation of ARM [62].

Discretization of numerical values is used to overcome this problem [28,43,44]. When a numeric column is divided into useful target groups, it becomes easier to identify and generate association rules, i.e. discretization helps to understand the numeric columns better. The discretized groups are useful only if the variables in the same group do not have any objective difference. Discretization minimizes the impact of trivial variations between values. Discretization can be performed using fuzzifying, clustering and *partitioning and combining* [8]. In Table 4, we summarize some selected discretization algorithms used in NARM.

6.1　Fuzzifying

Fuzzy logic is a suitable way of handling numeric value columns for association rule mining systems [50]. A straightforward method is in grouping numeric values of a column by fuzzy sets [8]. Here, *fuzzifying* is the technique of illustrating numeric values as fuzzy sets [29] which can help to rectify the *sharp boundary problem* of association mining [50,60]. Sometimes, endpoint values of discretized groups have more or less influence on the result than the midpoint values: this phenomenon is known as a sharp boundary problem. Fuzzy Class Association Rule (FCAR) is a model proposed by Kianmehr et al. in [29] to get the fuzzy class association rules.

6.2　Clustering

Clustering is one of the popular methods of discretizing a numerical column in an unsupervised manner [8]. In clustering, a numerical column is segregated into different groups according to properties of each value; in this method, the probability of having values in the same group depends on the degree of similarity or dissimilarity of the values [23,54]. To obtain maximum results in clustering, the degree of similarity and dissimilarity needs to be well defined [21]: *"In other words, the intra-cluster variance is to be minimized, and the inter-cluster variance is to be maximized"* [62]. Two-step clustering [54] is the most common clustering method.

DRMiner Algorithm. Lian et al. [35] have proposed the DRMiner algorithm which exploits the notion of "density" to capture the characteristics of numeric attributes and an efficient procedure to locate the "dense regions". DRMiner scales up well with high-dimensional datasets. When mapping a database to a multidimensional space, the data points (transactions) are not distributed evenly throughout the multidimensional space. For this kind of distribution, the density measure was introduced and the problem of mining quantitative association rules transformed into the problem of finding dense regions to map them to find quantitative association rules. Weaknesses of this method were the prior requirement of many thresholds and, unsolving the dimensionality curse. It was noted that the algorithm may not perform well for data sets with uniform density between minimum density threshold and low density.

DBSMiner. DBSMiner is a density-based sub-space mining algorithm using the notion of density-connected to cluster the high-density sub-space of numeric attributes and gravitation between grid/cluster to deal with the low-density cells

[22]. DBSMiner employs an efficient high dimension clustering algorithm CBSD (Clustering Based on Sorted Dense unit) to deal with high dimensional data sets. The algorithm has a unique feature to deal with low-density sub-spaces and there is no need to scan the whole space just check the neighbor cell. It can find interesting association rules.

MQAR. MQAR (Mining Quantitative Association Rules based on a dense grid) is a novel algorithm that was proposed by Yang and Zhang [69]. The main objective of this algorithm was to mine the numeric association rules using a tree structure, DGFP-tree to cluster dense space. This algorithm is helpful to eliminate noise and redundant rules by transforming the problem into finding regions with enough density and to map them to quantitative association rules. A novel subspace clustering algorithm was also proposed which is based on searching DGFP-tree and inserts the dense cell in the database space into DGFP-tree as a path from a root node to a leaf node. MQAR has the advantage that DGFP-tree compresses the database and there is no need to scan the database several times.

ARCS. The Association Rule Clustering System [34] was presented by Lent et al. together with a new geometric-based clustering algorithm, BitOP. In this paper the problem of clustering of association rules like $(A \wedge B) => C$ where L.H.S. having quantitative attributes and R.H.S. having a categorical attribute was discussed and a two-dimensional grid is formed where each axis represents one of the L.H.S. attributes. ARCS is an automated system to compute a clustering of two-attribute spaces in large databases. In ARCS framework Binner, For a given partitioning of the input attributes, the algorithm makes only one pass through the data and allows the support or confidence thresholds to change without requiring a new pass through the data. BitOp algorithm enumerates the clusters. To locate clusters within bitmap grids the algorithm performs bit-wise operations.

6.3 Partitioning and Combining

In [55], Srikant and Agrawal discussed the problems of numeric attributes in databases. The authors addressed the problem of mining association rules from large databases containing both numerical and categorical attributes. To deal with this problem, a partitioning method was introduced but before partitioning, a measure of partial completeness was introduced which decided whether or not to partition a numeric attribute and number of partitions. The number of required partitions is computed by the following formula.

$$number\ of\ intervals = \frac{2n}{m(K-1)} \tag{6}$$

where n is number of numeric attributes, m is the minimum support and K is the partial completeness level.

Table 4. An overview of discretization-based algorithms for NARM.

Algorithm	Proposer	Concept
ARCS [34]	B. Lent et al. (1997)	Based on segmenting clusters using the geometric-based BitOp algorithm
DRMiner [35]	W. Lian (2005)	Based on finding density regions in a multidimensional space.
DBSMiner [22]	G. Yunkai et al. (2008)	Based on clustering of high density sub-spaces using a density- and grid-based cluster algorithm
MQAR [69]	Y. Junrui et al. (2010)	Based on finding dense sub-spaces using structure DGFP-tree

7   Conclusion

In this paper, a study of 24 NARM algorithms has been discussed. We briefly discussed different solutions and problems in optimization, discretization and distribution methods of solving the NARM problem. As per our findings, many algorithms have been proposed in the optimization method but there is less focused research in the area of discretization and distribution methods. NARM has huge potential to extend dimensions of classical ARM and it may be used for mining association rules in different types of data(categorical, quantitative, text, etc.).

Acknowledgments. This work has been conducted in the project "ICT programme" which was supported by the European Union through the European Social Fund.

References

1. Agbehadji, I.E., Fong, S., Millham, R.: Wolf search algorithm for numeric association rule mining. In: 2016 IEEE International Conference on Cloud Computing and Big Data Analysis (ICCCBDA), pp. 146–151. IEEE (2016)
2. Agrawal, R., Imieliński, T., Swami, A.: Mining association rules between sets of items in large databases. ACM SIGMOD Rec. **22**(2), 207–216 (1993). https://doi.org/10.1145/170036.170072
3. Agrawal, R., Srikant, R.: Fast algorithms for mining association rules in large databases. In: Proceedings of VLDB 1994 - the 20th International Conference on Very Large Data Bases, pp. 487–499. Morgan Kaufmann (1994)
4. Alatas, B., Akin, E.: Rough particle swarm optimization and its applications in data mining. Soft Comput. **12**(12), 1205–1218 (2008)
5. Alatas, B., Akin, E.: Chaotically encoded particle swarm optimization algorithm and its applications. Chaos Solitons Fract. **41**(2), 939–950 (2009)
6. Alatas, B., Akin, E.: Multi-objective rule mining using a chaotic particle swarm optimization algorithm. Knowl. Based Syst. **22**(6), 455–460 (2009)

7. Alatas, B., Akin, E., Karci, A.: MODENAR: multi-objective differential evolution algorithm for mining numeric association rules. Appl. Soft Comput. **8**(1), 646–656 (2008)
8. Altay, E.V., Alatas, B.: Performance analysis of multi-objective artificial intelligence optimization algorithms in numerical association rule mining. J. Amb. Intel. Hum. Comp. **11**, 1–21 (2019)
9. Altay, E.V., Alatas, B.: Intelligent optimization algorithms for the problem of mining numerical association rules. Physica A Stat. Mech. Appl. **540**, 123142 (2020)
10. Álvarez, V.P., Vázquez, J.M.: An evolutionary algorithm to discover quantitative association rules from huge databases without the need for an a priori discretization. Expert Syst. Appl. **39**(1), 585–593 (2012)
11. Aumann, Y., Lindell, Y.: A statistical theory for quantitative association rules. J. Intell. Inf. Syst. **20**(3), 255–283 (2003)
12. Beiranvand, V., Mobasher-Kashani, M., Bakar, A.A.: Multi-objective PSO algorithm for mining numerical association rules without a priori discretization. Expert Syst. Appl. **41**(9), 4259–4273 (2014)
13. Can, U., Alatas, B.: Automatic mining of quantitative association rules with gravitational search algorithm. Int. J. Softw. Eng. Knowl. Eng. **27**(03), 343–372 (2017)
14. Cui, Y., Geng, Z., Zhu, Q., Han, Y.: Multi-objective optimization methods and application in energy saving. Energy **125**, 681–704 (2017)
15. Deb, K., Pratap, A., Agarwal, S., Meyarivan, T.: A fast and elitist multiobjective genetic algorithm: NSGA-II. IEEE Trans. Evol. Comput. **6**(2), 182–197 (2002)
16. Djenouri, Y., Bendjoudi, A., Djenouri, D., Comuzzi, M.: GPU-based bio-inspired model for solving association rules mining problem. In: 2017 25th Euromicro International Conference on Parallel, Distributed and Network-Based Processing (PDP), pp. 262–269. IEEE (2017)
17. Eshelman, L.J.: The CHC adaptive search algorithm: how to have safe search when engaging in nontraditional genetic recombination. In: Foundations of Genetic Algorithms, vol. 1, pp. 265–283. Elsevier (1991)
18. Fister, I., Iglesias, A., Galvez, A., Del Ser, J., Osaba, E., Fister, I.: Differential evolution for association rule mining using categorical and numerical attributes. In: Yin, H., Camacho, D., Novais, P., Tallón-Ballesteros, A.J. (eds.) IDEAL 2018. LNCS, vol. 11314, pp. 79–88. Springer, Cham (2018). https://doi.org/10.1007/978-3-030-03493-1_9
19. Fonseca, C.M., Fleming, P.J., et al.: Genetic algorithms for multiobjective optimization: formulation discussion and generalization. In: ICGA, vol. 93, pp. 416–423. CiteSeer (1993)
20. Ghosh, A., Nath, B.: Multi-objective rule mining using genetic algorithms. Inf. Sci. **163**(1–3), 123–133 (2004)
21. Grabmeier, J., Rudolph, A.: Techniques of cluster algorithms in data mining. Data Mining Knowl. Disc. **6**(4), 303–360 (2002)
22. Guo, Y., Yang, J., Huang, Y.: An effective algorithm for mining quantitative association rules based on high dimension cluster. In: 2008 4th International Conference on Wireless Communications, Networking and Mobile Computing, pp. 1–4. IEEE (2008)
23. Han, J., Pei, J., Kamber, M.: Data Mining: Concepts and Techniques. Elsevier, Amsterdam (2011)
24. Hirasawa, K., Okubo, M., Katagiri, H., Hu, J., Murata, J.: Comparison between genetic network programming (GNP) and genetic programming (GP). In: Proceedings of the 2001 Congress on Evolutionary Computation (IEEE Cat. No. 01TH8546), vol. 2, pp. 1276–1282. IEEE (2001)

25. Holland, J.H.: Adaption in Natural and Artificial Systems. An Introductory Analysis with Application to Biology, Control and Artificial Intelligence. MIT Press, Cambridge (1975)
26. Ke, Y., Cheng, J., Ng, W.: MIC framework: an information-theoretic approach to quantitative association rule mining. In: 22nd International Conference on Data Engineering (ICDE 2006), p. 112. IEEE (2006)
27. Kennedy, J., Eberhart, R.: Particle swarm optimization. In: Proceedings of ICNN 1995-International Conference on Neural Networks, vol. 4, pp. 1942–1948. IEEE (1995)
28. Khade, R., Patel, N., Lin, J.: Supervised dynamic and adaptive discretization for rule mining. In: 2015 in SDM Workshop on Big Data and Stream Analytics (2015)
29. Kianmehr, K., Alshalalfa, M., Alhajj, R.: Fuzzy clustering-based discretization for gene expression classification. Knowl. Inf. Syst. **24**(3), 441–465 (2010)
30. Kim, H., Adeli, H.: Discrete cost optimization of composite floors using a floating-point genetic algorithm. Eng. Opt. **33**(4), 485–501 (2001)
31. Koza, J.R., Koza, J.R.: Genetic Programming: On the Programming of Computers by Means of Natural Selection, vol. 1. MIT press, Cambridge (1992)
32. Kuo, R., Gosumolo, M., Zulvia, F.E.: Multi-objective particle swarm optimization algorithm using adaptive archive grid for numerical association rule mining. Neural Comput. Appl. **31**(8), 3559–3572 (2019)
33. Kwaśnicka, H., Świtalski, K.: Discovery of association rules from medical data-classical and evolutionary approaches. Annales Universitatis Mariae Curie-Sklodowska, sectio AI-Informatica **4**(1), 204–217 (2006)
34. Lent, B., Swami, A., Widom, J.: Clustering association rules. In: Proceedings 13th International Conference on Data Engineering, pp. 220–231. IEEE (1997)
35. Lian, W., Cheung, D.W., Yiu, S.: An efficient algorithm for finding dense regions for mining quantitative association rules. Comput. Math. Appl. **50**(3–4), 471–490 (2005)
36. Liu, H., Abraham, A., Li, Y., Yang, X.: Role of chaos in swarm intelligence — a preliminary analysis. In: Tiwari, A., Roy, R., Knowles, J., Avineri, E., Dahal, K. (eds.) Applications of Soft Computing. AISC, vol. 36, pp. 383–392. Springer, Heidelberg (2006). https://doi.org/10.1007/978-3-540-36266-1_37
37. Liu, H., Hussain, F., Tan, C.L., Dash, M.: Discretization: an enabling technique. Data Min. Knowl. Disc. **6**(4), 393–423 (2002)
38. Lud, M.-C., Widmer, G.: Relative unsupervised discretization for association rule mining. In: Zighed, D.A., Komorowski, J., Żytkow, J. (eds.) PKDD 2000. LNCS (LNAI), vol. 1910, pp. 148–158. Springer, Heidelberg (2000). https://doi.org/10.1007/3-540-45372-5_15
39. Martín, D., Rosete, A., Alcalá-Fdez, J., Herrera, F.: A multi-objective evolutionary algorithm for mining quantitative association rules. In: 2011 11th International Conference on Intelligent Systems Design and Applications, pp. 1397–1402. IEEE (2011)
40. Martínez-Ballesteros, M., Troncoso, A., Martínez-Álvarez, F., Riquelme, J.C.: Mining quantitative association rules based on evolutionary computation and its application to atmospheric pollution. Integr. Comput. Aid. Eng. **17**(3), 227–242 (2010)
41. Mata, J., Alvarez, J., Riquelme, J.: Mining numeric association rules with genetic algorithms. In: Kůrková, V., Neruda, R., Kárný, M., Steele, N.C. (eds.) Artificial Neural Nets and Genetic Algorithms, pp. 264–267. Springer, Vienna (2001). https://doi.org/10.1007/978-3-7091-6230-9_65

42. Mata, J., Alvarez, J.-L., Riquelme, J.-C.: Discovering numeric association rules via evolutionary algorithm. In: Chen, M.-S., Yu, P.S., Liu, B. (eds.) PAKDD 2002. LNCS (LNAI), vol. 2336, pp. 40–51. Springer, Heidelberg (2002). https://doi.org/10.1007/3-540-47887-6_5
43. Mlakar, U., Zorman, M., Fister Jr., I., Fister, I.: Modified binary cuckoo search for association rule mining. J. Intell. Fuzzy Syst. **32**(6), 4319–4330 (2017)
44. Moreland, K., Truemper, K.: Discretization of target attributes for subgroup discovery. In: Perner, P. (ed.) MLDM 2009. LNCS (LNAI), vol. 5632, pp. 44–52. Springer, Heidelberg (2009). https://doi.org/10.1007/978-3-642-03070-3_4
45. Arakkal Peious, S., Sharma, R., Kaushik, M., Shah, S.A., Yahia, S.B.: Grand reports: a tool for generalizing association rule mining to numeric target values. In: Song, M., Song, I.-Y., Kotsis, G., Tjoa, A.M., Khalil, I. (eds.) DaWaK 2020. LNCS, vol. 12393, pp. 28–37. Springer, Cham (2020). https://doi.org/10.1007/978-3-030-59065-9_3
46. Poli, R., Kennedy, J., Blackwell, T.: Particle swarm optimization. Swarm Intell. **1**(1), 33–57 (2007)
47. Qodmanan, H.R., Nasiri, M., Minaei-Bidgoli, B.: Multi objective association rule mining with genetic algorithm without specifying minimum support and minimum confidence. Expert Syst. Appl. **38**(1), 288–298 (2011)
48. Rashedi, E., Nezamabadi-Pour, H., Saryazdi, S.: GSA: a gravitational search algorithm. Inf. Sci. **179**(13), 2232–2248 (2009)
49. Rashedi, E., Rashedi, E., Nezamabadi-pour, H.: A comprehensive survey on gravitational search algorithm. Swarm Evol. Comput. **41**, 141–158 (2018)
50. Russell, S., Norvig, P.: Prentice Hall Series in Artificial Intelligence. Prentice Hall, Englewood Cliffs (1995)
51. Salleb-Aouissi, A., Vrain, C., Nortet, C., Kong, X., Rathod, V., Cassard, D.: Quant-Miner for mining quantitative association rules. J. Mach. Learn. Res. **14**(1), 3153–3157 (2013)
52. Seki, H., Nagao, M.: An efficient java implementation of a GA-based miner for relational association rules with numerical attributes. In: 2017 IEEE International Conference on Systems, Man, and Cybernetics (SMC), pp. 2028–2033. IEEE (2017)
53. Sharma, R., Kaushik, M., Peious, S.A., Yahia, S.B., Draheim, D.: Expected vs. unexpected: selecting right measures of interestingness. In: Song, M., Song, I.-Y., Kotsis, G., Tjoa, A.M., Khalil, I. (eds.) DaWaK 2020. LNCS, vol. 12393, pp. 38–47. Springer, Cham (2020). https://doi.org/10.1007/978-3-030-59065-9_4
54. Shih, M.Y., Jheng, J.W., Lai, L.F.: A two-step method for clustering mixed categroical and numeric data. Tamkang J. Sci. Eng. **13**(1), 11–19 (2010)
55. Srikant, R., Agrawal, R.: Mining quantitative association rules in large relational tables. In: Proceedings of the 1996 ACM SIGMOD International Conference on Management of Data, pp. 1–12 (1996)
56. Srinivas, N., Deb, K.: Muiltiobjective optimization using nondominated sorting in genetic algorithms. Evol. Comput. **2**(3), 221–248 (1994)
57. Storn, R., Price, K.: Differential evolution: a simple and efficient adaptive scheme for global optimization over continuous spaces. J. Glob. Optim. **23** (1995)
58. Storn, R., Price, K.: Differential evolution-a simple and efficient heuristic for global optimization over continuous spaces. J. Glob. Optim. **11**(4), 341–359 (1997)
59. Taboada, K., Gonzales, E., Shimada, K., Mabu, S., Hirasawa, K., Hu, J.: Association rule mining for continuous attributes using genetic network programming. IEEJ Trans. Electr. Electron. Eng. **3**(2), 199–211 (2008)

60. Taboada, K., Mabu, S., Gonzales, E., Shimada, K., Hirasawa, K.: Genetic network programming for fuzzy association rule-based classification. In: 2009 IEEE Congress on Evolutionary Computation, pp. 2387–2394. IEEE (2009)
61. Tahyudin, I., Nambo, H.: The combination of evolutionary algorithm method for numerical association rule mining optimization. In: Xu, J., Hajiyev, A., Nickel, S., Gen, M. (eds.) Proceedings of the Tenth International Conference on Management Science and Engineering Management. AISC, vol. 502, pp. 13–23. Springer, Singapore (2017). https://doi.org/10.1007/978-981-10-1837-4_2
62. Tan, S.C.: Improving association rule mining using clustering-based discretization of numerical data. In: 2018 International Conference on Intelligent and Innovative Computing Applications (ICONIC), pp. 1–5. IEEE (2018)
63. Tang, R., Fong, S., Yang, X.S., Deb, S.: Wolf search algorithm with ephemeral memory. In: Seventh International Conference on Digital Information Management (ICDIM 2012), pp. 165–172. IEEE (2012)
64. Telikani, A., Gandomi, A.H., Shahbahrami, A.: A survey of evolutionary computation for association rule mining. Inf. Sci. **524**, 318–352 (2020)
65. Triguero, I., García, S., Herrera, F.: Differential evolution for optimizing the positioning of prototypes in nearest neighbor classification. Pattern Recognit. **44**(4), 901–916 (2011)
66. Yamany, W., Emary, E., Hassanien, A.E.: Wolf search algorithm for attribute reduction in classification. In: 2014 IEEE Symposium on Computational Intelligence and Data Mining (CIDM), pp. 351–358. IEEE (2014)
67. Yan, D., Zhao, X., Lin, R., Bai, D.: PPQAR: parallel PSO for quantitative association rule mining. Peer-to-Peer Netw. Appl. **12**(5), 1433–1444 (2019)
68. Yan, X., Zhang, C., Zhang, S.: Genetic algorithm-based strategy for identifying association rules without specifying actual minimum support. Expert Syst. Appl. **36**(2), 3066–3076 (2009)
69. Yang, J., Feng, Z.: An effective algorithm for mining quantitative associations based on subspace clustering. In: 2010 International Conference on Networking and Digital Society, vol. 1, pp. 175–178. IEEE (2010)

Applying Peer-to-Peer Networks for Decentralized Customer-to-Customer Ecommerce Model

Tu Kha Huynh[1], Hai-Duong Le[2(✉)], Sinh Van Nguyen[1], and Ha Manh Tran[2(✉)]

[1] International University–HCMC Vietnam National University, Block 6, Linh Trung Ward, Thu Duc District, Ho Chi Minh City, Vietnam
{hktu,nvsinh}@hcmiu.edu.vn
[2] Hong Bang International University, 215 Dien Bien Phu, Ward 15, Binh Thanh District, Ho Chi Minh City, Vietnam
{duonglh,hatm}@hiu.vn

Abstract. Among four ecommerce business models, the customer-to-customer (C2C) model allows customers to exchange goods or services, and get their money through fully or partly direct transactions. This model is usually dependent on mediate companies, e.g. eBay or Craigslist, for solving the main challenges of technology maintenance and quality control. This paper presents a decentralized C2C ecommerce model based on mobile peer-to-peer (P2P) networks. Several advantageous characteristics of the mobile P2P network including autonomy in control and administration, scalability and reliability in peers and resources not only avoid centralized servers and technology maintenance but also facilitate quality control by selecting various quality peers and resources using flexible search mechanisms on mobile devices. We have provided the design of Book Trading Service (BTS) using Gnutella protocol and the prototype of the BTS application on Android mobile platform. The experimental results show the feasibility and effectiveness of the decentralized C2C ecommerce model and the BTS application that can also be applied to several application domains.

Keywords: Decentralized C2C ecommerce · P2P network · Gnutella protocol · Mobile computing · Android platform

1 Introduction

The rapid growth of Internet technology and use has become main driving forces for ecommerce explosion. Several types of ecommerce including online stores, online retailers, online auction places, online market places, etc., take advantage of web, content and mobile technologies to facilitate online services and bring a lot of conveniences for sellers and buyers. Four ecommerce business models are business-to-business (B2B) such as Alibaba [1] selling services or goods to other

© Springer Nature Singapore Pte Ltd. 2020
T. K. Dang et al. (Eds.): FDSE 2020, CCIS 1306, pp. 21–34, 2020.
https://doi.org/10.1007/978-981-33-4370-2_2

businesses, business-to-consumer (B2C) such as Amazon [2] and Walmart [3] selling services or goods to consumers, consumer-to-consumer (C2C) such as eBay [4] and Craigslist [5] enabling consumers to sell goods or services to other consumers, and consumer-to-business (C2B) enabling consumers to sell their own products or services to businesses.

The B2C ecommerce model has widely been prevailing with a large number of online services, while the C2C ecommerce model has recently gained much attraction from companies and users due to the flexibility of executive management and business rule. Sharing economy services are an example of the B2C ecommerce model that facilitates interactions between customers. The new taxi service, namely Uber or Grab, solves several limitations of the traditional taxi service, such as poor quality control, low passenger and driver communication, wrong directions, etc. This service cooperates mobile computing and P2P technology to enhance passengers and drivers communication with determined information in advance, and also reduce the involvement of central management and control. The eBay and Craigslist companies provide C2C ecommerce services that allow customers to become either sellers or buyers in their business. These models are usually dependent on mediate companies for solving the main challenges of technology maintenance and quality control.

In this study, we apply P2P networks to propose a decentralized C2C ecommerce model. This model not only inherits remarkable characteristics of P2P networks, but also eliminates mediate issues including technology maintenance, central servers, mobile platform porting as technical issues and quality control, additional cost, mediate payment service as non-technical issues. The idea behind this model comes from advertising and trading activities on Facebook. Buyers contact directly sellers for service transactions without the involvement of Facebook that only plays a role of a marketing platform. However, these activities still depend on Facebook servers. Our study aims to propose a purely decentralized model that is independent on the above issues, supports mobile platforms and allows customers to evaluate and control quality by themselves. The contribution of this study is therefore threefold:

1. Propose a decentralized C2C ecommerce model using unstructured P2P networks.
2. Provide a design of Book Trading Service (BTS) using Gnutella protocol [6].
3. Experiment a prototype of the BTS application on Android mobile platform.

The rest of the paper is structured as follows: the next section presents some background of centralized, structured and unstructured P2P networks, C2C ecommerce applications based on P2P networks. Section 3 introduces a decentralized C2C ecommerce model based on an unstructured P2P network. Section 4 provides an architecture design of C2C ecommerce application that uses Gnutella protocol to trade books on mobile devices. The BTS architecture inherits remarkable characteristics of an unstructured P2P network. Sections 5 presents a BTS prototype and some experiments on Android mobile platform before the paper is concluded in Sect. 6.

2   Background

P2P networks have been widely studied and applied to multiple application domains ranging from files and resources sharing to voip, distributed computing. A P2P network is a collection of networked computers and mobile devices referred as peers. Peers acting as both client and server share computing resources including file, storage, bandwidth and processor power through consuming and provisioning services, respectively. The P2P network is established by a special communication process that allows peers to join and leave dynamically with some degree of self-administration, fault-tolerance and scalability. Considering the mechanisms of searching and sharing resources, P2P networks can be divided into three categories: centralized, structured and unstructured networks (Fig. 1).

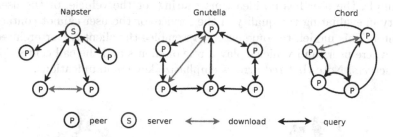

Fig. 1. Searching and sharing resources on Napster, Gnutella and Chord

A centralized P2P network uses a centralized server to index resources from peers. A peer searches the resource indexes and corresponding peers from the server and directly downloads the resources from the corresponding peers. The typical network includes Napster [7]. A structured P2P network uses Distributed Hash Table (DHT) to generate uniquely consistent identifiers for peers and resources such that the peers hold the resource indexes if their identifiers are in the same identifier space. Peers forward queries to other peers closer to the resource indexes in the identifier space to figure out the corresponding peers. The typical structured networks include CAN [8], Chord [9], and Kademlia [10]. An unstructured P2P network maintains resource indexes on peers. Peers search resources by flooding queries to other peers on the network, and the peers holding the resources send back their information for the download process. The typical unstructured P2P systems include Gnutella [6], Freenet [11], and BitTorrent [12]. In addition, a super peer P2P network is a hybrid network that combines the characteristics of the P2P network with the client-server network to address the problem of heterogeneous peers, i.e., peers possess various capability of storage, bandwidth and processing power. The study of Yang et al. [13] has presented guidelines for designing the super peer network to take advantage of peer capabilities. The super peer network comprises many clusters connected to each other to form either structured or unstructured P2P networks, in which each cluster contains a super peer and a set of clients. The clients submit queries to, and also obtain queryhits from, their super peer while the super peers forward the queries and receive the queryhits on the super peer network.

P2P networks have recently been applied to sharing economy or C2C ecommerce applications. Sharing economy applications such as Uber [14], Airbnb [15] contain a P2P-based architecture design. The key point of this design is to facilitate direct communication between peers and reduce centralized control. We consider Uber as an example. The traditional taxi company contains call centers and a large number of vehicles. A user calls the call center to book a vehicle, then the call center sends a vehicle to the user's location. The user uses the service provided the taxi vehicle and pay the bill. This taxi service model, as shown in Fig. 2 on the left side, emphasizes communications between the user and the call center, and the call center and the vehicle, but ignores communication between the user and the vehicle. This model contains several limitations, for example, the user has no idea time waiting for the vehicle, or the user has difficulty in evaluating the quality of the service, or the user cannot contact the call center. This model, to some extent, resembles the client-server architecture model, where users and vehicles play a role of clients and the call centers play a role of servers. Note that red arrows emphasize key communications.

Fig. 2. Traditional taxi model (left); Uber taxi model (right)

The Uber company has recently succeeded in taking advantage of the digital platform and sharing economy model. The Uber model provides a virtual space to connect users for offering and seeking rides. Different from the traditional taxi service, the Uber company only possesses the platform without vehicles. The operation of the Uber service is shown in Fig. 2 on the right side. A user uses a mobile application provided by the Uber company to request a vehicle. The application communicates the Uber service to obtain an appropriate offer. The Uber service collects the real time information of vehicles, seeks the most appropriate offer for the user, and pass the request to the vehicle. The vehicle contacts the user for the service. The application provides the detailed information of user's and vehicle's locations, price and route. The user also evaluates the quality of the service using the application. This model, to some extent, resembles the P2P architecture model, where users and vehicles play a role of peers and the data centers only serve registration and management purposes. This model also facilitates the P2P provision of a service [16]. Many sharing economy applications share the same design with Uber.

3   Decentralized C2C Model

Online marketplace applications such as Craigslist [5] and eBay [4] pioneer this model in the early days of the internet. There is a Web application platform serving as an online marketplace or emarket for buyers and sellers. Sellers post selling items to the emarket, while buyers look for items from the emarket and obtain items from the sellers through indirect transactions. In this model as shown in Fig. 3, the centralized emarket servers play an important role in connecting buyers and sellers. These servers provide a mediate mechanism for performing transactions to guarantee quality control, i.e., after a buyer and a seller agree on trading an item, the buyer transfers money to the mediate company, the seller sends the item to the buyer, then the seller receives money from the company if there is no any complaint from the buyer. The server must be powerful in computing, storage, bandwidth and technology to keep services running efficiently. This model can also be considered as a centralized C2C model because the dependence of the centralized servers, similar to the centralized P2P network.

Suppliers

Consumers

Online Marketplace
with or without Warehouse

Fig. 3. Centralized C2C ecommerce model

A decentralized C2C model allows buyers and sellers to trade items through direct transactions. The centralized servers only act as the bootstrapping servers to form a network of sellers and buyers. On this network, sellers and buyers can dynamically join and leave, search items, and perform transactions through a P2P application. The motivation of this model comes from online trading activities on Facebook where sellers advertise items on their pages, and buyers search appropriate items, then transactions occur directly between sellers and buyers without the participation of Facebook. Facebook is only a platform for the decentralized C2C model. However, the disadvantages of this platform include Facebook server dependency, limited search capability, advertisement fee, etc.

We propose a decentralized C2C model based on an unstructured P2P network as shown in Fig. 4. This model takes advantage of remarkable characteristics of unstructured P2P networks. Buyers and sellers act as peers in this network; they directly connect and trade items to each other without centralized servers; the network is self managed when peers join and leave dynamically. The centralized servers are only used for network bootstrapping and user rating purposes. Since there is no centralized servers, sellers can only advertise their items when they get online, and this network provides a flexible search mechanism that allows buyers to look for items on several sellers' stores. This model eliminates the mediate company, cost is thus reduced compared to the above model. However, this model also suffers some limitations from unstructured P2P networks, such as search scalability, peer heterogeneity, peer reliability, etc., discussed in the below section.

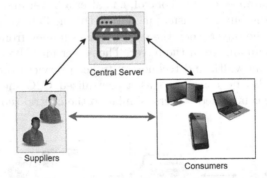

Fig. 4. Decentralized C2C ecommerce model

4   Application Design

This section presents a design of a mobile P2P application that can be applied to Book Trading Service within a university as a prototype. This application allows students to trade used books easily and conveniently through their smart phones. The application uses the Gnutella protocol to build the unstructured P2P network on Android mobile platform.

4.1   Gnutella Protocol

The Gnutella protocol has been used to build purely decentralized P2P networks. There is no central coordination of the activities in the networks and users connect to their peers directly through an application that acts both as a client and a server. To locate a file in such a network, a peer uses the flooding algorithm to send a request to neighboring peers that in turn forwards the request to their

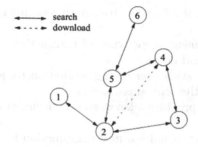

Fig. 5. Flooding algorithm in Gnutella network

neighboring peers and so on. This algorithm floods (broadcasts) the network to distribute the request. Any peer holding the file sends a reply back to the sending route. There are five types of types of messages used in this protocol [17]:

1. Ping – A request to certain hosts to announce itself.
2. Pong – A reply to a ping request contains IP and port of the responding host and number and size of the sharing file.
3. Query – A search request contains a search string and the minimum speed requirements of the responding host.
4. QueryHit – A reply to a query request contains the IP, port, and speed of the responding host, the number of matching files found, and their indexed result set.
5. Push – A download request for peers behind firewall.

Figure 5 explains how the flooding algorithm works in the Gnutella network. Each request from a peer is passed directly to connected peers, which in turn flood their peers, until the request is answered, or a maximum number of flooding steps occur by applying a time-to-live (TTL) value stored in the header of the message [18]. According to the figure, peer (2) wants to query a file to download. It first broadcasts to peers (1), (5), and (3). The message is flooded until reaching peer (4) that keeps the file. After peer (4) returns the result, peer (2) can contact peer (4) to download the file.

4.2 BTS Architecture

The proposed BTS architecture contains two main parts: (i) the bootstrapping servers store a list of peers permanently available on the P2P network and a list of peer rating values; (ii) the core functions of a BTS mobile application allow peers to connect to the network and perform activities. The architecture contains an unstructured P2P network that ignores centralized servers as much as possible. The mobile application possesses several components as shown in Fig. 6:

– *User Management* stores user information including user contact, IP address that are public for sharing.

– *Inventory Management* advertises user resources including selling books and wishlist books.
– *Transaction Management* keeps track of transaction history including a list of transacted peers and books.
– *Rating Management* sends peer rating evaluation to, and also retrieves peer rating update, from the centralized server.
– *Search Management* provides a keyword search function for peers to look for book titles.
– *Message Management* includes a message function for peers to contact each other directly after successfully matching books.

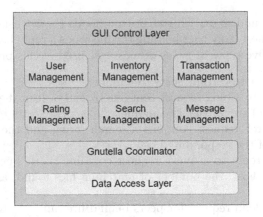

Fig. 6. BTS application components

4.3 Gnutella Coordinator

The BTS application or peer uses a list of recently connected peers to join the network. A new peer without this list first connects to the bootstrapping servers to receive a list of neighboring peers, then connects to the neighboring peers to join the network. When a peer get online, its books in a local shared directory are publicly advertised to the network. Each book contains an XML file storing book information, price, contact information, IP address, etc.

When receiving a query message, a peer looks for a matching file in the local shared directory. If there is such a book, the peer returns a queryhit message to the sending peer following the sending route, then the peer forwards the message to its neighboring peers. The sending peer uses information from the message to download directly the XML file from the returning peer, then both peers get sufficient information to perform a transaction directly. Figure 7 presents the general idea of how resource is advertised, how a peer sends a query for a book, gets queryhits from some peers and then downloads an XML file from the selected peer.

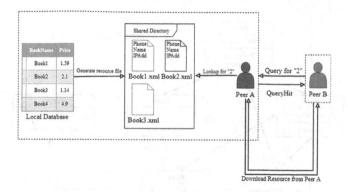

Fig. 7. Book searching process on peers

The BTS prototype application also includes a package holding necessary components for mobile peers to join the Gnutella network and look up for books. These components contain three types of functions based on client, server and networking sides.

- Client:
  - Obtain user preference from a text file called *preference.txt*.
  - Launch a *Pinger* to check regularly neighboring peers alive.
  - Launch a *Connector* to connects to peers in the list and new peers.
  - Work with layout resource and activities to display query messages and download results through *GnutellaCoordinator*.
- Server:
  - Launch a *Listener* to catch incoming connections.
  - Launch a downloading service that looks up the upload directory when a Query is received and creates a QueryHit for the sending peer to download resource.
  - Handle different package types.
- Networking:
  - Contain a *NetworkManager* to keep track of live neighboring peers.
  - Each packet sent among peers contains a header with: payload descriptor (packet type), payload length, TTL (Time to Live), Hops, Message ID (to create a QueryHit for a Query).
  - Each packet possesses a corresponding *Handler* to keep the information of routing, capability and requirement for each packet types.

The application also includes three functions that extend the Gnutella protocol, as follows:

- Book advertisement: Upload book files to *SharedDirectory* from the local database; launch *Listener* for the download server and lookup function in SharedDirectory for incoming query messages.

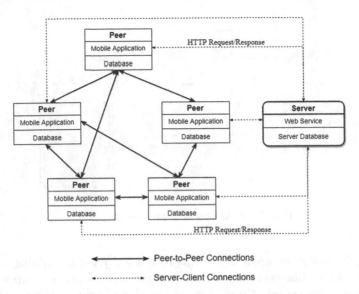

Fig. 8. BTS network deployment

- Target search: Create a query message from user's keywords and send the message to the neighboring peers; each neighboring peer, after receiving the message, seeks a book in SharedDirectory; the peer returns a queryhit message if the book exists, and then the peer forwards the message to its neighboring peers.
- Target message: Modify query and queryhit messages to adapt the required function, e.g., *Chat* and *ChatHit* messages perform similarly to query and queryhit messages, except for searching and forwarding processes.

4.4   BTS Deployment

The BTS network contains mobile peers and desktop peers that connect to each other and exchange data in a purely decentralized way, as shown in Fig. 8. The peers uses a Gnutella protocol to form an unstructured P2P network, where peer functions including *ping, pong, query, queryhit, push* only occur between peers without a central server. The arrows between peers indicate data exchange within the P2P network.

The central server offers web services for bootstrapping and rating activities. Peer rating values are stored in a central database that all peers can set and get these rating values. When a peer wants to know a targeted peer's rating value, it sends an HTTP GET request to the server with the targeted peer's phone number, and the server returns a message with the targeted peer's rating value. When a transaction completes, a peer wants to submit a targeted peer's rating value to the server, it sends an HTTP POST request including the targeted peer's phone number and a rating value. When receiving the HTTP POST request, the server uses a rating algorithm to compute and update the new rating value to the database and then return a successful HTTP message as an acknowledgment. The dot arrows between peers and the central server indicate HTTP message exchange within the client and server network.

5   Experimental Evaluation

We have implemented the BTS application and established the mobile P2P network with a web server for bootstrapping and rating activities. The BTS application can be installed on an Android emulator, thus both mobile and desktop applications possibly connect to the network as peers. Note that the connectivity between peers requires the activation of peer wifi.

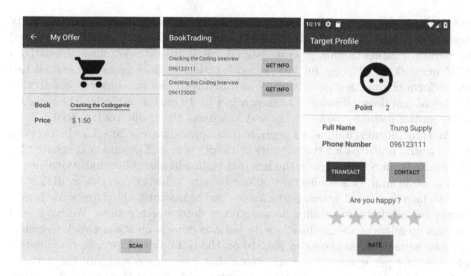

Fig. 9. BTS mobile application

Figure 9 depicts the graphical user interface of the BTS application. As getting the IP addresses of neighboring peers, the BTS application as a peer connects to these IP addresses to reach the maximum number of neighboring peers, and periodically ping them to update status. The processes of advertising and seeking books then occur as mentioned above. Since the experimental network is relatively small, time consumption for searching books is also small. The web server plays an important role in storing permanent peers and retrieving peer rating values. Two functions allow peers to contact with the web server, as follows:

- Retrieving peer rating values from peer phone number by using HTTP GET request.
- Posting new rating values to the server by using HTTP POST request.

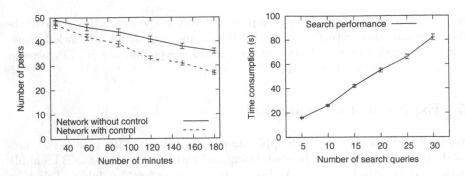

Fig. 10. Connection failure of peers over various time periods (left); Time consumption of book search over various numbers of search queries (right)

We have also examined service availability on the network. Service availability heavily depends on the connectivity of mobile applications that might be affected by several reasons including power, signal, capability, etc. We have simulated a P2P network of 50 peers on virtual workstations. While peers are established to perform communication activities automatically, we measure the connection failure of mobile applications, as shown in Fig. 10 on the left side. The network with control includes packet delay and loss using the traffic control tool.

Within 180 min, number of peers reduce approximately 20% for the network with control and 10% for the network without control. The same experiment for the limited number of peers on the Internet results in unstable connections for the period of 30 min. This connection failure heavily influences service availability.

We have measured search performance on the network. Quick response is necessary for service survivability because peers need search results. We have used various numbers of search queries with various criteria on the network to collect time consumption, as shown in Fig. 10 on the right side. A peer approximately obtains 2.6 s per query on average. Note that peers leave and join the network automatically during the execution of book search. There is a trade-off between time consumption and peer reachability (resulting in the increasing number of queryhits). As the number of neighboring peers increases, the number of peers receiving a query increases, the possibility of returning queryhits also increases, and therefore time consumption per query increases while responding time might decrease.

6   Conclusion

The B2C ecommerce model has successfully been applied to many application domains, while the C2C ecommerce model has recently attracted to companies and users, e.g., sharing economy applications, Facebook online retails. These models contain a main problem of centralized control and management. We have proposed the decentralized C2C ecommerce model that takes advantage of remarkable characteristics of P2P networks to eliminate this problem, thus improving several issues including technology maintenance, central servers, mobile platform porting, quality control, additional cost, mediate payment service, etc. We have provided the design of Book Trading Service using Gnutella protocol and the prototype of the BTS application on Android mobile platform. The proposed model and design can be applied to several application domains, where trading books in an university is only an experiment. We have demonstrated typical application functions and evaluated service availability and search performance on the mobile P2P network. The experimental results show the feasibility and effectiveness of the proposed C2C ecommerce model and the BTS application. However, this model lacks solutions for some problems when applying to specific application domains, for example, controlling malicious sellers and buyers, handling conflicts between sellers and buyers or providing effective transaction mechanisms. Future work focuses on improving and applying the proposed model and design for real application domains.

Acknowledgments. We thank Pham Le Trung for implementing the prototype of the BTS application. This research activity is funded by Hong Bang International University under the grant number GVTC14.1.01.

References

1. Alibaba Group (1999). https://www.alibabagroup.com/. Accessed Aug 2020
2. Amazon Company (1994). https://www.amazon.com/. Accessed Aug 2020
3. Walmart Company (1962). https://www.walmart.com/. Accessed Aug 2020
4. eBay Company (1995). https://www.ebay.org/. Accessed Aug 2020
5. Craigslist Company (1995). https://www.craigslist.org/. Accessed Aug 2020
6. Gnutella Protocol Specification (version 0.4) (2001). http://rfc-gnutella. sourceforge.net/developer/stable/. Accessed Jan 2017
7. Carlsson, B., Gustavsson, R.: The rise and fall of Napster - an evolutionary approach. In: Liu, J., Yuen, P.C., Li, C., Ng, J., Ishida, T. (eds.) AMT 2001. LNCS, vol. 2252, pp. 347–354. Springer, Heidelberg (2001). https://doi.org/10.1007/3-540-45336-9_40
8. Ratnasamy, S., Francis, P., Handley, M., Karp, R., Schenker, S.: A scalable content addressable network. In: Proceedings of the Conference on Applications, Technologies, Architectures, and Protocols for Computer Communications (SIGCOMM 2001), pp. 161–172. ACM Press, New York (2001)
9. Stoica, I., Morris, R., Karger, D., Kaashoek, M.F., Balakrishnan, H.: Chord: a scalable peer-to-peer lookup service for internet applications. In: Proceedings of the Conference on Applications, Technologies, Architectures, and Protocols for Computer Communications (SIGCOMM 2001), pp. 149–160. ACM Press, New York (2001)
10. Maymounkov, P., Mazières, D.: Kademlia: a peer-to-peer information system based on the XOR metric. In: Druschel, P., Kaashoek, F., Rowstron, A. (eds.) IPTPS 2002. LNCS, vol. 2429, pp. 53–65. Springer, Heidelberg (2002). https://doi.org/10.1007/3-540-45748-8_5
11. Clarke, I., Sandberg, O., Wiley, B., Hong, T.W.: Freenet: a distributed anonymous information storage and retrieval system. In: Federrath, H. (ed.) Designing Privacy Enhancing Technologies. LNCS, vol. 2009, pp. 46–66. Springer, Heidelberg (2001). https://doi.org/10.1007/3-540-44702-4_4

12. Cohen, B.: Incentives build robustness in Bittorrent. In: Proceedings of the 1st Workshop on Economics of Peer-to-Peer Systems (2003)
13. Yang, B., Garcia-Molina, H.: Designing a super-peer network. Technical report, Stanford University (2002). http://dbpubs.stanford.edu/pub/2002-13
14. Uber Company (2014). https://www.uber.com/. Accessed Aug 2020
15. Airbnb Company (2008). https://www.airbnb.com/. Accessed Aug 2020
16. Sundararajan, A.: What Airbnb Gets About Culture That Uber Doesn't. Harvard Business Review (2014). https://hbr.org/2014/11/what-airbnb-gets-about-culture-that-uber-doesn't
17. Androutsellis-Theotokis, S., Spinellis, D.: A survey of peer-to-peer content distribution technologies. ACM Comput. Surv. **36**(4), 335–371 (2004)
18. Milojicic, D., et al.: Peer-to-peer computing. Technical Report HPL-2002-57R1, HP Laboratories, Palo Alto, USA, April 2002

An Elastic Data Conversion Framework for Data Integration System

Tran Khanh Dang$^{(\boxtimes)}$, Manh Huy Ta, and Le Hoang Nguyen$^{(\boxtimes)}$

Ho Chi Minh City University of Technology, Vietnam National University
Ho Chi Minh City, 268 Ly Thuong Kiet, District 10, Ho Chi Minh City, Vietnam
{khanh,nlhoang}@hcmut.edu.vn, tamanhhuy@yahoo.vn

Abstract. Data nowadays is an extremely valuable resource. However, they are created and stored in different places with various formats and types. As a result, it is not easy and efficient for data analysis and data mining which can make profits for every aspect of social applications. In order to overcome this problem, a data conversion is a crucial step that we have to build for linking and merging different data resources to a unified data store. In this paper, based on the intermediate data conversion model, we propose an elastic data conversion framework for data integration system.

Keywords: Data conversion · Data integration system · Data transformation · Open data

1 Introduction

With the development of technology, data is becoming an extremely valuable resource. Data is being created, analyzed and used in a massive scale in every modern system. As a result, data analysis and data mining are very essential in each aspect of social applications. The value of data will be more useful if it can be linked and merged with other different data resources, especially for solving current social problems [1,4]. In order to make a reality of this big challenge, data transformation is a crucial step that we have to overcome.

Data transformation can be described as a task that can flexibly convert data among different models and formats, thereby supporting the combination of data from various resources to a unified one, in another word, a unified dataset. This problem is not easy even when converting traditional data with few data sources with simple structure. Usually, this process requires the participation of human to understand and correct the meaning of the data in each source to solve the data ambiguity problems, including semantic and data representation ambiguity.

In the age of big data, this problem becomes more and more challenging when data are not only heterogeneous, but are also produced continuously with enormous mass [15]. These three main characteristics of big data are known through the notation "3V":

T. K. Dang et al. (Eds.): FDSE 2020, CCIS 1306, pp. 35–50, 2020.
https://doi.org/10.1007/978-981-33-4370-2_3

– Volume: not only data sources contain a large amount of data but the number
of sources of the data also becomes very large
– Velocity: data are continuously generated and changed over time
– Variety: data from many different sources are diverse and heterogeneous

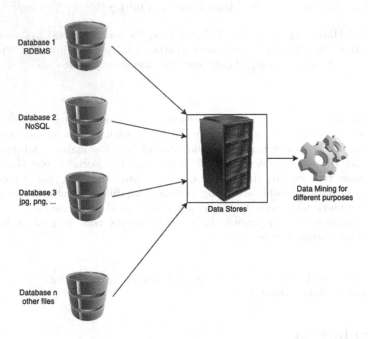

Fig. 1. Data Stores

Data transformation is an essential problem in many industries. For example, the traffic data integrated from the bus black boxes and the cameras on
the road will provide a comprehensive view of the traffic situation of the city.
If able to combined with data on population such as population density and
distribution, the management agencies and related departments will be able to
make appropriate decisions and policies such as traffic flow, reconstructing and
establishing traffic infrastructure, or navigating traffic to avoid traffic jams. The
problem is that departments often store data with completely different models
and formats. Hence, data transformation is an indispensable step in the integration, analysis, and decision-making process. In the US, transport agencies rely
on large amounts of data to support everyday tasks such as planning, design, and
construction [5]. Therefore, these agencies also need to gather and exchange a lot
of information. The speed of access together with the accuracy and consistency
of the information from these different platforms and targets lead to the problem
of data conversion. In addition, the converted data can be combined together
into a unified dataset and through data mining process, this can bring many
benefits to data analysis and management applications as well as can provide

potential and optimal value [2, 14]. Furthermore, this combined dataset is a rich resource in making predictions and supporting decision making. Data now can be collected and integrated to store and manage in data centers for a variety of purposes (Fig. 1).

However, the challenge in the data transformation problem is that this process need to interact with many different data sources in various structures and formats. Hence, it is necessary to do research and propose a data standard format to support storage in data centers and propose a framework supporting data transformation before integrating them into data centers. This research direction is also one of the research trends on Information Technology for the Ho Chi Minh City in the period of 2018–2023. In this paper, we propose a novel data conversion framework for data integration system. The rest of this paper is organized as follows, some related works and researches will be mentioned in Sect. 2 while the our proposed framework will be in Sect. 3. The summary and conclusion will be in Sect. 4.

2 Related Works

Since 2010, there have been a lot of researches and proposed methods for data conversion. Such as in 2013, Ivan et al. proposed a data transformation system based on a community contribution model [8]. As depicted in Fig. 2, the data shared on the publicdata.eu portal includes data from many different organizations of various formats. The system will make initial mappings, then let the community contribute by creating new mappings, re-editing existing mappings, transforming the data, and using the data. The accuracy in data conversion will improve over time with the contribution of the community.

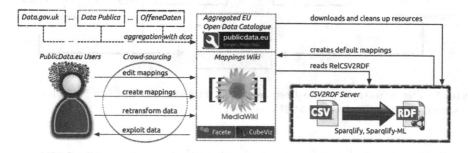

Fig. 2. Data transformation system based on a community contribution model (Ivan et al., 2013)

In 2015, Rocha et al. proposed a method to support the migration of data from relational databases RDBMS to NoSQL [16]. This method includes 2 main modules which are data migration and data mapping.

– The data migration module (Fig. 3) is responsible for automatically identifying all elements from the original relational databases (e.g. tables, properties, relationships, indexes, etc.), then creates equivalent structures using the
NoSQL data model and then exports the data to the new model
– The data mapping module (Fig. 4) consists of an abstract class, designed
as an interface between the application and the DBMS, which oversees all
SQL transactions from the applications, and translates these operations then
moves to the NoSQL model that was created in previous module

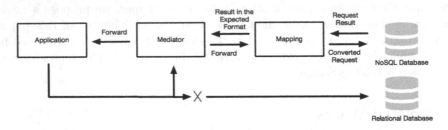

Fig. 3. The migration of data from relational databases RDBMS to NoSQL - Data
migration module (Rocha et al., 2015)

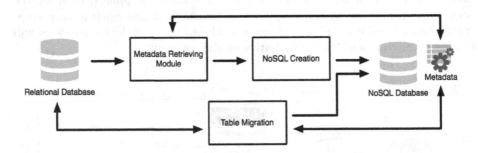

Fig. 4. The migration of data from relational databases RDBMS to NoSQL - Data
mapping module (Rocha et al., 2015)

Hyeonjeong et al. developed a semi-automatic tool for converting ecological
data in Korea in 2017 [6]. The goal of this tool is to gather data in different
formats from various research organizations and institutes specializing in environment in Korea and then convert to a shared standard ecological dataset. To
accomplish this goal, the authors propose 4 transformation steps as described in
Fig.5 including:

– Step 1 - Data File & Protocol Selection: selecting data from the source file
and the corresponding protocol

- Step 2 - Species Selection: choosing which species in the data to be converted
- Step 3 - Attribute Mapping: mapping attributes from source data to normalized attributes defined in the protocol
- Step 4 - Data Standardization: converting mapped data to a shared standard

However, this tool currently only converts data for few species from the original data. Another limitation is that it only supports data sources stored in **.csv** format whereas the actual data is usually represented in many different formats.

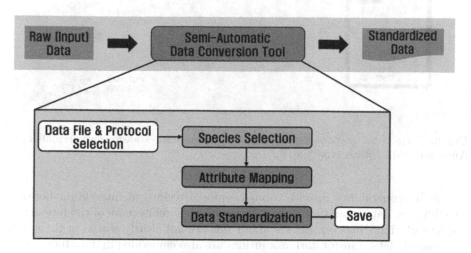

Fig. 5. Semi-automatic tool for converting ecological data in Korea (Hyeonjeong et al., 2017)

In 2017, Milan et al. looked to the context of factory integration through the use of the data transformation toolkit for AutomationML (AML), an open standard XML-based data format for storage and exchange of technical information of the plant [13].

In this context, factory automation requires the participating and collaborating in a variety of fields from automation control, mechanical engineering, electronics, and software engineering. These domains all have different support tools, and the tools manipulate different data structures. Therefore, the authors propose a model integrating these tools with AML by using a process engineering transformation tool. This model will convert the data described by the AML into the appropriate formats corresponding to the technical tools of different disciplines as depicted in Fig. 6. Although the model can work well, the input of the process is stored only in AML standard.

In 2017, Luis et al. developed a data conversion framework to support energy simulation [10]. The goal of this framework is to convert data in different formats to enable communicating and interacting among different systems in an automated environment. This approach designs an intermediate component defined

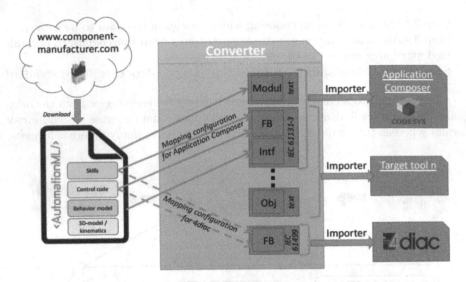

Fig. 6. Factory integration through the use of the data transformation toolkit for AutomationML (Milan et al., 2017)

as the Interoperability Specification to enforce reciprocal interaction between two different data formats. Figure 7 illustrates the architecture of the interactive implementation. However, details about this are not clearly stated in the study.

Besides, data transformation solutions are also embedded in data integration systems. Dong and Srivastava in [3], by based on traditional data integration architectures as depicted in Fig. 8, highlight challenges for big data integration with the following three main phases

– Schema Alignment: solving semantic ambiguity challenges
– Record Linkage: solving ambiguity challenges of data representation
– Data Fusion: solving data quality challenges

In another work of Marek et al. in 2015 [11], the authors describe different types of data inconsistencies, especially semantic inconsistencies. From there, the integration problem is classified according to two different challenges: low level and high level integration. In an approach aimed at reducing semantic heterogeneity, the authors used Semantic Web Technology for data integration and proposed architectural model called Semantic Big Data Historian (SBDH) with four main components as follows

– Data Acquisition Layer: data collected from sensors, additional internal data sources, or from external data sources. The problem of heterogeneity of platforms related to different systems will be solved in this layer.
– Data Transformation Layer: converting data into integrated semantic form based on the proposed semantic network (SHS Ontology). This class will also correct the corrupted data if necessary. Semantic inconsistencies will be resolved in this class.

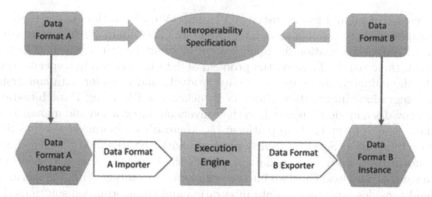

Fig. 7. Data conversion framework to support energy simulation (Luis et al., 2017)

Fig. 8. Challenges for big data integration (Dong et al., 2015)

- Data Storage Layer: data storage based on three systems: 4Store1, Cumulus-RDF, Hadoop and Jena Elephas.
- Analytic Layer: providing direct access to the storage layer for compost data analysis or user query processing. Selected analytical framework options include: KNIME, Mahout.

Knoblock and Szekely developed the Karma system, an integrated data system in the cultural heritage domain [9]. This system will integrate data with high data heterogeneity from different museums. The process is described through four main stages:

- Data import phase: importing data from any different source including databases, spreadsheets, or web services provided in XML or JSON format
- Data cleansing and normalization phase: identifying unusual data components and normalizing the data according to similar formats of related sources
- Modeling phase: creating a semantic description of each resource
- Phase integration: converting the data into a single format using a description on semantics and data integration in an unified framework

However, the above integrated system only focuses on integrating the data source at the schema level, not the data link problem. Moreover, this system only considers the data heterogeneity factor (Variety), while the other two factors of big data are the data volume (Volume) and the rate of data generation (Velocity) have not been mentioned.

There are also some studies related to data transformation and integration in Vietnam. For example, the PhD thesis on integrating data models in the data center of oil and gas industry in Vietnam (Vu, 2016), the Master thesis on geographic data conversion tools integrated into GIS (Pham, 2016), or workshop on health data integration for management of smart health (Nguyen, 2016). In general, these studies focus on the problem of data integration in a specific field.

In the industry, there are also many products and tools for data conversion and integration. Information Builders launched the iWay Big Data Integrator that provides a modern approach to the conversion, integration and management of data based on the Hadoop platform [7]. Microsoft Corporation also has SQL Server Integration Services (SSIS) products with services able to extract and transform data from various data sources such as XML, files, and relational data sources, and load the data into one or more data storages [12]. Furthermore, Talend provides tools for big data integration and transformation solutions [17]. However, these tools perform the transformation of data directly through user interaction without the standard conversion data specification.

In Vietnam, the problem of data conversion has not been given adequate attention. Currently, almost data sources are stored individually at different departments, branches. Therefore, utilizing the value of this data source is very limited when it is difficult to combine data since each place often stores data in different formats and models. Although there are data centers in the infrastructure; however, these centers have not really combined data to create a unified data source to serve the needs of data mining and data analysis.

In the next section, we propose a framework that converts data from many different sources and formats into a common format called standard data format. Furthermore, we propose a data conversion framework based on this standard one.

3   Proposed Framework

3.1   Approaching Method for Data Conversion

The data conversion methods can be divided into two categories: direct conversion and intermediate conversion.

> Direct conversion: The data is converted directly from source to target format. This conversion method is the most popular conversion method due to its simplicity and ease of implementation. However, this method is only effective when the number of source and target formats is small. As this number increases, the complexity of the system increases rapidly (Fig. 9).
> Intermediate conversion: Data will be converted to intermediate data format and this data will be converted to the format that the user wants. This method has the advantage that it will reduce the complexity of the system and make the system expandable (Fig. 10).

Most studies and works mainly use the direct conversion model [6,10]. The reason for the usefulness of this model is due to the natural factor of the goal or project: the need to convert data from one or several specific forms to one or

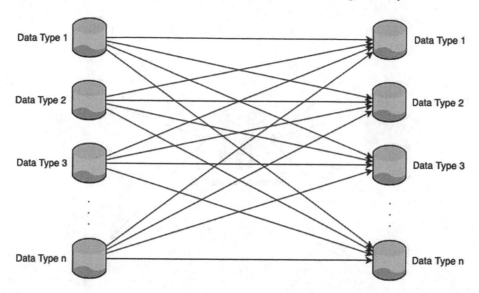

Fig. 9. Direct Data Conversion

several specific forms. However, with the goal of designing an extensible system having the framework can work with a variety of input and output formats, the direct transformation model creates a lot of complexity when adding more data types for the system. In the direct conversion model, if we add a new input format to the system including n outputs of the system, it is required to manually programmatically extend n functions.

However, if the intermediate conversion model is used, only one additional function is needed for the system. Therefore, the direct conversion model is not suitable for the needs of a large and extensible data conversion system. In this paper, we use the intermediate conversion for our proposed framework. For this type of approaching method, one of the most significant problems is finding the most suitable intermediate data type for the system.

3.2 Proposed Intermediate Data Type

The framework is designed to use an intermediate data type or standard data format in the transformation process. In fact, this standard format of data will also be stored in the storage block, for later needs and purposes. This data standard format must meet the following criteria

- Flexible structure
- Efficient storage
- Good scalability

According to the above standards, only formats such as JSON, XML and BSON do meet the above needs since traditional database models will not meet

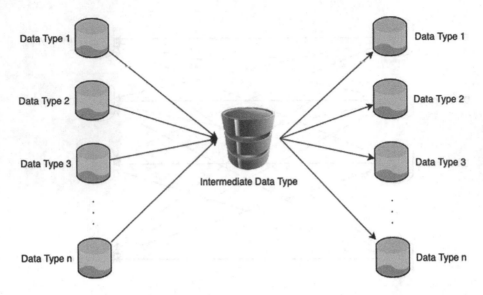

Fig. 10. Intermediate data conversion

the need for flexible structure. There are other standard data formats that can be used here; however, we only consider JSON format for our proposed framework because the JSON format has several advantages

- Require small storage
- Widely used in reality
- Fully-supported community and technology
- Easy to learn for new users

3.3   Framework Components

The framework contains 6 components (Fig. 14) as follows

- I/O: this component will be in charge of the input and output processes of the system
- Data Stores: saving and storing data of the system
- Schema Detection: when a new data is input, this component will detect and recognize the structure and schema of this data
- Schema Conversion: this part will convert the original schema into the intermediate data structure
- Data Conversion: this will create a mapping for converting each original data record to intermediate data format
- Validation: checking the input to ensure the data convertible and validate the correctness of output before sending to user

```
{
  "type": "object",
  "properties": {
    "first_name": { "type": "string" },
    "last_name": { "type": "string" },
    "birthday": { "type": "string", "format": "date" },
    "address": {
      "type": "object",
      "properties": {
        "street_address": { "type": "string" },
        "city": { "type": "string" },
        "state": { "type": "string" },
        "country": { "type" : "string" }
      }
    }
  }
}
```

Fig. 11. The JSON format will use JSON schema for storing meta-data

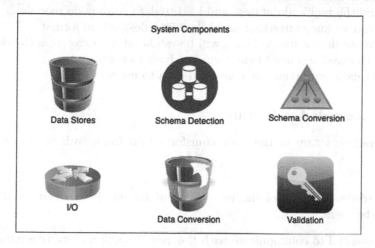

Fig. 12. Core Components of Framework

3.4 The Working Flow of the System

The data conversion system performs in the two phases: from input to data storages and from data storages to output. Figure 14 describes these two processes, the big arrows perform the input process while the small arrows show the output. The first phase is described as follows

1. Input user's data: In this step, the data will be provided by the user to the system through the open data portal.
2. Validation: this data will be checked whether it is suitable for converting or not. If yes, a back-up file will be created then saved to the corresponding storage. If no, process stops.
3. Schema Detection: this part plays a core role in the whole process; it will read and understand the input's data structure and schema
4. Schema Conversion: this will convert current data schema into intermediate format
5. Data Conversion: this step creates a mapping from the detected schema to the converted schema, the whole dataset will be converted through this mapping to intermediate data format
6. Save data to data stores: once the conversion is finished, both the schema and the converted data will be saved in the data stores

The second phase can be describe as follows

1. Load data from data stores: when receiving demands from users, the system will find the required datasets and load to data conversion module
2. Data conversion: converting saved data into destination format
3. Validation: final converted data will be validated its correctness (by comparing with saved schemas) before sending back to users
4. Export data: exporting the converted data to users

3.5   Framework Architecture

The overall structure of the data transformation framework is shown in the Fig. 13.

I/O Module. The job of the Input/Output module is to receive and return data to the users:

- It is essential to communicate with the user through an intuitive interface
- It is more convenient if we can use an open data communication portal for this I/O module. This will help the system more flexible and extensible
- It is possible to use a direct connection to user database system or raw uploaded files
- For some large or big data, there must be a module to ensure the integrity of the data

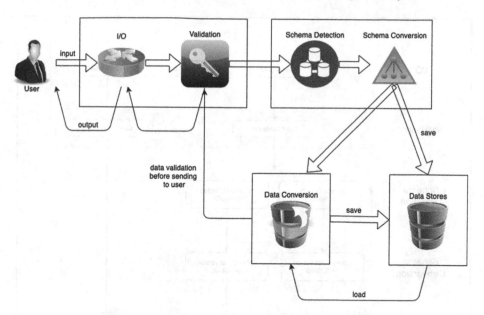

Fig. 13. Framework Architecture

Validation. Every data must be checked before inputing to the system or out-putting to users. For input data:

- The data must be in some specific formats that can be converted
- For a set of files such as images, videos, etc., this module can check and ensure the data harmless to the system

  Before sending output data to users, the validation should do

- Ensure the output data is similar to the original data
- Ensure that current user having the right to access the output or part of the output

Schema Detection. This component is responsible for extracting and searching the schema of the data provided by the user. According to the design of the framework, input data will include two types of data: structured data and NoSQL data. Therefore, the schema detection component must be able to handle both structured data and NoSQL data.

Schema Conversion. This module will convert the detected schema into the intermediate data formats. This step requires the schema conversion module to understand and able to recognize the meanings of original schema.

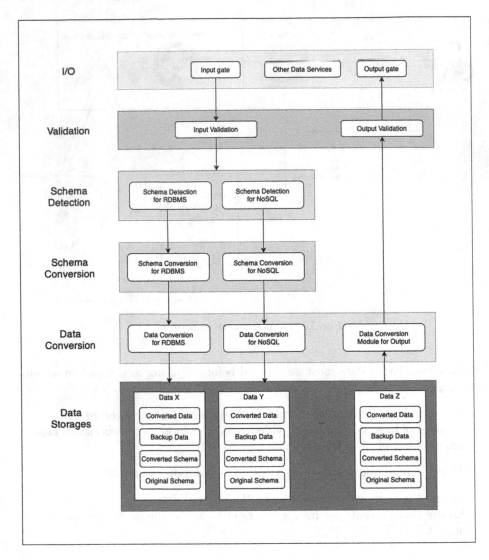

Fig. 14. Work flow of the system

Data Conversion. This component is responsible for transforming the data according to the schema outlined in the previous step. Therefore, this component is only active when the schema-related modules have finished. The input of this component is the extracted schema, converted by the schema conversion and the original user data. The output is the data after converted.

As shown in the Fig. 13, this component also converts intermediate data in data stores back to destination formats. This is an inverted process but much more simple.

For big data, this process will take a lot of time. Parallel processing with big data frameworks such as Hadoop or Spark will make this task faster and more efficiently.

Data Stores. For each input data, the data stores will save

- Backup data: original dataset. This is used for backup in case users need the original data
- Converted data: data in intermediate data format
- Original schema: the schema receiving from schema detection module. This is used for validating process to ensure the output data is similar to the original data schema
- Converted schema: the schema from schema conversion module

Furthermore, the data stores must satisfy these following conditions

- Systematic data storage: for helping users to create, store, search and use data accurately and quickly
- Data safety: ensuring data integrity and security is one of the most important concerns in the public data storage
- Simultaneous access of multiple users on data

4   Conclusions

Data conversion is an emerging topic closely related to various fields, including open data, Internet of Things. Recent studies have shown the important role and usefulness of data conversion task in data integration systems. However, these current data converter tools are still relatively simple, not fully considered the diversity of input data sources and data formats or the challenging context of big data. In particular, there are few researches that have the ability to expand in order to deal with new and various data formats, that's why in this paper, we propose a data transformation framework that allows users to declare the characteristic of new data and enables to convert the data into the desired formats. The novelty of our framework is the openness of our framework: users can add or change the data formats in our framework.

Furthermore, there are many related challenges such as schema conversion, schema mapping, efficiency data conversion, distributed data conversion techniques, ontology mapping between schema, incremental data conversion, remote data conversion, etc. Other than aforementioned problems, there are even more challenges in how to use the data: how to protect the privacy of the users who provide the data, how to prove the provenance of the data or how to use the data in a system. All these problems can be considered as interesting research topics for us to gradually solve in future.

Acknowledgments. This work is supported by a project with the Department of Science and Technology, Ho Chi Minh City, Vietnam (contract with HCMUT No. 42/2019/HD-QPTKHCN, dated 11/7/2019).

References

1. Lai, C.S., et al.: A review of technical standards for smart cities. Clean Technol. **2**(3), 290–310 (2020)
2. Dang, T.K., Nguyen, Q.P., Nguyen, V.S.: Evaluating session-based recommendation approaches on datasets from different domains. In: Dang, T.K., Küng, J., Takizawa, M., Bui, S.H. (eds.) FDSE 2019. LNCS, vol. 11814, pp. 577–592. Springer, Cham (2019). https://doi.org/10.1007/978-3-030-35653-8_37
3. Dong X.L., Srivastava, D.: Big Data Integration, p. 198. Morgan & Claypool Publishers (2015)
4. McLaren, D., Agyeman, J.: Sharing Cities: A Case for Truly Smart and Sustainable Cities. MIT Press, Cambridge (2015)
5. Federal Highway Administration, U.S. Department of Transportation. Data Integration Primer (2010). https://www.fhwa.dot.gov/asset/dataintegration/if10019/dip00.cfm
6. Lee, H., Jung, H., Shin, M., Kwon, O.: Developing a semi-automatic data conversion tool for Korean ecological data standardization. J. Ecol. Environ. **41**(11), (2017)
7. Information Builders: Real World Strategies for Big Data - Tackling The Most Common Challenges With Big Data Integration - A white paper (2016)
8. Ermilov, I., Stadler, C., Martin, M., Auer, S.: CSV2RDF: User-driven CSV to RDF mass conversion framework. In: Proceedings of the 9th International Conference on Semantic Systems (2013)
9. Knoblock, C.A., Szekely, P.: Exploiting semantics for big data integration. AI Mag. **36**(1), 25–38 (2015)
10. Paiva, L., et al.: Interoperability: A data conversion framework to support energy simulation. Proceedings **1**(7), 695 (2017). ISSN: 2504–3900
11. Obitko, M., Jirkovský, V.: Big data semantics in industry 4.0. In: Mařík, V., Schirrmann, A., Trentesaux, D., Vrba, P. (eds.) HoloMAS 2015. LNCS (LNAI), vol. 9266, pp. 217–229. Springer, Cham (2015). https://doi.org/10.1007/978-3-319-22867-9_19
12. Microsoft: SQL Server Integration Services (2017). https://docs.microsoft.com/en-us/sql/integration-services/sql-server-integration-services
13. Vathoopan, M., Brandenbourger, B., George, A., Zoitl, A.: Towards an integrated plant engineering process using a data conversion tool for AutomationML. In: IEEE International Conference on Industrial Technology, pp. 1205–1210 (2017)
14. Nguyen, L.H., Le, H.T., Dang, T.K.: A comparative study of the some methods used in constructing coresets for clustering large datasets. SN Comput. Sci. 1(4), 215 (2020). Online ISSN: 2661–8907
15. Barnaghi, P., Bermudez-Edo, M., Tonjes, R.: Challenges for quality of data in smart cities. ACM J. Data Inf. Qual. **6** (2015)
16. Rocha, L., et al.: A framework for migrating relational datasets to NoSQL1. Procedia Comput. Sci. **51**, 2593–2602 (2015)
17. Talend: Talend Data Integration (2017). https://www.talend.com/

A Novel Model Using CDN, P2P, and IPFS for Content Delivery

Tien-Thao Nguyen and Ba-Lam Do[⊠]

School of Information and Communication Technology,
Hanoi University of Science and Technology, Hanoi, Vietnam
`thao.nguyen@v-chain.vn`, `lamdb@soict.hust.edu.vn`

Abstract. The use of multimedia data is increasingly popular due to their outstanding advantages compared to traditional textual data. The demand for live streaming and the proliferation of new standards such as Full High Definition (FHD) and Ultra High Definition(UHD) makes it increasingly difficult to satisfy users. To overcome this challenge, content providers can utilize a hybrid architecture relying on a Content Delivery Network (CDN) and Peer-to-Peer communications. Many efforts have been conducted in order to evaluate and improve the performance of this architecture. However, research on applying blockchain-related technologies to the problem of content delivery is still scarce. In this context, our paper aims to investigate the ability of applying InterPlanetary File system (IPFS) - one of the salient technologies related to blockchain to the traditional hybrid architecture. We conduct different experiments to provide preliminary evaluations of the performance of the proposed system. Experimental results show that the proposed architecture is promising and effective in providing content delivery service.

Keywords: Content Delivery Network · Peer-to-Peer · InterPlanetary File system · Video · Hybrid model

1 Introduction

In recent years, advances in storage, compression, and communication have encouraged the proliferation of multimedia data on the Web. Users are provided not only valuable text-based content, but also videos, images, songs which transfer facts, statistics, and information in an effective and quick manner. According to a report published by Cisco [5], in 2020, video data are predicted to reach 82% of total network traffic in the world. Data quality is also improving significantly with the rapid popularity of new standards such as Full High Definition (FHD) and Ultra High Definition (UHD) in videos. As a result, content providers always need to extend the bandwidth and improve the system to provide better and more comfortable user experiences.

T. K. Dang et al. (Eds.): FDSE 2020, CCIS 1306, pp. 51–62, 2020.
https://doi.org/10.1007/978-981-33-4370-2_4

Currently, the providers can consider four main system design approaches as follows: (i) Unicast and multicast models [10, 21, 24] are traditional architectures providing many advantages for easy deployment and centralized management. In this approach, users receive all contents through packets from a single machine (i.e., server). Consequently, these architectures expose a serious drawback, which is a single point of failure when the system entirely depends on the server's availability. Indeed, internal reasons or an increase in demands on special occasions leading to the server failure can cause the whole system to collapse unexpectedly; (ii) Content Delivery Network (CDN) [23, 36] has been used to enhance the availability and performance of the system. By utilizing multiple geographically distributed servers to store a cached version of the content, CDN allows visitors to quickly connect to a nearby server to receive desired content. However, the CDN-based approach also contains significant limitations because of the limited number of deployed servers and the sharing of these servers between different content providers. Indeed, a massive demand from users can still overload the system and negatively affect other providers. For example, ESPN video streaming service crashed when more than 1.4 million users utilized this service to watch a football match between the USA and Germany in the 2014 FIFA World Cup [12, 32]; HBO also encountered the same problem when millions of Game of Thrones fans expected to watch the premiere of season 4 [11, 22]; (iii) Next, peer-to-peer (P2P) model [2, 27] has been emerged as an efficient approach for content delivery. This model allows users can act as both client and server when they can download data from other users and continue to share their data with others. This mechanism is especially important in delivering video because of two main reasons. First, videos using tremendous traffic are typically those having a huge number of people watching at the same time. Besides, Internet traffic in the busy hour is rapidly growing and is predicted to reach 7.2 petabytes per second in 2020, seven-fold than the average traffic [4, 5]. As a result, the P2P model for video delivery can effectively address the unpredictable demand from users and liberate the server from overload at peak hours. However, it barely ensures the service quality because the distribution depends heavily on the number of connected peers and their Internet speed; (iv) Final, a hybrid model using CDN and P2P combines the advantages from both existing models [15, 34, 35]. On the one hand, this model makes use of CDN to leverage the availability and downloading speed of the system. On the other hand, the P2P-based hybrid model allows providers to reduce the dependency on a limited number of data hosts, economize on bandwidth, as well as liberate the obstruction of a huge number of requests.

The development of blockchain technology [30, 33] in recent years has opened a great opportunity to address existing problems. For example, data providers typically store their contents on traditional data repositories such as cloud-based systems, private servers. These centralized data systems pose a threat of a single point of failure, as well as privacy issues of data loss, data leakage, etc [3, 16]. As a result, there is a need to move from centralized storage systems to decentralized ones. In this context, the InterPlanetary File system (IPFS) has emerged as an effective approach to address this issue. IPFS makes use of the P2P model and salient technologies in encryption, version control, routing, etc. to allow users to store data in a secure, decentralized, and convenient manner. Furthermore, to implement the hybrid model, content providers need to use a collection of different technologies such as real-time communication, request routing, load balancing, etc., which are available on IPFS. As a result, IPFS is a promising approach for integrating into the traditional hybrid architecture. However, visible research to apply IPFS in this architecture is scarce.

In this paper, we introduce a hybrid architecture using CDN, P2P, and IPFS for content delivery. To the best of our knowledge, our work is the first effort to provide preliminary results of the feasibility of applying IPFS in the hybrid architecture. Our system, named DWS (Decentralized Web Service), relies on three main components, i.e., a CDN, a DWS tracker, and P2P connectors. The CDN is implemented based on an IPFS cluster to effectively provide data transmission at different geographical locations. The DWS tracker plays a role as a mediator between peers, which analyzes peers' performance and behavior to select suitable peers to a specific peer. Meanwhile, the P2P connectors allow IPFS to run on the browsers without installing any extension or plugin; hence, these browsers (i.e., peers) can directly send data chunks to others.

The remainder of this paper is organized as follows. In Sect. 2, we discuss related work. Section 3 presents the design of DWS, and Sect. 4 illustrates the system through detailed experiments. We conclude in Sect. 5 with an outlook of future work.

2   Related Work

We classify related efforts into two main categories, namely research on hybrid CDN-P2P model and research on IPFS.

Within the first group, a significant number of researchers have proposed and evaluated hybrid CDN-P2P architectures for content delivery. Tran et al. [31] made use of the hybrid model for live video streaming on the Web to reduce the number of requests to CDN servers and enhance the system's scalability. The experimental results showed that the proposed system is promising and useful. Sanguankotchakorn et al. [26] introduced a hybrid Pull-Push method in CDN-P2P architecture to decrease the latency in a live video system. Compared to the traditional method, this method helps reduce the end-to-end delay but increase startup delay. Ha et al. [14] also introduced a novel hybrid CDN-P2P architecture for live streaming. This architecture relies on a special mechanism to effectively manage buffers at peers in order to balance the bandwidth between CDN servers and these peers. Abdallah et al. [1] proposed a hybrid architecture that uses Ftree system - a name resolution system. This system proves its effectiveness by reducing the traffic and waiting time of clients.

Recently, research on IPFS - a protocol and network designed based on the P2P model, has attracted a remarkable interest of researchers. Instead of identifying data by location, IPFS addresses each input file by a unique content identifier (CID), which is the result of hashing the content by SHA-256 function [13]. As a result, IPFS can easily eliminate duplication across the network. Moreover, IPFS utilizes the advantages of numerous existing technologies such as Distributed Hash Table (DHT) for routing [7,28], Merkle Distributed Acyclic Graphs (DAG) for building a tree of data [8], Bitswap for exchanging data blocks [6], etc. In particular, the use of DHT allows nodes share data to each other without any central coordination whereas Merkle DAG enables permanent and tamper-resistant data storage. Bitswap can be used to encourage peers to join and contribute resources for content delivery through reward. In addition, IPFS helps to build networks that can operate independently without depending on Internet connection. This can be applied to the livestream problem, for example, only playing a video in a LAN when all computers are not connected to the Internet. Nowadays, many existing efforts focus on a combination of IPFS and blockchain networks to obtain characteristics of decentralization, trust, and transparency for proposed systems. In these systems [17,18,29], IPFS stores large-size data such as documents, videos, images, etc., whereas blockchain networks are responsible for storing hash values of input data.

Compared to related attempts, our work aims to apply IPFS on the traditional hybrid model with two main differences. (i) First, we utilize an IPFS cluster including multiple IPFS nodes to deploy the CDN, instead of using a network of traditional servers; (ii) Next, relying on IPFS's protocol, peers, i.e., users' browsers, can share data chunks with other browsers instead of using the existing popular technologies, e.g., WebRTC [20], Bittorrent protocol [9,25], etc.

3   System Design

We first introduce the system architecture in Sect. 3.1. Next, we explain the communication between components in DWS through an activity flow in Sect. 3.2. Final, Sect. 3.3 introduces an algorithm used in DWS to identify paired peers.

3.1   System Architecture

Figure 1 illustrates the system architecture, which consists of three main components: a CDN, a DWS tracker, and IPFS connectors.

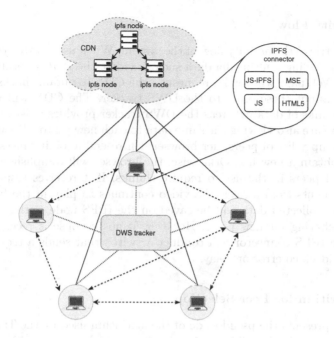

Fig. 1. System architecture

(i) CDN: We use an IPFS cluster with nodes distributed in different geographical locations to act as a CDN. In fact, IPFS cluster is a decentralized network that has the advantage of data orchestration among IPFS nodes through mechanisms of allocating, replicating, and tracking data. Therefore, the use of IPFS cluster simplifies data synchronization between CDN nodes and increases efficiency for version management of data on the system.

(ii) DWS tracker: This component is responsible for managing peers participating in the system, including joining, leaving, and pairing. It depends on peers' information, including location, browser type, operating system, and especially Internet speed and ISP provider to select suitable peers that can be paired to a peer who has just joined the system. We make use of salient technologies, including Node.js, Socket, and Redis, to ensure scalability and high load capacity of the system.

(iii) IPFS connectors: They operate in the end-users' browsers to collect necessary information from the peers, then send this information to the Tracker to receive a list of suitable peers to pair before performing the exchange of chunks with other peers. This component is built using modern technologies, including HTML5, JavaScript, Media Source Extensions (MSE), and JS-IPFS library. MSE is a JavaScript API designed to manage and play video from chunks of media data. This technology has already been adopted by popular browsers such as Google Chrome, Mozilla Firefox, etc. and is used by default by Netflix and YouTube. JS-IPFS [19] is a JavaScript library that allows running IPFS node on the browser.

3.2   Activity Flow

Figure 2 illustrates the activity flow of the system. When users' browsers access a Web page, including multimedia data such as video, the P2P connector embedded on this Web page will send a request to the CDN to obtain chucks and send information about these users to the DWS tracker. The CDN will return the beginning chunks of data, whereas the DWS tracker provides a list of appropriate peers who are also viewing the same data to each new visitor. If a new visitor receives an empty list of peers, her browser will resend a joining message to the Tracker to obtain a new list. Otherwise, the browser will establish connections to all related peers in the list to require chunks. If it receives responses such as video segments from a peer, the video continues to play in the browser. In addition, the collected data will be saved on the IPFS node of this browser to extend the sharing for new peers. However, if no response is received after a timeout, the IPFS connector will conduct a switch that sends a request to the CDN to avoid video error or delay.

3.3   Algorithm for Peer Selection

Algorithm 1 presents the pseudocode of the algorithm used by the Tracker component for peer selection. From a list of all peers who are watching the same video, the Tracker will identify a list of suitable peers to a specific peer. For a

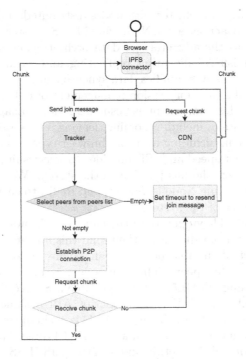

Fig. 2. Flow of activity

new user, the Tracker will calculate the PeerScore for each available peer. To avoid getting all appropriate peers, which can lead to a time-consuming process, we utilize a threshold and set a maximal number of paired peers in the returned list. Currently, we set these parameters to five and three, respectively.

Algorithm 1: Peer Selection

$peers \leftarrow []$;
while $peer$ in $peerList$ **do**
    $peerScore \leftarrow PeerScore(peer)$;
    if $peerScore \geq threshold$ **then**
        | $peers \leftarrow insert(peer)$;
    end
    if $size(peers) \geq maxConnection$ **then**
        | **return** peers
    end
end
return peers

$$PeerScore() = \begin{cases} speed + 0.1 * (100 - distance) + 5 & distance < 100 \text{ and same ISP} \\ speed - 0.1 * distance + 5 & distance > 100 \text{ and same ISP} \\ speed - 0.1 * (100 - distance) & distance < 100 \text{ and different ISP} \\ speed - 0.1 * distance & distance > 100 \text{ and different ISP} \end{cases}$$

Units: speed in Mbps; distance in km.

4 Evaluations

We first introduce experimental environment in Sect. 4.1. Next, we conduct different experiments to evaluate the proposed system in terms of performance, offload, and relationship between offload and video length. Experimental results are introduced in Sects. 4.2, 4.3 and 4.4.

4.1 Experiment Setup

Our setups contain three settings. First, we utilize an IPFS cluster, including three nodes version 0.4.23, each node has 4 CPUs, 8 GB RAM. These nodes are located in Singapore (two nodes) and London, United Kingdom (one node). Next, the DWS tracker is implemented on a server located in Singapore, having 2 CPUs and 4 GB RAM. Final, we conduct experiments in three cases of users, including: (i) a user uses different tabs on a browser to access the Website; (ii) multiple users in the same network; and (iii) multiple users in two different networks, each network has the same number of users. Each experiment is conducted three times to calculate the average value.

4.2   Evaluation of DWS Tracker Performance

The purpose of this experiment is to evaluate the performance of the DWS tracker in terms of time-consuming for identifying suitable peers for a specific peer. We compare the performance in the two cases of peers, i.e., on the same network and on different networks. For each case, the same video will be downloaded, and the number of peers will change from two to sixty-four peers. Figure 3 describes the experimental results, which show that the higher the number of peers watching the same video, the faster the ability to find corresponding peers to exchange chunks. They also illustrate the system's tendency to be stable when the number of peers is higher than thirty-two.

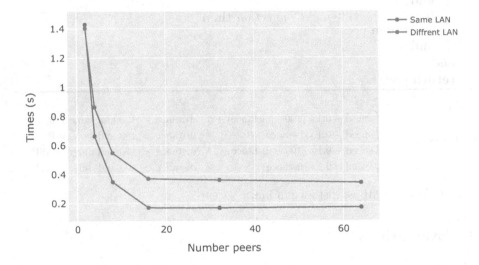

Fig. 3. Processing time for identifying peers

4.3   Evaluation of CDN Offload

The purpose of the experiment is to evaluate the contribution of directly exchanging data between peers when changing the number of peers watching the same video. The experiment conducts on the same 5-min video with two segments divided by five seconds and ten seconds, respectively. For each case, the number of peers in the same LAN is changed from two to six peers. Figure 4 shows that the bigger number of participating peers, the larger proportion of data transferred from peers, instead of the CDN. For instance, in the first case, data size exchanged between peers increases from approximately 30 MB to 42 MB when the number of peers changes from two to six. In the second case, this change is from 30 MB to around 50 MB. Furthermore, for each case, we also see that the first peer always has the highest rate of getting data from the CDN because it is the first peer watching the video. The proportion of data taken from peers between two videos with different segment lengths also share some similarities.

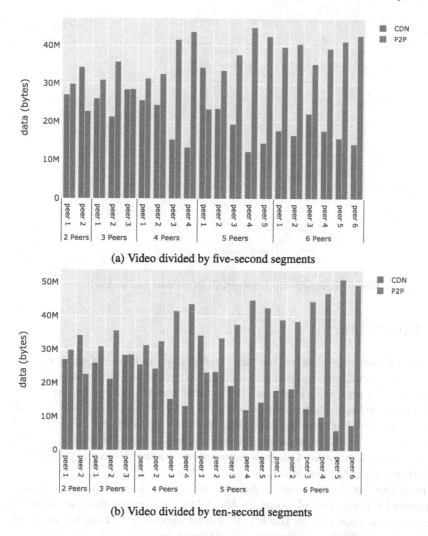

(a) Video divided by five-second segments

(b) Video divided by ten-second segments

Fig. 4. Evaluation of CDN Offload

4.4 Relationship Between CDN Offload and Video Length

This experiment aims to evaluate the effect of video length on the proportion of data taken from other peers. We experiment with two cases, i.e., using the same computer and using two computers in the same LAN, and with the duration of the video changed from one minute to five minutes. Figure 5 shows that with the same computer, the load rate from P2P is higher than that of other computers. In addition, in both cases, the load rate from P2P escalates when the video duration increases. In particular, this proportion for one-minute video is around 34%–37% whereas for five-minute video is till 45%–48%. This is understandable because the longer the video gets, the easier it is to request segments from other peers.

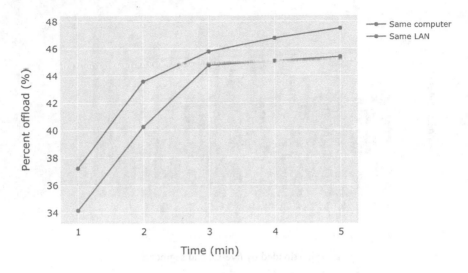

Fig. 5. Relationship between CDN offload and video length

5 Conclusion

Nowadays, the explosion of Internet traffic and multimedia data makes content delivery challenging. In this context, our paper aims to introduce a novel model relying on CDN, P2P, and IPFS for content delivery. In particular, our architecture relies on three components, i.e., a CDN, a Tracker server, and P2P connectors. Two components, including the CDN and P2P connectors, are developed based on IPFS - a protocol and network for decentralized data storage with many salient advantages. Our experimental results show that the proposed architecture is promising and effective.

In future work, we aim to extend the system's implementation, such as increasing the number of nodes in the CDN and improving the algorithm of peer selection used by the Tracker. It will be necessary to conduct more experiments to evaluate the system in many different aspects, such as user experience, privacy, and bandwidth cost that is saved.

Acknowledgments. This research is supported by the Vietnamese MOET's project "Researching and applying blockchain technology to the problem of authenticating the certificate issuing process in Vietnam", No. B2020-BKA-14.

References

1. Abdallah, H.B.H., Louati, W.: Ftree-CDN: hybrid CDN and P2P architecture for efficient content distribution. In: Euromicro International Conference on Parallel, Distributed and Network-Based Processing (PDP), pp. 438–445. IEEE (2019)
2. Buford, J., Yu, H., Lua, E.K.: P2P Networking and Applications. Morgan Kaufmann, Burlington (2009)

3. Cadwalladr, C., Graham-Harrison, E.: Revealed: 50 million facebook profiles harvested for cambridge analytica in major data breach. Guard. **17**, 22 (2018)

4. Cisco: Cisco visual networking index predicts annual internet traffic to grow more than 20% (reaching 1.6 zettabytes) by 2018 (2014). https://newsroom.cisco.com/press-release-content?type=webcontent&articleId=1426270. Accessed 01 Aug 2020

5. Cisco: Cisco predicts more IP traffic in the next five years than in the history of the internet (2018). https://newsroom.cisco.com/press-release-content?type=webcontent&articleId=1955935. Accessed 01 Aug 2020

6. Docs, I.: Bitswap (2020). https://docs.ipfs.io/concepts/bitswap/. Accessed 01 Aug 2020

7. Docs, I.: Distributed hash tables (DHTs) (2020). https://docs.ipfs.io/concepts/dht/. Accessed 01 Aug 2020

8. Docs, I.: Merkle distributed acyclic graphs (DAGs) (2020). https://docs.ipfs.io/concepts/merkle-dag/. Accessed 01 Aug 2020

9. Fan, B., Chiu, D., Lui, J.C.: The delicate tradeoffs in bittorrent-like file sharing protocol design. In: IEEE International Conference on Network Protocols, pp. 239–248. IEEE (2006)

10. Floyd, S., Handley, M., Padhye, J., Widmer, J.: Equation-based congestion control for unicast applications. ACM SIGCOMM Comput. Commun. Rev. **30**(4), 43–56 (2000)

11. Forbes: Game of thrones premier brings HBO more customers despite episode crash (2014). https://www.forbes.com/sites/brandindex/2014/05/06/game-of-thrones-premier-brings-hbo-more-customers-despite-episode-crash/#46fb36141327. Accessed 01 Aug 2020

12. Friedman, R., Libov, A., Vigfussony, Y.: Distilling the ingredients of P2P live streaming systems. In: International Conference on Peer-to-Peer Computing (P2P), pp. 1–10 (2015)

13. Gilbert, H., Handschuh, H.: Security analysis of SHA-256 and sisters. In: Matsui, M., Zuccherato, R.J. (eds.) SAC 2003. LNCS, vol. 3006, pp. 175–193. Springer, Heidelberg (2004). https://doi.org/10.1007/978-3-540-24654-1_13

14. Ha, D.H., Silverton, T., Fourmaux, O.: A novel hybrid CDN-P2P mechanism for effective real-time media streaming. Master's thesis, Université Pierre et Marie Curie (2008)

15. Huang, C., Wang, A., Li, J., Ross, K.W.: Understanding hybrid CDN-P2P: why limelight needs its own red swoosh. In: International Workshop on Network and Operating Systems Support for Digital Audio and Video, pp. 75–80 (2008)

16. Isaak, J., Hanna, M.J.: User data privacy: facebook, cambridge analytica, and privacy protection. Computer **51**(8), 56–59 (2018)

17. Krejci, S., Sigwart, M., Schulte, S.: Blockchain- and IPFS-based data distribution for the Internet of Things. In: Brogi, A., Zimmermann, W., Kritikos, K. (eds.) ESOCC 2020. LNCS, vol. 12054, pp. 177–191. Springer, Cham (2020). https://doi.org/10.1007/978-3-030-44769-4_14

18. Kumar, R., Marchang, N., Tripathi, R.: Distributed off-chain storage of patient diagnostic reports in healthcare system using IPFS and blockchain. In: International Conference on COMmunication Systems & NETworkS (COMSNETS), pp. 1–5. IEEE (2020)

19. Labs, P.: A full P2P protocol written entirely in javascript (2020). https://js.ipfs.io/

20. Loreto, S., Romano, S.P.: Real-Time Communication with WebRTC: Peer-to-Peer in the Browser. O'Reilly Media, Inc., Newton (2014)

21. Majumda, A., Sachs, D.G., Kozintsev, I.V., Ramchandran, K., Yeung, M.M.: Multicast and unicast real-time video streaming over wireless lans. IEEE Trans. Circuits Syst. Video Technol. **12**(6), 524–534 (2002)
22. Mukerjee, M.K., et al.: Enabling near real-time central control for live video delivery in CDNs. In: ACM Conference on SIGCOMM, pp. 343–344 (2014)
23. Peng, G.: CDN: content distribution network. arXiv preprint cs/0411069 (2004)
24. Pizzi, S., Condoluci, M., Araniti, G., Molinaro, A., Iera, A., Muntean, G.M.: A unified approach for efficient delivery of unicast and multicast wireless video services. IEEE Trans. Wirel. Commun. **15**(12), 8063–8076 (2016)
25. Rai, V., Sivasubramanian, S., Bhulai, S., Garbacki, P., Van Steen, M.: A multi-phased approach for modeling and analysis of the bittorrent protocol. In: International Conference on Distributed Computing Systems (ICDCS 2007), pp. 10–10. IEEE (2007)
26. Sanguankotchakorn, T., Krueakampliw, N.: A hybrid pull-push protocol in hybrid CDN-P2P mesh-based architecture for live video streaming. In: Asia-Pacific Network Operations and Management Symposium (APNOMS), pp. 187–192. IEEE (2017)
27. Schollmeier, R.: A definition of peer-to-peer networking for the classification of peer-to-peer architectures and applications. In: International Conference on Peer-to-Peer Computing, pp. 101–102. IEEE (2001)
28. Steichen, M., Fiz, B., Norvill, R., Shbair, W., State, R.: Blockchain-based, decentralized access control for IPFS. In: IEEE International Conference on Internet of Things (iThings) and IEEE Green Computing and Communications (GreenCom) and IEEE Cyber, Physical and Social Computing (CPSCom) and IEEE Smart Data (SmartData), pp. 1499–1506. IEEE (2018)
29. Sun, J., Yao, X., Wang, S., Wu, Y.: Blockchain-based secure storage and access scheme for electronic medical records in IPFS. IEEE Access **8**, 59389–59401 (2020)
30. Swan, M.: Blockchain: Blueprint for a New Economy. O'Reilly Media, Inc., Newton (2015)
31. Thi Thu Ha, T., Kim, J., Nam, J.: Design and deployment of low-delay hybrid CDN-P2P architecture for live video streaming over the web. Wirel. Pers. Commun. **94**(3), 513–525 (2017)
32. Todd, S.: ESPN live stream crashes during USA-Germany world cup match (2014). https://variety.com/2014/digital/news/espn-video-streaming-service-crashes-during-usa-germany-world-cup-match-1201251221/. Accessed 01 Aug 2020
33. Underwood, S.: Blockchain beyond bitcoin (2016)
34. Xu, D., Kulkarni, S.S., Rosenberg, C., Chai, H.K.: Analysis of a CDN-P2P hybrid architecture for cost-effective streaming media distribution. Multimed. Syst. **11**(4), 383–399 (2006)
35. Yin, H., et al.: Design and deployment of a hybrid CDN-P2P system for live video streaming: experiences with LiveSky. In: ACM International Conference on Multimedia, pp. 25–34 (2009)
36. Zhao, J., Liang, P., Liufu, W., Fan, Z.: Recent developments in content delivery network: a survey. In: Shen, H., Sang, Y. (eds.) PAAP 2019. CCIS, vol. 1163, pp. 98–106. Springer, Singapore (2020). https://doi.org/10.1007/978-981-15-2767-8_9

Course Recommendation with Deep Learning Approach

Tran Thanh Dien(✉), Luu Hoai-Sang, Nguyen Thanh-Hai,
and Nguyen Thai-Nghe(✉)

Can Tho University, Can Tho, Vietnam
{thanhdien,lhsang,nthai.cit,ntnghe}@ctu.edu.vn

Abstract. Course selection is a crucial task which may affect greatly on student performance. Because of poor performances, numerous students have been receiving formal warnings and expulsions from universities. Clearly, a good strategy for study progress which can come from course recommendation methods really holds an important role to obtain a good study performance. In addition, early warnings that release on challenging courses enable students to prepare better for such courses. The current course recommendation systems are usually conducted from marks prediction and factor analysis on marks of courses based on advancements of machine learning approaches. In this study, we propose a course recommender system by using deep learning techniques with MultiLayer Perceptron and pre-processing methods. The prediction tasks are performed on approximately four million of mark records at Can Tho University, Vietnam to provide recommendations on course selection to students. The proposed method reveals promising results and is expected to apply in practical cases.

Keywords: Course selection · Deep learning · MultiLayer Perceptron · Student performance prediction · Course recommendation

1 Introduction

Student performance is an important task of higher educational institutions because it is a criteria for high quality universities that are based on excellent profile of their academic achievements. According to [1], student performance can be obtained by measuring the learning assessment and curriculum. However, most of the studies mentioned that student performance based on the measurement of students' success [2].

Several situations of student performance in the universities are released to student and family's student to warn in the case that students got poor performance. Taking an example from Can Tho University, in the first semester of the academic year 2018–2019, there were more than 800 released warnings for one-poor-performance semester and more than 100 for the two-consecutive-poor-performance semesters cases. These numbers are rising with 986 and 196

© Springer Nature Singapore Pte Ltd. 2020
T. K. Dang et al. (Eds.): FDSE 2020, CCIS 1306, pp. 63–77, 2020.
https://doi.org/10.1007/978-981-33-4370-2_5

respectively for the academic year 2019–2020[1]. One of the main reasons for the students' poor performance is that they have not selected appropriate courses to their competencies. These results in extension of learning term and increase of cost for their families, higher educational institutions and society as well. Therefore, predicting students' performance is an important research topic in exploiting educational data, which is of interest to many researchers [3].

In order to students to obtain the best academic performance, recommender systems is needed for course selection to predict the best courses that should be selected by students. There are the existing recommender systems for selecting courses. For example, data mining is one of the most popular approaches to be widely applied in educational area. One of the most popular techniques to predict student performance is classification. There are several algorithms used for classification task such as Decision Tree, Artificial Neural Networks, Naive Bayes, K-Nearest Neighbor and Support Vector Machines [2]. However, the existing researches are primarily based on learning results of previous semesters to predict student performance of next semester or Current Grade Point Average (GPA), but do not analyze additional factors such as English entrance testing grades, activity incentive grades, etc. that affect their performance. Moreover, the researchers have not sufficiently compared among techniques, especially deep learning techniques with other traditionally machine learning techniques.

This study proposes a course selection recommendation system by using deep learning techniques [4], especially the multi-layer perceptron (MLP) to build a student's performance prediction model for predicting student performance in next semesters based on the course's achievement results of the previous semesters. In addition, in order to improve the predictive results, we also consider other additional factors such as entrance English testing grades, activity incentive grades etc. for the proposed model. Moreover, a comparison between deep learning techniques and traditionally machine learning ones is also conducted. Experiential data is collected from the student information system of a Vietnamese multidisciplinary university. The results show that the proposed model provides rather accurate prediction and it can be applied in practical other cases.

2   Related Work

Course recommendation is really important to build a good study strategy for students. Mark prediction tasks are required to provide valuable advices for course recommendation. Numerous studies have attempted to propose efficient methods for student performance. The authors in [5], introduced an approach implementing Tensor Factorization (TF) to predict student performance. The proposed method enabled us to personalize the prediction for specific student. The authors reported promising experiential results on two large datasets.

---

[1] Can Tho University, 2020. Management Information System, accessed on 12/5/2020. Available from https://htql.ctu.edu.vn/.

Recently, open source libraries have been more used for predictive work. [6] developed a student performance prediction system using the open source recommendation system called *MyMediaLite*. For the grade databases collected from the academic management system of a university, the authors proposed using Biased Matrix Factorization (*BMF*) technique to predict the learning results. This results can help students choose more appropriate courses. The authors in [7] proposed a novel approach which uses recommender system techniques for educational data mining, especially for predicting student performance. For validating this approach, the recommender system techniques were compared with traditional regression methods such as linear regression by using educational data for intelligent tutoring systems. The experimental results showed that the proposed approach can improve prediction results.

The work in [8] presented an approach to boost student performance prediction in interactive online question pools through considering student interaction features and the similarity between questions. The proposed approach evaluated on the dataset from a real-world interactive question pool using four typical machine learning models. The result showed that the approach can achieve a much higher accuracy for student performance prediction in interactive online question pools than the traditional way using the statistical features in various models.

The authors in [9] evaluated exhaustively the prediction performance based on all possible combinations of four types of attributes including behavioral features, demographic features, academic background, and parent participation. Using support vector machine and feature selection, the authors concluded that the behavioral feature is so crucial because of the optimal prediction performance. In [10], the authors proposed a method of predicting student performance in computing majors. This method is based on collaborative filtering using enhanced similarity and yields personalized predictions of student grades in courses required for each computing major. Prediction accuracy is enhanced by analyzing computing major-specific course characteristics, such as core courses, course prerequisites, and course levels.

The authors with the research in [11] proposed a methodology in which the process of data collection and pre-processing is carried out, then the grouping of students with similar patterns of academic performance was carried out. The authors selected the most appropriate supervised learning algorithm. The experimental results showed the effectiveness of machine learning techniques to predict the performance of students. The authors in [12] used the efficacy of Matrix Factorization as a technique for solving the prediction problem. The study uses Singular Value Decomposition (SVD), a Matrix Factorization technique that has been successfully used in recommender systems. The performance of the technique was benchmarked against the use of student and course average marks as predictors of performance. The results obtained suggests that Matrix Factorization performs better than both benchmarks. The work in [13] proposed a direct search of the optimal value of latent factors where the calculation for each number of latent factors is driven by a metaheuristic that select, at the same time, the optimal values of learning rate and regularization factor. Using this method, authors can determine the best number of latent factors to be applied in further predictions for the similar databases.

Another study in [14] introduced a supervised content-aware matrix factorization for mutual reinforcement of academic performance prediction and library book recommendation. The proposed model was evaluated on three consecutive years of book-loan history and cumulative grade point average of 13047 undergraduate students in one university. The results showed that the proposed model outperforms the competing baselines on both tasks, and that academic performance not only is predictable from the book-loan history but also improves the recommendation of library books for students.

An optional course recommendation system based on score prediction was introduced in [15] using a novel cross-user-domain collaborative filtering algorithm to accurately predict the score of the optional course for each student by using the course score distribution of the most similar senior students. The experimental results showed that the proposed method is able to accurately recommend optional courses to students who will achieve relatively high scores. Another work of [16] proposed a method to predict student performance using various deep learning techniques. Several techniques for data pre-processing used such as Quantile Transforms, MinMax Scaler before fetching them into well-known deep learning models such as Long Short Term Memory and Convolutional Neural Networks to do prediction tasks. The experiential results showed that the proposed method provides good prediction results, especially using data transformation.

Some studies also introduced methods for course recommendation. [17] proposed a collaborative recommender system that recommends university elective courses to students by exploiting courses that other similar students had taken. The system used an association rules mining algorithm to discover patterns between courses. The experiments were conducted with real datasets to assess the overall performance of the proposed approach.

In order to support students choose their subjects as per their capability, [18] used data mining and natural language processing techniques that helps in conversion of human-readable format to machine-readable format, both of which are vastly emerging fields to propose a collaborative recommendation system. In addition, [19] proposed a novel course recommendation system based collaborative filtering considering the case of repeating a course and students' grades in the course for each repetition. The authors experimented different Ordered Weighted Averaging operators which aggregates grades for each student's repeated courses to enhance the recommendation quality. [20] developed an optional course recommendation system based on score prediction. A novel cross-user-domain collaborative filtering algorithm is designed to accurately predict the score of the optional course for each student by using the course score distribution of the most similar senior students. After generating the predicted scores of all optional courses, the top t optional courses with the highest predicted scores without time conflict will be recommended to the student.

Based on the previous research results, we propose an approach of deep learning techniques using a MLP to build a student's performance prediction model. Beside course grades, additional factors such as entrance English testing grades, activity incentive grades, etc. also considered to improve the proposed prediction model.

3   Proposed Approach

General framework of the prediction models in the proposed approach is described in detail in Fig. 1. First, we collect real data sets at the Student Management System of a university, then data is pre-processed to remove noise, redundant attributes, etc. Traditional approaches usually used full dataset to build one prediction model (presented in the bottom of Fig. 1) to predict all of the students (denoted as **MLP**), however, we realize that this approach does not fit to the data since we should not use a "very good performance student" to predict a "poor performance student" or vise versa. In this work, we propose using four prediction models for four group of students which have similar performance based on their marks (as presented in the top of Fig. 1). The proposed approach is called **GroupMLP**.

3.1   Data Pre-processing

For evaluating the proposed model, we have collected real data at Can Tho University, Vietnam; however, the model can be used for other case studies such as other universities, schools, colleges as well. The collected data relates to students, courses, marks, and other information from the year 2007 to 2019 with 3,828,879 records, 4,699 courses (subjects), and 83,993 students. Data distributions are described in Fig. 2.

The considered data set is collected from Student Management system and pre-processed as described in Algorithm 1.

After carefully analyzing the data, we have selected the input attributes for learning model as described in Table 1. This selection based on pre-experimental results and previous analysis in predicting student performance [6,21].

3.2   Deep Learning Architecture

The proposed model is presented in Fig. 3 that was used in the work of [22]. The input attributes are selected from Table 1 and the output (prediction) of the model having eight classes which are the four-grading system (i.e., the output belongs to [0, 1, 1.5, 2, 2.5, 3, 3.5, 4]).

The proposed MLP architecture includes 6 layers. The first layer contains 18 input features while the last layer consists of 1 output exhibiting the predicted mark. The first four hidden layers contain 256 neurons, but they are followed by different activation functions. The first hidden and the fourth hidden layer use Rectified Linear Unit (ReLU) while other hidden layers are followed by Sigmoid

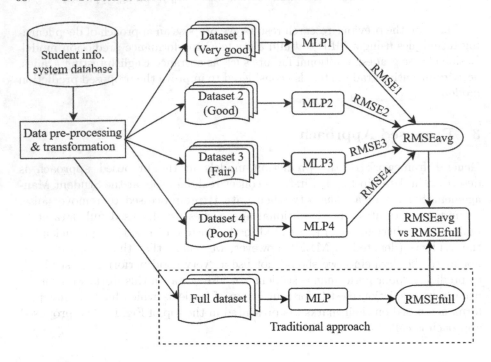

Fig. 1. General diagram of the proposed approach

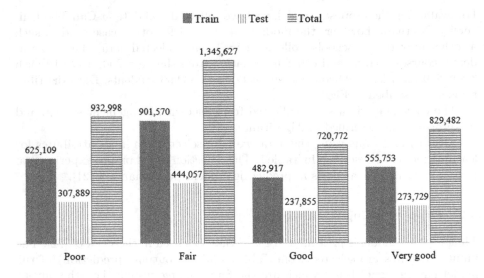

Fig. 2. Data set distribution by grading score

function. Before producing predicted score, we implement the fifth hidden layer containing 8 nodes using ReLU.

Algorithm 1. Algorithm for pre-processing and filtering features from student management system

---

Begin

Step 1: Redundant attributes such as Student Name, Course Name, Lecturer Name, etc. are eliminated from the original set of features collected from the Can Tho University's student management system.

Step 2: For each student, mark entries which did not contain a specific value (for example, null or empty values) or was exemption courses, etc. were removed.

Step 3: Transform features which is text type to numeric values.

End

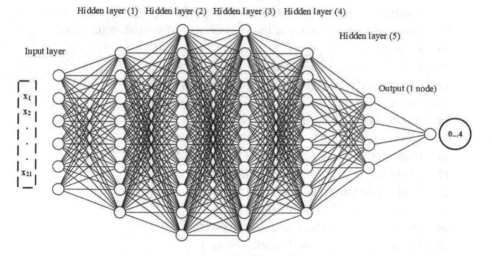

Fig. 3. The proposed MLP architecture [22].

The Sigmoid function [23] usually appears in the output layers of Deep learning architectures. It transforms the input values which lie in the domain $\mathbb{R}$ to outputs have the domain in [0, 1]. The Sigmoid function is also called "squashing" because this function squashes any input in the range of (-inf, -inf) to range of [0, 1]. When we shifted to gradient based learning, the Sigmoid was considered as a natural selection due to its smooth and differentiable approximation to a thresholding unit. The Sigmoid function is given by the formula:

$$Sigmoid(x) = \frac{1}{1 + e^{-x}} \tag{1}$$

where, x denotes data after being computed by the preceded neural layer.

Table 1. Input attributes

No.	Attribute name	Description
1	studentID	Student ID
2	Gender	Student gender
3	Hometown	Student hometown
4	EntranceMark1	Entrance mark for Course 1
5	EntranceMark2	Entrance mark for Course 2
6	EntranceMark3	Entrance mark for Course 3
		(The students take an entrance test with 3 courses)
7	FoS	Field of study
8	Faculty	Student belongs to a faculty (e.g. IT, Agriculture,..)
9	TrainingNumber	Course of the student, e.g. 2000–2004, 2002–2006,
10	Semester	
11	GPA	Current Grade Point Average
12	CGPA	Cumulative Grade Point Average
13	TotalCredits	Total of taken credits by student
14	AVGMark	Average of previous marks
15	LecturerID	The lecturer who taught the course
16	CourseID	ID of the course
17	CreditNo	Number of credit of the course
18	MarkEntryDate	The date when the mark is entered
19	BSC1	Basic English Course 1
20	BSC2	Basic English Course 2
21	BSC3	Basic English Course 3

Another activation namely, ReLU [24], is also implemented in our architecture. ReLU follows the formula:

$$f(x) = max(0, x) \tag{2}$$

where, x denotes data after being processed by the preceded neural layer.

ReLU is the most widely used activation function for deep learning architectures with state-of-the-art results to date. ReLU helps models to produce the better performance and generalization in deep learning compared to the Sigmoid and Tanh activation functions. It represents a nearly linear function, so this activation function preserves the properties of linear models that made them easy to optimize, with gradient-descent method [25, 26].

In order to reduce overfitting issues, dropout technique is deployed with a rate of 0.015. In addition, we also consider using Early Stopping with a patience epoch of 5. If the loss cannot be improved after 5 consecutive epochs, the learning will be stopped. Otherwise, the learning will be continued to run to 500 epochs. The network is implemented with Adam optimizer function, use a batch size of 255 and a default learning rate of 0.001.

4   Evaluation

To evaluate results of the proposed model, we describe some baselines and state-of-the-art for comparison and two popular metrics for measuring the performance. We have not applied cross validation since the data are in order, i.e., using the students' marks of previous semesters to predict the marks of current semester.

4.1   Baseline Methods

In this work, to compare with other methods, we have used two baselines which are User Average and Item Average. Furthermore, we also compared with Collaborative Filtering methods since previous works [5,27] showed that using Collaborative Filtering such as state-of-the-art Matrix Factorization [28] provided very good results in predicting student performance.

Let denote u as the student, i as the course, and r as the mark of the student on that course. The User Average method, which can be known as Student Average in this work, generates prediction mark ($\hat{r}_{ui}$) for student u on course i by using formula 3.

$$\hat{r}_{ui} = \frac{\sum_{(u',i,r) \in \mathcal{D}^{train}|u'=u} r}{|\{(u',i,r) \in \mathcal{D}^{train}|u' = u\}|} \tag{3}$$

The Item Average is Course Average in this work, which predicts the mark for the student u on course i by using formula 4.

$$\hat{r}_{ui} = \frac{\sum_{(u,i',r) \in \mathcal{D}^{train}|i'=i} r}{|\{(u,i',r) \in \mathcal{D}^{train}|i' = i\}|} \tag{4}$$

Matrix Factorization is a well-known method in recommender systems, it decomposes a matrix X (each row of X is a user/student, each column is an item/course, and each element is a mark for the student on that course, respectively) to two small matrices W and H such that we can reconstruct X from these two matrices

$$X \approx WH^T$$

where $W \in \mathbb{R}^{|U| \times K}$; $H \in \mathbb{R}^{|I| \times K}$; K is number of latent factors, $K << |U|, K << |I|$. The latent factors W and H can be obtained from optimizing the function:

$$\mathcal{O}^{MF} = \sum_{(u,i) \in \mathcal{D}^{train}} \left(r_{ui} - \sum_{k=1}^{K} w_{uk} h_{ik} \right)^2 + \lambda \cdot (||W||_F^2 + ||H||_F^2)$$

$\lambda \in (0..1)$ is a regularization and $|| \cdot ||_F$ is the Frobenius norm.

One benefit of the Matrix Factorization approach is its flexibility in dealing with various data aspects. However, the variation in the rating values are due to effects associated with either users or items, known as biases. Thus, researchers extended the previous work as Biased Matrix Factorization.

Biased matrix factorization [31], an improvement of MF, models the characteristics of each user and each item and the global tendency that are independent of user-item interactions.

At that time, the optimizing the function described as follows:

$$\mathcal{O}^{BMF} = \sum_{(u,i) \in \mathcal{D}^{train}} \left(r_{ui} - \mu - b_u - b_i - \sum_{k=1}^{K} w_{uk} h_{ik} \right)^2 + \lambda \cdot (||W||_F^2 + ||H||_F^2)$$

where:

- μ is the global average (average performance of all students and tasks in $\mathcal{D}^{train}$) as shown in Eq. 5.
- b_u (exhibited in Eq. 6) is student bias (average performance of student u deviated from the global average).
- b_i (Eq. 7) is mark bias (average performance on mark i deviated from the global average).

$$\mu = \frac{\sum_{(u,i,r \in D^{train})} r}{|D^{train}|} \tag{5}$$

$$b_u = \frac{\sum_{(u',i,r \in D^{train})|u'=u|} (r - \mu)}{|\{(u',i,r \in D^{train})|u' = u|\}|} \tag{6}$$

$$b_i = \frac{\sum_{(u,i',r \in D^{train})|i'=i|} (r - \mu)}{|\{(u,i',r \in D^{train})|i' = i|\}|} \tag{7}$$

Details of these methods are described in [5, 27–31].

4.2   Evaluation Metrics

The root mean squared error (RMSE) and mean absolute error (MAE) are used to evaluate the models. They are calculated by Eqs. (8) and (9), respectively.

$$\sqrt{\frac{1}{n} \sum_{i=1}^{n} (y_i - \hat{y}_i)^2} \tag{8}$$

$$\frac{1}{n} \sum_{i=1}^{n} |y_i - \hat{y}_i| \tag{9}$$

where, y_i is the true value, and $\hat{y}_i$ is the predicted value.

4.3   Experimental Results

Experimental results of MAE and RMSE are presented in Fig. 4. The GroupMLP presents for using four different models for four groups of student performances and the MLP means using one model to predict the result of all the students, as mentioned in Fig. 1. Clearly, by using different prediction models for different student performances, the results are significantly improved.

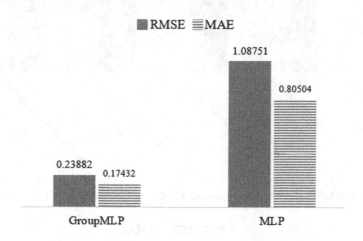

Fig. 4. RMSE and MAE comparisons between GroupMLP and MLP

Figure 5 presents the comparison results between the proposed GroupMLP and other baselines in Recommender Systems. This result shows that the GroupMLP works better than other baselines, however, using train (67%)/test(33%) split by time, the recommender system techniques may suffer from the "cold-start problem", i.e., new-users and new-items may happen in the test set.

Figure 6 presents the results for each model in the group (as presented in Fig. 1). The results show lower errors where levels of Very Good and Good exhibit promising performance. However, with lower levels of marks such as Fair and Poor reveals high errors both in MAE and RMSE in the prediction.

Moreover, while analyzing the results, we obtain that the English skill of the students is very important attribute. For example, without using English marks (the $BSC1$, $BSC2$, $BSC3$ in Table 1) the MAE of the MLP model is 0.24564, while using these attributes with english courses, the MAE is dropped to 0.23882 as shown in Table 2. This result implies that for the students having better English, they can read learning resources (mostly in English) better.

Deep learning approach may take more times for training the models, however, this is not a problem since models are trained every one or two times in the semester when the marks are changed in mid-term and final examination.

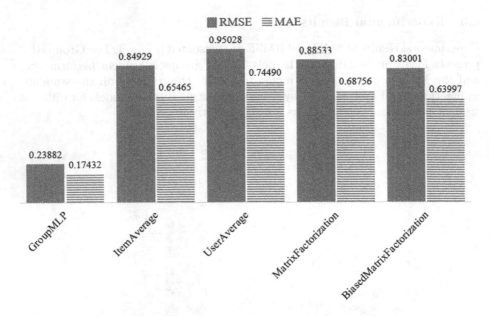

Fig. 5. RMSE and MAE comparisons between GroupMLP and baselines

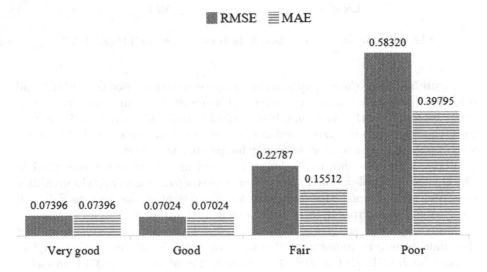

Fig. 6. Performance comparison with mark levels in MAE and RMSE

Table 2. Feature analysis on English skill

	MAE	RMSE
Without using English marks	0.24564	0.18064
Using English marks	**0.23882**	**0.17432**

4.4 Model for Early Warning and Course Recommendation

After evaluating the model, we have attempted to apply the proposed method for the real case study as in Fig. 7. Given the student information (or a list of students) and the course information as described in Table 1, the model can generate prediction results for the student on that course. We can use the result in two cases:

- **Case 1**: If the prediction result is less than 1.0 (or other selected threshold in the four-grading system, from 0 to 4), that would be the warning case.
- **Case 2**: If the prediction result is more than 3.25 (or other selected threshold) for the elective/selection course, that would be the recommendation course for the student to select.

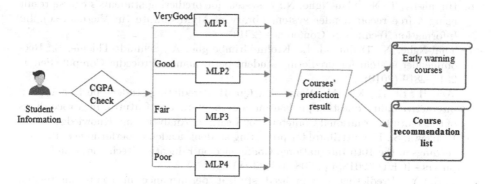

Fig. 7. The proposed early warning and course recommendation model for students

5 Conclusion

In this study, we proposed a method to predict student performance using deep learning techniques for prediction tasks on the data collected from a Vietnamese multidisciplinary university's information system. We analyze and propose some techniques for data pre-processing before fetching them into a MLP to do prediction tasks. The proposed method provides good prediction results and is expected to apply in practical cases. Using these results, we can help the educational managers or the academic advisors and the students to know early warning results so that the students can have better plan for studying. Moreover, evaluating on various training courses to help the managers to propose appropriate policies.

We continue to perform experiments on other published data sets and to change the model settings for better performance. Further research should investigate more on groups based on student performance to support better students' course selection and enhance the prediction tasks performance.

References

1. Mat, U., Buniyamin, N., Arsad, P., Kassim, R.: An overview of using academic analytics to predict and improve students' achievement: a proposed proactive intelligent intervention. In: 2013 IEEE 5th Conference on Engineering Education (ICEED) (2013)
2. Shahiri, A., Husain, W., Rashid, N.: A review on predicting student's performance using data mining techniques. Procedia Comput. Sci. **72**, 414–422 (2015)
3. Guo, B., Zhang, R., Xu, G., Shi, C., Yang, L.: Predicting students performance in educational data mining. In: 2015 International Symposium on Educational Technology (ISET) (2015)
4. LeCun, Y., Bengio, Y., Hinton, G.: Deep learning. Nature **521**, 436–444 (2015). https://doi.org/10.1038/nature14539
5. Thai-Nghe, N., Horvath, T. and Schmidt-Thieme, L.: Factorization models for forecasting student performance. In: Educational Data Mining (2011)
6. Huynh-Ly, T.-N., Thai-Nghe, N.: A system for predicting students's course result using a free recommender system library of MyMediaLite (in Vietnamese). In: Information Technology Conference (2013)
7. Thai-Nghe, N., Drumond, L., Krohn-Grimberghe, A., Schmidt-Thieme, L.: Recommender system for predicting student performance. Procedia Comput. Sci. **1**, 2811–2819 (2010)
8. Wei, H., Li, H., Xia, M., Wang, Y., Qu, H.: Predicting student performance in interactive online question pools using mouse interaction features. In: Proceedings of the Tenth International Conference on Learning Analytics and Knowledge (2020)
9. Hirokawa, S.: Key attribute for predicting student academic performance. In: Proceedings of the 10th International Conference on Education Technology and Computers - ICETC 2018, pp. 308–313 (2018)
10. Park, Y.: Predicting personalized student performance in computing-related majors via collaborative filtering. In: Proceedings of the 19th Annual SIG Conference on Information Technology Education (2018)
11. Buenaño-Fernández, D., Gil, D., Luján-Mora, S.: Application of machine learning in predicting performance for computer engineering students: a case study. Sustainability **11**, 2833 (2019)
12. Jembere, E., Rawatlal, R., Pillay, A.: Matrix factorisation for predicting student performance. In: 2017 7th World Engineering Education Forum (WEEF) (2017)
13. Duran-Dominguez, A., Gomez-Pulido, J., Rodriguez-Lozano, D., Pajuelo-Holguera, F.: Selecting latent factors when predicting student performance in online campus by using recommender systems. In: 2018 13th Iberian Conference on Information Systems and Technologies (CISTI) (2018)
14. Lian, D.-F., Liu, Q.: Jointly recommending library books and predicting academic performance: a mutual reinforcement perspective. J. Comput. Sci. Technol. **33**(4), 654–667 (2018). https://doi.org/10.1007/s11390-018-1847-y
15. Huang, L., Wang, C., Chao, H., Lai, J., Yu, P.: A score prediction approach for optional course recommendation via cross-user-domain collaborative filtering. IEEE Access **7**, 19550–19563 (2019)
16. Dien, T.T., Sang, L.H., Thanh-Hai, N., Thai-Nghe, N.: Deep learning with data transformation and factor analysis for student performance prediction. Int. J. Adv. Comput. Sci. Appl. **11**(8), 711–721 (2020)
17. Al-Badarenah, A., Alsakran, J.: An automated recommender system for course selection. Int. J. Adv. Comput. Sci. Appl. **7**, 3 (2016)

18. Naren, J., Banu, M.Z., Lohavani, S.: Recommendation system for students' course selection. In: Somani, A.K., Shekhawat, R.S., Mundra, A., Srivastava, S., Verma, V.K. (eds.) Smart Systems and IoT: Innovations in Computing. SIST, vol. 141, pp. 825–834. Springer, Singapore (2020). https://doi.org/10.1007/978-981-13-8406-6_77

19. Bozyigit, A. et al.: Collaborative filtering based course recommender using OWA operators. In: 2018 International Symposium on Computers in Education (SIIE) (2018)

20. Huang, L., et al.: A score prediction approach for optional course recommendation via cross-user-domain collaborative filtering. IEEE Access 7, 19550–19563 (2019)

21. Thai-Nghe, N., Janecek, P., Haddawy, P.: A comparative analysis of techniques for predicting academic performance. In: 2007 37th Annual Frontiers in Education Conference - Global Engineering: Knowledge Without Borders, Opportunities Without Passports (2007)

22. Sang, L.H., Dien, T.T., Thai-Nghe, N., Thanh-Hai, N.: Predicting student's performance through deep learning using a multi-layer perceptron (in Vietnamses). Can Tho Univ. J. Sci. 56(3), 20–28 (2020)

23. Nwankpa, C., Ijomah, W., Gachagan, A., Marshall, S.: Activation functions: comparison of trends in practice and research for deep learning. ArXiv:1811.03378 (2018)

24. Nair, V., Hinton, G.E.: Rectified linear units improve restricted Boltzmann machines. In: ICML (2010)

25. Zeiler, M., et al.: On rectified linear units for speech processing. In: 2013 IEEE International Conference on Acoustics, Speech and Signal Processing, pp. 3517–3521 (2013)

26. Dahl, G., Sainath, T., Hinton, G.E.: Improving deep neural networks for LVCSR using rectified linear units and dropout. In: 2013 IEEE International Conference on Acoustics, Speech and Signal Processing, pp. 8609–8613 (2013)

27. Iqbal, Z., Qadir, J., Mian, A., Kamiran, F.: Machine learning based student grade prediction: a case study. ArXiv:1708.08744 (2017)

28. Khanal, S.S., Prasad, P.W.C., Alsadoon, A., Maag, A.: A systematic review: machine learning based recommendation systems for e-learning. Educ. Inf. Technol. 25(4), 2635–2664 (2019). https://doi.org/10.1007/s10639-019-10063-9

29. Thai-Nghe, N., Schmidt-Thieme, L.: Factorization forecasting approach for user modeling. Journal of Computer Science and Cybernetics. 31(2), 133–148 (2015)

30. Koren, Y., Bell, R., Volinsky, C.: Matrix factorization techniques for recommender systems. Computer 42, 30–37 (2009)

31. Koren, Y., Bell, R.: Advances in collaborative filtering. In: Ricci, F., Rokach, L., Shapira, B., Kantor, P.B. (eds.) Recommender Systems Handbook, pp. 145–186. Springer, Boston, MA (2011). https://doi.org/10.1007/978-0-387-85820-3_5

Py_ape: Text Data Acquiring, Extracting, Cleaning and Schema Matching in Python

Bich-Ngan T. Nguyen[1](✉), Phuong N. H. Phạm[1], Vu Thanh Nguyen[1](✉),
Phan Quoc Viet[1], Le Dinh Tuan[2], and Vaclav Snasel[3]

[1] Ho Chi Minh City University of Food Industry, Ho Chi Minh City, Vietnam
{nganntb,phuongpnh,nguyenvt}@hufi.edu.vn, viet20304@gmail.com
[2] Long an University of Economics and Industry, Tân an, Vietnam
le.tuan@daihoclongan.edu.vn
[3] VSB-Technical University of Ostrava, Ostrava, Czech Republic
vaclav.snasel@vsb.cz

Abstract. Py_ape is a package in Python that integrates a number of string and text processing algorithms for collecting, extracting, and cleaning text data from websites, creating frames for text corpora, and matching entities, matching two schemas, mapping and merging two schemas. The functions of Py_ape help the user step-by-step perform data integration and data preparation, based on some popular Python libraries. Especially in the entity matching function of the schema matching and merging phase, we used the Hamming distance algorithm to identify similar string pairs, and the longest common substring similarity algorithm to map data between the columns of schemas. These algorithms help to increase the accuracy of the schema matching process. In addition, in the article, we present experimental results using Py_ape to scrape, clean, match, and merge two sets of data related to aviation crashes, taken from different sources of Kaggle and Wikipedia. The result of the experiment will be evaluated in detail in the rest of the paper.

Keywords: Text data preparation · Text data integration · Scraping data · Cleaning data · Schema matching · Entity matching

1 Introduction

Nowadays, most of the machine learning problems require dataset, especially the clean and useful dataset. Data is crucial in training, experimentation, analysis, evaluation, or statistics. One of the challenges that may be faced by this problem is to collect and build a clean and useful data set for the requirement of problem [3]. The industry and academia face to long-standing issues, that is data preparation and integration. Nowadays, there are many data sources, such as websites, social networking communities, data of e-commerce sites, big data systems [4, 6],… but there is one difficulty that we have to face is finding support tools for this vital data preparation and integration need, according to AnHai Doan et al. [2], the underlying architecture of a general data integration system.

T. K. Dang et al. (Eds.): FDSE 2020, CCIS 1306, pp. 78–89, 2020.
https://doi.org/10.1007/978-981-33-4370-2_6

Data sources can be tuples, XML, or any store that contains structured data [3]. The wrappers or loaders request and parse data from the sources. The mediated schema or central data warehouse abstracts all source data, and the user poses queries over this. Between the sources and the mediated schema, source descriptions and their associated schema mappings, another case a set of transformations, are used to convert the data from the source schemas and values into the global representation.

We propose a tool that supports end-to-end to collect structured, unstructured text data from sources on the website, then do the retrieval, clean up processing and build into structured data. It is possible to match entities, match two schemas and merge them into a clean dataset containing useful data. We built Py_ape[1], which includes supportive functions such as: scraping web, removing HTML tags, normalizing text data, counting and deleting duplicate records, mapping data, matching entities, and merging data sources, etc.

To the best of our knowledge, BigGorilla[2] is currently an open-source ecosystem for data preparation and integration and is currently supported in Python [1, 7]. However, it provides discrete library packages that perform each task, such as information extraction, schema matching, schema matching and entity matching [8, 9]. In this paper, we aim to build general functions for the user to step by step in order of collecting, extracting, cleaning, building dataset, matching, and merging data.

The rest of this paper is organized as follows. Section 2 presents related works. Section 3 presents the Py_ape package. Section 4 presents the model of data collection and integration using the Py_ape, and the similar string algorithm in the entity matching phase. Section 5 presents datasets, experiments, and results. Finally, we conclude the paper in Sect. 6.

2 Related Works

In the data analysis research community, Scikit-learn (Sklearn) is a familiar tool for this research work for almost a decade. This is a library for machine learning algorithms written in the Python language. It provides a set of tools for processing machine learning and statistical modeling problems including classification, regression, clustering, and dimensionality reduction [17].

In recent years, BigGorilla, the ecosystem of open-source libraries that supports the collection, preparation, and processing of text data, has been created by Chen Chen, AnHai Doan et al. [1]. BigGorilla is a community of libraries, a place to introduce, share and encourage people to contribute projects related to each different stage in the collection and processing of data [1]. Some typical libraries are as follows: (1) To acquire data from other sources or extract structured data from text, there are some packages, such as: Scrapy[3], Usagi[4], pandas[5], Koko[6], etc.; (2) To identify when two entities are the same

---

[1] https://pypi.org/project/py-ape.

[2] https://www.biggorilla.org.

[3] https://scrapy.org/.

[4] https://github.com/biggorilla-gh/usagi.

[5] http://pandas.pydata.org/.

[6] https://github.com/biggorilla-gh/koko.

entity, there are some packages, such as: pydeduple[7], febrl[8], Magellan[9], etc.; (3) To match two schemas, there are some packages, such as: schema-matching[10], wit[11]; (4) To contain additional data preparation tools, there are some packages, such as: Apache Airflow[12] and Luigi[13]. The Fig. 1 displays the BigGogrilla components and their functions [24].

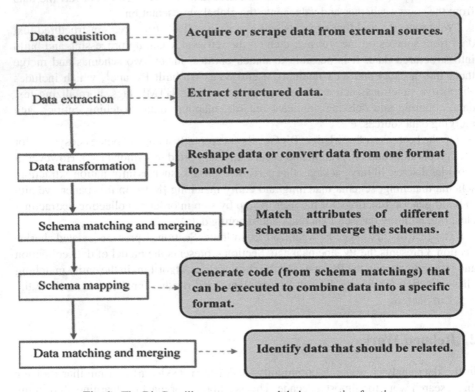

Fig. 1. The BigGogrilla components and their respective functions

Beside there is an important tool at the disposal of Data Scientists and Analysts working in Python today, that is the Pandas package. The powerful machine learning and glamorous visualization tools may get all the attention, but Pandas is the backbone of most data projects. Pandas is built on top of the NumPy[14] package, meaning a lot of the structure of NumPy is used or replicated in Pandas. Data in pandas is often used to

---

[7] https://github.com/gpoulter/pydedupe.

[8] https://sourceforge.net/projects/febrl/.

[9] https://sites.google.com/site/anhaidgroup/projects/magellan.

[10] https://github.com/davidfoerster/schema-matching.

[11] https://github.com/bkj/wit.

[12] https://airflow.apache.org/.

[13] https://github.com/spotify/luigi.

[14] https://numpy.org/.

feed statistical analysis in SciPy[15], plotting functions from Matplotlib[16], and machine learning algorithms in Scikit-learn.

The tools above have become very popular and useful for data scientists. However, each of their library packages performs specific functions, can executes on many types of data, and requires users to search and install multiple packages to meet their needs. Our Py_ape package supports a step-to-step process of collecting, cleaning, and matching text data. In the building process the Py_ape, we based on the basic Python libraries, such as: pandas, Numpy, CSV[17], BeautifulSoup[18]. However, we have built string handler functions to clean up raw data, convert to structured data, and match strings in matching entities and schemas.

3 Py_ape Package

The Py_ape package is the result that our team has aggregated, built, and is supported in Python. It contains functions that help to collect, mine, and aggregate textual data from the web, or structured dataset. Up to this point, the Py_ape package consists of six main processing groups, such as: collecting text data from resources and preprocessing, normalizing data, converting data into structured data, removing redundant data sets, and mapping data. They include methods that perform the core functions as follows: searches HTML tags of the data was scraped from the web, deletes the HTML tags in the text in order to gain the necessary text data, normalize the text data, join data of tables, scan and remove duplicate records, evaluate similarity between multiple tables, calculates the similarity of the strings to match entities, import and export data from CSV file, mapping data, processing raw data, etc.

To use the Py_ape package, users can install as python packages, as in pip with the command: "pip install Py_ape"After installing the library successfully, users need to perform a simple operation which is to add the command line: "import Py_ape". Currently, the Py_ape library is only compatible with Python versions 2.7 and above.

4 Proposed Method

4.1 Implementation Model

In this section, we cover the process of scraping, retrieving, cleaning, and building frame data set from text scraping data of a web page using the Py_ape.

---

[15] https://www.scipy.org/.

[16] https://matplotlib.org/.

[17] https://docs.python.org/3/library/csv.html.

[18] https://pypi.org/project/beautifulsoup4/.

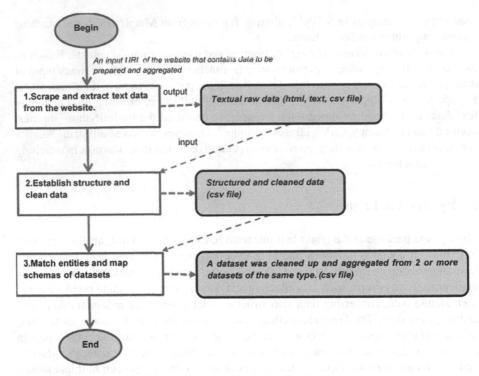

Fig. 2. The execution is based on Py_ape

As in Fig. 2, the Py_ape which we have been build, that supports the implementation of text data preparation and integration includes three main steps as follows:

- **Step 1:** From an input URL of the website that contains data to be prepared and aggregated, we scrape and extract text data from this website to create a textual raw data (called output1). The output1 can be a html, txt, json or csv file.

  There is a note to users at this step, which is the difference in content structure of different websites. Therefore, for each web page, the user needs to define the structure before scraping and extracting the data. The Py_ape provides some of functions to find and remove html tags, find, and collect matching data according to the regex specified by the user.

- **Step 2:** After we received the output1, we proceed to determine the structure and information in it, remove redundant data, define a new table structure, and extract data to put into the table. Before finishing this step, we have deleted duplicates, deleted columns containing redundant information. The Py_ape provides some of functions to support in the above operations.

- **Step 3:** If we have multiple datasets of the same type, we can match the entities and schemas to get a data set that is the intersection of the originals. The result of this intersection process of these tables is similar to the full outer join. Naturally, then you must find and delete the duplication, delete the redundant attributes to get the result that a table has been cleaned and it contains lots of useful information that users want. Specifically, this step should be done in the following order:

- To define the properties as the primary key of each table. This step is done manually by the user.
- To identify pairs of attributes in each table that contain the same entity information. Of course, the primary key must also belong to these attributes, on the contrary, this means that these 2 data frames do not contain data of the same type.
- To find records to perform entity matching of the above table. Specifically, we compare the value of the key attribute of the records in data frames. If they have a high similarity, they belong to one entity.

In order to determine the similarity of strings, Wael H. Gomaa and Aly A. Fahmy had a survey of Text Similarity Approaches. This survey displayed the existing works on text similarity through partitioning them into three approaches, which includes: String-based, Corpus-based, and Knowledge-based similarities [22].

Because we needed to compute similarity between values in columns of schemas, we interested string-based measures. String-like measures work on chain and character composition. String metric is a measure of the similarity or dissimilarity (distance) between two text strings to match or compare an approximate string. There are many algorithms which is well known and widely used [22, 23], such as: Damerau Levenshtein, Longest Common SubString, Hamming distance, Levenshtein distance, Jaro-Winkler, Jaccard index, Sorensen-Dice, etc. Each algorithm has features that suit the specific needs of each problem. In our entity matching problem, because the values in the columns of the schema belong to the same entity, they must be of high similarity or the longest generic substring also takes up a high percentage in the series. Therefore, in the Py_ape, we chose the Hamming distance algorithm [20] and the Longest common substring algorithm [21] to find similar strings. These algorithms will be presented in Sect. 4.2.

4.2 The Similar String Algorithm in the Matching Entity

Schema matching is a technique in data processing. This technique helps to find the association between the parts (attributes or relationships) of the two schemas. Schema matching has been recognized as one of the basic steps in the data integration process [18], so the results of schema matching will have a huge effect.

In schema matching, there is one of the stages, that is entity matching. This step helps to find and match the values of the attributes that have been determined to be equivalent in the above two schemas. If the records in the two schemas have similarities in the same properties as much, it is considered the same entity.

The Py_ape supports entity matching for attributes that contain string values. There are many algorithms that support the same sequence problem [19]. After we studied and analyzed, the data characteristics of the columns identified in the schemas, which belong to two cases: the first case, if they contain a value of one word, these values differ by only a few characters, otherwise if they contain a string value, they will have a common substring.

To solve the problem in the first case, we choose the Hamming distance algorithm[19]. It belongs to the Edit distance-based algorithms. This distance is computed by overlaying one string over another and finding the places where the strings vary. The logic is to find the total number of places one string is different from the other. The result must be less than or equal to 2 to be able to accept the same. We chose this ratio because we were based on Alberto Apostolico et al.'s Hamming distance algorithm similarity analysis [20].

We showcase an example as follows:

```
Hamming_similarity('flight', 'flight#') >> 1
Hamming_similarity('airline', 'operator') >> 8
```

Algorithm 1: Hamming Distance

Input: word and matching word.
Output: count (the total number of places one string is different from the other)
1: count = 0
2: i = 0
3: **if** word.Length == matching_word.Length **then**
4:     **while** i <= word.Length
5:         **if** word.toLowerCase ()[i] != matching_word.toLowerCase ()[i] **then**
6:                     count = count +1
7:         **end if**
8:         i = i + 1
9:     **end while**
10:    **return** count
11: **end if**
12: **return** 0

To solve the other, we find the longest common substring to identify pairs of similar values. The longest common substring must occupy 80% of the length of the original string, then we can define them as similar. This ratio is chosen because we use the results of the research of Gusfield and Dan [21].

---

[19] https://itnext.io/string-similarity-the-basic-know-your-algorithms-guide-3de3d7346227.

Algorithm 2: The longest common substring

Input: String X and String Y.
Output: Z (the longest common substring of X and Y)
1: maxlen = 0   // *stores the max length of Z*
2: endingIndex = X.Length   // *store the ending index of Z in X*
3: int lookup [X.Length + 1][y.Length + 1]
4: initialize all cells of lookup table to 0
5: **for** i =1 **to** m **do**
6:     **for** j =1 **to** n **do**
7:         **if** X[i-1] == Y[j-1] **then**
8:             lookup[i][j] = lookup[i-1][j-1]+1
9:             **if**   lookup[i][j] > maxlen **then**
10:                 maxlen = lookup[i][j];
11:                 endingIndex = i
12:             **end if**
13:         **end if**
14:     **end for**
15: **end for**
16: Z = X.subString (endingIndex – maxlen, maxlen)
17: **return** Z

---

5 Experiment

In this section, we introduce two data sources that we experiment with using Py_ape, describe in detail the experimental process and evaluate the results obtained.

5.1 Dataset

The first dataset is a list of the accidents and incidents involving commercial aircraft extracted from Wikipedia[20], which includes notable events that have a corresponding Wikipedia[21] article. Entries in this list contain passenger or cargo aircraft that are operating commercially and meet this list's size criteria—passenger aircraft with a seating capacity of at least 10 passengers or commercial cargo aircraft of at least: 20,000 lb (ca. 9,072 kg). The list is grouped by the year in which the accident or incident occurred, from 1919 to the present. This data is aggregated from the Aircraft Crash Record Office[22], AirDisaster.com Accident Database[23], Jet Airliner Crash Data Evaluation Center[24], and PlaneCrashInfo.com[25] systems.

---

[20] https://www.wikipedia.org.
[21] https://en.wikipedia.org/wiki/List_of_accidents_and_incidents_involving_commercial_aircraft.
[22] http://www.baaa-acro.com.
[23] http://www.airdisaster.com/cgi-bin/database.cgi.
[24] https://www.jacdec.de.
[25] http://www.planecrashinfo.com.

The second dataset is taken from Kaggle[26]—Kaggle is the world's largest data science community with powerful tools and resources to help you achieve your data science goals. This is "Air Passengers, Departures and Crashes Data" dataset, that contains civil and commercial aviation accidents of scheduled and non-scheduled passenger airliners worldwide[27], from Sep 1908 to Mar 2020. This file includes 4983 rows and 17 columns. Each line contains information for an accident including Date, Time, Location, Operator, Flight#, Route, AC Type, Registration, cn/ln, Total Aboard, Passengers, Aboard, Crew Aboard, Total Fatalities, Passengers Fatalities, Crew Fatalities, Ground, Summary.

Our experimental purpose is scraping information about plane crashes on Wikipedia, then extracting and cleaning them up and forming a data frame containing their information. The next, to perform entity matching and schema mapping with the second dataset. The result we get a dataset contains matching sets between the first two datasets, which contains more useful information. The statistical results will be presented in the next section.

5.2 Implementation Process

After scraping and extracting text data in step 1 at the URL[28] of "List of accidents and incidents involving commercial aircraft" on Wikipedia (as of August 10, 2020), we obtained a raw data file containing the corresponding 1257 lines of information 1257 crashes. Each line contains the information of the month, day, year of the accident and description as shown in Fig. 3.

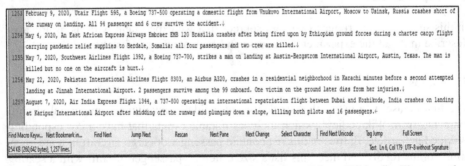

Fig. 3. The structure of a crash after being scraped and cleaned from Wikipedia. These are the last 5 records of the file.

The text data are not structured. To facilitate further data processing, it would be better if we convert text into a structured data, such as a data frame. This work is done in step 2. Converting text to a structured data frame, that contains information in the order of columns: {'Date', 'Airline', 'Flight', 'Location', 'Text'}. The Fig. 3 illustrates

---

[26] https://www.kaggle.com.

[27] https://www.kaggle.com/imdevskp/air-passengers-and-departures-data-from-19702018.

[28] https://en.wikipedia.org/wiki/List_of_accidents_and_incidents_involving_commercial_airc raft.

the results of printing the first 5 lines of the structure when converted to a data frame. In step 2, the result is a table with 1257 rows and 5 columns.

In Fig. 4, we see that some of the records that have the value in Flight are NULL because there is no mention in the description data. In addition, in this data sheet, information about Operator, Route, AC Type, Registration, Total Aboard, Passengers Aboard, Crew Aboard, Total Fatalities, Passengers Fatalities,... mentioned but is challenging for us to handle in order to get this information from text. This is a problem in natural language processing. In this article, we follow the mapping schema and entity matching method of this dataset with another dataset (the 2nd dataset introduced in Sect. 5.1. Dataset) and talk about trip accident information. fly around the world, to map and merge them, to enrich the matching data set information between them. This is the work will be done in step 3.

	Date	Airline	Flight	Location	Text
0	July 21, 1919	the Illinois Trust and Savings Building		Chicago, Illinois	July 21, 1919, The Goodyear dirigible Wingfoot Air Express catches fire and crashes into the Ill...
1	15			Verona, Italy, Venice, Taliedo, Milan	August 2, 1919, A Caproni Ca.48 crashes at Verona, Italy, during a flight from Venice to Taliedo.
2	December 14, 1920	Golders Green		London	December 14, 1920, A Handley Page Transport Handley Page O/400 hits a tree and crashes at Golder...
3	April 7, 1922	CGEA		the Thieulloy-St. Picardie, France	April 7, 1922, In the first mid-air collision of airliners, a de Havilland DH.18A, G-EAWO, opera...
4	May 14, 1923	Goliath		Monsures, Somme, France	May 14, 1923, An Air Union Farman F.60 Goliath crashes near Monsures, Somme, France, due to the...
...	...	...	...	...	...
1252	February 9, 2020	Boeing	Flight 595	Moscow, Usinsk, Russia	February 9, 2020, Utair Flight 595, a Boeing 737-500 operating a domestic flight from Vnukovo In...
1253	May 4, 2020	An East African Express Airways Embraer		Berdale, Somalia	May 4, 2020, An East African Express Airways Embraer EMB 120 Brasilia crashes after being fired...
1254	May 7, 2020	Austin-Bergstrom International Airport	Flight 1392	Austin, Texas	May 7, 2020, Southwest Airlines Flight 1392, a Boeing 737-700, strikes a man on landing at Austi...
1255	May 22, 2020	Airbus	Flight 8303	Karachi	May 22, 2020, Pakistan International Airlines Flight 8303, an Airbus A320, crashes in a resident...
1256	August 7, 2020	Air India Express	Flight 1344	Dubai, Kozhikode, India	August 7, 2020, Air India Express Flight 1344, a 737-800 operating an international repatriation...

1257 rows × 5 columns

Fig. 4. The data frame of result in step 2.

When we performed the entity matching, perform a mapping between *['Airline', 'Flight']* of the first dataset with *['Operator', 'Flight #']* of dataset 2, we got 40 matching records.

The result of this dataset has only 40 records, because in the first dataset, extracted from Wikipedia which just only 717/1257 records contains the Flight value. Meanwhile, the second dataset (crashed.csv) has 1320/4983 records with the value Flight. Therefore, the actual number of matching sets of these 2 data sets may be larger, but because the lack of key information for matching leads to low match result. This issue will be our team's upcoming development direction to improve the functionality for this shortcoming.

6   Conclusion

We studied the data preparation and integration process, based on the BigGorilla library and built the Py_ape tool supported in Python, helping to build the process of gathering, retrieving, cleaning, schema mapping and merging data frames. This tool supports a step-by-step, step-by-step format. At the same time, we also give the experimental steps and evaluate its results. Although the lack of data of the datasets, the accuracy of the results is low. Our next interests are improving the processing of the records of the datasets to increase the correct rate of matching.

References

1. Chen, C., Golshan, B., Halevy, A., Tan, W.-C., Doan, A.H.: BigGorilla: an open-source ecosystem for data preparation and integration. Comput. Sci. IEEE Data Eng. Bull. (2018)
2. Doan, A., Halevy, A., Ives, Z.: Principles of Data Integration, 1st edn. Morgan Kaufmann (2012)
3. Golshan, B., Halevy, A.Y., Mihaila, G.A., Tan, W.: Data integration: after the teenage years. In: PODS (2017)
4. Miller, R.J.: The future of data integration. In: KDD, p. 3 (2017)
5. Pedregosa, F., et al.: Scikit-learn: machine learning in Python. J. Mach. Learn. Res. **12**, 2825–2830 (2011)
6. Doan, A., Halevy, A.Y.: Semantic integration research in the database community: a brief survey. AI Mag. **26**(1), 83–94 (2005)
7. Pessig, P.: Entity matching using Magellan - matching drug reference tables. In: CPCP Retreat (2017). http://cpcp.wisc.edu/resources/cpcp-2017-retreat-entity-matching
8. Mudgal, S., et al.: Deep learning for entity matching: a design space exploration. In: SIGMOD-18 (2018)
9. Konda, P., et al.: Magellan: toward building entity matching management systems. PVLDB **9**(12), 1197–1208 (2016)
10. Wang, S., Jiang, J.: A compare-aggregate model for matching text sequences. In: ICLR (2017)
11. Yu, M., et al.: String similarity search and join: a survey. Front. Comput. Sci. **10**(3), 399–417 (2016)
12. Bloor Research International: Self-Service Data Preparation and Cataloguing (2016). https://www.bloorresearch.com/research/self-service-data-preparation-cataloguing/. Accessed 14 May 2018
13. Heer, J., Hellerstein, J., Kandel, S.: Predictive interaction for data transformation. In: Proceedings of the Conference on Innovative Data Systems Research (CIDR) (2015)
14. Jin, Z., et al.: Foofah: transforming data by example. In: Proceedings of the 2017 ACM International Conference on Management of Data, pp. 683–698. ACM (2017)
15. Kopelowitz, T., Porat, E.: A simple algorithm for approximating the text-to-pattern hamming distance. In: 1st Symposium on Simplicity in Algorithms (SOSA 2018) (2018)
16. Ho, T., Oh, S., Kim, H.: New algorithms for fixed-length approximate string matching and approximate circular string matching under the Hamming distance. J. Supercomput. **74**, 1815–1834 (2018). https://doi.org/10.1007/s11227-017-2192-6
17. Pedregosa, F., et al.: Scikit-learn: machine learning in Python. JMLR **12**, 2825–2830 (2011)
18. Bernstein, P.A., Melnik, S.: Metadata management. In: Proceedings of the IEEE CS International Conference on Data Engineering. IEEE Computer Society (2004)
19. Mittal, S., Nag, S.: A survey of encoding techniques for reducing data-movement energy. J. Syst. Arch. **97**, 373–396 (2019)
20. Apostolico, A., et al.: Sequence similarity measures based on bounded hamming distance. Theoret. Comput. Sci. **638**, 76–90 (2016)
21. Gusfield, D.: Algorithms on Strings, Trees and Sequences: Computer Science and Computational Biology, pp. 125–128. Cambridge University Press, Cambridge (1999). ISBN 0-521-58519-8

22. Gomaa, W.H., Fahmy, A.A.: A survey of text similarity approaches. Int. J. Comput. Appl. (0975–8887). **68**(13) (2013)
23. Yu, M., Li, G., Deng, D., Feng, J.: String similarity search and join: a survey. Front. Comput. Sci. **10**(3), 399–417 (2015). https://doi.org/10.1007/s11704-015-5900-5
24. Recruit Holdings Co., Ltd.: Recruit's Artificial Intelligence Laboratory Releases BigGorilla: An Open-source Data Integration and Data Preparation Ecosystem (2019). https://recruit-holdings.com/news_data/release/2017/0630_7890.html

Security and Privacy Engineering

Improving ModSecurity WAF with Machine Learning Methods

Ngoc-Tin Tran[1,2], Van-Hoa Nguyen[2], Thanh Nguyen-Le[2], and Khuong Nguyen-An[1(✉)]

[1] University of Technology (HCMUT), VNU-HCM, Ho Chi Minh City, Vietnam
{1613575,nakhuong}@hcmut.edu.vn
[2] Verichains Lab, Ho Chi Minh City, Vietnam
{tintn,vanhoa,thanh}@verichains.io
https://verichains.io

Abstract. Web Application Firewall (WAF) is a security technology that helps mitigate and prevent common attacks in web applications. Designed as a barrier between the web server and the user (possibly an attacker), the WAF analyzes, detects, and early warns of possible attacks. However, the current techniques for detecting web application attacks are still mainly based on available attack signatures. This method has the advantage of being simple and easy to apply in most cases, a typical implementation of this method is ModSecurity (`ModSecurity`: open source web application firewall, https://modsecurity.org.) with ModSecurity CRS (`ModSecurity CRS`: a set of generic attack detection rules for use with ModSecurity, https://coreruleset.org.). The main weakness of this approach is that it is unable to detect new attack vectors and mistakenly detects a normal user as an attacker also. In response to these issues, the goal of this paper is to develop a WAF system based on ModSecurity with ModSecurity CRS, which focuses on reducing the false-positive rate of ModSecurity CRS based on machine learning methods. Specifically, this is a method that combines ModSecurity CRS and machine learning.

Keywords: Web Application Firewall · ModSecurity · Machine learning · Security

1 Introduction and Related Work

With the rapid development of technology accompanied by sophistication and diversity in the types of cyber-criminal attacks, web application security has a more and more important role today. In order to combat the risk of attacks as well as data theft, organizations, businesses, etc. need to pay attention and have a proper investment in the level of security in their products, especially in web applications. However, in order to build and maintain a team of security experts to continually perform risk assessments in all products, a business needs to have a relatively high financial investment. This may not be affordable sometimes,

© Springer Nature Singapore Pte Ltd. 2020
T. K. Dang et al. (Eds.): FDSE 2020, CCIS 1306, pp. 93–107, 2020.
https://doi.org/10.1007/978-981-33-4370-2_7

especially for small and medium businesses. There are two popular solutions today that can be applied separately or simultaneously for most cases.

Performing Security Testing. To ensure the system's safety before release, the web application should be performed vulnerability checking by third-party security companies or independent security experts in many bug bounty platforms.

Deploy a Defense System. In the course of operation, although security checks have already been performed, the remains of a few security vulnerabilities inside the application are surely inevitable. In addition, the process of patching new security bugs will take a long time to verify before being put into production. During this time, the web application can be completely exploited and compromised. To overcome this problem, WAF was deployed to temporarily fix existing security holes without interfering with the application source code. This is also our main research topic.

The main problem of WAF is detecting whether the input request is valid or not. For solving this problem, many research results have been published, in which two main approaches are rule-based and anomaly detection. Typical examples of the rule-based approach have been mentioned in [7] by Roger Meyer and Carlos Cid, wherein this study they have shown how to detect common attack vectors from OWASP Top 10 (2007) [11] through web server log file analysis. Next, Ryan Barnett published a paper [2] discussing how to use ModSecurity to *virtual patch* web applications, which clearly shows the usage of ModSecurity for applying in real cases. These rule-based approaches have the advantage of being easy to implement, but the downside of rule-based methods is that they have a high rate of false positives and cannot detect new attacks, typically zero-day attacks.

Several approaches based on anomaly detection using machine learning methods are also proposed. Specifically, Christopher Kruegel et al. mentioned an anomaly detection method based on the statistical properties of HTTP requests in [6]. This is an anomaly detection-based method, but this method only takes input from the access log, which mainly analyzes the request's URI. Thus, this method will omit some malicious requests, which may include attack vectors inside the request body (POST requests). Besides, Tammo Krueger et al. proposes a WAF system called TokDoc [1] that automatically replaces abnormal parts in the request to turn the malicious one into the normal one using various abnormally detection methods based on n-gram and Markov Chain models.

Some approaches based on neural network models have also been proposed as in [10,13], etc. Using neural network models, these WAF systems will have the ability to detect some new types of attacks that rule-based methods cannot. However, the more blocked attacks, the higher the false-positive rate will be, and the system availability will decrease. Moreover, the downside of using neural network models is that our WAF's behavior will become more unpredictable. In our opinion, a request should only be blocked if it contains a clear attack signature and not by its strangeness. So, we still prefer a rule-based method when approaching this kind of problem. Also, Vartouni et al. [12] proposes an exciting approach that combines a Stacked-AutoEncoder neural network (SAE) for feature extraction and an Isolation Forest model for anomaly detection. The approach that combines of ModSecurity and machine learning algorithms is not a new one either. Betarte et al. [3] proposes a method that combines a one-class classifier for anomaly detection and ModSecurity CRS when deciding the outcome. In this study, we approach this problem as a two-class classification problem with the goal of classifying the input request as normal or attack based on the labeled training dataset and the ruleset of ModSecurity CRS.

2   Background

ModSecurity is an open-source, cross-platform WAF engine developed by Spider-Labs at Trustwave. This engine provides a simple and powerful syntax, allows us to quickly write security rules to protect web applications from various types of attacks, perform real-time analysis on HTTP requests. With over 10,000 installations worldwide, ModSecurity is arguably the most used WAF right now[1]. Below is an example rule, written in ModSecurity rule syntax, which will block (**deny**) any request whose uri (**REQUEST_URI**) matches the regular expression **<script>** and return a 403 status code.

```
SecRule REQUEST_URI "@rx <script >" "t:lowercase ,log ,deny ,
    status :403"
```

In general, any ModSecurity rule syntax written with **SecRule** directive can be expressed as follows (there are many more directives in ModSecurity).

```
SecRule VARIABLES OPERATOR [TRANSFORMATIONS ,ACTIONS]
```

Four components in SecRule syntax are **VARIABLES**, **OPERATOR**, **ACTIONS**, and **TRANSFORMATIONS**. **VARIABLES** is a set of input variables extracted from the request where the rule is checked, which can be the request headers, URI, form inputs, etc. For each value in the rule's variables, a list of transformation functions in **TRANSFORMATIONS** will be applied for preprocessing before further checks. **OPERATOR** defines how the rule is checked, which can be regular expression matching, or simple substring matching, etc. The remaining component, **ACTIONS**, is a list of actions that ModSecurity will execute if this rule matches the input request; a valid action can be logging, blocking, setting the returned status code, etc. These things are just some basic syntax of ModSecurity to introduce how ModSecurity works briefly; more details can be found in ModSecurity Handbook [9].

Combined with ModSecurity CRS, a set of generic attack detection rules, ModSecurity can help prevent the majority of common attacks listed in [11]. The principle of ModSecurity CRS is quite simple; when a request is analyzed, each rule in CRS will generate a corresponding score for that request, also known

---

[1] https://github.com/SpiderLabs/ModSecurity/wiki.

as anomaly-score. When the total score of this request exceeds a pre-configured threshold, it will be blocked. The score of each rule is decided based on the Paranoia Level. In ModSecurity CRS, there are four Paranoia Levels with increasing security levels from low to high (1 to 4). A rule with a higher Paranoia Level will have a more strict checking condition, which can easily be triggered with the normal request. The higher the Paranoia Level increases, the more the number of rules will be checked; in some cases, the false-positive rate can reach to 40% as mentioned in [4], which makes ModSecurity CRS challenging to apply to web applications in practice. We can say that ModSecurity CRS is a set of rules with a relatively high false-positive rate. For that reason, in the next section, we will propose a method that uses two machine learning models, Decision Tree and Random Forest, to reduce the false-positive rate of the ModSecurity CRS.

3   Our Proposed Method

The reason for the false detection of a normal HTTP request into attack one mainly comes from some quite strict rules in ModSecurity CRS. For illustration, we will consider the rule with id 920272 in the ModSecurity CRS, which has content as follows.

```
SecRule  REQUEST_URI | REQUEST_HEADERS | ARGS | ARGS_NAMES |
    REQUEST_BODY    " @validateByteRange 32-36,38-126 " \
    "id:920272,\
    phase:2,\
    block,\
    t:none,t:urlDecodeUni,\
    msg:'Invalid character in request (outside of printable
chars below ascii 127)',\
    logdata:'%{MATCHED_VAR_NAME}=%{MATCHED_VAR}',\
    tag:'application-multi',\
    tag:'language-multi',\
    tag:'platform-multi',\
    tag:'attack-protocol',\
    tag:'OWASP_CRS',\
    tag:'OWASP_CRS/PROTOCOL_VIOLATION/EVASION',\
    tag:'paranoia-level/3',\
    ver:'OWASP_CRS/3.2.0',\
    severity:'CRITICAL',\
    setvar:'tx.anomaly_score_pl3=+%{tx.critical_anomaly_score
}'"
```

This rule will check the value of some fields in the HTTP request through ModSecurity variables such as uri (REQUEST_URI), headers (REQUEST_HEADERS), request inputs (ARGS), etc. If any of the checked values that contain characters whose ASCII value is not between 32 and 36 or 38 to 126, this rule will be triggered, meaning the chance of being suspected as an attack of this request will be higher. However, while observing the actual daily traffic, we realized this rule is triggered by many normal requests, which means that the false-positive rate of this rule is very high. Therefore, we think that ModSecurity CRS needs a more precise decision formula based on the triggered rules instead of the total score of each rule, which is pre-configured entirely manually. Assigning the abnormal score for each rule is not straightforward and inaccurate, so we should not do it manually, but let the machine learning models decide based on real data instead.

3.1 Data Preparation

At present, the most widely used dataset for this problem is HTTP CSIC 2010 [5]. However, during the initial experiment, we realized a few limitations of this dataset through a manual verification process as well as referencing the origin of the dataset.

- An anomaly request should not always be considered as an attack. There are many anomaly requests in the attack-label part of this dataset, which not really be attack requests and should have a normal-label; these wrong cases may produce a significant negative impact on the training results of the machine learning model.
- This dataset is entirely generated by an automation tool, and information is filled randomly. Therefore, the dataset is somewhat unrealistic and only suitable for research purposes.
- All generated HTTP request data belongs to a single e-commerce website. Therefore, this dataset is somewhat not generic, so trained machine learning models might not be appropriate for real cases since the characteristics of websites on the Internet are hugely diverse. For example, the HTTP request data of an e-commerce website will have completely different properties from social network websites. The diversity may come from user behavior, the technology used, or the type of website; if the training data is not generic enough, it will easily misunderstand the regular user's request into the attack.

In general, the input data of this problem is HTTP requests from the user, which can contain user sensitive data such as email, password, access token, etc. Therefore, having a free dataset generated from real websites available on the Internet is extremely difficult. If so, there is a high chance that the dataset is illegally published. Furthermore, data collected from actual operating websites will be completely unlabeled. Labeling HTTP requests as normal or attack will take much time; finding someone to label the dataset is also a difficult problem. It requires the labeler to have a certain level of knowledge about web application security. Therefore, this type of data will be much more challenging to handle than typical data such as images, voices, handwriting texts, etc. which most people are capable of labeling.

With the goal of building a new dataset for practical application, we have been setting up a proxy server and redirect all HTTP traffic in the local computer to the WAF system. Specifically, we have been redirected all of our daily web traffic to a previously configured WAF system. The goal is to use our own HTTP traffic to train the machine learning models, which can solve the problem of HTTP traffic belongs to only one website so that the generated data will be more generic and realistic than the original dataset, HTTP CSIC 2010.

In order to build a WAF system that can analyze, monitor HTTP requests, and store them in a log database for further use, we propose a system architecture, as shown in Fig. 1. According to the proposed system architecture, we divide the system into many small services, in which each service only does a specific task; the use of each service can be briefly described as follows.

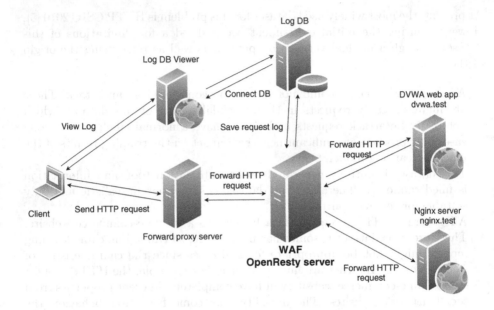

Fig. 1. Proposed system architecture

- OpenResty server with ModSecurity and CRS installed, all HTTP requests will be redirected to it for analyzing. This is the core component of the system, in which trained machine learning models will be integrated later.
- A server with DVWA[2] installed (dvwa.test), protected by the WAF server, which provides a testing environment for the WAF system.
- An empty Nginx server (nginx.test), used as a target for the data generation process.
- LogDB server with MongoDB[3] installed, this server is responsible for saving HTTP requests sent from the OpenResty server, which will be used to train the machine learning models.

---

[2] `Damn Vulnerable Web App (DVWA)`: http://www.dvwa.co.uk/.
[3] `MongoDB`: a document-based database, https://www.mongodb.com.

- LogDB viewer with Mongo Express[4] installed, this server provides a web-based user interface, making it easy to manage and manipulate the LogDB database.
- Forward proxy server, this server allows the client to redirect all HTTP traffic through the WAF server without the need to change local DNS config (via /etc/hosts file).

With the proposed system architecture above, we divide the data collection process into two steps as follows.

Generating Data with Normal-Label. At this step, we will first configure ModSecurity to be in the detection-only mode. In order to generate normal requests, we redirect all traffic from our browser to the WAF server through the proxy configuration. Next, we start browsing as many websites on the Internet as possible, like a typical user. Depending on daily web traffic, the number of recorded requests may be more or less. Currently, we have been capturing our web traffic data within five days and obtained a total of 182,103 normal HTTP requests on a total of 1,405 different websites (calculated according to the Host header in HTTP requests). The statistical result of 15 domains with the most number of requests in the dataset is shown in Table 1. In the next step, we will show the way we generate attack data.

Generating Data with Attack-Label. Currently, the simplest way to generate attack data is to use available open-source web application security tools such as SQLMap, WPScan, MetaSploit, etc. However, there are some notable characteristics and mechanisms of these tools. Most of these tools will conduct a scanning process to find some information about the target website before actually launching an attack. Therefore, among these attack requests, it is possible to mix quite a lot of normal requests, which will lead to mislabeling of request data. In order to use the above tools, first of all, it is necessary to have a particular mechanism to eliminate normal requests contained in it. After careful consideration, finally, the only tool we chose to generate attack data was FTW[5]. This tool was initially used for writing the unit test suite for ModSecurity CRS. Using this tool and the available attack test cases in the CRS test suite, we can quickly generate a large number of attack requests. Below is an example of a PHP Command Injection attack test case in ModSecurity CRS test suite.

```
...
tests:
- desc: PHP Injection Attack (933100) from old modsec
    regressions
  stages:
  - stage:
```

---

[4] **Mongo Express**: web-based MongoDB admin interface, https://github.com/mongo-express/mongo-express.

[5] **FTW**: a framework for testing WAFs, https://github.com/coreruleset/ftw.

```
input:
   dest_addr: nginx.test
   headers:
      Accept: text/xml,application/xml,application/xhtml+
xml,text/html;q=0.9,text/plain;q=0.8,image/png,*/*;q=0.5
      Accept-Charset: ISO-8859-1,utf-8;q=0.7,*;q=0.7
      Accept-Encoding: gzip,deflate
      Accept-Language: en-us,en;q=0.5
      Host: nginx.test
      Keep-Alive: '300'
      Proxy-Connection: keep-alive
      User-Agent: Mozilla/5.0 (Windows; U; Windows NT
5.1; en-US; rv
   method: GET
   port: 80
   uri: /?foo=<?exec('wget%20http://r57.biz/r57.txt%20-0
   version: HTTP/1.0
 output:
   response_contains: 403 Forbidden
test_title: 933100-1
...
```

With our method of automatic data generation, as mentioned above, the initial results that we achieved are relatively satisfactory. Currently, we have collected 182,103 normal requests on a total of 1,405 different websites. As for attack data, we can only generate attack requests on our own web apps with a limitation of attack tools. Tools that only generate purely attack requests without being mixed with the normal ones are relatively rare. Furthermore, it is entirely illegal to use automatic tools to attack websites on the Internet arbitrarily without the owner's permission. Due to the above limitations, the number of attack requests in our dataset will be pretty much less than normal requests, only about 2,313 attack requests. Details of the generated dataset can be found in Table 2.

From the current datasets that we have, for normal data, we will use our generated data completely; the normal-labeled part of the HTTP CSIC 2010 dataset will not be used. Due to the lack of attack data, we will combine the attack dataset we generated with the attack-label part of the HTTP CSIC 2010 dataset. In short, the dataset used to train the models is summarized in Table 3.

Due to the privacy and sensitive nature of recorded data (which may contain access tokens, cookies, private information, login passwords, etc.), we will show our data generation method only but not the collected dataset. However, using our proposed data generation method, the readers can easily generate labeled data supporting their future research on this topic.

Table 1. List of 15 domains with the most number of requests

Host name	Number of requests
mail.google.com	28,644
www.youtube.com	22,776
www.google.com	15,535
static.xx.fbcdn.net	10,072
www.messenger.com	9,115
play.google.com	4,947
beacons.gcp.gvt2.com	4,886
github.com	4,224
github.githubassets.com	1,894
i.ytimg.com	1,818
calendar.google.com	1,568
r3---sn-n5pbvoj5caxu8-nbos.googlevideo.com	1,565
20.client-channel.google.com	1,468
www.google-analytics.com	1,453
edge-chat.messenger.com	1,360

Table 2. Summary of our datasets

Source	Type	Number of requests
Generated	Attack	2,313
Generated	Normal	182,103
CSIC 2010	Attack	21,451
CSIC 2010	Normal	66,958

Table 3. The dataset used to train the models

Source	Type	Number of requests	Ratio (%)
Generated, CSIC 2010	Attack	23,764	11,54%
Generated	Normal	182,103	88,46%

3.2 Proposed Model

Our original basic idea was to keep the entire ruleset of ModSecurity CRS, while also discovering which rules would often block ordinary users in order to reduce the impact of these rules. According to the way ModSecurity works, when a request is being analyzed, a particular set of rules in the ModSecurity CRS will be triggered for that request. From there, with this set of matched rules from ModSecurity CRS along with the HTTP method, we will take it as features for model training. With the above idea, we propose a method combining the

ModSecurity CRS with a classification algorithm (for example, Decision Tree), as illustrated in Fig. 2. Many machine learning algorithms can be applied in this case. Currently, we only experiment with two algorithms, Decision Tree and Random Forest. The Decision Tree is a fairly effective model for the classification problem. With fast training and prediction speeds, Decision Tree is the top choice for such problems, which requires real-time processing on each input request. Furthermore, the Decision Tree can help us identify which combinations of rules in the ModSecurity CRS are often triggered with normal requests as well as attack requests, which cannot be achieved via simple linear functions (for example, the sum of rules' scores).

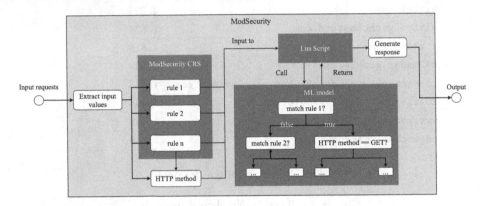

Fig. 2. Combining ModSecurity CRS with Decision Tree

In the current version of ModSecurity CRS that we use, there are a total of 156 rules denoted as $r_1, r_2, ..., r_{156}$. For each of the above rules, we will map it as a feature in the training dataset. If a request x causes a rule r_i to be triggered, we will have feature $x_{r_i} = 1$, otherwise $x_{r_j} = 0$ for all rule r_j in the set of non-triggered rules. Additionally, we also use the HTTP request method as a training feature. The possible values of the HTTP request method in our collected dataset include GET, POST, HEAD, OPTIONS, PUT. For an input request x, which has the HTTP method GET, we will have the following feature $x_{method} = $ GET and so on.

Using these extracted features, we apply two machine learning algorithms, Decision Tree and Random Forest, into the training dataset. To integrate the trained machine learning models into ModSecurity, we use the SecRuleScript directive syntax in ModSecurity. This feature allows us to write our custom rules using Lua script and invoke the compiled machine learning models as a shared library through Lua C API, which gains a relatively high performance. However, ModSecurity does not support retrieving triggered rules using the Lua C API currently. Hence, we have made a few small modifications to the ModSecurity library. The `m.getTriggeredRules()` function has been implemented to get all the triggered rules of the current request. Below is a simple example that calls the `m.getTriggeredRules()` function from the Lua script to get all triggered rules and passing features to the compiled model. The implementation details can be found in our source code[6].

```
local ml_model = require("ml_model")

function main()
    -- logging
    m.log(1, "Starting Lua script")

    -- get all triggered rules
    local rules = m.getTriggeredRules()

    -- transform rules to model features
    local features = transform(rules)

    -- evaluate with ML model
    local ml_result = ml_model.predict(features)

    return ml_result > 0
end
```

4   Experimental Result

To start the process of training the machine learning models, we split the training dataset into two parts for training and testing with a 2:1 ratio. Due to the imbalance between the ratio of the two classes in the dataset, as shown in Table 3, we will split the dataset using the stratified train-test split technique. The first model that we experimented is the Decision Tree, which is a model where outputs are determined based on the tree data structure. Each node in a tree corresponds to a question; the result of that question will lead us to the corresponding sub-tree. This process continues until the leaf node is met; the value of the leaf node will decide which class the input data belongs to. There are many variations of the Decision Tree algorithm, such as ID3, C4.5, C5.0, and CART. Here, we only experiment with the CART algorithm according to the implementation version of the scikit-learn library [8]. After the training process, we obtained the following Decision Tree, as shown in Fig. 3.

---

[6] https://github.com/ngoctint1lvc/waf.

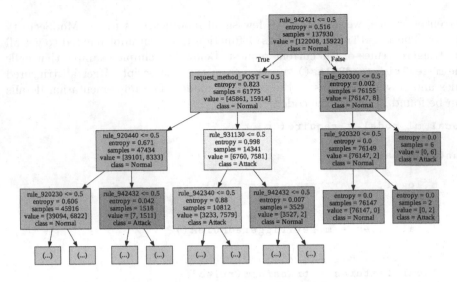

Fig. 3. The Decision Tree after training

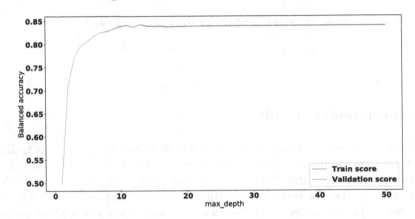

Fig. 4. Decision Tree validation curve with `max_depth` parameter

Additionally, to improve the Decision Tree model, we experimented with a popular ensemble model, Random Forest. Essentially, Random Forest is a model which makes the decision based on the average result of multiple Decision Trees. Figures 4 and 5 respectively show the validation curves of the max depth parameter of the Decision Tree model and the number of estimators of the Random Forest model compared to the balanced accuracy score. The balanced accuracy score here is the average of true-positive rate and false-positive rate, as shown in Eq. (1).

$$BAC \ (Balance \ Accuracy \ Score) = \frac{TPR + FPR}{2}. \tag{1}$$

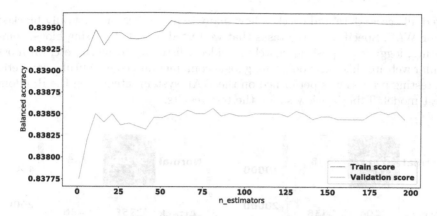

Fig. 5. Random Forest validation curve with n_estimators parameter

This type of score is suitable for the classification problem when two classes are sample imbalance, so we used this score to evaluate our models. Based on the validation curves in Figs. 4 and 5, we can see that the balanced accuracy score does not improve much with the max depth greater than 15 for the Decision Tree model and the number of estimators greater than 75 for Random Forest. With these parameters, our model evaluation results are shown in Table 4, and the confusion matrixes are shown in Figs. 6 and 7.

Based on the experimental results, they show that our proposed method has significantly improved the initial false-positive rate of the ModSecurity CRS. However, in order to reduce the false-positive rate to this level (about 1.26%), the true-positive rate had to decrease to 69.96% (with Random Forest model). It means that our WAF can only protect about 69.96% of attacks on web applications. The reason may come from the noisy training dataset, as mentioned in Subsect. 3.1, that many abnormal requests have been labeled attack in the CSIC dataset. Also, the ruleset in ModSecurity CRS still does not characterize between normal and attack requests well. An attack that does not trigger any rules in ModSecurity CRS will easily bypass the WAF system. Therefore, a more generic ruleset is required, which can easily be triggered by most types of attacks to prevent various tricky bypasses from hackers.

In addition to evaluating the models on the available dataset, we also tested our WAF system when accessing to real websites, which is called the *false-positive test*. The testing process is similar to the normal data collection process. Here, we

Table 4. Model evaluation results

Model	FPR	TPR (Recall)	TNR	BAC	Precision	F1-Score
Decision Tree	0.0128	0.6934	0.9872	0.8403	0.8762	0.7742
Random Forest	0.0126	0.6996	0.9874	0.8435	0.8788	0.7790

logged all access data and checked how many requests were accidentally blocked by our WAF. Specifically, the tasks that we tested include browsing blogs, commenting, logging in, posting, watching videos, listening to music, etc. on most popular websites like facebook.com, google.com, medium.com, youtube.com, etc. The testing process was performed on the WAF system integrating the Random Forest model. Table 5 below shows the test results.

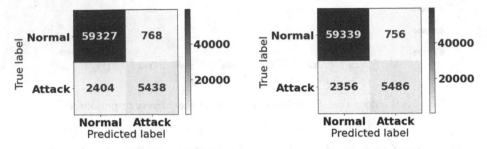

Fig. 6. Confusion matrix of Decision Tree model

Fig. 7. Confusion matrix of Random Forest model

Table 5. False-positive test

Model	Passed requests	Wrong blocked requests
Random Forest	16,784 (99,71%)	48 (0,29%)

5   Conclusion and Future Work

In this research, we have proposed a relatively efficient method for generating labeled data so that it can easily be applied in future research on this topic. Based on the generated dataset together with the available data, we also proposed a method that combines Decision Tree and Random Forest machine learning models with ModSecurity and ModSecurity CRS. With the trained model, we have been significantly reducing the false-positive rate of ModSecurity CRS and thereby making it more suitable for practical use. However, the proposed models basically only improve the false-positive rate in ModSecurity CRS's final decision formula, not the ability to detect any new types of attacks. In future work, we can improve it by adding a more generic ruleset which better characterizes the input requests and returns a more detailed value rather than 1 or 0. For example, a rule that returns the number of SELECT * keyword inside the request, which may indicate a malicious SQL Injection attack from the user. Besides, we can conduct more experiments that combine this generic ruleset with many other deep learning and machine learning methods. These approaches are extremely exciting and promising. In the near future, we will proceed to deploy our WAF system to protect our blog websites in order to evaluate its capabilities in practice.

Acknowledgments. The authors would like to thank Mr. Van Minh Hao for his comments helping to improve the manuscript significantly.

References

1. Ammo, K., Christian, G., Konrad, R., Pavel, L.: TokDoc: a self-healing web application firewall. In: SAC'10, Sierre (2010)
2. Barnett, R.: WAF virtual patching challenge: securing WebGoat with modsecurity. Breach Security (2009)
3. Betarte, G., Giménez, E., Martínez, R., Pardo, Á.: Machine learning-assisted virtual patching of web applications. arXiv preprint arXiv:1803.05529 (2018)
4. Folini, C.: Handling false positives with the OWASP modsecurity core rule set. https://www.netnea.com/cms/nginx-tutorial-8_handling-false-positives-modsecurity-core-rule-set (2016). Accessed 04 Oct 2020
5. Giménez, C.T., Villegas, A.P., Marañón, G.Á.: HTTP data set CSIC 2010. Information Security Institute of CSIC (Spanish Research National Council) (2010)
6. Kruegel, C., Vigna, G., Robertson, W.: A multi-model approach to the detection of web-based attacks. Comput. Netw. **48**(5), 717–738 (2005)
7. Meyer, R., Cid, C.: Detecting attacks on web applications from log files. Sans Institute (2008)
8. Pedregosa, F., et al.: Scikit-learn: machine learning in Python. J. Mach. Learn. Res. **12**, 2825–2830 (2011)
9. Ristic, I.: ModSecurity Handbook. Feisty Duck, London (2010). GBR
10. Rong, W., Zhang, B., Lv, X.: Malicious web request detection using character-level CNN. In: Chen, X., Huang, X., Zhang, J. (eds.) ML4CS 2019. LNCS, vol. 11806, pp. 6–16. Springer, Cham (2019). https://doi.org/10.1007/978-3-030-30619-9_2
11. Stock, A., Williams, J., Wichers, D.: Owasp top 10. OWASP Foundation (2007)
12. Vartouni, A.M., Kashi, S.S., Teshnehlab, M.: An anomaly detection method to detect web attacks using stacked auto-encoder. In: 2018 6th Iranian Joint Congress on Fuzzy and Intelligent Systems (CFIS), pp. 131–134. IEEE (2018)
13. Zhang, M., Xu, B., Bai, S., Lu, S., Lin, Z.: A deep learning method to detect web attacks using a specially designed CNN. In: Liu, D., Xie, S., Li, Y., Zhao, D., El-Alfy, E.-S.M. (eds.) ICONIP 2017. LNCS, vol. 10638, pp. 828–836. Springer, Cham (2017). https://doi.org/10.1007/978-3-319-70139-4_84

An Elastic Anonymization Framework for Open Data

Trung Hieu Le[1,2] and Tran Khanh Dang[1,2(✉)]

[1] Ho Chi Minh City University of Technology (HCMUT),
268 Ly Thuong Kiet Street, District 10, Ho Chi Minh City, Vietnam
{1670222,khanh}@hcmut.edu.vn
[2] Vietnam National University Ho Chi Minh City (VNU-HCM), Linh Trung Ward,
Thu Duc District, Ho Chi Minh City, Vietnam

Abstract. Open data is a vast resource that is waiting for being utilizing. To publish data to an open environment, the privacy preserving requirement is a must. Different solutions are applied to privacy protection, and data anonymization is one of the prominent ones. This paper proposed a framework flexibly applying different anonymization models to work with an arbitrary open data management platform. An experimental setup was implemented with a heterogeneous service architecture using two datasets vary in the data volume and the number of dimensions. The measured results show that the proposed method produces anonymized data in an acceptable time using different anonymization techniques and settings, giving high quality outputs.

Keywords: Data anonymization · Open data · Privacy preservation

1 Introduction

Contemporary, many individuals, organizations, and governments have been collecting a tremendous amount of data, which belong to different types and domains, to serve their jobs. Many of those data have to be public by law, which creates a vast resource that mostly untapped. As more and more organizations (especially governments) provide open data sources, many open data applications have shown tangible benefits in practice.

As defined by the Open Knowledge Foundation (OKF), open data can be used, edited, and shared by anyone for any purpose [9]. The essential characteristics of OKF's interpretation of this definition are:

- Availability and accessibility: all data must be available and accessible without charge except the fee of operating the system. Besides, data must exist in forms that can be conveniently edited and used.
- Reuse and redistribution: data must be provided under licenses that allow for reuse, redistribution and combination with other data sets.

T. K. Dang et al. (Eds.): FDSE 2020, CCIS 1306, pp. 108–119, 2020.
https://doi.org/10.1007/978-981-33-4370-2_8

- Universal participation: everyone has the right to use, reuse, and redistribute the data in any form, for any purpose. This means that the definition of open data does not prevent its commercial use or any other purpose of causing harm to others, leading to concerns about protecting the privacy of individuals who have faced an open dataset.

While open data promises to be beneficial in various ways, the above principle of universal participation makes it possible to use the data for purposes of violating ethical or legal standards. Currently, most countries and regions have laws to protect data privacy. These reasons ensure that privacy is one of the top imperatives when opening data [34].

There are many approaches to protecting data privacy:

- Data encryption: leads to expensive to operate, especially with large and diverse data such as open data.
- Access control: becomes cumbersome and challenging to control in an open environment with many individuals and organizations participating in contributing to the shared data warehouse.
- Data anonymization: has been considered an indispensable step in disclosing data, has been studied for a long time [18].

Our research proposed a framework to preserve the dataset's privacy in the open data environment via data anonymization. The framework resolves some challenges:

- There may be multiple anonymization algorithms applied to the data, based on the data experts' requirements. A better alternative solution can replace the default output of the selected anonymization algorithm.
- The open data management tools and the data anonymization engines are usually implemented in several technologies, to satisfy different standards. In a production system, the computation power for managing the data and anonymizing it may be different.

In this paper, we first review related works about open data management and data anonymization. The paper presents different open data management systems and data anonymization techniques. Then, we introduce a framework to connect different anonymization approaches and open data management systems. The proposed framework allows data experts and data providers to create anonymized datasets based on different settings and requirements before publishing them to the public catalog. Some sample data are used with the experimental setup to see the feasibility of the proposed method and the quality of the anonymization process. Last, we mention some possible future studies and give a conclusion.

2   Related Work

2.1   Open Data Management Systems

Open data is usually large in volume, diverse in structure and generated continuously from many sources. Open data management, storage, and distribution systems are indispensable requirements to ensure the availability and accessibility of data as well as improve the ease of usage.

CKAN[1] (The Comprehensive Knowledge Archive Network) is an open source system used to manage and distribute open data. Currently, CKAN is used by government systems of many countries such as the United Kingdom[2], Netherlands[3], and the USA[4]. The architecture of CKAN includes:

- Routing: direct user requests from the internet to appropriate APIs or interfaces to process those requests.
- Communication (views): read data, edit data with action functions before returning the results.
- Logic: include action functions, authentication and authorization functions, background tasks, and business logic.
- Model: data in CKAN can be stored by different database management systems that default is PostgreSQL. The organization of the model class in CKAN allows hiding the underlying implementation of the database and extending the utilization of various database management systems, including NoSQL.

The architecture of CKAN is highly scalable. Extensions can add business logic or new features to different components of the system.

DSpace[5] is another open source solution for open data systems used by many organizations such as the World Bank[6], Cambridge University[7], MIT University[8], ... The operation of the DSpace system includes the following principal components:

- Submission: Data providers will upload data files into the system via a web interface. DSpace supports a variety of formats, from text to images and videos.
- Data files and metadata are organized into related groups. The smallest unit of data storage operations in DSpace is called an "item" that includes the data files and the information related to them. "Items" are organized into collections based on their logical relevance.
- Communities are the highest hierarchy in the content hierarchy of DSpace. Usually, each DSpace community corresponds to a department or sub unit of a large organization.

The DSpace architecture allows the system to be organized into many individual components that can be deployed separately for each department and

---

[1] https://ckan.org/.
[2] https://data.gov.uk/.
[3] https://data.overheid.nl.
[4] https://www.data.gov.
[5] https://duraspace.org/dspace/.
[6] https://openknowledge.worldbank.org/.
[7] https://www.repository.cam.ac.uk/.
[8] https://dspace.mit.edu/.

sub-unit. DSpace is committed to ensuring that files stored in the system can be accessed from time to time, even when the number of new data formats is added later. End users can access the system through web browsers. The appropriate data formats will be displayed directly in the browser while other formats can be downloaded to the end users computer.

CKAN and DSpace are popular open data management systems. Both of them provide extensible platforms that satisfy the requirements of storing and publishing different kinds of data. However, there is no straightforward approach to anonymized data with a different technique in those platforms.

2.2   Data Anonymization

Anonymizing data is a transformative process that applies to data related to personal data, in which an individual cannot be identified from this data set directly or indirectly, even by combining this data with other data sets. This helps reduce the risks of disclosing undesirable personal information while ensuring that the data can be reused and distributed among participants to share data, thereby ensuring data availability.

Latanya Sweeney introduced the k-anonymity model in 2002 [29]. So far, this model is one of the most famous in anonymizing data [10,15,16,29]. Let $RT(A_1, ..., A_n)$ be a data table, and QI_{RT} is its quasi-identifier attributes. RT is said to satisfy k-anonymity if each value chain in $RT[QI_{RT}]$ has at least k occurrences in $RT[QI_{RT}]$. By this definition, data has the k-anonymity attribute if a person's record in the publication cannot be distinguished from at least $k-1$ other individual whose data is also published in the same release. If a record in the table has some QID values, then at least $k - 1$ other record also has a QID value.

To modify an initial data into a form that satisfies k-anonymity, many methods have been investigated: sampling [26], global and local recording [22,30], micro aggregation [6], adding noise [3], condensation [2], substitution [25] ... The above methods can be applied individually but often applied in combination to anonymize a data table. Figure 1 illustrates examples of different methods on one dataset.

The k-anonymity model may be subjected to hacking and disclosure of private information. l-diversity [17] is proposed to solve this problem. In k-anonymity, each equivalence class is a group of records with the same set of quasi-identifiers with at least k records. l-diversity proposes an additional request for equivalent groups. In particular, each group needs to have at least l different well representations for sensitive attributes. Machanavajjhala presented several ways to describe what is a "good representation" in his research [17]:

- Distinct l-diversity or p-sensitive k-anonymity: Each sensitive attribute has at least p distinct values for each equivalence class.
- Entropy l-diversity: use an entropy function for each sensitivity attribute. The more evenly distributed the values of sensitivity properties are, the higher the entropy, the more extensive the value for l. It becomes more challenging to use probability to find a person's real sensitive value when the l value is high.

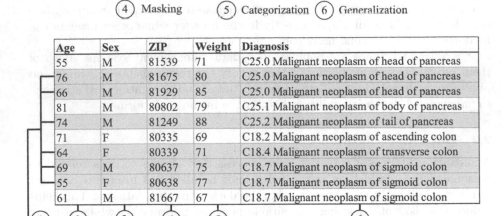

Fig. 1. Example of different data transformation methods [20]. (1) Some records are sampled from the original dataset. (2) Numbers are aggregated based on the average value of the range. (3) The values of the "Sex" attribute of some records are suppressed. (4) The "ZIP" attribute is masked, hiding a part of its values. (5) Values of the "Weight" attribute are categorized into different ranges. (6) The "Diagnosis" attribute is generalized to more abstract values.

– Recursive (c, l) diversity: this criterion ensures that the frequency of occurrence of the most common attribute within each sensitive attribute is not too high and that the frequency of occurrence of the least common value is not too low, compared with the frequency of occurrence of different values of that sensitive attribute.

Although l-diversity overcomes some weaknesses in k-anonymity, this model still has some weaknesses before knowledge base attacks, probability inference attacks. The principle of t-closeness [1, 28, 32] introduced in the study of Ninghui and colleagues adds constraint on data anonymity. Accordingly, in each equivalence class, in addition to specifying sensitive attributes that need at least good representation, this principle also requires the distance between the distribution of the sensitive attribute in this group and the distribution of the sensitive properties throughout the data table cannot be greater than a threshold t. To measure this distance, the original study used Earth Mover's Distance (EMD) [21]. Recently, Sei introduced a novel model with an attribute that can be both quasi-identifier and sensitive [24].

Dwork introduced Differential Privacy [7] as another approach to prevent the attacker from disclosing user data. With this approach, if an individual record is removed from a statistical release of the dataset, that individual privacy is still not compromised. The more one individual data contributes to the dataset, the more noises needed to preserve that individual's privacy. Another research created a k-anonymity dataset then adding noises to each equivalence class to achieve a Differential Privacy [27]. Sanchez et al. [23] reduce the information loss of this process with an improved method. Recently, Differential Privacy is a trendy topic that is investigated in multiple researches [11, 12, 33].

3   Methodology

3.1   Flexible Data Anonymization

This research proposes an engine of data anonymization, as shown in Fig. 2. A client creates a request then delivers it to the engine. The *data provider* component produces the dataset for the rest of the process. The *config provider* also receives the input request then prepares the configuration for other components. The core of the engine is anonymization and utility models. The *anonymization models* transform the provided dataset into different ones, which are inturned processed by the *utility models* to find the best candidates. The candidate output datasets which satisfy the anonymization models form the solution space. Along with the utility models' metrics, the solution space is delivered to different *result consumers*, which decide what to do with the output data.

With the variety of anonymization and utility models [31], it is apparent that we cannot find the best candidate by simply browse all the solution space. Multiple heuristics and clustering solutions were proposed [4, 19, 28]. The engine model presented in this paper allows us to develop different strategies to utilize different anonymization models in multiple combinations. The *config provider* can also be improved to let the user chose an alternative strategy instead of the default one.

3.2   Heterogeneous Services Architecture

The complete framework proposed in this paper insists on not only the anonymization engine but also the open data management platform and the front-end service. The author uses the Enterprise Service Bus (ESB) [5] to connect those components. Therefore, the components can be implemented in different programming languages, deployed in different machines with different scaling levels. Instead of communicating directly to each other, the components publish and subscribe to the service bus to produce and consume appropriate messages.

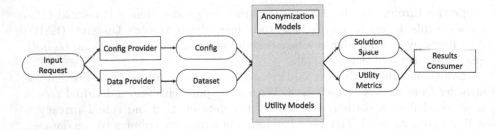

Fig. 2. The overview of the proposed data anonymization engine

Direct messages between components are limited to exchanging data that is too large to be transferred on the bus. Figure 3 represents the overview of this architecture.

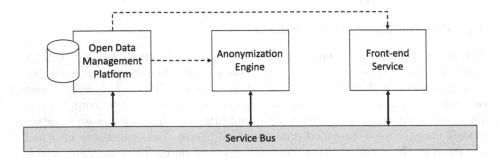

Fig. 3. The Enterprise service bus linked with different services

Several components take part in the whole system of anonymization for open data. However, this paper pays attention to the three essential building blocks: the open data management platform, the anonymization engine and the front-end service. The open data management platform provides the data source for other parts of the system and hosting the final anonymized dataset. The anonymization engine runs different strategies to produce a privacy-preserved version of the input data. The front-end service is the interface for end-users (mostly data experts) to interact with the whole system. The front-end service itself may use internal data storage to cache the data between different requests and do initial analyses.

The open data management platform notifies the service bus every time a new dataset is uploaded. By subscribing to the bus, the front-end service adds a new entry to its local database with the reference back to the open data management platform. The front-end service may fetch a copy of the dataset using the HTTP endpoint of the open data manager, then build the metadata to support the data expert configuration process. After the expert submitting the anonymization configuration, the front-end service publishes a new message, including the original dataset reference, the anonymization configuration, and additional data to the service bus. The anonymization engine listens to the bus and invokes the anonymization process when a new message from the front-end service comes. The engine may communicate with the open data manager to retrieve the dataset or push the anonymized data to the central catalog.

4   Results

An experimental implementation was build based on the proposed framework, as depicted in Fig. 4. RabbitMQ[9] is chosen to implement the service bus, while CKAN is selected as the open data management platform. Users can use a command line utility to dispatch the anonymization process directly. A message listener is also implemented so that the anonymization process can be triggered via a new message sent to the service bus.

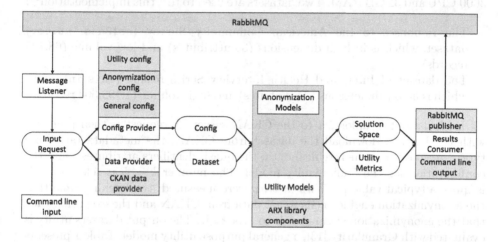

Fig. 4. The experimental implementation of the anonymization engine

The CKAN data provider implements the data provider interface fetches the data from the open data catalog and stores in the memory during the anonymization process. Different config providers also parse the provided request: the application standard configurations and metadata, the anonymization models configurations (the values of k, l, t, ..., the hierarchical generalization data, suppression values), and the utility models configurations. In the engine's core, a default strategy was implemented and utilized anonymization model implementations from the ARX [14,20] library. This strategy currently supports k-anonymity, l-diversity and t-closeness models, and different combinations that can be configured from the initial request. The anonymized data and the utility metric

---

[9] https://www.rabbitmq.com/.

Table 1. The metrics measured during evaluation of experimental setup

Dataset	ss13acs_int.csv				ihis_int.csv			
Number of QIs	1	5	10	20	1	2	4	8
Fetching time (ms)	871	895	904	899	2,113	2,350	1,998	1,981
Execution time (ms)	180	804	1,537	4,955	2,565	5,103	20,010	41,597
Utility value	0.9999	0.9888	0.9671	0.8830	0.9999	0.9999	0.9990	0.8565

then delivered to two different consumers: a command line output that prints the results to screen; and a RabbitMQ publisher module that pushes the output to another RabbitMQ queue so that other components can process it.

Components are run inside Docker containers on a computer with Ryzen 5 3600 CPU and 32 GB RAM. Two datasets are used to test this implementation[10]:

- The responses to the American Community Survey (ss13acs_int.csv) dataset, which is in high dimensions (30 attributes) and low volume (68,725 records).
- The dataset of Integrated Health Interview Series results (ihis_int.csv), which is in low dimensions (9 attributes) and high volume (1,193,504 records).

Each dataset is uploaded to the CKAN server. A request is then prepared with the URL to download the dataset from CKAN, the metadata (attribute types, generalization hierarchical data, the quasi-identifiers attributes), and the configuration for the 5-anonymity model. The number $k = 5$ is selected as it is quite a typical value [8]. Two metrics were measured: the fetching time that the anonymization engine needs to get data from CKAN and the execution time that the anonymization engine needs to process it. The output datasets utility is evaluated with Granularity [13], a general purpose utility model. Table 1 presents the results with different numbers of QI.

It is easy to understand that the fetching time is similar between trials of the same dataset because the data is delivered to the anonymization engine in the same way. In other experiments, some local caching methods are used. Data is only fetched once, and the following iteration fetching time is nearly eliminated. The execution time increases quickly when there are more quasi-identifier attributes. With a large dataset, it may take nearly a minute to complete the anonymization process. This supports the selected architecture with service bus and asynchronous processing. The utility values of the anonymized datasets are close to one in most cases. When testing with a low number of quasi-identifier attributes, the metrics are more significant than 0.9. These results show that the proposed framework produce high quality outputs.

---

[10] https://github.com/letrunghieu/transformation-benchmark/tree/master/data.

5   Conclusion and Future Work

We have presented results from our research to propose a framework of data anonymization for open data. The introduced framework supports utilizing varying models of anonymization and utility with various combinations. All components in the framework (the open data management platform, the anonymization engine, and the front-end service) communicate via a service bus, allowing them to be implemented with different technologies and operated in different environments. When a new anonymization message arrives, the engine is triggered and starting parsing the message to retrieve the dataset from the open data catalog as well as building the configuration for the rest of the process. The data is then manipulated by different strategies, which include several anonymization and utility models. At the end of the process, there may be multiple results consumers using the solution space and utility metrics.

An experimental implementation was built based on the proposed framework. Two sample datasets vary in volume and the number of dimensions was used to measure the implementation's performance. The anonymized datasets were published to the open data catalog with high utility value. While the time to retrieve the data from the open data management platform can be reduced with a local caching mechanism, the anonymization engine's execution time increased significantly with the number of quasi-identifier attributes. These results show that the method introduced in this paper successfully resolved the problem of data anonymization in an open data environment.

New strategies can utilize a better combination of anonymization in the core engine to produce better results in the future. More implementation of anonymization and utility models can also be added to the framework easily with the current abstraction. New components can also be introduced, such as logging or security monitoring. A deep learning module can be added to the framework to suggest the data expert in the front-end service configuration phase.

Acknowledgments. This work is supported by a project with the Department of Science and Technology, Ho Chi Minh City, Vietnam (contract with HCMUT No. 08/2018/HĐQKHCN, dated 16/11/2018). We also thank all members of AC Lab and D-STAR Lab for their great supports and comments during the preparation of this paper.

References

1. t-Closeness: privacy beyond k-anonymity and l-diversity. In: Proceedings - International Conference on Data Engineering (3), pp. 106–115 (2007)
2. Aggarwal, C.C., Yu, P.S.: A condensation approach to privacy preserving data mining. In: Bertino, E., et al. (eds.) EDBT 2004. LNCS, vol. 2992, pp. 183–199. Springer, Heidelberg (2004). https://doi.org/10.1007/978-3-540-24741-8_12
3. Agrawal, R., Srikant, R.: Privacy-preserving data mining. ACM SIGMOD Rec. **29**(2), 439–450 (2000)

4. Babu, K.S., Reddy, N., Kumar, N., Elliot, M., Jena, S.K.: Achieving K-anonymity using improved greedy heuristics for very large relational databases. Trans. Data Privacy **6**(1), 1–17 (2013)
5. Curry, E.: Message-oriented middleware. In: Middleware for Communications, pp. 1–28. Wiley, Chichester, UK (2005)
6. Domingo-Ferrer, J., Mateo-Sanz, J.: Practical data-oriented microaggregation for statistical disclosure control. IEEE Trans. Knowl. Data Eng. **14**(1), 189–201 (2002)
7. Dwork, C.: Differential privacy. In: Bugliesi, M., Preneel, B., Sassone, V., Wegener, I. (eds.) ICALP 2006. LNCS, vol. 4052, pp. 1–12. Springer, Heidelberg (2006). https://doi.org/10.1007/11787006_1
8. El Emam, K., Dankar, F.K.: Protecting privacy using k-anonymity (Appendix A : Risk Estimates). J. Am. Med. Inform. **15**(5), 1–5 (2008)
9. Open Knowledge Foundation: The Open Definition. https://opendefinition.org/
10. Guo, N., Yang, M., Gong, Q., Chen, Z., Luo, J.: Data anonymization based on natural equivalent class. In: Proceedings of the 2019 IEEE 23rd International Conference on Computer Supported Cooperative Work in Design, CSCWD 2019, pp. 22–27 (2019)
11. Ha, T., Dang, T.K., Dang, T.T., Truong, T.A., Nguyen, M.T.: Differential privacy in deep learning: an overview. In: Proceedings - 2019 International Conference on Advanced Computing and Applications, ACOMP 2019, pp. 97–102 (2019)
12. Ha, T., Dang, T.K., Le, H., Truong, T.A.: Security and privacy issues in deep learning: a brief review. SN Comput. Sci. **1**(5), 253 (2020)
13. Iyengar, V.S.: Transforming data to satisfy privacy constraints. In: Proceedings of the ACM SIGKDD International Conference on Knowledge Discovery and Data Mining, pp. 279–288 (2002)
14. Kohlmayer, F., Prasser, F., Eckert, C., Kuhn, K.A.: A flexible approach to distributed data anonymization. J. Biomed. Inform. **50**, 62–76 (2014)
15. LeFevre, K., DeWitt, D.J., Ramakrishnan, R.: Incognito: efficient full-domain K-anonymity. In: Proceedings of the ACM SIGMOD International Conference on Management of Data, pp. 49–60 (2005)
16. LeFevre, K., DeWitt, D.J., Ramakrishnan, R.: Mondrian multidimensional K-anonymity. In: Proceedings - International Conference on Data Engineering 2006, p. 25 (2006)
17. Machanavajjhala, A., Gehrke, J., Kifer, D., Venkitasubramaniam, M.: L-diversity: privacy beyond k-anonymity. In: 22nd International Conference on Data Engineering (ICDE'06), p. 24. IEEE (2006)
18. Murthy, S., Abu Bakar, A., Abdul Rahim, F., Ramli, R.: A comparative study of data anonymization techniques. In: Proceedings - 5th IEEE International Conference on Big Data Security on Cloud, BigDataSecurity 2019, 5th IEEE International Conference on High Performance and Smart Computing, HPSC 2019 and 4th IEEE International Conference on Intelligent Data and Securit, pp. 306–309 (2019)
19. Nergiz, M., Clifton, C.: Thoughts on k-anonymization. In: 22nd International Conference on Data Engineering Workshops (ICDEW'06), p. 96. No. 0428168. IEEE (2006)
20. Prasser, F., Eicher, J., Spengler, H., Bild, R., Kuhn, K.A.: Flexible data anonymization using ARX–current status and challenges ahead. Softw. - Pract. Exp. **50**(7), 1277–1304 (2020)
21. Rubner, Y., Tomasi, C., Guibas, L.J.: Earth mover's distance as a metric for image retrieval. Int. J. Comput. Vis. **40**(2), 99–121 (2000)
22. Samarati, P.: Protecting respondents' identities in microdata release. IEEE Trans. Knowl. Data Eng. **13**(6), 1010–1027 (2001)

23. Sánchez, D., Domingo-Ferrer, J., Martínez, S., Soria-Comas, J.: Utility-preserving differentially private data releases via individual ranking microaggregation. Inf. Fus. **30**, 1–14 (2016)
24. Sei, Y., Okumura, H., Takenouchi, T., Ohsuga, A.: Anonymization of Sensitive Quasi-Identifiers for l-Diversity and t-Closeness. IEEE Trans. Dependable Secure Comput. **16**(4), 580–593 (2019)
25. Singh, A., Yu, F., Dunteman, G.: MASSC: a new data mask for limiting statistical information loss and disclosure. In: Work Session on Statistical Data (23), pp. 1–13 (2004)
26. Skinner, C., Marsh, C., Openshaw, S., Wymer, C.: Disclosure control for census microdata. J. Off. Stat. **10**(1), 31–51 (1994)
27. Soria-Comas, J., Domingo-Ferrer, J., Sánchez, D., Martínez, S.: Enhancing data utility in differential privacy via microaggregation-based k-anonymity. VLDB J. **23**(5), 771–794 (2014)
28. Soria-Comas, J., Domingo-Ferrer, J., Sánchez, D., Martínez, S.: t-Closeness through microaggregation: strict privacy with enhanced utility preservation. IEEE Trans. Knowl. Data Eng. **27**(11), 3098–3110 (2015)
29. Sweeney, L.: k-anonymity: a model for protecting privacy. Int. J. Uncertain. Fuzziness Knowl.-Based Syst. **10**(05), 557–570 (2002)
30. Takemura, A.: Local recoding by maximum weight matching for disclosure control of microdata sets. In: ITME Discussion Paper (40), pp. 1–14 (1999)
31. Wagner, I., Eckhoff, D.: Technical privacy metrics: a systematic survey. ACM Comput. Surv. **51**(3), 1–38 (2018)
32. Wang, R., Zhu, Y., Chen, T.S., Chang, C.C.: Privacy-preserving algorithms for multiple sensitive attributes satisfying t-Closeness. Journal of Computer Science and Technology **33**(6), 1231–1242 (2018)
33. Wood, A., et al.: Differential privacy: a primer for a non-technical audience. SSRN Electron. J. **21**, 209 (2019)
34. Zhang, K., Ni, J., Yang, K., Liang, X., Ren, J., Shen, X.S.: Security and privacy in smart city applications: challenges and solutions. IEEE Commun. Mag. **55**(1), 122–129 (2017)

A Computer Virus Detection Method Based on Information from PE Structure of Files Combined with Deep Learning Models

Vu Thanh Nguyen[1][✉], Vu Thanh Hien[2], Le Dinh Tuan[3], Mai Viet Tiep[4],
Nguyen Hoang Anh[5][✉], and Pham Thi Vuong[6]

[1] Ho Chi Minh City University of Food Industry, Ho Chi Minh City, Vietnam
nguyenvt@hufi.edu.vn
[2] Ho Chi Minh City University of Technology, Ho Chi Minh City, Vietnam
vt.hien@hutech.edu.vn
[3] Long an University of Economics and Industry, Tan an, Long an Province, Vietnam
le.tuan@daihoclongan.edu.vn
[4] Academy of Cryptography Techniques, Ho Chi Minh City, Vietnam
vtiepbcy@gmail.com
[5] Ho Chi Minh City Tax Department, Ho Chi Minh City, Vietnam
nhanh.hcm@gdt.gov.vn
[6] Sai Gon University, Ho Chi Minh City, Vietnam
vuong.pham@sgu.edu.vn

Abstract. In this paper, we demonstrate a new approach to virus detection. Extract information from a file's Portable Executable (PE) structure to save storage costs compared to other types of features such as signatures, opcodes, or file strings, while still detect unknown malicious code. Use a deep learning network, namely the Deep Belief Network (DBN) model to classify and train data. The results show that the accuracy of the method is quite high, can reach over 97% for ten properties and over 95% for 15 properties, respectively.

Keywords: Portable executable (PE) · PE structure · Computer virus detection · Deep learning · Deep belief network (DBN)

1 Introduction

At present, most computer security software often uses typical digital patterns to identify known malicious codes and update the database containing new ones on a daily basis. The advantage of this method is that it is fast, less resource-consuming in malicious code analysis, and highly-accurate because it has been analyzed manually by security experts in a virtual environment.

However, the number of malicious codes skyrockets day by day, with metamorphic and self-variant malware lines after each replication, which causes the solution ineffectively.

© Springer Nature Singapore Pte Ltd. 2020
T. K. Dang et al. (Eds.): FDSE 2020, CCIS 1306, pp. 120–129, 2020.
https://doi.org/10.1007/978-981-33-4370-2_9

Typically in 2017, the WannaCry malware event attacked more than 300,000 computers in 150 countries within 24 h. Therefore, many different approaches have been being studied based on data mining, machine learning, statistics, and artificial immune system that scientists are interested.

By adopting these approaches, this paper will propose a virus detection approach based on a deep learning model combined with information extracted from the PE Structure of files on the Windows operating system. We hope to contribute more with a new approach, including the method using deep learning model (under reinforcement learning).

2 Related Works

Invincea Labs [3] study on the efficiency of using neural networks to detect malicious codes. They used 400,000 software binary files, including clean files and virus files, to feed into the deep learning network, which consisted of an input layer, two hidden layers, and an output layer. The results show that the malware detection rate using Deep Learning has a zero-day malware detection rate of about 95% with a low rate of false positives of 0.1%.

Jung et al. [4] applied a deep learning network to detect zero-day malware. The method used the Deep Feed-forward Neural Network, extracted the properties by static analysis and dynamic analysis (API) then converted them into digital form. Finally, they applied deep learning networks to classify malware.

Bai et al. [5] used the information in the .EXE executable to detect new malware. The study used CfsSubsetEval and WrapperSubsetEval methods to extract 197 properties in the executable. Then, they used algorithm J48 and random forest (random forest) to classify viruses. The results obtained a 97.6% rate of detection and a 1.3% rate of false positives.

3 The Proposed Approach

We decide to choose a deep belief network as our training model because of its efficiency in classification problems.

The proposed method will contain the following main phases: data collection, feature statistics, feature extraction, training, and testing. An overview of the implementation steps of the proposed approach is shown in Fig. 1.

Data collection phase: Data is collected from Windows file and dowload.cnet.com for a clean file. Virusshare and Malicia for file virus. Then, it is verified with Virustotal to make sure that the data set matches the collected label.

Typical statistical stage: Next is the typical statistics stage, all the information in the PE file is extracted and saved in .txt format. Then, select a set of features where the difference between a clean file and a virus file is significant. Moreover, the paper reuses some of the features taken from research articles related to PE information. The selected features are saved for the next phase.

Feature extraction stage: The feature extraction system is based on a feature set that selectively forms sets of vectors where each vector represents a file. Next, the system

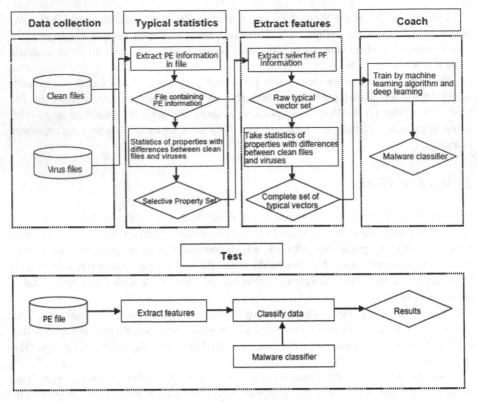

Fig. 1. The implementation steps

uses the Min-Max method to standardize the raw vectors to create a complete set of feature vectors.

Training phase: The complete feature vector set is trained by the machine learning algorithm that creates malicious classifier.

Test phase: The system extracts features from the tested PE file, then uses the malicious classifier taken from the training phase to predict whether the file's label is clean or virus.

3.1 Extract and Process Data

Process Data: According to the overall model shown in the previous section, .EXE files are processed duplicated, and PE non-extractable files are removed using tools written in python. Then, extract the parameters in the PE header of the file with the help of the official Microsoft tool Dumpbin [15] of the Visual C++ standard tool.

PE Header: In our proposed work, we consider the PE files for the experiment since they are one of the most used file formats of Windows operating system and secondly the most common files submitted to VirusTotal are PE files. Figure 2 shows the number

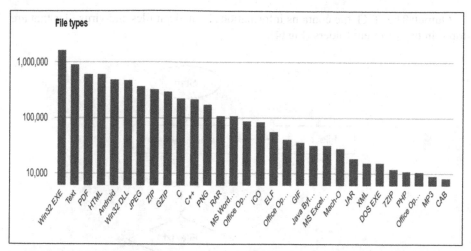

Fig. 2. The figure for file types submitted to VirusTotal (8 August 2018), (Last Accessed: August 8, 2018) (https://virustotal.com/en/statistics/)

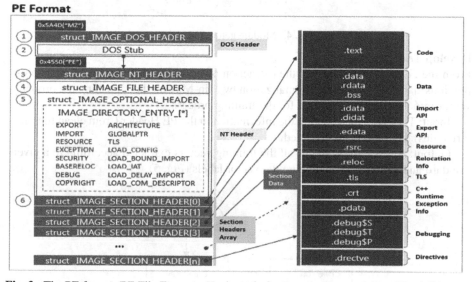

Fig. 3. The PE format (PE File Format – Kevin Attic for Security Research http://dandylife.net/blog/archives/388 August 8, 2018)

of different file types submitted to VirusTotal and Fig. 3 describes the structure of a portable execute file.

Extract Information in PE Header from .EXE Files (Clean Files and Virus Files)
This is the first stage in data extraction and processing. Use Microsoft's dumpbin tool to perform information extraction in PE Header from clean files and virus files. The results are recorded in 2 .txt files corresponding to 2 types of clean files and virus files.

Input: The path to the .EXE files have been selected, including a clean file and virus file.

Output: The .TXT file contains information about clean files and virus files that are stored in two different folders (Fig. 4).

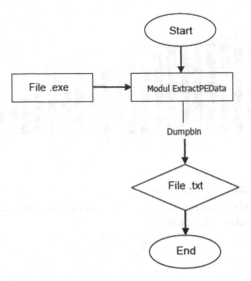

Fig. 4. Module general model

Develop Training Data:

From the .TXT files obtained in the extraction of information in the PE Header in the previous stage, we conducted normalization by Min-Max method, pushing the property vector into it.CSV file to prepare for the training process.

Input: The .TXT files contain the information in the PE Header (from clean files and virus files) that have been extracted.

Output: A .CSV file contains all the training vectors extracted according to a given standard and a .CSV file containing the vector labels (Fig. 5).

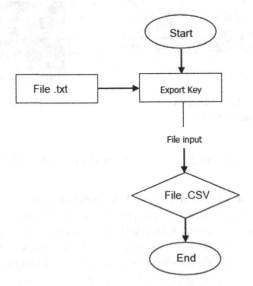

Fig. 5. Module general model

3.2 Feature Selection

The specific selection criteria in the paper use statistical methods and use the scatter graph in excel to examine and select the features with the most different values between the clean file and the virus file (Table 1).

Table 1. The following are the 15 critical features of PE information

Priority value	Feature name
1	Size of headers
1	DLL characteristics
1	File alignment
1	RVA [size] of certificates directory
1	RVA [size] of debug directory
2	.data
2	.reloc
2	Size of initialized data
2	Size of image
2	Characteristics
3	Size of uninitialized data
3	Number of symbols
3	Image version
3	Subsystem version
3	File pointer to symbol table

3.3 Classification

After all, features are extracted and selected, standardization is carried out using the Min-Max method, followed by classification using the Deep Belief Network (DBN) network model. The result of this process is a model used for subsequent virus detection.

Develop Classifier

Input: Training data
Output: Detector (Fig. 6).

Assess the Classification Model

The paper uses precision, recall, F-score, and overall accuracy as an indicator of classifier performance using the Deep Belief Network.

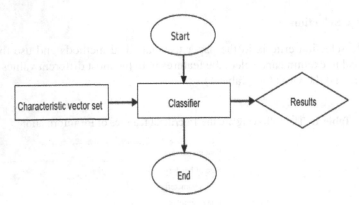

Fig. 6. Module general model

3.4 Test

In the test step, the test files are extracted from the PE structure, as presented. Next, use the malware classifier from the training phase predicts whether the file's label is clean or virus.

4 Experiments

In this article, we will train and test with five different test datasets. For each data set, the ratio between the number of training files and the number of test files is 7: 3. Here are the parameters of the five sets of datasets (Table 2):

Table 2. The number of files in each dataset

Dataset	Training files		Testing files	
	Benign	Virus	Benign	Virus
Dataset 1	400	600	171	257
Dataset 2	600	800	257	342
Dataset 3	700	900	300	385
Dataset 4	700	1200	300	514
Dataset 5	800	1300	342	557

Each data set is tested for 10 and 15 features, respectively, using the DBN classifier. After performing many tests with different sets of parameters, we have selected the last set of parameters for low error rate and high detection rate epoch = 10, learning_rate = 0.1, number of iterations = 500, batch_size = 128 (Tables 3 and 4).

Table 3. Experimental results for ten properties (priority 1, 2)

Dataset	Deep belief network			
	Accuracy	Precision	Recall	F-Score
Dataset 1	0.9825	0.9882	0.9766	0.9824
Dataset 2	0.9664	0.9654	0.9678	0.9664
Dataset 3	0.9684	0.9705	0.9662	0.9683
Dataset 4	0.9688	0.9706	0.9669	0.9688
Dataset 5	0.9657	0.9615	0.9659	0.9637
Average	**0.9704**	**0.9712**	**0.9687**	**0.9699**

Table 4. Experimental results for a set of 15 properties (priority 1, 2, 3)

Dataset	Deep belief network			
	Accuracy	Precision	Recall	F-Score
Dataset 1	0.9592	0.9438	0.9766	0.9599
Dataset 2	0.9513	0.9393	0.9649	0.9519
Dataset 3	0.9454	0.9254	0.9688	0.9466
Dataset 4	0.9708	0.9707	0.9708	0.9708
Dataset 5	0.9657	0.9573	0.9749	0.9660
Average	**0.9585**	**0.9473**	**0.9712**	**0.9590**

Experiments showed the accuracy of over 97% for 10 properties and over 95% for 15 properties.

The result uses 10 high properties, and it is more stable than 15 properties because the ability to distinguish between clean file and virus file of set 10 properties is more apparent when adding the last five ones to the property set, leading to dilute detection results.

5   Conclusion and Future Research Orientation

The paper proposes a method to extract information in the PE of the executable in the Windows operating system, then remove the features, combined with deep learning network, Deep Belief Network (DBN), to create a classifier to identify clean files and files that contain viruses. The study also showed a classification system with positive results with unknown malware, which is very practical in the current computer security situation. The results of the DBN classification system partly show the effectiveness of the approach. In the future, we will investigate further as following:

- Select more high-specific property fields to support the classifier more accurately and expand the program's ability to detect and diagnose malicious codes.
- Add supporting tools to self-infer approximate parameters for classifier development.
- Compare with other deep learning networks to refine the classifier and perfect the solution.
- Supplement to the data set many other types of viruses to improve the quality of the classifier.
- Detect viruses on all files of the Windows operating system.

References

1. Vu, T.N., Nguyen, T.T., Phan Trung, H., Do Duy, T., Van, K.H., Le, T.D.: Metamorphic malware detection by PE analysis with the longest common sequence. In: Dang, T.K., Wagner, R., Küng, J., Thoai, N., Takizawa, M., Neuhold, E.J. (eds.) FDSE 2017. LNCS, vol. 10646, pp. 262–272. Springer, Cham (2017). https://doi.org/10.1007/978-3-319-70004-5_18
2. Tobiyama, S., Yamaguchi, Y., Shimada, H., Ikuse, T., Yagi, T.: Malware detection with deep neural network using process behavior. In: 2016 IEEE 40th Annual Computer Software and Applications Conference (COMPSAC), vol. 2, pp. 577–582. IEEE (2016)
3. Saxe, J., Berlin, K.: Deep neural network based malware detection using two dimensional binary program features. In: 2015 10th International Conference on Malicious and Unwanted Software, Fajardo, Puerto Rico, pp. 11–20 (2015)
4. Jung, W., Kim, S., Choi, S.: Deep learning for zero-day flash malware detection. In: In 36th, IEEE Symposium on Security and Privacy (2015)
5. Bai, J., Wang, J., Zou, G.: A malware detection scheme based on mining format information. Hindawi Sci. World J. **2014** (2014). Article ID 260905
6. Kop, L.M.: Bứ c tranh toàn cảnh vụ tấn công đòi tiền chuộc WannaCry đang làm đau đầu giới bảo mật trên toàn thế giới, 14 May 2017. http://cafef.vn/buc-tranh-toan-canh-vu-tan-cong-doi-tien-chuoc-wannacry-dang-lam-dau-dau-gioi-bao-mat-tren-toan-the-gioi-201705 14212143119.chn. Accessed 8 July 2017
7. Wikipedia: Máy học (2016). https://vi.wikipedia.org/wiki/Học_máy
8. Veen, F.V.: The Nơ-ron Network Zoo, 14 September 2016. http://www.asimovinstitute.org/ no-ron-network-zoo. Accessed 28 Oct 2016
9. Sejnowski, T.J., Hinton, G.E.: Learning, and relearning in Boltzmann machines (1986)
10. Bengio, Y., Lamblin, P., Popovici, D., Larochelle, H.: Greedy layer-wise training of deep networks (2007)
11. He, K., Zhang, X., Ren, S., Sun, J.: Deep residual learning for image recognition (2015)

12. Brownlee, J.: Classification accuracy is not enough: more performance measures you can use, 21 March 2014. http://machinelearningmastery.com/classification-accuracy-is-not-eno ugh-more-performance-measures-you-can-use/. Accessed 8 July 2017
13. Antonio, N., Zubair, R.M., Juan, C.: The MALICIA dataset: identification and analysis of drive-by download operations. Int. J. Inf. Secur. **14**, 15–33 (2015)
14. Microsoft Corporation: Desktop App Technologies. Microsoft Corporation (2017). https://msdn.microsoft.com/library/windows/desktop/bg126469.aspx. Accessed 2 Jan 2018
15. Wikipedia: x86 Disassesembly/Windows Excuteable Files. Wikipedia (2017). https://en.wik ibooks.org/wiki/X86_Disassembly/Windows_Executable_Files. Accessed 2 Jan 2018

Automatic Attendance System Based on Face Recognition Using HOG Features and Cosine Distance

Thanh-Hai Nguyen$^{(\boxtimes)}$, Cong-Tinh Dao, Nguyen-Minh-Thao Phan,
Thi-Ngoc-Cham Nguyen, Tan-Tai Phan, and Huynh-Ngoc Pham

College of Information and Communication Technology,
Can Tho University, Can Tho, Vietnam
{nthai,pttai}@cit.ctu.edu.vn,
dcongtinh@gmail.com, pnmthaoct@gmail.com, ntncham0109@gmail.com,
phngoc.ct@gmail.com

Abstract. Advancements in machine learning have been applying deeply and widely in numerous fields. Especially, computer vision tasks for object detection in recent years have achieved great performances which are even better than human recognition ability. This work leverages machine learning methods and information systems to present a framework for student attendance combining machine learning-based face recognition algorithm and relational databases to store, recognize, and record student attendance. The proposed method is tested on various scenarios and is expected to apply in practical cases. We investigate the Histogram of Oriented Gradients (HOG) for face detection and to use cosine distance to recognize faces. The purpose of this study is face recognition in real-time i.e. using a webcam, camera of the mobile device, and from a photograph or from a set of faces tracked in a video. We measured the distance between the landmarks and compared the test image with different known encoded image landmarks in the recognition stage. Face Recognition includes extracting features and then recognizing it, in any case, such as brightness, transformations as translation, rotation, and scale image. We recognized that using the HOG algorithm to detect faces improves more and more efficient model and avoids time-consuming.

Keywords: Student attendance · Face recognition · Relational databases · Cosine distance · Histogram of Oriented Gradients · Recognition in real-time

1 Introduction

In recent years, the rapid development of artificial intelligence has created a driving force for scientists to research smart applications to meet the needs of people in modern society. Artificial Intelligence in general and image processing or computer vision, in particular, have been promoting and developing strongly

© Springer Nature Singapore Pte Ltd. 2020
T. K. Dang et al. (Eds.): FDSE 2020, CCIS 1306, pp. 130–148, 2020.
https://doi.org/10.1007/978-981-33-4370-2_10

with advancements in all domains of society such as security, medicine, government, e-commerce, retailing, education and many other fields. One of the significant applications in image processing is Face Recognition that becomes more and more concerning [1]. Therefore, face recognition has gradually become not only an important field but also a popular field with many beneficial applications. There is a wide range of relevant applications of image analysis such as disease diagnosis, film production, human-machine interaction, security, and defense, etc. are especially applied in attendance.

Attendance is a very practical job doing in schools, agencies, and enterprises. However, it is still quite inadequate. By manually attendance using reading the name, it is time-consuming and inaccurate because one person may take attendance instead of the other person. In addition, using scanning fingerprints or swiping the card that is possible to transmit infectious diseases, especially in the context of the Coronavirus disease (COVID-19) pandemic. One of the most emerged methods about identifying and authenticating a person currently is Biometrics, especially face recognition. With the purpose to save labor, increase the accuracy and to ameliorate our lives, scientists are looking forward to inventing the automated attendance system replacing traditional attendance one. Automated attendance systems based on face recognition techniques were demonstrated to reduce time and ensure secured. For this reason, timekeeping by face recognition is one of the most trusted and appreciated measures to contribute to the prevention of current infectious diseases. The automated system makes a record of students whose attendance in the classroom. Besides, it provides for lecture the facilities function to manage individuals present in class easily [2]. Therefore, the attendance method is a better approach, easier to apply, more effective, helps to prevent fake attendance that is the automatic attendance system based on face recognition.

Face Recognition is a technique providing features that identify people's identity in the input image when face images were existed in the database [3]. This is automatically detected as a face and recognizes a specific person from a photo or video [4]. One way to do this is to compare the facial features with the images in the database. There are two techniques for face detection as model-based and feature-based [5]. Over the years, there have been many studies on the problem of identifying human faces from black and white, gray, and color. The research went from the simple problem that the image only contains a human face looking directly at the camera and the head in an upright position, to a color image with many human faces in the same photo, the face has a rotation small corners or partially obscured with background images of outdoor photos to meet the needs of people really needed. The problem of determining the human face is a computer technique to determine the position and size of faces in digital photos. This technique recognizes facial features and ignores contextual things like buildings, trees, roads, etc. There are many stages in the facial recognition system including image acquisition, building database, face detection, pre-processing, feature extraction, and classification stage [6]. With the extraction of human faces as mentioned above, it was collected from images by cameras and identified the objects in the system based on the face images that were extracted. Thus, by using a camera in a room or just a picture that was photographed, the system could automatically attend to people with scans and access the information of individuals to manage.

In this study, our study provides some contributions:

- We propose a Data Augmentation, a data-space solution to the problem of limited data. Data Augmentation enhances the size and quality of training datasets such that better deep learning models can be built using them. Besides, it also improves the performance of their models and expands limited datasets to take advantage of the ability of big data.
- One of the effective approaches in face detection is the Histogram of Oriented Gradients (HOG) is presented to encode images. In the recognition stage, we deploy the Cosine Distance method for face recognition. The cosine distance compares the feature vectors of two images by returning the cosine of the angle between two vectors.

For the remaining parts, we described the related work in Sect. 2. Next, we illustrate how to approach the issue in the Method Section (Sect. 3). The experimental Results of our proposed methods are provided in Sect. 4 with some scenarios exhibited. We conclude important closing remarks for the work in Sect. 5.

2   Related Work

In many state-of-the-art methods, Deep learning investigates as an approach to extract the hierarchical description of data in the context of face recognition. Deep learning is a significant framework in machine learning that is related to a bunch of algorithms that solve different issues including images, texts and voice to achieve high results [7]. The parallel of developing deep learning and convolutional neural networks, the accuracy and reducing the time of face recognition has gotten great along [8]. During the past two decades, face recognition has experienced considerable notice [9]. Researchers proposed numerous face recognition algorithms such as Eigenfaces [10], Fisherfaces (PCA+LDA) [11], independent component analysis [12], local feature analysis [13], elastic bunch graph matching (EBGM) [14] and so on.

As mentioned above, face recognition is a vital research topic. Besides, solving the complex context issue by using the best algorithms dealing with was computational high-priced for processing real-time. The face recognition approach has provided a great deal of observing in a variety of applications image analysis. A wide range of competitive projects in biometric innovation takes place, especially facial recognition at present. The largest companies in the world such as Google, Apple, Facebook, Amazon, and Microsoft that discover rapidly to implement the intelligent analysis of the video stream in real-life conditions.

In 2018, the US Homeland Security Science and Technology Directorate presented the potential results of the best face recognition system. Besides, The Chinese University of Hong Kong remarked successfully in the face of identifying by Discriminative Gaussian Process Latent Variable Model (DGPLVM) named GaussianFace [15] that the figure for better scores compared with the humans was great progress. Furthermore, Facebook developed a famous program, namelyDeepFace, which can determine whether two faces belong to the same individuals. On the one hand, Google went one better with FaceNet used Labeled Faces in the Wild (LFW) dataset, FaceNet gets an achieved a record accuracy of 99.63%. OpenFace is developed by Mountain View that demonstrated importance in the biometrics context.

Face recognition state of the art Face recognition error rates have decreased over the last twenty years by three orders of magnitude [16] when recognizing frontal faces in still images taken in consistently controlled (constrained) environments. Many vendors deploy sophisticated systems for the application of border-control and smart biometric identification [17]. Face recognition consists of two steps, in the first step faces are detected in the image and then these detected faces are compared with the database for verification. A number of methods have been proposed for face detection i.e. Ada Boost algorithm, the Float Boost algorithm, the S-Ada Boost algorithm Support Vector Machines (SVM), and the Bayes classifier. The efficiency of face recognition algorithms can be increased with the fast face detection algorithm. In all the above methods. SURF is the most efficient. Author in [18] system utilized this algorithm for the detection of faces in the office room image. Authors in [19] proposed a method for student attendance systems in the classroom using face recognition technique by combining Discrete Wavelet Transforms (DWT) and Discrete Cosine Transform (DCT). These algorithms were used to extract the features of a student's face followed by applying Radial Basis Function (RBF) for classifying the facial objects. This system achieved an accuracy rate of 82%.

3   Method

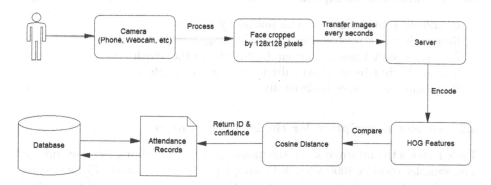

Fig. 1. The architecture of Face recognition based attendance system using HOG features and cosine distance

The given diagram illustrates the architecture system of our proposed method that is using HOG features and cosine distance for the attendance system by face recognition in Fig. 1. At the first stage of our pipeline, we collect the data by a specialist device having a camera such as a mobile phone, webcam, and so on. In the next step, we crop the image to detect face by 128×128 pixels. Following that, the photos will be transferred to the server. The next stage is encoding data and then using HOGs features to detect faces. After that, we recognize faces by applying cosine distance with the encoded and stored datasets. In the subsequent step, the system returns the ID and confidence of the predicted person. Then, this information will be sent to the attendance records system to be written down into the database. Simultaneously, the system returns the list of people who successfully attended at the end of the process.

3.1 Data Collection by Taking a Photo and Data Augmentation

Collecting a large database is extremely expensive and time-consuming. Therefore, we collect by taking a photo per person. In order to avoid the overfitting problems, we need to expand artificially our dataset. Augment image by rotating $10°$, flipping horizontal, brightness adjustment. With one image, we augment 128 images. So, we have 129 images per person. Some general augmentations are horizontal flips, rotations, grayscales, vertical flips, random crops, color jitters, translations, and much more. The idea is to change the training data with small transformations to reproduce the variations. The methods that change the training data in ways that alter the array representation while remaining the label the same are known as data augmentation techniques. This method is a very useful technique for constructing better datasets. Data Augmentation is preventable or at least dramatically reduced in several cases of biases such as brightness, occlusion, scale, background, and many more. Moreover, overfitting may not be as much of a problem with handling big data. Data Augmentation prevents overfitting by altering limited datasets to possess the features of big data. We can easily enhance the number of training examples and create a very robust model by applying just a couple of these transformations to our training data. For the data augmentation, we experimented to:

- Randomly rotate some training images by $15°$
- Randomly zoom by 10% some training images
- Randomly shift images horizontally by 10% of the width
- Randomly shift images vertically by 10% of the height
- Randomly flip images horizontally.

3.2 Images Description for the Face Recognition

Table 1 shows the information of the image dataset for training face recognition. The samples total is 4690 with 4515 samples for encoding and 175 for testing. The information is stored on a server in the repository, the structure of which includes in Fig. 2.

Table 1. Information on image dataset

Class	Encode	Validation
Samples	4515	175

```
datasets
├── augmented
│   ├── B1605247
│   │   ├── B1605247_1.jpg
│   │   └── B1605247_2.jpg
│   └── B1709632
│       ├── B1709632_1.jpg
│       └── B1709632_2.jpg
└── validation
    ├── B1605247
    │   └── B1605247.jpg
    └── B1709632
        └── B1709632.jpg
```

Fig. 2. Dataset directory structure

- As shown in Fig. 2, it can be seen that both /*augmented* folder and /*validation* folder contain sub-folders B1605247, B1709632, ... which is a student ID number. Each folder contains images with the extension of .*jpg* which are numbered as $B1709632\_1.jpg$, $B1709632\_2.jpg$, etc.
- The Folder namely /*validation*, in which photos of new people are added in order to do attendance tasks. For each student, there will be a folder, which is the student ID number, containing the student's photo. This folder is also the director of the raw data collected.
- Next, the folder /*augmented* contains whole photos that were augmented from th face's image and were cropped by 128 × 128 pixels.

3.3 Face Detection by HOG

At the early stages, Histogram of Oriented Gradients (HOG) descriptor was applied to detect humans, in parallel it achieved great success in computer vision. The HOG has been recently applied to face recognition. Object recognition in general and face recognition in particular, HOGs have recently illustrated to be an effective descriptor. HOGs are image descriptors invariant to 2D rotation which have been usual in many different issues in computer vision for the purpose of detecting the objects [20]. We investigated the representational strength of HOG features for face recognition, and to build robust HOG descriptors. An example of the HOG-structure of the face is shown below in Fig. 3. To provide

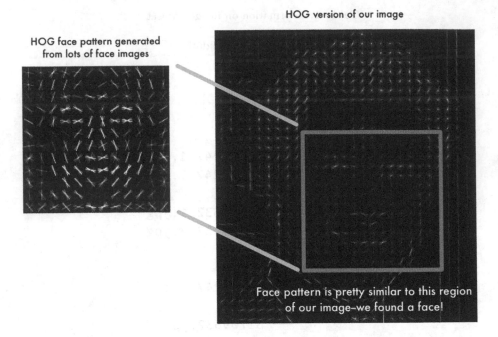

HOG version of our image

HOG face pattern generated from lots of face images

Face pattern is pretty similar to this region of our image—we found a face!

Fig. 3. Overview of finding faces in images with HOG [22]

robustness to facial feature detection by uniformly sampling the HOG features, to remove redundancy in the data, improve computational efficiency and avoid overfitting. We propose to use dimensionality reduction in the HOG representation. Results using HOG features extracted from different image patch sizes significantly improves on choosing a single best patch size. Firstly, the image is divided into small connected cells for each scale and rotation may be also enforced by extracting descriptors from only key points in the scale-space of the image after a rotation normalization. The steps related are Scale Invariant Feature Transform (SIFT) to achieve scale invariance, orientation assignment to find the dominant gradient orientation, and descriptor extraction.

3.4 Face Encode Using Dlib Library

To encode a face, we first detect each face in the image. Then, we will train a machine learning algorithm to be able to find 68 specific points (called **landmarks**) that exist on every face such as the top of the chin, the outside edge of each eye, the inner edge of each eyebrow, the straight line of nose and lip (as shown in Fig. 4). We use the model "face_recognition_model_location" in dlib [21] to train it to generate 128 features for each face128-dimension face encoding for each face in the image.

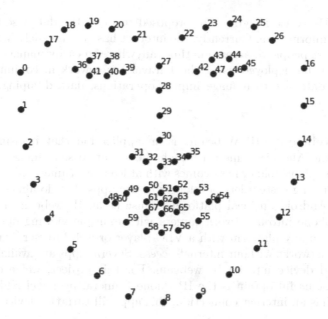

Fig. 4. Detecting face based on 68 landmarks [26]

3.5 Model for Attendance Checking

Compare the image by cosine distance with the saved encoding array. Cosine distance is represented follow by Eq. 1. Given two vectors of attributes, A and B, the cosine distance, $\cos(\theta)$, is represented using a dot product and magnitude as exhibited in Eq. 1.

$$distance = cos(\theta) = \frac{\text{A.B}}{\|A\|\,\|B\|} = \frac{\sum_{i=1}^{n} A_i B_i}{\sqrt{\sum_{i=1}^{n} A_i^2}\sqrt{\sum_{i=1}^{n} B_i^2}}, \tag{1}$$

where A·B is the dot product of A and B, A_i and B_i are components of vector A and B respectively. However, to increase accuracy, we put out tolerance. Tolerance is a real constant equal to 0,6. If the distance is less than or equal to tolerance, it is considered correct. Otherwise, it will not be determined.

3.6 Attendance Records System

The system consists of components such as inputs, processing components, outputs. In which, the system input includes practice management process, catalog data system such as lecturers, students (including photo data), subjects, practice rooms, weekday, etc. Along with the system, outputs are identification results, attendance results, attendance statistics report forms and classroom use. In addition, the information system processing component includes database management for practice and attendance. Conceptual Data Model, Logical Data

Model, and Use Case Diagram are proposed to build the database to manage the required information. Currently, the internet has grown widely, web applications will assist people to access anytime, anywhere to easily manage data. The databases will be deployed using the Laravel Framework in conjunction with the MySQL database to manage import operations, data dumping, and data monitoring.

3.6.1 IP Webcam: IP Webcam[1] is an application that transmits images taken from the Android camera through the server to send images. A typical Android smartphone, old or new, comes with at least one camera. Meanwhile, the Android operating system lets developers create apps that do almost anything. This makes Android an ideal platform for use as an IP webcam. IP Webcam turns your phone into a network camera with multiple viewing options. View your camera on any platform with a VLC player or web browser. Stream video inside WiFi networks without internet access. Several apps are available to turn your Android device into an IP webcam. For this project, we've determined that the most useful option is the IP Phone Camera, by Pavel Khlebovich. If your phone has an internet connection, this app will turn the device into an IP camera.

When faces are detected on the video stream, they are compared with those already present in the database. When faces are detected on the video stream, they are compared with those already present in the database. If the distance between the vectors of the received face image from the video stream and the face image from the database does not exceed the determined threshold value, then the person is detected in the database and must be stored into attendance records. The final step is a data processing application that provides the necessary processing of the information received and then stores it to the database, for example, information about the time of student detection.

3.6.2 The Conceptual Data Model for Attendance System: Provides a map of concepts and their relationships used for databases consists of identifying principal entities, entity types, entity instances, attributes, entity key, relationship, relation types to describe entirely attendance records system.

In Fig. 5, the ATTENDANCE entity inherits properties from the parent entities STUDENT, SCHEDULE. The JOIN entity inherit properties from the parent entities STUDENT, GROUP, and other entities linked through a one-to-many relationship.

Besides, we need to constraint the integrity specifications for the system. For instance, each subject must have its own subject code. Also, each class must have a private class code and class symbol. A group has one or more practice groups (based on class size). A group has a unique code, symbol, semester, and year. Each group practice one or more sessions per week. Each student only joins one practice group of a class (as shown in Fig. 6).

---

[1] http://ip-webcam.appspot.com/static/doc.html.

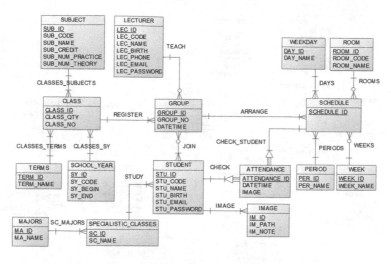

Fig. 5. Conceptual data model of attendance system

In addition, the Use Case Diagram is the means of showing the necessary use cases of an attendance system, used to describe relationships between actors, use cases, and the system. Accordingly, the system has 3 main actors that are administrator user, lecturer user, and schedule manage user. For an actor, each Use Case will perform a sequence of actions performed by the system and produce a result that a certain actor can observe.

Figure 7 shows that the Administrator user is responsible for importing the list of catalogs includes by students, lecturers, school year, term, period, weekday, so on. Lecturers is specialized in 2 groups, namely theory instructors and practice instructors. Lecturers in charge of teaching practice are responsible for creating practice groups and importing a list of students for all classes. Meanwhile, lecturers inherit all of their duties such as view the practice schedule, statistic attendance, check attendance (as shown in Fig. 8).

The Schedule Manager Users are in charge of arranging rooms for practical groups, updating software for each practical room, importing a list of classes by term and school year, viewing list of the practical group, viewing list of the student by practical group, statistics student attendance by classes, view practical schedule entirely (as shown in Fig. 9)

3.6.3 Major Interfaces of the Automated Attendance System: For the illustrations, we introduce some interfaces of the automatic attendance system for the functions of setting the practical schedule and recording the attendance of the students who attended the class.

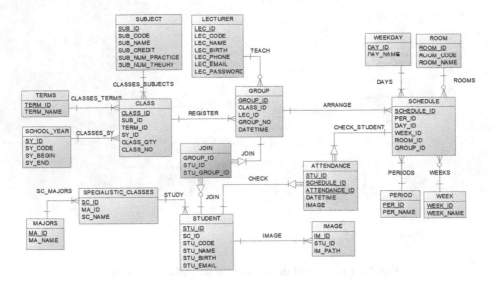

Fig. 6. Logical data model of attendance system

Practical Schedule for courses with some step as follows:

- Step 1: User chooses "Practical Schedule"
- Step 2: The system displays the practice schedule by the system date. In addition, the user is able to review another practice schedule by filtering follow on attributes including "School Year, Term, Week" and then choose to Find to execute this task.
- Step 3: The system ends the series.

Automated Attendance with some step as follows:

- Step 1: User selects "Attendance"
- Step 2: The system displays a list of the student's practical group followed by School Year, Term, Subject Code, Subject Name, Class No, and Group No.
- Step 3: User selects "School Year, Term, Subject Code, Subject Name, Class No, and Group No".
- Step 4: User selects "Find" button to view the expected list of the student's practical group.
- Step 5: The system displays a list of practice group students which was searched.
- Step 6: User selects an image file by "Choose" button.
- Step 7: User selects "Automated Attendance" button.
- Step 8: User sticks into the checkbox to check students who attend the class on system date.
- Step 9: User chooses "Save".
- Step 10: The system ends the series.

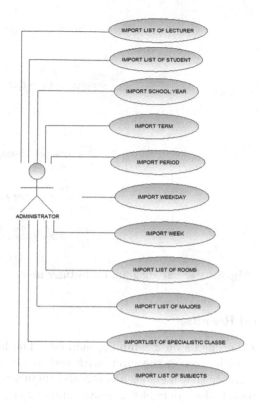

Fig. 7. Use case diagram for administrator user

4 Results

4.1 Experimental Setup

There are many libraries for solving the problems of classification and identification of people's faces. One of these libraries that are written in a high-level programming language Python [24] is face_recognition [23]. This library uses dlib [25] that was written in C++. Using dlib library to classify all regions by HOG descriptors to detect faces. To select the data after finding faces on the image by the face_recognition library. It supports the face_encoding() function to encode all the regions found in a 128-dimensional vector. To find a person in the database of known persons, use the compare_faces() function of the face_recognition library, which uses the Cosine Distance as a proximity metric to compare two 128-dimensional vectors. For each identified person, its name is added to the face_names array. We use a camera which is put in front of the door. Before a class begins, students will look at the camera to attend.

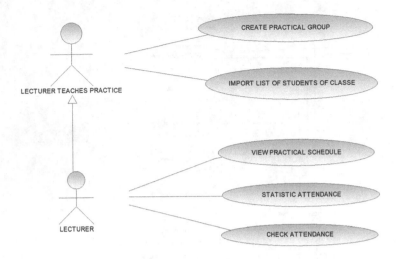

Fig. 8. Use case diagram for lecturer user

4.2   Experimental Results

We performed the experiments on 2 sampling methods. The first one is carried
out on video_recog which receives the input with 600 frames over video 1 min.
Another one is photo_recog that includes a photo and augments 128 more photos
as input for recognition tasks. We deploy 2 above sampling cases, and enconding
whole the input images. Next, the output is then saved into the file with the
extension of .*npy*, we get the following results as presented in Table 2.

Table 2. Results of encoding whole data by cosine and euclidean distance

#method	#distance	#time(s)	#accuracy(%)
video_recog	Cosine	9555.23	99.90
video_recog	Euclid	9813.89	99.87
photo_recog	Cosine	125.44	99.25
photo_recog	Euclid	134.97	99.25

Both methods reveal positive results. Method video_recog gives higher accuracy than photo_recog, however, it is not significantly. Besides that the encode
time of method video_recog is much higher than the photo_recog method about
20x. Therefore, we strongly proposed the photo_recog method with cosine distance to use for this paper.

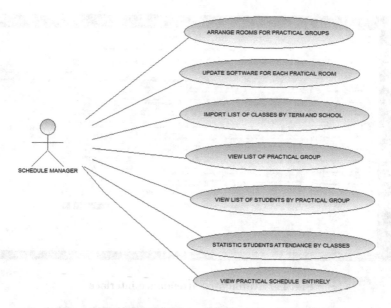

Fig. 9. Use case diagram for schedule manager user

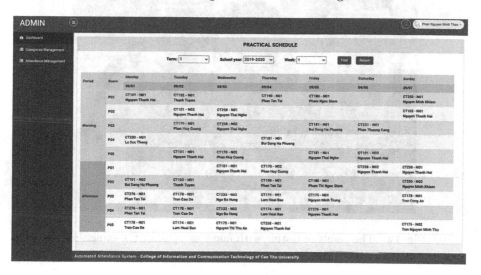

Fig. 10. Practical schedule interface

We present four scenarios as follows:

- **Scenario 1: With respect to test with samples which validation images.**
  Using HOG features with cosine distance reaches accuracy up to 99.25%. In fact, attendance is also affected by environmental conditions such as lighting, people, camera angle, and so on.

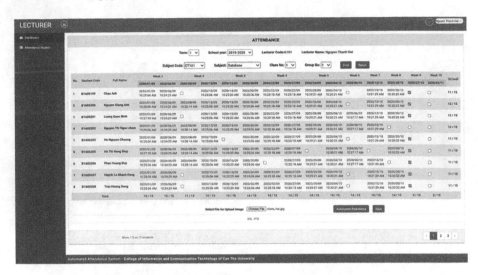

Fig. 11. Automated attendance interface

Fig. 12. The result of testing with many samples at the same time

– **Scenario 2: With respect to test with samples together.**
  The attendance at the same time shown in Fig. 12 is similar to Scenario 1. The
  disadvantage of this context is predicting the outcome when it is necessary
  to detect the people in the photograph and in parallel is predicting who they
  are. Therefore, the prediction will take longer and the rendered video will not
  be real-time and lagging. The predicted time will depend on the number of
  people in the photo for this case.
– **Scenario 3: With respect to test with noise.**
  In this case, we recognize faces with some noises such as wearing glasses,

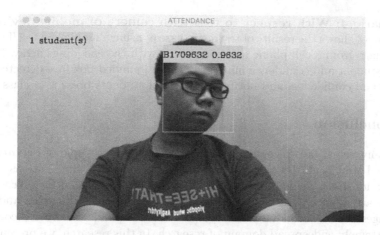

Fig. 13. The result of testing with some noises that is particularly wearing glasses

wearing a hat, light condition, face rotation and so on. However, if the face is covered with a face mask of 50% surface area, our system may not recognize, overfit and return something wrong results. Factors influencing identification results such as lighting, distance from the camera, facial expressions, standing posture, clothing. Represents the intensity of a digital image of an object, so when the light changes, information about the subject is affected. Besides, the object distance from the camera will determine the number of image pixels that define the face. Moreover, the emotional expressions on the face cause noise. Changing in posture will change most of the information about the object, resulting in false identification. Identification results can be greatly affected if the subject has different costumes than the sample includes glasses, hats, etc. We experienced to test within case of wearing glasses in Fig. 13.

Fig. 14. The result of testing with camera of mobile device

– **Scenario 4: With respect to test with camera of mobile device.**
Figure 14 shows the results of testing in case of using a mobile device. Through an image from a cell phone and compare it with the encodings array. Return ID's student and confidence number. Draw a bounded box face detected with label and confidence, and notify a number of students present in class.

5   Conclusion

Over many years, face recognition has been a significant topic of research that originated way back. Its relevance owing to its potential applications that it supports for many fields in human life. In addition, integrated face recognition into the attendance system will be huge contributor to automation and more advantages in the Coronavirus disease (COVID-19) pandemic. Face recognition is an extremely widespread domain of research. In this research, we presented an automatic face recognition based attendance system where the image or video containing a person's face might have been captured from a mobile device or webcam.

Our study was based on combining two approaches HOG for face detection and calculating distance by cosine for face recognition. HOG features with fewer dimensions have better performance than the LBP features under complex changes of light and time environments. HOG features have benefits over VGG16, VGG19, etc. With less computational time of feature extraction and a smaller number of feature vector dimensions. Computing HOG features less time than CNNs and speeds up for real-time face recognition. In addition, we propose storing encrypted data sets to reuse. Because the encoding process takes a lot of time while the data is large. Archiving data avoids a waste of time for the next time. Our research investigated that the encoding time depends on the input image size. In essence, the image encoding is detecting the face and encoding it, so we consider the face which exists in the image rather than the entire image. Therefore, we also recommend cropping faces by 128×128 pixels or lower to reduce the time it takes to encode the datasets.

In the future, our research is concentrated on improving more and more prediction performance and the classification algorithm. Moreover, the influence of each particular landmark on the recognition rate will be investigated to make landmarks that can be precisely weighted or resized.

Acknowledgments. This work is funded by Can Tho University under grant number TSV2020-44.

References

1. Li, Y., Cha, S.: Face Recognition System (2019)
2. Bhattacharya, S., Nainala, G.S., Das, P., Routray, A.: Smart attendance monitoring system (SAMS): a face recognition based attendance system for classroom environment. In: 2018 IEEE 18th International Conference on Advanced Learning Technologies (2018). https://doi.org/10.1109/ICALT.2018.00090

3. Wagh, P., Chaudhari, J., Thakare, R., Patil, S.: Attendance system based on face recognition using Eigen face and PCA algorithms. In: 2015 International Conference on Green Computing and Internet of Things (ICGCIoT) (2015). https://doi.org/10.1109/ICGCIoT.2015.7380478

4. Kar, N., Debbarma, M.K., Saha, A., Pal, D.R.: Study of implementing automated attendance system using face recognition technique. Int. J. Comput. Commun. Eng. 1(2), 100–103 (2012). https://doi.org/10.7763/IJCCE.2012.V1.28

5. Ranganatha, S., Gowramma, Y.P.: Face recognition techniques: a survey. Int. J. Res. Appl. Sci. Eng. Technol. (IJRASET) 4(23), 4979–4990 (2012)

6. Chintalapati, S., Raghunadh, M.V.: Automated attendance management system based on face recognition algorithms. In: 2013 IEEE International Conference on Computational Intelligence and Computing Research (2013). https://doi.org/10.1109/ICCIC.2013.6724266

7. AbdAlmageed, W., et al.: Face recognition using deep multi-pose representations. In: Proceedings of IEEE Winter Conference on Applications of Computer Vision (WACV) (2016). https://doi.org/10.1109/WACV.2016.7477555

8. Xi, M., Chen, L., Polajnar, D., Tong, W.: Local binary pattern network: a deep learning approach for face recognition. In: 2016 IEEE International Conference on Image Processing (ICIP) (2016). https://doi.org/10.1109/ICIP.2016.7532955

9. Zhao, W., Chellappa, R., Phillips, P., Rosenfeld, A.: Face recognition: a literature survey. ACM Comput. Surv. 35(4), 399–458 (2003)

10. Turk, M., Pentland, A.: Eigenfaces for recognition. J. Cogn. Neurosci. 3(1), 71–86 (1991)

11. Belhumeur, P.N., Hespanha, J.P., Kriegman, D.J.: Eigenfaces against Fisherfaces: recognition using class specific linear projection. IEEE Trans. Patt. Anal. Mach. Intell. 19(7), 711–720 (1997). https://doi.org/10.1109/34.598228

12. Bartlett, M., Movellan, J., Sejnowski, T.: Face recognition by independent component analysis. IEEE Trans. Neural Netw. 13(6), 1450–1464 (2002). https://doi.org/10.1109/TNN.2002.804287

13. Penev, A., Atick, J.: Local feature analysis: a general statistical theory for object representation. Netw. Comput. Neural Syst. 7(3), 477–500 (1996)

14. Wiskott, L., Fellous, J., Kruger, N., Malsburg, C.: Face recognition by elastic bunch graph matching. IEEE Trans. Patt. Anal. Mach. Intell. 19(7), 775–779 (1997). https://doi.org/10.1109/ICIP.1997.647401

15. Lu, C., Tang, X.: Surpassing human-level face verification performance on LFW with GaussianFace. In: 29th AAAI Conference on Artificial Intelligence. AAAI Publications (2015)

16. Phillips, P.J., et al.: An introduction to the good, the bad, & the ugly face recognition challenge problem. IEEE (2011). https://doi.org/10.1109/FG.2011.5771424

17. Taigman, Y., Yang, M., Ranzato, M., Wolf, L.: DeepFace: closing the gap to human-level performance in face verification. In: 2014 IEEE Conference on Computer Vision and Pattern Recognition (2014). https://doi.org/10.1109/CVPR.2014.220

18. Selvi, K.S., Chitrakala, P., Jenitha, A.A.: Face recognition based attendance marking system. Int. J. Comput. Sci. Mob. Comput. 3(2), 337–342 (2014)

19. Lukas, S., et al.: Student attendance system in classroom using face recognition technique. In: 2016 International Conference on Information and Communication Technology Convergence (ICTC). IEEE (2016). https://doi.org/10.1109/ICTC.2016.7763360

20. Déniz, O., Bueno, G., Salido, J., De la Torre, F.: Face recognition using Histograms of Oriented Gradients (2011). https://doi.org/10.1016/j.patrec.2011.01.004

21. https://github.com/davisking/dlib-models
22. Voronov, V., Strelnikov, V., Voronova, L., Trunov, A., Vovik, A.: Faces 2D-recognition and identification using the HOG descriptors method. In: Proceedings of the 24th Conference of FRUCT Association (2019)
23. Face Recognition and Identification Library "face_recognition". https://github ubcom/ageitgey/face_recognition
24. High Level Python Programming Language. https://www.python.org
25. Machine learning library "dlib". http://dlib.net
26. Rosebrock, A.: Facial landmarks with dlib, OpenCV, and Python. https://www.pyimagesearch.com/2017/04/03/facial-landmarks-dlib-opencv-python/

Industry 4.0 and Smart City: Data Analytics and Security

Ontology-Based Shrimp and Fish Diseases Diagnosis

An C. Tran[1(✉)] and M. Fukuzawa[2]

[1] Can Tho University, Can Tho, Vietnam
tcan@cit.ctu.edu.vn
[2] Kyoto Institute of Technology, Kyoto, Japan
fukuzawa@kit.jp

Abstract. Shrimp and fish farming industry is one of the major productions that contributes importantly to the Vietnam economy. It provides hundreds of thousands of jobs and the hundred millions of U.S. dollars in revenues. However, this is also considered as a high-risk industry as shrimp and fish are very sensitive to the environmental changes. In addition, the development of diseases on these species is very fast. Any late treatment may cause serious problems to the species and consequently the reduction of revenues. Therefore, in this research, we propose an approach to diagnosing shrimp and fish diseases based on ontology. It helps the farmers making early predictions on shrimp and fish diseases from their morphological symptoms. The ontology is created manually based on the experts' knowledge. The proposed system has been validated using a set of test cases. The validation result shows that the knowledge base and a set of rules have been implemented accurately.

Keywords: Ontology · Shrimp diseases · Fish diseases · Symptoms · Diagnosis

1 Introduction

Shrimp farming industry is one of the most important industries providing hundreds of thousands of jobs and billions of U.S. dollars in revenues [12]. In Vietnam, shrimp farming is a major production that contributes to the country's economy. In recent years, this industry achieved great success in production, contributing positively to the country's economy. It is one of the industries that has the fastest growth rate as illustrated in Fig. 1 [14].

However, this is also considered as a high-risk industry as the shrimp and fish are very sensitive to the environment. Any changes in the environment may cause them to be infected with some kinds of diseases. In addition, the development of diseases on fish and shrimp is very fast, which may result in a sudden death after they are infected.

A report of the Ministry of Agriculture and Rural Development of Vietnam [14] shows that the widespread shrimp diseases caused a total lost of hundreds

© Springer Nature Singapore Pte Ltd. 2020
T. K. Dang et al. (Eds.): FDSE 2020, CCIS 1306, pp. 151–165, 2020.
https://doi.org/10.1007/978-981-33-4370-2_11

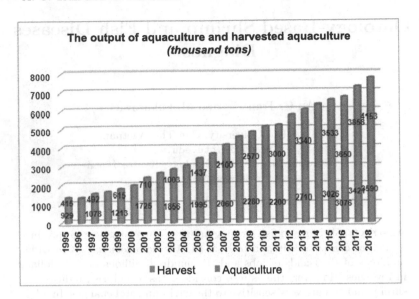

Fig. 1. Aquaculture and harvest output in Vietnam from 1995 to 2018 [14]

of billion dollars. For example, in 2011, the shrimp diseases damaged about 97.000 ha of shrimp farm in Bac Lieu and Soc Trang and caused a loss of about 648 billion VND in revenues. In 2012, the damaged area increased to more than 100.700 ha. Fish is also a major target of widespread diseases. A widespread Tilapia disease caused by bacteria Streptococcus sp. also occurred in the North of Vietnam in 2014.

One of the reasons causing such damages is changes in the feeding environment. Another important reason is the lack of knowledge about farming techniques of farmers [13]. Therefore, to reach large sustainable production levels and reduce any damage caused by diseases, it requires a significant improvement in the farm management methodology and in the development of tools to help the farmers' decision of appropriate treatments against the diseases.

Since the morphological symptom is a simple and conventional form of early disease detection for shrimp and fish, it had been helped farmers to have appropriate treatments [20]. This may help to prevent the disease outbreak from resulting in farm-level damages. There are some studies that many shrimp and fish diseases can be diagnosed in advance by identifying their specific symptoms [6,22]. For example, the shrimps infected by white spot disease will have the following signs:

– Rapid reduction in feed consumption,
– White spot of up to 2 mm diameter appear on the head and/or tail,
– The cuticle becomes loose, etc.

Early detection of diseases allows farmers to select appropriate action such as to avoid its widespread or to have them early treatment to reduce damages.

However, some symptoms present commonly in some diseases, thus causing difficulties for the farmers to diagnose the potential disease. For example, both White
Spot Disease (WSD) and Hepatopancreatic Parvo-like Virus Diseases may cause
the infected shrimps to reduce feeding. Therefore, lacking detailed knowledge of
disease may result in incorrect diagnosis and then leads to inappropriate treatment.

In this research, a diagnosis support system, relying on semantic technologies,
has been proposed to help farmers diagnose the correct disease and then, to
carry out the right treatment, thus avoiding the disease outbreak. The typical
architecture of a disease diagnosis system is shown in Fig. 2. It consists of two
main components namely disease ontology and a rule-based engine. The proposed
approach uses the ontology as a form of knowledge representation and combines
with a rule system for disease diagnosis.

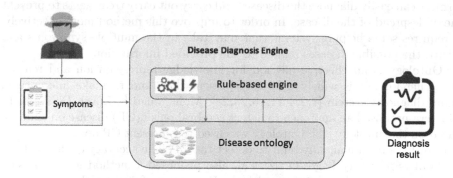

Fig. 2. A typical diagnosis system architecture

2   Related Work

Shrimp and fish farming is an important industry, particularly in developing
countries. However, these species are very sensitive to the environment and diseases. Therefore, early disease detection is a crucial problem for this industry.
Several studies undertook shrimp and fish disease determination. These studies
can be classified into two categories. The first approach is to perform some tests
on the species to check the appearance of the etiologic agents such as viruses
or bacteria. For example, Timothy W. Flegel used PCR technique to check several types of viruses on shrimps such as white-spot syndrome virus (WSSV),
yellow-head virus, etc. [7]. Tomoya Kono et al. developed a diagnostic procedure based on the Loop-mediated isothermal amplification (LAMP) method to
detect the presence of WSSV on shrimps [10]. This is a sensitive and rapid technique in principle and highly sensitive for WSSV detection in particular. Some
studies used several methods to examine the existence of the etiologic agents to
detect the aquatic diseases such as in [24,26,27]. The methods are considered
as effective and accurate methods for aquatic diseases detection. However, these

methods require special tools as well as the experts in this area to conduct tests and confirm the results. The shrimp or fish farmers may not have the required knowledge to perform the tests.

The other approach to detect shrimp and fish diseases is based on some signs on the appearance of species. Some studies showed that the diseases on shrimp and fish result in special signs on their appearance [5,6,22]. Discovering these symptoms can help to identify the diseases. Since this method does not require any special tool, it seems applicable to shrimp and fish farmers as well as experts. However, this method has a disadvantage that a kind of disease may have many symptoms and a certain symptom may commonly appear on many different diseases. Therefore, it causes difficulty for the farmers to diagnose the disease correctly, and the diagnosis accuracy is strongly rely on the individual skill. In spite of such disadvantages, this method has a great potential in the convenience and instantaneousness. If it becomes accurate without the individual skill, the farmers can easily diagnose the diseases and carry out early treatments to prevent the widespread of the disease. In order to improve this method more effectively, it requires some helping systems that may take in the multiple symptoms and return the possible diseases related to the provided information.

Ontology is an effective method for knowledge representation and reasoning. Therefore, it is widely used to represent data and to make inference in many diagnosis system [1,2,4,11,15,23,28]. Mohammad S. Zurob Dr. Wael F. Al Sarra proposed an approach to detect cerebral palsy (CP) disease on children based on the ontology [28]. Ontology was used to represent CP domain and a set of rules have been manually built to detect the CP. The accuracy of this method is about 85%. Katty Lagos-Ortiz et al. also proposed a method for diagnosing plant diseases based on ontology with the F-measure of 79% for the diagnosis of diseases [11]. Valerie Bertaud-Gounot et al. used ontology for knowledge modeling and reasoning in their medical diagnosis [4]. Other research work listed above also used ontology for knowledge representation combined with a rule system for reasoning. These research showed that ontology method is suited to this sort of problem.

3   Ontology-Based Shrimp and Fish Diseases Diagnosis

3.1   Technical Background

The term *ontology* was originally coined from philosophy. In that context, it is the name of a subfield of philosophy that studies the nature of existence, concerned with identifying the kinds of things that actually exist and how to describe them [18,25].

However, in recent years, *ontology* has given a technical meaning in computer science that is rather different from the original one. The most accepted definition of *ontology* was introduced by T. Gruber [8] and then refined by R. Studer [21] as follow: *An ontology is an explicit and formal specification of a conceptualization.*

In general terms, an ontology is a formal specification of the concepts within a domain and their relationships describing formally a domain of discourse. It is a methodology for describing the domain of knowledge structure in a specific area. Typically, an ontology consists of a finite list of terms (classes) and the relationships (properties) between these terms. This is also a useful tool for sharing and reusing knowledge of a domain.

Following are the core components of an ontology:

- **Classes:** describe the concepts in the domain. This is the focus of most ontologies. For example, a class of diseases represents all diseases. A class can have subclasses that represent concepts that are more specific than the superclass. For example, we can organize the cause of disease into viruses and bacteria. Or we can divide species into fish and shrimp. Shrimp then can be divided into Dendrobranchiata and Pleocyemata, etc. (Fig. 3).

- **Properties:** describe the relationships between things (concepts, literals, instances, etc.) in the ontologies. The properties are classified into two categories:

  - **Object properties:** describe the relationships between instances. For example, between instances of Shrimp and Symptom may exist the relationship *hasSymptom*.

  - **Data properties:** describes the relationships between instances and data values (literals). For example, the class Species has a property *hasName* that describes the relationship between this class and a string value (the name).

- **Individuals:** are instances or assertion of classes and properties which include specific or real objects in the domain such as people, animals, diseases, etc.

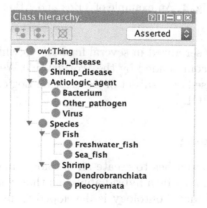

Fig. 3. Super class—Subclass example

A knowledge base is composed of two elements called TBox (terminological box) and ABox (assertion box). TBox is the terminological box which describes the domain in term of classes and properties. This part of the knowledge base contains the classes and properties. On the other hand, the ABox contains the assertions or instances of classes and properties established in TBox.

Knowledge in ontology is represented in triples, based on the Resource Description Framework (RDF) [17]. A RDF triple contains three components, i.e. a subject, a predicate, and an object. A subject must be an instance in the ontology. A predicate corresponds to a property that describes the relationship between a subject and an object. Meanwhile, an object may be an instance or a data value. Figure 4 demonstrates a part of TBox and ABox of the shrimp and fish disease ontology represented using RDF graph.

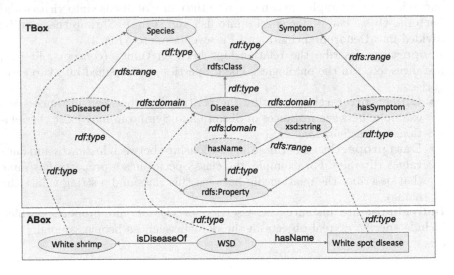

Fig. 4. An example of TBox and ABox

An ontology can be serialized in several formats, in which the Ontology Web Language (OWL) is recommended by the World Wide Web Consortium (W3C) [3]. This language is based on a subset of Description Logic, a decidable fragment of First Order Logic (FOL).

3.2 Ontology Building

There are two basic approaches to create an ontology: manually and automatically. In addition, there may be a hybrid approach that combines both the above approaches. In this research, ontology is developed from information gathered by domain experts.

There are several well-established methodologies to develop an ontology [16,19,21]. For the manual construction of ontology, we mainly follow Noy and McGuinnes methodology [16]. In practical terms, developing an ontology includes the following tasks:

– Defining classes in the ontology.
– Arranging the classes in a taxonomic (subclass—superclass) hierarchy.
– Defining properties and describing allowed values for these properties.
– Filling in the values for properties for instances.
– Defining the properties of classes.

The process of developing an ontology is an iterative process which includes seven steps:

1. Determining the domain and scope of the ontology.
2. Considering reusing existing ontology.
3. Enumerating important terms in the ontology.
4. Defining the classes and the class hierarchy.
5. Defining the properties of the classes.
6. Defining the facets of the properties.
7. Creating instances.

From what we discussed earlier, ontology developing method, with the shrimp and fish disease knowledge mainly based on three books of Thai T. Binh et al. [22], Bui Q. Te [5], and the Central Institute of Brackishwater Aquaculture, India [6], the resulting ontology encompasses 17 classes, 10 object properties, and 3 data properties. We also inserted some instances for demonstration. The result of ontology is described as follows:

– Classes:
  • **AetiologicAgent:** the class of agents which cause or may cause diseases. There are three subclasses (i.e. three kinds of aetiologic agent) that are **Bacterium**, **Virus** and **OtherAetiologicAgent** (other aetiologic agents).
  • **Disease:** the class of shrimp and fish diseases, including two subclasses **ShrimpDisease** (shrimp diseases) and **FishDisease** (fish diseases).
  • **Position:** the class of positions in species such as mouth, tail, fin, etc.
  • **Species:** the class of species considered in the research, that are shrimp and fish. This class has two subclasses which are **Shrimp** and **Fish**. Moreover, class **Shrimp** has two subclasses, i.e. **Dendrobranchiata** and **Pleocyemata**, and class **Fish** has also two subclasses **FreshwaterFish** and **SeaFish**.
  • **Symptom:** the subjective evidences of diseases.
  • **SymptonPosition:** this is a mediate class for the ternary relationship between **Disease**, **Symptom** and **Position** classes. A disease may have symptoms at a particular position. However, in an ontology, the information is described in triples, each of them describes the relationship between only two subjects. Therefore, we use a mediate class to model this ternary relationship. Class **SymptomPosition** describes a symptom at a particular position and it can be defined as follow (in N3 language):

```
:SymptomPosition
    a owl:Class ;
```

```
rdfs:subClassOf
    [a owl:Restriction ;
     owl:someValuesFrom :Symptom ;
     owl:onProperty :hasSymptom
    ] ;
rdfs:subClassOf
    [ a owl:Restriction ;
     owl:allValuesFrom :Position ;
     owl:onProperty :hasPosition
    ] .
```

Figure 5 describes the hierarchical structure of the classes in the ontology.

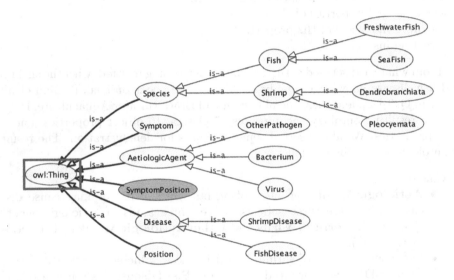

Fig. 5. Concepts/classes in the shrimp and fish disease ontology

– Object properties:
  - **causedBy:** describes the relationship between diseases and aetiologic agents. A disease is caused by one or more aetiologic agents.
  - **causes:** this is an inverse property of the **causedBy** property. It describes the relationship between aetiologic agents and diseases.
  - **isDiseaseOf:** describes the relationship between a disease and a species. A disease may occur on a particular species.
  - **hasDisease:** descries the relationship between a species and a disease. A species may have certain kind of diseases.
  - **hasSymptom:** describes the relationship between a disease and a symptom. A disease may have certain symptoms.
  - **hasSymptomOf:** this is an inverse property of **hasSymptom** property which describes the relationship between a disease and a symptom.

- **isSymptomAt:** describes that relationship between a disease and a position. A disease may have a symptom at particular position.
- **hasSymptomAtPosition:** describes the ternary relations between a disease, a symptom and a position. A disease may a have a symptom at a particular position.

Table 1. Object properties in the shrimp and fish disease ontology

Property	Domain	Range	Notes
causedBy	Disease	Aetiologic agent	Inverse property: causes
causes	Aetiologic agent	Disease	Inverse property: causedBy
isDiseaseOf	Disease	Species	Inverse property: hasDisease
hasDisease	Species	Disease	Inverse property: isDiseaseOf
hasSymptom	Disease	Symptom	Inverse property: isSymptomOf
isSymptomOf	Symptom	Disease	Inverse property: hasSymptom
isSymptomAt	Disease	Position	
hasSymptomAt_Position	Disease	SymptomPosition	

- Table 1 describes more details about the object properties.
- Data properties:
  - **hasDescription:** used to assign description of some concepts in the ontology, i.e. the **Disease** and **Symptom**. Datatype of this property is **xsd:string**.
  - **hasID:** used to assign the ID to diseases. Datatype of this property is also xsd:string.
- Individuals: based on the two books of Thai T. Binh et al. and the Central Institute of Brackishwater Aquaculture, India, we created 8 instances of class Fish, 5 instances of class Shrimp, 4 kinds of disease on fish, 5 kinds of disease on shrimp, 17 symptoms, 6 kinds of virus, 5 kinds of bacterium, 8 positions on shrimp and fish, and 68 combinations of symptoms and positions. Figure 6 demonstrates the individuals of class Bacterium visualized by Protege, an ontology editor developed by Stanford University[1].
- Rules: are used to infer new knowledge from the existing ontology knowledge base. In general, the semantic reasoners, such as Pallet[2], FaCT++[3], and Her-

---

[1] https://protege.stanford.edu/.

[2] https://github.com/stardog-union/pellet.

[3] http://owl.cs.manchester.ac.uk/tools/fact/.

miT[4] can perform ontology reasonings such as classification, retrieval, check for consistency, etc. However, a rule system may extend the reasoning capability. For example, if the shrimps have the following signs: rapid reduction in feed consumption, minute white spots up to 2 mm appear on the head and/or tail, the cuticle becomes loose, and the body and appendages show reddish discoloration, then they are said to be infected to the White Spot Disease.

Fig. 6. Individuals of class Bacterium

Based on such information, a set of rules for diagnosing diseases can be developed. In this research, the Semantic Web Rule Language (SWRL) is used to implement the rules in the ontology. This is the most popular semantic web rule language that combines OWL and RuleML [9]. This rule language is also supported by most of the popular semantic reasoners such as Pallet, HermiT, and FaCT++. For example, the SWRL rules to detect the White Spot Disease described above is as follow:

```
Shrimp(?x)
    ∧ hasSymptom(?x, reduction_in_feed_consumption)
    ∧ hasSymptomAtPosition(?x, white_spot_head)
    ∧ hasSymptonAtPosition(?x, loose_cuticle)
    ∧ hasSympton(reddish_discoloration)
⇒ hasDisease(?x, white_spot_disease)

Shrimp(?x)
    ∧ hasSymptom(?x, reduction_in_feed_consumption)
    ∧ hasSymptomAtPosition(?x, white_spot_tail)
    ∧ hasSymptonAtPosition(?x, loose_cuticle)
    ∧ hasSympton(reddish_discoloration)
⇒ hasDisease(?x, white_spot_disease)
```

---

[4] http://www.hermit-reasoner.com/.

3.3   Ontology-Based Diagnosis System

Based on the ontology created, a web-based shrimp and fish disease diagnosis application has been developed. The application is implemented in PHP that uses ARC library[5] to work with ontology. The system architecture is described in Fig. 7.

This application supports two diagnosis modes: the multi-step diagnosis and the one-step diagnosis. In multi-step mode, the users provide the symptoms one-by-one. When a symptom is provided, the system will select all diseases that have the provided symptom. The list of possible symptoms will also be restricted to the remaining diseases. Then, the users can continue to choose further symptoms to eliminate the possible disease. The more symptoms are selected, the more accurate the diagnosis is. The diagnosis in this circumstance is an iterative process which is described in Fig. 8.

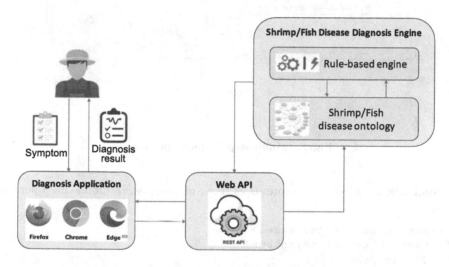

Fig. 7. Shrimp and fish disease diagnosis system architecture

To select the diseases for a given symptom, the following SPARQL query is used:

```
//input: <symptom>
//output: a set of <diseases> and their <descriptions>
SELECT ?disease ?description
WHERE {
   ?disease a Disease ;
      hasSymptom <symptom> .
   OPTIONAL {
      ?disease hasDescription ?description
   }
}
```

---

[5] https://github.com/semsol/arc2.

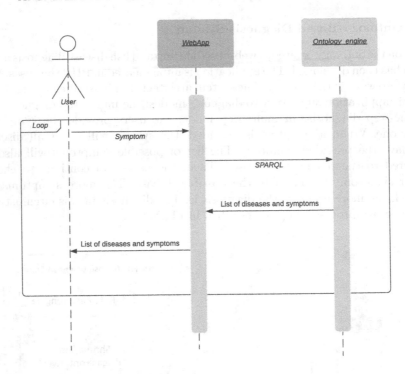

Fig. 8. Muilti-step diagnosis process

Similarly, to select all symptoms of a set of diseases, the following query is used:

```
//input: a set of <diseases>
//output: a set of <symptoms>
SELECT ?symptom
WHERE {
   ?disease in diseases .
   ?symptom isSymptomOf ?disease
}
```

On the other hand, the one-step diagnosis method gets a full set of symptoms, then it will produce the diagnosis result, i.e. the possible diseases corresponding to the given symptoms. In this method, an instance of the selected species and the observed symptoms will be added to the ABox of the ontology. Then, the SWRL rules will be used to reason about the possible diseases that the shrimp or fish may be infected.

4   Result and Discussion

Five test cases have been designed and tested to validate the diagnosis system, as noted. Table 2 shows the test results.

Table 2. Object properties in the shrimp and fish disease ontology

No	Test case	Inputs	Expected output	Actual output	Test result
1	WSD	All WSD disease symptoms	WSD	WSD	Success
2	IHLN	All IHLN disease symptoms	IHLN	IHLN	Success
3	Overlapped symptom	Reduced feeding	WSD, HPV and MBV	WSD, HPV and MBV	Success
4	Multiple overlapped symptoms	Reduced feeding, gill fouling	HPV and MBV	WSD, HPV and MBV	Success
5	Non-related symptoms	Some symptoms that are not in the ontology	None	None	Success

When designing the test cases, the coverage has been considered. In test cases 1 and 2, all symptoms of 2 selected diseases were provided. The system is expected to return only these 2 diseases, i.e. WSD and IHLN respectively. In test case 3, a common symptom of WSD, HPV, and MBV were provided and it is expected to return all three diseases. Test case 4 is also for testing the overlap. However, 2 common symptoms of HPV and MBV were fed into the system, one of them is a symptom of another disease. It is expected to return only HPV and MBV in this case. Finally, in test case 5, a symptom that is not related to any diseases in the ontology was provided. It is expected not to return any disease.

The validation result shows that all test cases are successful. That means the ontology and rule set had been implemented correctly.

5   Conclusion

This research has proposed an ontology-based diagnosis system for shrimp and fish diseases from their appearance expression. An ontology was developed based on the method proposed by Noy and McGuinnes. The ontology consists of 17 classes, 10 object properties, 3 data properties and 128 individuals. A set of SWRL rules for inferring diseases was also created. The web-based diagnosis application has been developed using PHP programming language that uses ARC library for accessing the ontology from PHP. The system was validated based on 5 test cases. The validation results show that the system returned the correct result for all test cases. This implies the disease ontology and the rules were designed correctly.

Acknowledgments. This study is funded in part by the Can Tho University Improvement Project VN14-P6, supported by a Japanese ODA loan.

References

1. Alagha, H.M.: Diagnosing Heart Diseases Using Ontology and SWRL Rules. Master's thesis, The Islamic University (2017)

2. Alharbi, R.F., Berri, J., El-Masri, S.: Ontology based clinical decision support system for diabetes diagnostic. In: 2015 Science and Information Conference (SAI), pp. 597–602. IEEE (2015)
3. Antoniou, G., Van Harmelen, F.: Web ontology language: Owl. In: Handbook on ontologies, pp. 67–92. Springer, Berlin (2004)
4. Bertaud-Gounot, V., Duvauferrier, R., Burgun, A.: Ontology and medical diagnosis. Inf. Health Soc. Care **37**(2), 51–61 (2012)
5. Bui Quang, T.: Aquatic pathology. Research Institute for Aquaculture No. 1 (2006)
6. Central Institute of Brackishwater Aquaculture: Shrimp Diseases: Symptoms, causes, diagnosis, prevention and control. Central Institute of Brackishwater Aquaculture (2000)
7. Flegel, T.W.: An overview of PCR techniques for shrimp disease diagnosis in Asia, with emphasis on Thailand. In: Disease Control in Fish and Shrimp Aquaculture in Southeast Asia-Diagnosis and Husbandry Techniques: Proceedings of the SEAFDEC-OIE Seminar-Workshop on Disease Control in Fish and Shrimp Aquaculture in Southeast Asia-Diagnosis and Husbandry Techniques, 4–6 December 2001, Iloilo City, Philippines, pp. 34–64. Aquaculture Department, Southeast Asian Fisheries Development Center (2002)
8. Gruber, T.: What is an ontology? 1993. http://www-ksl.stanford.edu/kst/what-is-an-ontology.html (2013)
9. Horrocks, I., Patel-Schneider, P.F., Boley, H., Tabet, S., Grosof, B., Dean, M., et al.: Swrl: A semantic web rule language combining OWL and RuleML. W3C Member Submission **21**(79), 1–31 (2004)
10. Kono, T., Savan, R., Sakai, M., Itami, T.: Detection of white spot syndrome virus in shrimp by loop-mediated isothermal amplification. J. Virol. Methods **115**(1), 59–65 (2004)
11. Lagos-Ortiz, K., Medina-Moreira, J., Paredes-Valverde, M.A., Espinoza-Morán, W., Valencia-García, R.: An ontology-based decision support system for the diagnosis of plant diseases. J. Inf. Technol. Res. (JITR) **10**(4), 42–55 (2017)
12. Ling, B.H., Leung, P., Shang, Y.C.: Overview of the world shrimp industry. In: Leung, P.S., Sharma, K.R. (eds.) The Farm Performance Study on which these Research Papers were Based was Funded by the Asian Development Bank under RETA 5534, and Implemented by the Network of Aquaculture Centres in Asia-Pacific in 1994–1995, p. 3. University of Hawaii at Manoa, Honolulu, Hawaii, USA (2001)
13. Lundin, C.G.: Global attempts to address shrimp disease. World Bank Environment Department, Land, Water and Natural Habitats Division (1996)
14. Ministry of Agriculture and Rural Development of Vietnam: Environment monitoring for aquaculture farming project. Agriculture Publishing House (2014)
15. Mukabunani, A.: Ontology-Based Clinical Decision Support System Applied on Diabetes. Master's thesis, University of Agder (2017)
16. Noy, N.F., McGuinness, D.L., et al.: Ontology development 101: A guide to creating your first ontology (2001)
17. Pan, J.Z.: Resource description framework. In: Handbook on Ontologies, pp. 71–90. Springer (2009)
18. Pollock, J.T.: Semantic Web for Dummies. Wiley, New York (2009)
19. Roussey, C., Pinet, F., Kang, M.A., Corcho, O.: An introduction to ontologies and ontology engineering. In: Ontologies in Urban Development Projects, pp. 9–38. Springer (2011)
20. Selvin, J.: Shrimp Disease Management. Ane Books Pvt Ltd (2010)

21. Staab, S., Studer, R.: Handbook on Ontologies. Springer Science & Business Media, Berlin (2010)
22. Thai Thanh, B., Nguyen Thi, Q., Do Trung, K., Bui Quang, T., Truong Van, T.: Fast Diagnosis and Treatment Diseases Caused by Parasites on Aquatic Animals. Agriculture Publishing House (2015)
23. Thangaraj, M., Gnanambal, S.: A rule based decision support system for aiding vitamin d deficiency management. Indian J. Sci. Technol. **7**(1), 48–52 (2014)
24. Tinwongger, S. et al.: Development of PCR diagnosis for shrimp acute hepatopancreatic necrosis disease (AHPND) strain of vibrio parahaemolyticus. Fish Pathol. **49**(4), 159–164 (2014)
25. Van Harmelen, F.: A Semantic Web Primer. MIT Press, Cambridge (2008)
26. Xiong, J., Zhu, J., Dai, W., Dong, C., Qiu, Q., Li, C.: Integrating gut microbiota immaturity and disease-discriminatory taxa to diagnose the initiation and severity of shrimp disease. Environ. Microbiol. **19**(4), 1490–1501 (2017)
27. Yu, W., Cao, J., Dai, W., Qiu, Q., Xiong, J.: Quantitative PCR analysis of gut disease-discriminatory phyla for determining shrimp disease incidence. Appl. Environ. Microbiol. **84**(18), e01387-18 (2018)
28. Zurob, M.S., Al Sarraj, W.F.: Towards cerebral palsy diagnosis: an-ontology based approach. Int. J. Softw. Eng. Appl. (IJSEA) **9**(3), 17–24 (2018)

Deep Learning-Based Methods for Plant Disease

Vu Thanh Nguyen[1]([⊠]), Triet Quang Duong[2]([⊠]), Tuan Dinh Le[3],
and Anh Thi Dieu Nguyen[2]

[1] Ho Chi Minh City University of Food Industry, Ho Chi Minh City, Vietnam
nguyenvt@hufi.edu.vn
[2] Van Hien University, Ho Chi Minh City, Vietnam
trietdq@vhu.edu.vn, anhntdgm@gmail.com
[3] Long An University of Economics and Industry, Tan An, Long An Province, Vietnam
tuan@daihoclongan.edu.vn

Abstract. Plant diseases are one of the main factors that can cause significant crop damages and yield losses. Deep learning has recently attracted a lot of attention to use for plant disease identification. The recent studies used deep learning techniques to diagnose plant diseases in an attempt to identify plant diseases. This paper evaluates the performance of different deep learning methods, including YOLO, RetinaNet, Faster RCNN, and Mask RCNN, for plant disease-identification problem. The real dataset of 5,180 leaves and 42 types of leaf samples (disease or not) from different crops were used for evaluation.

Keywords: Crop diseases · Deep learning · YOLO (You Only Look Once) · Batch normalization · Dropout · RetinaNet · Faster RCNN · Mask RCNN

1 Introduction

Plant diseases are a significant threat to production and quality, and many researchers have made various efforts to control these diseases. In the last few years, traditional machine-learning algorithms have been widely used to realize disease detection. Deep learning refers to the use of artificial neural network architectures that contain quite a large number of processing layers. Deep learning has recently attracted a lot of attention intending to use for plant disease identification such as YOLO [1], RetinaNet [4], Faster RCNN [2], and Mask RCNN [3].

This paper's main contribution is as follows: Collecting the fact data set includes 55,180 leaves images 42 types of leaf samples (disease or not) from different crops. Images were collected from various sources, including data from the Plant Village contest data from agriculture sites. The data set we have built is a challenging one for local and foreign research teams and a useful reference source for application developers. Data is public at this link address with providing purpose for subsequent researches.

The four most advanced deep learning-based methods for plant disease identification are YOLO, Faster RCNN, Mask RCNN, and RetinaNet. The accuracy, the processing speed, and the computing resources were the main criteria, which are used for our evaluation. Besides, for each method, we also investigated different settings to find suitable

© Springer Nature Singapore Pte Ltd. 2020
T. K. Dang et al. (Eds.): FDSE 2020, CCIS 1306, pp. 166–177, 2020.
https://doi.org/10.1007/978-981-33-4370-2_12

parameters. Comparative analysis of experimental results showed that when developing practical applications with the need to balance between factors, the YOLO method would be an appropriate choice because it gives the best results with high accuracy.

The rest of this paper is organized as follows: Sect. 2 presents a brief review of the related work. Sections 3 describes our experimental setup, and the experimental results are further discussed subsequently in Sect. 4. Section 5 concludes the paper recommending future works.

2 Related Work

The problem's input is the image of their leaves, which is used to identify the disease. In contrast, the output is the object's position. If it is available, the position is shown through a rectangle surrounding the object-bounding box (Fig. 1).

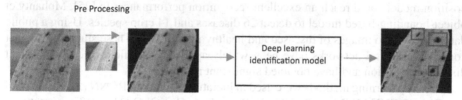

Fig. 1. Outline of input and output data on leaf disease recognition system

Previous studies in this area are listed as follows:

In [17], Qin et al. proposed a feasible solution for lesion image segmentation and image recognition of alfalfa leaf disease. The relief method was first used to extract 129 features, and then an SVM model was trained with essential elements. The results indicated that image recognition of the four alfalfa leaf diseases could be implemented. In [18], Rothe et al. presented a pattern recognition system for identifying and classifying three cotton leaf diseases. An active contour model was used for image segmentation, and Hu's moments were extracted as features for the training of an adaptive neuro-fuzzy inference system. In [19], Islam et al. presented an approach that integrated image processing and machine learning to diagnose diseases from leaf images. This automated method classifies diseases on potato plants from 'Plant Village,' which is a publicly available plant image database. The segmentation approach and utilization of an SVM demonstrated disease classification in over 300 images.

In [20], Gupta proposed an autonomously modified SVM-CS (Cuckoo Search) model to identify the healthy portion and disease. Using a dataset of diseases containing plant leaves suffering from Alternaria Alternate, Cercospora Leaf Spot, Anthracnose, and Bacterial Blight, along with healthy leaf images, the proposed model was trained and optimized the concept of a cuckoo search. However, these studies' identification and classification approaches are semiautomatic and complex and deal with a series of image processing technologies. Simultaneously, it is challenging to accurately detect the specific disease images without extracting and designing the appropriate classification features depending heavily on expert experience. Recently, several researchers have studied plant disease identification based on deep learning approaches.

In [21], Lu et al. proposed a novel identification approach for rice diseases based on deep convolutional neural networks. Using a dataset of 500 natural images of diseased and healthy rice leaves and stems, CNNs were trained to identify ten common rice diseases. In [22], Tan et al. presented an approach based on CNN to recognize apple pathologic images and employed a self-adaptive momentum rule to update CNN parameters. In [23], the cucumber leaf's disease detection system was presented based on convolutional neural networks. Under the fourfold cross-validation strategy, the proposed CNN-based system achieved an average 94.9% accuracy in classifying cucumbers into two typical disease classes and a healthy type. The experimental results indicate that a CNN-based model can automatically extract important classification features and obtain optimal performance. In [24], Sladojevic et al. proposed a novel approach based on deep convolutional networks to detect plant disease. By discriminating the plant leaves from their surroundings, 13 different common types of plant diseases were recognized by the proposed CNN-based model. The experimental results showed that the object's position model could reach an excellent recognition performance. In [25], Mohanty et object-bounding-based model to detect 26 diseases and 14 crop species. Using a public dataset of 54,306 images of diseased and healthy plant leaves. These studies show that convolution neural networks have been widely applied to the field of crop and plant disease recognition and have obtained significant results.

The deep learning methods were used in literature, including RCNN [5], Fast RCNN [6], Faster RCNN [2], Mask RCNN [3], RetinaNet [4], YOLO [1], etc. These methods are divided into two main approaches [7]: the two-stage approach - that is, region-based proposals are results from another technique such as Selective Search [8] or Region Proposal Network [3], and the one-stage approach - that is, within the network structure itself, the method includes the operation of making the proposed area. In our study, both the two-stage approach, including the Faster RCNN and Mask RCNN and the one-stage approach, including YOLO and RetinaNet, were adopted for evaluation.

2.1 Faster RCNN [2]

The faster RCNN method is one method to detect objects using a deep learning network with high accuracy on standard data sets such as COCO [9]. Faster RCNN is improved based on two previous methods, RCNN [5] and Fast RCNN [6]. In Faster RCNN, the authors used the Region Proposal Network (RPN) to create the proposed areas. After acquiring in-depth features from the first convolutional layers, the RPN network uses the sliding window on the feature map to extract features for each proposed region. RPN is considered a fully associative network is simultaneously performing two tasks to predict coordinates for objects and reliability for that object. Compared to the previous methods, Faster RCNN has higher results and faster processing time, but the speed cannot meet real-time processing.

2.2 Mask RCNN [3]

The RCNN Mask method performs both object segmentation (Instance Segmentation) and object detection. RCNN Mask is an improved method from Faster RCNN [2], in which RCNN Mask recommends using the RoI Align layer instead of RoI pooling in

Faster RCNN using RoI Align helps RCNN Mask to improve significantly in selecting extracting areas. This approach improves the accuracy of object detection and a reasonable basis for object partitioning problems. RCNN Mask performs two issues simultaneously, so the RCNN Mask network has two parallel branches. The branch detection branch's task is similar to Faster RCNN, and the branching is to calculate the features from the RoI Align layer to give partition masks to the objects. Although the RCNN Mask has improved the accuracy more than Faster RCNN, it has not improved the calculation, so the RCNN Mask time is still considerably low.

2.3   RetinaNet [4]

RetinaNet is a one-stage approach. RetinaNet performs the calculation based on the default anchor boxes at each location instead of using the proposed areas created from another study. RetinaNet input data is passed through a network model called FPN [10] to extract specific matrices with the same scale but in many different sizes. The characteristic matrix is used for calculating the regions to export. Finally, the proposed areas are passed over two subnets to calculate the bounding boxes' position and the object's class that the bounding box surrounds.

2.4   You Only Look Once (YOLO) [1]

YOLO is the first method to process data in real-time and with high accuracy. YOLO's main idea is that instead of using the proposed regions to extract characteristics, YOLO uses local information from training data to learn the features of interest by dividing the image of the input data. Grid (grid view) is to exploit features on the grid. If the object's focus falls on any cell in the grid, that cell is responsible for detecting the object. The size of the grid depends on the version of YOLO because YOLO currently has three versions, including YOLOv1 [1], YOLOv2 [11], YOLOv3 [12], and each version has different meshing and implementation. Featured in these three versions is YOLOv3. Although the speed is slower than YOLOv2, its accuracy is significantly better than that of the YOLOv2.

Empirical results on the standard data sets of object detection problems show that two-stage methods tend to have higher accuracy than one-stage methods. However, in terms of execution time, the one-stage approach is usually faster and can use real-time. However, the methods' performance varies depending on the size, attributes, complexity, and variety of data sets used for training and the design of the Deep learning network. Therefore, assessing these factors' influence when applying the methods listed above on the actual data set will help developers choose the most appropriate for their requirements.

3   Experimental Settings

To evaluate the methods according to the Deep learning approach on actual data, we conducted data collection and labeling 42 classes, including different types, diseased and disease-free leaves from multiple sources. We then evaluated the methods on various factors, including the accuracy, time, and computational resources to be processed. Besides, we considered many different settings for each approach ind the most appropriate parameters for each method. Accordingly, in this content, we will describe the criteria and the metrics used in the evaluation, detailed information about the data set collected, and the different settings corresponding to each method.

3.1 Evaluation Metrics and Datasets

In our study, we use the following metrics for evaluation:
Accuracy of the methods on actual data:
The accuracy is calculated as follows:

$$mAP = \sum_{q=1}^{Q} \frac{AP(q)}{Q} \tag{1}$$

Where Q is the number of object classes in the data set, A.P. is the average of each class calculated by the following formula:
In this case, we use 42 object classes:

$$AP = \frac{1}{42} \sum_{r \in \{0,0.1,...,42\}} P_{inter}p(r) \tag{2}$$

With $P_{inter}p(r)$ is calculated as follows:

$$P_{inter}p(r) = \max_{\tilde{r}:\tilde{r} \geq r} p(\tilde{r}) \tag{3}$$

Inside $p(\tilde{r})$ is precision measured at recall $\tilde{r}$:

$$\tilde{r} = \frac{TP}{TP + FN} \tag{4}$$

TP is True positive, and F.N. is False Negative.

The Speed and Processing Time: The speed and processing time play an essential role in plant disease identification problems [16].

For recording the computation time for a single epoch of a deep network, we can first compute the time which requires for a forward and backward pass on a single batch:

$$T_b = \sum_{i=0}^{l} b_{M(i)} \tag{5}$$

Where l is the number of layers in the deep neural network, and bM(i) is the batch execution time estimate, generated by the prediction approach, for I layer, where M(i) is of type of I layer. It should be noted here that bM(i) should also be parameterized by the other features we use when training our network; however, we have not listed those for simplicity. Then to compute the total execution time for a single epoch of the deep learning network, we can calculate:

$$E = p.Tb \tag{6}$$

Where p is the number of batches required to process the data;

To evaluate these factors, we use the standard measures of the object detection problem. In particular, with exact criteria, we use the mAP (mean average precision) according to the evaluation standard of PASCAL VOC [13] as the formula below. Measure the model training time in hours and determine the resources used for each model by the GPU's RAM capacity during the training and running predictions.

3.2 The Dataset

The collected data included 55,180 diseased leaves images 42 types of leaf samples (disease or not) from different crops. The images were collected from various sources, including data from the Plant Village contest data from agriculture sites. We do this collection for supporting has a leafy library of a wide range of diseases and leaves for plant-related research. Most images were captured and resized at 256 × 256, with a vertical and horizontal resolution of 96 dpi (Table 1 and Fig. 2).

Table 1. The type of leaf samples

1	Apple scab	22	Potato healthy
2	Apple black rot	23	Potato late blight
3	Apple cedar rust	24	Raspberry healthy
4	Apple healthy	25	Soybean healthy
5	Blueberry healthy	26	Squash powdery mildew
6	Cherry healthy	27	Strawberry healthy
7	Cherry powdery mildew	28	Strawberry leaf scorch
8	Corn gray leaf spot	29	Tomato bacterial spot
9	Corn common rust	30	Tomato early blight
10	Corn healthy	31	Tomato late blight
11	Corn northern leaf blight	32	Tomato leaf mold
12	Grape black rot	33	Tomato septoria leaf spot
13	Grape black measles (Esca)	34	Tomato two spotted spider mite
14	Grape healthy	35	Tomato target spot
15	Grape leaf blight	36	Tomato mosaic virus
16	Orange huanglongbing (citrus greening)	37	Tomato yellow leaf curl virus
17	Peach bacterial spot	38	Tomato healthy
18	Peach healthy	39	Rice bacterial-leaf light
19	Bell pepper bacterial spot	40	Rice blast
20	Bell pepper healthy	41	Rice brown spot
21	Potato early blight	42	Rice leaf smut

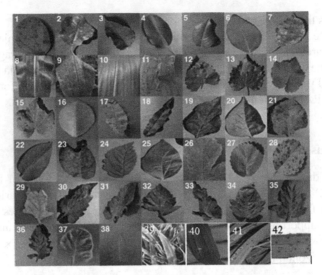

Fig. 2. The dataset of 55,180 diseased leaves images.

After the manual labeling process, we divide the construction data set according to the following ratio: photo-training accounts for 60%, the number of validating photos is 20%, and test files account for a 20% submission process.

3.3 Evaluation Settings

For object detection methods, each method has its settings corresponding to the model's parameters, such as learning rate, iteration, input image size, etc. Besides, the choice of model for the backbone extraction process also plays an essential role in running the method. All of these settings affect factors such as accuracy, speed, processing time, and system resources. Accordingly, in the empirical part and comparing different methods, we also set various parameters in each method to give the best parameters. The models we evaluated included YOLOv3, RetinaNet, RCNN Mask, Faster RCNN with a backbone, including FPN [10], ResNet [14].

We train these Deep learning network models with transfer learning method - that is, using weight sets that have been trained before on large data sets such as ImageNet [15], and then by using weights, have been learned on the real dataset of the problem. Training in this way helps us solve the problem of lack of data in training Deep learning networks.

For YOLO, we use K-means, as the author mentioned, to recalculate the size and ratio of the anchors. Empirically after recalculating the anchors, the result on YOLOv3 gives worse results than the default anchors, so we decided to use nine default anchors including [10, 13], [16, 30], [33, 23], [30, 61], [62, 45], [59, 119], [116, 90], [156, 198], [373, 326]. The remainder related to the super parameters is shown in Table 2.

We train models totaling 30 epochs. From the results, we will compare each other based on the three criteria set out to find each method's advantages and limitations.

Table 2. Detailed statistical information about the parameters when training the model

Method	Learning rate	Batch size	Weight decay	Max iteration	Step size	Image size
Mask RCNN	0.001	2	0.0001	135000	60000, 120000	256,256
Faster RCNN	0.001	2	0.0001	135000	60000, 120000	
RetinaNet	0.001	2	0.0001	135000	60000, 120000	
YOLOv3	0.001	32	0.0005	422202	40000	

4 Experimental Results

In this section, we describe the experimental results. The trained models were run on Google Colab Linux 64 bits Colab machine with an Nvidia Tesla K80 GPU and 25 G.B. of RAM.

4.1 The Accuracy

Table 3 shows the accuracy of the evaluated methods. The results indicate that for the two-stage approach, the RCNN Mask model achieves the highest mAP, especially the RCNN Mask, with the mechanical network when compared to other methods. The resNet50-FPN version is 82.9%, which is about 2.4% higher than the basic network of ResNet101-FPN, reaching 80.5%. The results show that using a network with multiple layers is unlikely to have better results. The more classes a network has, the larger the number of parameters it needs to learn. The parameters' value will be updated in the training process by adopting optimal algorithms such as Gradient Descent. If the method we use does not handle well when extracting characteristics from data, the results when classifying and predicting the objects' coordinates will be affected.

Table 3. Experimental results on data collection

Method Name									
	YOLO v3	RetinaNet ResNet50	ReitnaNet ResNet101	Mask ResNet50 C4	Mask ResNet50 FPN	Mask ResNet101 FPN	Faster ResNet50 C4	Faster ResNet50 FPN	Faster ResNet101 FPN
Medium (mAP %)	**60.5**	79	80.2	78.3	**82.9**	80.5	81.6	80.4	80.1

Similarly, in the Faster RCNN method, the basic network of ResNet50-FPN reaches 80.4%, and ResNet101-FPN reaches 80.1%. In this case, the difference between the two basic networks is insignificant, only 0.3%. Although the Faster RCNN achieves about

2% lower than the RCNN Mask, the difference between the two basic networks shows that the combination of basic networks with Faster RCNN has better results than the RCNN Mask.

For the one-stage methods, the YOLOv3 model achieved the lowest result of 60.5%. In contrast, for the RetinaNet, when combined with the basic network, the ResNet 101 performed 80.2%, which results in 1.2% better than ResNet-50. This because the RetinaNet uses Focal Loss to calculate the error level that Focal Loss is proposed to use in cases where data between layers is not equal between foreground and background, so in cases like data sets. Our RetinaNet data gives stable results when combined with the underlying network.

The results showed that the accuracy of the model significantly affects the baseline when extracting the feature. The back network is used to handle the characteristics and the function of calculating error in the training method.

4.2 Computational Resources

As shown in Fig. 3, the average amount of RAM needed when using model training by using the RetinaNet method with ResNet50 backbone-The FPN is the lowest (3.13 GB), the YOLOv3 method consumes the most resources when using up to twice the resources than those of other methods required. YOLOv3 uses more resources because of using the darknet19 basic network as in the previous two versions. YOLOv3 uses the Darknet53 basic network with 3 locations for predicting results with three different conversion rates instead of just one predictable location for all subjects like the previous two versions. Behind the Retinanet in terms of resource usage is the 3.9 GB RCNN Mask with the basic network is ResNet50-C4, and combined with the accuracy of 76.3%, RetinaNet is somewhat superior. Meanwhile, when comparing RetinaNet ResNet50-FPN with RCNN Mask ResNet50-FPN, RCNN Mask uses about 4.14 GB larger than 1 GB to increase accuracy 2%. When comparing Faster RCNN with RetinaNet and RCNN Mask in the case of resources used in combination with accuracy, RetinaNet with RCNN Mask will have better performance.

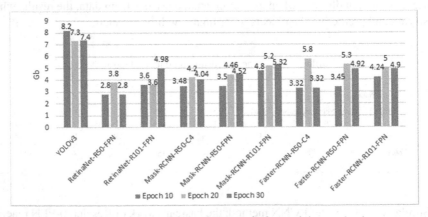

Fig. 3. The rating is based on the RAM used when training on the dataset

4.3 Speed

As shown in Fig. 4, when considering the methods' training time parameters, the YOLOv3 method is a model with a fast average training time of only about 1.5 h, compared to the common ground of other models is time-consuming. In particular, the Faster RCNN method with the basic ResNet101-FPN networks is up to 3 days for every ten different epochs. Simultaneously, when combined with Faster RCNN, other basic networks also take a lot of time to train. The RCNN mask is the second-fastest training method, combined with the accuracy and resources used; the RCNN Mask is the method that works when we focus on accuracy. Compared to the speed of training and the rate of data processing, YOLOv3 is still the leading method, although the amount of resources used for training is relatively high.

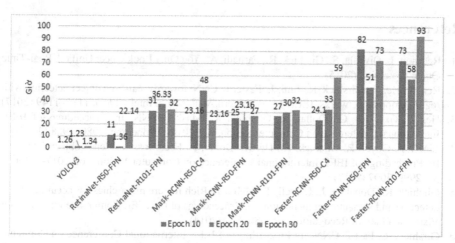

Fig. 4. The evaluation parameters are based on the time when training on a standard dataset.

As shown in Table 4, YOLO is the fastest processing method, while RCNN Mask is the slowest. Overall, including the processing time and accuracy, YOLO is the method that owns quite a lot of advantages despite consuming many RAM resources.

Table 4. The time when using models to detect disease on leaves

Name of method	Time (s/image)
YOLO	0.05
RetinaNet-Resnet50-FPN	0.12
RetinaNet-Resnet101-FPN	0.15
Mask RCNN-Resnet50-C4	0.43
Mask RCNN-Resnet50-FPN	0.12
Mask RCNN-Resnet101-FPN	0.14
Faster RCNN-Resnet50-C4	0.43
Faster RCNN-Resnet50-FPN	0.12
Faster RCNN-Resnet50-FPN	0.14

5 Conclusion

The study's content focused on evaluating four methods of object detection, including YOLO, RetinaNet, Faster RCNN, and Mask RCNN, on actual data collection and labeling. We evaluated, compared, and analyzed three main factors, including accuracy, processing speed, and resources to be calculated - these are essential factors to consider when applying calculation results to practical applications. The evaluation results show that YOLO is the fast data processing speed method, but the accuracy is not high (mAP = 60.5%). Simultaneously, RCNN Mask is the best accuracy (mAP = 82.9), but processing time extends. YOLO is the best choice for application development to balance speed, time, and resources used. The actual data set of 42 types of leaf samples of about 55,180 leaves images collected and labeled.

References

1. Redmon, J., Divvala, S., Girshick, R., Farhadi, A.: You Only Look Once: Unified, Real-Time Object Detection (2015)
2. Ren, S., He, K., Girshick, R., Sun, J.: Faster R-CNN: towards real-time object detection with region proposal networks. IEEE Trans. Pattern Anal. Mach. Intell. **39**(6), 1137–1149 (2017)
3. He, K., Gkioxari, G., Dollar, P., Girshick, R.: Mask R-CNN. In: Proceedings of IEEE International Conference on Computer Vision, vol. 2017-October, pp. 2980–2988 (2017)
4. Lin, T.Y., Goyal, P., Girshick, R., He, K., Dollar, P.: Focal loss for dense object detection. In: Proceedings of IEEE International Conference on Computer Vision, vol. 2017-October, pp. 2999–3007 (2017)
5. Girshick, R., Donahue, J., Darrell, T., Malik, J.: Rich feature hierarchies for accurate object detection and semantic segmentation. In: Proceedings of the IEEE Conference on Computer Vision and Pattern Recognition, pp. 580–587 (2014)
6. Girshick, R.: Fast R-CNN. In: Proceedings of IEEE International Conference on Computer Vision, ICCV 2015, vol. 2015, pp. 1440–1448 (2015)
7. Liu, L., et al.: Deep learning for generic object detection: a survey. Int. J. Comput. Vision **128**(2), 261–318 (2019). https://doi.org/10.1007/s11263-019-01247-4
8. Uijlings, J.R., Van De Sande, K.E., Gevers, T., Smeulders, A.W.: Selective search for object recognition. Int. J. Comput. Vision **104**(2), 154–171 (2013). https://doi.org/10.1007/s11263-013-0620-5
9. Lin, T.-Y., et al.: Microsoft COCO: common objects in context. In: Fleet, D., Pajdla, T., Schiele, B., Tuytelaars, T. (eds.) ECCV 2014. LNCS, vol. 8693, pp. 740–755. Springer, Cham (2014). https://doi.org/10.1007/978-3-319-10602-1_48
10. Lin, T.Y., Dollár, P., Girshick, R., He, K., Hariharan, B., Belongie, S.: Feature pyramid networks for object detection. In: Proceedings - 30th IEEE Conference on Computer Vision Pattern Recognition, CVPR, 2017, vol. 2017-January, pp. 936–944 (2017)
11. Redmon, J., Farhadi, A.: YOLO9000: better, faster, stronger. In: Proceedings - 30th IEEE Conference on Computer Vision Pattern Recognition, CVPR, 2017, vol. 2017-January, pp. 6517–6525 (2017)
12. Redmon, J., Farhadi, A.: YOLOv3: An Incremental Improvement (2018)
13. Everingham, M., Van Gool, L., Williams, C.K.I., Winn, J.: The PASCAL visual object classes (VOC) challenge. Int. J. Comput. Vision **88**, 303–338 (2010)
14. He, K., Zhang, X., Ren, S., Sun, J.: Deep Residual Learning for Image Recognition (2015)

15. Krizhevsky, A., Sutskever, I., Hinton, G.E.: ImageNet classification with deep convolutional neural networks. In: Pereira, F., Burges, C.J.C., Bottou, L., Weinberger, K.Q. (eds.) Advances in Neural Information Processing Systems 25, pp. 1097–1105. Curran Associates, Inc. (2012)
16. Justus, D., Brennan, J., Bonner, S., McGough, A.S.: Predicting the Computational Cost of Deep Learning Models (2018)
17. Qin, F., Liu, D.X., Sun, B.D., Ruan, L., Ma, Z., Wang, H.: Identification of alfalfa leaf diseases using image recognition technology, p. 11 (2016)
18. Rothe, P.R., Kshirsagar, R.V.: Cotton leaf disease identification using pattern recognition techniques. In: International Conference on Pervasive Computing, Pune, India, pp. 1–6 (2015)
19. Islam, M., Dinh, A., Wahid, K., Bhowmik, P.: Detection of potato diseases using image segmentation and multiclass support vector machine. In: Proceedings of the 30th IEEE Canadian Conference on Electrical and Computer Engineering, pp. 1–4 (2018)
20. Gupta, T.: Plant leaf disease analysis using image processing technique with modified SVM-CS classifier. Int. J. Eng. Manag. Technol. **5**, 11–17 (2018)
21. Lu, Y., Yi, S.J., Zeng, N.Y., Liu, Y., Zhang, Y.: Identification of rice diseases using deep convolutional neural networks. Neurocomputing **267**, 378–384 (2017)
22. Tan, W.X., Zhao, C.J., Wu, H.R.: CNN intelligent early warning for apple skin lesion image acquired by infrared video sensors. High Technol. Lett. **22**, 67–74 (2016)
23. Kawasaki, Y., Uga, H., Kagiwada, S., Iyatomi, H.: Basic study of automated diagnosis of viral plant diseases using convolutional neural networks. In: Proceedings of the 12th International Symposium on Visual Computing, Las Vegas, NV, USA, pp. 638–645, December 2015
24. Sladojevic, S., Arsenovic, M., Andela, A., Culibrk, D., Stefanovic, D.: Deep neural networks based recognition of plant diseases by leaf image classification. Comput. Intell. Neurosci. (2016)
25. Mohanty, S.P., Hughes, D.P., Marcel, S.: Using deep learning for image-based plant disease detection. Front. Plant Sci. **7**, 14 (2016)

Uberwasted App for Reporting and Collecting Waste Using Location Based and Deep Learning Technologies

Binh Thanh Nguyen[1]([✉]), Dat Ho Tan[2]([✉]), Hien Vo Thi Dieu[2], Dat Nguyen Khac[2], and Huy Truong Dinh[2]

[1] International Institute for Applied Systems Analysis (IIASA), Laxenburg, Austria
nguyenb@iiasa.ac.at
[2] Duy Tan University, Da Nang, Vietnam
datht2311@gmail.com

Abstract. Nowadays, waste becomes one of the main air pollution sources. In this context, Uberwasted app is studied and developed as a mobile app that allows volunteers to report and to take part in waste collection based on location based technology and deep learning algorithms. First, a waste data management system has been built to store waste photo and descriptions, which are submitted by using the app. Furthermore, waste are classified by applying convolutional neural network model called "Resnet34", then reported to network of volunteers the place to be collected based on location based technology. To proof of our conceptual approach, several typical implementation results will be illustrated.

Keywords: Waste · Data collection · Volunteer · Mobile app · CNN · Resnet34

1 Introduction

Increasing in availability of mobile phones in societies around the world, even in the remote areas has led to the use of mobile technologies in data collection [1]. Furthermore, current technology, such as smartphones and "apps", allows time-use research to be set up in a completely different way. Smartphone users have (almost) permanently access to this device, so respondents can report their activities at multiple times per day, resulting in less recall problems. In [1], smartphones enable the collection of auxiliary data, such as the GPS location or usage of the respondents' mobile phone at the time of the activities. Also other information can easily be reported. In this context, the popularization of smartphones has brought about substantial changes in location-based services (LBS) [19].

On another hand, [23] artificial Intelligence has been witnessing a monumental growth in bridging the gap between the capabilities of humans and machines [14]. The agenda for this field is to enable machines to view the world as humans do, perceive it in a similar manner and even use the knowledge for a multitude of tasks such as Image & Video recognition, Image Analysis and Classification, Media Recreation,

© Springer Nature Singapore Pte Ltd. 2020
T. K. Dang et al. (Eds.): FDSE 2020, CCIS 1306, pp. 178–188, 2020.
https://doi.org/10.1007/978-981-33-4370-2_13

Recommendation Systems, Natural Language Processing, etc. The advancements in Computer Vision with Deep Learning has been constructed and perfected with time, primarily over one particular algorithm—a Convolutional Neural Network. According to [18], convolutional neural network (CNN) is a class of artificial neural networks that has become dominant in various computer vision tasks, is attracting interest across a variety of domains, including image processing.

In this paper, we first introduce conceptual model of based on location based and deep learning algorithms to allow a community of environmental lovers (volunteers) to report and to take part in collecting waste. In this application framework, volunteers will use the Uberwasted app to report the contaminated place of waste by taking picture and provide information about the waste, including *waste location, waste type, waste size and whether it biodegradable or not* by retrieving data from the Waste data management. Then, Uberwasted app will send the notification of the newly reported waste to volunteer(s) nearby by using the Uberwasted map. Hereafter, by selecting a contaminated place from the data collection points, Volunteer(s) can view the information of that location and can register to cleanup the polluted place through the Uberwasted app, after the cleanup process volunteer will report back the cleaning progress to confirm whether the waste on that location is clean or not. Those result will be store directly into the Uberwasted data management system, the concepts of which have been introduced in our previous publications [7, 10–12]. To proof our concepts, some typical implementation results of the Uberwasted app will be presented.

The remainder of this paper is organized as follows: Sect. 2 introduces some approaches and projects related to our work; then an introduction of the Uberwasted concepts is provided in Sect. 3, Sect. 4 presents the results of the Uberwasted implementation, and lastly, Sect. 5 gives a summary of what has been currently achieved and future work.

2 Related Work

Mobile apps have become powerful tools for collecting data in the context of crowd-sourcing campaigns [17, 20], each of which is an open data collection call and refers to a distributed problem-solving model to solve a complex problem through [5].

First, according to [19] most mobile information services, such as portals, maps, and online yellow pages, provide requested information based on the users' location information. [2] reported that mobile LBS are already achieving mainstream market acceptance in Europe and North America. Moreover, about one-third of mobile subscribers use LBS applications regularly in North America, while 20 percent of mobile users do so in Europe.

In the context of image processing based on deep learning technique, according to [18] the most established algorithm among various deep learning models is convolutional neural network (CNN), a class of artificial neural networks that has been a dominant method in computer vision tasks since the astonishing results were shared on the object recognition competition known as the ImageNet Large Scale Visual Recognition Competition (ILSVRC) in [9, 16]. In the field of medical research, CNN has been achieved as expert-level performances in various subjects. [3, 4, 6] demonstrated the potential of deep learning for diabetic retinopathy screening, skin lesion classification, and lymph node metastasis detection, respectively.

Familiarity with this state-of-the-art methodology would help not only researchers who apply CNN to their tasks in imaging processing, but also, especially in waste reporting and collection by using mobile app. This paper focuses on the basic concepts of CNN and their application to various waste collection tasks.

3   Uberwasted Concepts

In this section, we first describe the parameters of the reported contaminated location, including *waste picture, waste longtitude, waste latitude, waste type, biodegradable/nonbiodegradable and waste size*. Those parameters is being provided by volunteer through report function. In this function, after user taking a picture, the application then automatically recommend *waste location, waste type, waste size and whether it biodegradable or not* back to the volunteer device's screen by using Deep Learning, volunteer can choose between edit the recommended parameters or can report the waste right away. Hereafter, based on the *waste longtitude* and *waste latitude*, which is automatically receive after volunteer report the waste, the reported contaminated place then being displayed on the Uberwasted map. For further description on the Deep Learning refer to Sect. 3.2 and 3.3. Figure 1 shows the Uberwasted system architecture and the data collection workflow.

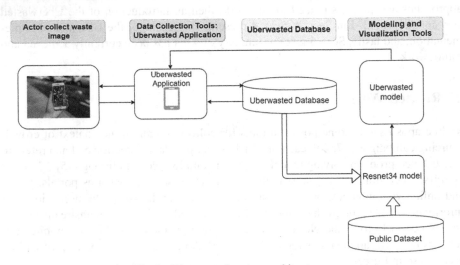

Fig. 1.   Uberwasted system architecture.

3.1 Waste Data Object Definition Based on Location Based and AI Technology

The key data object of our application is *Waste*, which can be denoted as follows:
$w = \langle p, l, t, m, s \rangle$, where:

- p: is a photo of w, based on p 's information the next parameters can be retrieved and classified.
- l: waste location (*Latitude, Longitude*)
- t: waste type, i.e. *biodegradable, non-biodegradable*
- m: waste material, e.g. *plastic, glass, metal, cardboard*, etc.
- s: waste size (*small, medium, big*)

3.2 Volunteers

The second data object is used to define volunteers, who collect report and collect waste. The location based technology is also used not only for reporting position of waste, but also to call volunteer(s), who are in the near and willing to collect the waste. As a result, we define volunteer data object as:

$$v = <vid, email, password, gender, job, score, avatar>$$

where:

- *vid: id* of the volunteer, which is the current phone number of the volunteer

Furthermore, the position of a volunteer can be specified by the app based on the location based technology, in our case which is Fused Location Provider API [26].

3.3 Reports and Waste Collections

Waste w_i can be reported by using Uberwasted if it has been recognised by a volunteer v_r who takes photo p_i of w_i at timestamp t_i therefore we define a report r as:

$$r_i = <w_i, v_r, t_i>$$

Afterwards, based on the report information r_i, a nearest group of volunteer(s) *{vc1,..vcn}* who are willing to collect the waste can be found. So, we can define the groups as:

$$gv_i = <\{vc1, ..vcn\}, r_i>$$

3.4 Training the Model

Convolutional is a process where we take a small matrix of numbers (called kernel or filter) [21, 24], we pass it over our image and transform it based on the values from filter with the aim to extract features from image into sub-feature such as detect edges, sharpen, color, etc. by applying the following equation [15, 25]:

$$O(H, W) = \frac{I(H, W) + 2 * P - K}{S} + 1$$

$$O(C) = I(F)$$

Where:

- C: Number of channels
- H: Height of input
- W: Width of input
- S: Number of Stride
- P: Number of Padding
- F: Number of Feature map
- O: Output value
- I: Input Value

In this context, *Rectified Linear Unit (ReLU)* [21] is a type of activation function where it returns 0 if it receives any negative input, but keep the same value when receives positive input: $y = max(0, x)$, where x is the input to a neuron. Figure 2 shows an example how to use Resnet34 for specifying multiple layers to train our model.

Our training cycle (1 epoch) can be described as follows:

– Calculate Prediction:

1. Initialize the parameters (Only once at epoch 1)
2. Provide input image into convolution layer (Fig. 3), apply filters with strides, padding. Then, perform convolution on the image and apply *ReLU* activation to the matrix.
3. *Perform Max Pooling* [15], which is the layer that select maximum value from each region of the kernel.
4. Continue going through the other layers by perform *Convolution + Batch Normalization* [13] *+ ReLU.*
5. After Layer 4, perform *Average pool + Flattern + Fully Connected + Dropout + Batch Normalization.* More detail:

   - *Average Pool* is the layer which calculating the average for each patch of the feature map [8].
   - *Flatten* [25] is the layer which flatten the input matrix
   - *Linear Layer (Fully Connected Layer)* [24] connect every neuron in one layer to every neuron in another layer by applies a linear transformation to the incoming data.

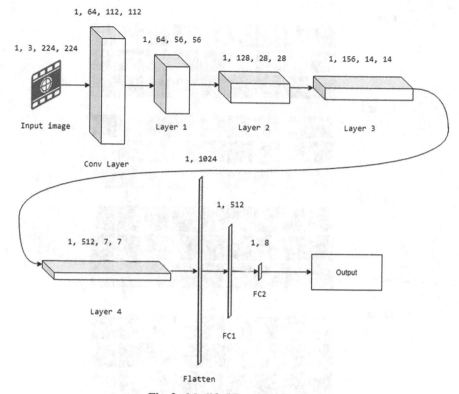

Fig. 2. Modified Resnet34 layers

- *Dropout* [27] is the technique which purpose is to reduce the possibility of over-fitting by randomly drop units (along with their connections) from the neural network during training.

6. Using *Back-propagation* [22] to fine-tuning the weights by computes the gradient with respect to the loss function. The Back-propagation can be break down to the following steps:

- Using *Cross Entropy* [23] loss function to calculate loss of the model. The Cross Entropy can be considered of two part:

  - Softmax is a type of activation function that change the results in the output layers into probabilities that sum to one by using the following equation:

$$p_i = \frac{e^{x_i}}{\sum_j^n e^{x_j}}$$

- Conv1:

- Layer 1:

- Layer 2:

- Layer 3:

- Layer 4:

- Flatten Layer:

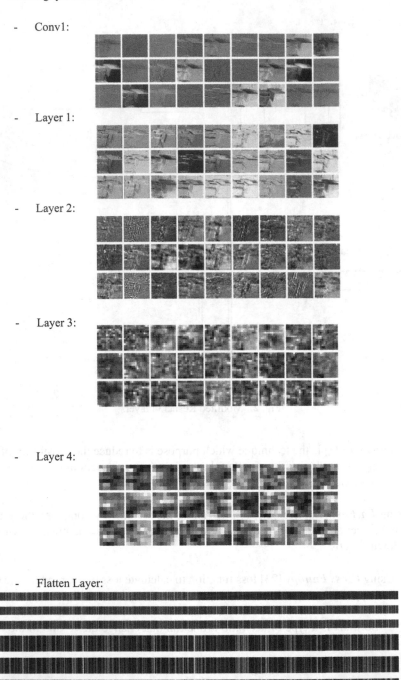

Fig. 3. Running example of Resnet34 layers

Where:

- p: Probabilities of the results.
- n: Length of the elements in the output result.
- x: Element of the output result.

- Negative log likelihood is an another type of loss function telling us how bad our model is performing. Negative log likelihood equation can be express as follows:

$$- \log \frac{e^{x_i}}{\sum_j^n e^{x_j}}$$

Where:

- x: Element of the output result.
- n: Length of the elements in the output result.

- Stochastic gradient descent algorithm (SGD) will be used to minimize the loss function by taking the derivative of the loss function from each mini-batch, the weight then being updated by using this equation:

$$w = w - lr * \frac{\partial L}{\partial w}$$

Where:

- w: Weight
- lr: Learning rate
- L: Loss function

The following figures shows a running example of *Resnet34* layers.

4   Uberwasted App

The Uberwasted app is a tool that uses data collection based on location base technology to collect and store waste's information into the database. It focuses on the use of internet and mobile phones allowing participants to easily identify, report and clean up waste. In this section, Uberwasted use cases are introduced with one main actor, namely *Volunteer*. According to those use cases, some typical implementation results will be introduced to proof our concepts.

4.1   Uberwasted Use Cases

Uberwasted app is designed to collect, handle data completely based on volunteers willingness. The Data Collection package: aimed to collect information about waste with the help of Deep Learning to assist volunteers with the report process and create the simplicity in the waste cleanup process (Fig. 4).

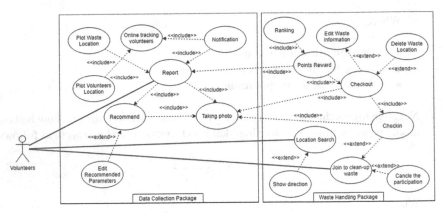

Fig. 4. Uberwasted use case diagram

4.2 Uberwasted Implementing Results

Google Map API and Mapbox API are used as an instance of location based technologies to support data collection. Map-related function such as *Locate Volunteer Location, Mark Waste Location, Search, etc.* have been developed in this context. Figure 5 provides some screenshots to illustrate the Uberwasted map.

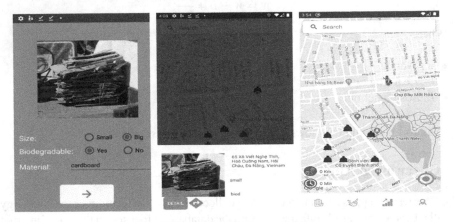

Fig. 5. Examples of Uberwasted app

Thereafter being redirect, volunteers now can participate in the clean-up a waste's in a location by tap on the join button after they choose their desire location. Hereafter, volunteers can start to clean-up the waste by taking a picture when they arrived at the location. When they finished cleaning, volunteer will take another picture as a proof that the location is waste-free, then the system will reward with points to all of the participants and remove the location from the map. Volunteers can also report the waste by using the report function, right when volunteers taking a picture, the Uberwasted app will automatically predict the waste parameters back to volunteers device, volunteer has the ability to edit the information in case the volunteers is willing to correct the information.

5   Conclusion

This paper introduced the concepts and implementation results of the Uberwasted app, which allows a community of environmental lovers (volunteers) to report waste and to take part in collecting waste by using location based technology and deep learning algorithms. First, waste photo and descriptions are collected by volunteers and stored in the waste data management system. In this context, waste are classified by applying convolutional neural network model called "Resnet34", then reported to the network of environmental lover community, who are willing to collected the reported waste The implementation results of Uberwasted app have been represented to proof of our conceptual approach.

Future work of our approach could then be able to support big and multimedia data analysis in the context of crowdsourcing and social networks. Waste data patterns will be studied and used for mining of big collected data. This tool will also allow local people to engage in projects, thus making them more aware of the environmental and health issues that could affect their wellbeing if not appropriate regulation, in this case related to reduce pollution, is implemented.

References

1. Barzilay, M.: Data collection and mobile technologies (2019). https://doi.org/10.13140/rg.2.2.31541.93929
2. Berg Insight: Mobile Location-Based Services (2012). http://www.berginsight.com/Report PDF/ProductSheet/bi-lbs4-ps.pdf
3. Bejnordi, B.E., et al.: Diagnostic assessment of deep learning algorithms for detection of lymph node metastases in women with breast cancer. JAMA **318**, 2199–2210 (2017)
4. Esteva, A., Kuprel, B., Novoa, R.A., et al.: Dermatologist-level classification of skin cancer with deep neural networks. Nature **542**, 115–118 (2017)
5. Chatzimilioudis, G., Konstantinidis, A., Laoudias, C., Zeinalipour-Yazti, D.: Crowdsourcing with Smartphones. IEEE Internet Comput. **16**(5), 36–44 (2012)
6. Gulshan, V., Peng, L., Coram, M., et al.: Development and validation of a deep learning algorithm for detection of diabetic retinopathy in retinal fundus photographs. JAMA **316**, 2402–2410 (2016)
7. Hoang, D.T.A., Ngo, N.S., Nguyen, B.T.: Collective cubing platform towards definition and analysis of warehouse cubes. In: Nguyen, N.-T., Hoang, K., Jędrzejowicz, P. (eds.) ICCCI 2012. LNCS (LNAI), vol. 7654, pp. 11–20. Springer, Heidelberg (2012). https://doi.org/10.1007/978-3-642-34707-8_2
8. Brownlee, J.: A Gentle Introduction to Pooling Layers for Convolutional Neural Networks. https://machinelearningmastery.com/pooling-layers-for-convolutional-neural-networks/
9. Krizhevsky, A., Sutskever, I., Hinton, G.E.: ImageNet classification with deep convolutional neural networks. In: Advances in Neural Information Processing Systems 25 (2012). https://papers.nips.cc/paper/4824-imagenet-classification-with-deep-convolutional-neuralnetworks.pdf. Accessed 22 Jan 2018
10. Nguyen, T.B., Ngo, N.S.: Semantic cubing platform enabling interoperability analysis among cloud-based linked data cubes. In: Proceedings of the 8th International Conference on Research and Pratical Issues of Enterprise Information Systems, CONFENIS 2014, 2014, ACM International Conference Proceedings Series (2014)

11. Nguyen, T.B., Wagner, F., Schoepp, W.: GAINS-BI: business intelligent approach for greenhouse gas and air pollution interactions and synergies information system. In: Proceedings of the International Organization for Information Integration and Web-Based Application and Services IIWAS 2008, Linz (2008)

12. Nguyen, T.B., Wagner, F., Schoepp, W.: Federated data warehousing application framework and platform-as-a-services to model virtual data marts in the clouds. Int. J. Intell. Inf. Database Syst. **8**(3), 280 (2014). ISSN 1751-5858, 1751-5866. https://doi.org/10.1504/ijiids. 2014.066635

13. Kumar, N.: Batch Normalization and Dropout in Neural Networks with Pytorch. https://tow ardsdatascience.com/batch-normalization-and-dropout-in-neural-networks-explained-with-pytorch-47d7a8459bcd

14. Ruiz, P.: Understanding and visualizing ResNets. https://towardsdatascience.com/understan ding-and-visualizing-resnets-442284831be8

15. Skalski, P.: Gentle Dive into Math Behind Convolutional Neural Networks. https://towardsda tascience.com/gentle-dive-into-math-behind-convolutional-neural-networks-79a07dd44cf9

16. Russakovsky, O., et al.: ImageNet large scale visual recognition challenge. Int. J. Comput. Vision **115**(3), 211–252 (2015). https://doi.org/10.1007/s11263-015-0816-y

17. Using mobile phones in data collection: Opportunities, issues and Challenges. http://blogs. worldbank.org/edutech/using-mobile-phones-data-collection-opportunities-issues-and-cha llenges. Accessed Sept 2018

18. Yamashita, R., Nishio, M., Do, R.K.G., Togashi, K.: Convolutional neural networks: an overview and application in radiology. Insights Imaging **9**(4), 611–629 (2018). https://doi. org/10.1007/s13244-018-0639-9

19. Yun, H., Han, D., Lee, C.C.: Understanding the use of location-based service applications: do privacy concerns matter? J. Electron. Commer. Res. (2013)

20. Szabó, Z., Bilicki, V., Berta, Á., Jánki, Z.R.: Smartphone-based data collection with stunner using crowdsourcing: lessons learnt while cleaning the data. In: Twelfth International Multi-Conference on Computing in the Global Information Technology (2017)

21. Agarap, A.F.M.: Deep Learning using Rectified Linear Units (ReLU). https://arxiv.org/pdf/ 1803.08375.pdf

22. Kostadinov, S.: Understanding Backpropagation Algorithm. https://towardsdatascience.com/ understanding-backpropagation-algorithm-7bb3aa2f95fd

23. Understand Cross Entropy Loss in Minutes. https://medium.com/data-science-bootcamp/und erstand-cross-entropy-loss-in-minutes-9fb263caee9a

24. Fully Connected Layers in Convolutional Neural Networks: The Complete Guide. https:// missinglink.ai/guides/convolutional-neural-networks/fully-connectedlayers-convolutional-neural-networks-complete-guide/

25. SuperDataScience Team. Convolutional Neural Networks (CNN): Step 3 – Flattening. https:// www.superdatascience.com/blogs/convolutional-neural-networks-cnn-step-3-flattening

26. Fused Location Provider API https://developers.google.com/location-context/fused-location-provider

27. Srivastava, N., Hinton, G., Krizhevsky, A., Sutskever, I., Salakhutdinov, R.: Dropout: A Simple Way to Prevent Neural Networks from Overfitting. http://jmlr.org/papers/v15/srivastava14a

A Flexible Internet of Things Architecture for Data Gathering and Monitoring System

Khuat Duc Anh, Le Dinh Huynh, and Phan Duy Hung[✉]

FPT University, Hanoi, Vietnam
{anhkdmse0105,huynhldmse0083}@fpt.edu.vn, hungpd2@fe.edu.vn

Abstract. The advances in technology and impressive opportunities Internet of Things (IoT) promises are encouraged the development of IoT products. The enthusiasm ideas are legible and won the investor's heart. However, it appears much arduous to be achieved in reality, given the scale of devices, the inlet new features. The data collecting and monitoring system are premises, marketable, and variety. While the architecture in the industry is quite rigid, complex, expensive for small and medium problems, flexible architectures appear to be superior in both software and hardware design. The flexible architecture still might lack overall architectural knowledge, is an obstacle to be extended and integrated. In other words, the problem of establishing a well thought out architecture of the Internet of Things inevitably enters the first place. This article provides a flexible, open, and custom architecture in design and deployment. The product variant design from the original in accordance with the real world is also proposed.

Keywords: IoT architecture · Data gathering system · Monitoring system

1 Introduction

The term Internet of Things (IoT) wasn't officially named until 1999 by Professor Kevin Ashton in the MIT Auto-ID Center, enables the physical objects (things) in the world that connect to the internet and other related devices [1, 2]. It is now the time of the IoT era, where billions of devices are connected follow several studies such as Gartner [3] and Cisco [4]. The diversity of applications, techniques, business purpose, and the scale-out over time is the challenge of designing an IoT system.

Data gathering and monitoring are the astounding pieces of works in IoT. Huge amounts of data from sensors, actuators are transferred through networks protocols such as Wi-Fi, Bluetooth, ZigBee or Z-Wave to the data center (Fig. 1) [5, 6].

According to lots of studies about conventional IoT architecture, it can be considered as three layers:

- Perception Layer: also call recognition layer [7] is the lowest layer. The main responsibility is to collect useful information and transform them into a digital signal.
- Network Layer: collect information from the Perception layer and transmit to the Application layer insecure form. This layer also setup addressing and routing.

© Springer Nature Singapore Pte Ltd. 2020
T. K. Dang et al. (Eds.): FDSE 2020, CCIS 1306, pp. 189–199, 2020.
https://doi.org/10.1007/978-981-33-4370-2_14

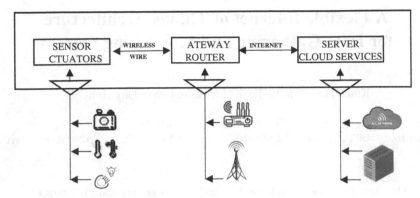

Fig. 1. IoT standard architecture

- Application Layer: the top of conventional IoT architecture. This layer also integrates with various services and components. It should fill the gap between user and machine. The essence of users is here.

The three layers above can be transposed to five layers in Fig. 2, following the study from B. N. Silva, M. Khan, and K. Han [8].

IoT STANDARD ARCHITECTURE	SERVICE ORIENTED ARCHITECTURE
Server Cloud services	Applications
	Service Composition
	Service Management
Gateway / Router	Object abstraction
Sensor / Actuators	Objects

Fig. 2. The comparing of 5 layers of an IoT architecture.

In five layers above, the objects or things are as the Perception layer. It holds the different categories of things, such as the sensor of temporary, humidity, light intensity, and or the status, power consumption, and so on. The Object abstraction layer is the network layer. It deals with communication technologies like RFID, Bluetooth LE, Wi-Fi, 4G 5G. The top layer is divided into Business layer, Application layer, and Service management. The Service Management is responsible for paring with requestor, the application layer provides smart service and the topmost layer establishes the business model and graphical representations.

The architectures are very colorful and then also have a lot of variations, both in hardware and software design. Over the time, the Service Oriented Architecture (SOA) is a more powerful framework for support development [9]. In the author's perspective, the SOA and the 5 layers' design are more adaptive with data gathering and monitoring. The development team can take advantage of open source to build a system at a fast rate. The hardware is modular as it can be plug and play more easily, the software is based on API and micro-services [10].

Take in the sights of authors country Vietnam, an emerging nation with the developing of commercial activities and services become wider [11–13]. A lot of things become possible by the IoT technologies, such as structural health monitoring for large-scale bridges, food truck refrigeration system in logistics field and integrated security at public policy service agencies. This study proposes an IoT architecture and applies it in actual works. Through project implementation, architecture has proved its flexibility and stability.

The remainder of this paper is as follows: the proposed architecture is introduced in Sect. 2. The real products are presented in Sect. 3. The conclusion and future work are in Sect. 4.

2   Proposed Architecture

The studies demonstrate that a flexible, low-cost architectural model for small and medium IoT problems is necessary. Also, the solution must ensure ease of deployment and stable operation in the real environment. This work proposes a flexible architecture for simple IoT problems to collect, control and monitor signals. The architecture is compared with the standard IoT architecture as shown in Fig. 3. Components that are solutions for each class are also proposed in Fig. 4.

IoT STANDARD ARCHITECTURE	PROPOSED IoT ARCHITECTURE		
Server Cloud services	Application Layer		
	Monitoring	Controlling	Acquisition
Gateway / Router	Communication Layer		
Sensor / Actuators	Field Layer		

Fig. 3. Comparison between standard IoT architecture and proposed architecture.

The first layer of the system consists of sensing devices, control devices, alarm devices, and monitor device. The devices in this class were packaged based on the STM 32, AVR, Arduino board, ESP 8266, ESP 32 chip. Several types such as temperature sensors, accelerometer, etc. are supported and integrated. The device in the second layer supports sensors connected to the internet and connects any devices in the next layer. In the third class, popular and varied embedded computer options are available. They are not expensive, open-source, and easy to use, e.g.: Orange Pi, Raspberry, O DROID, Rock 64, Asus Tinker Board, Pine A 64, Banana Pi. In our projects, embedded computers are

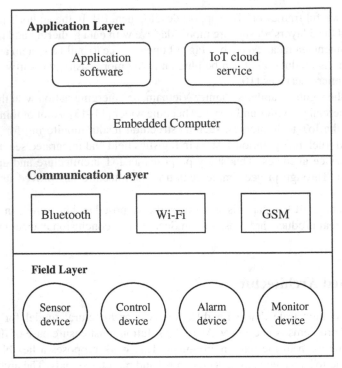

Fig. 4. Components overview.

used as data backup, visual, and monitoring. The application layer is on the top where all services in the server or cloud that support tracking data, testers, and check alerts on mobile phones or websites.

3 Some Practical Deployment Applications

3.1 Food Truck Refrigeration System (FTRS)

The Food Truck Refrigeration plays a significant role in transporting and logistics. The cooling agent of refrigerator trucks could be ice-cooled or equipped with any one of a variety of mechanical refrigeration systems, designed to carry perishable freight at specific temperatures. The quality of fruits and vegetables depends much on the refrigerated boxes and tanks. The agricultural product is very diverse in terms of storage as well as transportation in many conditions. The error rate is existent and the manager is hard to find out where and why the responsibility lies with the driver. To solve this problem, engineers have flexibly integrated the basic components, build a solution that allows managers to continuously monitor parameters, temperature, humidity, vehicle status, graphical representation over time, recommend human actions and warnings in some cases.

ThingSpeak cloud [14] is used to aggregate, visualize, and analyze live data streams in the cloud. Users can on both the smart-phone and the website easily. The system identifies errors, severity and gives warning as well as the next steps such as the quality of the air conditioner which are classified as Severity Level 1 (critical), and need to check as soon as possible (next action). The alert to the driver through the ringing bell, flash-light, sending a message, gossip with the manager if the alerts are not removed.

The black box records all relevant data on the journey. At first for the backup purpose, managers can always take it back for any inspection, the pill works for plan B in case of losing mobile signal, lost internet connection, and data mining. The storage could be a very small SD card, hdd, ssd, or a rack.

The proof of concept FTRS is delivered to Viet - Net Computer Solution Joint Stock Company [15]. The system consists of three main parts: the hardware device, the local system (collecting data into a black box), and the cloud service monitoring (Fig. 5).

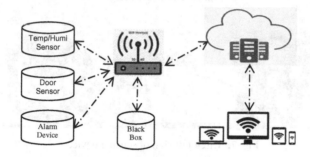

Fig. 5. Architectural overview of the food truck refrigeration system.

The Hardware

The hardware consists of 3 modules: Sensor and Alarm device, Black box (Data Storage box), and Connection box.

Sensor and Alarm Device. The sensing/alarm device was attached to the refrigerated truck. The device transmits and receives incoming commands via Wi-Fi signal to the local system inside the truck. The central control circuit is the ESP 8266 [16], 1-wire bus is used for communication between SoC and sensor. The detail design is shown in Fig. 6 and Fig. 7.

Black Box (Fig. 8): This module is attached to the cockpit of refrigerated truck. After the transportation process, the manager can easily retrieve data from the storage box device, research, analyze and check the data. On the road, it may encounter the phone range of poor quality, may lose internet connection, observation data will be lost and managers do not see the goods parameters. The architects have integrated storage box feature, record all data from sensors and simultaneously send data via the internet to the cloud.

Connection Box. The designed system could work locally, data could synchronize manually via USB port soldered in Black box, but it might be too late for the competitive

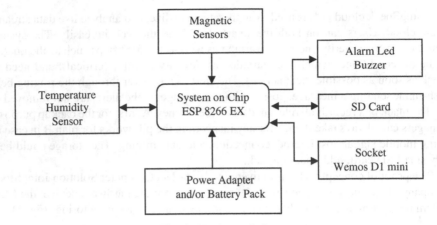

Fig. 6. Hardware design.

Fig. 7. Circuit design of sensing device.

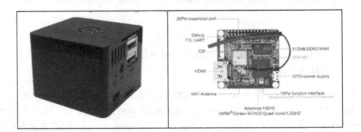

Fig. 8. Black box structure

advantage and the handwork is not efficient, leading to the use of Connection box. The Connection box could deal with both design system and installed infrastructural network interface. If the business is creating new, architect could design a suitable solution without redundancy. For the available infrastructural, the Box have to integrate to running system, it could configurable based on which protocol is feasible such as Wi-Fi, Ethernet, cellular network or WAN for outside communication and Wi-Fi, Bluetooth, wired for inside system (locally). FTR System used a packing solution available on the market named Wireless Wi-Fi Router Mobile Power Bank with UPS, Cellular SIM and Wi-Fi installed (Fig. 9). An universal device, simple to use, low cost, with many brands with good quality on the market, well compatible with the telecommunications infrastructure.

Fig. 9. System 3G 4G wireless, Wi-Fi router mobile power 10000 mAh

Mechanical Design of Shell

The current product does not need an anti-electromagnetic interference so the POM plastic is considered for use. Plastic material is enough for heat exchanger efficiency and door closing/opening detector (installed magnetic sensor inside). Figure 10 shows the mechanical design of the sensor. The finished aluminum model, tested with good Wi-Fi, anodized plating technology is used to increase the durability and quality of the case. The design is convenient for manufacturing the cover with a 3d printer.

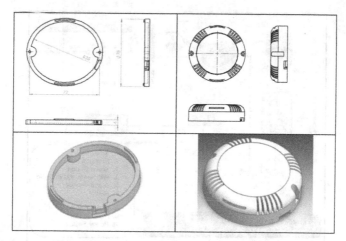

Fig. 10. Mechanical design of the sensing device.

Firmware Function

The device is designed to incorporate with sensors, communication outside world and to Black box via Connection box. The program can become complicated when dealing with 1-wire interface (sensors), Wi-Fi (ESP 8266), TCP/IP (Black box), UDP (warning server system, to manager) and ensure secure with Cloud server through HTTP protocol. And it also supports deep sleep mode for power consumption. In which open-source electronics platform that satisfy inexpensive, cross-platform, simple, clear programing environment, extensible software, extensible hardware, Arduino.

3.2 Hospital Warning System (HWS)

Every hospital wants to provide a safe environment for staff and patients. In every hospital there is a possibility that an angry or unstable patient, a distraught family member, a mental illness or a thief will cause or threaten violence in the facility. In emergency departments, it is also necessary to have a quick reaction to critical patients such as accident or stroke [17]. The system is designed to help alert the problematic locations, complicated situations such as overcrowding, violent inciting acts. In the manner with banking alter system, there are a lot of "button" panic button and nurse call button allocations in campus and clinics. The security guard could monitor all the status areas through installed screen and when the "button" is activate, an emergency signal will be sent to the security center, regional police, and perimeter guards. The security system will rely on that alert to mobilize the necessary support force for problem areas [18].

HWS could work 24/7 to solve problems that old systems could not perform, for instance false alarms due to interference signals, signal interruption (cable transmitter too long, or affected by weather), flexible Activate alarm playback time in security units [19]. The solution for HWS could describe in Fig. 11. The system has been transferred technology to AtSol Vietnam technology joint stock company to deploy and operate.

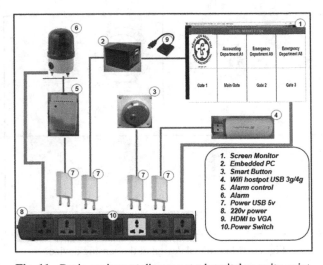

Fig. 11. Basic equipment diagram at a hospital security point.

3.3 Vibration Data Collection for Bridge Health Monitoring System Under Random Traveling Vehicle Loads

The bridge was constructed to include "smart bridge" electronic monitoring system [20]. The system includes a lot of accelerometers continuously provide data for analyzing bridge structural defects early. The system integrated MPU 6050 accelerometer sensor, ESP 8266 main processor chip, vibration data sent to data center via UDP protocol (Fig. 12). A large amount of data has been collected from the bridge for researchers to establish the vibratory fingerprint. This system is cooperated with AtSol Vietnam Technology Joint Stock Company and a private vibration research group, experiments at Nhat Tan Bridge, Vietnam [21] (Fig. 13).

Fig. 12. Vibration measurement experiment at Nhat Tan Bridge.

Fig. 13. Accelerometer sensor, developed and customize from hardware design.

The collected data could be shown in the Fig. 14.

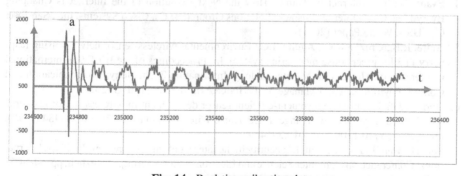

Fig. 14. Real-time vibration data.

4 Conclusion and Perspectives

The paper introduced a flexible architecture, used basic equipment, successfully applied some practical problems and shared them to the community.

This system architecture has been customized to build the Food Truck Refrigeration System. A monitoring system for refrigerated vehicles during transportation at a low cost, expandable and easy to deploy was established. In this article, we introduce a number of application solutions for warning systems in hospitals, mechanical vibration measurement systems in construction. The system meets variety of customer needs, from small to large scale. Components in the system operate stably, with high reliability. The results have proven to be flexible and easy to implement in practice.

The proposed architecture continues to promote by authors and IoT open source communities. The current and or further product could improve by adding Class 1 certificate and design, proposing the selection of industrial Grade 2 and Grade 3. The design integrates Layer 1 and Layer 2 functions to build compact devices that deploy rapidly. In addition, it adds options to develop remote collection and monitoring functions in clouds like AWS, Azure, Google Cloud Platform. This paper is also a good reference for research directions of IoT [22, 23], Embedded Systems [24, 25].

References

1. Bilal, M.: A Review of Internet of Things Architecture, Technologies and Analysis Smartphone-based Attacks Against 3D printers. arXiv preprint arXiv:1708.04560 (2017)
2. Wang, S., Hou, Y., Gao, F., Ji, X.: A novel IoT access architecture for vehicle monitoring system. In: Proceedings of the IEEE 3rd World Forum on Internet of Things (WF-IoT), Reston, VA, pp. 639–642 (2016). https://doi.org/10.1109/wf-iot.2016.7845396
3. Gartner. https://www.gartner.com/en/newsroom/press-releases/2015-11-10-gartner-says-6-billion-connected-things-will-be-in-use-in-2016-up-30-percent-from-2015. Accessed 04 June 2020
4. Evans, D.: The Internet of Things: How the Next Evolution of the Internet Is Changing Everything. Cisco Internet Business Solutions Group (IBSG), Cisco Systems, Inc., San Jose, CA, USA, White Paper (2011)
5. Anire, R.B., Cruz, F.R.G., Agulto, I.C.: Environmental wireless sensor network using raspberry Pi 3 for greenhouse monitoring system. In: Proceedings of the IEEE 9th International Conference on Humanoid, Nanotechnology, Information Technology, Communication and Control, Environment and Management (HNICEM), Manila, pp. 1–5 (2017)
6. Guo, J., Jafarkhani, H.: Movement-efficient sensor deployment in wireless sensor networks with limited communication range. IEEE Trans. Wirel. Commun. **18**(7), 3469–3484 (2019). https://doi.org/10.1109/twc.2019.2914199
7. Suo, H., Wan, J., Zou, C., Liu, J.: Security in the internet of things: a review. In: IEEE International Conference on Computer Science and Electronics Engineering, Hangzhou, pp. 648–651 (2012). https://doi.org/10.1109/ICCSEE.2012.373
8. Silva, B.N., Khan, M., Han, K.: Internet of things: a comprehensive review of enabling technologies, architecture, and challenges. IETE Tech. Rev. 116 (2017)
9. Uviase, O., Kotonya, G.: IoT Architectural Framework: Connection and Integration Framework for IoT Systems. arXiv preprint arXiv:1803.04780 (2018)

10. Datta, S.K., Bonnet, C.: Next-generation, data centric and end-to-end IoT architecture based on microservices. In: Proceedings of the IEEE International Conference on Consumer Electronics - Asia (ICCE-Asia), Jeju, pp. 206–212 (2018). https://doi.org/10.1109/icce-asia.2018. 8552135
11. Vietnam for Growth and Shared Prosperity Development Report 2019. http://documents.wor ldbank.org/curated/en/590451578409008253/pdf/Vietnam-Development-Report-2019-Con necting-Vietnam-for-Growth-and-Shared-Prosperity.pdf. Accessed 04 June 2020
12. Efficient Logistics a Key to Vietnam's Competitiveness. http://documents.worldbank.org/cur ated/en/646871468132885170/pdf/Efficient-logistics-a-key-to-Vietnams-competitiveness. pdf. Accessed 04 June 2020
13. Agriculture, forestry, and fishing. https://www.britannica.com/place/Vietnam/Agriculture-for estry-and-fishing. Accessed 2020/06/04
14. ThingSpeak for IoT Projects. https://thingspeak.com
15. Viet - Net Computer Solution Joint Stock Company, Hanoi, Vietnam (2018)
16. Datasheet ESP266EX https://www.espressif.com/sites/default/files/documentation/0a-esp 8266ex_datasheet_en.pdf
17. Security and safety at hospital. https://www.betterhealth.vic.gov.au/health/servicesandsupp ort/security-and-safety-at-hospital. Accessed 24 June 2020
18. Zurn, P., Dal-Poz, M.R., Stilwell, B., Adams, O.: Imbalance in the health workforce. Hum. Resour. Health (2004). https://doi.org/10.1186/1478-4491-2-13
19. Sullivan, M., Robertson, G., Nibbelink, S., et al.: How an intelligent Infrastructure can help optimize hospital safety and Security. Schneider Electric Inc (2011) www2.schneiderele ctric.com/documents/support/white-papers/wp-HealthcareIntelligent-InfrastructureSafety. pdf. Accessed 24 June 2020
20. Xu, Y.-L.: Making good use of structural health monitoring systems of long-span cable-supported bridges. J. Civil Struct. Health Monit. 8(3), 477–497 (2018). https://doi.org/10. 1007/s13349-018-0279-2
21. AtSol Vietnam Technology Joint Stock Company, lane 155, Truong Chinh street, Phuong Liet Ward, Thanh Xuan District, Hanoi, Vietnam (2019)
22. Hung, P.D., Vinh, B.T.: Vulnerabilities in IoT devices with software-defined radio. In: Proceedings of the 4th International Conference on Computer and Communication Systems (ICCCS 2019), Singapore, 23–25 February 2019 (2019)
23. Hung, P.D., Giang, T.M., Nam, L.H., Duong, P.M., Van Thang, H., Diep, V.T.: Smarthome control unit using vietnamese speech command. In: Vasant, P., Zelinka, I., Weber, G.-W. (eds.) ICO 2019. AISC, vol. 1072, pp. 290–300. Springer, Cham (2020). https://doi.org/10.1007/ 978-3-030-33585-4_29
24. Hung, P.D., Nam, L.H., Van Thang, H.: Flexible development for embedded system software. In: Solanki, V.K., Hoang, M.K., Lu, Z., Pattnaik, P.K. (eds.) Intelligent Computing in Engineering. AISC, vol. 1125, pp. 873–883. Springer, Singapore (2020). https://doi.org/10.1007/ 978-981-15-2780-7_93
25. Hung, P.D., Chin, V.V., Chinh, N.T., Tung, T.D.: A flexible platform for industrial applications based on RS485 networks. J. Commun. 15(3), 245–255 (2020). https://doi.org/10.12720/jcm. 15.3.245-255

Recognition and Quantity Estimation of Pastry Images Using Pre-training Deep Convolutional Networks

An C. Tran[1]([✉]), Nghi C. Tran[2], and Nghia Duong-Trung[3]

[1] Can Tho University, Can Tho city, Vietnam
tcan@ctu.edu.vn
[2] Department of Computer Science and Information Engineering, National Central University, Taoyuan City, Taiwan
tcnghivn@gmail.com
[3] Can Tho University of Technology and FPT University, Can Tho city, Vietnam
duong-trung@ismll.de

Abstract. It has recently been demonstrated that food recognition systems opened to an exciting challenge for computer vision and machine learning. These systems' actual benefit depends on the recognition capacity of models in unconstrained environments and application scenarios. In this paper, the authors collect a real-world dataset for the evaluation of object recognition algorithms. The images have been taken in a real bakery shop with cakes arranged in many different ways on a tray. Each tray can have zero or many cakes. The authors have collected a set of 1289 bakery trays for a total of 16 different categories. Then we evaluate several off-the-shelf deep architectures to recognize pastry tray and take into account the recognition accuracy and operation time. Excellent accuracy of 100% is achieved within 20 frames per second. Finally, we integrate the best approach into our self-developed website that (i) recognizes the cakes on the tray and (ii) makes the invoice. This work is the first regarding our collected dataset and the application scenario.

Keywords: Food recognition · Pastry/Cake · Convolutional networks · YOLO

1 Introduction and Motivation

In general, food plays an essential role in everyday life, and the understanding of food intake relates to much research on the field of computer vision. Current advances in machine learning and deep learning boosts this research direction's success to a high level. Previous works in the literature have focused on different tasks of the food recognition system. Many works have developed some public food image datasets for food-related tasks and applications [4,6,7]. Then a range of approaches has been applied to address the task of feature engineering and classification. The work of [15] investigates features and their combinations for

© Springer Nature Singapore Pte Ltd. 2020
T. K. Dang et al. (Eds.): FDSE 2020, CCIS 1306, pp. 200–214, 2020.
https://doi.org/10.1007/978-981-33-4370-2_15

food image analysis and a classification approach based on k-nearest neighbors and vocabulary trees. First, they use image segmentation methods to locate object boundaries for food items in the image. Then color, texture, and local region features are extracted from each segmented area for food classification. We can find an evaluation of different classification methods in [2]. Furthermore, solutions based on convolutional neural networks have already been addressed in the context of food classification [3, 16].

Other works in the literature focus on the application aspect, such as a diet monitoring system in a real scenario. FoodCam is a mobile food recognition system that enables real-time food image recognition on a consumer smartphone and estimates the calorie and nutrition of foods and recording a user's eating habits [17]. FoodLog is a web application for food logging to extract information that facilitates people's beneficial knowledge about their dietary habits [18].

Another interesting topic in food recognition is quantity estimation. An image of a plate with food is taken then a systematic mechanism is developed to recognize the food location. Then depending on the reference information, the quantity of food on the plate is estimated [7, 20].

In this paper, the authors also address quantity estimation but in different scenarios and output. This scenario happens in a bakery shop where the owner wants to automate the final control at checkout. A customer comes to the shop, select desired cakes, and put them on a plate. At the checkout, an image of the plate is taken, and an underlying process works as follows: (i) it recognizes cakes and the equivalent amount, and (ii) produces invoice automatically. The developed system boosts the overall performance and impression of the bakery shop. This work is the first regarding our collected dataset and the application scenario.

2   Technical Background

2.1   Deep Learning and Convolutional Neural Networks (CNNs)

Deep-learning-based models have recently achieved remarkably in a wide range of different image-related tasks, including image recognition and detection. Deep learning is a collective term for methods building on a deep architecture that solves complex problems by automatically extracting the level of abstraction layers by layers. Convolutional Neural Networks satisfy the requirement of a deep learning approach. CNNs initially attending several large-scale image classification challenges [8, 14, 24], is a class of deep, feed-forward artificial neural networks that are applied to the vast majority of machine learning problems due to the outstanding performance. The architecture of CNNs is usually a composition of layers that can be grouped by their functionalities. The high performance of CNNs is achieved by (i) their ability to learn rich level image representations and (ii) leveraging a tremendous amount of data. It can take millions of estimated parameters to characterize the network. Recently, deep convolutional neural networks have gained outstanding performance in vast majority ranging from image classification [21], transfer learning [9–11] and object detection [1, 5].

Compared to other image-related tasks, object detection is a more challenging problem that requires a combination of different methods to solve. First, several candidate object regions must be processed. Second, these proposed regions must be refined to achieve accurate localization. Fortunately, many researchers have endeavored to achieve state-of-the-art solutions that combine speed, accuracy, and simplicity.

2.2   Region Proposal Networks (RPN)

RPN [23] is an algorithm used to find the position of an object in an image. The algorithm will output a box shape, along with a classification of what the objects are inside. RPN inherits and improves from region-based convolutional network (R-CNN) [13] and Fast R-CNN [12]. Thus, some papers refer to it as Faster R-CNN. An RPN takes an image with any size as the input, and a set of rectangular object proposals is the output. Each proposal associates with an objectiveness score. The proposals are generated by sliding a network of small windows with an anchor over the last shared layer's convolutional feature map. Then the network is converted into a representative vector 256-d. Next, it is fed into two fully-connected layers. One is a box-classification layer (*cls*) while the other layer is a box-regression (*reg*). The RPN core is illustrated in Fig. 1.

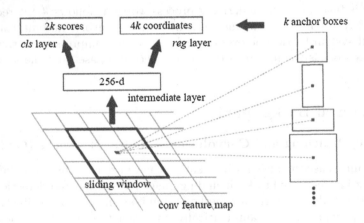

Fig. 1. The illustration of RPN core.

Each anchor is labeled by either having an object (positive) or not having an object (negative). Suppose the anchor has the highest Intersection over Union (IoU) overlap with a ground-truth rectangle, or the value of IoU is more significant than 0.7. In that case, it is assigned as a positive label. Otherwise, should the IoU value of an anchor be less than 0.3, its class is negative. The anchors with neither positive nor negative do not contribute to the training objective.

We denote i, and p_i is the index of an anchor in a mini-batch and the predicted probability of i as an object. $\hat{p}_i$ is the ground-truth label, which has the value of 0 if the anchor is negative and 1 otherwise. t_i and $\hat{t}_i$ are a tuple containing four coordinates of the predicted bounding box and the ground-truth box, respectively. Then the loss function is as follows:

$$L(\{p_i\}, \{t_i\}) = \frac{1}{N_{cls}} \sum_i L_{cls}(p_i, \hat{p}_i) + \lambda \frac{1}{N_{reg}} \sum_i \hat{p}_i L_{reg}(t_i, \hat{t}_i) \qquad (1)$$

where L_{cls} is log classification loss over two classes (not object vs. object). $L_{reg}(t_i, \hat{t}_i) = R(t_i - \hat{t}_i)$ is the smooth L_1 loss function [12]. λ is a balancing weight between L_{cls} and L_{reg}. RPN is optimized by back-propagation and stochastic gradient descent. The position of RPN is a convolutional neural network is presented in Fig. 2.

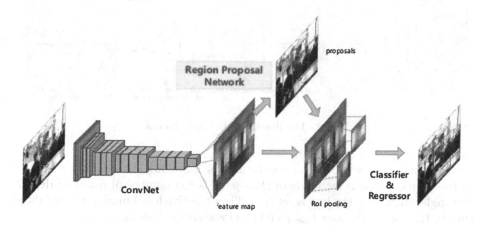

Fig. 2. The illustration of RPN model.

2.3   Single Shot Detection (SSD)

The SSD model [19] contains a convolutional-based network, e.g., VGG-16 or any standard architecture used for high-quality image classification auxiliary structure to produce object detection. SSD's input is an image and ground-truth rectangles of each object during training. The model evaluates a small set of default rectangle of different aspect ratios of each location in several feature maps with different shapes, e.g., 8×8 and 4×4. For each default rectangle, the model predict both the offsets and the confidences for all object classes $(c_1, c_2, \ldots, c_p)$. The default rectangles are matched to the ground-truth squares in training. The loss is calculated by weighting summation between the confidence loss and the localization loss. The key features of the added auxiliary structure at the end of the network are (i) multi-scale feature maps for detection, (ii) convolutional predictors for detection, and (iii) default boxes and aspect ratios. We present the SSD core is Fig. 3. The model of SSD is presented in Fig. 4.

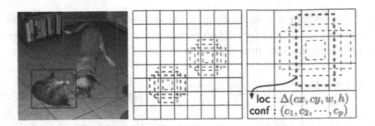

Fig. 3. The illustration of SSD core.

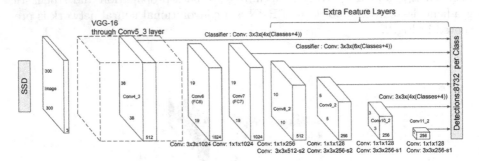

Fig. 4. The illustration of SSD model.

We denote $x_{i,j}^p = \{1, 0\}$ as an indicator for matching the i default rectangle to the j ground-truth rectangle of class p. N is the number of matched default rectangles. If $N = 0$, the loss is set to 0. The objective loss function is a weighted sum of the confidence loss L_{conf} and the localization loss L_{loc}:

$$L(x, c, l, g) = \frac{1}{N}(L_{conf}(x, c) + \alpha L_{loc}(x, l, g)) \tag{2}$$

The confidence loss is the softmax loss over multiple classes' confidence (c).

$$L_{conf}(x, c) = -\sum_{i \in Pos}^N x_{i,j}^p \log\left(\frac{\exp(c_i^p)}{\sum_p \exp(c_i^p)}\right) - \sum_{i \in Neg} \log(\hat{c}_i^0) \tag{3}$$

The localization loss is a Smooth L1 loss [12] between the ground-truth rectangle g and the predicted rectangle l parameters. We denote cx, cy as the offsets center of the default bounding rectangle d and its height h and width w.

$$L_{loc}(x, l, g) = \sum_{i \in Pos}^N \sum_{m \in \{cx, cy, w, h\}} x_{i,j}^k \text{smooth}_{L1}(l_i^m - \hat{g}_i^m) \tag{4}$$

where for each $m \in \{cx, cy, w, h\}$, we calculate

$$\hat{g}_j^{cx} = \frac{g_j^{cx} - d_i^{cx}}{d_i^w} \tag{5}$$

$$\hat{g}_j^{cy} = \frac{g_j^{cy} - d_i^{cy}}{d_i^h} \tag{6}$$

$$\hat{g}_j^{w} = \log\left(\frac{g_j^w}{d_i^w}\right) \tag{7}$$

$$\hat{g}_j^{h} = \log\left(\frac{g_j^h}{d_i^h}\right) \tag{8}$$

2.4 You only Look once (YOLO)

YOLO [22] is a single convolutional network that predicts multiple bounding rectangles and the probability of classes for those rectangles. The model is trained on full images and optimized for detection performance. The object detection is viewed as a single regression problem, from image pixels to bounding rectangle coordinates and their probability of classes. The input image is divided into a $S \times S$ grid, which is used to detect an object if the center of it falls into a grid cell. Let denote B is the bounding box. Then each grid cell predicts B and its confidence, defined as $\Pr(\text{Obj}) * \text{IoU}_{pred}^{truth}$, that a box consists of an object. Each B contains five predicted values: coordinates x, y presenting the center of the box relative to the bounds of the grid cell, width w and height h relative to the whole image, and confidence. We denote $\Pr(\text{Class}_i)|\text{Obj})$ as conditional class probability.

$$\Pr(\text{Class}_i)|\text{Obj}) * \Pr(\text{Obj}) * \text{IoU}_{pred}^{truth} = \Pr(\text{Class}_i) * \text{IoU}_{pred}^{truth} \tag{9}$$

which results in class-specific confidence scores for each box. The YOLO core is presented in Fig. 5.

YOLO predicts multiple bounding rectangles per grid cell. One predictor is assigned to predict an object based on the highest IoU score with the ground-truth. It leads to specialization among the bounding box predictors, which turns out to improve recall scores. Hence, the objective loss of YOLO is as follows.

$$L = \lambda_{coord} \sum_{i=0}^{S^2} \sum_{j=0}^{B} \mathcal{O}_{ij}^{obj}[(x_i - \hat{x}_i)^2 + (y_i - \hat{y}_i)^2]$$

$$+\lambda_{coord} \sum_{i=0}^{S^2} \sum_{j=0}^{B} \mathcal{O}_{ij}^{obj}[(\sqrt{w_i} - \sqrt{\hat{w}_i})^2 + (\sqrt{h_i} - \sqrt{\hat{h}_i})^2]$$

$$+\sum_{i=0}^{S^2} \sum_{j=0}^{B} \mathcal{O}_{ij}^{obj}(C_i - \hat{C}_i)^2 + \lambda_{noobj} \sum_{i=0}^{S^2} \sum_{j=0}^{B} \mathcal{O}_{ij}^{noobj}(C_i - \hat{C}_i)^2 \tag{10}$$

$$+\sum_{i=0}^{S^2} \mathcal{O}_i^{obj} \sum_{c \in C} (p_i(c) - \hat{p}_i(c))^2$$

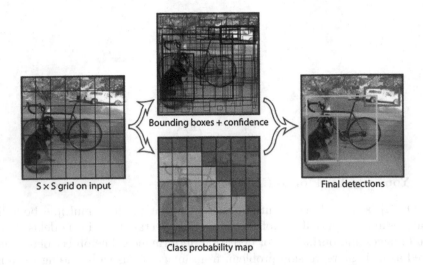

S × S grid on input   Bounding boxes + confidence   Final detections

Class probability map

Fig. 5. The illustration of YOLO core.

where $\lambda_{coord} = 5$ and $\lambda_{noobj} = 0.5$ are hyperparameters that control the loss from bounding box coordinate predictions and the loss from confidence predictions. $\mathcal{O}_i^{obj}$ denotes if an object exists in cell i. $\mathcal{O}_{ij}^{obj}$ denotes if the j bounding box predictor in cell i. The model of YOLO is presented in Fig. 6.

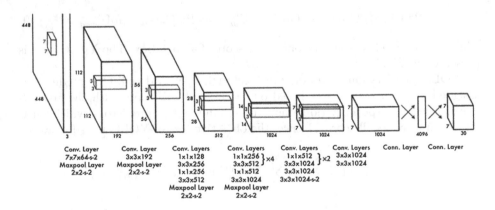

Fig. 6. The illustration of YOLO.

3   Experiments

3.1   Datasets

Theoretically, to create a data set for training object recognition and classification models, we need many images of objects and diversity. It can be said that this is the most critical stage to lead the good results of the model. One thing to note is that one must consider the capture environment must be close to the actual deployment to increase the model accuracy. In this topic's content, the authors have assumed that the cake will be placed in a white tray; the camera is located in a fixed distance with enough exposure. We present some typical pictures in Fig. 7.

Fig. 7. Images of cakes taken.

We collect 1289 1080px × 1080px images using a regular camera as our implemented dataset. Then cakes images are annotated by using labelImg[1] tool. A total of 16 different cake categories are identified. We randomly split data into 90% training and 10% test portions. An example of an input image and its predicted detection is presented in Fig. 8.

3.2   Evaluation Metrics

We denote TP, FP, and FN as true positive, false positive, and false negative. With the classification problem where the classes' data sets are very different, there is a logical operation commonly used as Precision-Recall. First of all, consider the problem of binary classification. We also consider one of the two classes to be positive and the other to be negative. With a way of determining a class to be positive, Precision is defined as the ratio of the number of true positive points to those classified as positive (TP + FP). The recall is defined as the ratio of the number of true positive points to positive (TP + FN). Mathematically, Precision and Recall are two fractions with equal numerators but different denominators:

---

[1] https://github.com/tzutalin/labelImg.

Fig. 8. Input image (left) and predicted detection (right).

$$\text{Precision} = \frac{\text{TP}}{\text{TP} + \text{FP}} \tag{11}$$

$$\text{Recall} = \frac{\text{TP}}{\text{TP} + \text{FN}} \tag{12}$$

We combine Eqs. 11 and 12 to compute F1-score as follows:

$$\text{F1-score} = 2\frac{\text{Precision} \times \text{Recall}}{\text{Precision} + \text{Recall}} \tag{13}$$

3.3   Experimental Results

After successfully training the models from the collected data set, the authors perform models testing and evaluate results to propose the best model to solve the detection problem. The most appropriate model should meet the following conditions

1. it accurately identifies all objects included in the input image,
2. the accurate identification of objects' location,
3. objects that do not exist in the input image should be ignored, and
4. operation speed should be high.

Table 1 presents the comparison on detection accuracy while Table 2 shows that of operation speed.

Table 1. Comparison of detection accuracy.

	RPN	SSD	YOLO
F1-score (%)	100	99.54	100
# False Positive	0	0	0
# True Positive	331	328	331
# False Negative	0	3	0
# True Negative	0	0	0

Table 2. Comparison of operation speed in frame per second (Fps).

No. test	RPN (Fps)	SSD (Fps)	YOLO (Fps)
1	0.923	16.442	21.329
2	0.873	16.545	21.232
3	0.874	16.542	21.316
4	0.876	16.605	21.472
5	0.877	16.481	21.095
6	0.864	16.073	20.211
7	0.867	16.046	20.656
8	0.875	15.902	20.219
9	0.872	16.100	19.930
10	0.874	16.067	20.407
Average	**0.877**	**16.280**	**20.828**

3.4   Remarks

After performing the training of cake recognition models, evaluating the experimental results, we can conclude that the models work well on the collected data set. Models make predictions quickly and accurately, in which the SSD model still has some cases of wrong identification. We see that the accuracy of two models RPN and YOLO, is quite impressive. However, in terms of speed, YOLO shows the best of the three algorithms. Therefore, we consider that YOLO is the most suitable model for deploying into our software application.

4   Application Deployment

Our application software is a website that (i) recognizes the cakes on the tray, and (ii) makes an invoice. This software makes the payment and cake management easier, reducing human resources and time for the shop owner. The application is written on a website interface that communicates with a server through the Django framework's support, runs well on Chrome browser and other JavaScript-enabled browsers. Client-Server is a well-known architecture in

210   A. C. Tran et al.

computer networks and is widely applied. The idea of this architecture, see Fig. 9, is that a client sends a request to a server to process and return the results to the client. The software uses the sqlite3 database management system to store data. Since this is just a relatively simple application, it only needs a small database with two tables to store data: BILL to save customer invoices and PASTRY to store cakes, including in the invoice, see Fig. 10. A regular camera or webcam takes images as the input of the system. Besides, the software also integrates many libraries for image processing. The several functions are as follows. The usecase diagram is presented in Fig. 11.

- Invoice calculation
- Add/Adjust/Remove cake(s) to invoice
- Bill management
- Manage cake information
- Revenue statistics

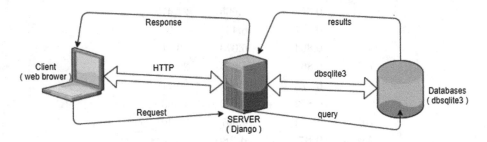

Fig. 9. Client - Server architecture used in our solution.

Fig. 10. Database design.

A customer enters a bakery, selects as many cakes he/she needs, and put them on a tray. The tray is scanned by a fix-position camera attached to a desktop computer via USB cable at check-out. The image of that tray is captured. Cakes are recognized together with how much the customer needs to pay. The whole technical process performs in real-time. Several screenshots are presented in Figs. 12, 13, and 14.

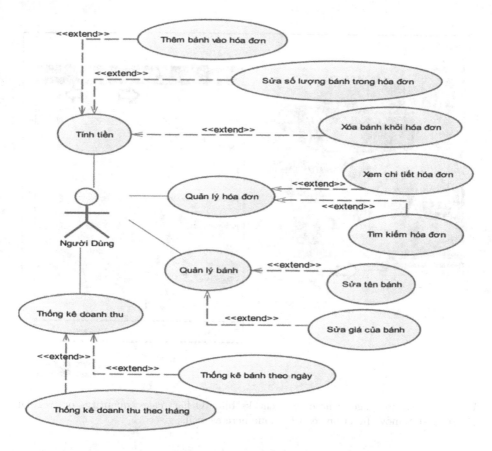

Fig. 11. Usecase diagram.

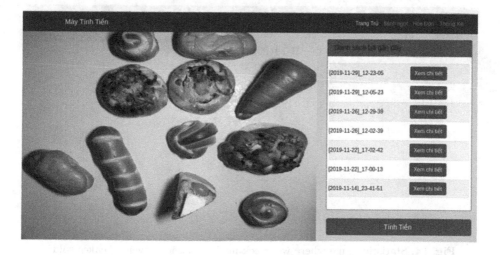

Fig. 12. Homepage where image is taken.

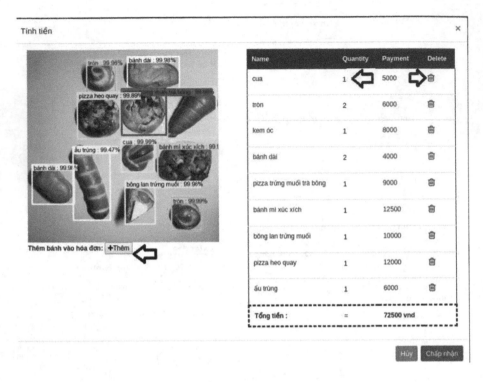

Fig. 13. Invoice page where we check bill. Other cake quantity or regular add/adjust/remove functions can be done here as well.

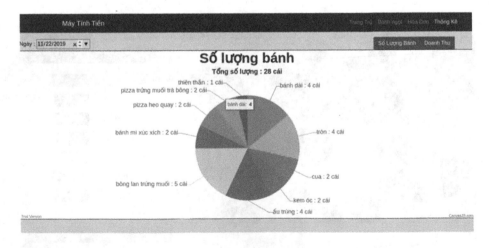

Fig. 14. Statistics page where we check invoice history, revenue, cakes sold.

5 Conclusion

In this work, we have proposed a pipeline of CNNs for pastry image detection and software development. First, we collect a cake image dataset from a local bakery. Second, we evaluate several CNNs models for the task of object detection in images. We achieve an accuracy of 100% on our collect dataset with an operation speed of 20 frames per second. The most appropriate approach is selected based on considering operation time and performance. Third, we develop a website integrating the CNNs model. The payment process, management, and statistics are easily managed. This work is the first to develop this kind of software used in a bakery shop.

References

1. Agarwal, S., Terrail, J.O.D., Jurie, F.: Recent advances in object detection in the age of deep convolutional neural networks. arXiv preprint arXiv:1809.03193 (2018)
2. Anthimopoulos, M.M., Gianola, L., Scarnato, L., Diem, P., Mougiakakou, S.G.: A food recognition system for diabetic patients based on an optimized bag-of-features model. IEEE J. Biomed. Health Inform. **18**(4), 1261–1271 (2014)
3. Attokaren, D.J., Fernandes, I.G., Sriram, A., Murthy, Y.S., Koolagudi, S.G.: Food classification from images using convolutional neural networks. In: TENCON 2017–2017 IEEE Region 10 Conference, pp. 2801–2806. IEEE (2017)
4. Bossard, L., Guillaumin, M., Van Gool, L.: Food-101 – mining discriminative components with random forests. In: Fleet, D., Pajdla, T., Schiele, B., Tuytelaars, T. (eds.) ECCV 2014. LNCS, vol. 8694, pp. 446–461. Springer, Cham (2014). https://doi.org/10.1007/978-3-319-10599-4_29
5. Cai, Z., Fan, Q., Feris, R.S., Vasconcelos, N.: A unified multi-scale deep convolutional neural network for fast object detection. In: Leibe, B., Matas, J., Sebe, N., Welling, M. (eds.) ECCV 2016. LNCS, vol. 9908, pp. 354–370. Springer, Cham (2016). https://doi.org/10.1007/978-3-319-46493-0_22
6. Chen, X., Zhu, Y., Zhou, H., Diao, L., Wang, D.: ChinesefoodNet: a large-scale image dataset for Chinese food recognition. arXiv preprint arXiv:1705.02743 (2017)
7. Ciocca, G., Napoletano, P., Schettini, R.: Food recognition: a new dataset, experiments, and results. IEEE J. Biomed. Health Inform. **21**(3), 588–598 (2016)
8. Deng, J., Dong, W., Socher, R., Li, L.J., Li, K., Fei-Fei, L.: ImageNet: a large-scale hierarchical image database (2009)
9. Duong-Trung, N., Quach, L.D., Nguyen, C.N.: Learning deep transferability for several agricultural classification problems. Int. J. Adv. Comput. Sci. Appl. **10**(1), 58–67 (2019)
10. Duong-Trung, N., Quach, L.D., Nguyen, M.H., Nguyen, C.N.: Classification of grain discoloration via transfer learning and convolutional neural networks. In: Proceedings of the 3rd International Conference on Machine Learning and Soft Computing, pp. 27–32 (2019)
11. Duong-Trung, N., Quach, L.D., Nguyen, M.H., Nguyen, C.N.: A combination of transfer learning and deep learning for medicinal plant classification. In: Proceedings of the 2019 4th International Conference on Intelligent Information Technology, pp. 83–90 (2019)
12. Girshick, R.: Fast R-CNN. In: Proceedings of the IEEE International Conference on Computer Vision, pp. 1440–1448 (2015)

13. Girshick, R., Donahue, J., Darrell, T., Malik, J.: Rich feature hierarchies for accurate object detection and semantic segmentation. In: Proceedings of the IEEE Conference on Computer Vision and Pattern Recognition, pp. 580–587 (2014)
14. Griffin, G., Holub, A., Perona, P.: Caltech-256 object category dataset (2007)
15. He, Y., Xu, C., Khanna, N., Boushey, C.J., Delp, E.J.: Analysis of food images: features and classification. In: 2014 IEEE International Conference on Image Processing (ICIP), pp. 2744–2748. IEEE (2014)
16. Kagaya, H., Aizawa, K., Ogawa, M.: Food detection and recognition using convolutional neural network. In: Proceedings of the 22nd ACM International Conference on Multimedia, pp. 1085–1088 (2014)
17. Kawano, Y., Yanai, K.: FoodCam: a real-time food recognition system on a smartphone. Multimedia Tools Appl. **74**(14), 5263–5287 (2015)
18. Kitamura, K., Yamasaki, T., Aizawa, K.: FoodLog: capture, analysis and retrieval of personal food images via web. In: Proceedings of the ACM Multimedia 2009 Workshop on Multimedia for Cooking and Eating Activities, pp. 23–30 (2009)
19. Liu, W., et al.: SSD: single shot MultiBox detector. In: Leibe, B., Matas, J., Sebe, N., Welling, M. (eds.) ECCV 2016. LNCS, vol. 9905, pp. 21–37. Springer, Cham (2016). https://doi.org/10.1007/978-3-319-46448-0_2
20. Pouladzadeh, P., Kuhad, P., Peddi, S.V.B., Yassine, A., Shirmohammadi, S.: Food calorie measurement using deep learning neural network. In: 2016 IEEE International Instrumentation and Measurement Technology Conference Proceedings, pp. 1–6. IEEE (2016)
21. Rawat, W., Wang, Z.: Deep convolutional neural networks for image classification: a comprehensive review. Neural Comput. **29**(9), 2352–2449 (2017)
22. Redmon, J., Divvala, S., Girshick, R., Farhadi, A.: You only look once: unified, real-time object detection. In: Proceedings of the IEEE Conference on Computer Vision and Pattern Recognition, pp. 779–788 (2016)
23. Ren, S., He, K., Girshick, R., Sun, J.: Faster R-CNN: towards real-time object detection with region proposal networks. In: Advances in Neural Information Processing Systems, pp. 91–99 (2015)
24. Russakovsky, O., et al.: ImageNet large scale visual recognition challenge. Int. J. Comput. Vision **115**(3), 211–252 (2015)

Forecasting Sensor Data Using Multivariate Time Series Deep Learning

Nguyen Thai-Nghe[(⊠)] and Nguyen Thanh-Hai

College of Information and Communication Technology, Can Tho University,
Can Tho city, Vietnam
{ntnghe,nthai}@cit.ctu.edu.vn

Abstract. Vietnam is a country that has a long coastline, stretching from its North to its South. This has many advantage for aquaculture and fisheries, however, the Global climate change and water pollution have caused problems to the farmers in fish/shrimp raising. Tackling the problem of monitoring and managing quality of the water to help the farmers is very necessary. By monitoring the real-time indicators of salinity, temperature, pH, and dissolved oxygen which are produced by sensor networks, and forecasting them to get early warning, we can help the farmers in shrimp/fish raising. In this work, we propose model for forecasting the water quality indicators by using deep learning (Long-Short Term Memory) with Multivariate Time Series. Experimental results on several data sets show that the proposed approach works well and can be applied to real systems.

Keywords: Deep learning · Multivariate Time Series Forecasting · LSTM (Long-Short Term Memory) · Sensor data · Water quality

1 Introduction

Vietnam is a country which has many advantages in aquaculture and fishery since its sea adjoins the North thorough the South. However, the farmers still have many problems in fish raising because of the Global climate change and water pollution effects. Climate change not only causes great impacts on all regions, resources, environment and socio-economic, but also affects water resources, agriculture and rural development, health and the coastal areas. Economic losses due to the impact of climate change combined with the costs of recovering from the damage reduce the economic growth of many countries and globally. Especially, Agricultural/Aquaculture countries have been suffering great losses because of Global climate change. For example, fishery is one of the key economic sectors of Vietnam's agriculture, with billions of dollars in exports. It also creates jobs for millions of workers, contributing to stabilizing social security and developing the country. Shrimp is a seafood product in the top export of billion US dollars. However, shrimp nursery is too difficult because they are particularly sensitive to water. Polluted water environment is a great concern for numerous fishermen

© Springer Nature Singapore Pte Ltd. 2020
T. K. Dang et al. (Eds.): FDSE 2020, CCIS 1306, pp. 215–229, 2020.
https://doi.org/10.1007/978-981-33-4370-2_16

and Agricultural managers. However, these farmers do not have enough technique and media to forecast environment factors, so they cannot manage risks which they are facing. Thus, how to manage and monitor the water quality, especially in aquaculture and fisheries such as fish raising management is really necessary.

Recently, techniques in the Internet of Things (IoT) can help users to build the monitoring systems which can monitor the water quality to help reducing pollution. There are many applications of IoT such as automatic door systems (smart-home), aircraft and self-driving cars (smart-city), etc. [1]. This adds a level of digital intelligence to passive devices, allowing us to communicate real-time data without human involvement, effectively integrating the digital and physical world. When something is connected to the internet, it is able to send or receive information, or both. Leveraging IoT techniques, the ability to send or receive this information makes everything smarter, and that is also our target.

This work proposes an approach to monitor and forecast the water quality (such as indicators of salinity, temperature, pH, and dissolved oxygen - DO) for the IoT systems in aquaculture and fisheries. These data are collected from the sensors every day and ordered by time, they can be considered as time series or sequential data. Previous works show that deep learning with LSTM (Long-Short Term Memory) could be an appropriate method for time series data [2], thus, we propose LSTM model with multivariate time series for forecasting these water quality indicators.

2   Related Work

A full-fledged IoT system related to several sides such as sensor networks, hardware circuits, energy, etc., and software for analysis. One of the important tasks in the environmental monitoring IoT system is finding the suitable methods to analyze data and forecast. In this section, we focus on reviewing the literature related to the forecasting methods. There are several researches in this field.

The authors in [3] proposed a water quality predictive model based on a combination of Kernal Principal Component Analysis (kPCA) and Recurrent Neural Network (RNN) to forecast the trend of dissolved oxygen. Data collected from Burnett River, Australia, was used to evaluate their kPCA-RNN model. Results showed that the kPCA-RNN model achieved better performance than the data-driven methods. In [4], the water, temperature, pH and DO levels are measured and integrated with aerating and water supply pumps using Arduino. The user could receive information at predetermined intervals on preferred communication. The authors tested on a sample of two days measurements of temperature, pH and DO levels. Results show that with this integration system, farmer need not hire worker at their site, consequently drive down operating costs and improve efficiency.

The authors of [5] developed a web-based system which monitor the pH and salinity values. The workings of the monitoring and control system send data on pH and salinity sent by the sensor and then stored and in database hosting.

They said that for the value of a dangerous salt content worth less than 160 and more than 210, if for a pH of less than 6.5 and more than 7.5. Darmalim et al. in [6] proposed an IoT solution to automatically monitor the environmental factors. The system had five sensors to measure each parameter. It is developed using a Python framework with a web application to present information from the IoT device. [20] presented a feasible model for the daily average temperature on the area of Zhengzhou and apply it to weather derivatives pricing.

The study in [7] used recurrent neural networks with its Long Short-Term Memory to predict the ambient temperature. The prediction is based on sensor data retrieved from IoT stations such as temperature, humidity and some gases in the air. The proposed network architecture consists of two types of hidden layers: LSTM layer and full connected dense layer. Results showed that the proposed method worked fine. In [8], the authors proposed a deep learning and image-based model for air quality estimation. The model extracts image feature from the camera and then classifies them to estimate air quality levels. The experimental results show that proposed method produces accurate results for air quality classification. The analysis in [9] used univariate and multivariate techniques namely Autoregressive Integrated Moving Average and Vector Autoregression models to forecast the Air Quality Index. The authors in [10] uses deep Gated Recurrent Units to forecast multivariate time series in parking lots setting. Other researches can be found in [11–15].

The book of [16] offered information on the theory, models and algorithms involved in state-of-the-art multivariate time series analysis and highlights several of the latest research advances in climate and environmental science. Other Time Series Analysis—Univariate and Multivariate methods can be found in [17].

In this work, we propose using multivariate time series forecasting for sensor data with Deep Learning. This forecasting module is part of an IoT system which monitors the water quality (such as indicators of salinity, temperature, pH, and DO) in aquaculture and fishery. Since these data are collected every day (ordered by time), we propose deep learning with Long-Short Term Memory (LSTM) model for forecasting these time series data.

The remaining of this study is presented as follows. Section 3 introduces the proposed architectures for the forecast problems. In Sect. 4, we present the data sets used in the experiments and do some investigations, comparisons, explain the experimental results. Finally, we discuss and summarize our work in Sect. 5.

3   Proposed Method

3.1   System Architecture

The system architecture is presented in Fig. 1. In this system, we have implemented the sensors for monitoring water quality indicators such as salinity, temperature, pH, and dissolved oxygen (DO) in the fish/shrimp ponds. Data from sensors is daily transferred to a cloud database (in this work, we have used the cloud database provided by the DigitalOcean[1]). These data will be collected to a server for analyzing and forecasting.

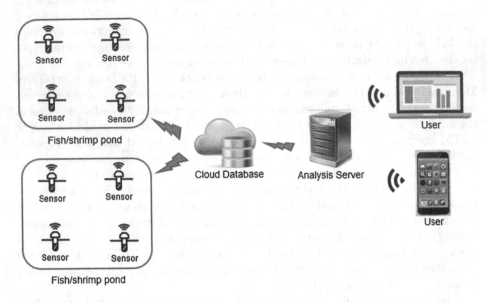

Fig. 1. System architecture for shrimp/fish pond monitoring

Using this system, the users can visualize all of the indicators via mobile devices or pc/laptop. The system automatically send the messages to the users (farmers) when the indicators are lower or higher the threshold values. Moreover, based on historical data, the system can forecast the values of each indicator for the next dates (or other selected time).

The system infrastructure is implemented by another group in our team. In this paper, our task is to develop a forecasting model which can provide the forecast values to send early warning to the users. Thus, in the rest of this work, we focus on developing the forecasting models, especially Deep Learning with LSTM for forecasting multivariate time series data.

3.2 The Proposed Multivariate Time Series Forecasting with LSTM

For using Multivariate Time Series Forecasting with Long Short-Term Memory (LSTM), we need to transform data. Instead of using only one feature (variable), in this work we utilize all other features by transforming their values at time (t-1) as input values at time t. An example of this transformation is presented in Fig. 2.

In this example, the original dataset have 5 features (DateTime, Salinity denoted as sal, temperature denoted as temp, pH, and dissolved oxygen denoted

---

[1] https://www.digitalocean.com.

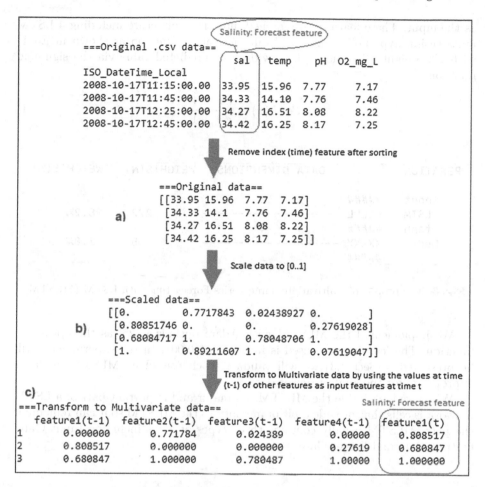

Fig. 2. An example of Multivariate data transformation

as O2_mg_L). After sorting the data, we remove the index/time column as in Fig. 2a). Next, we scale the data to the range of [0..1] as in Fig. 2b). Finally, a new dataset is created by using the values at time (t-1) as the values at time t for each feature, as presented in Fig. 2c). Since this process is automatically performed, the features are also renamed for general purpose (for any dataset). In this case, the mapping as "feature1:sal", "feature2:temp", "feature3:pH", "feature4:O2_mg_L".

After transforming data, we propose using LSTM (Long Short-Term Memory) for forecasting. The LSTM is well-known deep learning method which widely-used in forecast models and can be used to avoid the long-term dependency problem [2,21]. The proposed LSTM for multivariate time series data is called **MLTSM**. Its architecture is presented in Fig. 3. The network receives the 12 features (consisting of a time feature with a time step in the architecture) as the input. These features are fetched into an architecture including 4 LSTM units (using hyperbolic tangent (Tanh) activation function as shown in Eq. 1) with 272 weights. The network provides one predicted value via the signmoid function.

$$Tanh(x) = \frac{e^{2x} - 1}{e^{2x} + 1} \tag{1}$$

OPERATION	DATA DIMENSIONS			WEIGHTS(N)	WEIGHTS(%)
Input	#####	1	12		
LSTM	LLLLL	----------------------		272	98.2%
tanh	#####		4		
Dense	XXXXX	----------------------		5	1.8%
	#####		1		

Fig. 3. The proposed Multivariate Time Series Forecasting with LSTM (MLSTM)

We implemented the MLSTM with Adam optimizer [25] as the optimized function. The learning rate used is initiated at 0.001. In the experiments (will be presented in Sect. 4.3) we will validate to choose which MLSTM model is appropriate for the kind of sensor data.

When we look inside the MLSTM, its major and important part of a LSTM network is cells that provide a bit of memory to the MLSTM so it can remember the past. MLSTM usually contains three types of gates including Input Gate, Output Gate and Forget Gate.

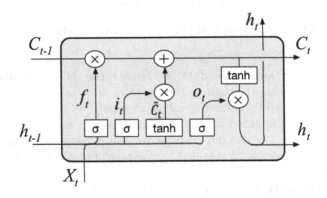

Fig. 4. An illustration of LSTM cell [24].

Gates in LSTM consist of sigmoid activation functions. In most of the cases, the value is either 0 or 1. The sigmoid function (Eq. 2) is used widely for gates because we want a gate to give only positive values and should be able to give us a clear cut answer whether, we need to keep a particular feature or we need to discard that feature. LTSM architectures are also deployed some other activation functions such as hyperbolic tangent function (Eq. 1) or as the peephole LSTM paper proposed in [26,27].

$$Sigmoid(x) = \frac{1}{1+e^{-x}} \qquad (2)$$

The Sigmoid function is popularly considered as the gate types of in, out, forget (as illustrated in Fig. 4) since it produces a value ranging from 0 to 1 and it can either let no flow (value $= 0$) or complete flow (value $= 1$) of information throughout the gates. In order to overcome the problem of the vanishing gradient [21], we need a function (Tanh) whose second derivative can sustain for a long range before going to zero.

The followings are formulas for three gate types:

$$i_t = \sigma(w_i[h_{t-1}, x_t] + b_i) \qquad (3)$$

$$f_t = \sigma(w_f[h_{t-1}, x_t] + b_f) \qquad (4)$$

$$o_t = \sigma(w_o[h_{t-1}, x_t] + b_o) \qquad (5)$$

With:

$$C_t = f_t \times C_{t-1} + i_t \times \tilde{C}_t \qquad (6)$$

$$\tilde{C}_t = tanh(WC.[h_{t-1}, x_t] + b_C) \qquad (7)$$

$$h_t = o_t \times tanh(C_t) \qquad (8)$$

Where:

- i_t denotes input gate.
- f_t reveals output gate.
- o_t represents forget gate.
- w_m shows weights for the respective $gate(m)$.
- h_{t-1} denotes the output of the preceded LSTM block at the timestamp t $-$ 1.
- h_t exhibits the current unit state.
- x_t is the input at the current timestamp.
- $\tilde{C}_t$ is the state of x_t involving the hidden state value h_{t-1} from the preceded block at time $t-1$.
- C_t is the current unit state controlled by f_t and i_t.
- b_m exhibits the biases of the respective $gate(m)$.

Equation 3 reveals what new information will be stored in the cell state while Eq. 5 aims to provide the activation to the final output of the LSTM block at timestamp t. The forget gate at Eq. 4 give us the information on which information to throw away from the cell state.

As described details in [21–24], the key to the Long Short Term Memory model is the cell state C_t. C_t (Eq. 6, 7, 8) is characterized by only a small amount of linear interaction during the entire operation while it can effectively record history information for a long time through the three such gates.

4   Experimental Results

4.1   Data Sets for the Experiments

In the proposed architecture in Fig. 1, the sensors' implementation is deployed by another group in our team. However, this system is just started and we do not have enough data for training the model. Luckily, there are several published data sets which have the structures similar to our data structure, so we have used them to test the proposed forecasting approach.

Table 1. Published datasets

No.	Dataset	#Records	#Variables	Variable name
1	Water quality - Tomales Bay, CA	245	5	Datetime, dissolved oxygen (O2_mg_L), pH, salinity, temperature, percentage of dissolved oxygen (O2_sat_pcnt)
2	NSW Estuary Temperature, pH and salinity data	6,271	22	Datetime, pH, Salinity, Temperature, Turbidity, Days_Elapsed, Latitude, Longitude, Seagrass_area, Mangrove_area, Total_estuary_area, Estuary_volume, total_sa_vol, Total_area_saltmarsh, Average_depth, Perimeter, openwater_SA.volume, Total_flush_time, Retention_factor, Propn_increase_N, percent_cleared, percent_urban, Catchment_area
3	Temperature and DO from the EGIM, EMSO-Azores observatory, 2017–2018	38,657	10	Datetime, Temperature, Oxygen, SATURATION, CALPHASE, TCPHASE, C1RPH, C2RPH, C1AMP, C2AMP, RAWTEMP

The first data set is published by the BCO-DMO[2], located at the Woods Hole Oceanographic Institution, US. This data set includes water quality parameters (e.g., pH, salinity, temperature, and dissolved oxygen - DO) in Tomales Bay, CA which is a monthly time series through sampling every 2 km.

The second data set is published by Australian Government, which is the sensor data of Temperature, pH and salinity at New South Wales Estuary[3].

The third data set is published by the European Multidisciplinary Seafloor and water column Observatory[4]. This dataset contains temperature and dissolved oxygen concentrations and the associated sensor raw data acquired between July 2017 and August 2018 on EMSO-Azores observatory by the EGIM.

These datasets were accessed on August, 2020. After pre-processing by removing missing data, the remaining number of observations, input variables (features), and forecast variables are presented in Table 1. The "Variable name" column includes all of the attributes in the dataset. When we forecast for one variable (e.g., salinity), it is dropped out and the remaining are input variables.

The data sets are sorted based time series and then divided into 2 parts. The first one (earlier) is for training with 66.67% of samples of the full data set. The remaining (test set) occupies 33% for test.

4.2   Evaluation Metrics and Baselines

Root mean squared error (RMSE) is used to evaluate the models. The RMSE for n observations is calculated by Eq. (9).

$$\sqrt{\frac{1}{n}\sum_{i=1}^{n}(y_i - \hat{y}_i)^2} \tag{9}$$

where, y_i is the true value, and $\hat{y}_i$ is the forecasted value.

We have used regression version of the Support Vector Machines (SVM) and a well-known method in forecasting called **Holt** [28] as a baseline for comparison. **Holt** extended single exponential smoothing to allow the forecasting of data with a trend. The forecast value at time $t + h$ is calculated by

Forecast value	$\hat{y}_{t+h} = \ell_t + hb_t$
Level equation	$\ell_t = \alpha y_t + (1 - \alpha)(\ell_{t-1} + b_{t-1})$
Trend equation	$b_t = \beta(\ell_t - \ell_{t-1}) + (1 - \beta)b_{t-1},$

where h is the h-step-ahead forecast (in this work we use one-step-ahead), and ℓ_t is an estimation of the level of the series at time t, b_t denotes is an estimation of the trend (slope) of the series at time t, y_t is the true value at time t, α is the smoothing parameter for the level ($0 \leq \alpha \leq 1$), and β is the smoothing parameter for the trend ($0 \leq \beta \leq 1$).

---

[2] https://www.bco-dmo.org/dataset-deployment/455476.
[3] https://data.gov.au/dataset/ds-nsw-c2041218-0496-453a-ac22-9e974fdebf89/ distribution/dist-nsw-5154e497-647f-4e2a-a2ad-151fa293b0da/details?q=.
[4] https://www.seanoe.org/data/00453/56501.

4.3   Evaluation Results

On the collected datasets, the MSLTM took aroud 100 epochs to get good value of RMSE as examples presented in Fig. 5. It just needs a couple of minutes to complete the training stage on Google Colab environment[5].

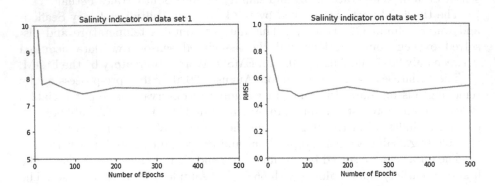

Fig. 5. Number of epochs

Table 2. RMSE comparison between MLSTM and others. The results formatted in bold and red are the best results corresponding the each indicator.

No.	Data set	Indicator	#Records	RMSE		
				SVM	Holt	MLSTM
1	Water quality - Tomales Bay, CA	Salinity	245	7.266	7.318	**6.623**
		pH	245	**0.171**	0.255	0.226
		Temperature	245	2.232	**1.092**	1.275
		DO (mg)	245	**0.293**	1.232	1.281
2	NSW Estuary Temperature, pH and salinity data	Salinity	6,271	7.590	7.535	**7.481**
		pH	6,271	3.199	3.208	**3.156**
		Temperature	6,271	2.908	2.555	**2.550**
3	Temperature and DO from the EGIM, EMSO-Azores observatory, 2017-2018	DO	38,657	4.000	4.015	**3.872**
		Temperature	38,657	0.385	0.385	**0.384**

The final RMSE results are presented in Table 2. There are four considered indicators which include salinity, pH, temperature, and dissolved oxygen (DO). As shown from Table 2, most of the cases, the MLSTM has lower error (RMSE) than the baseline SVM, thus it can produce better forecasting results. However,

---

[5] https://colab.research.google.com/.

the MLSTM does not work well on small datasets (e.g., dataset 1) since it has not enough data to learn as presented in Fig. 6. This figure shows that, on large dataset (the right side), the MLSTM could fit to the data after several epochs while it could not fit on small data (the left side).

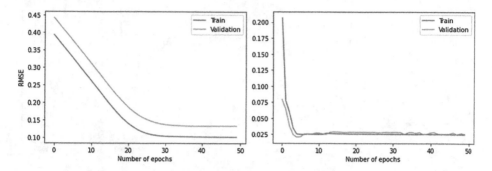

Fig. 6. RMSE during training and validation phases. Small dataset (DO indicator in dataset1) vs. larger dataset (DO indicator in dataset 3)

Figures 7, 8, 9, and 10 visualize some samples of the true values and the forecast values for the temperature, salinity, and dissolved oxygen indicators. Although data distributions for the temperature of dataset 1 and dataset 2 look quite different, the proposed model could fit well as presented in the Figs. 7 and 8. These results show that the forecast values of the proposed model are nearly approached to the true values, thus the proposed model could be appropriate for sensor data with time series, and it could be applied to the real world.

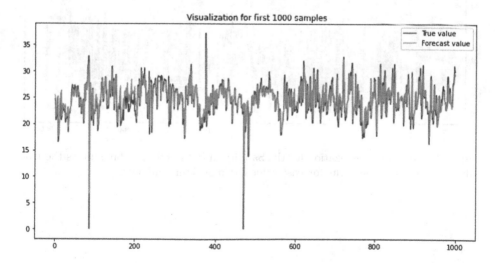

Fig. 7. Forecasting visualization for the temperature in dataset 1. The blue line is the true values, the orange line is the forecast values (Color figure online)

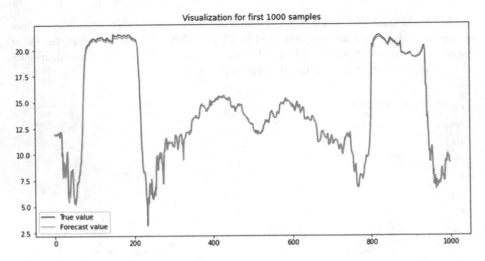

Fig. 8. Forecasting visualization for the temperature in dataset 2. The blue line is the true values, the orange line is the forecast values. (Color figure online)

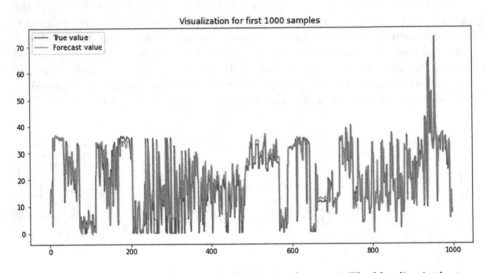

Fig. 9. Forecasting visualization for the Salinity in dataset 1. The blue line is the true values, the orange line is the forecast values. (Color figure online)

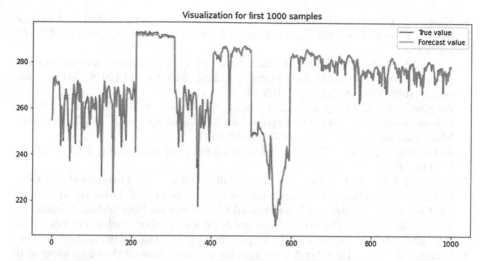

Fig. 10. Forecasting visualization for the Dissolved Oxygen (DO) in dataset 3. The blue line is the true values, the orange line is the forecast values (Color figure online)

5 Conclusion

In this work, we propose the model for forecasting the water quality indicators in aquaculture and fisheries (salinity, temperature, pH, and dissolved oxygen) by using deep learning (Long-Short Term Memory) with multivariate time series. Experimental results on the considered data sets with 4 indicators show that the proposed approach can produce acceptable forecasting values and can be applied for the real system.

By monitoring these real-time indicators and getting early warning, the system can help the farmers to manage the quality of the water, thus collecting both quality and quantity in shrimp/fish raising. In the future, we will collect the data provided in our system to retrain the model for implementing to the real world. Also, some sophisticated models are taken into account to improve the forecast performance.

Acknowledgments. This study is funded in part by the Can Tho University Improvement Project VN14-P6 supported by a Japanese ODA loan.

References

1. Shafique, K., Khawaja, B., Sabir, F., Qazi, S., Mustaqim, M.: Internet of Things (IoT) for next-generation smart systems: a review of current challenges, future trends and prospects for emerging 5G-IoT scenarios. IEEE Access, p. 1 (2020). https://doi.org/10.1109/ACCESS.2020.2970118
2. Lim, B., Zohren, S.: Time series forecasting with deep learning: a survey. arXiv preprint arXiv:2004.13408 (2020)

3. Zhang, Y.-F., Fitch, P., Thorburn, P.: Predicting the trend of dissolved oxygen based on the kPCA-RNN model. Water **12**, 585 (2020). https://doi.org/10.3390/w12020585
4. Harun, Z., Reda, E., Hashim, H.: Real time fish pond monitoring and automation using Arduino. IOP Conf. Ser.: Mater. Sci. Eng. **340**, 012014 (2018). https://doi.org/10.1088/1757-899X/340/1/012014
5. Preetham, K., Mallikarjun, B.C., Umesha, K., Mahesh, F.M., Neethan, S.: Aquaculture monitoring and control system: an IoT based approach. Int. J. Adv. Res. Ideas Innovat. Technol. **5**(2), 1167–1170 (2019)
6. Darmalim, U., et al.: IoT solution for intelligent pond monitoring. E&ES **426**(1), 012145 (2020)
7. Ikram, B.A.O., Abdelhakim, B.A., Abdelali, A., Zafar, B., Mohammed, B.: Deep learning architecture for temperature forecasting in an IoT LoRa based system. In: Proceedings of the 2nd International Conference on Networking, Information Systems & Security (NISS19). Association for Computing Machinery, New York, NY, USA, Article 43, 1–6 (2019). https://doi.org/10.1145/3320326.3320375
8. Zhang, Q., Fu, F., Tian, R.: A deep learning and image-based model for air quality estimation. Sci. Total Environ. **724**, 138178 (2020). ISSN 0048–9697 https://doi.org/10.1016/j.scitotenv.2020.138178
9. Sethi, J.K., Mittal, M.: Analysis of air quality using univariate and multivariate time series models. In: The 10th International Conference on Cloud Computing, Data Science & Engineering (Confluence), Noida, India, 2020, pp. 823–827 (2020). https://doi.org/10.1109/Confluence47617.2020.9058303
10. Almuammar, M., Fasli, M.: Deep learning for non-stationary multivariate time series forecasting. In: 2019 IEEE International Conference on Big Data (Big Data), Los Angeles, CA, USA, pp. 2097–2106 (2019). https://doi.org/10.1109/BigData47090.2019.9006192
11. Licata, R.J., Tobiska, W.K., Mehta, P.M.: Benchmarking forecasting models for space weather drivers. arXiv: Space Physics (2020)
12. Dong, J., Wang, G., Yan, H., Xu, J., Zhang, X.: A survey of smart water quality monitoring system. Environ. Sci. Pollut. Res. **22**(7), 4893–4906 (2015). https://doi.org/10.1007/s11356-014-4026-x
13. Siddiqui, N.A., Tauseef, S.M., Dobhal, R. (eds.): Advances in Water Pollution Monitoring and Control. STCEE. Springer, Singapore (2020). https://doi.org/10.1007/978-981-32-9956-6
14. Thai-Nghe, N., Thanh-Hai, N., Chi Ngon, N.: Deep learning approach for forecasting water quality in IoT systems. Int. J. Adv. Comput. Sci. Appl. (IJACSA), **11**(8) (2020). https://doi.org/10.14569/IJACSA.2020.0110883
15. Dien, T.T., Luu, S.H., Thanh-Hai, N., Thai-Nghe, N.: Deep learning with data transformation and factor analysis for student performance prediction. Int. J. Adv. Comput. Sci. Appl. (IJACSA) **11**(8) (2020). https://doi.org/10.14569/IJACSA.2020.0110886
16. Zhang, Z.: Multivariate Time Series Analysis in Climate and Environmental Research. Springer, Heidelberg (2018). ISBN 978-3-319-67340-0 https://doi.org/10.1007/978-3-319-67340-0
17. Wei W.W.S.: Multivariate Time Series Analysis and Applications, Wiley Series in Probability and Statistics. Wiley, Hoboken (2019). ISBN 111-950-2853
18. Kanjo, E., Younis, E.M.G., Ang, C.S.: Deep learning analysis of mobile physiological, environmental and location sensor data for emotion detection. Inf. Fus. **49**, 46–56 (2019). ISSN 1566–2535, https://doi.org/10.1016/j.inffus.2018.09.001

19. Wang, Z.J., Mazharul Mujib, A.B.M.: The weather forecast using data mining research based on cloud computing. Phys.: Conf. Ser. **910**, 012020 (2017)
20. Wang, Z., Li, P., Li, L., Huang, C., Liu, M.: Modeling and forecasting average temperature for weather derivative pricing. Advances in Meteorology (2015)
21. Suresh, H.: The Vanishing Gradient Problem (2016). http://harinisuresh.com/2016/10/09/lstms/
22. Gago, J.J., et al.: Sequence-to-sequence natural language to humanoid robot sign language. In: The 10th EUROSIM Congress on Modelling and Simulation. ISBN978-3-901608-92-6 (2019). https://arxiv.org/abs/1907.04198
23. Olah, C.: Understanding LSTM Networks (2015). http://colah.github.io/posts/2015-08-Understanding-LSTMs/
24. Li, H., Zhu, L., Gong, H., Sun, H., Yu, J.: Land subsidence modelling using a long short-term memory algorithm based on time-series datasets. In: Proceedings of the International Association of Hydrological Sciences, vol. 382, pp. 505–510. IAHS (2020). https://doi.org/10.5194/piahs-382-505-2020
25. Kingma, D.P., Ba, J.L.: Adam: a method for stochastic optimization. arXiv:1412.6980v9 (2014)
26. Gers, F.A., Schmidhuber, J.: LSTM recurrent networks learn simple context free and context sensitive languages. IEEE Trans. Neural Networks **12**(6), 1333–1340 (2001). PMID 18249962, https://doi.org/10.1109/72.963769
27. Gers, F., Schraudolph, N., Schmidhuber, J.: Learning precise timing with LSTM recurrent networks. J. Mach. Learn. Res. **3**, 115–143 (2002)
28. Hyndman, R.J., Athanasopoulos, G.: Forecasting: principles and practice. OTexts (2014). ISBN:0987507109

A Template-Based Approach for Generating Vietnamese References from Flat MR Dataset in Restaurant Domain

Dang Tuan Nguyen[✉] and Trung Tran

Sai Gon University, Ho Chi Minh City, Vietnam
dangnt@sgu.edu.vn, ttrung@nlke-group.net

Abstract. In recent years, researchers in natural language generation (NLG) focus on corpus-based systems on specific or across domains. The training data should consist of meaning representations (MRs) paired with Natural Language (NL) references. In the first content of the article, we introduce a Vietnamese Flat MR dataset which is the first Vietnamese dataset for training end-to-end, data-driven NLG systems in restaurant domain. We establish a method of generating references on this dataset. The core of the method are two important stages: (i) sentence planning which determine semantic template of the output text; (ii) surface realization which selecting appropriate Vietnamese phrases to replace the corresponding predicates (slot-value) of the Flat MR in the semantic template. The evaluation results show that the dataset and proposed generating method have contributed well to the development of the NLG research direction.

Keywords: Flat Meaning Representation · Natural language generation · End-to-end data-driven system · Corpus-based system · Semantic template · Sentence planning · Surface realization · Restaurant domain

1 Introduction

Natural language generation (NLG) plays a critical role in recent spoken dialogue systems [1–5, 8, 10, 12, 13, 18, 19, 22, 25, 26, 32, 33, 38]. So far, end-to-end NLG methods [6, 28, 40] were limited to small, de-lexicalized data sets. For new application domain, the corpus-based NLG systems should be re-developed so that they can replicate the rich dialogue and discourse phenomena. The dataset for training end-to-end, data-driven systems should require costly semantic alignment between meaning representations (MRs) paired with Natural Language (NL) references instead of non-aligned data [14, 15, 23, 29, 37, 40, 41].

The overall aim of this article is to present our research for Vietnamese language from building dataset to develop a domain-dependent NLG system. Based on the idea of crowd-sourcing English dataset [16, 17, 30, 31], we hired Vietnamese people to create <Flat MR – NL Reference> pairs in restaurant domain. This is the first Vietnamese dataset for training end-to-end, data-driven NLG systems for specific domain. So far we created 3516 unique Flat MRs and 42061 corresponding descriptions. Table 1 shows an

© Springer Nature Singapore Pte Ltd. 2020
T. K. Dang et al. (Eds.): FDSE 2020, CCIS 1306, pp. 230–245, 2020.
https://doi.org/10.1007/978-981-33-4370-2_17

example of a Flat MR with eight slots-values aligning with different human-written NL References.

Table 1. An example of a Flat MR aligning with different human-written NL References

Flat MR	NL References
name[Hi Caphe],	• Hi Caphe là một quán cà phê được đánh giá cao gần Công Viên Tao Đàn và Quận 1 thân thiện với gia đình và chưa đến 60.000đ cho các món ăn Nhật Bản.
eatType[quán cafe], food[Món Nhật],	• Hi Caphe là một quán cà phê Nhật Bản cung cấp thực phẩm với mức giá dưới 60.000đ cho gia đình và nằm ở Quận 1 gần Công Viên Tao Đàn và có tỷ lệ khách hàng đánh giá cao
priceRange[thấp hơn 60.000đ], customer rating[cao],	• Một quán cà phê được đánh giá cao gần Công Viên Tao Đàn và Quận 1 là Hi Caphe và thân thiện với gia đình và ít hơn 60.000đ cho thực phẩm Nhật Bản.
area[Quận 1], familyFriendly[có],	• Nằm ở trung tâm thành phố, Hi Caphe gần Công Viên Tao Đàn. Đó là một quán cà phê thân thiện với gia đình với giá rẻ và xếp hạng cao.
near[Công Viên Tao Đàn]	• Hi Caphe là một quán cà phê thân thiện với gia đình gần Công Viên Tao Đàn ở trung tâm thành phố. Họ phục vụ các món ăn Nhật Bản có giá dưới 60.000đ và có tỷ lệ khách hàng cao.

We then establish a method of generating Vietnamese references on this dataset. At the first sub-task called *sentence planning* [35], we analyze the input Flat MR and determine appropriate semantic template from warehouse. Each template in warehouse is a structure-type string of a reference which contains slots (predicates of Flat MR) and connection words. At the second sub-task called *surface realization* [35], we determine the exact word forms and linearizing the structure into a string. The automatic evaluation shows that the output texts consist of most of the information from input Flat MR and have suitable Vietnamese grammars.

The structure of this article is as follows. In Sect. 2, we brief introduce the Flat Meaning Representation and Vietnamese dataset in restaurant domain. The two main stages of template-based NLG method will be presented in Sect. 3. We setup the experiment in Sect. 4 and express the results of automatic evaluation with popular metrics. Finally, the conclusion will be presented in Sect. 5.

2 Vietnamese Flat MR Dataset in Restaurant Domain

2.1 Flat Meaning Representation

A Flat MR [16, 17, 30, 31] is an unordered set of predicates/slots with their corresponding values. Each predicate/slot has a specific meaning in restaurant domain. Each Flat MR has three to eight predicates which express different aspects of an agent. Table 2 shows the meaning of all 8 defined predicates and the example Vietnamese values.

Table 2. Meaning and example values of each predicate

Slot/Predicate	Meaning	Example Value
name[]	Name of the agent – where to eat or drink	"Hi Caphe"; "Coffee Bean"; …
eatType[]	Type of the agent (restaurant, coffee house, pub)	"quán café"; "quán rượu"; "nhà hàng"; …
familyFriendly[]	Is agent good for whole family or not	"không"; "có"
priceRange[]	Range of price of food	"trung bình"; "cao"; "60.000đ–100.000đ"; …
food[]	Type of food	"Món Trung Quốc"; "Món Ấn Độ", …
near[]	The place that near the agent	"Nhà Hát Thành Phố"; "Chợ Bến Thành"; …
area[]	The bigger place where the agent is located	"Quận 1"
customer rating[]	The rating of the customer for the agent	"1 trên 5", "cao"; "trung bình"; …

In fact, the key predicate of a Flat MR is "name[]" which indicates the name of the agent. The other predicates are modifiers of "name[]" and indicate different aspects of the agent. Therefore, each NL Reference – group of sentences – is the description the relationships between predicates. We present the relationships between "name[]" and other predicates in Fig. 1.

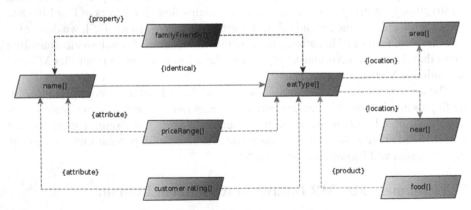

Fig. 1. Relationships between predicates

2.2 Building Vietnamese Flat MR Dataset in Restaurant Domain

So far, studies in [9, 28, 36, 42] showed that collecting NLG data via crowdsourcing have proven to be successful in related tasks. The MRs and corresponding human-crafted NL texts that are collected by this way have sufficient quantity and high quality for training NLG systems. Based on the idea of building English Flat MR dataset in restaurant domain [16, 17, 30, 31], we build the first Vietnamese dataset through following steps.

- **Step 1.** We collected some random places in District 1, Ho Chi Minh City, for predicates "name[]"/"near[]"/"area[]": 34 restaurants/coffee house/pubs; 19 places for "near[]"; 01 area is "Quận 1" (District 1).
- **Step 2.** With predicates "eatType[]"/"familyFriendly[]"/"food[]", we defined the values which have the same meaning with the corresponding values in English dataset [16, 17, 30, 31]. With predicate "priceRange[]", we defined values: "trung bình" (average)/"thấp hơn 60.000đ" (less than 60 k VND)/"cao" (high)/"cao hơn 100.000đ" (higher than 100 k VND)/"rẻ" (cheap)/"60.000đ–100.000đ" (60 k–100 k VND). With predicate "customer rating[]", we defined values: "1 trên 5" (1 out of 5)/"3 trên 5" (3 out of 5)/"5 trên 5" (5 out of 5)/"cao" (high)/"trung bình" (average)/"thấp" (low).
- **Step 3.** We hired 10 Vietnamese people who have good English skills. In fact, they do not need to know much information about places to eat or drink. We asked them to carefully consider above slots-values and English dataset [16, 17, 30, 31]. We provided them with clear and concise instructions about the goal of the data collection. At first, they should defined Flat MRs according to structure-type string in English dataset [16, 17, 30, 31] but with above Vietnamese values. They then had to create the Vietnamese NL descriptions for each Flat MR. They were free to do these things: (i) produce the Vietnamese reference that has similar meaning as English texts if the Vietnamese Flat MR has the same group of predicates as in English dataset; (ii) produce the brand new references; (iii) modify/delete/add new sentences for each reference. The requirements for this task are: (i) the NL references must contain most information in Flat MRs; (ii) express the relationships between slots-values; (iii) have correct Vietnamese grammars and naturalness in common Vietnamese communications.

By performing the above steps, we finally built the whole Vietnamese Flat MR dataset. In Table 3 and Table 4 we summarize the descriptive statistics of linguistic and computational adequacy of dataset: References per Flat MR is the average number of NL references per one Flat MR; Slots per Flat MR is the average number of slot-value pairs per Flat MR; Tokens per Reference is the average number of tokens per one description; Tokens per Sentence is the average number of tokens per single sentence; Sentences per Reference is the number of NL sentences per reference.

Table 3. Overall size statistics for the dataset

Total Flat MR	Total references	Total sentences	Total slots	Total tokens
3516	42061	64189	18808	1051990

Table 4. The average statistics of the dataset

References per Flat MR	Tokens per reference	Sentences per reference	Tokens per sentence	Slots per Flat MR
11.96	25.01	1.53	16.39	5.35

We also calculate the total number of most common n-grams in Table 5. In Vietnamese, a word can be a single token or a compound of some tokens. Therefore, we consider four types of n-gram: bigram, trigram, 4-gram, 5-gram. We also investigate the distribution of the top most frequent n-grams in our dataset (see Fig. 2, Fig. 3, Fig. 4, Fig. 5). The majorities of these n-grams are only used once in the dataset (49.43%, 58.05%, 65.09%, 71.1% respectively).

Table 5. Total number of most common n-grams

No. of 2-grams	No. of 3-grams	No. of 4-grams	No. of 5-grams
36558	100709	196378	310945

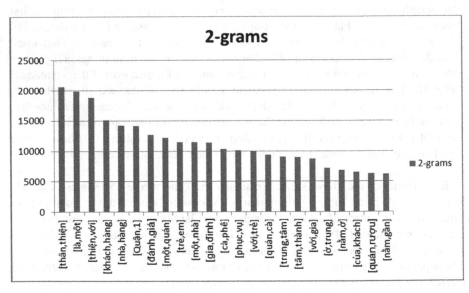

Fig. 2. The most frequent 2-grams in the dataset

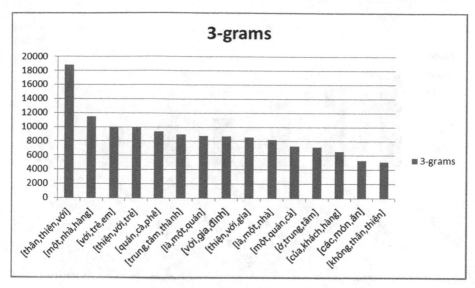

Fig. 3. The most frequent 3-grams in the dataset

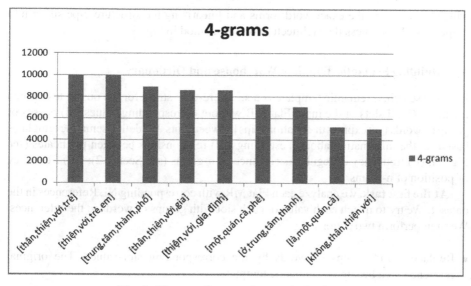

Fig. 4. The most frequent 4-grams in the dataset

3 Template-Based Approach for Generating Vietnamese Reference

The main content of this Section is to present our method for generating Vietnamese NL reference from input Flat MR. Based on traditional approach [35], our method consists of two main phases: (i) *sentence planning* which analyzing the input Flat MR and determine appropriate semantic template from warehouse; (ii) *surface realization*

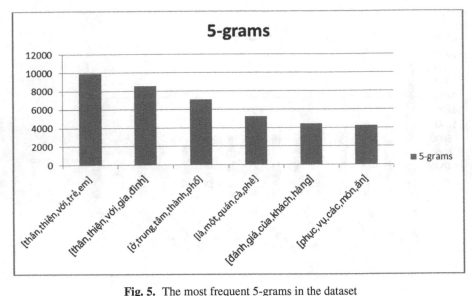

Fig. 5. The most frequent 5-grams in the dataset

which determining the exact word forms and linearizing the structure-type string into output text. We express the architecture of our method in Fig. 6.

3.1 Building Semantic Template Warehouse and Dictionary

In this research, a semantic template is a structure-type string for the output text which includes: (i) all slots of the input Flat MR without corresponding values; (ii) phases or group of words that express the relationships between slots. We define semantic templates based on the information about these things: (i) relationships between predicates (see Fig. 1); (ii) frequency of regular occurrence of n-grams (see Sect. 2.2); (iii) frequency of position of n-grams.

At the first task, we analyze each Flat MR with corresponding NL References in the dataset. We try to match each value of each slot with groups of words in the references. We then perform two actions:

- Replace found groups of words by the corresponding slot-values. The original reference then becomes a semantic template.

As an example, consider Flat MR "name[Above Skybar], eatType[quán rượu], priceRange[cao hơn 100.000đ], customer rating[5 trên 5], near[Union Square]". We have two NL references:

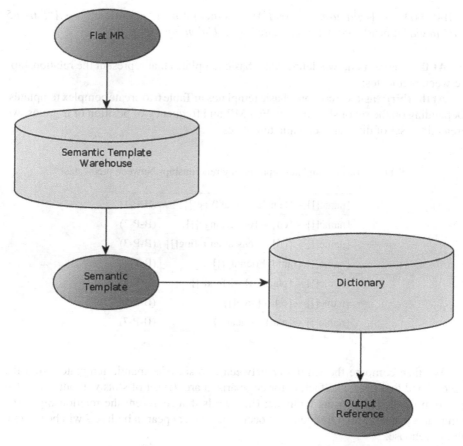

Fig. 6. Architecture of template-based NLG method

NL Reference: *"Above Skybar là một quán rượu có giá hơn 100.000đ và có 5 trên 5 đánh giá. Quán này gần Union Square."* (English: Above Skybar is a pub that costs over 100,000 VND and has 5 out of 5 reviews. This shop is near Union Square.)

⇨ Semantic template: "{name[]} {là một} {eatType[]} {có} {priceRange[]} {và} {có} {customer rating[]} {.} {Quán này} {gần} {near[]}"

NL Reference: *"Above Skybar có giá hơn 100.000đ và có 5 trên 5 đánh giá. Đó là một quán rượu nằm gần Union Square."* (English: Above Skybar is priced over 100,000 VND and has 5 out of 5 reviews. It is a pub located near Union Square.)

⇨ Semantic template: "{name[]} {có} {priceRange[]} {và} {có} {customer rating[]} {.} {Đó} {là một} {eatType[]} {gần} {near[]}"

- Put the found groups of words into dictionary. Consider the above example, we found the groups of words for each slot-value: name[] → "Above Skybar" → {*Above Skybar*}; eatType[] → "quán rượu" → {*quán rượu*}; priceRange[] → "cao hơn

100.000đ" → {"*giá hơn 100.000đ*"}; customer rating[] → "5 trên 5" → {"*5 trên 5 đánh giá*"}; near[] → "Union Square" → {"*Union Square*"}.

At the second task, we define some basic templates that represent the relationships between predicates:

At the third task, we combine basic templates in Table 6 to create complex templates. Depending on the set of slots in each Flat MR and frequency of position of n-grams, we created the set of different semantic templates.

Table 6. Basic templates representing relationships between predicates

{name[]} – {là một} – {eatType[]}	(B-P-1)
{name[]} – {có} – {priceRange[]}	(B-P-2)
{name[]} – {có} – {customer rating[]}	(B-P-3)
{name[]} {familyFriendly[]}	(B-P-4)
{name[]} – {phục vụ} – {food[]}	(B-P-5)
{name[]} – {ở} – {area[]}	(B-P-6)
{name[]} – {gần} – {near[]}	(B-P-7)

We then compare the similarity between two set of semantic templates from the second and first task. The factors for comparison are: (i) set of slots without value; (ii) position of each slot in the template; (iii) words that represent the relationships. The templates that have high frequency of occurrence and appear in both sets will be put into the warehouse.

3.2 Generating NL Reference from Input Flat MR

After building the warehouse and dictionary, we can perform the generation task with following steps:

- Consider predicates of the input Flat MR in the order: familyFriendly[] > customer rating[] > food[] > priceRange[]. For predicate "eatType[]"/"area[]"/"near[]", we check to see if the predicate appears.
- We analyze the relationships between each above predicate with "name[]". We then browse in the warehouse to determine the appropriate semantic template that covers all these relationships.
- With each slot in the semantic template, we find the corresponding groups of words in dictionary that satisfy: (i) express the value of slot; (ii) have the highest frequency of occurrence.

As the first example, consider Flat MR having three predicates: "name[Begin Coffee], area[Quận 1], familyFriendly[không]". We see that there is no "eatType[]" in the Flat

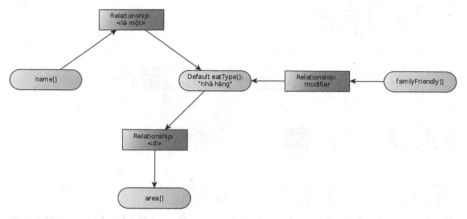

Fig. 7. Example of determining the semantic template of input Flat MR without "eatType[]"

Table 7. Example of generating output NL Reference from input Flat MR without "eatType[]"

Flat MR	name[] → "Begin Coffee", familyFriendly[] → "không", area[] → "Quận 1"
Semantic Template	{name[]} {là một} {nhà hàng} {familyFriendly[]} {ở} {area[]} {.}
NL Reference	Begin Coffee là một nhà hàng không thân thiện với gia đình ở trung tâm thành phố.

MR. Therefore, we set the default type for this place is "nhà hàng" (restaurant). Figure 7 and Table 7 express the semantic template created from this Flat MR.

As the second example, consider Flat MR having six predicates: "name[Coffee Bean], eatType[quán cafe], food[Món Trung Quốc], customer rating[3 trên 5], area[Quận 1], familyFriendly[có]". Figure 8 and Table 8 express the semantic template created from this Flat MR.

The general algorithm for determining the semantic template from input Flat MR:

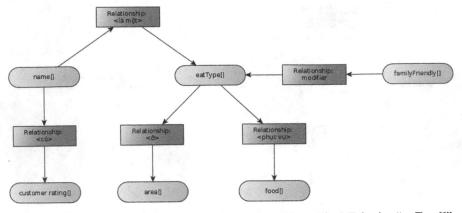

Fig. 8. Example of determining the semantic template of input Flat MR having "eatType[]"

Table 8. Example of generating output NL Reference from input Flat MR having "eatType[]"

Flat MR	name[] → "Coffee Bean", eatType[] → "quán cafe", food[] → "Món Trung Quốc", customer rating[] → "1 trên 5", area[] → "Quận 1", familyFriendly[] → "có"
Semantic Template	{name[]} {là một} {eatType[]} {familyFriendly[]} {phục vụ} {food[]} {ở} {area[]} {.} {Quán này} {có} {customer rating[]} {.}
NL Reference	Coffee Bean là một quán cà phê thân thiện với gia đình phục vụ các món ăn Trung Quốc ở khu vực Quận 1. Quán này có đánh giá của khách hàng là 3 trên 5.

Algorithm 1. Select output semantic template.

Input. Slot-values.

Output. Semantic template.

```
1: check (¬∃familyFriendly[]) ‖ ((∃familyFriendly[]) && (value of
   familyFriendly[]))
2:    check (¬∃customer rating[]) ‖ ((∃customer rating[]) &&
      (value of customer rating[]))
3:      check (¬∃food[]) ‖ ((∃food[]) && (value of food[]))
4:        check (∃eatType[]) ‖ (∃area[]) ‖ (∃near[])
5:          output ← select_from_warehouse();
6:        end check
7:      end check
8:    end check
9: end check
```

4 Experiment and Evaluation

With the same idea of building dataset in Sect. 2, we setup the experiment process as follows:

- At first, we asked the hiring people to define Flat MRs and corresponding NL References based on development part of English dataset [16, 17, 30, 31]. The value for each slot was taken randomly from Vietnamese training dataset in Sect. 2. The human-crafted descriptions were created carefully so that they should be appropriate in Vietnamese grammars and naturalness in common Vietnamese communications. Table 9 expresses the overall size statistics for the testing set.

Table 9. Overall size statistics for the testing set

Number of Flat MRs	Number of references	Number of sentences	Number of slots	Number of tokens
362	4672	7871	2229	113315

- We then run our method and generated one Vietnamese text for each Flat MR in the testing set. The collection of system references will be compared to set of human references to determine the overall quality and naturalness.

By far, there are two ways of evaluating a NLG system: (i) using automatic metrics; (ii) taking human evaluation. Sometime they express the different pictures and the results of human evaluation are often more sensible and give more exact quality and naturalness in domain-specific language. However, using automatic metrics is popular for evaluating NLG systems [20] because this way is cheaper and faster to run than hiring people to evaluate.

In this research, we can only use the automatic metrics to measure word-overlap between system output and NL references in testing set. The popular metrics that were used in this research are: (i) BLEU [34] and NIST [11] calculating n-gram precisions and how informative a particular n-gram is; (ii) METEOR [24] is based on the harmonic mean of unigram precision and recall, aligns the system output with the human-crafted references; (iii) ROUGE-L [27] considers sentence level similarity and determines the longest common subsequences between the system output and human-crafted references; (iv) CIDEr [39] calculates the average cosine similarity between the system output and human-crafted on the level of n-grams.

Table 10 presents the results of automatic evaluation phase:

Based on cursory checks, the output texts from our method seem mostly fluent and contain all information in the input Flat MR. Moreover, our method was able to generate long, grammatical, meaningful, multi-sentence output, as illustrated by the example in Table 8: *"Coffee Bean là một quán cà phê thân thiện với gia đình phục vụ các món ăn Trung Quốc ở khu vực Quận 1. Quán này có đánh giá của khách hàng là 3 trên 5."*

Table 10. Results of automatic evaluation

BLEU	NIST	METEOR	ROUGE-L	CIDEr
0.7121	8.0101	0.4782	0.7215	2.2424

(English: Coffee Bean is a family-friendly cafe serving Chinese food in the District 1 area. It has a customer rating of 3 out of 5.).

Deeper analyzing the testing results, we notice some remaining points. First, as we see that with one idea, a person can generate different texts which consist of different number of sentences with different structure types. These situations happen depending on the context of the real communication and the psychology of that person in this context. These constraints were already mentioned in [35] when talking about challenges that a NLG system should deal with. However, we only considered some aspects such as syntactic, semantic and pragmatic which are discussed in [7, 21]. Second, there are some applied semantic templates of some concrete Flat MR entries are not commonly used in reality contexts.

5 Conclusion

We described the first Vietnamese Flat MR dataset in restaurant domain for training end-to-end, data-driven NLG systems. Each instance consists of a Flat MR paired with a NL reference. Based on the idea of English dataset in [16, 17, 30, 31], the Vietnamese people created the different complex Flat MRs and corresponding description texts that have lexical richness and syntactic variation.

On the created dataset, we proposed a domain-dependent method for generating Vietnamese references from input Flat MRs. For surface realization task, we performed two stages: (i) determine hand-written grammars with semantic templates; (ii) align between slot-value and NL words. Although this method followed the traditional approach, the automatic evaluation shows that the output texts consist of most of the information from input Flat MR and have suitable Vietnamese grammars. Taking the further looks, the references have the naturalness in the cognitive of Vietnamese people.

In future works, we will use the collected data to further develop corpus-based NLG methods, combining the idea of building semantic templates with techniques in Deep Learning. This approach promises to be able to learn NLG strategies across domains and languages.

References

1. Androutsopoulos, I., Lampouras, G., Galanis, D.: Generating natural language descriptions from OWL ontologies: the natural OWL system. J. Artif. Intell. Res. **48**, 671–715 (2013)
2. Ballesteros, M., Bohnet, B., Mille, S., Wanner, L.: Data-driven sentence generation with non-isomorphic trees. In: Proceedings of NAACL-HTL 2015, pp. 387–397 (2015)
3. Bangalore, S., Stent, A.: Natural Language Generation in Interactive Systems. Cambridge University Press, Cambridge (2014)

4. Bernardi, R., et al.: Automatic description generation from images: a survey of models, datasets, and evaluation measures. J. Artif. Intell. Res. **55**, 409–442 (2016)
5. Chen, X., et al.: Microsoft COCO Captions: Data Collection and Evaluation Server (2015)
6. Chen, D.L., Mooney, R.J.: Learning to sportscast: a test of grounded language acquisition. In: Proceedings of the 25th International Conference on Machine learning (ICML), Helsinki, Finland, pp. 128–135 (2008)
7. Chomsky, N.: Syntactic Structures, 2nd edn. Mouton de Gruyter (2002)
8. Colin, E., Gardent, C., Mrabet, Y., Narayan, S., Beltrachini, P.L.: The webNLG challenge: generating text from DBPedia data. In: Proceedings of INLG 2016, pp. 163–167 (2016)
9. Dethlefs, N., Hastie, H., Rieser, V., Lemon, O.: Optimising incremental dialogue decisions using information density for interactive systems. In: Proceedings of the 2012 Conference on Empirical Methods in Natural Language Processing, EMNLP, pp. 82–93 (2012)
10. Dethlefs, N.: Context-sensitive natural language generation: from knowledge-driven to data-driven techniques. Lang. Linguist. Compass **8**(3), 99–115 (2014)
11. Doddington, G.: Automatic evaluation of machine translation quality using n-gram cooccurrence statistics. In: Proceedings of the 2nd International Conference on Human Language Technology Research, San Diego, CA, USA, pp. 138–145 (2002)
12. Dong, L., Huang, S., Wei, F., Lapata, M., Zhou, M., Xu, K.: Learning to generate product reviews from attributes. In: Proceedings of EACL 2017, pp. 623–632 (2017)
13. Dusek, O., Jurcicek, F.: Sequence-to-sequence generation for spoken dialogue via deep syntax trees and strings. In: Proceedings of the 54th Annual Meeting of the Association for Computational Linguistics, Berlin, Germany, pp. 45–51 (2016a)
14. Dusek, O., Jurcicek, F.: A context-aware natural language generator for dialogue systems. In: Proceedings of the 17th Annual Meeting of the Special Interest Group on Discourse and Dialogue, Los Angeles, CA, USA, pp. 185–190 (2016b)
15. Dusek, O., Jurcicek, F.: Training a natural language generator from unaligned data. In: Proceedings of the 53rd Annual Meeting of the Association for Computational Linguistics and the 7th International Joint Conference on Natural Language Processing, Beijing, China, pp. 451–461 (2015)
16. Dusek, O., Novikova, J., Rieser, V.: Findings of the E2E NLG challenge (2018)
17. Dusek, O., Novikova, J., Rieser, V.: Evaluating the state-of-the-art of end-to-end natural language generation: the E2E NLG challenge (2019)
18. Gatt, A., Krahmer, E.: Survey of the state of the art in natural language generation: core tasks, applications and evaluation. J. Artif. Intell. Res. **61**, 65–170 (2018)
19. Gardent, C., Beltrachini, P.L.: A statistical, grammar-based approach to microplanning. Comput. Linguist. **43**(1), 1–30 (2017)
20. Gkatzia, D., Mahamood, S.: A snapshot of NLG evaluation practices 2005–2014. In: Proceedings of the Fifteenth European Workshop on Natural Language Generation (ENLG), pp. 57–60. Association for Computational Linguistics, Brighton, UK (2015)
21. Halliday, M., Matthiessen, C.: An Introduction to Functional Grammar, 3rd edn. Hodder Arnold, London (2004)
22. Herzig, J., Shmueli-Scheuer, M., Sandbank, T., Konopnicki, D.: Neural response generation for customer service based on personality traits. In: Proceedings of INLG 2017, pp. 252–256 (2017)
23. Lampouras, G., Vlachos, A.: Imitation learning for language generation from unaligned data. In: Proceedings of COLING 2016, the 26th International Conference on Computational Linguistics: Technical Papers, Osaka, Japan, pp. 1101–1112 (2016)
24. Lavie, A., Agarwal, A.: METEOR: an automatic metric for MT evaluation with high levels of correlation with human judgments. In: Proceedings of the Second Workshop on Statistical Machine Translation, Prague, Czech Republic, pp. 228–231 (2007)

25. Lebret, R., Grangier, D., Auli, M.: Generating Text from Structured Data with Application to the Biography Domain. CoRR, 1603.07771 (2016)
26. Lepp, L., Munezero, M., Granroth-Wilding, M., Toivonen, H.: Data-driven news generation for automated journalism. In: Proceedings of INLG 2017, pp. 188–197 (2017)
27. Lin, C.Y.: ROUGE: a package for automatic evaluation of summaries. In: Proceedings of the Workshop on Text Summarization Branches Out, Post-Conference Workshop of ACL 2004, Barcelona, Spain, pp. 74–81 (2004)
28. Mairesse, F., et al.: Phrase-based statistical language generation using graphical models and active learning. In: Proceedings of the Forty-Eighth Annual Meeting of the Association for Computational Linguistics, Uppsala, Sweden, pp. 1552–1561 (2010)
29. Mei, H., Bansal, M., Walter, M.R.: What to talk about and how? Selective generation using LSTMs with coarse-to-fine alignment. In: Proceedings of NAACL-HLT, San Diego, CA, USA (2016)
30. Novikova, J., Lemon, O., Rieser, V.: Crowd-sourcing NLG data: pictures elicit better data. In: Proceedings of the 9th International Natural Language Generation Conference, Edinburgh, UK, pp. 265–273 (2016)
31. Novikova, J., Dusek, O., Rieser, V.: The E2E dataset: new challenges for end-to-end generation. In: Proceedings of the 18th Annual Meeting of the Special Interest Group on Discourse and Dialogue, Saarbrücken, Germany, pp. 201–206 (2017a)
32. Novikova, J., Dusek, O., Rieser, V.: Data-driven Natural Language Generation: Paving the Road to Success. arXiv preprint arXiv:1706.09433 (2017b)
33. Novikova, J., Dusek, O., Curry, A.C., Rieser, V.: Why we need new evaluation metrics for NLG. In: Proceedings of the 2017 Conference on Empirical Methods in Natural Language Processing, Copenhagen, Denmark, pp. 2241–2252 (2017c)
34. Papineni, K., Roukos, S., Ward, T., Zhu, W.-J.: BLEU: a method for automatic evaluation of machine translation. In: Proceedings of the 40th Annual Meeting of the Association for Computational Linguistics, Philadelphia, PA, USA, pp. 311–318 (2002)
35. Reiter, E., Dale, R.: Building Natural Language Generation System. Cambridge University Press, Cambridge (1997)
36. Rieser, V., Lemon, O., Keizer, S.: Natural language generation as incremental planning under uncertainty: adaptive information presentation for statistical dialogue systems. IEEE/ACM Trans. Audio Speech Lang. Process. **22**(5), 979–993 (2014). https://doi.org/10.1109/TASL. 2014.2315271
37. Sharma, S., He, J., Suleman, K., Schulz, H., Bachman, F.: Natural language generation in dialogue using lexicalized and delexicalized data. CoRR, abs/1606.03632 (2016)
38. Tran, T.: Phương pháp xác định nhữ ng câu hỏi tương đương nghĩa cho hệ thống tìm kiếm thư viện b`ăng truy vấn tiếng Việt [The method of identifying questions having the equivalent meaning for the library finding system by Vietnamese queries]. M.S. Thesis. University of Information Technology, VNU-HCM, Vietnam (2011)
39. Vedantam, R., Zitnick, C.L., Parikh, D.: CIDEr: consensus-based image description evaluation. In: Proceedings of the 2015 IEEE Conference on Computer Vision and Pattern Recognition (CVPR), Boston, MA, USA, pp. 4566–4575 (2015)
40. Wen, T.-H., Gasic, M., Mrksic, N., Su, P.-H., Vandyke, D., Young, S.: Semantically conditioned LSTM-based natural language generation for spoken dialogue systems. In: Proceedings of the 2015 Conference on Empirical Methods in Natural Language Processing, Lisbon, Portugal, pp. 1711–1721 (2015)

41. Wen, T.-H., et al.: Multi-domain neural network language generation for spoken dialogue systems. In: Proceedings of the 2016 Conference of the North American Chapter of the Association for Computational Linguistics: Human Language Technologies, San Diego, CA, USA, pp. 120–129 (2016)
42. Zaidan, O.F., Callison-Burch, C.: Crowdsourcing translation: professional quality from non-professionals. In: Proceedings of the ACL, Portland, Oregon, USA, pp. 1220–1229 (2011)

Data Analytics and Healthcare Systems

A Synthetic Data Generation Model for Diabetic Foot Treatment

Jayun Hyun[1] , Seo Hu Lee[2] , Ha Min Son[1] , Ji-Ung Park[3] ,
and Tai-Myoung Chung[1(✉)]

[1] Department of Computer Science and Engineering,
Sungkyunkwan University, Suwon, Republic of Korea
{jayunhyun,sonhamin,tmchung}@skku.edu
[2] Department of Artificial Intelligence,
Sungkyunkwan University, Suwon, Republic of Korea
qwaszx6677@skku.edu
[3] Department of Plastic and Reconstructive Surgery,
Seoul National University Boramae Hospital,
Seoul National University College of Medicine, Seoul, Korea
alfbskan@gmail.com

Abstract. Generating synthetic sensor-based time-series medical data
is important when simulating machine learning-based digital therapeutics. Many existing approaches for generating synthetic sequence medical
data require sufficient amount of real data. The deficiency of the realistic
medical data poses a great challenge for developing artificial intelligence
(AI) based healthcare application or devices. To overcome the challenge,
we propose a time-series medical sensor-based data synthesis model especially designed for diabetic foot treatment system. Our proposed system
utilizes statistical methods and *Prophet* model - an open source API
provided by Facebook - to generate synthetic data required for the diagnosis of diabetic foot treatment while maintaining medical validity. We
also suggest systemic methods to evaluate the validity of the synthesized
data. The results shows that synthetic time-series data generated by our
system follows trends and tendencies of real data.

Keywords: Digital therapeutics · Deep learning · Data synthesis

1 Introduction

Diabetes has become a very common disease. According to the World Health
Organization, the number of people with diabetes has risen from 108 million
in 1980 to 422 million in 2014 [1]. Furthermore, a diabetic foot ulcer occurs in
approximately 15% of patients with diabetes and 14–24% of the patients with
diabetic foot ulcer will eventually require an amputation [2]. Therefore, warning
diabetic patients before an amputation is required will save many patients' legs.
There are several papers attempting to reveal the relationship between diabetes
and other diagnostic measure (e.g. foot temperature, transcutaneous oxygen,

T. K. Dang et al. (Eds.): FDSE 2020, CCIS 1306, pp. 249–264, 2020.
https://doi.org/10.1007/978-981-33-4370-2_18

blood pressure and etc.) [25–31]. These studies used one parameter to diagnose and predict diabetic foot ulcer. We, however, simultaneously use glucose levels, glycated hemoglobin (HbA1c), transcutaneous oxygen pressure (TcPO2), blood pressure, partial foot pressures, and foot temperature. The relationship between these parameters can be used for more accurate diagnosis and predictions through AI techniques. Unfortunately, AI applications require many medical sensor dataset that are rarely available and lack diversity. A possible solution is synthesizing more data for the training and validation of AI applications. However, the deterioration of medical efficacy is a serious concern when applying existing synthetic data generation methods to medical data.

In this paper, we introduce a new system for generating synthetic sensor data while maintaining medical validity. Our approach adopts statistical data augmentation and Facebook's *Prophet* model. Data augmentation helps create more robust data and allows *Prophet* to generate various realistic sensor data. *Prophet* is adequate for the problem of modeling time-series medical sensor data due to its sequential-predictive nature. We employ open source dataset and leverage medical research results to generate time-series medical sensor data as shown in Fig. 1. To evaluate the proposed system and the generated synthetic dataset, we propose metrics and a techniques in order to verify the medical validity of data.

The main contribution of this work is providing a data synthesis model for diabetic foot treatment system by using an open source machine learning model (Facebook's *Prophet*). This synthetic data can be used in the initial training and validation of developing AI based applications. Our main contributions of this paper are as follows:

1. We propose a method to apply medical criteria on data synthesis system.
2. We propose a multi-variated time-series medical data synthesis system for diabetic foot treatment system.
3. We introduce methods to accurately evaluate synthetic data.

The results on this paper will be deployed in digital therapeutics named *Diabetic Foot Ulcer Treatment Insole System* to simulate its performance. Synthetic datasets are beneficial for developing machine learning based healthcare applications, as it solves the problem of medical sensor data scarcity. The following sections are organized as follows. Section 2 describes related work. Section 3 includes open source dataset description and utilization of the medical research results. Section 4 details our synthesis model, the overall process of the data synthesis, and explanations of each procedure. Section 5 proposes the evaluation methods for synthetic data. Section 6 discusses about our system and the results. Finally, in Sect. 7, we conclude remarks on this paper.

2   Related Work

Collecting time-series medical data is costly, time consuming and has uncertain availability [3]. To solve these problems, some early researches on medical time-series data synthesis employed Generative Adversarial Networks (GANs). Saloni et al. succeeded in synthesizing patients records that sporadic and longitudinal.

And also *SynSys* and *Synthea* demonstrated their work on data synthesis for health care application [3,4]. But those of works employed medical records and IoT sensor based data.

Stephanie et al. successfully demonstrated synthesizing time-series real-valued multi-dimensional medical data from the intensive care unit (ICU) data [6]. They also showed novel approach on evaluating employed system [6]. Andrew et al. proposed *HealthGAN*, the frame work for medical data synthesis [5]. Stephanie et al. succeeded in generating the time-series synthetic medical data, but they used existing real data for synthesizing. *HealthGAN* intended to develop a framework that generate the discrete medical data rather than multi-variated time-series data.

Previous studies have succeeded in synthesizing data using actual data with all parameters. However, this approach did not address data deficiencies. Therefore, this paper introduces the data synthesis system to solve these problems. The system utilizes the medical research results data and UCI dataset to generate medical data. Medical research results show that TcPO2, Blood Pressure, foot temperature, and HbA1c values, distributions, and patterns can be obtained from the data. The values can be processed through preprocessing and augmentation process and put into the synthesis system to obtain the synthetic data. For the glucose level data, UCI Dataset Open Source Dataset is utilized. But the problem is that the dataset is not in form of 5-min interval of blood glucose measurement data that we employ to diagnose diabetes. The UCI data was recorded the glucose levels six to eight times a day. Therefore, rather than utilizing the actual UCI data as it is, instead, we enrich the data through preprocessing and data augmentation processes. Then the results are fed into the synthesis system. Unlike other parameters, glucose levels are synthesized using UCI data because the value greatly varies from person to person depending on the patient's lifestyle (e.g., insulin time, insulin dosage, diet habits, exercise habits). Therefore, this system guarantee diversity in data pattern by utilizing the glucose level data that has diversity in time domain.

When adopting the existing algorithms, scarcity of medical data and missing values lead inconsistencies with real medical data [21]. To address the challenges, Facebook introduced *Prophet*. *Prophet* is an open source time-series data analysis and forecasting model. It has better accuracy than other time-series forecasting methods [21]. It also has innate error tolerance properties that combat the problem of medical inconsistency. For these reasons, our system adopts *Prophet* to deal with data scarcity and missing values problem [32].

3   Dataset

The data which are examined in this work are essential for diagnostic measuring diabetic foot ulcer and referred to as parameter in this paper. Those parameters are - **glucose level, transcutaneous oxygen pressure (TcPO2), foot temperature, blood pressure (APG; Acceleration Plethysmogram)**, and **glycated hemoglobin (HbA1c)**; each in a time-series sequence. Certainly, this kind of data does not exist now. To address this problem while keeping consistent with medical statistic criteria, we combine UCI open source dataset and results from our own medical research as the input data for our synthesis model. The form of data is shown in Fig. 1.

05-17-2020	9:20:00	276	57.5	58	60	33	32.4	29.4	38.4	6.49	0
05-17-2020	9:22:00	7	38.8	33	33	35	33.6	39.2	32.4	6.49	3
05-17-2020	9:24:00	10	39.2	35	64	57	31.8	31.7	39.9	6.49	2
05-17-2020	9:26:00	188	31.6	57	70	61	32	35.4	41.3	6.49	2
05-17-2020	9:28:00	190	38.4	57	33	33	31.7	33.9	35.4	6.49	2
05-17-2020	9:30:00	44	33.7	57	35	62	31.4	30.8	41.6	6.49	1
05-17-2020	9:32:00	324	32.1	58	58	33	31.1	30.9	41.3	6.49	1
05-17-2020	9:34:00	6	41.0	33	33	35	30.8	38.4	37.6	6.49	2
05-17-2020	9:36:00	10	28.2	35	35	58	30.5	32.8	29.8	6.49	2
05-17-2020	9:38:00	337	33.3	60	60	33	30.2	35.0	41.9	6.49	3
05-17-2020	9:40:00	8	30.2	33	33	34	31.7	39.1	36.9	6.49	2
05-17-2020	9:42:00	348	36.0	64	64	60	32.2	33.6	41.4	6.49	4
05-17-2020	9:44:00	0	41.0	70	33	33	31.9	27.9	29.3	6.49	4
05-17-2020	9:46:00	12	28.2	33	35	62	33.2	32.3	31.6	6.49	1
05-17-2020	9:48:00	10	28.3	35	58	33	33.7	35.9	27.9	6.49	2

Fig. 1. An example of a dataset employed in the diabetic foot treatment system

3.1 UCI Dataset

The time-series glucose level data we utilize in our implementation is the *Diabetes Dataset* from *UC Irvine Machine Learning Repository*. The data in this dataset are obtained from automatic electric recording devices and paper records of patients [33]. Each record in the dataset consists of four fields: data (in MM:DD:YYYY format), time (XX:YY), code, and the value of glucose level [33]. The values of the code field indicates a specific action of influencing factor that may affect glucose level. The *Prophet* model makes use of the code field to generate the synthetic glucose level data. However, a problem with this dataset is that time-stamps of paper recordings are unreliable [33]. To deal with this problem, we preprocessed the data to solve any disparity.

3.2 Medical Research Results

This section describes the reason why and the way how we employ the medical criteria and research results. Utilization of medical research results is our novel approach to maintain the validity of medical sensor data. Medical criteria has been established empirically and scientifically over a long period time of development process. However, utilizing only traditional medical criteria is insufficient for digital therapeutics system. Because traditional medical criteria only contains the rough wide ranges of medical inspection results. So that we employ informative medical research results in order to enrich the rough data.

Since we aim to develop a digital therapeutics for diabetic foot, one of chronic diseases, consistent observation is essential under time-series analyzing system. To synthesize the valid time-series medical sensor data, synthetic data must follow their own medical criteria.

Utilization method of the medical diagnosis criteria and research results are as follows. Transcutaneous oxygen pressure (TcPO2) values were divided into five levels as shown in Table 1 [24–30]. Fluctuation flow of TcPO2 value in time-series shows an irregular waveform within range [24–30]. Foot temperature was divided into three levels as derived from the medical research as shown in Table 2 [18,19]. Blood pressure was divided into seven levels by referencing vascular disease progression [18–20]. The waveform of vascular disease progression levels are shown in Table 3. The higher the level, the worse the vascular condition is. HbA1c values, however, are different from the other parameters. Researchers found mathematical models between HbA1c and glucose level [31]. As such, the values of HbA1c in our dataset are obtained through accumulated values of glucose level from the same instance.

Table 1. TcPO2 severity grades and range.

TcPO2 severity grade	Value range (mmHg)	Deviation
1. Critical Ischemia	0 to 30	±15
2. Impaired	30 to 45	±7
3. Cautious	45 to 55	±12
4. Normal	55 to 60	±10
5. Healthy	From 60	±3

Table 2. Foot temperature severity grades and range.

Foot temperature severity grades	Value range (mmHg)	Temperature difference between right and left foot
1. Healthy	30.6 ± 2.6 °C	±1.78
2. Neuropathy	32.89 ± 1.02 °C	±2.89
3. Inflammation	36.8 ± 2.86 °C	N/A

Without following medical criteria derived from medical research results, the synthesis system may generate distorted data. Moreover, following statistics of the medical research result would not harm the distributions of the dataset.

4   Synthesis Model

Our proposed synthesis model is shown in Fig. 2. This figure describes the overall process as well as inputs and outputs of each sub-process. We define raw data as data that is obtained through the UCI dataset and medical research results. The raw data is first preprocessed by clustering similar data and excluding redundancies. After preprocessing the raw data, the output is named preprocessed data.

Table 3. Vascular disease progression levels and waveform.

Vessel Disease Progression Levels	APG Wave Form
1. Level 1	
2. Level 2	
3. Level 3	
4. Level 4	
5. Level 5	
6. Level 6	
7. Level 7	

The preprocessed data undergoes statistical data augmentation to increase sample size and diversity. After data augmentation, the output is combined with preprocessed data results in a combined dataset. The combined dataset is input to *Prophet* to generate synthetic datasets. We now explain each stage in detail.

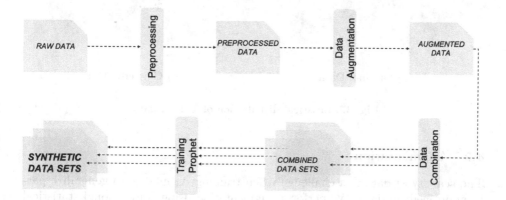

Fig. 2. Data synthesis process

4.1   Preprocessing

Our dataset consists of multiple parameters. Each parameter, however, do not belong to the same patient as they are a combination of multiple data sources. As a result, it would be difficult to trust any trends seen with time-series analysis. Thus, we employ a statistical method of preprocessing within our dataset. The statistical distribution of TcPO2 data is shown in Fig. 3a. We define 5 centroids according to the average of the ranges presented in Table 1. We then cluster these data points by calculating the shortest distance from each point to one of the centroids. The result of our clustering algorithm is shown in Fig. 3b. We apply this clustering algorithm to each parameter in our dataset according to value ranges suggested by medical professionals, effectively splitting our data into 5 classes. In addition, we exclude certain redundant data values with equivalent timestamps on *Diabetes Dataset* to avoid sections of data gaining unnecessary weight advantages. This step help us properly train the *Prophet* in later. Lastly, we linearly interpolate data in sections where the time between data points are uneven.

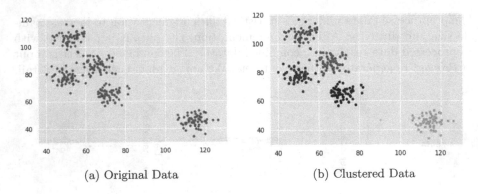

(a) Original Data   (b) Clustered Data

Fig. 3. Statistical distribution of TcPO2 data

4.2   Augmentation

The scarcity of data is a challenge when training AI models to generalize patterns in medical data. We perform augmentation using conventional statistical methods. The equation for a Gaussian distribution is shown in Eq. 1. Here, μ represents the statistical mean and Σ represents the covariance matrix. We modify the distribution to create an isotropic Gaussian distribution by simplifying the covariance matrix to be the variance multiplied by an identity matrix as shown in Eq. 2. This limits the computational cost required by the quadratic growth of the original covariance matrix. Moreover, employing isotropic Gaussian distribution results in statistical distributions more diverse compared to a distribution biased towards a particular axis. Lastly, we create noise in the form of outliers by increasing the standard deviation of the new data being introduced to each cluster. As such, we create a more diverse and robust dataset as shown in Fig. 4.

$$N(\mu, \Sigma) \tag{1}$$

$$\Sigma = \sigma^2 * I \tag{2}$$

4.3   Data Generation Model

Facebook's *Prophet* is an open source times-series prediction model. Predictions from *Prophet* have proven to be more accurate compare to ETS methods, TBATS model, etc. [21].

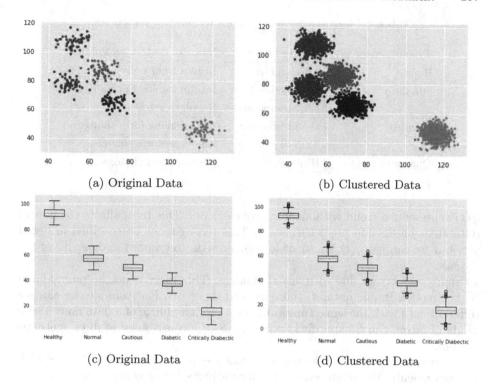

(a) Original Data   (b) Clustered Data

(c) Original Data   (d) Clustered Data

Fig. 4. Data augmentation visualization

There are three main components in *Prophet* - trend, seasonality, and holidays - and a sub component [21]. Equation 3 represents the components of *Prophet*.

$$y(t) = s(t) + h(t) + g(t) + e_t \tag{3}$$

Here, **s(t)** represents the seasonality of a parameter. This refers to the length of time required for a parameter to show cyclic trends. With our data, changes in glucose level due to insulin can be specified as an 'Hourly Seasonality'. Regular insulin intake, eating habit, and regular exercise can be specified as 'Sub-daily Seasonality'. Changes in APG waves(represents blood pressures) and TcPO2 can be specified as 'Monthly Seasonality'. Lastly, the changes of HbA1c can be specified as 'Quarterly Seasonality' and can be used to predict future glucose levels. Table 4 shows the custom seasonality types of each parameter.

h(t) represents the holidays in our dataset. There are irregular effects on time-series data flow. We cannot merely apply this to the medical field, so defining $h(t)$ is an important to guarantee the diversity of the synthetic data. We can, for example, set vascular procedures as $h(t)$.

Table 4. Custom specified seasonality for each parameter

Type of seasonality	Affected data	Name of custom seasonality
Hourly	Glucose level	Insulin from body
Sub-daily	Glucose level	Insulin intake, Eating habit
	Foot temperature	Regular exercises
Monthly	Blood pressure	APG waving form changes
	TcPO2	Blood pressure changes
Quarterly	HbA1c	Glucose level changes

g(t) represents a trend without iterative elements. This term affects the flow of data changing in non-predicting ways. This term cannot be specified in detail yet, but we can use $g(t)$, linear or logistic growth, to ensure the diversity of the dataset.

e_t represents errors due to unusual changes. This term is not accommodated by the model. In our dataset, there are certain errors. For example, we can see different data with the same timestamp or a sudden plunge of a data flow. These kinds of errors can be specified to guarantee the consistency of data synthesis system.

Facebook's *Prophet* model can sufficiently express the medical changes with its components. Its innate error tolerance aspects (error component e_t and an outlier) will help the system maintain its performance. *Prophet* analyzes the trends and effectively predicts the values of the target parameter. The predicted data by *Prophet* from augmented data is sufficiently accurate that we can term it as the synthetic data.

5 Evaluation

This section introduce our proposed evaluation method for generated synthetic data. The most difficulty is that we could not acquire an authentic real dataset that contains set of our parameters to compare with generated data because they do not exist.

5.1 Pattern and Distribution Similarity

To deal with the lack of real medical data, we employ 'Pattern and Distribution Similarity' comparison to visually compare the synthetic data and augmented data which is considered equivalent to real data in this study. Figure 5 shows data pattern similarity comparison between the augmented data and the synthetic data of glucose level.

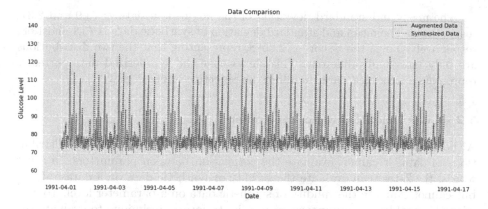

Fig. 5. Data pattern comparison of the synthetic data and augmented data

Although augmented data follows medical criteria advised by medical professionals, we cannot guarantee that the augmented data correctly represents the real data. Thus, we examine the distribution of the data to assure its validity.

We use 'Kernel Density Estimation' (KDE) to visualize the distributions of data. The result of KDE represents the frequency of values in a time-series sequence. Figure 6 shows the KDE of synthetic data and augmented data.

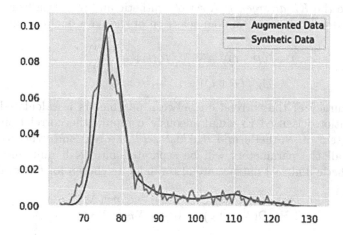

Fig. 6. Result of Kernel Density Estimation of the synthetic data and augmented data

To evaluate the similarity of these distributions, we employ the Z-test, a common method to compare distributions. The equation of the Z-test is shown in Eq. 4. Here, $\overline{x_1}$ and $\overline{x_2}$ represent the sample mean of each distribution, and σ_{x1}^2 and σ_{x2}^2 represent the standard deviation of each sample.

$$Z = \frac{(\overline{x_1} - \overline{x_2})}{\sqrt{\sigma_{x1}^2 + \sigma_{x2}^2}} \qquad (4)$$

The mean and standard deviation of the augmented data is 74.9 and 2.31, respectively. The mean and standard deviation of synthetic data is 73.1 and 1.68, respectively. Thus, the z-score is 2.2678, representing that the two distributions are only marginally different. This shows that the synthesized data correctly represents augmented data, fulfilling the objective of our study.

5.2   Correlation Between Parameters

Although we can utilize *KDE* and *Z-test* to visualize and evaluate the distributions of data, it cannot evaluate the correlation between parameters. In other words, the Z-test can evaluate the validity of synthetic data on a dataset level, but cannot evaluate the validity of synthetic data on a parameter level. To deal with this problem, we propose two metrics to form a technique to evaluate the correlation between multiple parameters simultaneously.

By utilizing both Eqs. 5 and 6, we can evaluate the distributions of a separate parameter and correlation of multiple parameter at the same time. The two employed criteria are **Kullback-Leibler (KL) divergence** and **Pairwise Correlation Difference (PCD)**.

The accuracy of each separate parameter is calculated through the *KL divergence*. Equation 5 is used to compute the distributions between both real data and synthetic data. The real and synthetic data are separated on a 24-h unit and put into the *KL divergence*. A set of synthetic and real data from a parameter are randomly chosen. Random selection of the data enables fair and valid evaluation.

$$D_{KL}(P \parallel Q) = \sum_{t=1}^{p} P_p(t) \log \frac{P_p(t)}{Q_p(t)}$$

$$D_{KL}(P \parallel Q) = 0 \longrightarrow P \approx Q$$

(5)

The accuracy of the correlation between parameters is calculated through PCD. Equation 6 is used to simultaneously compute the correlation between the parameters of synthetic and real dataset. The real and synthetic dataset containing all the parameters will be separated into 24-h unit and input to *PCD*. Synthetic and real dataset are also randomly chosen for fair evaluation.

$$PCD(X_R, X_s) = \parallel Corr(X_R) - Corr(X_s) \parallel_F$$

$$PCD(X_R, X_S) = 0 \longrightarrow X_R \approx X_S$$

(6)

With both equations, a lower result suggests less discernible differences between synthetic and real data. In summary, low *KL divergence* and *PCD* suggests that the synthetic data resembling the real data. There are two steps in this evaluation technique. We first validate the data of each separate parameter by applying *KL divergence* using Eq. 2. This ensures that each synthesized parameter value represent real data. If the *KL divergence* of each parameter is sufficiently close to zero, we can assure that each separate parameter is similar with the real data. We then validate fully comprised multiple dataset by applying *PCD* using Eq. 3 between the parameters of synthetic data and real data.

The accuracy of the complete dataset is determined by how well the correlation between the parameters of the synthesized data, which is respective to the correlation between the parameters of real data. If the *PCD* is sufficiently close to zero, the synthesized dataset is deemed to accurately represent real data. Figure 7 shows the schema of an evaluation.

Separate parameter | Multiple parameters

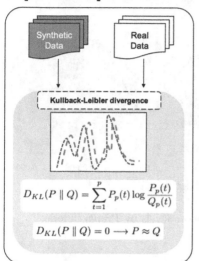
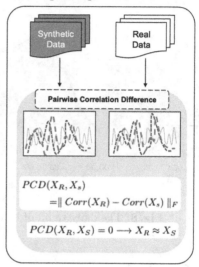

Fig. 7. Evaluation schema including *Kullback-Leibler Divergence* for separate parameter evaluation and *Pairwise Correlation Difference* for dataset level Correlation evaluation

6   Discussion

Currently, its quite difficult to apply more sophisticated evaluation methods on the synthetic data generated by our proposed model, as real data corresponding to our examined data does not exist for comparing.

Nevertheless, the result from *Prophet* shows promising results. Figure 8 shows the daily trend of blood glucose levels predicted by *Prophet*. We have validated that our model correctly recognizes sharp increases in blood glucose level during meal times and decreases throughout the rest of the day. Though not a mathematical proof like the *KL divergence* and *PCD* methods, this was seen as the only available form of validity. In the future, we will develop evaluation strategies to prove the validity of our data in term of mathematics.

We are developing diabetic foot treatment insole and will use the data synthesis system presented in this paper. Generated synthetic data will be used to train artificial intelligence systems for diabetic foot ulcer analysis system. We expect that synthetic data may accelerate the developing process. Because making use of synthetic data enables us to develop the hardware and AI-based software at the same time.

After we get real data from the diabetic foot ulcer treatment insole which is developing, we can improve our system more sophisticated. Mathematical model of each parameters and correlation between each parameter can be revealed from the real dataset. From that revelation, adequate and efficient algorithms can be applied for the further sophistication.

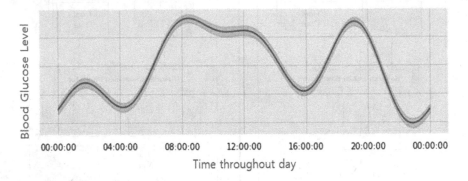

Fig. 8. The daily trend of blood glucose levels by *Prophet* model

7   Conclusion

We proposed a time-series medical sensor data synthesis model for diabetic foot treatment system combining data augmentation methods and Facebook's *Prophet*. The most beneficial characteristic is this system can overcome the real data scarcity. We also showed systematic approach on how to generate the medical data by following medical criteria. The benefits of synthesis system in this paper save us from wasting time and helps us to deal with shortage of the data. The limitation, however, is that evaluation of the synthetic dataset needs real dataset. In the future, we hope to precisely demonstrate the validity of this system after obtaining sufficient amount of real dataset. And also we hope to generate the time-series multi-variated in general purpose.

Acknowledgement. This work was supported by Institute of Information & communications Technology Planning & Evaluation (IITP) grant funded by the Korea government (MSIT) (No. 2020-0-00990, Platform Development and Proof of High Trust & Low Latency Processing for Heterogeneous typical Large Scaled Data in 5G-IoT Environment).

References

1. World Health Organization. https://www.who.int/news-room/fact-sheets/detail/diabetes. Tue, 01 Sep 2020 09:04:12 GMT
2. APMA Homepage. https://www.apma.org/diabeticwoundcare. Tue, 01 Sep 2020 09:10:54 GMT
3. Walonoski, J., et al.: Synthea: an approach, method, and software mechanism for generating synthetic patients and the synthetic electronic health care record. J. Am. Med. Inform. Assoc. **25**(3), 230–238 (2018)
4. Dahmen, J., Cook, D.: SynSys: a synthetic data generation system for healthcare applications. Sensors **19**, 11–81 (2019)
5. Yale, A., Dash, S., Dutta, R., Guyon, I., Pavao, A., Bennett, K.P.: Generation and evaluation of privacy preserving synthetic health data. Neurocomputing **416**, 244–255 (2020)
6. Esteban, C., Hyland, S.L., Rätsch, G.: Real-valued (Medical) Time Series Generation with Recurrent Conditional GANs. esteban2017realvalued 1706.02633 (2017)
7. Li, W., Chen, C., Zhang, M., Li, H., Du, Q.: Data augmentation for hyperspectral image classification with deep CNN. IEEE Geosci. Remote Sens. Lett. **16**(4), 593–597 (2019)
8. Advancing foot and ankle medicine and surgery. https://www.apma.org/Patients/content.cfm?ItemNumber=1108&navItemNumber=24202. Thu, 20 Aug 2020 07:51:14 GMT
9. Goodfellow, I.J., et al.: Generative adversarial nets. In: Proceedings of the 27th International Conference on Neural Information Processing Systems, vol. 2, pp. 2672–2680 (2014)
10. Frid-Adar, M., Klang, E., Amitai, M., Goldberger, J., Greenspan, H.: Synthetic data augmentation using GAN for improved liver lesion classification. In: 2018 IEEE 15th International Symposium on Biomedical Imaging, ISBI 2018, pp. 289–293 (2018)
11. Shin, H.-C., et al.: Medical Image Synthesis for Data Augmentation and Anonymization using Generative Adversarial Networks. arXiv:1807.10225 (2018)
12. Nie, D., Trullo, R., Petitjean, C., Ruan, S., Shen, D.: Medical Image Synthesis with Context-Aware Generative Adversarial Networks. arXiv:1612.05362 (2016)
13. Nie, G.D., et al.: Medical image synthesis with deep convolutional adversarial networks. IEEE Trans. Biomed. Eng. **65**(12), 2720–2730 (2018)
14. Fawaz, H.I., Forestier, G., Weber, J., Idoumghar, L., Muller, P.A.: Data augmentation using synthetic data for time series classification with deep residual networks. arXiv:1808.02455 (2018)
15. Derungs, A., Amft, O.: Estimating wearable motion sensor performance from personal biomechanical models and sensor data synthesis. Sci. Rep. **10**(11450) (2020)
16. Abri, H., Aalaa, M., Sanjari, M., Amini, M.R., Mohajeri-Tehrani, M.R., Larijani, B.: Plantar pressure distribution in diverse stages of diabetic neuropathy. J. Diab. Metab. Disord. **18**(1), 33–39 (2019). https://doi.org/10.1007/s40200-019-00387-1
17. Wyss, C.R., Robertson, C., Love, S.J., Harrington, R.M., Matsen 3rd, F.A.: Relationship between transcutaneous oxygen tension, ankle blood pressure, and clinical outcome of vascular surgery in diabetic and nondiabetic patients. Surgery **102**, 56–62 (1987)
18. Lavery, L.A., et al.: Home monitoring of foot skin temperatures to prevent ulceration. Diab. Care **27**(11), 2642–2647 (2004)

19. Gordon, I.L., Rothenberg, G.M., Lepow, B.D., et al.: Accuracy of a foot temperature monitoring mat for predicting diabetic foot ulcers in patients with recent wounds or partial foot amputation. Diab. Res. Clin. Pract. **161**, 108074 (2020)
20. Elgendi, M.: On the analysis of fingertip photoplethysmogram signals. Curr. Cardiol. Rev. **8**(1), 14–25 (2012)
21. Rotună, C., Cohal, A., Sandu, I., Dumitrache, M.: New tendencies in linear prediction of events. Rom. J. Inf. Technol. Autom. Control **29**(3), 19–30 (2019)
22. Goncalves, A., Ray, P., Soper, B., Stevens, J., Coyle, L., Sales, A.P.: Generation and evaluation of synthetic patient data. BMC Med. Res. Methodol. **20**, 1–40 (2020)
23. Rashid, K.M., Louis, J.: Times-series data augmentation and deep learning for construction equipment activity recognition. Adv. Eng. Inform. **42**, 100944 (2019)
24. Benhamou, Y., et al.: Detection of microcirculatory impairment by transcutaneous oxymetry monitoring during hemodialysis: an observational study. BMC Nephrol. **15**(4), 1–8 (2014)
25. Azuma, N.: The diagnostic classification of critical limb ischemia. Ann. Vasc. Dis. **11**(4), 449–457 (2018)
26. Wyss, C.R., Matsen 3rd, F.A., Simmons, C.W., Burgess, E.M.: Transcutaneous oxygen tension measurements on limbs of diabetic and nondiabetic patients with peripheral vascular disease. Surgery **95**(3), 339–346 (1984)
27. de Meijer, V.E., van't Sant, H.P., Spronk, S., Kusters, F.J., den Hoed, P.T.: Reference value of transcutaneous oxygen measurement in diabetic patients compared with nondiabetic patients. J. Vasc. Surg. **48**(2), 382–388 (2008)
28. Cliff, M.: TRAMUL: TRAnscutaneous oxygen Measurement and diabetic foot ULceration. Diab. Foot J. **22**(2), 5–67 (2019)
29. Yang, C., Weng, H., Chen, L., et al.: Transcutaneous oxygen pressure measurement in diabetic foot ulcers: mean values and cut-point for wound healing. J. Wound Ostomy Cont. Nurs. **40**(6), 585–589 (2013)
30. Kalani, M., Brismar, K., Fagrell, B., Ostergren, J., Jörneskog, G.: Transcutaneous oxygen tension and toe blood pressure as predictors for outcome of diabetic foot ulcers. Diab. Care **22**(1), 147–151 (1999)
31. Makris, K., Spanou, L., Jörneskog, G.: Is there a relationship between mean blood glucose and glycated hemoglobin? J. Diab. Sci. Technol. **5**(6), 1572–83 (2011)
32. Facebook Open Source. https://facebook.github.io/prophet/. Wed, 19 Aug 2020 21:27:47 GMT
33. Dua, D., Graff, C.: UCI Machine Learning Repository, vol. 2, no. 5. University of California, Irvine, School of Information and Computer Sciences (2017). http://archive.ics.uci.edu/ml

An Approach for Skin Lesions Classification with a Shallow Convolutional Neural Network

Hiep Xuan Huynh[1]([✉]), Loan Thanh Thi Truong[2,3], Cang Anh Phan[3], and Hai Thanh Nguyen[1]([✉])

[1] College of Information and Communication Technology,
Can Tho University, Can Tho 900000, Vietnam
hxhiep@ctu.edu.vn, nthai@cit.ctu.edu.vn
[2] Cai Nhum Town High School, Vinh Long, Vietnam
tttloan906@gmail.com
[3] Faculty of Information Technology, Vinh Long University of Technology Education,
Vinh Long, Vietnam
cangpa@vlute.edu.vn

Abstract. Skin is the largest and fastest-growing organ in the human body, which protects the body from the effects of the external environment. The skin is frequently exposed to the outside environment, so the possibility of the skin lesion is high. In recent years, the incidence of skin diseases is increasing rapidly. Some skin lesions develop into malignant tumours, sometimes we can see or feel, but others only detect through diagnostic imaging tests. The medical examination of skin lesions is not a simple task, as there is a similarity between lesions and medicals experience that can result in inaccurate diagnoses. Many cases of cancer are misdiagnosed as another disease with injurious consequences. In this article, we propose a method for classifying skin lesions using a shallow convolutional neural network (CNN). We perform the prediction tasks on a public International Skin Imaging Collaboration (ISIC) 2019 dataset and achieve a ROC-AUC of 0.782 for an eight-class classification of eight various types of skin.

Keywords: Skin lesions · Classification · Convolutional neural networks · Skin diagnosis

1 Introduction

Skin lesions are a severe disease globally [1]. A skin lesion is a condition that occurs in one patient for many different reasons. One of them could be due to abnormal skin tissue growth. It could be melanoma that was the cause of death. However, correctly classification skin lesions are very hard due to the low contrast between skin lesions and the surrounding skin, visual similarities among melanoma lesions, and not malignant tumors, changes in skin condition.

T. K. Dang et al. (Eds.): FDSE 2020, CCIS 1306, pp. 265–280, 2020.
https://doi.org/10.1007/978-981-33-4370-2_19

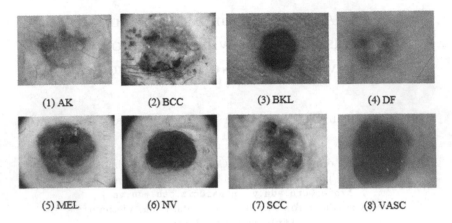

(1) AK   (2) BCC   (3) BKL   (4) DF

(5) MEL   (6) NV   (7) SCC   (8) VASC

Fig. 1. One sample of each class from the ISIC 2019. From left to right: actinic keratosis, basal cell carcinoma, benign keratosis, dermatofibroma, melanoma, melanocytic nevus, squamous cell carcinoma, and vascular lesion.

Previous studies performed a classification with some classes. The methods are proposed in [2–4] to classify skin lesion images using traditional hand-crafted feature sets. Automatic skin cancer classification has lacked generalization [5,6]. The 2017 ISBI Competition for Skin Lesions Analysis Towards Melanoma Detection [7] examined methods for a deep neural network image classification problem. The classification accuracy of the different solutions is almost equal. When the dimensions of the set of images are used for training divergent it can lead to small differences in performance. In [8,9] CNN-based features were also considered; however, the trained neural network model applies only to a limited number of images.

We can see that most of the works only looked at some types of skin lesions: melanoma, squamous cells, and benign keratosis. But there are several other diseases of equal importance in the medical field. Therefore, we conduct a full classification of skin lesions. In this paper, we will propose a model of skin lesion classification based on the shallow convolutional neural network, which can automatically classify with multiple skin lesions. For our test results with images on the ISIC [17] 2019 dataset. The main contributions of this paper can be summarized as follows: We present a learning model on the CNN architecture to support classifying skin lesions with CNN. By using the softmax, the proposed model can work through the binary and multi-class.

The rest of this paper is organized as follows. Section 2 presents a learning model classify skin lesions with CNN. Section 3 we give a short description of the dataset, tools, performance evaluation metrics, and our experimental results. Finally, we conclude in Sect. 4 and point out future work directions.

2 Skin Lesions Classification with CNN

2.1 A Framework for the Skin Classification

To develop a system that classification from skin lesions, we need first to preprocess the images (Fig. 2 – Preprocessing). In the classification system, we used a dataset with samples of skin lesions from ISIC 2019, randomly divided into two sets of train and test with a ratio of 3: 1.

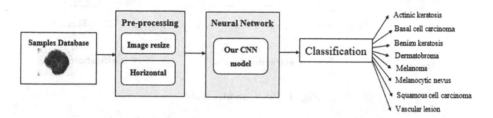

Fig. 2. The proposed diagram for skin classification

In the preprocessing stage, to reduce the computational cost, we preprocess skin lesion samples using Keras ImageDataGenerator [19]. The skin lesions samples in the dataset were downscaled to 150×150 pixels resolution from the original size. ISIC 2019 dataset has an unbalance distribution of samples among the eight classes. Deep learning models require a large amount of data to produce good results [13], increase the data for train models to help prevent overfitting. In our training set, we have applied many geometric transformations to the increased by data. We use vertical and horizontal flip, random rotation of some training patterns 30°, random zoom 20% of some training samples, randomly changing samples horizontally 10%, vertical 10%.

In the classification system shown in Fig. 2 (Neural Network), we use our CNN model as the feature extractor. Skin lesion characteristics can be extracted to obtain classification information. The system has output layers covering eight types of skin lesions.

2.2 Learning Model with a Shallow Convolutional Neural Network

In the classification system, CNN has shown performance for classifying images in many areas [10]. The structure of CNN usually consists of two parts as Fig. 3: automatic feature extraction and full connection layer, in which feature extraction includes the convolution layer and pooling layer. We can get a good classification model without through to manually selecting features, this is the advantage of CNN.

The CNN architectures vary with the type of image and especially when the input image size is different. In this article, we recommend a shallow Convolutional Neural Network for detecting damage on skin images. The proposed

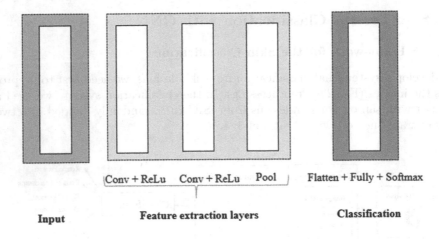

Fig. 3. CNN architecture.

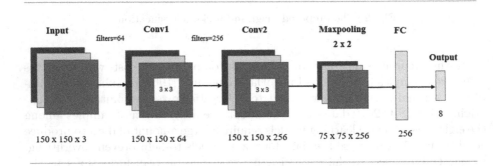

Fig. 4. Our CNN architecture.

method provides insight into the medical image and explains in detail the model supports the diagnosis. The proposed architecture is described in Fig. 4.

The input image has an input of size $150 \times 150 \times 3$ (color images). CNN contains two convolutional layers, followed by the max-pooling class and the full connected class. To be more specific, the convolution layer is involved in feature extraction, which creates feature mappings by performing convolution operations between the input and the filter.

Our convolution layer contains 256 filters or kernels, the filters itself is a 3×3 integer matrix. The max-pooling layer is used to reduce data size but retains main properties. The reduced data size helps reduce computations in the model. We used the max-pooling class of size 2×2, activation used is ReLU. Softmax is used for multiple classifications in the logistic regression models. I used the optimizer Adam [11] with a default learning rate = 0.001, then after a few epochs, the training model had a "loss:nan" problem. I solved using the learning rate = 0.0001.

Softmax is a common learning algorithm for multiple linear classification functions. The softmax value for output z_j is calculated as follows:

$$\sigma(z_j) = \frac{e^{z_j}}{\sum_{k=1}^{K} e^{z_k}} \tag{1}$$

where $\sigma(z_j)$ is the softmax value, z is a vector of inputs to the output layer and j indexes the output units from 1, 2,..., K.

3 Experimental Results

In this section, our method's performance is evaluated on a dataset of skin lesion images from the ISIC 2019 database. This work is presented as follows. Subsect. 3.1 presents the experimental dataset. Subsect. 3.2 presents the evaluation metrics. Subsect. 3.3 presents the using tools. We formulate scenarios to predict and test our results in Subsects. 3.4 and 3.5 respectively.

3.1 Dataset Description

Samples used for experimentation in this study are acquired from the ISIC 2019 with 25331 images of skin lesions as Table 1.

Table 1. The number of samples for each class in the training dataset.

Diagnostic	Samples
Melanoma	4522
Melanocytic nevus	12875
Basal cell carcinoma	3323
Actinic keratosis	867
Benign keratosis	2624
Dermatofibroma	239
Vascular lesion	253
Squamous cell carcinoma	628
Total	**25331**

The ISIC 2019 dataset contains samples of HAM10000 [14] and the BCN_20000 [15]. HAM10000 contains samples with a size of 600×450 that was centered and cropped around the lesion. This dataset was the older challenge of ISIC 2018. While the BCN_20000 contains samples of size 1024×1024. This dataset is particularly challenging as many samples are uncropped, and lesions in difficult and uncommon locations are present. The skin samples are RGB samples in JPG format classified into eight class: Melanoma (MEL), melanocytic nevus (NV), basal cell carcinoma (BCC), actinic keratosis (AK), benign keratosis (BKL), dermatofibroma (DF), the vascular lesion (VASC), and squamous cell carcinoma (SCC).

3.2 Evaluation Metrics

The overall performance of the model evaluated with several evaluation metrics: A confusion matrix [18] is a robust result exhibition tool for measuring the quality of a classification system. Each column of the matrix represents the number of occurrences of a predefined class, while each line represents the number of occurrences of a reference class. A simple form of a confusion matrix is the example below Table 2.

Table 2. Confusion matrix.

	Actual class	
Predicted class	*Positive*	*Negative*
Positive	*TP*	*FP*
Negative	*FN*	*TN*

Accuracy: The measure/indicator to evaluate the accuracy of the model by the ratio of the number of correctly detected skin images (with skin lesions and no skin lesions) to the total number of skin images.

$$Accuracy = \frac{TP + TN}{TP + TN + FP + FN} \tag{2}$$

Where TP (True Positive): the number of damaged labeled skin images correctly classified into the damaged layer. FP (False Positive): the number of non-damaged labeled skin images that were misclassified into damaged layers. FN (False Negative): the number of injures label skin photos that are layered incorrectly into non-damaged layers. TN (True Negative): the number of skin images bearing no skin lesions that are layered properly into layers without skin lesions.

The results of the proposed network simulation also presented with the help of the receiver operating characteristic (ROC) curve [12]. The measurement of diagnostic test validity is linked to the area placed under the ROC curve.

3.3 Tools for the Experiments

Our method was implemented with Python-based on Tensorflow [16]. Keras [20], a deep learning framework for Python, was utilized to implement the neural network architecture. Keras provides a layer of abstraction on top of Theano, which is used as the prime neural network framework. Moreover, Keras works on a Python environment, which gives users the freedom to use additional Python dependencies, including SciPy [21] and PIL [22]. Machine learning algorithms using the programming language Python 3.6 on the Jupyter Notebook [23] web-based application for interactive computing.

3.4 Experimental Scenarios

The ratio for training data to test data is approximately 3:1. Then the images are resized to 150×150 for fetc.hing into the proposed CNN model. The results as following:

Scenario 1: Classification of Two Classes.   The study investigated 4775 samples of two classes: melanoma (4522 samples), and vascular lesion (253 samples). The dataset is divided into two parts, 2143 of the dataset for training and 1056 for testing. The number of epochs for the method (chosen based on checking the behavior of exact accuracy/loss compared to the number of epochs) is 18. The confusion matrix of the testing in this experiment is shown in Fig. 5(b).

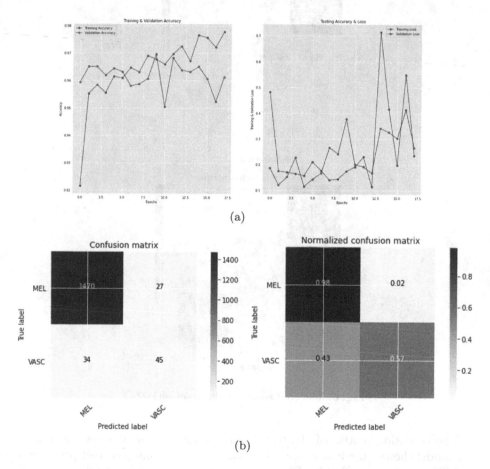

(a)

(b)

Fig. 5. a) Accuracy and Loss vs epoch b) Confusion Matrix of the CNN model for scenario 1

The best classification result for the melanoma class is Fig. 5. The results of the testing phase reach 0.961 accuracies and 0.874 of Area under Roc Curve (AUC).

Scenario 2: Classification of Three Classes. The study was performed with 5403 samples of three classes: melanoma (4522 samples), squamous cell carcinoma (628 samples), and vascular lesion (253 samples). The dataset is divided into two parts, 3620 of the dataset for training and 1783 for testing. The number of epochs for the method is 30.

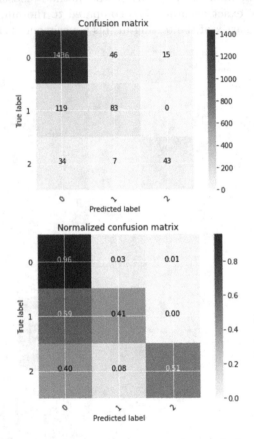

Fig. 6. The confusion matrix of scenario 2

The confusion matrix of the testing in this experiment is shown in Fig. 6. Our model showed the best result for melanoma by making a correct prediction for 1436 samples out of 1497. The vascular lesion and squamous cell carcinoma have correctly determined for 43 samples out of 84 and for 83 samples out of 202. The results of the testing phase reach 0.876 accuracies and 0.868 of Area under Roc Curve (AUC).

Scenario 3: Classification of Four Classes. The study investigated 5642 samples of four classes: melanoma (4522 samples), squamous cell carcinoma (628 samples), the vascular lesion (253 samples), and dermatofibroma (239 samples). The dataset is divided into two parts, 3780 of the dataset for training and 1862 for testing. The number of epochs for the method is 40.

	precision	recall	f1-score	support
MEL (Class 0)	0.88	0.94	0.91	1501
SCC (Class 1)	0.46	0.32	0.38	206
VASC (Class 2)	0.62	0.51	0.56	79
DF (Class 3)	0.42	0.22	0.29	76
accuracy			0.82	1862
macro avg	0.59	0.50	0.53	1862
weighted avg	0.80	0.82	0.81	1862

Fig. 7. Multi-class classification report showing macro average and weighted average for precision, recall and F1-score of scenario 3

The best classification result for the melanoma, by making a correct prediction for 1413 samples out of 1501. The lowest predicted success is the dermatofibroma class. The Multi-Class Classification Report showing Macro Average and Weighted Average for Precision, Recall, and F1-Score are represented in Fig. 7. The results of the testing phase reach 0.825 accuracies and 0.849 of Area under Roc Curve (AUC).

Scenario 4: Classification of Five Classes. The study investigated 6509 samples of five classes: melanoma (4522 samples), squamous cell carcinoma (628 samples), the vascular lesion (253 samples), dermatofibroma (239 samples), and actinic keratosis (867 samples). The dataset is divided into two parts, 4361 of the dataset for training and 2148 for testing. The number of epochs for the method is 20.

The best classification result for the MEL, by making a correct prediction for 1270 samples out of 1496. The lowest predicted success is the squamous cell carcinoma class in Fig. 9. The results of the testing phase reach 0.702 accuracies and 0.813 of Area under Roc Curve (AUC).

Scenario 5: Classification of Six Classes. The study investigated 9133 samples of six classes: melanoma (4522 samples), squamous cell carcinoma (628 samples), the vascular lesion (253 samples), dermatofibroma (239 samples), actinic keratosis (867 samples), and benign keratosis (2624 samples). The dataset is divided into two parts, 6119 of the dataset for training and 3014 for testing. The number of epochs for the method is 30.

The best classification result for the melanoma, by making a correct prediction for 1123 samples out of 1489. The lowest predicted success is the squamous cell carcinoma class, the squamous cell carcinoma has correctly determined for

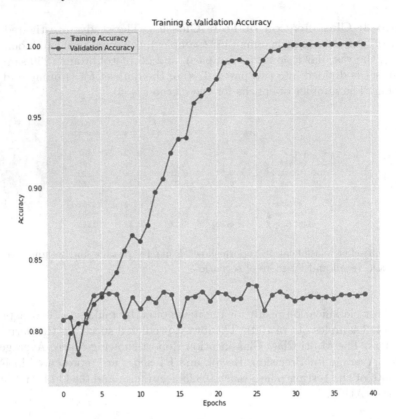

Fig. 8. Skin lesions classification performance in training and testing phases of the CNN model for scenario 3.

33 samples out of 216 in Fig. 10. The results of the testing phase reach 0.581 accuracies and 0.808 of Area under Roc Curve (AUC).

Scenario 6: Classification of Seven Classes. The study investigated 12456 samples of seven classes: melanoma (4522 samples), squamous cell carcinoma (628 samples), the vascular lesion (253 samples), dermatofibroma (239 samples), actinic keratosis (867 samples), benign keratosis (2624 samples), and basal cell carcinoma (3323 samples). The dataset is divided into two parts, 8345 of the dataset for training and 4111 for testing. The number of epochs for the method is 30.

The best classification result for the melanoma, by making a correct prediction for 986 samples out of 1522. The lowest predicted success is the dermatofibroma class, the dermatofibroma has correctly determined for 5 samples out of 82 in Fig. 11. The results of the testing phase reach 0.528 accuracies and 0.774 of Area under Roc Curve (AUC).

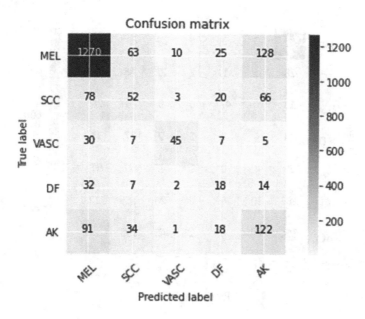

Fig. 9. The confusion matrix of scenario 4

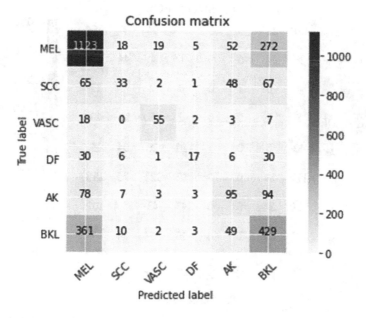

Fig. 10. The confusion matrix of scenario 5

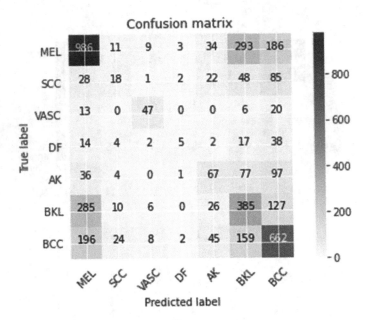

Fig. 11. The confusion matrix of scenario 6

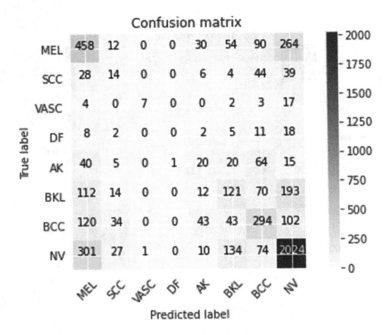

Fig. 12. Classification results on the eight classes

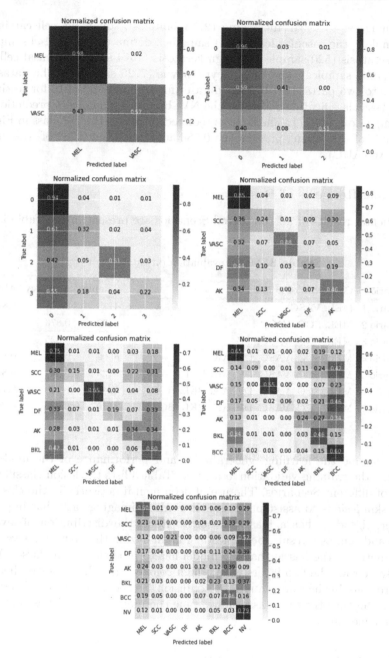

Fig. 13. The confusion matrix results of experiments with various numbers of classes

Scenario 7: Classification of Eight Classes. From the ISIC 2019 training set of 25331 samples, divided into eight classes as Table 1, we take 60% of the training set to learn: melanoma (2713 samples), squamous cell carcinoma (376 samples), the vascular lesion (151 samples), dermatofibroma (144 samples), actinic keratosis (520 samples), benign keratosis (1574 samples), basal cell carcinoma (1994 samples), and melanocytic nevus (7725 samples). The dataset is divided into two parts, 10181 of the dataset for training and 5016 for testing.

The best classification result for the NV, by making a correct prediction for 2024 samples out of 2571. The lowest predicted success is the DF class in Fig. 12. The results of the testing phase reach 0.586 accuracies and 0.782 of Area under Roc Curve (AUC).

3.5   Some Remarks of Results

Experimental results of all considered Scenarios are present in the Table 3.

Table 3. Model evaluation on the test set

Scenario	Categories of lesion	Samples	Accuracy	AUC
Scenario 1	MEL, VASC	4775	0.961	0.874
Scenario 2	MEL, SCC, VASC	5403	0.876	0.868
Scenario 3	MEL, SCC, VASC, DF	5642	0.825	0.849
Scenario 4	MEL, SCC, VASC, DF, AK	6509	0.702	0.813
Scenario 5	MEL, SCC, VASC, DF, AK, BKL	9133	0.581	0.808
Scenario 6	MEL, SCC, VASC, DF, AK, BKL, BCC	12456	0.528	0.774
Scenario 7	MEL, SCC, VASC, DF, AK, BKL, BCC, NV	15197	0.586	0.782

To examine the learning, generalizing, and performance of the model, we computed the training-validation loss curve. Table 3 lists the lesion classification results of different Scenarios. The use of deep neural networks in the classification of skin lesions to assist physicians in medical imaging tasks has improved. However, this data has a bias attached to it, as the distribution of layers is uneven and can, as a result, be misleading in analyzing this data. One weakness of this matrix is the hassle that the model has to predict several classes. When in the same row, the two layers have a high color value, which means there is a high error rate in the rows, caused by confusion between these layers. Therefore, it may mean that the two classes have some common characteristics that cause this phenomenon.

4   Conclusion

In this paper, we proposed a model for the classification of skin lesions with the hope that the model will help and accelerate the diagnosis of skin lesions. Our study gives a useful contribution to the research area of skin lesion images classification. This work is related to the steps needed for the development of an automatic diagnostic system for skin lesions detection and classification. Moreover, the proposed CNN model was tested on different use cases and produced good AUC-ROC results.

In the future, we are going to increase the size of the dataset and using sophisticated models to enhance the classification performance of skin lesions images.

References

1. Li, Y., Shen, L.: Skin lesion analysis towards melanoma detection using deep learning network. Sensors **18**(2), 556 (2018)
2. Faziloglu, Yunus., et al.: Colour histogram analysis for melanoma discrimination in clinical images. Skin Res. Technol. **9**(2), 147–156 (2003)
3. Stoecker, W.V., et al.: Detection of asymmetric blotches (asymmetric structureless areas) in dermoscopy images of malignant melanoma using relative color. Skin Res. Technol. **11**(3), 179–184 (2005)
4. Celebi, M.E., et al.: A methodological approach to the classification of dermoscopy images. Comput. Med. Imaging Graph. **31**(6), 362–373 (2007)
5. Burroni, M., et al.: Melanoma computer-aided diagnosis: reliability and feasibility study. Clin. Cancer Res. **10**(6), 1881–1886 (2004). https://doi.org/10.1158/1078-0432.CCR-03-0039
6. Masood, A., Al-Jumaily, A.A.: Computer aided diagnostic support system for skin cancer: a review of techniques and algorithms. Int. J. Biomed. Imaging (2013) 323268 http://dx.doi.org/10.1155/2013/323268
7. Codella, N., et al.: Skin lesion analysis toward melanoma detection: a challenge at the 2017 international Symposium on Biomedical Imaging (ISBI), Hosted by the International Skin Imaging Collaboration (ISIC) (2017). arXiv preprint arXiv:1710.05006
8. Yu, L., Chen, H., Dou, Q., Qin, J., Heng, P.A.: Automated melanoma recognition in dermoscopy images via very deep residual networks. IEEE Trans. Med. Imaging **36**(4), 994–1004 (2017)
9. Esteva, A., et al.: Dermatologist-level classification of skin cancer with deep neural networks. Nature **542**(7639), 115–118 (2017)
10. LeCun, Y., Bengio, Y., Hinton, G.: Deep Learn. Nature **521**(7553), 436–444 (2015). https://doi.org/10.1038/nature14539. PMID: 26017442
11. Kingma, D.P., Lei Ba, J.: Adam: a method for stochastic optimization. arXiv:1412.6980v9 (2014)
12. Park, S.H., Goo, J.M., Jo, C.H.: Receiver operating characteristic (ROC) curve: practical review for radiologists. Korean J. Radiol. **5**(1), 11–18 (2004)
13. Chen, X.W., Lin, X.: Big data deep learning: challenges and perspectives. IEEE access **2**, 514–525 (2014)
14. Tschandl, P., Rosendahl, C., Kittler, H.: The HAM10000 dataset, a large collection of multi-source dermatoscopic images of common pigmented skin lesions. Scientific Data **5**, 180161 (2018). https://doi.org/10.1038/sdata.2018.161
15. Combalia, M., et al.: BCN20000: dermoscopic lesions in the wild (2019). arXiv:1908.02288
16. Abadi, M., et al.: (Google Brain), TensorFlow: a system for large-scale machine learning. In: Proceedings of the 12th USENIX Conference on Operating Systems Design and Implementation, OSDI 2016, pp. 265–283 (2016)

17. ISIC Homepage. https://challenge2019.isic-archive.com/. Accessed 20 July 2020
18. Confusion_matrix. https://en.wikipedia.org/wiki/Confusion_matrix
19. Image Preprocessing. https://keras.io/preprocessing/image/. Accessed 26 July 2020
20. Keras documentation. https://keras.io/
21. Scipy Python Library. https://www.scipy.org/
22. Python Imaging Library (PIL). http://www.pythonware.com/products/pil/
23. Jupyter. https://jupyter.org/

Detection and Classification of Brain Hemorrhage Using Hounsfield Unit and Deep Learning Techniques

Anh-Cang Phan[1](✉), Hung-Phi Cao[1], Thanh-Ngoan Trieu[2], and Thuong-Cang Phan[2]

[1] Vinh Long University of Technology Education, Vinh Long, Vietnam
{cangpa,caohungphi}@vlute.edu.vn
[2] Can Tho University, Can Tho, Vietnam
{ptcang,ttngoan}@cit.ctu.edu.vn

Abstract. Stroke is a dangerous disease with a complex disease progression and a high mortality rate just behind cancer and cardiovascular disease. To diagnose brain hemorrhage, the doctors check CT/MRI images and rely on the Hounsfield Unit to determine the region, duration and level of bleeding. Due to the increasing number of brain haemorrhages, it will put pressure on the treating doctors. Therefore, the construction of an automatic system of segmentation and identification of brain hemorrhage with fast processing time and high accuracy is essential. In this paper, we propose a new approach based on Hounsfield Unit and deep learning techniques. It not only determines the level and duration of hemorrhage but also segments the brain hemorrhagic regions on MRI images automatically. From experiments, we compared and evaluated on three neural network models to select the most suitable model for classification. As a result, the proposed method using Hounsfield Unit and Faster RCNN Inception is time-effective and high accuracy with mean average precision (mAP) of 79%.

Keywords: Brain hemorrhage · CT/MRI image · Hounsfield unit · Deep learning

1 Introduction

Stroke is a dangerous disease progressing quickly in case of not having prompt treatment. According to statistics from the World Health Organization, stroke is the second leading cause of death and the first leading cause of disability affecting patients' daily life. In Vietnam, stroke is the seventh leading cause of death with 0.64 deaths per 100,000 cases [11]. Stroke has two main types: hemorrhagic stroke and ischemic stroke with a ratio of 85% and 15% respectively. This disease has a serious complication after recovery with 92% carrying movement sequelae, 27% severe movement sequelae, and cognitive disorders [13]. To diagnose the disease, a doctor might prescribe a CT/MRI of the cranial region. The diagnosis

© Springer Nature Singapore Pte Ltd. 2020
T. K. Dang et al. (Eds.): FDSE 2020, CCIS 1306, pp. 281–293, 2020.
https://doi.org/10.1007/978-981-33-4370-2_20

is then based on the Hounsfield Unit (HU) of the cerebral hemorrhage area in the CT/MRI image [10, 12]. However, with a large number of patients, doctors have more pressure that can affect the accuracy of diagnosis and treatment planning.

The advancement of computer vision has benefits in many different fields, especially medical images. The study [14] in 2017 used a convolutional neural network (CNN) with three models including LeNet, GoogLeNet, and Inception-ResNet to diagnosing brain hemorrhage. The dataset for experiments consisted of 100 cases of brain hemorrhage with CT/MRI images collected from Hospital 115 (Ho Chi Minh City, Vietnam). The research results indicated that the three models are relevant to the diagnosis of brain hemorrhage with the F1 score of LeNet, GoogLeNet, and Inception-ResNet are 0.997, 0.983, and 0.989, respectively. In 2018, experts from the University of California, Berkeley, and the University of California, San Francisco (UCSF) [8] trained a convolutional neural network called PatchFCN. This model is trained on a dataset of 4,000 CT images from hospitals affiliated with UCSF. The results show that PatchFCN has the capability of intracranial hemorrhage detection.

In general, these methods [8, 14] use the CNN technique to classify medical images without considering the HU values. This can cause effects on the accuracy of the segmentation and classification of cerebral hemorrhage because HU values are often used by medical specialists to identify bleeding areas and duration of damages in reality. On the other hand, there is a lack of comparison and evaluation of neural network models on medical data. In this paper, we propose a new approach for detection and classification of brain hemorrhage based on HU values using the techniques of deep learning. Experiments were conducted to compare and evaluate the results of the four common types of cerebral hemorrhage [10, 12]: epidural hematoma (EDH), subdural hematoma (SDH), subarachnoid hemorrhage (SAH), and intracerebral hemorrhage (ICH) (as in Fig. 1). Our contributions are as follows: 1) Collect medical images of cerebral hemorrhage for classification; 2) Apply HU values in automatic segmentation of cerebral hemorrhage regions to assist experts in labeling the dataset; 3) Train the multi-layer classifier of brain hemorrhage on three deep learning network models: Faster R-CNN Inception ResNet v2, and SSD MobileNet v2, and SSD Inception v2; 4) Detect, segment and quantify the time and level of cerebral hemorrhage based on HU values; 5) Compare and evaluate the classification results on these 3 models.

The remaining of the paper is organized as follows: Sect. 2 details the related work for the detection and classification of cerebral hemorrhage. Our proposed methods are described in Sect. 3. We show and compare experimental results of our methods in Sect. 4. Finally, we draw the conclusion in Sect. 5.

2   Related Work

2.1   Hounsfield Unit (HU) in Brain Hemorrhage Segmentation

The diagnosis of cerebral hemorrhage needs a high accuracy because any error can affect the treatment regimen and the patient's recovery. In this study, we calculate the HU values, which are often used by specialists to diagnose CT/MRI hemorrhagic images [10,12] for accurately determining the hemorrhage area, bleeding time, and the extent of bleeding. This is also a new approach proposed in our approach. We analyze input CT/MRI images in the standard DICOM format [7] without converting them to other formats, such as JPG, BMP, and PNG. The input information includes patient information, hospital information, and image data. Currently, modern CT/MRI scanners have the grayscale of −1000 to +4000 [12] while digital devices such as computer screens have the grayscale of 0 to 255. Thus, displaying the CT/MRI images on those devices will not be correct. In order to properly display the gray level on computer screens, it is necessary to convert the values by the linear transformation as in formula 1.

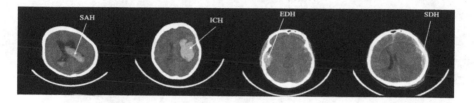

Fig. 1. Illustration of four types of brain hemorrhage on CT/MRI image [3,4]

$$HU = Pixel\_value * Rescale_{slope} * Rescale_{intercept} \qquad (1)$$

where:

- *Pixel_value*: is the value of each pixel
- *Rescale_{slope}* and *Rescale_{intercept}*: are the values stored in DICOM images

Specifically, a cranial DICOM image will be converted to a digital image according to the HU value. Types of tissue, water and air show different HU values, which are illustrates in Table 1. The Hounsfield scale of tissue density is based on two values: air as −1000 HU (minimum HU value) and water as 0 HU. Density of other tissues is related to this range, usually from −1000 to +1000 HU

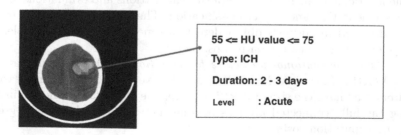

55 <= HU value <= 75
Type: ICH
Duration: 2 - 3 days
Level   : Acute

Fig. 2. Difference between bleeding and non-bleeding areas [3,4]

[1,3]. The hemorrhagic/hematoma region has the HU values in the range from 40 to 90 (as in Fig. 2 and Table 1). We use image thresholding techniques [17] and the contours detection technique [2] to define the contours connecting all adjacent points with the same/approximately color value or contrast value. We later define a convex hull [6] surrounding the contours. The brain hemorrhagic regions are identified in this way and this is also the area for classification.

Table 1. X-ray absorption was measured on a CT/MRI image by hounsfield unit (HU) [1,3,12]

Matter	Density (HU)
Water	0
Bone	1,000
Air	−1,000
Gray matter	35–40
White matter	20
Hematoma	40–90

2.2 Convolutional Neural Network (CNN) for Training and Classifying

The choice of the appropriate deep learning models and the quality dataset plays an important role in improving classification accuracy. With many powerful deep learning models for images, we decide to take the advantage of two effective deep learning models, SSD [9] and Faster R-CNN [15]. After preparing the training dataset, we perform a training phase on these two models including SSD and Faster R-CNN with three neural networks consisting of Inception v2, MobileNet v2, Inception ResNet v2 for feature extraction. Below is a brief description of the models we applied in the proposed methods.

2.2.1 Single Shot MultiBox Detector Architecture (SSD)

The SSD model [9] comes up with the idea of bounding boxes to create boxes in multiple locations of the image. It performs calculations and evaluations on each box for segmentation and object classification. The SSD architecture shown in Fig. 3 is designed to optimize object detection time as quickly as possible. The SSD model consists of two main phases.

Phase 1 - Convolutional predictors for detection: SSD uses basic networks such as VGG16, Inception, MobileNet, and ResNet to extract image features. The filters used have the size of $3 \times 3 \times p$ over the layers for prediction instead of using the fully connected layer as in other network models. This is greatly reducing computation costs.

Phase 2 - Multi-scale feature maps for detection: The size of feature maps will decrease along with the depth of the network when using filters. This helps

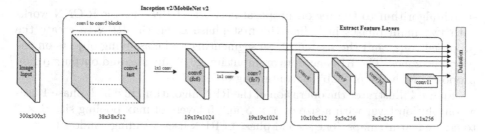

Fig. 3. Single shot MultiBox detector architecture [9]

in detecting objects at different sizes and different scales. In this study, we conduct experiments of the SSD model with two basic networks, Inception and MobileNet. The architecture of the SSD model is presented in Fig. 3.

SSD has the objective loss function with localization loss and confidence loss. The localization loss is used to evaluate the detection task and the confidence loss is used to evaluate the classification task. The localization loss is a Smooth L1 loss [5] between the predicted box (l) and the ground truth box (g). Let $x_{ij}^p = \{1, 0\}$ corresponds to the i-th box that matches the ground truth box j-th of class p. The Loss function is a weighted sum of the localization loss (loc) and the confidence loss ($conf$), as in Eq. 2.

$$L_{loc}(x, c, l, g) = \frac{1}{N}(L_{conf}(x, c) + \alpha L_{loc}(x, l, g)) \tag{2}$$

where:

$$- L_{loc}(x, l, g) = \sum_{i \in Pos}^{N} \sum_{m \in \{cx, cy, w, h\}} x_{ik}^k smooth_{L1}(l_i^m - g_j^m)$$

$$- L_{conf}(x, c) = - \sum_{i \in Pos}^{N} x_{ij}^p log(\hat{c}_i^p) - \sum_{i \in Neg} log(\hat{c}_i^0)$$

2.2.2 Faster R-CNN Architecture

The Faster Region-based Convolutional Network model (Faster R-CNN) [15] is improved from the Fast R-CNN model [5] with the replacement of the selective

RPN Phase 1: Feed-forward the input image through DNN to obtain convolutional features

RPN Phase 2: Use a convolutional sliding window up

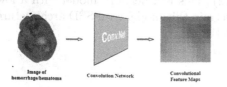

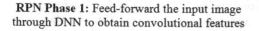

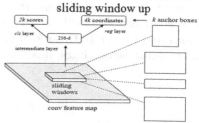

Fig. 4. Two main phases of RPN [15]

search algorithm to the region proposal network (RPN). Faster R-CNN works with two main phases including the first phase using the RPN to create the proposed zones and the second phase segmenting and classifying objects on the proposed zones. The RPN accepts an input image of any size and outputs region proposals with the probability containing objects.

Figure 4 illustrates the operation of the RPN algorithm, in which phase 1 uses a convolution layer with a size of 3×3 and 5 layers of max pooling size 2×2 to create feature maps. The second phase of RPN uses a sliding window ($n \times n$) on the feature maps. The results achieved are the positions of the objects and the probability containing the objects on the feature maps. The Loss function is measure by formula 3 and 4 [15].

$$Loss(\{p_i\}, \{t_i\}) = \frac{1}{N_{cls}} \Sigma_i L_{cls}(p_i, p_i^*) + \lambda \frac{1}{N_{reg}} \Sigma_i p_i * L_{reg}(t_i, t_i^*) \qquad (3)$$

$$SmoothL1Loss(x, y) = \begin{cases} 0.5(x_i - y_i)^2 & \text{if } |x_i - y_i| < 1 \\ |x_i - y_i| - 0.5 & \text{otherwise} \end{cases} \qquad (4)$$

where:

- i: is the index of anchor in mini-batch
- p_i: is the predicted probability of anchor i is an object
- p_i^*: is the ground-truth label value, 1: if anchor is positive and 0: if anchor is negative
- t_i: is a 4-dimensional vector representing the coordinate values of the predicted bounding box
- t_i^*: is a 4-dimensional vector representing the coordinate values of the ground-truth box corresponding to the positive anchor.
- L_{cls}: is the log loss of 2 classes (object and non-object)
- L_{reg}: is the SmoothL1Loss

2.3 CNN Models for Feature Extraction

2.3.1 Inception V2

The Inception v2 network [19] is an artificial neural network made up of multiple layers of CNN networks with the architecture described in Fig. 5 . The Inception v2 network is trained on more than 10 million images of 1,000 different classes of objects (ImageNet database version 2012). This is a network model with a low error rate (3.46%). In this research, we retrain this model with SSD architecture on the brain hemorrhagic image dataset [19].

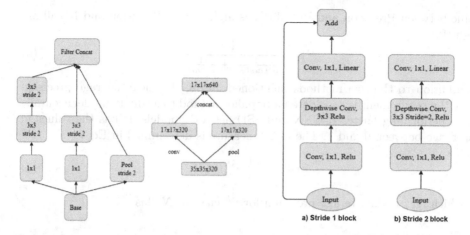

Fig. 5. Architecture of the inception v2 [19]

Fig. 6. Architecture of the MobileNet v2 [16]

2.3.2 MobileNet V2

MobileNet v2 network [16] is an artificial neural network designed to be optimized for low configuration devices with limited computing power but still ensuring accuracy (as shown in Fig. 6). Comparing with the VGG network model, the MobileNet v2 network reduces up to 75% of the parameters with a total of 30 computational layers. In this study, we retrain the MobileNet v2 network model together with the Inception v2 network for comparison and evaluation.

2.3.3 Inception Resnet V2

Inception Resnet v2 [19] is a network model built on a combination of the Inception and Residual Network architectures. Inception Resnets overall architecture is evaluated as a deep learning architecture network and trained with more than 1000 layers on ImageNet-2012 image set. The input of the model is 299 × 299 images and the output is a list of the predicted results.

2.4 Measurements for Evaluating the Accuracy of Classification

It is necessary to have a suitable method to evaluate and compare the use of network models. The commonly used method for multi-class classification problems is Precision-Recall [18], as in formula 5. High precision relates to the low False Positive rate, i.e, the proportion of the negatives having positive outcomes. High recall means a high True Positive rate, i.e., the rate of omitting objects that are actually positive is low.

$$precision = \frac{TP}{TP + FP} \qquad recall = \frac{TP}{TP + FN} \qquad (5)$$

F1 is a combination of Precision and Recall, which is the harmonic mean value of the Precision and Recall. F1 tends to get the value, which is closer to the lower value between Precision and Recall. F1 is high if both Precision and Recall are high [18].

$$F1 = \frac{1}{\frac{1}{precision} + \frac{1}{recall}} \tag{6}$$

In addition to the two methods mentioned above, the mean average precision (mAP) measurement is considered a popular method to evaluate model accuracy when performing Faster R-CNN and SSD network models. It has the values in the range between 0 and 1. The mAP measure is determined in Eq. 7.

$$mAP = \frac{1}{N} \Sigma_{i=1}^{N} AP_i \tag{7}$$

in which AP_i is the average precision for i^{th} class in N class.

3   Proposed Method

In this paper, we propose the implementation consists of two processing phases: the training phase of the network model and the testing phase. We perform these two phases on the three network models (Faster R-CNN Inception ResNet v2, and SSD MobileNet v2, and SSD Inception v2) so that we can evaluate and choose a suitable model for applying in brain hemorrhage detection and classification. Specifically, the training phase consists of 5 stages described in Fig. 7.

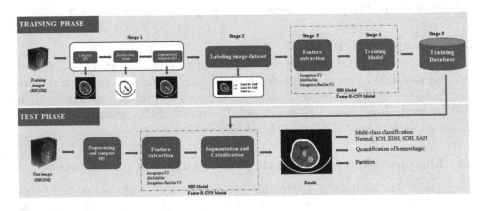

Fig. 7. General model of the proposed method

Stage 1- Data Preprocessing and Automatic Hemorrhage Segmentation Based on HU: A DICOM file captured from the CT/MRI scanner will be converted to a digital image (.jpg). The extent, duration, and location of cerebral hemorrhage were determined based on the HU values calculated by formula 1 and Table 1 as shown in Sect. 2.1. The results of stage 1 is a digital image dataset with the brain hemorrhage regions highlighted.

Stage 2- Labeling Image Dataset With the Support of Experts: Each digital image will be automatically labeled based on the location of the brain hemorrhage areas under the supportive supervision of specialists. At the end of stage 2, the outcome is the labeled brain hemorrhage image dataset.

Stage 3 - Feature Extraction: To reduce the computation time and classify hemorrhage quickly, this stage is to perform feature extraction. We extract the features using the three network models including Inception v2, MobileNet, and Inception ResNet v2 (presented in Sect. 2.3).

Stage 4- Training: The extracted features in Stage 3 are used to train in three network models SSD Inception v2, SSD MobileNet v2, and Faster R-CNN Inception ResNet v2. We monitor the training process based on the Loss value of each network architecture presented in Sect. 2.2. This process will be done until the Loss value does not improve (not decrease) after a certain number of iterations. We stop training the model and move to the testing phase to compare and evaluate the model.

Stage 5 - Storing Features and Training Parameters: At the end of stage 4, we receive the features, labels, and training parameter values. Those will be stored in the database for classification of cerebral hemorrhage. Next, we compare and evaluate the network models through the testing dataset to evaluate the accuracy with mAP, presented in Sect. 2.4.

4   Experimental Results

The experiments were conducted on the three models SSD Inception v2, SSD MobileNet v2, Faster R-CNN Inception ResNet v2 in the same Google Colab environment with Ubuntu 18.04. The configuration of the computer is 32 GB RAM and Nvidia Tesla P100 GPU. The library used to support the training of the network model is TensorFlow GPU version 1.5. Since there are no public datasets for labeled cerebral hemorrhage images, we collected a dataset from several hospitals with 479 MRI images with size 512×512, including 79 images of EDH type, 54 images of SDH type, 90 images of SAH type and 256 images of ICH type. Based on HU values, the dataset is automatically partitioned and labeled under the support of experts to contribute to the high reliability training dataset. The dataset will be randomly divided into a training dataset and a testing dataset at the rate of 80% (382 images) and 20% (97 images) respectively. Since pretrained weights for medical images are not available, we do not use transfer learning and train all the layers. The weights of these models are initialized using "COCO dataset" and a sigmoid output layer has been added to get our final output labels. In addition, during training, we tweak the parameters of these models to obtain high accuracy.

Figure 9 shows the results after performing detection and segmentation of the brain hemorrhage. Compared with the results of the FBB method [4] as shown in Fig. 8, the proposed method has accuracy 100% for detecting the contours of the entire hemorrhage region. Especially, our proposed method can detect all bleeding types on the same CT/MRI image.

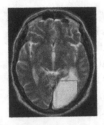 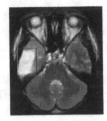 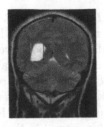 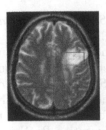

Fig. 8. Hemorrhage segmentation results using FBB algorithm [4]

We evaluate the accuracy and identification time of the three network models. First, the three models need to be assessed on the accuracy of cerebral hemorrhage classification. We determine the Loss value of the three network models to decide to stop training the model and move to the testing phase. Figure 10 shows the results comparing the Loss value of the three network models after a number of iterations with the Learning_rate of 0.0003. Figure 10.c shows the Loss value of the Faster R-CNN is very low below 10% (Loss_value < 0.01) compared to the other models (Fig. 10.a and Fig. 10.b) after 60,000 training times. This means that the error rate in predicting hemorrhage types and training frequency of Faster R-CNN model is lowest compared to the other models. Figure 11 shows the classification accuracy of the three network models by two measurements Average Precision (AP) and mean Average Precision (mAP). In terms AP, the Faster R-CNN Inception ResNet v2 model has the most stable classification results in comparison with the other two models (Fig. 11.a). Similarly, when evaluating the models with mAP, Faster R-CNN Inception ResNet v2 gives the highest result with mAP = 0.79 for all 4 classes of brain hemorrhage (Fig. 11.b). SSD Inception v2 and SSD MobileNet v2 have the lower mAP results of 0.72 and 0.75, respectively.

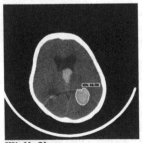 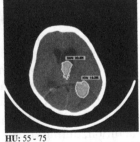 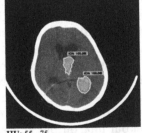

HU: 55 - 75
Hemorrhagic type: ICH (42.1%)
Duration: 2-3 days
Level: Acute
Model: SSD Inception v2

HU: 55 - 75
Hemorrhagic type: ICH (13.3%), SAH (22.8%)
Duration: 2-3 days
Level: Acute
Model: SSD MobileNet v2

HU: 55 - 75
Hemorrhagic type: ICH (100%), SAH (100%)
Duration: 2-3 days
Level: Acute
Model: Faster R-CNN

Fig. 9. Hemorrhage segmentation results of the proposed method

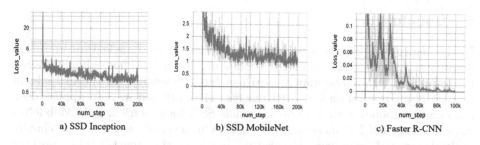

a) SSD Inception b) SSD MobileNet c) Faster R-CNN

Fig. 10. Comparison of the loss values of three network models

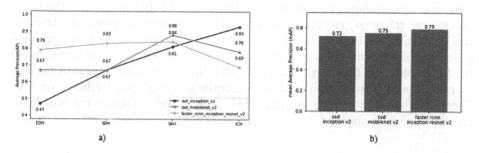

a)   b)

Fig. 11. Comparing the metrics of AP and mAP of the three network models for 4 classes

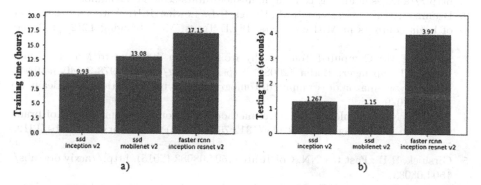

a)   b)

Fig. 12. Comparing training time (a) and testing time (b) of the three network models

In the same environment, the training time is quiet different with 17 h 15 min of the Faster R-CNN Inception ResNet v2, 13 h 08 min of the SSD MobileNet v2, and 9 h 93 min of the SSD Inception v2. We can see that the SSD Inception v2 has the fastest training and reasonable classification time compared to other models but the mAP measurement is the lowest (see Fig. 11.b and Fig. 12). The Faster R-CNN network model has longer training time but mAP is the highest at 79%.

5   Conclusion

In this paper, we propose a new approach based on Hounsfield Unit and deep learning techniques. Based on Hounsfield Unit, our method not only determines the levels and duration of brain hemorrhage but also supports in automatic hemorrhage segmentation on CT/MRI images. The proposed method applies deep learning techniques with 3 network models SSD Inception v2, SSD MobileNet v2, and Faster R-CNN Inception ResNet v2. Our method can detect and classify multiple types of brain hemorrhages that appear on the same CT/MRI image of the patient. The experimental results show that the proposed method can detect multiple types of brain hemorrhage on the same CT/MRI image and the automatic hemorrhage segmentation achieves 100% accuracy. In which, the training model with Faster R-CNN Inception ResNet v2 achieves the mean average precision of 79% for the four types of hemorrhage. This research can be extended to the problem of collecting cranial CT/MRI images from the hospitals for segmentation and classification of brain hemorrhages automatically based on HU. Specialists and doctors can be supported to accurately diagnose cerebral hemorrhage and offer appropriate treatment regimens.

References

1. http://radclass.mudr.org/content/hounsfield-units-scale-hu-ct-numbers
2. Brummer, M.E., Mersereau, R.M., Eisner, R.L., Lewine, R.R.: Automatic detection of brain contours in MRI data sets. IEEE Trans. Med. Imaging **12**(2), 153–166 (1993)
3. Buzug, T.M.: Computed Tomography from Photon Statistics to Modern Cone-Beam CT. Springer, Berlin (2008). https://doi.org/10.1007/978-3-540-39408-2. http://www.amazon.de/Computed-Tomography-Photon-Statistics-Cone-Beam/dp/3540394079
4. Fazli, S., Nadirkhanlou, P.: A novel method for automatic segmentation of brain tumors in MRI images. CoRR abs/1312.7573 (2013). http://arxiv.org/abs/1312.7573
5. Girshick, R.B.: Fast R-CNN. CoRR abs/1504.08083 (2015). http://arxiv.org/abs/1504.08083
6. Graham, R.L., Yao, F.F.: Finding the convex hull of a simple polygon. J. Algorithms **4**(4), 324–331 (1983)
7. ISO12052:2017: Health informatics Digital imaging and communication in medicine (DICOM) including workflow and data management. International Organization for Standardization (ISO) (2017)
8. Kuo, W., Häne, C., Yuh, E.L., Mukherjee, P., Malik, J.: Patchfcn for intracranial hemorrhage detection. CoRR abs/1806.03265 (2018). http://arxiv.org/abs/1806.03265
9. Liu, Wei., et al.: SSD: single shot MultiBox detector. In: Leibe, Bastian, Matas, Jiri, Sebe, Nicu, Welling, Max (eds.) ECCV 2016. LNCS, vol. 9905, pp. 21–37. Springer, Cham (2016). https://doi.org/10.1007/978-3-319-46448-0_2
10. Ly, N.L., Dong, V.H.: Brain Injury. Medical Publishing House (2013)
11. Pham, L.T., Nguyen, N.L., Phan, L.T.H.: Health Statistics Yearbook. Medical Publishing House (2015)

12. Pham, N.H., Le, V.P.: CT Head Injury. Medical Publishing House (2011)
13. Phan, A.C., Phan, T.C., Vo, V.Q., Le, T.H.Y.: Automatic detection and classification of brain hemorrhage on CT/MRI images. In: Twentieth National Conference: Selected Issues of Information and Communication Technology, pp. 246–252 (2017)
14. Phong, T.D., et al.: Brain hemorrhage diagnosis by using deep learning. In: Proceedings of the 2017 International Conference on Machine Learning and Soft Computing, pp. 34–39. ACM (2017)
15. Ren, S., He, K., Girshick, R.B., Sun, J.: Faster r-CNN: Towards real-time object detection with region proposal networks. In: Cortes, C., Lawrence, N.D., Lee, D.D., Sugiyama, M., Garnett, R. (eds.) In: NIPS, pp. 91–99 (2015)
16. Sandler, M., Howard, A., Zhu, M., Zhmoginov, A., Chen, L.C.: Mobilenetv 2: inverted residuals and linear bottlenecks. In: Proceedings of the IEEE Conference on Computer Vision and Pattern Recognition, pp. 4510–4520 (2018)
17. Sezgin, M., Sankur, B.: Survey over image thresholding techniques and quantitative performance evaluation. J. Electron. Imaging **13**(1), 146–166 (2004)
18. Simon, L., Webster, R., Rabin, J.: Revisiting precision and recall definition for generative model evaluation. CoRR abs/1905.05441 (2019), http://arxiv.org/abs/1905.05441
19. Szegedy, C., Ioffe, S., Vanhoucke, V., Alemi, A.A.: Inception-v4, inception-resnet and the impact of residual connections on learning. In: Thirty-first AAAI Conference on Artificial Intelligence, AAAI (2017)

Inflammatory Bowel Disease Classification Improvement with Metagenomic Data Binning Using Mean-Shift Clustering

Nhi Yen Kim Phan and Hai Thanh Nguyen[(✉)]

College of Information and Communication Technology, Can Tho University,
Can Tho, Vietnam
nhipky.cto@gmail.com, nthai@cit.ctu.edu.vn

Abstract. In the human body, where the greatest concentration of bacteria is the gastrointestinal tract, it is considered to be a diverse and complex microbial population, involving many different diseases. The development of metagenomics has many achievements in evolution and biodiversity. The application of machine learning algorithms to solve metagenomics problems has helped researchers make new advances in the field of personalized medicine, especially the diagnosis and improvement of human health people. In this study, we propose an unattended binning approach combined with Mean-shift algorithm to improve predictive performance. We performed on the Inflammatory Bowel Disease (IDB) dataset with 6 subclasses. This clustering method has improved results when applying deep learning techniques and shows the promising potential of data preprocessing methods when applied on different datasets.

Keywords: Mean-shift clustering algorithm · Metagenomics · Personalized medicine · Classic machine learning · Deep learning · Clustering-based binning

1 Introduction

In recent years, people have increasingly focused on health care and protection. Therefore, many health services have been created to meet the needs of the people and the correct medicine - the right treatment for the right people, the right medicine, the right dose and the tendency for everyone to follow. This requires high accuracy in diagnosis and examination through the use of modern medical equipment and tools with many different diseases. One of the most common diseases and the current spike rate is Inflammatory Bowel Disease. Inflammatory Bowel Disease (IDB) is a term for chronic diseases related to the human digestive system, including two main types: Ulcerative colitis and Crohn's disease. The main cause of the disease is mainly due to living environment, family factors, age problems, smoking. The number of people infected is currently on the rise, with 1.3% of adults (about 3 million) in 2015 estimated to have IBD

T. K. Dang et al. (Eds.): FDSE 2020, CCIS 1306, pp. 294–308, 2020.
https://doi.org/10.1007/978-981-33-4370-2_21

in the United States while in 1999, it was estimated that there were about 0.9% (1.8 million), data offered from National Health Interview Survey (NHIS) [1]. A common cure nowadays is that there is a single treatment that is applicable to all patients. Although some patients recover through this method, we need to study genetic diversity in order to cure their patients' root diseases. The concentration of metagenomics research and development by scientists has proved the importance of metagenomics to human health, and the strong development of deep learning algorithms has helped to propose. Many models and methods support effective diagnosis and treatment of diseases.

Personalized medicine impacts on key factors such as environment, genes, etc. Collaboration with modern techniques has been remarkably effective for the group of patients used. One of the most outstanding techniques of precision medicine is metagenomics, this method will capture genetic material directly without culturing them by applying DNA sequencing techniques of microorganisms. In this study, we looked at the human gut environment, where the most diverse population of microorganisms is concentrated. It is this variety that helps us learn more about diseases, so that predictions become easier and more effective. However, we still have a difficult time because IBD is very complicated but we only have a certain number of samples to test. Powerful algorithms have been studied to solve the problem related to metagenomics, thereby helping scientists test and propose predictive models and support treatment.

2   Related Work

As mentioned above, scientists are making efforts to study methods of precision medicine with the aim of increasing prognostic performance, disease diagnosis and metagenomics as the most noticeable method. Metagenomics is a modern genetic research method that uses information extracted from microorganisms in the natural environment. This technique is widely used in the natural environment with the purpose of exploring the diversity of microorganisms in the environment and finding new ways to diagnose and treat diseases.

According to research by Derek Reiman et al. [3], they introduced the PopPhy-CNN architecture that is able to effectively exploit phylogentic structures in microbiological classification. They used genetically engineered plants and based on the proposed model to explore the spatial relationship of taxonomic annotations on plants and their quantitative characteristics in metagenomics data. The results of this study, showed that PopPhy-CNN effectively trained models without requiring data, visualizing the phynogenetic tree classification. Authors in [4] introduces machine learning workflow that is effective in predicting server type from all shotgun metagenomes by analogy preserving the compact representation of genetic material. Nathan LaPierre et al. [5] research on a number of in-depth methods and feature extraction to focus on analysis, improve disease prediction performance, particularly diabetes and obesity Type 2 from metagenomic sequencing data.

The MetaSUB International Association has collected and sequenced metagenomics from metro stations of different cities around the world. To distinguish the motagenomic profile and predict these unknown patterns, Harris et al. proposed using two methods based on machine learning techniques, a read-based taxonomy profiling of each sample and prediction method or another method is a reduced representation assembly-based method. Applying this method to the Random Forest model has shown promising results, the method of reading each sample reaches 91% accuracy, the method based on assembly reaches 90% accuracy. They demonstrate that metagenomic samples can be traced back to their position by creating careful features from the bacterial composition and using machine learning algorithms [6].

These studies have demonstrated the potential of metagenomics in particular and personalized medicine in general in the present life. The selection of algorithms to build a machine learning model with positive results is very important, greatly contributed to the diagnosis, treatment and Mean-shift is the algorithm that we propose in our research.

Mean-shift is an unsupervised clustering algorithm. The number of clusters assigned by Mean-shift is not given as the K-means algorithm but it will be automatically detected based on the number of central densities found in the dataset. From the dataset, the algorithm will calculate the centroids and the location of the centroid will be updated. The process will be repeated, move to a higher density area and this process will stop until centroids reach a position where it cannot move further.

The application of Mean-shift clustering algorithm has been widely applied in many studies to solve clustering problems. We can use clustered clusters to experiment with different models before applying them to all data. Many scientists have studied this algorithm to apply it to the field of biology. However, up to now, there are quite a few studies in bioinformatics using meanshift algorithm. In the study [7] proposed MeShClust, this is one of the applications of the average displacement algorithm in bioinformatics. The authors have demonstrated the ability of MeShClust to sequence DNA sequences with great accuracy even when the same sequence parameters provided are not very accurate. D. Barash and D. Comaniciu [8] has proposed the implementation of Mean-shift clustering algorithm to apply microarray expression data analysis to improve the performance of local search mode.

In the remainder of the study, we will briefly describe the IBD dataset in Sect. 3. Our proposed methodology will be presented in Sect. 4. The test results of the proposed method will be illustrated in detail in Sect. 5. Section 6 will discuss the results, summarizing key points in this study.

3   Data Benchmarks for Metagenomic Analysis

We work on metagenomic abundance data, that is OTU (Operational taxonomic unit) indicates how present (or absent) in human gut. We look at the IBD disease dataset, which is the Sokol's lab dataset which is described in detail in [9].

Based on the phenotype of the disease, we have divided it into two types, namely Ulcerative colitis (UC), Crohn's disease (CD). For Crohn's disease, the dataset is partitioned into 2 subsets ileal Crohn's disease (iCD) and colon Crohn's disease (cCD) [10]. Each condition will be divided into two conditions (flare (f) if the patient's disease worsens or symptoms appear, remission (r)). Each dataset includes 4 main information: (1) the number of features, (2) the number of samples, (3) the number of infected samples, (4) the number of healthy samples.

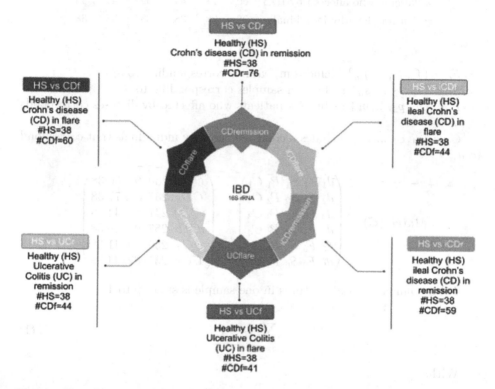

Fig. 1. Classification tasks on IDB dataset. The six learning tasks discriminating HS versus different stages of IBD patients [10]

CDf dataset consists of 60 patients and 38 healthy individuals out of 98 samples. Review the CDr dataset with a total of 237 features and a total of 114 samples including 77 patients and 38 controls. For iCDf dataset, the number of positive cases is 44 out of 82. iCDr datasets include 257 features with the number of samples is 97, of which 59 patients and 38 healthy people. UCf disease dataset with a total of 79 samples and 41 cases positive for the disease. The last dataset considered is UCr with the number of features is 237 and number of samples is 82.

The data of the 6 datasets is shown in detail in Table 1. In which, each sample, species has the total number of abundance of all species is 1 and this is a relative proportion for the species abundance datasets.

Let D be the set of considered datasets, D = $\{d_1, d_2, d_3, d_4, d_5, d_6\}$, d = 1..6, with: d_1 = CDf, d_2 = CDr, d_3 = iCDf, d_4 = iCDr, d_5 = UCf, d_6 = UCr

Table 1. Information on six considered datasets.

	CDf	CDr	iCDf	iCDr	UCf	UCr
#Features	259	237	247	257	250	237
#Samples	98	115	82	97	79	82
#Patients who affected by IDB	60	77	44	59	41	44
#Controls/healthy individuals	38	38	38	38	38	38

$F_i = \{f_1, f_2, ..., f_m\}$ includes m features corresponding to d_i

$S_i = \{s_1, s_2, ..., s_n\}$ includes n samples corresponding to d_i

$P_i = \{p_1, p_2, ..., p_k\}$ includes k patients who affected by diseases corresponds to d_i

$C_i = \{c_1, c_2, ..., c_x\}$ includes x controls / healthy individuals that correspond to d_i

$$Matrix(C) = \begin{pmatrix} d_1 & F_1 & S_1 & P_1 & C_1 \\ d_2 & F_2 & S_2 & P_2 & C_2 \\ d_3 & F_3 & S_3 & P_3 & C_3 \\ d_4 & F_4 & S_4 & P_4 & C_4 \\ d_5 & F_5 & S_5 & P_5 & C_5 \\ d_6 & F_6 & S_6 & P_6 & C_6 \end{pmatrix} = \begin{pmatrix} CDf & 259 & 98 & 60 & 38 \\ CDr & 237 & 114 & 77 & 38 \\ iCDf & 247 & 82 & 44 & 38 \\ iCDr & 257 & 97 & 59 & 38 \\ UCf & 250 & 79 & 41 & 38 \\ UCr & 237 & 82 & 44 & 38 \end{pmatrix}$$

Total abundance of all features in one sample is sum up to 1:

$$\sum_{i=1}^{k} f_i = 1 \tag{1}$$

With:

- k is the number of features for a sample.
- f_i is the value of the i-th feature.

The next section, based on the binning approach, we will introduce pre-processing methods on these metagenomic datasets.

4   Metagenomic Data Binning

4.1   Binning Approaches for Metagenomic Data

Data binning or Data Discretization is a method of converting continuous values into discrete. Select values as "breaks", this is the boundary to define. Put continuous values in "bins". Each bins will contain elements in the range of values in two boundaries. For example, consider a group of elements from 0.2 to 0.4. Assuming a break of 0.3, there are 2 bins: from 0.2 to 0.3 and from 0.3 to 0.4.

To see the difference, we explored a number of different binning approaches as a basis for comparing results. These binning methods are introduced in [11].

Equal Width binning (EQW) is a fairly simple and popular approach. This technique divides data into equal segments based on the arithmetic mean ($\frac{Max\_value - Min\_value}{number of bin}$) of the range under consideration. Suppose, in the range [Min $= 0$, Max $= 0.5$], we want to provide 5 bins of equal width, then the width of each bins will be 0.1, which means the boundary of the enclosures $Min + w, Min + 2 \times w, ..., Min + (k-1) \times w$. This way will give same breaks in case number of bins is equal. Figure 2 and Fig. 3 describe the division of different breaks between EQW and Mean-shift approaches.

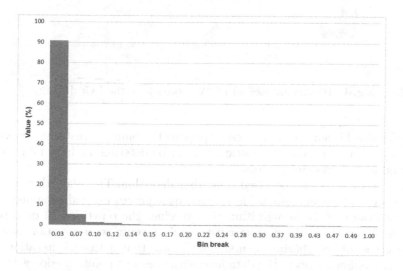

Fig. 2. Histogram uses an Mean-shift approach on the UCr dataset.

EQual Frequency binning (EQF) is the binning method based on the frequency of the values. This technique divides groups with equal frequency, where the breaks depend entirely on data distribution so the dimension plus the buckets can change significantly. For example, the breaks could be 0.1, 0.13, 0.14, 0.2, 0.5 depending on the data distribution.

Species Bins (SPB) is an approach taken from the distribution based on the abundance of bacterial species in the six metagenomics datasets mentioned in relation to different diseases. This method was observed by the authors in [12] and showed that the original species abundance almost follows the zero-inflated distribution.

4.2   Binning Based on Mean-Shift Algorithm

The clustering algorithm is an important tool in distributing different data with the goal of defining groups of data. Clustering algorithms have been widely

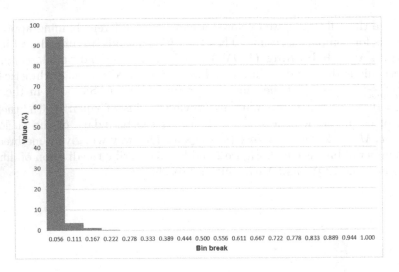

Fig. 3. Histogram uses an EQW approach on the UCr dataset.

applied and achieved certain success. Applying the binning clustering algorithm, we expect to improve the diagnostic efficiency by determining how data is delivered and high data density areas.

Mean-shift is an unsupervised clustering algorithm. This algorithm has been applied successfully in many fields such as image processing and computer vision [13,14]. Mean-shift is an algorithm that specifies the repetition of data points towards the center of the nearest cluster and its centripetal direction based on the positions of neighboring points. That means that with each iteration, each data point either moves to the data area with the most points needed with it, or leads to the cluster center. When the algorithm ends, each point will belong to a corresponding cluster. With this approach, Mean-shift is called search algorithm mode (mode is understood as the highest data point density in the area) [15].

Suppose, given a dataset of n points in a d-dimensional space Rd. Select a kernel K with bandwidth parameter h. The formula for multiplying density is:

$$f_K(u) = \frac{1}{nh^d} \sum_{i=1}^{n} K \frac{u - u_i}{h} \qquad (2)$$

The kernel function needs to satisfy 2 conditions:

1. $\int K(u)du = 1$
2. $K(u) = K(|u|)$ for all values of u

Using binning with Mean-shift clustering algorithm, we will get improved results compared to the methods mentioned earlier. The algorithm will automatically find the appropriate cluster number for each dataset. This method is performed by the algorithm below.

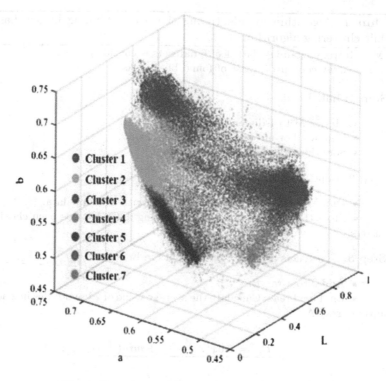

Fig. 4. Description of Mean-shift algorithm [15].

5   Experimental Results

For the comparison to be effective, we see the predictive performance improvements of the IBD datasets on different machine learning models, each of which we present separately. Table 2 and Fig. 5, 6, 7 show the results when applying the Random Forest model and compare the results mentioned in [10] that is detailed in Table 3 and Fig. 8. The dataset used is the set of types of IBD disease presented in Sect. 3.

5.1   Learning Model for Comparison

We recommend 1 popular machine learning models for evaluation and comparison. Random Forest (RF) as a traditional neural network, is run the tests on the dataset. Random Forest (RF) is a popular model, the most successful methods of metagenomic datasets also often apply RF and this is usually the algorithm that achieves the best results of the algorithms considered.

5.2   Metrics for Comparison

The performances are assessed by 10-fold cross validation. We use 3 measures of AUC, ACC and MCC to evaluate the accuracy of the proposed study. Average

Algorithm 1. Algorithm for identifying the list of binning breaks based on Mean-shift clustering algorithm

Input: M - Matrix containing data 1 of 6 datasets is considered
Output: B - Array contains the list of found bin breaks
Begin

   Step 1: Initialize data

   - Matrix M to 1-dimensional array.
   - Remove 0 or uncountable values in array.
   - Sort the array in ascending values

   Step 2: Implement Mean-shift algorithm

   - Run Mean-shift clustering algorithm with M array data.
   - Store the results in array A containing data that has been classified by n clusters.

   Step 3: Constructs array B containing n bin breaks

   - Add 0 to array B.
   - Find bin break: Calculate the average value of 2 boundaries in 2 adjacent groups in array A

$$B[i] = \frac{max(A[i-1]) + min(A[i])}{2} \tag{3}$$

   - Sort the array in ascending values

End

Accuracy and Average Matthews Correlation Coefficient (MCC) is calculated by us as a measure of the performance for overestimation of classifiers. We can say that the same creases are used for all of these classifiers, which means that the training and test suites are exactly the same for each classifier. Based on this technique, changes when comparing the performance of any of the 2 classifiers can be directly calculated as differences in per-test readings.

Accuracy is a common measure of model performance. MCC is considered as a good tool to evaluate performance and progressing model for metagenomic datasets. The authors in [19] said that "among the common performance evaluation scores, MCC is the only one which correctly takes into account the ratio of the confusion matrix size". Matthews correlation coefficient score is computed as following formula:

Matthews Correlation Coefficient score is computed by:

$$MCC = \frac{TN.TP - FN.FP}{\sqrt{(TN+FN).(TP+FP).(TP+FN).(TN+FP)}} \tag{4}$$

With:

- TN stands for True Negative
- TP stands for True Positive
- FN stands for False Negative
- FP stands for False Positive

5.3   Evaluation Binning Approaches with Random Forest (RF)

We are considering 6 diseases CDf, CDr, iCDf, iCDr, UCf, UCr using Random Forest model. The results are evaluated on 3 measures: ACC, AUC, MCC and using popular binning methods for comparison such as: EQF, EQW, SPB. These experimental results are described in detail in Table 2.

Table 2. Performances in ACC, AUC and MCC of various binning approaches on six considered datasets. The Mean-shift algorithm whose performances are formatted with bold text are the best result corresponding to each dataset.

Datasets	Metrics	CDf	CDr	iCDf	iCDr	UCf	UCr
EQF	ACC	0.899	0.796	0.902	0.824	0.893	0.804
EQW		0.860	0.786	0.900	0.822	0.877	0.703
SPB		0.897	0.801	0.910	0.833	0.904	0.790
Mean-shift		0.870	**0.806**	**0.919**	**0.843**	0.902	0.732
EQF	AUC	0.956	0.899	0.960	0.925	0.936	0.891
EQW		0.934	0.884	0.939	0.923	0.921	0.828
SPB		0.959	0.896	0.963	0.928	0.943	0.886
Mean-shift		0.953	0.894	**0.965**	**0.93**	0.932	0.843
EQF	MCC	0.807	0.526	0.819	0.646	0.802	0.627
EQW		0.727	0.490	0.815	0.641	0.775	0.413
SPB		0.809	0.547	0.836	0.673	0.828	0.598
Mean-shift		0.750	**0.551**	**0.855**	**0.689**	0.820	0.468

In general, the binning approach with Mean-shift showed quite positive results. In 3 diseases CDr, iCDf, iCDf the values are higher than other approaches, EQW, EQW, SPB at 2 degrees of ACC, MCC. For AUC measurement, the results reached the highest value in 2 CDr and iCDf diseases. Of the 3 measurements that we use, the AUC with the highest and lowest value is the MCC. To have a visualization, we have drawn the result description graph in 3 Fig. 5, 6, 7.

For ACC measurement, CDr disease using Mean-shift approach will have the highest value and 0.806 value. Considering iCDf and iCDr, we have ACC value of Meanshift of 0.919, 0.843 and this value is higher than other approaches, EQW, EQF, SPB.

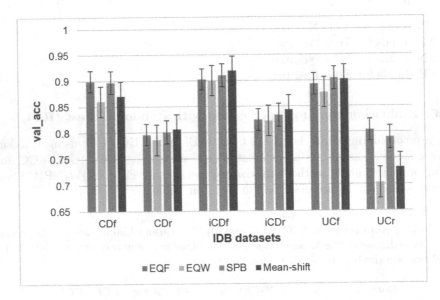

Fig. 5. Different Methods and Measurements Comparison using Random Forest with Average Accuracy (ACC).

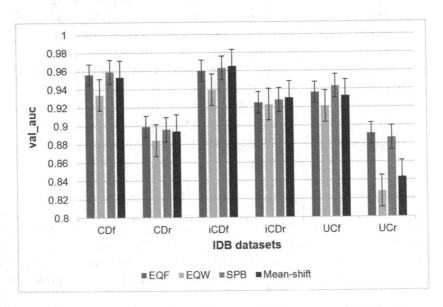

Fig. 6. Different Methods and Measurements Comparison using Random Forest with Area under the ROC Curve (AUC).

For AUC measurement, iCDf also gives the highest value when applying Mean-shift approach which is 0.965. Similarly, iCDr disease also gave the highest value of 0.93 when using Mean-shift.

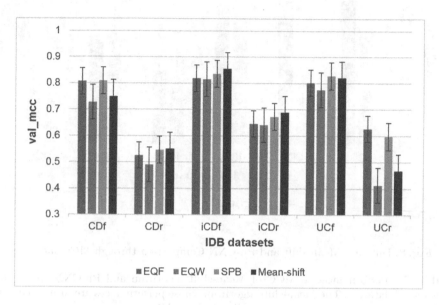

Fig. 7. Different Methods and Measurements Comparison using Random Forest with Matthews correlation coefficient (MCC).

For MCC measurement, Mean-shift also gives the best results for 3 diseases CDr, iCDf, iCDr similar to the ACC measurement. These values are 0.551, 0.855, and 0.689 respectively. CDr disease when using Mean-shift has significantly better results when using binning method with EQW ($val_m cc = 0.490$).

5.4 Comparison of MCC Value Between Mean-Shift and Ph-CNN Approach

Phylogenetic convolutional neural networks (Ph-CNN) is the solution proposed by the group of authors in [10]. They showed that, when applying this method, the results will be better than previous methods. In this study, we have compared the value of the MCC measurement when using binning with Mean-shift and using Ph-CNN. The comparison table and chart are shown in detail in Table 2 and Fig. 5, 6, 7. In six datasets, when comparing values with MCC measurements, we found that there are 3 diseases: iCDf (val_mcc = 0.855), iCDr (val_mcc = 0.689), UCf (val_mcc = 0.820) reached better results than Ph-CNN. This shows the potential development of the algorithm we have proposed.

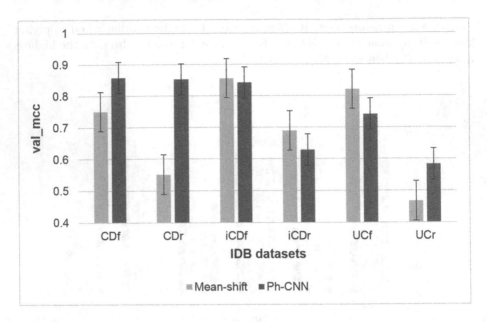

Fig. 8. Different Mean-shift and Ph-CNN Comparison through MCC measure

Table 3. Performances in MCC of Mean-shift algorithm and Ph-CNN [10] on six considered datasets. The Mean-shift algorithm whose performances are formatted with bold text are the best result corresponding to each dataset.

Datasets	CDf	CDr	iCDf	iCDr	UCf	UCr
Mean-shift	0.750	0.551	**0.855**	**0.689**	**0.820**	0.468
Ph-CNN	0.858	0.853	0.842	0.628	0.741	0.583

6   Conclusion

In this study, we propose a binning approach using the Mean-shift algorithm. With these approaches, the results are encouraging when comparing them to other binning approaches such as binning based on width, base on frequency and base on species distribution.

We train on machine learning models that is Random Forest (RF). When comparing these models, the results showed that the Random Forest model seemed to outperform the remaining models. When compared with previous studies, it is clear that the proposed method has quite satisfactory results.

This study provides a prerequisite for further research on algorithms and models to improve performance. However, our datasets are quite small so we need to do more on other datasets to have a different view. Experimental results show the potential when applying pretreatment to Mean-shift, promising positive results when applying other data sets and in-depth studies.

References

1. Dahlhamer, J.M., Zammitti, E.P., Ward, B.W., Wheaton, A.G., Croft, J.B.: Prevalence of inflammatory bowel disease among adults aged $\geq$ 18 years - United States. MMWR Morb Mortal Wkly Rep **2016**(65), 1166–1169 (2015). https://doi.org/10.15585/mmwr.mm6542a3

2. Andreani, J., Million, M., Baudoin, J., et al.: Klenkia terrae resistant to DNA extraction in germ-free mice stools illustrates the extraction pitfall faced by metagenomics. Sci. Rep. **10**, 10228 (2020). https://doi.org/10.1038/s41598-020-66627-0

3. Reiman, D., Metwally, A.A., Dai, Y.: PopPhy-CNN: Ation Neural Networks for Metage- nomic D Phylogenetic Tree Embedded Architecture for Convoluata, (2018). https://doi.org/10.1101/257931

4. Anna, P.C., Will, P.M.R., Martyn, W., Edward, O.P.-K.: A Fast Machine Learning Workflow for Rapid Phenotype Prediction from Whole Shotgun Metagenomes. vol. 33, No. 01: AAAI-19, IAAI-19, EAAI-20, (2019). https://doi.org/10.1609/aaai.v33i01.33019434

5. Nathan, L., Chelsea, J.-T., Ju, G.Z., Wei, W.: MetaPheno: a critical evaluation of deep learning and machine learning in metagenome-based disease prediction. Methods, vol. 166, pp. 74–82, ISSN 1046–2023 (2019). https://doi.org/10.1016/j.ymeth.2019.03.003

6. Harris, Z.N., Dhungel, E., Mosior, M., et al.: Massive metagenomic data analysis using abundance-based machine learning. Biol. Direct. **14**, 12 (2019). https://doi.org/10.1186/s13062-019-0242-0

7. James, B.T., Luczak, B.B., Girgis, H.Z.: MeShClust: an intelligent tool for clustering DNA sequences. Nucleic Acids Res. **46**(14), e83 (2018). https://doi.org/10.1093/nar/gky315

8. Barash, D., Comaniciu, D.: Meanshift clustering for DNA microarray analysis. In: Proceedings of the 2004 IEEE Computational Systems Bioinformatics Conference. CSB 2004, Stanford, CA, USA, 2004, pp. 578–579 (2004). https://doi.org/10.1109/CSB.2004.1332503

9. Sokol, H., Leducq, V., Aschard, H., et al.: Fungal microbiota dysbiosis in IBD. Gut. **66**(6), 1039–1048 (2017). https://doi.org/10.1136/gutjnl-2015-310746

10. Diego, F., et al.: Phylogenetic convolutional neural networks in metagenomics. **19**(2), 49 (2018). https://doi.org/10.1186/s12859-018-2033-5

11. Le Chatelier, E., Nielsen, T., Qin, J., et al.: Richness of human gut microbiome correlates with metabolic markers. Nature **500**, 541–546 (2013). https://doi.org/10.1038/nature12506

12. Thanh, H.N., et al.: Disease classification in metagenomics with 2d embeddings and deep learning. In: Proceedings of CAp, France (2018)

13. Girgis, H.Z., Mitchell, B.R., Dassopoulos, T., Mullin, G.: Hager G: An intelligent system to detect Crohn's disease inflammation in Wireless Capsule Endoscopy videos. In: Proceedings IEEE International Symposium Biomed Imaging, pp. 1373–1376 (2010). https://doi.org/10.1109/ISBI.2010.5490253

14. Hai, T.N., Toan, B.T., Huong, H.L., Trung, P.L., Nghi, C.T.: Improving disease prediction using shallow convolutional neural networks on metagenomic data visualizations based on mean-shift clustering algorithm. Int. J. Adv. Comput. Sci. Appl. (IJACSA), **11**(6) (2020). https://doi.org/10.14569/IJACSA.2020.0110607

15. Xing, L., Zhang, J., Liang, H., Li, Z.: Intelligent recognition of dominant colors for Chinese traditional costumes based on a mean shift clustering method. J. Textile Inst. (2018). https://doi.org/10.1080/00405000.2018.1423896

16. Thanh H.N., Jean-Daniel, Z.: Enhancing metagenome-based disease prediction by unsupervised binning approaches. In: The 2019 11th International Conference on Knowledge and Systems Engineering (KSEIEEE), pp 381–385, ISBN: 978-1-7281-3003-3, (2019). https://doi.org/10.1109/KSE.2019.8919295
17. Lo, C., Marculescu, R.: MetaNN: accurate classification of host phenotypes from metagenomic data using neural networks. BMC Bioinform. **20**, 314 (2019). https://doi.org/10.1186/s12859-019-2833-2
18. Rodriguez-Valera, F.: Environmental genomics, the big picture? FEMS Microbiol Lett. **231**, 153–158 (2004). https://doi.org/10.1016/S0378-1097(04)00006-0
19. Edwards, R., Rohwer, F.: Viral metagenomics. Nat. Rev. Microbiol. **3**, 504–510 (2005). https://doi.org/10.1038/nrmicro1163
20. Baghban, H., Rahmani, A.M.: A Heuristic on job scheduling in grid computing environment. In: 2008 Seventh International Conference on Grid and Cooperative Computing, Shenzhen, pp. 141–146 (2008). https://doi.org/10.1109/GCC.2008.22

Machine Learning-Based Big Data Processing

Additional Learning on Object Detection: A Novel Approach in Pornography Classification

Hoang-Loc Tran[1,2]([⊠]), Quang-Huy Nguyen[1,2], Dinh-Duy Phan[1,2],
Thanh-Thien Nguyen[1,2], Khac-Ngoc-Khoi Nguyen[1,2], and Duc-Lung Vu[1,2]([⊠])

[1] University of Information Technology, Vietnam National University Ho Chi Minh
City, Ho Chi Minh City, Vietnam
{locth,duypd,thiennt,lungvd}@uit.edu.vn
{15520306,15520386}@gm.uit.edu.vn
[2] Vietnam National University Ho Chi Minh City, Thu Duc Dist.,
Ho Chi Minh City, Vietnam

Abstract. In this paper, we proposed a new approach for pornographic classification by recognizing sensitive objects on images. To handle the misdetection and wrong judgment, a novel training strategy named additional learning was developed to help object detection model learns from mistakes, therefore increasing the method performance. Furthermore, a separate SVM classifier was trained to classify pornography and benign images from sexual object detected using Mask R-CNN model. Benchmarked by the NPDI-800 dataset, our proposed method achieved an accuracy of 84.625% and 90.125%, before and after applying additional learning strategy respectively. Besides, our proposed model also improves the false positive rate from 22.16% to 3.56% in our manually collected dataset.

Keywords: Computer vision · Image processing · Object detection algorithms · Pornographic content recognition and classification

1 Introduction

Pornography has been a long-lasting problem in society nowadays. Not only it brings a huge negative impact toward the young generation but also provokes the ratio of commit crime, especially sexual crime. Although extensively studied and researched, recognizing pornographic images and videos remains a challenging problem in computer vision. The difficulties of addressing pornographic content often due to various factors, such as people's definition of pornography, the variation exhibited in scenario, person pose, background, lightning, scales, especially the highly similar between some certain pornographic images and normal ones.

To address the problem, various methods have been proposed based on different definition toward pornography. With the base hypothesis that pornographic

Supported by Vietnam National University Ho Chi Minh City.

image often portray a large ratio of explicit body, skin based approaches focus on determining the ratio of skin and face of the image, therefore conclude the safety of that image based on a custom threshold. Low level-based approaches develop description model to specify a visual codebook represent hand-crafted features extracted from pornographic images, then using a classifier model such as SVM to classify pornographic image under the robustness of machine learning algorithms. One of the finest approaches in pornographic visual content identification problem belongs to deep learning approaches, modifying pre-train neural networks models to learn the global features from obscene images automatically. However, these approaches comes with some certain weakness. Determining explicit pornographic images from skin and face ratio have been known for the large ratio of misdetection and wrong judgement [1], while the various features that describe pornographic images make it quite a challenging problem to determine appropriate features presenting visual low-level codebooks [2]. While deep learning method is the state-of-the-art, the lack of public pornographic dataset and the rich diversity and complexity of pornographic content that make the creation of a "standard" dataset with quantity and quality for training pornographic model become difficult. By the lack of data for training, many deep learning method often suffer from high rate false-positive classification [3].

As we recognized, there is a significant part of pornographic content describe sexual body parts, textually and visually. Extremely rarely it has a pornographic content without sexual objects description, as these parts play a significant role to cause people's euphoria. Hence, recognizing sexual objects in content means identifying pornography. In other words, detecting sexual objects is one of the root of the pornographic content classification problem. In the light of that conclude, our study proposed a method that focused on recognizing pornographic image and video-based on detecting sensitive objects such as anus, breast, or genitals. Our proposed method included all the advantages of the existing methods, which are modifying the neural network model to study low-level features from images and identifying obscene objects on images automatically. After that, to transfer from pornographic object detection to pornographic classification problem, a separated discriminative model SVM was trained based on the predicted results from object detection model to identify sensitive images.

One of the most crucial problem of object detection is wrong detection i.e. the false-positive rate. To deal with wrong detection problem as well as to improve the performance of our detection model, we proposed a binary-training-phase strategy called additional learning. The initial training phase worked as a classic strategy which learned to recognize sexual objects, and the additional training phase, which is our novel approach, served to learn again with the combination between the original training set and false recognized objects, thus improved the total accuracy and strengthened the model's performance.

In summary, this paper proposed a method to detect pornographic content based on human sensitive objects. It took images as input and gave classification results as output which let us know if an image is benign or pornographic. To discriminate pornographic content from the normal one, the proposed method focused on detecting human sensitive objects. If the model found anus, women nude breast, or genitals in images, it identified that image as pornography and vice versa. This led to the root problem which we were dealing with turned into the sensitive object detection. To reduce the false-positive rate, this paper proposed the train-booster strategy which contain two phases of training. Finally, an SVM is applied to determine whether the content is pornography or not. In the experiment, our additional training strategy helped boost the total accuracy of Mask R-CNN model from 84.625% to 90.125% on the open NPDI-800 dataset [4], proving the effectiveness of our method. Our main contribution lies in the new strategy to reduce the false-positive rate hence boosting the performance of the model.

The rest paper is organized as follows. Section 2 describes in details some relevant approaches in pornographic detection. After that, the detail of our proposed method is presented in Sect. 3. Section 4 provides the details of our experiments and the results, while in Sect. 5, we discuss our study and our future work in details.

2   Related Works

One of the earliest approaches for recognizing pornography image is calculated the ratio of human body skin exposure on that image, hence conclude the safety of the image. Since skin cell identification and segmentation involve color and texture information, color-spaces are often applied to identify whether the pixel is skin or not, therefore segment the areas of human skin. Balamurali et al. [5] proposed a binary model consist of skin extraction using YCbCr color space and face identification with Viola-Jones algorithms to calculate the ratio of face and skin areas on the image. If the percentage between human face and skin body lesser than 30% or the skin areas detected is half an image, this picture is declared as pornographic explicit and vice versa. Although Zaidan et al. [1] praised the skin-based approaches for its effectiveness in classifying between obscene and benign images, there are still some certain problems, mainly because of the quality and resolution that affect the performance of images. Moreover, wrong decisions can be made when it comes to images with skin-like objects or athletic images, which have a vast amount of exposed skin.

Another approach for recognizing pornographic images is using feature descriptors to extract hand-crafted features from images, then develop a classifier to determine whether the image is pornography or not based on extracted features. Avila et al. [4] presented a descriptor named BossaNova to represent the conceptual point of view in visual content. Extended from Bag-of-Visual-Work model, BossaNova computing histogram of distances between descriptors found in image and the visual dictionary in order to preserve essential information about the distribution of Hue-SIFT descriptor. Developing an open pornographic video dataset named NPDI-800, the research team extracted key-frames from every video and applied a binary model consist of BossaNova and SVM to detect labels for each video via a major voting scheme. Moreira et al. [6] introduced a space-temporal detector and descriptor called Temporal Robust Features

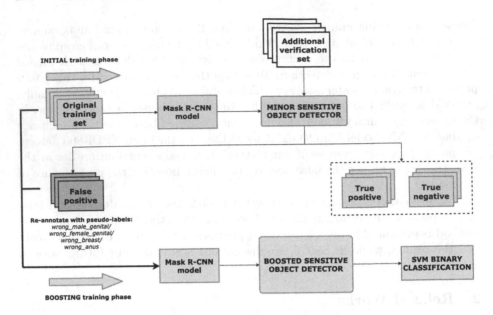

Fig. 1. Proposed method's training procedure

which was a custom-tailor for effective and efficient description to extract local information on the image. Then, these features are aggregate into a mid-level representation using a state-of-the-art Bag-of-Visual-Words model named Fisher Vectors. To benchmark the method, an extension of NPDI-800 named NPDI-2k was developed.

Taking into account of the remarkable results achieved by deep learning architectures on various computer vision tasks, recent advances in pornography detection applied deep learning convolutional neural networks (ConvNet) to learn pornographic features from images automatically. Moustafa et al. [7] remodeled two pre-trained neural networks architectures AlexNet (ANet) and GoogLeNet (GNet) for pornographic images detection. By feeding a two-way Softmax with the output from the last layer of two architectures respectively, the models yielded a probability that pointed out whether the input image is pornographic or normal. Eventually, the two new architectures are combined together to developed new classifying models called AGNet and AGbNet with distinct metrics. In AGNet, the final score was determined by calculating the average between two probabilities, while in AGbNet, the result was choosing max. Mahadeokar et al. [8] developed an NSFW classification model by replicated ResNet 50-layer networks using half number of filters in each layer. For training the pre-trained residual network on ImageNet 1000 class dataset, the authors applied scaled augmentation to avoid over fitting. The last layer of every networks was replaced with two fully-connected layers and fine-tuned with an NSFW dataset. Furthermore, CaffeOnSpark, an open source deep learning framework developed by Yahoo, was applied for training NSFW model on Hadoop and Spark cluster. Vitorino et al. [9] adopted a transfer learning approach, training GoogLeNet model to classify a large scale everyday object dataset ImageNet. Then, the model was fine-tuned to learn pornographic features from NPDI-2k dataset. Finally, the last layer of the model architecture was replaced with an SVM with RBF kernel as a discriminative model to identify pornographic images. Wehrmann et al. [3] proposed ACORDE, a deep learning architecture comprised of separate ConvNet for image feature extraction and LSTM recurrent networks for sequence learning on video, thus optimise the performance of ACORDE on adult video.

Although the advantage of deep learning helps neural network models learn the common global features from explicit sexual images, these approaches do not identify sexual body parts specifically on images as a major part of pornographic photos often include sensitive organs. Fortunately, with the robust development of object detection algorithms, this is no longer a difficult problem. Shen et al. [2] developed a combine model called EFUI (Ensemble Framework using Uncertain Inference) consist of SSD [20] to identify sensitive semantic components included genital, breast, ass, nude body and sexual action. While SSD model has a slight possibility of false detection in practical, the training dataset is prepared with slight noisy data to incorporate the prior global confidence. Wang et al. [10] located female breast and sex organs on image using Multiple Instance Learning model, applying a generic pornographic content detector to recognise a pornographic image if it contains at least one exposed sexual organs. Comparing with the transitional pornographic classification methods such as image retrieval or bag-of-features, multi-instance generic detector achieved more accurate results. Notably, in Tabone et al. study [11], a multi-class ConvNet was applied to divide sensitive organs into five main classes: buttock, female breast, female genital, male genital and sex toy, which has a significant similar to the genital to be ignored. As female genital appearance was recognized quite different between obscene posing and sexual activities, this class was divided into two sub-classes: female genital posing and female genital active. Moreover, the authors proposed an extra class named benign to define the concept of normal body parts, thus strengthen the recognition performance.

3   Proposed Method

When examined the nature of the problem, we found that if an image is called as pornography, it must "describe or show naked people and sexual acts in order to make people feel sexually excited"[1]. In other words, pornography must show off the sensitive objects of human. These objects usually are male or female genitals, breast, and anus. From this observation, sensitive body parts detection could be used as a potential approach for the pornography recognition problem. In general, the proposed method is presented in Fig. 1. Different from the existing methods which usually trained the model only one time, the proposed method trained the model up to two times in binary-training phase. To obtain the sensitive object detector, Mask R-CNN was selected (Fig. 2).

---

[1] https://www.oxfordlearnersdictionaries.com/definition/english/pornography.

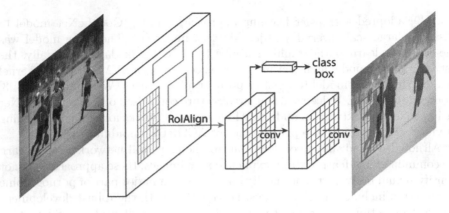

Fig. 2. Mask R-CNN main architecture [12]

Mask R-CNN [12] has been well known as one of the most effective and efficient method to deal with object detection and instance segmentation problem. Created as the extension of the famous architecture Faster R-CNN, Mask R-CNN can detect multiple objects with high performance. With the combination of Residual Network (ResNet) [13] and Feature Pyramid Network [14] architecture as the main backbone as well as the Fully Convolutional Network as an extended mask branch, Mask R-CNN is able to describe segmentation mask for object instances in the pixel-level. For the core operation of local features extraction, an unique pooling algorithms called RoIAlign [12] is applied to help Mask R-CNN to achieve the pixel-to-pixel alignment, therefore improves the bounding box localization and instance mask segmentation to predict object in high detail.

The reason for choosing Mask R-CNN models for this paper mainly because it is a noticeable algorithm for both object detection and instance segmentation tasks. Our target of recognizing private body parts, not only because it could identify whether the image is safe or not, but also it could lead to censoring inappropriate visual content automatically in the future. Because of that, Mask R-CNN is the most suitable choice as it is considered to be one of the most significant models which have the ability to recognize objects in the pixel-level. However, due to the lack of data as well as the complexity of training parameters, Mask R-CNN model is quite easy to suffer from over-fitting, thus leads to wrong judgment and misdetection. To improve the prediction's performance, the proposed two-phase training strategy is developed alongside with model's parameters improvement. While the labeling process in pixel level for Mask R-CNN training is quite a tedious task, this is a crucial step for developing the automatic censoring pornographic visual content that we are currently working on.

The sensitive object detector, which had been trained by the Mask R-CNN model, was used to detect if human expose their sensitive part in an image, thus gave the conclusion whether that image is pornography or not. Not like other methods that usually stop training after achieving the model, our proposed

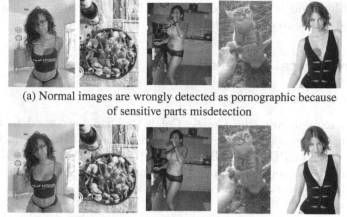

(a) Normal images are wrongly detected as pornographic because
of sensitive parts misdetection

(b) No sensitive object found in normal images

Fig. 3. (a) Results from initial training phase with no augmentation and (b) results
after augmenting Mask R-CNN model with additional learning strategy

method had an extra step to validate and re-train the model which called the
additional learning phase.

The purpose of this additional training was that we wanted to improve the
false-positive rate. Since Mask R-CNN had a great advantage in detecting sensitive objects, it was also too sensitive with normal images. This leads to the high
rate of false positive when benign objects were wrongly detected as sensitive
parts of human (Fig. 3).

To deal with this problem, an additional verification set, which contained
all normal images, was used to improve the performance of the sensitive object
detector. As shown in Fig. 1, if any normal images in the verification set were
classified as pornography, which meant that normal objects have been detected
wrongly in these images, it will be re-annotated with pseudo-negative-labels
included wrong-male-genitals, wrong-female-genitals, wrong-breast, and wrong-
anus. Based on this proposal, there were a total of 8 labels in the additional
training phase: four real labels to detect sensitive objects and the four corresponded pseudo-labels to avoid misdetection. Because the number of training
class was different from the initial phase, the model had to be re-trained completely. The training set of the additional training phase is the combination of
original training set and false-positive images from the initial validation set.
This combination came with pseudo labels that helped the proposed model to
discriminate features from pornographic images and normal ones hence reducing
the false-positive rate and increasing the total accuracy.

The final step of the training phase has been done with the help of the Support Vector Machine [15] (SVM) binary classification model. Using the results
from the sensitive object detector, which included the number of each kind of

sensitive object and its highest confidence, the SVM finally trains a classifier that has the ability to distinguish pornography from normal images.

4   Experimental Results

4.1   Experiment Environment

To conduct experiments, the Google Colab Pro had been used to train and test the proposed model. In specific, the computation's hardware included the Intel(R) Xeon (R) CPU @ 2.30 GHz came with 25 GB RAM and NVIDIA Tesla P40 with 16 GB memory. Python version 3.7 and TensorFlow version 1.15.2 had been used for the development environment.

4.2   Dataset Processing

Initially, in the first training phase, a small annotated dataset was created by collecting nearly 8.000 explicit pornographic images from the internet. These images was then annotated in polygon mask for four sexual body parts, including female breast, male/female genitals, anus and split into two sub-sets namely Original Train and Original Val for Mask R-CNN training.

Table 1. Distribution of annotated objects of two training phases in total

Objects Name	Training	Validating	Total
male_genital	2055	799	**2854**
female_genital	2079	298	**2377**
breast	7740	949	**8689**
anus	1046	110	**1156**
pseudo_male_genital	2367	329	**2696**
pseudo_female_genital	715	111	**826**
pseudo_breast	6342	1280	**7622**
pseudo_anus	224	34	**258**

Table 2. Quantity of each sub-set distributed on their labels

Name	Porn	Normal	Sexy	Pseudo	**Total**
Original Train	6.850	N/A	N/A	N/A	6.850
Original Val	1.107	N/A	N/A	N/A	1.107
Additional Verification	N/A	30.000	10.000	N/A	40.000
Combination Train	6.850	N/A	N/A	6.000	12.850
Combination Val	1.107	N/A	N/A	1.058	2.165
Final Test	20.000	15.000	5.000	N/A	40.000

In the additional training phase, the Additional Verification set had been built with 40.000 images. This set included all non-porn images and was also divided into two sub-directories namely: (i) normal subset which contained 30.000 images from usual social life, (ii) sexy subset which contained 10.000 images that show human with sexy pose and exposed skin. Based on the false-positive prediction on that verification set, we extracted an pseudo set with over 7.000 images which are annotated with pseudo-class corresponded with the four original class from the first training phase. From the segmentation masks and labels predicted by the minor sensitive object detection, we converted them into polygon coordinate information as well as renamed these labels into pseudo respective with the original ones for the additional training phase. Then, the pseudo set was combined with the original training set to create the Combination Set for the next training stage, which included 12.850 images for training and 2.165 images for validating. The Combination Set consisted of 8 annotated class including 4 original explicit sexual classes and their corresponding pseudo class, which distribution are described in detail in Table 1. Eventually, a 40.000-testing set included 15.000 normal, 20.000 pornography and 5.000 sexy images was developed as the final measurement to evaluate the object detection model after the binary-phase training. The quantity of each image-set is described in Table 2.

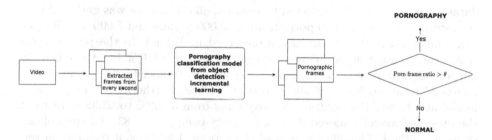

Fig. 4. Proposed method's training procedure

4.3   Experiment Detail

In the proposed method, the training phase has been split into two phases which used two different image sets. The first training phase use the Original Set to train and validate. These images helped the Mask R-CNN model learn features to detect sensitive objects of humans includes male and female genital, breast, and anus. To implement the Mask R-CNN model, ResNet101 + FPN backbone had been used while the learning rate had been set to 0.001. We trained our model with 100 epochs which included 500 training steps and 200 evaluation steps for every epoch. All the training images were resized into 512 × 512 and augmentation strategy was randomly flip. The initial step of our strategy was training data with the first 60 epochs with the head layer of Mask R-CNN network. After that, we fine-tuned the model with the 40 later epochs, using the whole network architectures. The result from the initial training phase was the sensitive object detector that could detect sensitive objects in images.

In the additional training phase, an Additional Verification set had been built with 40.000 non-porn images. All images in this set were not pornographic content because this verification set aimed to improve the sensitivity of the model. If any image in this set was detected as positive result, it was considered as false positive and then would be annotated with corresponding pseudo labels and used in the additional training phase. This step helped model discriminate between pornographic content and normal content which look like pornographic. The predicted and segmented results of Mask R-CNN can be seen in Fig. 5.

After the two phases of training, the model was completed with the help of an SVM binary classification. Through experiments with various settings, the linear kernel has been chosen since it had given the significant results from others.

4.4   Result and Evaluation

To evaluate the effectiveness of the proposed method, 2 testing sets had been used included a manually collected testing set and the NPDI-800 benchmark dataset. In the manually collected testing set, 40.000 images was gathered from the internet included 20.000 pornography, 15.000 normal and 5.000 sexy images. The evaluation results in detail are presented in Table 3. In the pornographic class, the accuracy slightly decreases from 89.03% to 84.43% but there is a significant improvement on normal and sexy classes. In specific, the accuracy has increased from 86.45% to 97.48% on normal class. Furthermore, the proposed model also boosts the accuracy on sexy class from 52.02% to 93.32%. In total, the proposed model achieved 90.43% accuracy compares to 83.44% from classic training method. The effectiveness of the proposed additional training on sensitivity and specificity is shown in Table 4. The proposed method has improved the total accuracy by reducing the false positive rate from 22.16% in classic training strategy to 3.56% in additional training strategy. In the other hand, the true positive rate is also affected by the novel training strategy which reduces from 89.03% to 84.43%. However, the true nature of this problem is not detecting pornographic content as much as possible but trying to discriminate the pornography and normal content. Being too sensitive may incur user experience in unpleasant way. Because of that, we focus on improving the total accuracy by reducing the false positive rate and accepting a little bit decrease in the true positive rate.

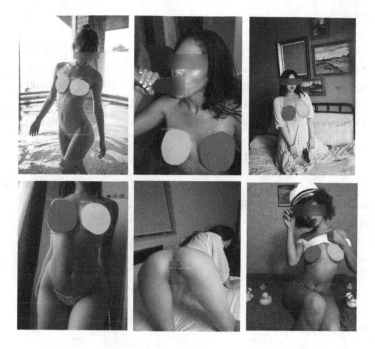

Fig. 5. Mask R-CNN performance

Beside the manually collected dataset, the NPDI-800 dataset was also used to evaluate the proposed model. This dataset consisted of 400 videos which are divided into 2 groups namely pornographic and normal. Because the testing data were videos, it was necessary to have a strategy to conduct the testing since the proposed model only works on image. Therefore, every second in each video of NPDI-800 was extracted as key-frames. For each extracted key-frame, the final model, which achieved from the SVM binary classification, made consideration and then gave the prediction. This strategy is graphically presented in Fig. 4, where

$$\text{porn frame ratio} = \frac{\text{porn frame}}{\text{total frame}}$$

In order to avoid wrong detection, a video is considered as pornography if only it contains at least θ percentage of porn frames. The selected value of θ will decide how sensitive the model be. If θ is too low i.e. a video will be treated as pornographic when it only have few predictably pornographic frames, the model becomes too sensitive since not all predictions are correct. This leads to high false-positive rate. In the other hand, if θ is too high, the threshold to identify if a video is pornographic become too high and easily lead to miss detection, in other words, high false-negative rate. In this paper, we choose θ by experimental results from Fig. 6. In this figure, the horizontal axis represents for the value of θ while the vertical axis represents for the accuracy, the blue line shows

Table 3. Custom dataset prediction results

Class	Classic training	Additional training	Quantity
Normal	86.45%	**97.48%**	15.000
Sexy	52.02%	**93.32%**	5.000
Porn	**89.03%**	84.43%	20.000
Total Accuracy	83.44%	**90.43%**	40.000

Table 4. Rate results

	TP	TN	FP	FN	Total accuracy
Classic training	**89.03%**	77.85%	22.16%	**10.97%**	83.44%
Train-boosting	84.43%	**96.44%**	**3.56%**	15.58%	**90.43%**

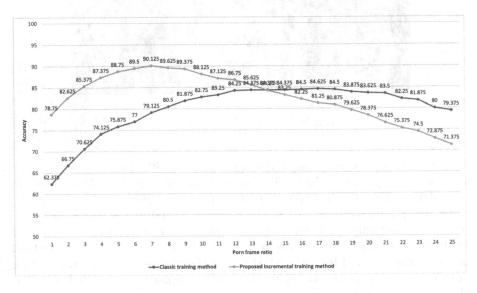

Fig. 6. NPDI-800 result (Color figure online)

the result from classic training strategy and the orange line shows the proposed method's result. To reach the peak performance, this value may be varied in two approaches. Based on experiments, $\theta = 7$ is chosen which means a video should have at least 7% porn frames over the total number of frames to be determined as pornographic video. Compare to the pure classification from object detection approach, the proposed additional learning gives a significant improvement whose result is **90.125%** compare to **84.625%** from original method.

5 Conclusion

In this paper, we proposed an approach for the pornography identification which applied a new training strategy call additional training. Our new strategy contained two phases of training named initial training phase which was the classic approach, and additional training phase which re-trained the model with pseudo labels from false-positive images. The proposed model had proven its performance by reducing the false positive rate hence increasing the total accuracy. The final result, which achieved from Mask R-CNN model combined with an SVM binary classification, had shown the better performance which is 90.125% compared to 84.625% from pure object detection approach on NPDI-800 dataset. On the manually collected dataset, the proposed method also showed the significant improvement in both accuracy and false positive rate which are 90.43% and 3.56% respectively.

Acknowledgments. This research is funded by Vietnam National University Ho Chi Minh City (VNU-HCM) under grant number B2019-26-02.

References

1. Zaidan, A.A., Karim, H.A., Ahmad, N.N., Bahaa, B., Sali, A.: An automated anti-pornography system using a skin detector based on artificial intelligence: a review. Int. J. Pattern Recogn. Artif. Intell. **27**, 561–625 (2013)
2. Shen, R., Zou, F., Song, J., Yan, K., Zhou, K.: EFUI: an ensemble framework using uncertain inference for pornographic image recognition. Neurocomputing. **322** (2018). https://doi.org/10.1016/j.neucom.2018.08.080
3. Wehrmann, J., Simões, G. S., Barros, R. C., Cavalcante, V. F., : Adult content detection in videos with convolutional and recurrent neural networks. Neurocomputing **272** (2018). https://doi.org/10.1016/j.neucom.2017.07.012
4. de Avila, S., Thome, N., Cord, M., Valle, E., Araújo, A.: Pooling in image representation: the visual codeword point of view. Comput. Vis. Image Understand. (CVIU) **117**, 453–465 (2013)
5. Balamurali, R., Chandrasekar, A.: Multiple parameter algorithm approach for adult image identification. Cluster Comput. **22**(5), 11909–11917 (2018). https://doi.org/10.1007/s10586-017-1510-3
6. Moreira, D., et al.: Pornography classification: the hidden clues in video space-time. Forensic Sci. Int. (Forensic Sci. Int.) **268**, 46–61 (2016)
7. Moustafa, M.N.: Applying deep learning to classify pornographic images and videos. In: 7th Pacific-Rim Symposium on Image and Video Technology (PSIVT) (2015)
8. Mahadeokar J., Pesavento G.: Open Sourcing a Deep Learning Solution for Detecting NSFW Images (2016). https://yahooeng.tumblr.com/post/151148689421/open-sourcing-a-deep-learning-solution-for
9. Vitorino, P., Avila, S., Perez, M., Rocha, A.: Leveraging deep neural networks to fight child pornography in the age of social media. J. Vis. Commun. Image Representation **50**, 303–313 (2018)
10. Wang, Y., Jin, X., Tan, X.: Pornographic image recognition by strongly-supervised deep multiple instance learning. In: International Conference on Image Processing (ICIP), pp. 4418–4422 (2016)

11. Tabone, A., Bonnici, A., Cristina, S., Farrugia, R., Camilleri, K.: Private body part detection using deep learning. Proceedings of the 9th International Conference on Pattern Recognition Applications and Methods (ICPRAM), pp. 205–211 (2020)
12. He, K., Gkioxari, G., Dollár, P., Girshick, R.B.: Mask R-CNN. In: IEEE International Conference on Computer Vision (ICCV), pp. 2980–2985 (2017)
13. He, K., Zhang, X., Ren, S., Sun, J.: Deep residual learning for image recognition. In: Proceedings of the IEEE Conference on Computer Vision and Pattern Recognition, pp. 770–778 (2016)
14. Lin, T.Y., Dollár, P., Girshick, R., He, K., Hariharan, B., Belongie, S.: Feature pyramid networks for object detection. In: Proceedings of the IEEE Conference on Computer Vision and Pattern Recognition, pp. 2117–2125 (2017)
15. Cortes, C., Vapnik, V.: Support-vector networks. Mach. Learn. **20**(3), 273–297 (1995)
16. Abdulla W.: Mask R-CNN for object detection and instance segmentation on Keras and TensorFlow. GitHub repository, GitHub (2017). https://github.com/matterport/Mask_RCNN
17. Redmon, R., Divvala, S., Girshick, R.B., Farhadi, A.: You only look once: unified, real-time object detection. In: 2016 IEEE Conference on Computer Vision and Pattern Recognition (CVPR), pp. 779–788 (2016)
18. Redmon, J., Farhadi, A.: YOLO9000:Better, Faster, Stronger. In: 2017 IEEE Conference on Computer Vision and Pattern Recognition (CVPR), pp. 7263–7271 (2017)
19. Redmon J., Farhadi A.: YOLOv3: An Incremental Improvement, Arxiv, arXiv:1804.02767 (2018)
20. Liu, W., Anguelov, D., Erhan, D., Szegedy, C., Reed, S., Fu, C.Y., Berg, A.C.: SSD: single shot multibox detector. In: European Conference on Computer Vision (ECCV), pp. 21–37 (2016)

Proposing the Development of Dataset of Cartoon Character using DCGAN Model

Phat Nguyen Huu[1]([✉]), Thuong Nguyen Thi Mai[1], Quang Tran Minh[2,3], and Hieu Nguyen Trong[4]

[1] School of Electronics and Telecommunications, Hanoi University of Science and Technology (HUST), Hanoi, Vietnam
phat.nguyenhuu@hust.edu.vn, thuong.ntm164021@sis.hust.edu.vn
[2] Faculty of Computer Science and Engineering, Ho Chi Minh City University of Technology, 268 Ly Thuong Kiet, District 10, Ho Chi Minh City, Vietnam
quangtran@hcmut.edu.vn
[3] Vietnam National University Ho Chi Minh City, Linh Trung Ward, Thu Duc District, Ho Chi Minh City, Vietnam
[4] National Institute of Patent and Technology Exploitation, Vietnamese Ministry of Science and Technology, Hanoi, Vietnam
nthieu@most.gov.vn

Abstract. In this paper, we propose to create animated images using the deep convolutional generative adversarial network (DCGAN) model for creative design of publications for entertainment applications. We have built a set of image data for machine learning with nearly 1000 images in order to increase their quality while reducing the machine learning execution time. The results show that the proposal model not only improves the accuracy of the image with 21 dB but also reduces the execution time to less than a week (with transposed convolution up to $stride = 2, kernel = 3$ and size of image from $64 \times 64 \times 32$ to $128 \times 128 \times 3$). The results meet for requirements of future real-time applications.

Keywords: Generative adversarial networks · Deep convolutional generative adversarial networks · Cartoon character

1 Introduction

Neural network is able to provide audio and visual recognition similar to humans. Previous models can instantly identify a person through learning and analyzing hundreds, even thousands, tens of thousands of images with many objects. However, these images are not able to use as a training dataset without labeling and classifying them. It takes more time and effort. Therefore, generative adversarial network (GAN) is developed with the expectation of creating highly accurate systems that require little human activity for training. Based on the anti-creation

© Springer Nature Singapore Pte Ltd. 2020
T. K. Dang et al. (Eds.): FDSE 2020, CCIS 1306, pp. 325–339, 2020.
https://doi.org/10.1007/978-981-33-4370-2_23

network model, they create two neural networks, namely distinguishing and fake image generation networks. Deep convolutional generative adversarial network (DCGAN) focuses on creating fake images that help create the images similar to reality. Based on advantages of DCGAN model, it is able to help the development of designers.

The goal of this paper is to build animation dataset for machine learning and to create new 2D cartoon character images based on existing data with the DCGAN model. The results show that the algorithm is promising for practical applications.

2   Related Work

Current technologies are evolving rapidly, especially artificial intelligence (AI). AI technology supports people for many difficult areas such as image processing and object recognition. Applying the AI technology for human creativity has been more focused in recent years. It is demonstrated by using DCGAN model for building movie characters [4,7,9,10,15,18].

The DCGAN model has achieved a lot of positive results for detecting human face [1,4,5,7–10,15,16,18]. Based on creating images to images and text to images, many algorithms have been proposed. However, it is difficult to create a satisfactory face since the facial features need lots of detail and color information. When creating sketches, we face many problems. In [18], the authors propose a more suitable network according to change of task. In addition, authors [18] also add attribute information to feature extraction and make better using of these advanced semantic information. In that network, they apply skills that create more realistic and closer to the photographer.

DCGAN is proposed to simulate process of human face and retain its unique characteristics. In [9], the authors propose two encoders to decompose characteristics and age. In this paper, they apply perceptions for aging simulations that create face images. The rationality of the method has been proved through analysis and comparison their diversity. The method of [9] can achieve a good effect for young age. However, it is not good for adult men.

In [2–4,10,15], the authors used DCGAN model and self-created dataset of nearly 800 images of *Kaggle* to generate images of 2D cartoon characters. The results show that this model is able to apply for applications in the future.

3   System Design

3.1   Overview of Generating Models

We will discuss the concept of generating and distinguishing models before introducing antagonistic generation networks (AGN). These two types of models are designed as follows.

1. **Distinguishing model:** Model is used to estimate the probability of conditional of y ($P(y\,|\bar{X}\,)$). An example of the model is the logistic regression.

2. **Generating model:** Model estimates the overall probability $(P(\bar{X}, y))$ that is used to generate a dataset. It is performed by using the Bayes rule as follows:

$$P(y \mid \bar{X}) = \frac{P(\bar{X}, y)}{P(\bar{X})} = \frac{P(\bar{X}, y)}{\sum_z P(\bar{X}, z)}. \tag{1}$$

We consider an example of generating model based on Naive Bayes as follows.

Distinguishing models can only be used to set up network while generating models are used for both setting up and performing networks. For example, they can create a generating model of one layer by specifying its division in a multi-layered installation. Similarly, they can create each point of the dataset by using a probability model. This approach is used for automating encoder to sample based on Gaussian division and then using them as input to the decoder to generate the data.

AGN performs with two neural network models simultaneously. The first model creates examples of objects similar to a real ones. The goal is to create real objects that a observer is not able to distinguish them. If we have a dataset, the generative network will use them to create car images. Finally, we will have both real and fake data about car images. The second type is a distinguishing network that has been trained on a dataset with the actual images. It takes the real data and tries to analyze them. We can see that the generative network is trying to create fake data and the discriminating network performs to catch them. Therefore, two networks will improve each other until a balanced state is reached.

When the network distinguishes correctly, we can flag for fake objects by modifying its weight. New samples are then created and the process is repeated. Therefore, the network becomes better when generating more fake data. Finally, other networks are not be able to distinguish between real and synthetic objects creating from them. In fact, it is a parameter setting based on the division of points generating by data samples. For the discriminator, it is important to build a model with a high capacity and access to a variety of data sources.

The created objects are often useful for machine learning algorithms and play a useful role for data enhancement. Moreover, it is possible to use the method to create objects with different properties. The created object is also used for artistic images. The method is used for image-to-image translation applications. In the applications, the missing characteristics of an image are completed. In the next section, we will discuss the details of using GANs to create image data.

3.2 Using GAN to Create Data

GAN is often used to create visual objects with different types of context. We have the DCGAN when adding its depth. DCGAN architecture is shown in Fig. 1.

In Fig. 1, we begins with the 100-dimensional noise Gaussian for the decoder. It is shaped into 1024 maps with 4×4 size. This is achieved with matrix multiplication that is completely connected to 100-dimensional. As a result, we have a tensor. The depth of each layer then decreases and increases according to the

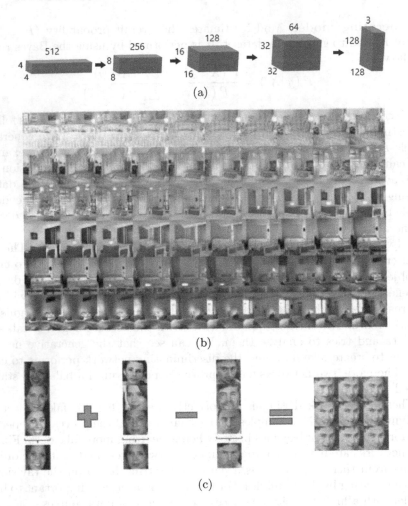

Fig. 1. DCGAN architecture and example image creation process a) generator of model, b) smooth image transition, and c) arithmetic operations [6,17].

length and width by factor of 2. For example, the second layer contains 512 feature maps while the third layer only contains 256 ones.

To increase the network length and width by factor 2, we use small segmented or transposed convolution with a fraction value of 0.5. If segmental steps are not much different from unit steps, it can be considered as a convolution after stretching the spatial input volume by inserting zeros between rows/columns or interpolation values. Since the input volume has been stretched, applying convolution with stride 1 on this input is equivalent to use segmented steps on the root.

An example of DCGAN is shown in Fig. 1. In Fig. 1 (a), we show the overall architecture of DCGAN. Figure 1 (b) shows examples of images using various

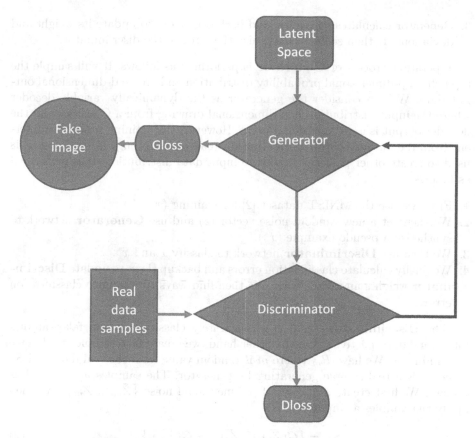

Fig. 2. Flowchart of data processing algorithm based on DCGAN [7]

patterns. In the figure, a room is transformed into a large window at 6th row. Smooth transitions are also observed in dynamically variable code. Figure 1 (c) shows the import of generator for a smiling man.

3.3   Overview of GAN

The training of AGN is performed by alternately updating the parameters of generator and discriminator as shown in Fig. 2. **Discriminator** is a neural network with d-dimensional input and a single output (0, 1) that indicates valuable probability. "1" and "0" represent real and fake values, respectively. The discriminator output with input $\widehat{X}$ is denoted $D(\widehat{X})$.

The process of **Discriminator** as shown in Fig. 2 is performed as follows:

1. The generator receives a new random noise vector z to synthesize a pseudo-sample x^*.
2. Generator uses the discriminator to classify x^*.

3. Generator calculates, classifies, and backs up errors to update its weight and deviations. It then seeks to maximize the error of the discriminator.

Operation process of **Generator** is performed as follows. It will sample the input from p-dimensional probability distribution and create d-dimensional output data. We can consider the generator as the dynamically variable decoder where the input distribution is p-dimensional drawing from a Gaussian and the decoder output is a d-dimensional point. However, the training process is different from the automatic transformation. Instead of using bugs for training, it is used to create other patterns similar to input data distribution. It is performed as follows.

1. First, we use the MNIST dataset [2] for training (x)
2. We then get a new random noise vector (z) and use **Generator** network to synthesize a pseudo example (x^*).
3. We then use **Discriminator** network to classify x and x^*.
4. We finally calculate classification errors and backup them to update **Discriminator** weights and deviations. We then find ways to minimize classification errors.

The **Discriminator**'s goal is to accurately classify real and fake samples into 1 and 0, respectively. On the other hand, we create fake samples to deceive discriminator. We have R_m where m is random value from the real data and S_n where n is a real sample generating by generator. The samples are created as follows. We first create a N_m set of p-dimensional noise $\{\bar{Z}_m \ldots \bar{Z}_m\}$. We then apply the samples as input as:

$$S_m = \{G(\overline{Z_1}), G(\overline{Z_2}), , ..., G(\overline{Z_m}),\}. \tag{2}$$

Therefore, the objective function J_D maximizes for **Discriminator** as follows:

$$Maximize_D J_D = \sum_{\overline{X} \in R_m} \log[D(\overline{X})] + \sum_{\overline{X} \in S_m} \log[1 - D(\overline{X})]. \tag{3}$$

We are able to verify the maximization of target function when the real and fake samples are classified correctly into 1 and 0, respectively. We then define that the target of generator function is to deceive discriminator. For generator, we don't care about real samples since the generator only cares about its sample. The generator generates m samples (S_m) to ensure that discriminator recognizes them. Therefore, the target of generator function (J_G) is to minimize the likelihood of mistakenly as follows:

$$Maximize_G J_G = \sum_{\overline{X} \in S_m} \log[1 - D(\overline{X})] = \sum_{\overline{Z} \in N_m} \log[1 - D(G(\overline{X}))]. \tag{4}$$

This objective function is minimized when the aggregating sample are miscategorized into 1. By minimizing the target function, we are trying to understand the parameters of generator. Another objective of generator function is to maximize the $\log\left[D(\overline{X})\right]$ for each $\log\left[D(\overline{X})\right]$ instead of $1-\log\left[D(\overline{X})\right]$. It will work better for several iterations.

Therefore, the optimization problem is built as a minimax game on J_D. We note that maximizing J_G on the different parameters of generator G is similar to maximize J_D since $J_D - J_G$ is not depend on generator G. As a result, we can be identified as follows [7]:

$$\nabla = Optimize(Maximize_D J_D \times Maximize_G J_G). \tag{5}$$

3.4 Designing Dataset

Firstly, the raw dataset of cartoon images are collected from various sources with different sizes as shown in Fig. 3.

The data is then automatically processed into the same 256×256 size with black border.

The data processing is shown in Fig. 2. The data after pre-processing will be put into the **Generator** block. They will be separated into two paths. In the first path, it is put into Gloss block to make fake data. In the second path, it will be put down the **Discriminator** block to make real data. The part of data will be put into Dloss block. The rest data will be return to the **Generator** block. The process will stop when number of epochs is limited.

3.5 Proposing Prediction Model

Predictive models include two networks, namely **Generator** and **Discriminator**. **Generator** block diagram is shown in Fig. 1 (a). In Fig. 1 (a), **Generator** network will create fake images. Input of network is noise, data, fake and real images ($128 \times 128 \times 3$). The layers are used as follows:

- Transposed convolution $stride = 2$, $kernel = 256$, $4 \times 4 \times 512 \rightarrow 8 \times 8 \times 256$,
- Transposed convolution $stride = 2$, $kernel = 128$, $8 \times 8 \times 256 \rightarrow 16 \times 16 \times 128$,
- Transposed convolution $stride = 2$, $kernel = 64$, $16 \times 16 \times 128 \rightarrow 32 \times 32 \times 64$,
- Transposed convolution $stride = 2$, $kernel = 32$, $32 \times 32 \times 64 \rightarrow 64 \times 64 \times 32$,
- Transposed convolution $stride = 2$, $kernel = 3$, $64 \times 64 \times 32 \rightarrow 128 \times 128 \times 3$.

Discriminator network are used to distinguish real images from dataset and fake images generating by **Generator**. The size of input image is $128 \times 128 \times 3$ and the output is fake image.

Discriminator network is symmetrical with the generator model as shown in Fig. 1 (a). The input image is passed through convolution with $stride = 2$ to reduce the image size as follows $128 \times 128 -> 64 \times 64 -> 32 \times 32 -> 16 \times 16 -> 8 \times 8 -> 4 \times 4$. Therefore, the depth of image also increases. Finally, the tensor $4 \times 4 \times 512$ is reshape to vector 4096 and uses a fully connected layer that changes from 4096 to 1 dimension.

Fig. 3. An example of original dataset.

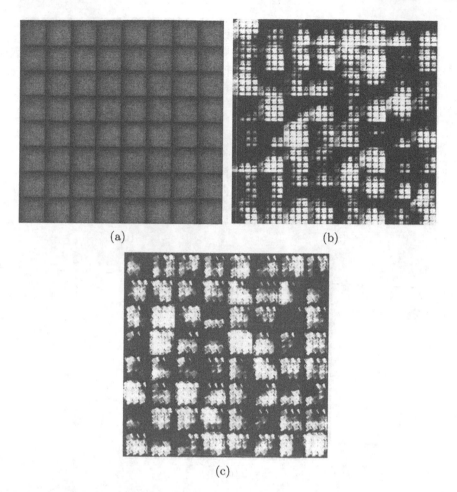

(a)   (b)

(c)

Fig. 4. Image is generated after a) 10 epochs (PSNR = 22.86 dB), b) 20 epochs (PSNR = 22.09 dB), and c) 30 epochs (PSNR = 21.96 dB).

4   Simulation and Result

We perform simulation with two datasets. The first dataset is built by ourselves. The second dataset is collected from [2,3] 800 Kaggle images (256 × 256) and PyTorch library. The results are shown as in Figs. 4, 5, 6, 7, 8, and 9.

1. Case 1: Results with self-built dataset
   At the first 30 epochs, the network only generates noise as shown in Fig. 4. After 200 epochs, the network has learned the properties of the images and can generate several basic cartoon. The result is shown in Fig. 5.
   However, the cartoon images become more clearly after 500 epoch. The result is shown in Fig. 6.

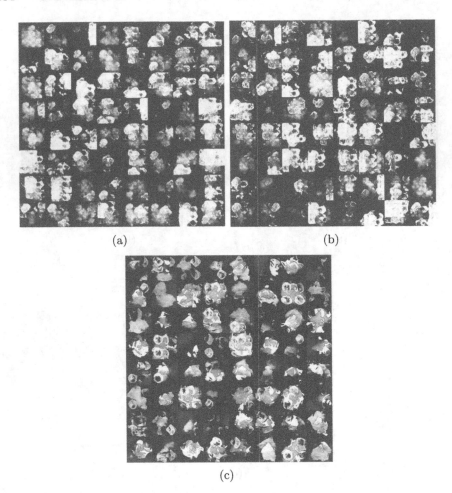

(a)   (b)

(c)

Fig. 5. Image is generated after a) 100 epochs (PSNR = 22.04 dB), b) 120 epochs (PSNR = 22.09 dB), and c) 200 epochs (PSNR = 22.28 dB).

2. Case 2: Results with dataset in [2]

For the dataset [2,3], we select the input images that is similar to our dataset as shown in Fig. 7.

We implemented an image generation model for data in [2,3]. The results are shown in Figs. 8 and 9.

For evaluating [3], we use Keras with 800 images on **Kaggle** [2]. The results of image production are shown in Fig. 9.

We realize that training phase takes a lot of time and independs on epochs. Algorithm in [3] shows sketched pokemon images after 45 epochs. However, the training time in [3] is equal to [2] with 150 epochs.

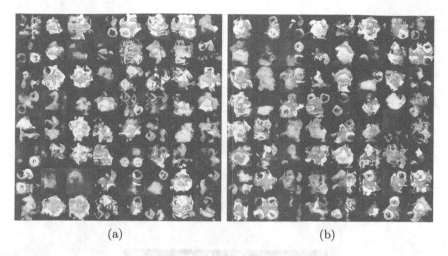

(a)   (b)

Fig. 6. Image is generated after 500 epochs for a) first time (PSNR = 22.22 dB) and b) second time (PSNR = 22.31 dB).

Besides, we also evaluate the image quality after generating by DCGAN model comparing to other methods. The peak signal-to-noise ratio (PSNR) (dB) is determined by:

$$PSNR = 10 \log \left(\frac{MAX_I{}^2}{MSE} \right),$$
$$MSE = \frac{1}{M \times N} \sum_{i=0}^{M} \sum_{j=0}^{N} [I(i,j) - K(i,j)]^2, \tag{6}$$

Fig. 7. Result of image with **Kaggle** dataset (PSNR = 21.42 dB).

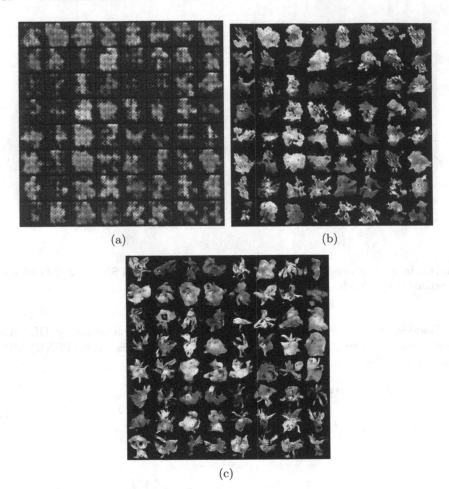

(a)   (b)

(c)

Fig. 8. Image [2] is generated after a) 50 epochs (PSNR = 21.42 dB), b) 150 epochs (PSNR = 20.78 dB), and c) 3700 epochs (PSNR = 22.76 dB).

where MAX_I is the maximum possible pixel value of image. When the pixels are represented using 8 bits per sample, it is 255. When samples are represented using linear with B bits per sample, MAXI is 2^B 1.

The results are shown in Table 1. We find that the image quality in our method is equivalent to [3] and [2] while the number of epochs is less.

Table 1. Comparing the quality of generating images with other methods.

Method	Number of epochs	PSNR (dB)
Our method	10	22.8682
Our method	20	22.0988
Our method	30	21.9611
Our method	100	22.0432
Our method	120	22.0924
Our method	200	22.2887
Our method	500	22.2205
Our method	500	22.3139
[2]	50	21.4202
[2]	150	20.7828
[2]	3700	20.7636
[3]	45	21.1261

Fig. 9. Image is generated after 45 epochs [3] (PSNR = 22.12 dB).

5   Conclusion

The paper focuses on the construction and improves the quality of cartoon characters while reducing the training time. In each step, we present the fundamental theory that is applied for proposal model. The results show that the proposal model not only improves the accuracy of the image with 21 dB but also reduces the execution time to less than a week (with transposed convolution up to *stride* =

2, $kernel = 3$ and size of image from $64 \times 64 \times 32$ to $128 \times 128 \times 3$). However, the quality of images is not good in several cases. Therefore, we will perform the steps in the next direction to

- optimize processing time,
- improve the accuracy of image output [14],
- building CNN models for evaluating images,
- develop a model of real images based on [11–13],

in order to improve the quality of image while optimizing the collecting data.

References

1. Cao, Y., et al.: Recent advances of generative adversarial networks in computer vision. IEEE Access **7**, 14985–15006 (2019)
2. Folkman, T.: How To create unique Pokéumon using GANs (2020). https://towardsdatascience.com/how-to-create-unique-pok. Accessed 4 Aug 2020
3. Ghanashyam: PokeGAN - a tf.keras implementation of deep convolutional generative adversarial networks (2020). https://github.com/ghanashyamvtatti/PokeGAN. Accessed 4 Aug 2020
4. Goodfellow, I.: NIPS 2016 tutorial: generative adversarial networks (2016)
5. Jaiswal, D.P., Kumar, S., Badr, Y.: Towards an artificial intelligence aided design approach: application to anime faces with generative adversarial networks. Procedia Comput. Sci. **168**, 57–64 (2020)
6. Kim, T.: carpedm20/DCGAN-tensorflow (2020). https://github.com/carpedm20/DCGAN-tensorflow. Accessed 4 Aug 2020
7. Langr, J., Bok, V.: GANs in Action: Deep Learning with Generative Adversarial Networks. Manning Publications, Shelter Island (2019)
8. Liu, B., Tan, C., Li, S., He, J., Wang, H.: A data augmentation method based on generative adversarial networks for grape leaf disease identification. IEEE Access **8**, 102188–102198 (2020)
9. Liu, X., Xie, C., Kuang, H., Ma, X.: Face aging simulation with deep convolutional generative adversarial networks. In: 2018 10th International Conference on Measuring Technology and Mechatronics Automation (ICMTMA), pp. 220–224 (2018)
10. Mehralian, M., Karasfi, B.: RDCGAN: unsupervised representation learning with regularized deep convolutional generative adversarial networks. In: 2018 9th Conference on Artificial Intelligence and Robotics and 2nd Asia-Pacific International Symposium, pp. 31–38 (2018)
11. Phat, N.H., Minh, Q.T., The, H.L.: An ANN-based gesture recognition algorithm for smart-home applications. KSII Trans. Internet Inf. Syst. **14**(5), 1967–1983 (2020)
12. Phat, N.H., The, H.L.: Proposing recognition algorithms for hand gestures based on machine learning model. In: 2019 19th International Symposium on Communications and Information Technologies (ISCIT), pp. 496–501 (2019)
13. Phat, N.H., Thu, H.N.T.: Proposal gesture recognition algorithm combining CNN for health monitoring. In: 2019 6th NAFOSTED Conference on Information and Computer Science (NICS), pp. 209–213 (2019)

14. Phat, N.H., Vinh, T.Q., Miyoshi, T.: Video compression schemes using edge feature on wireless video sensor networks. J. Electr. Comput. Eng. **2012** (2012). https://doi.org/10.1155/2012/421307
15. Radford, A., Metz, L., Chintala, S.: Unsupervised representation learning with deep convolutional generative adversarial networks (November 2015)
16. Roohi, A., Sheikhfaal, S., Angizi, S., Fan, D., DeMara, R.F.: ApGAN: approximate GAN for robust low energy learning from imprecise components. IEEE Trans. Comput. **69**(3), 349–360 (2020)
17. Yin, L.: DCGAN (2017). https://medium.com/@liyin2015/dcgan-79af14a1c247. Accessed 4 Aug 2020
18. Zhao, J., Xie, X., Wang, L., Cao, M., Zhang, M.: Generating photographic faces from the sketch guided by attribute using GAN. IEEE Access **7**, 23844–23851 (2019)

Feature Selection Using Local Interpretable Model-Agnostic Explanations on Metagenomic Data

Nguyen Thanh-Hai[1]([⊠]), Toan Bao Tran[2,3], An Cong Tran[1], and Nguyen Thai-Nghe[1]

[1] College of Information and Communication Technology, Can Tho University, Can Tho 900100, Vietnam
{nthai,tcan,ntnghe}@cit.ctu.edu.vn
[2] Center of Software Engineering, Duy Tan University, Da Nang 550000, Vietnam
tranbaotoan@dtu.edu.vn
[3] Institute of Research and Development, Duy Tan University, Da Nang 550000, Vietnam

Abstract. Metagenomics is one of the emerging concepts in personalized medicine approaches to take care of and improve human health. Numerous studies have revealed that metagenomic data can associate with a vast of human diseases. Recent advancements in machine learning techniques and computation resources enable us to speed up the data processing and also improve the performance in diagnosis accuracy. However, we face difficulties to process metagenomic data due to its complexities and high dimension. This work proposes an approach based on an explanation model to perform feature selection tasks. The proposed approach selects a small set of features from the original features with Interpretable Model-agnostic Explanations that can obtain better performances than feature selection based on importance scores generated from a robust learning machine learning such as Random Forests. We are expected that the approach can be an efficient feature selection method compared to classic feature selection techniques.

Keywords: Feature selection · Explanation · Metagenomic data · Disease prediction · Important features · Machine learning

1 Introduction

Personalized medicine is a medical model that proposes customized health care methods for individuals with medical decisions and medical products are designed based on the patient own genetic information and disease specificity. Based on each genetic map, personalized medicine applies the complex and dedicate diagnosis to achieve a better outcome and appropriate to each patient's genetic characteristics at the molecular level. Several studies indicate that genotype plays an important role and several diseases come from genotypic so this

© Springer Nature Singapore Pte Ltd. 2020
T. K. Dang et al. (Eds.): FDSE 2020, CCIS 1306, pp. 340–357, 2020.
https://doi.org/10.1007/978-981-33-4370-2_24

is an important step towards more effective treatment with fewer side effects. The traditional approach can be considered to a trial and error problem, the physicians make the most possible diagnosis and select the treatment based on the medical record, the symptoms, and the demographic. If the treatment is ineffective or has side effects, the physicians may change medicine instead and the cycle repeats until the desired cure effect is achieved. Whereas, the personalized medicine can easily propose a treatment regimen for patients with several criteria: right treatments, right person, right time and ensure the desired outcome. The authors in [1,2] stated that the microbial communities play an important role on human health and diseases, it also can be considered as a part of personalized medicine.

Metagenomics is the science of genetic material and used increasingly for research in personalized medicine approaches to improve the performance of health care protection. Recently, the experts conducted RNA sequencing to extract the first genome sequence of *SARS-CoV-2* [3]. Providing information about the evolutionary history of species is one of the advantages of metagenomics data. The studies in [4,5] explore several communities of microbial in the natural habitats and their contributions. Furthermore, the investigation of 16rRNA sequences from the undefined microorganisms discovered the vast new communities of microbial [6–8]. The communities of microbial are truly important to human health care, a lot of studies about microbiomes have been attracted numerous researchers to carry out the influence of biological communities in the human body. Several studies present the importance of metagenomics data in discovering microbes and viruses on earth. They evolve rapidly and with a massive majority of undetected microbes, the detection of them still challenge.

In this study, we consider using the Random Forest model [9] combining with model-agnostic for features extraction and investigate the performance on four datasets. Our contributions include:

- We use the Random Forest model to classify the colorectal cancer diseases and leverage the learned model for feature extraction on the original datasets with high dimensionality.
- We exploit the advantages of Local Interpretable Model-agnostic Explanations (LIME) [10] to screening the most important features on one dataset and use them for predicting the rest.
- The performance of the proposed method is investigated in several tasks. By comparing the performance of the proposed feature selection approach with features are selected randomly and the important features extracted from Random Forest. We also compare the performance of our method on the considered datasets.

In the rest of this study, the related studies are introduced in Sect. 2. We present the information on considered datasets in Sect. 3. The learning model and feature selection approach are described in Sect. 4. Our experimental results are presented in Accuracy, Area Under the Curve (AUC), and Matthews correlation coefficient (MCC) in Sect. 5. Section 6 conducts some closing remarks for the work.

Table 1. The further information on four considered datasets related to Colorectal Cancer in [16–18], and [19].

Dataset	Factors	Healthy samples	Patients	Total	Features
Feng	No. of samples	63	46	109	1981
	Average age	67.1	67.1	-	
	Gender	Male: 37	Male: 28	65	
		Female: 26	Female: 18	44	
Vogtmann	No. of samples	52	48	100	1976
	Average age	61.23	60.96	-	
	Gender	Male: 37	Male: 35	72	
		Female: 15	Female: 13	28	
Yu	No. of samples	92	73	165	1932
	Average age	58.51	65.90	-	
	Gender	Male: 51	Male: 47	98	
		Female: 41	Female: 26	67	
Zeller	No. of samples	64	88	152	1980
	Average age	58.75	68.44	-	
	Gender	Male: 32	Male: 53	85	
		Female: 32	Female: 35	67	

2   Related Work

The authors in [11] present a deep learning framework, namely Seeker for recognizing the phages in sequence datasets and cleaning the distinction of phage sequences. They supposed the existing approaches based on the similarity of bacteriophage sequences and obstructing the detection of bacteriophage families. The performance of unknown phages detection has been demonstrated the ability to identify the undetected phages from known phage families. The study [12] presented the advance of metagenomics data in identifying viruses via deep learning. The training data are collected from viral RefSeq and the performance is better in comparison with the state-of-the-art methods. The accuracy of underrepresented viral detection can be improved by using millions of viral sequences from metavirome samples. The authors also applied the proposed method on human gut metagenomic samples and detected vast viral sequences belonging to patients with colorectal carcinoma.

Identifying the viral genomes from representative of viral or viral and bacterial communities is the advantages of virMine [13]. The proposed approach can help the researchers seek their interest easily. The insufficient representation of viral variety in public data repositories is not the limitation of virMine like the alternative viral genome detection tools. Firstly, the non-viral sequences are

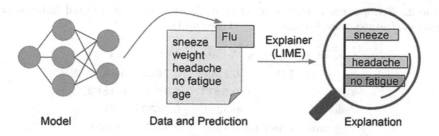

Fig. 1. Example of using LIME for explaining individual predictions [20].

removed and applying an iterative approach for identifying the viral genomes. Hence, the detection of related characterized viruses, novel species, eukaryotic viruses, and bacteriophages would be easier. The virMine is investigated the performance from three different habitats of microbial, namely the gut microbiota, the urinary microbiota, and freshwater viromes.

The authors in [14] presented the effective approach for feature selection with machine learning models based on the Amazon Fine Food Reviews dataset. The results revealed the effectiveness of the Gradient Boosting Trees and Random Forest model in extracting the meaning features from the dataset. Furthermore, the extracted features can be used for several classification tasks with promising results. The study [15] presented an approach for prediction based on the Random Forest model, maximum relevance minimum redundancy method, and incremental feature selection. The authors state that the results are significant in comparison with the existing prediction tools.

3   Dataset Benchmark

We investigated the performance on four metagenomic sequencing sequences datasets related to Colorectal Cancer from four cohorts namely Feng [16], Vogtmann [17], Yu [18], and Zeller [19]. The data were collected from 2014 to 2016 with a total of 255 patients and 271 healthy individuals. The further information are presented in Table 1. In specific, the Feng dataset contains 109 samples with 46 patients, Vogtmann includes 52 healthy individuals and 48 patients. Yu and Zeller datasets have more samples than the others, Yu and Zeller consist of 92, 64 Non-CRC patients, and 73, 88 CRC patients respectively. Four datasets are high dimensional, the Feng dataset dimension is of 109 × 1981, Vogtmann of 100 × 1976, 165 × 1932 and 152 × 1980 of Yu and Zeller datasets respectively.

Table 2. Performance of feature selection by LIME, randomly selected features, and important features from Random Forest based on Feng dataset.

Dataset	Features	Accuracy	AUC	MCC
Vogtmann	LIME	0.5189	**0.5623**	0.0321
Yu		**0.5811**	0.5925	**0.1882**
Zeller		0.5222	**0.5653**	0.0554
Vogtmann	Random	0.4200	0.4016	−0.1651
Yu		0.4027	0.4343	−0.2083
Zeller		0.4763	0.4560	−0.0511
Vogtmann	RF	**0.5400**	0.5595	**0.1022**
Yu		0.5600	**0.6193**	0.1189
Zeller		**0.5400**	0.4996	**0.0893**

Table 3. Performance of feature selection by LIME, randomly selected features, and important features from Random Forest based on the Vogtmann dataset.

Dataset	Features	Accuracy	AUC	MCC
Feng	LIME	**0.6000**	**0.5983**	**0.0773**
Yu		**0.5777**	**0.5119**	**0.0744**
Zeller		**0.6222**	**0.6425**	**0.2601**
Feng	Random	0.4200	0.4054	−0.2561
Yu		0.4800	0.3738	−0.0978
Zeller		0.4700	0.4613	−0.0771
Feng	RF	0.5000	0.4571	−0.0386
Yu		0.4700	0.4727	−0.0601
Zeller		0.5100	0.4772	−0.0219

The feature reveals species abundance which shows a proportion of speces bacterial in human gut of each sample. Total abundance of all features in the same sample is sum up to 1 which is exhibited by the formula as followings (Eq. 1):

$$\sum_{i=1}^{k} f_i = 1 \tag{1}$$

With:

- k is the number of features for a sample.
- f_i is the value of the i-th feature.

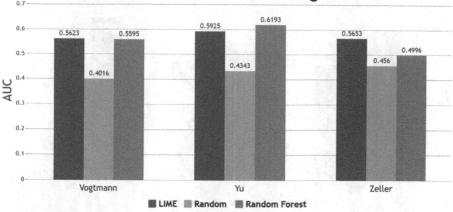

Fig. 2. Visualization of validation AUC of feature selection with LIME, random feature selection, and important feature selection with Random Forest method performed on Feng dataset. Y-axis shows the AUC of each method.

Algorithm 1. Algorithm for feature selection based on LIME method

Input:

- *model*: the learning model which trained on the considered datasets.
- *samples*: the samples on the considered datasets.

Output:

- *L*: an array containing a list of top 10 important features from all samples.

Begin

 Loop on whole samples:

 . Using LIME and *model* to generate the explanation for a prediction on each sample. The explanation contains the weight for each features on sample.

 . Rearrange the features based on the weight from LIME by the highest weight.

 . Select top 10 features and push to *L*.

 . Loop until the last sample.

 Return *L*

End

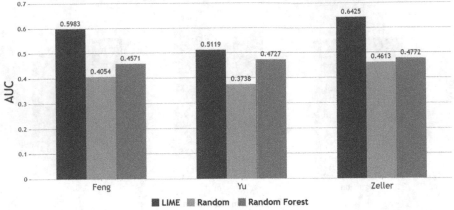

Fig. 3. Visualization of validation AUC of feature selection with LIME, random feature selection, and important feature selection with Random Forest method based on Vogtmann dataset. Y-axis shows the AUC of each method.

4 Feature Selection Based on Important Features Extracted from LIME

4.1 Learning Model

To investigate the performance of the Random Forest model on metagenomic datasets, we implemented the learning model with 500 trees, the maximum depth of each tree is 4, and measured the tree classifier quality with Gini impurity. Gini impurity is a measure of the frequency of choosing elements randomly from the labeled set incorrectly based on the distribution of labels in the subset. Furthermore, in the training section, we can compute the contribution of each feature that decreases the weighted impurity and obtain the feature importance of the sample.

We trained the learning model on 10-folds cross-validation and evaluated the error by Accuracy, AUC, and MCC. The best model is explained by LIME for effective feature selection. The Accuracy and MCC can be computed by the Eq. 2 and Eq. 3. The range value of both ACC and AUC is from 0 to 1 which higher is better. Whereas MCC is from -1 to $+1$, $+1$ represents for a good classifier, 0 means the model makes predictions randomly, and -1 denotes the disagreement between observations and predictions.

$$ACC = \frac{TN + TP}{TP + FN + TN + FP} \tag{2}$$

$$MCC = \frac{TP \times TN - FP \times FN}{\sqrt{(TP + FP)(TN + FP)(TP + FN)(TN + FN)}} \tag{3}$$

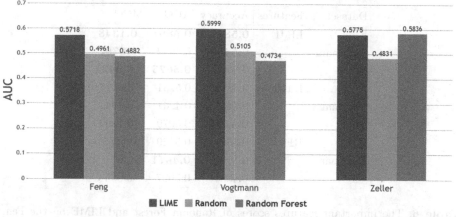

Fig. 4. Visualization of validation AUC of feature selection with LIME, random feature selection, and important feature selection with Random Forest method based on Yu dataset. Y-axis shows the AUC of each method.

Where

- FP stands for False Positive.
- FN stands for False Negative.
- TP stands for True Positive.
- TN stands for True Negative.

Table 4. Performance of feature selection by LIME, randomly selected features, and important features from Random Forest based on Yu dataset.

Dataset	Features	Accuracy	AUC	MCC
Feng	LIME	**0.5611**	**0.5718**	**0.1096**
Vogtmann		**0.5300**	**0.5999**	**0.0901**
Zeller		0.5088	0.5775	0.0349
Feng	Random	0.4199	0.4961	−0.0762
Vogtmann		0.4502	0.5105	−0.1272
Zeller		0.5439	0.4831	−0.0333
Feng	RF	0.4564	0.4882	−0.1632
Vogtmann		0.4702	0.4734	−0.0413
Zeller		**0.5858**	**0.5836**	**0.1363**

Table 5. Performance of feature selection by LIME, randomly selected features, and important features from Random Forest based on Zeller dataset.

Dataset	Features	Accuracy	AUC	MCC
Feng	LIME	**0.5811**	**0.5861**	**0.1348**
Vogtmann		**0.5400**	0.4932	**0.0792**
Yu		0.5065	**0.5625**	−0.0423
Feng	Random	0.4854	0.5251	−0.0118
Vogtmann		0.4401	0.4241	−0.1942
Yu		**0.5391**	0.5079	−0.1293
Feng	RF	0.5681	0.5129	0.0863
Vogtmann		0.4901	**0.4971**	−0.011
Yu		0.4801	0.5027	−0.055

Table 6. The important features scores of Random Forest and LIME on the Feng dataset.

Selected features by RF	Score	Selected features by LIME	Score
Otu0918	0.0208	Otu0307	0.2179
Otu0781	0.0181	Otu0309	0.2059
Otu0302	0.0175	Otu0918	0.1768
Otu0307	0.0136	Otu0302	0.1292
Otu0808	0.0120	Otu0308	0.1133
Otu0296	0.0113	Otu0310	0.1131
Otu0310	0.0111	Otu0915	0.1011
Otu0826	0.0099	Otu0306	0.0824
Otu0822	0.0098	Otu0238	0.0571
Otu0821	0.0094	Otu1113	0.0515

4.2 Feature Selection Approach with LIME

Local interpretable model-agnostic explanations (LIME) is a model-agnostic and can be applied by machine learning models. The main purpose of LIME is to focus on explaining individual predictions. In other words, LIME attempts to discover the model by perturbing the input samples and observe the changing of predictions. LIME also explains on a sample which features are important and contributed the most to the output. An explanation is created by approximating the underlying model locally by a machine learning model. In this study, we used Random Forest. Figure 1 visualized an example of using LIME for explaining the individual's prediction. In Fig. 1, the model predicts a patent has gotten the flu, and LIME focuses attention on the most important symptoms.

As mentioned above, we used four datasets to investigate the performance of this study. The feature selection is summarized in Algorithm 1. We selected

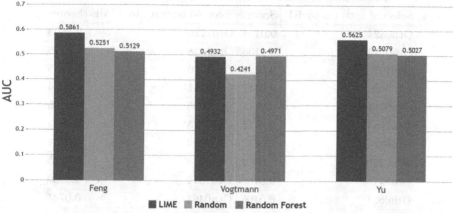

Fig. 5. Visualization of validation AUC of feature selection with LIME, random feature selection, and important feature selection with Random Forest method based on Zeller dataset. Y-axis shows the AUC of each method.

features on a specific dataset and used those features to predict the rest. On each dataset, we selected only 10 the most important features from thousands of original features. It could consider being a dimensionality reduction method effectively. For instance, we applied the LIME method on the Feng dataset and selected the most important features of the Feng. Then, used Feng's features to make predictions on Vogtmann, Yu, and Zeller. We repeated the feature selection progress on four datasets.

5 Experimental Results

We investigated the performance of the proposed method on several tasks on 10-fold cross-validation. We also compared the performance of selected features by LIME, randomly selected features, and important features from Random Forest by computing the average accuracy, AUC, and MCC.

In addition, we also revealed the important features score of each dataset extracted using the LIME and Random Forest models. The important scores comparison of Random Forest and LIME on Feng, Viogtmann, Yu, and Zeller datasets are presented in Table 6, Table 7, Table 8, and Table 9 respectively. We also visualized the important score in Fig. 6, Fig. 7, Fig. 8, and Fig. 9.

Table 7. The important features scores of Random Forest and LIME on the Vogtmann dataset.

Selected features by RF	Score	Selected features by LIME	Score
Otu0824	0.0154	Otu1116	0.1503
Otu0772	0.0135	Otu1138	0.1176
Otu1978	0.0127	Otu1680	0.1145
Otu0825	0.0117	Otu0111	0.0974
Otu0771	0.0117	Otu0995	0.0905
Otu1581	0.0116	Otu1113	0.0862
Otu0780	0.0113	Otu1859	0.0832
Otu0270	0.0112	Otu1938	0.0775
Otu0918	0.0109	Otu1612	0.0759
Otu0821	0.0106	Otu0464	0.0741

Table 8. The important features scores of Random Forest and LIME on the Yu dataset.

Selected features by RF	Score	Selected features by LIME	Score
Otu0291	0.0188	Otu0479	0.2246
Otu0858	0.0154	Otu0586	0.1188
Otu0849	0.0141	Otu1961	0.1051
Otu0826	0.0139	Otu0217	0.1038
Otu0795	0.0138	Otu1855	0.0967
Otu0817	0.0129	Otu1859	0.0845
Otu0808	0.0112	Otu1903	0.0834
Otu0314	0.0107	Otu0777	0.0754
Otu0915	0.0105	Otu1776	0.0706
Otu0821	0.0104	Otu0552	0.0689

5.1 The Performance of Feng Features on Vogtmann, Yu and Zeller Datasets

We presented the comparison between our selected features by the LIME method with randomly selected features and important features from Random Forest based on the Feng dataset. Table 2 contains 3 main contents. The Accuracy, AUC, and MCC of Vogtmann, Yu, and Zeller dataset with selected features by the LIME method is presented in the first row. The second and last row exhibits the performance of randomly selected features and important features from Random Forest respectively.

The selected features by LIME on the Feng dataset exhibits good performance in comparing with randomly selected features and important features by Random Forest. The Accuracy and MCC are good on the Yu dataset, whereas the AUC outperforms on both Vogtmann and Zeller datasets with 0.5623 and 0.5653 respectively. The visualization of the comparison between the AUC of each method is presented in Fig. 2. Otherwise, on both Vogtmann and Zeller datasets, the Random Forest selected features effectively. The Accuracy and MCC are better than features by LIME. The randomly selected features do not lead to good performance results, both Accuracy and AUC are under 0.5 and MCC are negative.

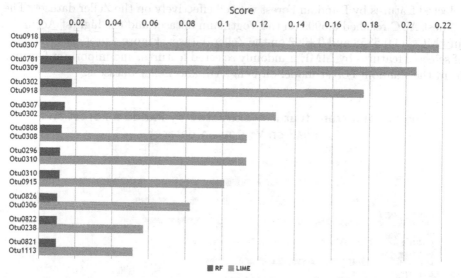

Fig. 6. Visualization of the important scores extracted by Random Forest and LME on the Feng dataset. Y-axis shows the name of the feature.

5.2   The Performance of Vogtmann Features on Feng, Yu and Zeller Datasets

We also presented a comparison of the performance of 3 feature selection methods in Table 3. The features are selected on the Vogtmann dataset and made predictions on Feng, Yu, and Zeller dataset. As observed from the results, the feature selection with LIME outperforms the others on three datasets. Furthermore, the performance of randomly selected features is still not good in comparison with the other methods. In specific, the accuracy on Feng, Yu, and Zeller of

0.6, 0.5777, and 0.6222 respectively. The highest AUC of 0.6425 on the Zeller dataset, whereas Feng and Yu reached 0.5983 and 0.5119. Furthermore, the MCC on Zeller is also good in comparison with the others. Generally, the selected features by LIME from Vogtmann show a good performance on the Zeller dataset. We also presented the AUC of three methods in Fig. 3.

5.3 The Performance of Yu Features on Feng, Vogtmann and Zeller Datasets

To investigate the performance of the selected features by LIME from Yu on the Feng, Vogtmann, and Zeller datasets, we computed the Accuracy, AUC, and MCC and compared with the randomly selected features and important features from Random Forest. Table 4 demonstrated the good performance of selected features by LIME on 2 out 3 datasets, namely Feng and Vogtmann, whereas the selected features by Random Forest worked effectively on the Zeller dataset. The highest AUC reached 0.5999 on the Vogtmann dataset and the highest Accuracy and MCC of 0.5858 and 0.1363 on the Zeller dataset. Figure 4 proposed the AUC of selected features by LIME, randomly selected features, and important features from the Random Forest model on Feng, Yu, and Zeller datasets.

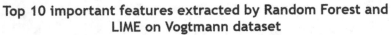

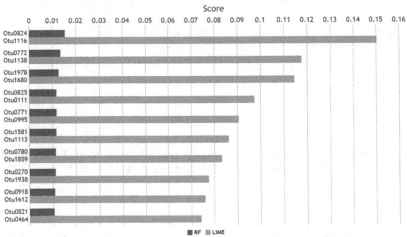

Fig. 7. Visualization of the important scores extracted by Random Forest and LIME on the Vogtmann dataset. Y-axis shows the name of the feature.

Table 9. The important features scores of Random Forest and LIME on the Zeller dataset.

Selected features by RF	Score	Selected features by LIME	Score
Otu0029	0.0241	Otu1612	0.0838
Otu0772	0.0201	Otu0915	0.0792
Otu0915	0.0161	Otu0302	0.0729
Otu0849	0.0156	Otu1129	0.0599
Otu0030	0.0146	Otu0918	0.0576
Otu0918	0.0134	Otu1879	0.0497
Otu0827	0.0133	Otu1777	0.0432
Otu0768	0.0126	Otu1706	0.0417
Otu0035	0.0123	Otu0639	0.0414
Otu0302	0.0122	Otu1178	0.0409

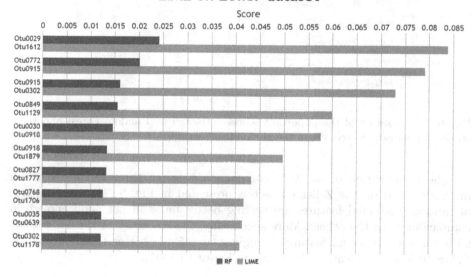

Fig. 8. Visualization of the important scores extracted by Random Forest and LME on the Zeller dataset. Y-axis shows the name of the feature.

5.4 The Performance of Zeller Features on Feng, Vogtmann, and Yu Datasets

The performance of selected features from the Zeller dataset are presented in Table 5. We applied the selected features on three other datasets, namely Feng, Vogtmann, and Yu. We also computed the Accuracy, AUC, and MCC for comparison. The selected features on the Zeller dataset carry out the same performance in comparison with the Vogtmann dataset. The Accuracy, MCC of selected features by LIME outperforms the random and important features from Random Forest. The AUC of Feng and Yu datasets are higher than the others and the AUC of Vogtmann is also close, 0.4932 of LIME features with 0.4971 of Random Forest features. Furthermore, the Feng dataset has the highest Accuracy, AUC, and MCC of 0.5811, 0.5861, and 0.1348.

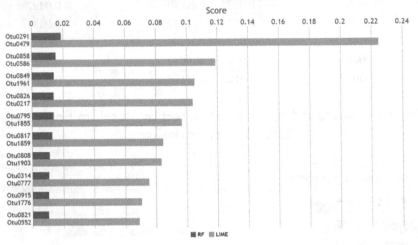

Fig. 9. Visualization of the important scores extracted by Random Forest and LME on the Yu dataset. Y-axis shows the name of the feature.

The visualization of an AUC comparison between three feature selection methods based on the Zeller dataset is presented in Fig. 5. The performance of randomly selected features are getting better but still not good enough in comparison with the others. More specifically, the Accuracy of the Yu dataset with randomly selected features is highest at 0.5391, better than features by LIME (0.5065) and features by Random Forest (0.4801).

5.5   The Comparison Between Original Dataset and LIME Method

We presented the Validation Accuracy of four original datasets which are Feng, Vogtmann, Yu, and Zeller in Fig. 10. The performance on the Feng dataset with original features is higher than the selected features by LIME, which is 0.7073 and 0.6511 respectively. The Vogtmann performance is quite lower in comparison with Feng. In specific, the accuracy obtained 0.6 and 0.5222. On the Yu dataset, the performance on original features and selected features by LIME is quite close, 0.6375, and 0.6067. The performance of selected features by LIME on the Zeller dataset reached 0.545 whereas 0.7762 of original features.

In general, the difference is not significant on Feng, Vogtmann, and Yu datasets with 0.0562, 0.0778, and 0.0308 respectively. The difference in the Zeller dataset is quite significant at 0.2313.

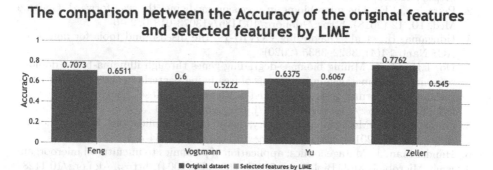

Fig. 10. Visualization of validation Accuracy four original dataset in comparison with selected features by LIME. The Y-axis shows the Accuracy of each method on specific datasets.

5.6   Discussion

In general, the proposed feature selection approach gives a better performance than the Random Forest method and can be considered as an effective dimensionality reduction technique on the metagenomic datasets. The selected features by LIME on the Vogtmann dataset work well on the other datasets and the performance is better in comparison with randomly selected features and important features from Random Forest. Furthermore, the performance of the selected features is also close in comparison with the original datasets.

6   Conclusion

We introduced a feature selection approach based on an explanation model with local interpretable model-agnostic explanations. The features were selected from one dataset, then these features are used for classification tasks on other datasets to evaluate the efficient on the chosen set of features. As revealed from the obtained results, the sets of selected attributes from the original features can achieve comparative performances comparing to the feature selection method using robust machine learning such as Random Forests.

Further studies can work on various data types to examine and select an optimal set of features for classification tasks.

References

1. Gilbert, J.A., Quinn, R.A., Debelius, J., et al.: Microbiome-wide association studies link dynamic microbial consortia to disease. Nature **535**(7610), 94–103 (2016). https://doi.org/10.1038/nature18850
2. Petrosino, J.F.: The microbiome in precision medicine: the way forward. Genome Med. **10**, 12 (2018). https://doi.org/10.1186/s13073-018-0525-6
3. Udugama, B., et al.: Diagnosing COVID-19: the disease and tools for detection. ACS Nano **14**(4), 3822–3835 (2020)
4. Do, T.H., et al.: Mining biomass-degrading genes through illumina-based de novo sequencing and metagenomic analysis of free-living bacteria in the gut of the lower termite Coptotermes gestroi harvested in Vietnam. J. Biosci. Bioeng. **118**(6), 665–671 (2014). https://doi.org/10.1016/j.jbiosc.2014.05.010
5. Chroneos, Z.C.: Metagenomics: theory, methods, and applications. Hum. Genomics **4**(4), 282–283 (2010). https://doi.org/10.1186/1479-7364-4-4-282
6. Handelsman, J.: Metagenomics: application of genomics to uncultured microorganisms. Microbiol. Mol. Biol. Rev. **68**(4), 669–685 (2004). https://doi.org/10.1128/MMBR.68.4.669-685.2004
7. Ma, B., France, M., Ravel, J.: Meta-pangenome: at the crossroad of pangenomics and metagenomics. Pangenome **205**, 205–218 (2020). https://doi.org/10.1007/978-3-030-38281-0_9
8. Jang, S.J., Ho, P.T., Jun, S.Y., Kim, D., Won, Y.J.: Dataset supporting description of the new mussel species of genus Gigantidas (Bivalvia: Mytilidae) and metagenomic data of bacterial community in the host mussel gill tissue. Data Brief **2020**(30), 105651 (2020). https://doi.org/10.1016/j.dib.2020.105651
9. Breiman, L.: Random forests. Mach. Learn. **45**(1), 5–32 (2001). https://doi.org/10.1023/A:1010933404324
10. Ribeiro, M.T., Singh, S., Guestrin, C.: Why should i trust you?: Explaining the predictions of any classifier. In: Proceedings of the 22nd ACM SIGKDD International Conference on Knowledge Discovery and Data Mining, 2016, pp. 1135–1144. ACM (2016)
11. Auslander, N., et al.: Seeker: alignment-free identification of bacteriophage genomes by deep learning. bioRxiv (2020). https://doi.org/10.1101/2020.04.04.025783
12. Ren, J., et al.: Identifying viruses from metagenomic data using deep learning. Quant. Biol. **8**(1), 64–77 (2020). https://doi.org/10.1007/s40484-019-0187-4
13. Garretto, A., Hatzopoulos, T., Putonti, C.: virMine: automated detection of viral sequences from complex metagenomic samples. PeerJ **7**, e6695 (2019). https://doi.org/10.7717/peerj.6695
14. Tran, P.Q., Trieu, N.T., Dao, N.V., Nguyen, H.T., Huynh, H.X.: Effective opinion words extraction for food reviews classification. Int. J. Adv. Comput. Sci. Appl. (IJACSA) **11**(7), 421–426 (2020). https://doi.org/10.14569/IJACSA.2020.0110755
15. Li, B.Q., Cai, Y.D., Feng, K.Y., Zhao, G.J.: Prediction of protein cleavage site with feature selection by random forest. PLoS One **7**(9), e45854 (2012). https://doi.org/10.1371/journal.pone.0045854
16. Feng, Q., et al.: Gut microbiome development along the colorectal adenoma-carcinoma sequence. Nat. Commun. **11**(6), 6528 (2015). https://doi.org/10.1038/ncomms7528. PMID: 25758642
17. Vogtmann, E., et al.: Colorectal cancer and the human gut microbiome: reproducibility with whole-genome shotgun sequencing. PLoS One **11**(5), e0155362 (2016). https://doi.org/10.1371/journal.pone.0155362. PMID: 27171425; PMCID: PMC4865240

18. Yu, J., et al.: Metagenomic analysis of faecal microbiome as a tool towards targeted non-invasive biomarkers for colorectal cancer. Gut **66**(1), 70–78 (2015). https://doi.org/10.1136/gutjnl-2015-309800. PMID: 26408641
19. Zeller, G., et al.: Potential of fecal microbiota for early-stage detection of colorectal cancer. Mol. Syst. Biol. **10**(11), 766 (2014). https://doi.org/10.15252/msb.20145645. PMID: 25432777; PMCID: PMC4299606
20. Ribeiro, M., Singh, S., Guestrin, C.: Local Interpretable Model-Agnostic Explanations (LIME): An Introduction. O'Reilly Media, Newton (2016). https://www.oreilly.com/

ORB for Detecting Copy-Move Regions with Scale and Rotation in Image Forensics

Kha-Tu Huynh[1,2(✉)], Tu-Nga Ly[1,2], and Thuong Le-Tien[3]

[1] International University, Ho Chi Minh City, Vietnam
{hktu, ltnga}@hcmiu.edu.vn
[2] Vietnam National University, Ho Chi Minh City, Vietnam
[3] University of Technology, Ho Chi Minh City, Vietnam
thuongle@hcmut.edu.vn

Abstract. The paper proposes a method to detect the forged regions in image using the Oriented FAST and Rotated BRIEF (ORB). In many previous researches in the field of copy-move forgery detection, algorithms mainly focus on objects or parts which are copied, moved and pasted in another places in the same image with the same size of the original parts or included the rotation sometimes, but the copied regions detection with different scale has not much interested in. By adding an oriented component to FAST and the rotation feature to BRIEF, ORB makes the proposed method more powerful and efficient to detect copy-move regions with both scale and rotation. In addition, the removing non-copied objects by calculating their sharpness improves the accuracy of the detection. The experiment is done on the datasets for copy-move images and some real images with the improved time and high accuracy.

Keywords: ORB (Oriented FAST and rotated BRIEF) · Image forgery detection (IFD) · Key-points · Copy-move forgery · Feature extraction · Feature descriptor

1 Introduction

Nowadays, with the rapid development of image processing softwares, processing and forging images for various purposes are done so perfectly that it is difficult to distinguish whether an image is fake or not by human eyes. According to the Wall Street Journal, at least 10% of all color images published in the US have actually been changed and intervened since 1989. The more diverse softwares develop, the more complicated detections are. The image authentication becomes more challenging if there is no information about the original image.

According to statistics from the IEEE and Science Direct websites, in the past ten years, the number of publications related to blind image forgery detection, generally called image forgery detection (IFD) in which information of the original image is completely unknown, has gradually increased (see Fig. 1). In IFD, the copy-move operation is more popular because that of copying and pasting information on the same image is easier to do but more difficult to detect. If they are copied from another images, many

© Springer Nature Singapore Pte Ltd. 2020
T. K. Dang et al. (Eds.): FDSE 2020, CCIS 1306, pp. 358–372, 2020.
https://doi.org/10.1007/978-981-33-4370-2_25

complicated steps are required to make them smooth and matched. Factually, also the above statistics for IFD, the number of copy-move publications has been a significant number (see Fig. 2).

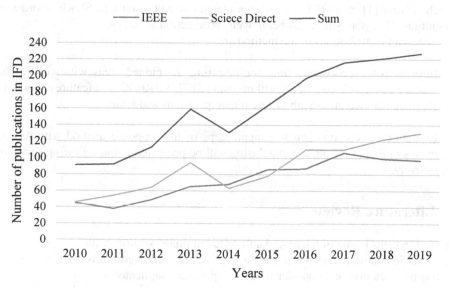

Fig. 1. Publications related to image forgery detection the past 10 years by IEEE and Science Direct. Statistics are performed at the website of IEEE Explore and Science Direct with the keyword "Image Forgery Detection".

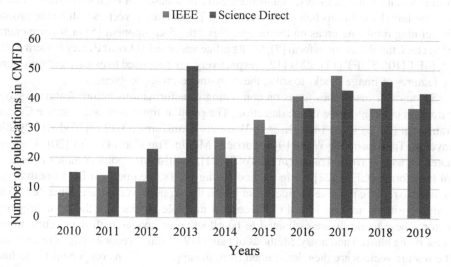

Fig. 2. Publications related to copy-move forgery detection the past 10 years by IEEE and Science Direct. Statistics are performed at the website of IEEE Explore and Science Direct with the keyword "Copy-Move Forgery Detection".

The paper proposes a method of detecting duplicated regions on the same image using ORB in which features extraction is performed by the oriented FAST (oFAST) with the directional element and the features description performed by the rotated BRIEF (rBRIEF) descriptor. The ORB is proved as a faster key-points and matching algorithm which is faster [1] than SIFT two order of magnitude and faster than SURF an order of magnitude ([2, 3])but still keeps being well on detection accuracy.

The main contributions of the method are:

1. Improving the processing time for detecting the cloned areas with/without the rotation compared to some algorithms using SIFT, SURF, ZMs in feature extraction.
2. Detecting copied areas with different manipulations and scales.

Literature review, problem statement, steps of the proposed method with related theories, simulation results and conclusion will be presented in the following sections, respectively.

2   Literature Review

Image forensics is one of the remarkable fields in image security with a lot of research being carried out in recent years. The basic principle of all algorithms is to find regions with similar features and consider if those regions are duplicated.

The first prominent in the field of Copy-Move images is a study by Alin C Popescu and Hany Farid published in a scientific report in the Department of Computer Science at Dartmouth College in 2004 by which demonstrated that PCA was effective in image features extraction. Each feature vector is called the basic component with values obtained from covariance matrix theory, eigenvalues and linear bases for each small image block with the initial conditions being zero-mean [4]. These feature vectors will be the proofs for defining duplicate areas on the image. Next, the 5-component [5] or 9-component [6] vectors, the Radon transform [7], the 8z affine variable [8] Local Binary Pattern-LBP [9], SIFT [10], SUFT [11], ZMs [12], respectively, are proposed to extract and represent the features of image blocks to solve the copy-move image problem.

Some other researches focus on combining transformations before feature vectors extraction in Copy-Move image detection. The popular transforms are Discrete Cosine Transform (DCT) ([13, 14]), Discrete Wavelets Transform (DWT) ([15–18]), Dyadic wavelets Transform (DyWT) [19], Fourrier –Mellin Transform (FMT) [20], Undecimated Dyadic Wavelet Transform (UDWT) [21], multi-radius polar complex exponential transform (PCET) [22], … In methods using DCTs, the quantum DCT coefficients are used to replace the pixels values from which the property vectors are generated. Correlated positions are considered in the case of multiple blocks with the same property vector. These methods are estimated to be effective in images with many copy-move areas, being blurred and noisy. Methods of using DWT aim to reduce image dimensions. The feature vectors are then determined from the approximation component LL to find similar regions. In addition, the identification of regions with different chroma/blur in sub-bands containing high frequency components such as LH, HL and HH is also suggested to identify tampered regions.

Although published techniques can solve the specific requirements, they still have their own limitations, discretely solving for different types of Copy-Move images. Therefore, it is always necessary to build the new or improve algorithms for Copy-Move problems.

3 Problem Statement

In a dataset of images including the original and copy-move images. The requirements of the problem are:

- Identifying copy-move images and locate duplicated areas, and among them, determine what is the area by copying and what is due to the composition of the image. Most of previous methods mainly stopped at the step of identifying similar regions and concluding that the image was copy-move operation intervention.
- Detecting cases of copy-pasting at many positions with many different operations with improved accuracy.

Problem solving:

- Based on the published methods and survey on copy-move image forgery detection, the authors recognize that the algorithms giving good results for the duplicated areas with rotation, scale manipulations have used feature extractions such as ZMs, SIFT and SUFT. Therefore, the author focus on using feature vectors on detecting the copy-move image problems.
- Studying on the algorithms of identifying and extracting features using ORB because this is a new method of feature extraction, outstanding, consistent with the problem.
- Implementing algorithm to extract features and identify similar regions based on ORB. Evaluating the performance of the proposed algorithm and comparing the simulation results with related algorithms in the same image set.
- Implementing the proposed algorithm for images with multiple copy regions with multiple different operations.

4 Proposed Algorithm

With a given image, the proposed method extracts key-points using oriented FAST (oFAST). That of adding a directional element to this step aims to enhance the orientation functionality in feature extraction because FAST itself cannot define the directional property. These key-points then identify binary features vectors and are described by rotated BRIEF (rBRIEF) descriptor. Regions with the same feature vectors will be detected using K-means clustering and the suspicious copied parts are defined.

However, for images on which there are many similar objects not being due to duplicated manipulations but by nature of the image, a question is "Among the suspicious regions detected above, how to determine whether the region is the replication or the inherent natural area of the image". If this problem is solved, the accuracy of the detection will be improved. Therefore, the paper proposes an algorithm to improve the accuracy based on the sharpness estimation at the corresponding positions of the suspicious regions at the HH sub-band of the image at which the high frequency components are concentrated. The fact that the sharpness of the edges at the pasted positions will be higher than that belonging to the composition of the image will support to remove the not-copied regions.

All steps of the proposed algorithm are shown in Fig. 3.

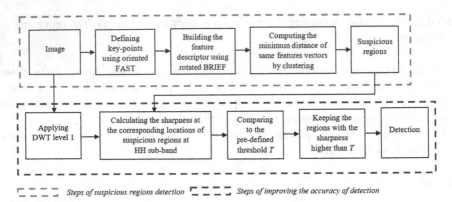

Fig. 3. Proposed algorithm (Color figure online)

4.1 ORB in Detecting Key-Points and Matching Image Regions

ORB is built on the combination of oriented FAST and oriented BRIEF. Compare to the related feature extraction such as SIFT and SURF, ORB is considered as a good alternative [2].

The oFAST Feature Points. Pixel i is defined as key-point if there are more than 8 pixels among 16 surrounding pixels i which brighter or darker than pixel i (see Fig. 4). Let I_i and I_j are respectively the intensity of pixel i and j, then pixel j is confirmed to be brighter than pixel i if I_j is greater than I_i by a predefined threshold T. Key-points are location at which the edges are represented. Each key-point are then assigned directions which aim to determine the intensity changes around that key-point. The intensity changes are detected based on the intensity centroid [23].

Intensity Centroid Method. Considering a pixel i having coordinates x, y and gray value $I(x, y)$. The moment and the centroid of a small image block B of pixels are defined by (1) and (2).

$$m_{pq} = \sum_{x,y \in B} x^p y^q I(x, y), \quad p, q = \{0, 1\} \tag{1}$$

$$C = \left(\frac{m_{10}}{m_{00}}, \frac{m_{01}}{m_{00}} \right) \tag{2}$$

where m_{00} and (m_{10}, m_{01}) are the mass and the centroid of B, respectively.

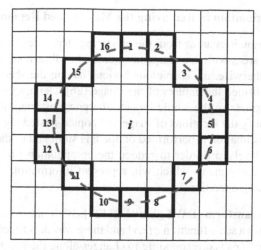

Fig. 4. Representation of 16 pixels around pixel i when defining a key-point

The direction vector is created by the geometric center O and the centroid C, then the direction of the key-point is defined by (3) [24].

$$\theta = arctan\left(\frac{m_{01}}{m_{10}}\right) \tag{3}$$

The rBRIEF Feature Descriptor. All key-points with assigned directions are calculated to create feature vectors or feature descriptors. BRIEF descriptor is a binary vector descriptor with vectors of 128 to 512 bits strings ([2, 24]).

BRIEF itself is not rotation invariant so the image information could be lost when rotating image. A rotation matrix R_θ in (4) is suggested to calculate the main direction for each feature points which is the solution to put the direction information into the descriptor.

$$R_\theta = \begin{pmatrix} cos\theta & sin\theta \\ -sin\theta & cos\theta \end{pmatrix} \tag{4}$$

The directional descriptor can be obtained by (5).

$$g_{N(p,\theta)} = f_N(p)|(x_i, y_i) \in Q_\theta \tag{5}$$

where Q_θ is defined based on the rotation correction

$$Q_\theta = R_\theta \begin{bmatrix} x_1, x_2, \ldots, x_N \\ y_1, y_2, \ldots, y_N \end{bmatrix}, N \; is \; numbers \; of \; pairs \; of \; pixel \; points \tag{6}$$

Clustering. A hierarchy of clusters is applied to detect the similar regions [25]. The OpenCV and Boost libraries support Kdsort in which the KD tree is used efficiently for detection the copied parts.

4.2 Sharpness Estimation in Removing the Mismatched Regions

After identifying suspicious areas from the clustering step, calculating the sharpness at these positions, the areas with the sharpness greater than threshold T are considered as the forged ones. Otherwise, the suspicious regions having the sharpness less than the threshold T are confirmed the natures of the image [26]. Defining a threshold depends on the average sharpness of the whole image. Sharpness estimation at high frequency components to identify the locations of suspected copied-pasted regions.

The sharpness estimation is performed on the HH sub-band of the Discrete Wavelet Transform (DWT) level 1 in order to reduce the computation time by focusing only the high frequency components which will represent information about the boundary regions if a cut-pasting operation.

Discrete Wavelet Transform (DWT) Level 1. [27] With a two-dimensional image $f(x,y)$, DWT generates a scale function $\varphi(x,y)$ and three wavelets functions with direction $\psi^H(x,y)$, $\psi^V(x,y)$, $\psi^D(x,y)$ corresponding to changes along the horizontal, vertical, and diagonal direction, respectively. These functions are identified by (7), (8), (9) and (10).

$$\varphi(x, y) = \varphi(x)\varphi(y) \tag{7}$$

$$\psi^H(x, y) = \psi(x)\varphi(y) \tag{8}$$

$$\psi^V(x, y) = \varphi(x)\psi(y) \tag{9}$$

$$\psi^D(x, y) = \psi(x)\psi(y) \tag{10}$$

where $\varphi(x)$, $\varphi(y)$ are scale functions and $\psi(x)$, $\psi(y)$ are one-dimensional wavelets functions.

In DWT, a scale function is used to produce an approximate component of an image and a factor of 2 in resolution is used to determine the differences between the closest approximate components while differences in information between the neighbor approximations is shown from the wavelets functions. The scale and shifted functions are defined by (11) and (12).

$$\varphi_{j,m,n}(x, y) = 2^{j/2}\varphi\left(2^j x - m, 2^j y - n\right) \tag{11}$$

$$\psi^i{}_{j,m,n}(x, y) = 2^{j/2}\psi^i\left(2^j x - m, 2^j y - n\right) \tag{12}$$

for j, $k \in \mathbf{Z}$, $m = n = 0,1,2, \ldots 2^j-1$.

In (12), $i = \{H,V,D\}$ defines wavelets with direction from (8), (9), (10). Then, the DWT of an image $f(x,y)$ having size MxN is performed by determining the approximation and directional coefficients as shown in (13) and (14).

$$W_\varphi(j_0, m, n) = \frac{1}{\sqrt{MN}} \sum_{x=0}^{M-1}\sum_{y=0}^{N-1} f(x, y)\varphi_{j_0,m,n}(x, y) \tag{13}$$

$$W_\psi^i(j, m, n) = \frac{1}{\sqrt{MN}} \sum_{x=0}^{M-1} \sum_{y=0}^{N-1} f(x, y) \psi^i{}_{j0,m,n}(x, y), i = \{H, V, D\} \quad (14)$$

where j_0 is any scale, $W_\varphi(j_0, m, n)$ is the approximation coefficients of the image $f(x,y)$ at the scale j_0 and $W_\psi^i(j, m, n)$ are the factors of details in the horizontal, vertical and diagonal directions for the scale $j \geq j_0$.

Mechanism of a DWT level 1 is shown in Fig. 5 and an example of DWT level 1 of an image is shown in Fig. 6.

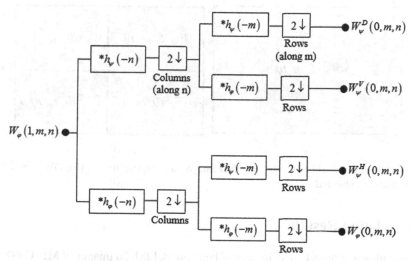

Fig. 5. Band-filter of DWT decomposition level 1

The HH sub-band $W_\psi^D{}_{(0,m,n)}$ component in Fig. 6(d) is used to filter the tampered positions by calculating sharpness.

The sharpness estimation is done on the regions which are suspicious to be copied moved.

Sharpness Estimation. At each image block, sharpness is calculated by using gradient amplitude. The gradient at the pixel with the coordinates (x, y) in the image block I is a vector of the first derivative determined by (15).

$$\nabla I(x, y) = \left[\frac{\partial I}{\partial x}(x, y) \frac{\partial I}{\partial y}(x, y) \right] \quad (15)$$

where $\frac{\partial I}{\partial x}(x, y)$, $\frac{\partial I}{\partial y}(x, y)$ are partial derivatives along x and y.

The gradient amplitude is then calculated in (16)

$$GM = |\nabla I(x, y)| = \sqrt{\left(\frac{\partial I}{\partial x}(x, y) \right)^2 + \left(\frac{\partial I}{\partial y}(x, y) \right)^2} \quad (16)$$

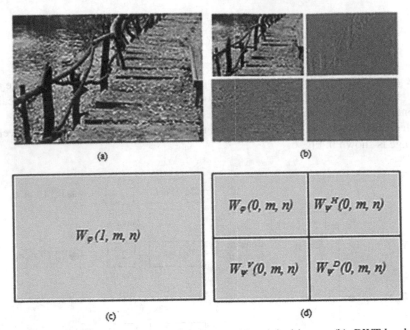

Fig. 6. DWT decomposition level 1 of a 2-D image, (a). original image; (b). DWT level 1; (c), (d). positions of sub-bands.

5 Simulation Results

The algorithm was tested on 35 images of benchmark [28], 20 images of MICC-600 [28] and 85 natural images which were created by Photoshop. Selected images for testing the proposed algorithm and comparing with related algorithms are diverse and meet the input requirements and the overall goal of the algorithms.

The proposed algorithm is compared with the interested algorithms using SIFT [10], SURF [11] and Zernike Moments [12] on the precision and processing time under specific image conditions. The values of precision, recall, F1 and processing time are calculated by average of images in group when doing comparison.

When processing an image, the precision, recall and F1 for each image are defined by (17), (18) and (19).

$$Precision = \frac{TP}{TP + FP} \tag{17}$$

$$Recall = TPTP + FN \tag{18}$$

$$F1 = 2 * \text{Recall} * \text{PrecisionRecall} + \text{Precision} \tag{19}$$

where

TP: the number of true tampered pixels,
FP: the number of false tampered pixels,
FN: the number of missed tampered pixels

With the implementations, the authors found that

(i).   For copy-move images in which the copy areas are duplicated and do not resize, with/without rotation, and the same areas due to collage only (not due to image's structure): In this case, 65 images are considered (including 20 images of benchmark, 20 images of MICC-600 and 30 images of natural images). The proposed algorithm only applies the step of detecting suspicious areas (see the steps belonging to the green box in Fig. 3) and confirm these are also copied areas. The results presented in Table 1 and Fig. 7 show that when performing the simulation on this group of images, the accuracy of the algorithms is not much different, and the ORB algorithm is slightly faster.

Table 1. The simulation results for copy-move images in which the copy areas are duplicated and do not resize, with/without rotation, and the same areas due to collage only (not due to image's structure)

Methods	The average of precision (%)	The average of Recall (%)	The average of F1 (%)	The average of processing time (x10 s)
SIFT [10]	90.07	88.25	89.15	32.19
SURF [11]	89.52	86.87	88.17	34.01
Zernike Moments [12]	88.96	83.08	85.92	35.62
ORB (proposed)	90.03	87.92	88.96	29.07

(ii).   For copy-move images in which areas of the copied image with/without resizing, rotating and the same areas due to collage only (not due to image's structure): In this case, 35 images are considered (including 15 images of benchmark and 20 of natural images). The proposed algorithm performs all steps as shown in Fig. 3. The results presented in Table 2 and Fig. 8 show that when performing simulation on this group of images, the accuracy of the algorithms is different. The proposed algorithm gives the highest accuracy, and the time is slower than others.

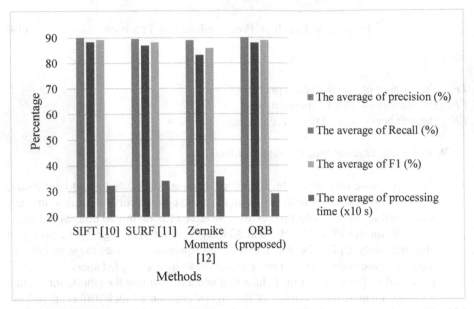

Fig. 7. Comparison of precision, recall, F1 and processing time for copy-move images in which the copy areas are duplicated and do not resize, with/without rotation, and the same areas due to collage only (not due to image's structure).

Table 2. The simulation results for copy-move images in which areas of the copied image with/without resizing, rotating and the same areas due to collage only (not due to image's structure)

Methods	The average of precision (%)	The average of Recall (%)	The average of F (%)	The average of processing time (x10 s)
SIFT [10]	87.35	87.52	87.43	37.25
SURF [11]	80.87	82.86	81.85	36.93
Zernike Moments [12]	82.06	85.91	83.94	39.17
ORB (proposed)	92.66	89.63	91.11	42.08

(iii). For copy-move images in which areas of the copied image are resized, rotated and the same areas may be due to collage or image's structure: In this case, only 40 natural images with the Photoshop operations are considered. The authors do not use the dataset of benchmark and MICC-600 image sets for this kind of images because their images do not meet the input requirements. The methods of using SIFT, SURF and Zernike Moments published have not yet seen mentioning

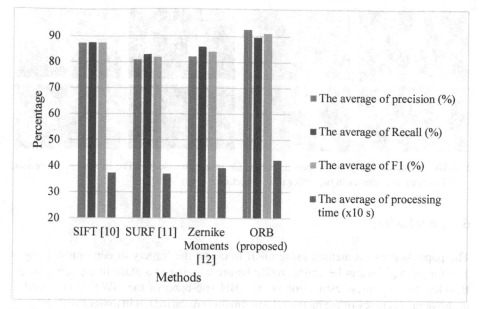

Fig. 8. Comparison of precision, recall, F1 and processing time for copy-move images in which areas of the copied image with/without resizing, rotating and the same areas due to collage only (not due to image's structure).

the identification of similar areas in case of image's structure. Therefore, only the proposed algorithm is applied to this case with positive results. The average precision of 92.67% proves the effectiveness of the algorithm.

Some simulations of the algorithm are shown in Fig. 9 and Fig. 10.

Fig. 9. Some results by the proposed method for images in case (i) and (ii). The images in above row: tested images, the images in the under row: detection.

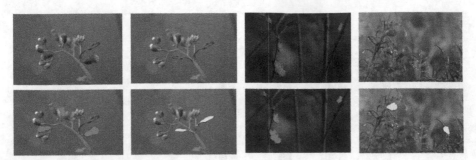

Fig. 10. Some results by the proposed method for image in case (iii) The images in above row: tested images, the images in the under row: detection.

6   Conclusion

The paper suggests a method using ORB to detect the forgery in copy-move images. The forged regions can be scaled, rotate before copying to a place in the same image. Besides, the sharpness estimation on the HH sub-band of the DWT is proposed to improve the accuracy of the method. Experiments are caried out in images with different kinds of operation in forging. With the simulations results and comparisons with related algorithms, the proposed method gives the average of accuracy at least 90% for image groups. This proves that ORB is an efficient method for detecting copy-move regions with scale and rotation in image forensics. However, the dataset is still limited on tempering operations.

References

1. Songtao, Z., Chao, L., Liqing, L.: An improved method for eliminating false matches. In: 2017 2nd International Conference on Image, Vision and Computing (ICIVC), pp. 133–137. IEEE, June 2017
2. Rublee, E., Rabaud, V., Konolige, K., Bradski, G.: ORB: an efficient alternative to SIFT or SURF. In: 2011 International conference on computer vision, pp. 2564–2571. IEEE, November 2011
3. Karami, E., Prasad, S., Shehata, M.: Image matching using SIFT, SURF, BRIEF and ORB: performance comparison for distorted images. arXiv preprint arXiv:1710.02726 (2017)
4. Popescu, A.C., Farid, H.: Exposing digital forgeries by detecting duplicated image regions. Dept. Comput. Sci., Dartmouth College, Technical Report TR2004–515, 1-11 (2017)
5. Luo, W., Huang, J., Qiu, G.: Robust detection of region-duplication forgery in digital image. In: 18th International Conference on Pattern Recognition (ICPR 2006), Vol. 4, pp. 746–749. IEEE, August 2006
6. Lin, H.J., Wang, C.W., Kao, Y.T.: Fast copy-move forgery detection. WSEAS Trans. Sig. Process. **5**(5), 188–197 (2009)
7. Nguyen, H.C., Katzenbeisser, S.: Detection of copy-move forgery in digital images using radon transformation and phase correlation. In: 2012 8th International Conference on Intelligent Information Hiding and Multimedia Signal Processing, pp. 134–137. IEEE, July 2012

8. Malviya, A.V., Ladhake, S. A.: Copy move forgery detection using low complexity feature extraction. In: 2015 IEEE UP Section Conference on Electrical Computer and Electronics (UPCON), pp. 1–5. IEEE, December 2015

9. Li, L., Li, S., Zhu, H., Chu, S.C., Roddick, J.F., Pan, J.S.: An efficient scheme for detecting copy-move forged images by local binary patterns. J. Inf. Hiding Multimedia Sig. Process. 4(1), 46–56 (2013)

10. Amerini, I., Ballan, L., Caldelli, R., Del Bimbo, A., Serra, G.: A sift-based forensic method for copy–move attack detection and transformation recovery. IEEE Trans. Inf. Forensics Secur. 6(3), 1099–1110 (2011)

11. Pandey, R.C., Singh, S.K., Shukla, K.K., Agrawal, R.: Fast and robust passive copy-move forgery detection using SURF and SIFT image features. In: 2014 9th International Conference on Industrial and Information Systems (ICIIS), pp. 1–6. IEEE, December 2014

12. Ryu, S.J., Lee, M.J., Lee, H.K.: Detection of copy-rotate-move forgery using zernike moments. In: Böhme, R., Fong, P.W.L., S.N, Reihaneh (eds.) IH 2010. LNCS, vol. 6387, pp. 51–65. Springer, Heidelberg (2010). https://doi.org/10.1007/978-3-642-16435-4_5

13. Fridrich, A.J., Soukal, B.D., Lukáš, A.J.: Detection of copy-move forgery in digital images. In: Proceedings of Digital Forensic Research Workshop (2003)

14. Cao, Y., Gao, T., Fan, L., Yang, Q.: A robust detection algorithm for copy-move forgery in digital images. Forensic Sci. Int. 214(1–3), 33–43 (2012)

15. Sutcu, Y., Coskun, B., Sencar, H.T., Memon, N.: Tamper detection based on regularity of wavelet transform coefficients. In: 2007 IEEE International Conference on Image Processing, vol. 1, pp. I-397. IEEE, September 2007

16. Bashar, M.K., Noda, K., Ohnishi, N., Kudo, H., Matsumoto, T., Takeuchi, Y.: Wavelet-based multiresolution features for detecting duplications in images. In: MVA, pp. 264–267, May 2007

17. Li, G., Wu, Q., Tu, D., Sun, S.: A sorted neighborhood approach for detecting duplicated regions in image forgeries based on DWT and SVD. In: 2007 IEEE international conference on multimedia and expo, pp. 1750–1753. IEEE, July 2007

18. Khan, E.S., Kulkarni, E.A.: An efficient method for detection of copy-move forgery using discrete wavelet transform. Int. J. Comput. Sci. Eng. 2(5), 2010 (1801)

19. Prathibha, O.M., Swathikumari, N. S., Sushma, P.: Image forgery detection using dyadic Wavelet transform. Int. J. Electron. Sig. Syst. 2, 41–43 (2012)

20. Bayram, S., Sencar, H.T., Memon, N.: An efficient and robust method for detecting copy-move forgery. In 2009 IEEE International Conference on Acoustics, Speech and Signal Processing (pp. 1053–1056). IEEE, April 2009

21. Yang, J., Ran, P., Xiao, D., Tan, J.: Digital image forgery forensics by using undecimated dyadic wavelet transform and Zernike moments. J. Comput. Inf. Syst 9(16), 6399–6408 (2013)

22. Wo, Y., Yang, K., Han, G., Chen, H., Wu, W.: Copy–move forgery detection based on multi-radius PCET. IET Image Process. 11(2), 99–108 (2016)

23. Rosin, P.L.: Measuring corner properties. Comput. Vis. Image Underst. 73(2), 291–307 (1999)

24. Luo, C., Yang, W., Huang, P., Zhou, J.: Overview of image matching based on ORB algorithm. In: Journal of Physics: Conference Series , vol. 1237, no. 3, p. 032020. IOP Publishing, June 2019

25. Wagstaff, K., Cardie, C., Rogers, S., Schrödl, S.: Constrained k-means clustering with background knowledge. In: ICML, vol. 1, pp. 577–584, June 2001

26. Tu, H.K., Thuong, L.T., Synh, H.V.U., Van Khoa, H.: Develop an algorithm for image forensics using feature comparison and sharpness estimation. In: 2017 International Conference on Recent Advances in Signal Processing, Telecommunications & Computing (SigTelCom), pp. 82–87. IEEE, January 2017

27. Gonzalez, R.C., Woods, R. E., Eddins, S.L.: Digital Image Processing using MATLAB. Pearson Education, India (2004)
28. Christlein, V., Riess, C., Jordan, J., Riess, C., Angelopoulou, E.: An evaluation of popular copy-move forgery detection approaches. IEEE Trans. Inf. Forensics Secur. 7(6), 1841–1854 (2012)

A Convex Optimization Based Method
for Color Image Reconstruction

Nguyen Thi Hong Anh[1], Nguyen Duy Viet Toan[2], and Le Hong Trang[2,3(✉)]

[1] Faculty of Information Technology, Saigon University, 370 An Duong Vuong,
Ho Chi Minh City, Vietnam
[2] Faculty of Computer Sicence and Engineering,
Ho Chi Minh University of Technology, 268 Ly Thuong Kiet,
Ho Chi Minh City, Vietnam
lhtrang@hcmut.edu.vn
[3] Vietnam National University Ho Chi Minh City (VNU-HCM),
Ho Chi Minh City, Vietnam

Abstract. In this paper, we present an efficient method for reconstructing color images based on the convex optimization. Current convex optimization methods are all applied to one channel images, so as the number of channels increases, the number of convex optimization problems increase. We present a solution to reconstruct color images represented by three color channels RGB by only one convex optimization problem and use a high-performance algorithm BFGS for solving the problem. We also perform several experiments to compare our method with others on reality datasets.

Keywords: Convex optimization · BFGS · Total variation · Color image reconstruction

1 Introduction

Image reconstruction is a field of image processing, try to solve the problem of finding an image that is closest to the original image from the damaged image. Due to presence of noise, blur, and overlap, possible further image processing tasks are adversely affected, so the image reconstruction techniques are necessary. Moreover, this general problem has many important applications, such as medical imaging, entertainment, and more.

One of fundamental problems in image reconstruction is denoising. A set of images collected by a camera or sensor systems usually contaminated by noise. Noisy images can also be created during transmission and compression. Denoising of images is thus required first before they are used for further analysis tasks. There are two approaches to image denoising, including spatial and transform domain filter methods. Spatial filters are traditional methods to remove noise from images. One of well-known methods is the mean filter (see [10]). This method was proposed for Gaussian noise in the sense of mean square error. It

T. K. Dang et al. (Eds.): FDSE 2020, CCIS 1306, pp. 373–383, 2020.
https://doi.org/10.1007/978-981-33-4370-2_26

tends to blur sharp edges, remove lines and other fine details. The mean filter typically is a linear one. Some nonlinear filters were also introduced for spatial filtering. In this approach, the noise can be removed without any attempts to identify it. A filter tries to remove the noise to a reasonable extent but ay the cost of blurring images that makes the edges in images invisible. Some of such filters were introduced such as weighted median [22], rank condition selection [9], and relaxed condition [8]. Regarding the transform domain filtering, wavelet based denoising has been received many attentions in the literature. These methods can be classified into some group such as linear filtering, non-linear threshold filtering, wavelet coefficient model, ans non-orthogonal wavelet transform. A brief review on these methods can be found in [13].

Recently, some modern approaches are studied for the image restoration. Jain et al. [11] presented a novel edge-preserving image denoising technique based on tetrolet transform (a Haar-type wavelet transform) and a locally adaptive thresholding method. On RGB-D images full of noise and text, Xue et al. [21] proposed a depth image inpainting method based on Low Gradient Regularization. Total variation approach also attracts much interest. Kim et al. [12] designed reconstruction and noise reduction algorithms based on inpainting method with decomposed sinusoid-like curve (S-curve) using total variation noise reduction algorithm in CT imaging system. Wali et al. [17] proposed a denoising and inpainting method using total generalized variation (TGV). The authors analyze three types of distortion including text, noise, and masks.

In this work, we aim to get confirmations about efficiency of convex optimization on image reconstruction field. We also present a solution to reconstruct color images based on the convex optimization. For a color image, three convex optimization formulations will be established for three color channels. We then combine them into only one formulation, so that the computational cost for solving the problem is decreased. The proposed method is implemented in Python with BFGS solver and tested for both synthetic and benchmark datasets. The results show that our method is efficient.

The rest of the paper is organized as follows. We recall some background on convex optimization and its formulation for the image denoising and deblurring problems. Section 3 presents our formulation proposed for the color images. We do experiments, comparisons and discussions in Sect. 4. Finally, some concluding remarks are given in Sect. 5.

2   Background

2.1   Convex Optimization Formulation

A convex optimization problem [3] is represented by the form:

$$x^* = \arg\min_x \; f_0(x)$$
$$\text{subject to } f_i(x) \le 0, \; i = 1, 2, \ldots, m,$$
$$h_j(x) = 0, \; j = 1, 2, \ldots, p, \tag{1}$$

where $f_0, f_1, ..., f_m$ are convex functions. Set x^* is solution or optimal point of problem $f(x)$. An important property of the convex optimization problem is every local minimum is a global minimum. Therefore, in order to solve a convex optimization problem, we will find all it's local minimums. There are many methods to find local minimums, for instance, interior point [18], gradient descent [5] or BFGS [14]. In this paper, BFGS algorithm is applied to solve the proposed convex optimization problem.

2.2 BFGS for Solving Convex Optimization

This section will focus on how to find the optimal point of a convex optimization problem by the BFGS algorithm [14]. The BFGS algorithm belongs to quasi-Newton method [16], an iterative method for solving unconstrained nonlinear optimization problems. In the situation that the full Newton's method [23] consumes amount of time to compute the Hessian matrix of second derivatives. Instead, the Hessian matrix is approximated using updates specified by gradient evaluations in quasi-Newton method. However, there are many solutions for the approximation at multi-dimensional problems. The BFGS method is one of the most popular solution of this class.

From an initial guess x_0 and an approximate Hessian matrix B_0. Note that B_0 should be positive-definite, the following steps are repeated as x_k converges to the solution:

1. $\Delta x_k = -\alpha_k B_k^{-1} \triangledown f(x_k)$, with α chosen to satisfy the Wolfe conditions.
2. $x_{k+1} = x_k + \Delta x_k$.
3. The gradient $\triangledown f(x_{k+1})$ computed, and $y_k = \triangledown f(x_{k+1}) - \triangledown f(x_k)$.
4. $B_{k+1} = B_k + \frac{y_k y_k^T}{y_k^T s_k} - \frac{B_k s_k s_k^T B_k}{s_k^T B_k s_k}$.

B_k matrix has not to be obtained because in first step of the algorithm is carried out using the inverse of it. Therefore the algorithm can apply the Sherman–Morrison formula to the step four, giving:

$$B_{k+1}^{-1} = B_k^{-1} + \frac{(s_k^T y_k + y_k^T B_k^{-1} y_k)(s_k s_k^T)}{(s_k^T y_k)^2} - \frac{B_k^{-1} y_k s_k^T + s_k y_k^T B_k^{-1}}{s_k^T y_k}.$$

2.3 Image Reconstruction Using Convex Optimization

Image reconstruction is one of the earliest and most classical inverse problems in imaging. In this class of problems, the connection between damaged image y and original image x is modeled as:

$$y = \mathbf{B}x + n, \tag{2}$$

where $\mathbf{B}$ is a matrix is the matrix representation of the direct operator and n is noise. Set u^* is reconstructed image, the problem applies the form of convex optimization [1, 15] in:

$$u^* = \arg\min_u \int_\omega \| \nabla u \|_2 du$$

$$\text{subject to } \int_\omega (\mathbf{B}u - y)^2 du - \epsilon \le 0, \tag{3}$$

where the total variation norm $\int_\omega \| \nabla u \|_2 du$ [4,15] is set as objective function. It is based on the principle that possible damaged signal has the high total variation, that means integral of the absolute gradient is high and reducing the total variation of the signal subject to it being a close match to the original signal. With the constraint function, $\int_\omega (\mathbf{B}u - y)^2 du - \epsilon$ is chosen to ensure y and $\mathbf{B}u$ are not very different.

In order that the formulation is appropriate with BFGS, an algorithm to solve unconstrained nonlinear optimization problems. By applying Lagrange multipliers [24], the problem (3) will transform to the unconstrained nonlinear problem:

$$u^* = \arg\min_u \int_\omega \| \nabla u \|_2 du + \frac{\lambda}{2} \int_\omega (\mathbf{B}u - f)^2 du. \tag{4}$$

Finally, image reconstruction is a subfield of signal processing. In this class, image(gray-scale) is represented by the 2-D signal. Therefore, in 2-D discrete space domain, problem (4) should be represented by :

$$u^* = \arg\min_u (\sum_{i,j} \sqrt{F_{i,j}^2 + G_{i,j}^2} + \frac{\lambda}{2} \sum_{i,j} (a_{i,j} - y_{i,j})^2), \tag{5}$$

where $F_{i,j} = |u_{i+1,j} - u_{i,j}|$, $G_{i,j} = |u_{i,j+1} - u_{i,j}|$, $a = \mathbf{B}u$.

3   Proposed Method

3.1   An Analysis of Using Convex Optimization for Color Image Reconstruction

This section will introduce the convex optimization formulation for color image reconstruction. In this research, color images are represented by RGB color space. Because the color image consists of three color channels instead one channel with gray-scale image. The problem can be solved by separating into three sub-problems and solving each formulation of sub-problem. However, we try to solve the color image reconstruction problem by only one formulation as follows:

$$u^* = \arg\min_u \sum_k \sum_{i,j} \sqrt{F_{i,j,k}^2 + G_{i,j,k}^2} + \frac{\lambda}{2} \sum_{i,j,k} (a_{i,j,k} - y_{i,j,k})^2, \tag{6}$$

where $F_{i,j,k} = |u_{i+1,j,k} - u_{i,j,k}|$, $G_{i,j,k} = |u_{i,j+1,k} - u_{i,j,k}|$, $a = \mathbf{B}u$. The regularization parameter λ is set to balance two sub-functions in the formulation. Before applying Lagrange multipliers [24], the problem (6) is represented by

$$u^* = \arg\min_u \sum_{i,j} \sqrt{F_{i,j}^2 + G_{i,j}^2}$$

$$\text{subject to } \sum_{i,j,k} (a_{i,j,k} - y_{i,j,k})^2 \le \epsilon, \tag{7}$$

where $F_{i,j,k} = |u_{i+1,j,k} - u_{i,j,k}|$, $G_{i,j,k} = |u_{i,j+1,k} - u_{i,j,k}|$, $a = \mathbf{B}u$. The objective function in problem (7) is

$$\sum_k \sum_{i,j} \sqrt{F_{i,j,k}^2 + G_{i,j,k}^2}.$$

As we have known that three color channels of the RGB image are independent with each others. At the same position the values of three channels could be very different. If a total variation norm is made for all three channels, we will get the inaccurate result. A solution using sum of 3 total variation norms is applied in here. The constraint ensures a and y are not too different, i.e.,

$$\sum_{i,j,k} (a_{i,j,k} - y_{i,j,k})^2 \le \epsilon.$$

4   Experiments

In this section, there are two types of experiment datasets to process, including generated and reality images. In Subsect. 4.1, we show some examples of the our generated damaged images in two standard problems, denoising and inpainting. In Subsect. 4.2, a table of denoising experiment results with the convex optimization method and some well-known methods is represented. Our proposed method was implemented using Python and SciPy framework, and tested on Window 10 platform, Intel Core i7 2.2 GHz and 8 GB memory.

4.1   Generated Datasets

During the denoising experiments in this section, we choose Gaussian noise because it is believed to be most similar to real-world noise. The probability p of a Gaussian random noise value z is given by:

(a) original image   (b) damaged image   (c) reconstructed image

Fig. 1. Reconstruct gaussian noisy image with $\sigma = 10$ by convex optimization.

$$p_z = \frac{1}{\sigma\sqrt{2\pi}}e^{-\frac{(z-\mu)^2}{2\sigma^2}}, \tag{8}$$

where μ represents the mean value, σ is a given standard deviation. The value of probability p depends on the value of σ.

We show first some examples of denoising noisy image generated by Gaussian noise with different sigma parameters. Figure 1 shows the example with $\sigma = 10$. The damaged image is showed in Fig. 1(b) which contains a less noise. Our method reconstructs the image as given in Fig. 1(c). For $\sigma = 30$, the noisy is increased. The reconstructed image is given in Fig. 2(c). For a large value of σ, the obtained result can be acceptable (see Fig. 3).

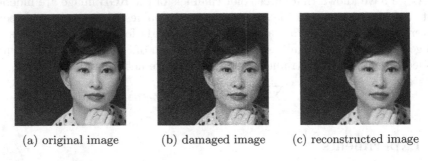

(a) original image   (b) damaged image   (c) reconstructed image

Fig. 2. Reconstruct gaussian noisy image with $\sigma = 30$ by convex optimization.

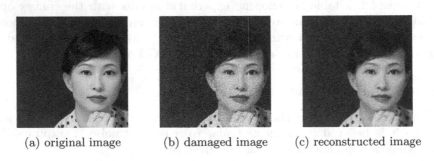

(a) original image   (b) damaged image   (c) reconstructed image

Fig. 3. Reconstruct Gaussian noisy image with $\sigma = 50$ by convex optimization.

For the inpanting images, the results of two situations of image overwritten by text are shown, a large amount of small letters and a few of large letters (see Fig. 4 and Fig. 5). The convex optimization seems to do better with the situation of a large amount of small letters. The reason in here is that when the overlapping area is too large, the neighborhoods of the locations in the overlapping area do not have right information to reconstruct the values. Similarly, the result of inpainting a long thin line (Fig. 6) is better than that with a large area (Fig. 7).

(a) original image

(b) damaged image

(c) reconstructed image

Fig. 4. Reconstruct painted image with the large area of small letters.

(a) original image

(b) damaged image

(c) reconstructed image

Fig. 5. Reconstruct painted image with the small area of big letters.

(a) original image

(b) damaged image

(c) reconstructed image

Fig. 6. Reconstruct painted image with the long thin line.

(a) original image

(b) damaged image

(c) reconstructed image

Fig. 7. Reconstruct painted image with the large area.

4.2   Reality Datasets

Due to the complex conditions of the inpanting problem solving by convex optimization, we can not find any appropriate benchmark dataset. Therefore we only report a table of denoising experiment results aimed at comparing the performance of the convex optimization method with current popular methods, for example, mean filter [6], median filter [7] and Fourier domain denoising [25] in three public benchmark datasets.

We tested first for the RENOIR[1] dataset [2]. This is a public dataset consisting of 500 images which are corrupted low-light noise together with pixel and intensity aligned clean images. Those images are captured in about 120 scenes and collected by three devices including Cannon T3i, Cannon S90, and a Xiaomi MI3 mobile phone. Figure 8 shows some examples of the dataset.

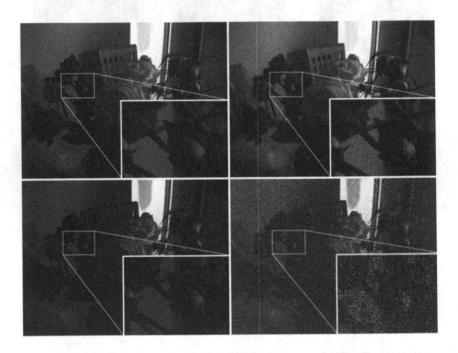

Fig. 8. The RENOIR dataset.

The second dataset which was tested in this work, is MCWNNM[2]. In this dataset, the noisy of images is generated by adding AWGN to each channel. The standard deviation of AWGN added to R, G, B channels are $40, 20$, and 30, respectively. Figure 9 shows an example of noisy images which was given in [19].

---

[1] https://github.com/lbasek/image-denoising-benchmark.
[2] https://github.com/csjunxu/MCWNNM-ICCV2017.

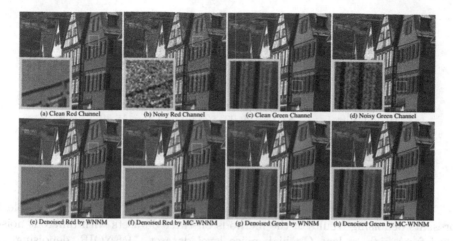

(a) Clean Red Channel   (b) Noisy Red Channel   (c) Clean Green Channel   (d) Noisy Green Channel

(e) Denoised Red by WNNM   (f) Denoised Red by MC-WNNM   (g) Denoised Green by WNNM   (h) Denoised Green by MC-WNNM

Fig. 9. The MCWNNM dataset.

The third dataset in our experiments is PolyU[3]. The dataset consists of images captured from 40 different scenes with different contents and objects [20]. The images in the dataset cover from different types of indoor scenes and facility objects, as shown in Fig. 10.

Fig. 10. The PolyU dataset.

---

[3] https://github.com/csjunxu/PolyU-Real-World-Noisy-Images-Dataset/tree/master.

Table 1. Comparison results between denoising image methods.

Method	RENOIR		MCWNNM		PolyU	
	MSE	PSNR	MSE	PSNR	MSE	PSNR
Noisy	163.55	25.99	33.56	32.87	18.54	35.45
Mean filter	72.86	29.5	23.86	34.35	16.77	35.85
Median filter	81.15	29.00	23.90	34.35	16.39	35.99
Fourier denoising	57.59	30.53	32.91	32.96	20.68	34.98
Our method	**45.60**	**30.62**	**23.66**	**34.39**	**15.32**	**36.28**

We evaluate algorithms by means of the MSE and PSNR indices. Table 1 presents denoising results of the methods on three datasets with different noise level from high to low. On high noise level dataset - RENOIR, denoising by convex optimization is significantly better than other methods. For the two other datasets (MCWNNM and PolyU) which have lower noisy levels, the convex optimization method still gives better results, while the difference with the other methods is very slight.

5   Conclusion

We presented a solution to reconstruct color images represented by three color channels RGB by only one convex optimization problem When comparing the convex optimization method with the popular color image denoising methods, the benchmark data results show that the method is appropriate and effective. It can be applied in the industry of image recovery or as a preprocessing step for other computer vision tasks.

For the inpanting images, the obtained results also indicate the effective of convex optimization method. However, a complete test for reality datasets is necessary to evaluate the convex models for this problem. This will be the topic in another work in the future.

References

1. Afonso, M.V., Bioucas-Dias, J.M., Figueiredo, M.A.T.: An augmented lagrangian approach to the constrained optimization formulation of imaging inverse problems. In: IEEE Transactions on Image Processing, vol. 20, no. 3 (2011)
2. Anaya, J., Barbu, A.: RENOIR - a dataset for real low-light image noise reduction. J. Visual Commun. Image Rep. **51**(2), 144–154 (2018)
3. Boyd, S., Vandenberghe, L.: Convex Optimization. Cambridge University Press, Cambridge (2004)
4. Clarkson, J.A., Adams, C.R.: On definitions of bounded variation for functions of two variables. Trans. Am. Math. Soc. **35**(1933), 824–854 (1933)
5. Curry, H.B.: The method of steepest descent for non-linear minimization problems. Quart. Appl. Math. **2**, 258–261 (1944)

6. Sundararajan, D.: Edge detection. Digital Image Processing, pp. 257–280. Springer, Singapore (2017). https://doi.org/10.1007/978-981-10-6113-4_9
7. Huang, T.S., Yang, G.J., Tang, G.Y.: In: IEEE Transactions on Acoustics, Speech, and Signal Processing, vol. 27, no. 1 (1979)
8. Hamza, A., Luque, P., Martinez, J., Roman, R.: Removing noise and preserving details with relaxed median filters. J. Math. Image Vision **11**(2), 161–177 (1999). https://doi.org/10.1023/A:1008395514426
9. Hardie, R.C., Barner, K.E.: Rank conditioned rank selection filters for signal restoration. IEEE Trans. Image Process. **3**, 192–206 (1994)
10. Jain, A.K.: Fundamentals of Digital Image Processing. Prentice-Hall, New Jersey (1989)
11. Jain, P., Tyagi, V.: An adaptive edge-preserving image denoising technique using tetrolet transforms. Vis.Comput. **31**(5), 657–674 (2014). https://doi.org/10.1007/s00371-014-0993-7
12. Kim, D., Park, S.W., Kim, D.H., Yoo, M.S., Lee, Y.J.: Feasibility of sinogram reconstruction based on inpainting method with decomposed sinusoid-like curve (S-curve) using total variation (TV) noise reduction algorithm in computed tomography (CT) imaging system: a simulation study. In: Optik, vol. 161, pp.270-277 (2018)
13. Motwani, M.C., Gadiya, M.C., Motwani, R.C., Harris, F.C.: Survey of image denoising techniques. In: GSPX (2004)
14. Nocedal, J., Wright, S.J.: Numerical Optimization, 2nd edn., pp. 136–143. Spinger, New York (2006)
15. Rudin, L.I., Osher, S., Fatemi, E.: Nonlinear total variation based noise removal algorithms. Physica D. **60**(1–4), 259–268 (1992)
16. Vandenberghe, L.: Quasi Newton Methods. http://www.seas.ucla.edu/~vandenbe/236C/lectures/qnewton.pdf. Accessed 1 Sep 2020
17. Wali, S., Zhang, H., Chang, H., Wu, C.: A new adaptive boosting total generalized variation (TGV) technique for image denoising and inpainting. J. Vis. Commun. Image Represent. **59**, 39–51 (2019)
18. Wright, M.II.: The interior-point revolution in optimization: History, recent developments, and lasting consequences. In: Bulletin of the American Mathematical Society (2004)
19. Xu, J., Zhang, L., Zhang, D., Feng, X.: Multi-channel Weighted Nuclear Norm Minimization for Real Color Image Denoising. In: International Conference on Computer Vision (ICCV), pp. 1105–1113. Venice, Italy (2017)
20. Xu, J., Li, H., Liang, Z., Zhang, D., Zhang, L.: Real-world noisy image denoising: a new benchmark. In: IEEE Conference Computer Vision and Pattern Recognition (2018)
21. Xue, H., Zhang, S., Cai, D.: Depth image inpainting: improving low rank matrix completion with low gradient regularization. IEEE Trans. Image Process. **26**(9), 4311–4320 (2017)
22. Yang, J., Yin, L., Gabbouj, M., Astola, J., Neuvo, Y.: Optimal weighted median filters under structural constraints. IEEE Trans. Signal Process. **43**, 591–604 (1995)
23. Encyclopedia of Mathematics. https://encyclopediaofmath.org/index.php?title=Newton_method. Accessed 1 Sep 2020
24. Lagrange Multiplier - Wolfram MathWorld. https://mathworld.wolfram.com/LagrangeMultiplier.html. Accessed 1 Sep 2020
25. Image denoising by FFT - Scipy lecture. http://scipy-lectures.org/intro/scipy/auto_examples/solutions/plot_fft_image_denoise.html

Emerging Data Management Systems and Applications

Cost Effective Control Plane Design for Service Assurance in Software Defined Service Function Chaining

Dokyung Lee[1], Syed Muhammad Raza[2], Moonseong Kim[3]([⊠]), and Hyunseung Choo[1]([⊠])

[1] Department of Software, Sungkyunkwan University,
Suwon, Korea
{dokyunglee,choo}@skku.edu
[2] Department of Electrical and Computer Engineering, Sungkyunkwan University, Suwon,
Korea
s.moh.raza@skku.edu
[3] Department of Liberal Arts, Seoul Theological University, Bucheon, Korea
moonseong@stu.ac.kr

Abstract. Service Function Chain (SFC) is an ordered list of dynamically deployed virtual service/network functions (SFs). In a software defined SFC, Network Function Virtualization (NFV) framework manages the lifecycle of SFs, and Software Defined Networking (SDN) control plane steers the traffic through the SFs in a given order to deliver a service. SFCs provide several benefits over conventional approaches through their agility and control, but also present new challenges. One of these challenges is service assurance that requires prompt resumption of a service in case of a SF unavailability due to traffic load, failure, maintenance or any other reasons. To ensure service availability, traffic from unavailable SF is migrated to a backup SF. Most of the studies deploy dedicated backup server for each SF in every SFC, which leads to needless consumption of resources. This paper exploits the fact that many instances of a SF are usually deployed in the network as part of different SFCs, and uses one of these instances as a backup SF in case of the primary SF unavailability. Selection of backup SF is done based on shortest detouring path to minimize the added delay due to altered path and the service disruption time. Emulation results from fat tree topology confirm that proposed mechanism reduces resource wastage by more than 20% comparing to conventional approaches while only adding 0.006 ms and 4 ms approximately in switching delay and transmission delay, respectively.

Keywords: Service assurance · Software defined networking · Service function chaining · Backup service function selection

© Springer Nature Singapore Pte Ltd. 2020
T. K. Dang et al. (Eds.): FDSE 2020, CCIS 1306, pp. 387–400, 2020.
https://doi.org/10.1007/978-981-33-4370-2_27

1 Introduction

Software Defined Networking (SDN) and Network Function Virtualization (NFV) technologies have been at the forefront of the softwarization transformation of conventional networking. SDN changes the distributed control in the conventional networks to a centralized control plane where a logically centralized SDN controller controls the network [1]. This enables global view of the network and provides flexibility to dynamically steer traffic as per changing conditions of the network. Meanwhile, NFV transforms the middle-boxes into virtual service/network functions (SFs) which can be dynamically deployed in the network, and a user service can comprise of one or multiple SFs. To define it formally, an ordered list of SFs in software-defined network to provide a user service is known as Software Defined Service Function Chain (SD-SFC).

Once a service request is received, the policy layer of NFV framework processes it and creates a logical SFC consist of SFs to render the requested service. Using the network monitoring data, NFV orchestrator determines which SFs require fresh deployment and which already existing SFs in the network can be used for requested service. SFs requiring the fresh deployment are embedded in the network through NFV infrastructure layer. This leads to one SF serving for multiple SFCs in the network [2]. SFC information along with the location of SFs is passed on to SDN controller and it installs the flow rules in the software-defined switches to steer the traffic through the SFs in the SFC. To fully benefit from the agility provided by the SD-SFC, service assurance is an essential attribute in case of any disruption. The whole SFC is vulnerable to disruption even with unavailability of a single SF due to link failure, server failure, over utilization, or even maintenance. To ensure service availability traffic must be migrated from primary unavailable SF to an operational backup SF. One of the challenges is to complete this migration within minimal time while curtailing the added computation and transmission delay cost.

The problem of traffic migration from primary unavailable SF to backup SF can be partitioned into three phases: 1) deployment of backup SF, 2) selection of backup SF, and 3) migration of traffic. The deployment of backup SF deals with the provisioning of backup SF or node (i.e., a device in which SF resides) at the time of network setup or dynamically at the runtime. Existing studies explore dedicated and shared backup approaches to achieve this. In dedicated approach, a backup SF or node for each primary SF or node is embedded in the network [3]. This causes serious underutilization of resources as backup SF or node remains idle until the primary SF become unavailable. Shared approach is used to curtail the underutilization by sharing a backup SF or node in case of unavailability of any primary SF of same type or a node [4–7]. Although this approach reduces the resource underutilization but does not solves it completely as dedicated backup SF or node still sits idle until unavailability.

At the instance of primary SF unavailability, SDN controller need to select the appropriate backup SF in the shared backup SF deployment scenario. Current load on shared backup SF [3], predictive load on shared backup SF, migration cost, and transmission cost are some of the conditions that can be used individually or in combination for the selection of backup SF. To maintain the Service Level Agreement (SLA) of SD-SFC, transmission are migration cost are the most critical conditions to be considered in backup SF selection. SFs represents intermediate destinations in a SFC which makes traffic steering much more challenging than conventional networks where there is a single destination for every communication. To migrate the traffic from primary SF to backup SF, SDN controller needs to find shortest paths to and from the backup SF, update/install flow rules in switches in those paths, and replace the primary SF with backup SF in the source routing [8, 9].

To provide service assurance and high availability in SD-SFC, this paper presents a control plane design which exploits the backup SF sharing in the deployment phase. Contrary to previous studies no exclusive or shared backup SFs are deployed. Instead, instances similar to unavailable SF in other SFCs are used as backup options. Rational behind this approach is that restoration time of unavailable SF to back to available is considerably less in SD-SFC, and for that short period traffic can piggy back on already available instance of same SF (i.e., backup SF). Once the primary SF is restored, the primary SFC path is restored as well. In the selection phase, we have used shortest detouring path as the individual selection condition to minimize the added transmission cost. Traffic migration phase employs the label stacking mechanism and flow table design from our previous study [9] to migrate traffic from unavailable primary SF to selected backup SF. The proposed control plane design for service assurance is evaluated on emulated datacenter fat-tree topology and results confirm minimum 20% improvement in resource utilization. Expectedly, the migration and transmission delays are higher than exclusively dedicated backup SF. However, the differences are negligible values of 0.006 ms and 4 ms for migration and transmission delays, respectively.

The remainder of this paper is organized as follows. Section 2 overviews the related studies for SD-SFC survivability using shared backup. Section 3 describes the architecture, operational details, and selection algorithm of the proposed service assurance the proposed solution and discusses the operational details and algorithm for backup SF selection. Performance evaluation and analysis is presented in Sects. 4 and 5 concludes the paper with future research directions.

2 Selected Existing Studies on SFC Survivability

Exclusive and dedicated backup SF is the most effective and most resource costly approach for service assurance in SFCs. Bifurcation of backup SFs into permanent and temporary backup SF salvage some of the resources [3]. Where, permanent dedicated backup SF are deployed at network setup time and one of the existing SFs in the network is selected based on load condition to serve as temporary backup SF. If no existing SF can serve as temporary backup then a new temporary backup SF is deployed at runtime. To give temporary backup preparation and embedding time to SDN controller, two level thresholds are used. SDN controller receives periodic load updates from each SF, and starts to select temporary backup SF among existing SFs or prepare new temporary backup SF when load of a primary SF crosses low-level threshold. Traffic is migrated to the backup SF when primary SF load crosses high-level threshold.

Shared dedicated backup SF is an alternate approach to exclusive dedicated backup. In this approach, one or multiple backup nodes are embedded in the network and all the primary nodes share them to deploy their dedicated backup SFs. Optimal placement of backup nodes is critical for efficient traffic migration, and it has been handled by

1-redundant and k-redundant algorithms in [4]. In the control plane, 1-redundant and k-redundant algorithms deploy 1 logical backup and k logical backup nodes, respectively, and connect them to primary nodes through virtual links. Embedding of logical backup node(s) and virtual links into the network is done to maximize computing and bandwidth resource sharing by formulating the problem as MILP and solving it through different heuristics. 1-redundant is resource efficient but is not enough to handle all backup SFs, and k-redundant again cases the same problem of excessive resource underutilization. Another downside to k-redundant algorithm is costly embedding [5]. In an improved solution, number of backup nodes, their placement in the network, and their connections to the primary nodes are all computed before the embedding phase and this not only simplifies the embedding but also reduces the backup resource footprint in the network [5].

To further reduce the shared backup nodes, one solution is to migrate the primary SF to shared backup node instead of deploying and using a backup SF [6]. Two heuristic algorithms are proposed to deploy as few backup SFs as possible to provide a backup for all SFs. Backup Sharing Pull (BS-PULL) sets one type j of SF and then looks for nodes that can provide backup to the most j-type SFs. Backup Sharing Push (BS-PUSH) finds nodes associated with the largest number of SFs, and then places the backup SF in search of the corresponding type j, which is the largest number of SFs around that node. Although these algorithms have effectively reduced backup SF deployment, there is room for improvement in terms of stability or resource usage since they are heuristic algorithms.

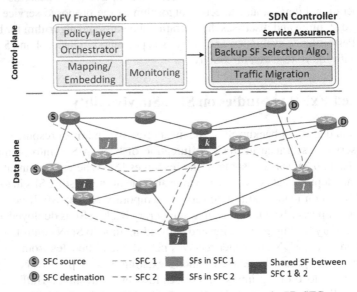

Fig. 1. System architecture for service assurance in SD-SFCs.

Performance of BS-PULL and BS-PUSH are updated in [7] by adding optimization steps before and after deployment. Migration After BS-PULL (MABS-PULL) migrates SFs after the execution of the BS-PULL algorithm. Optimized Backup Sharing (OBS) optimizes the number of backup SFs deployed through SF migration before and after the execution of the BS-PULL algorithm. Both algorithms have two stages. Physical nodes that fulfill the capacity and hops constraints with the SFs are found in the first step. Certain number of SFs are migrated to each candidate node in the second step. Between these two algorithms, MABS-PULL minimizes the number of SFs that are not backed up despite the execution of the BS-PULL algorithm. OBS, on the other hand, minimizes the backup SF deployment. OBS achieves 20% deployment resource savings instead of a slight run-time loss compared to BS-PULL. However, this is not a satisfactory figure, and this paper therefore presents a backup design without the use of additional resources and compares it with OBS.

3 Proposed Scheme for Service Assurance in SD-SFC

3.1 Architecture

The proposed service assurance mechanism for SD-SFCs exploits the fact that multiple instances of a particular SF are present in the network as part different SFCs. For example, SFC for security service may consists of firewall SF, Intrusion Detection System (IDS) SF, and anomaly detection SF, and SFC for access control service may include separate instance of anomaly detection SF as well. Moreover, a single instance of a particular SF can be part of different SFCs, for example, access control SFC can use the anomaly detection SF instance present in the security SFC. Figure 1 further explains these two scenarios in the control and data planes. The orchestrator in NFV framework, while creating a logical SFC for the requested service takes decision about deploying a new SF instance or reusing an existing one. Mapping/embedding algorithm determines the network locations where SFs in the logical SFC are actually deployed. Structural and mapping information of the SFC is forwarded to SDN controller to create paths for steering incoming service traffic through deployed SFs in the data plane.

NFV orchestrator is also responsible for monitoring the unavailability of SF due to any reasons, and relay the unavailability information to the SDN controller. The service assurance module in SDN controller receives the information and by using selection algorithm sub-module chooses another instance of the unavailable SF already existing in the network as backup. If no other instance is present, then a new backup SF instance is deployed using algorithm in [5]. This study focuses only on a scenario where multiple SF instances are available in the network, as shown in the Fig. 2. (d). This approach eliminates the need of deploying exclusively dedicated or shared dedicated backup SFs, as shown in Fig. 2. (b) and Fig. 2. (c), respectively. The traffic migration sub-module takes the information of the selected backup SF instance and updates the network to steer the traffic through it for service continuation. For efficient path creation and traffic steering, traffic migration sub-module uses mechanisms presented in our previous study [9].

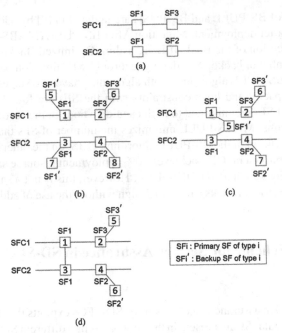

Fig. 2. Difference backup SF deployment scenarios in SD-SFC based network (a) Logical SFCs where each number means the type of SFs. (b) Exclusive dedicated backup method. (c) Shared dedicated backup when failure is occurred on SFC1's type 3 SF. (d) Shared backup SF without the need of any dedicated deployment.

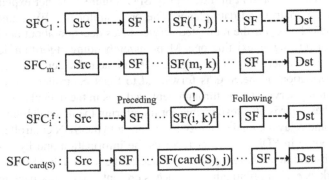

Fig. 3. Mathematical definition of SFCs in the proposed service assurance system.

3.2 Backup SF Selection

To describe the selection algorithm for backup SF, we first formally define SFCs and their components. In SD-SFC based network $S = \{SFC_1, SFC_2, \dots, SFC_{card(S)}\}$ is a set containing all SFCs, where SFC_i is itself a set of SFs. In particular, $SF(i, j)$ is an element in SFC_i of type j. In case of unavailability of type k SF in SFC_i, the unavailable SF is represented as $SF(i, k)^f$ and consequently the unavailable SFC as SFC_i^f. To restore the service, traffic from $SF(i, k)^f$ must be steered to $SFC_m \in R$ containing the function of type k, where $R = S \backslash \left\{ SFC_i^f \right\}$. Figure 3 shows formal definition of SFCs described above.

As described earlier, there can be multiple SFs of type k available in the network. SDN controller can restore the service by choosing any one of them and steer traffic to it. However, random selection of backup SF of type k can lead to higher migration delay due to additional flow tables updates in the data plane switches, and additional transmission delay due to added number of hops in the new path. High migration delay undermines the service assurance and leads to immense monetary cost. Increase in the transmission delay has devastating effects on user SLA. Therefore, this study prioritizes these factors while selecting the backup SF $SF(m, k) \in SFC_m$.

Algorithm 1 shows the selection of optimal $SF(m, k)$ from the set R as backup for the unavailable $SF(i, k)^f$. In order to do so, SFCs containing a SF of type k are pooled as candidate SFCs (Q) from R. In each $SFC_m \in Q$, candidate backup SF $SF(m, k)$ is sequentially searched and its detouring delay is calculated. Detouring delay is defined as cumulative number of hops from preceding SF of $SF(i, k)^f$ to $SF(m, k)$, and from $SF(m, k)$ to following SF of $SF(i, k)^f$. If the detouring delay of $SF(m, k)$ is lower than previously calculated detouring delays than $SF(m, k)$ is selected. Once all $SFC_m \in Q$ are searched, $SF(m, k)$ with minimum detouring delay is selected as the optimal backup SF.

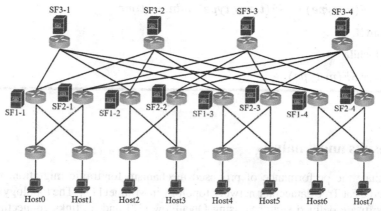

Fig. 4. Emulated fat tree topology in Mininet with multiple instances of SFs of different types.

The selection of backup SF based on minimum detouring delay ensures service continuity, as the number of switches to be updated for traffic migration are low. Similarly, the lowest hop count translates into lowest increment in the transmission delay. It is worth noting that current selection algorithm works under the assumption that the selected backup SF has enough capacity to accommodate the load of the unavailable SF. One of the potential improvements can be a joint detouring delay and load based selection algorithm. To complete the service assurance, the migration module in SDN controller updates the routing paths to migrate traffic to the selected backup SF.

Algorithm 1: Backup SF Selection Algorithm

Inputs: $SF(i, k)^f, SFC_i^f, S$

Variables: $R = S\{SFC_j^f\}, type$ = failed function type $k, Q \leftarrow \{\}, min$ = infinite

Output: $SF(m, type)$ in $SFC_m \in R$

1: **for** $m = 1$ to sizeof (R) **do**   // selecting candidate SFCs

2:    **if** $(SF(m, type) \in SFC_m)$

3:       Enqueue(Q, SFC_m) // Q is a set of candidate chains

4:    **end if**

5: **end for**

6: **while** length (Q) != 0

7:    $temp \leftarrow$ Dequeue(Q)

8:    $time \leftarrow$ DetourDelay$(SF(i, type)^f, SF(temp, type))$

9:    **if** $(time < min)$ **then**   // selecting SF which has the least transmission delay

10:       $SF(m, type) \leftarrow SF(temp, type), min \leftarrow time$

11:    **end if**

12: **end while**

13: **return** $SF(m, type)$

---

4   Results and Analysis

To evaluate the performance of proposed mechanism for traffic migration, we have emulated a Fat Tree datacenter network topology in Mininet [11]. The topology consists of 20 software-defined switches using OpenFlow [12] and 32 links connecting those switches, as shown in the Fig. 4. Service assurance module, consisting of selection algorithm and traffic migration sub-modules, is implemented on Ryu SDN controller [13] which has out-band connection with all the switches in the topology. The whole system is implemented on a system with Ubuntu 16.04 LTS OS, Intel Core i5-4690 CPU and 31.4 GiB RAM.

We have used up to eight SFCs in our experiments. Table 1 details the source, desti-nation, and ordered list of SFs for each emulated SFC, where first and second numbers after SF represents SF type and instance number of that SF type. For example, SF3-2 depicts second instance of type three SF. Different experiments use different configu-rations of SFCs, and we describe them while discussing each experiment. Evaluation criteria used in this paper are resource efficiency, transmission delay, and migration time, which are discussed in subsequent paragraphs.

Table 1. List of SFC details used

SFC	Ordered list of SFs	Source	Destination
1	{SF1-1, SF3-2}	Host0	Host7
2	{SF1-1, SF3-2}	Host7	Host2
3	{SF1-1, SF3-2}	Host6	Host0
4	{SF1-1, SF3-2}	Host3	Host5
5	{SF1-1, SF3-2}	Host2	Host1
6	{SF1-1, SF3-2}	Host1	Host4
7	{SF1-1, SF3-2}	Host1	Host3
8	{SF1-1, SF3-2}	Host2	Host6

The key contribution of this study is salvation of resources blocked by backup SFs. It is important to determine the amount of CPU and memory resources that become available as a result of proposed service assurance mechanism. For this purpose, we first install SFC1 and make SF3-2 temporarily unavailable, resultantly, backup selection algorithm chooses SF3-1 as the backup SF. By using reference values of average CPU and memory usage for a containerized SF on bare metal, shown in Table 2 [10], we measure the CPU and memory consumption of backup SF. Later, we incrementally install SFCs two to five, and they all share SF3-2. With the unavailability of SF3-2 all five SFCs become unavailable, and the results of CPU and memory consumption are shown in the Fig. 5. Comparison with OBS, currently the most resource-efficient backup sharing mechanism, shows that our proposed service assurance mechanism saves up to 20% of resources.

Table 2. CPU and memory usage values of a containerized sf on a bare metal

	CPU usage	Memory usage
Average	19.85	9.85
σ	4.61	0.33

The 20% improvement in resource usage comes at the cost of added transmission and migration cost. To prove the viability of the proposed service assurance mechanism in real systems, we compare the added transmission delay and migration delay with conventional backup (i.e., exclusive dedicated) and random selection methods. Here, conventional method serves as lower bound for transmission and migration delays because exclusive dedicated backup SF is deployed at the time of service creation and backup paths are pre-installed under protection mechanism. This enables conventional method to migrate traffic to backup SF with single message from SDN controller. Random selection method uses the shared backup SF same as the proposed scheme, but

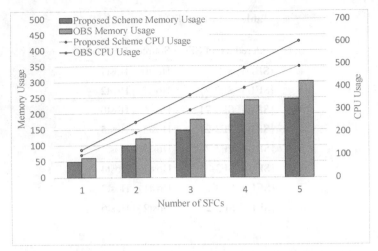

Fig. 5. Additional resource usage comparison between proposed solution and OBS to provide service assurance

randomly chooses the backup SF from the list of candidates. We use random selection for comparison to show the effectiveness of the proposed backup SF selection algorithm.

The added transmission delay comparison between proposed service assurance, conventional backup, and random selection mechanism is shown in Fig. 6. Added transmission delay refers to the time added in the end-to-end transmission delay of primary SFC path due to detouring after traffic migration. The experiments for each method are repeated 100 times and measurements are gathered for a single SFC with 500 Mbps network traffic. Expectedly, the conventional backup method shows the minimum added delay of 1–3 ms, because of the short detouring path resulting from the close proximity of the exclusive dedicated backup SF. Nevertheless, the proposed service assurance shows 5–8 ms added transmission delay, which is only ~4 ms more than conventional backup. Performance of random selection method is the worst and inconsistent because any of the candidate backup SFs can be selected for service assurance.

Service disruption time due to SF unavailability is the most important criterion to evaluate effectiveness of any service assurance method. In this study, service disruption time is represented by migration delay and it is defined as the time taken by a service assurance method to switch the traffic from unavailable SF to the backup SF. This includes searching for the backup SF, calculation of detouring path to and from backup SF, and installation of flow entries in the detouring path for steering of the traffic. Intuitively, the migration delay increases with more number of SFCs sharing the unavailable SF. To evaluate the migration delay of the proposed service assurance mechanism against reference schemes, we incrementally install one, three, and five SFCs that share the unavailable SF and their results are presented in Fig. 7. (a), (b), and (c), respectively. The experiments for each method are conducted 100 times and measurements are collected with 500 Mbps network traffic.

Expectedly, the migration delay of conventional backup mechanism is the lowest in all three cases shown in Fig. 7. (a), (b) and (c). This is because backup SF is installed at the

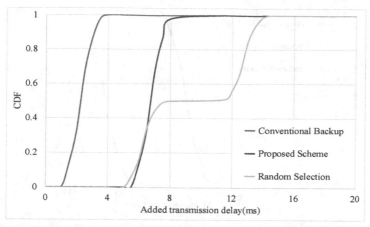

Fig. 6. Added transmission delay comparison between proposed service assurance, conventional backup, and random selection methods.

time of service setup which eliminates the need for searching algorithm, and detouring paths are pre-calculated. However, we see the increase in migration delay as the number of effected SFCs increase, and that is because of the increasing number of flows entries required to be installed to setup the detouring path. The backup SF selection algorithm in the proposed service assurance mechanism takes more time with increase in number of effected SFCs, but makes up for it by using the label switching technique presented in our previous work [9] to setup detouring path. This allows the proposed service assurance mechanism to have only slightly increased migration delay than conventional backup method. More specifically, the difference between conventional and proposed methods with one SFC in Fig. 7. (a) is ~0.006 ms, ~0.023 ms with three SFCs in Fig. 7. (b), and ~0.04 ms with five SFCs in Fig. 7. (c). The results of random selection are worst in all three cases as it suffers from delay in both backup SF selection and detouring path calculation. Also, the path setup delay is more for random selection mechanism due to often longer detouring paths.

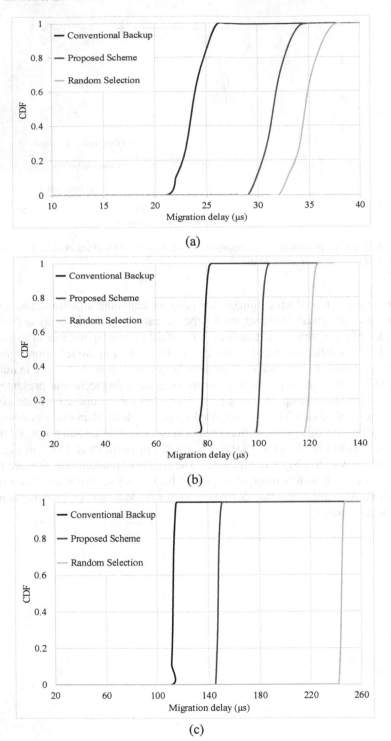

Fig. 7. Migration delay comparison between proposed service assurance, conventional backup, and random selection methods (a) results 1 SFC, (b) 3 SFCs, and (c) 5 SFCs

5   Conclusion and Future Work

This study proposes a service assurance mechanism in SD-SFCs through backup sharing with the aim to improve the resource usage. It exploits the fact that multiple instances of a same SF are deployed in the network as part of different SFCs, and use them as backup. To select the best suited backup SF among multiple candidates, we have proposed a selection algorithm based on shortest detouring path. Results show that our proposed mechanism saves as much as 20% resources comparing to current state-of-the-art backup sharing technique. This improvement comes at the cost of increased transmission and migration delays. However, the results show that this increase is very minimal and will have almost no effect on service performance. Specifically, the maximum increase in transmission and migration delays is ~4 ms and ~0.04 ms, respectively. We are currently working on improvements of backup SF selection algorithm by using current load of candidate SFs and detouring path as joint selection criteria. In future we look to further improve it by predicting the future load of candidate SFs, which will also help in reducing the number of migrations.

Acknowledgements. This work is partly supported by the Ministry of Education, IITP, and NRF, Korea, under the High-Potential Individuals Global Training Program(IITP-2019-0-01579), AI Graduate School Support Program (No.2019-0-00421), and mid-career support program (NRF-2020R1A2C2008447).

References

1. McKeown, N., et al.: 2008. OpenFlow: enabling innovation in campus networks. SIGCOMM Comput. Commun. Rev. **38**(2), 69–74, March 2008
2. Mijumbi, R., Serrat, J., Gorricho, J.L., Bouten, N., De Turck, F., Boutaba, R.: Network function virtualization: state-of-the-art and research challenges. IEEE Commun. Surv. Tutorials **18**, no. 1, pp. 236–262, Firstquarter 2016
3. Lee, J., Ko, H., Suh, D., Pack, S.: Overload and failure management in service function chaining. In: IEEE Conference on Network Softwarization (NetSoft), pp. 1–5 (2017)
4. Yu, H., Anand, V., Qiao, C., Sun, G.: Cost efficient design of survivable virtual infrastructure to recover from facility node failures. In: IEEE International Conference on Communications (ICC), pp. 1–6 (2011)
5. Ayoubi, S., Chen, Y., Assi, C.: Towards promoting backup-sharing in survivable virtual network design. IEEE/ACM Trans. Networking **24**(5), 3218–3231 (2016)
6. Aidi, S., Zhani, M.F. Elkhatib, Y.: On improving service chains survivability through efficient backup provisioning. In: International Conference on Network and Service Management (CNSM), pp. 108–115 (2018)
7. Aidi, S., Zhani, M.F. Elkhatib, Y.: On optimizing backup sharing through efficient VNF migration. In: IEEE Conference on Network Softwarization (NetSoft), pp. 60–65 (2019)
8. Dominicini, C.K., et al.: KeySFC: traffic steering using strict source routing for dynamic and efficient network orchestration. Comput. Netw., **167**, p. 106975 (2020)
9. Jeong, H., Raza, S.M., Nguyen, D.T., Kim, S., Kim, M., Choo, H.: Control plane design for failure protection in software defined service function chains. In: 14th International Conference on Ubiquitous Information Management and Communication (IMCOM), pp. 1–6 (2020)

10. Sheoran, A., Bu, X., Cao, L., Sharma, P., Fahmy, S.: An empirical case for container-driven fine-grained VNF Resource Flexing. In: IEEE Conference on Network Function Virtualization and Software Defined Networks (NFV-SDN), pp. 121–127 (2016)
11. Mininet – an instant virtual network on your laptop (or other PC). http://www.mininet.org/. Accessed 27 Oct 2020
12. OpenFlow Switch Specification Version 1.3.0. https://opennetworking.org/product-certification/. Accessed 27 Oct 2020
13. Ryu SDN Framework. https://ryu-sdn.org/. Accessed 27 Oct 2020

Using Fuzzy Time Series Model Based on Hedge Algebras and Relationship Groups Following Time Points for Forecasting Time Series

Nguyen Dinh Thuan[1](✉) and Hoang Tung[2](✉)

[1] University of Information Technology, Linh Trung Ward, Thu Duc Dist.
Ho Chi Minh City, Vietnam
thuannd@uit.edu.vn
[2] Dong Nai University, Tan Hiep Ward, Bien Hoa City, Dong Nai Province, Vietnam
tungh@grad.uit.edu.vn

Abstract. There are three problems when applying fuzzy time series (FTS) model for forecasting time series, the first, how to partition the universe of discourse, the second, determining effective relationships, and the third, setting up formula for calculating forecasting values. This paper introduces a new model of fuzzy time series based on hedge algebras (HA), developed from combining relationship groups and formulas using weighs following time points, to handle these problems. Experimental results show that the proposed method helps improving accuracy rate of forecasting results when comparing existing other methods.

Keywords: Forecasting · Fuzzy time series · Time series · Hedge algebras

1 Introduction

In many cases, applying the fuzzy time series model to forecast time series, which has the number of observations is not big enough or time series that its values are linguistic terms bring about good forecasting results compared to other methods [1–3]. Basically, when using this method, there are three problems affecting to forecasting quality.

The first problem is how to partition the universe of discourse of the time series need forecasting. Because the values belonging to the intervals are taken for computing forecasting values, so the more suitable intervals we have, the more better forecasting result we get. The second one is how to build relationship groups among the values of the fuzzy time series. The relationship groups closely relate to the formula used to determine forecasting values, hence this problem is also affecting to forecasting results. The third one is how to build defuzzification formula. This directly generates forecasting values.

In order to resolve the first problem, scholars have been suggested many approaches, such as distribution- and average-based length [4], ratio-based lengths [5], fuzzy c-means clustering method [7], information granules [8–10], modified genetic algorithm [11] and particle swarm optimization technique [12] and so on.

Paper [13] is the first study that proposed the concept of fuzzy relationship groups for handling the second problem. Since then, many scholars have applied in this study for

© Springer Nature Singapore Pte Ltd. 2020
T. K. Dang et al. (Eds.): FDSE 2020, CCIS 1306, pp. 401–410, 2020.
https://doi.org/10.1007/978-981-33-4370-2_28

their researches with some improvements such as [14] adding weighs after the terms referring to the number of the terms appearing at the right hand side in the fuzzy relationship.

With the third one, the work [13] is also the first study used arithmetic formula to calculate forecasting values. Based on this one, many papers suggested some changes, for example, [15] uses weighs in the formula, and [14] employed semantically quantifying value in the intervals to compute forecasting results.

Paper [12, 16] suggested group of fuzzy relationships following time points. The paper supposes that when forecasting time series at point t, then values of the time series of t backward affect on forecasting results. So only the values should participate forecasting formula. Study [14] proposed fuzzy time series based on Hedge algebras for forecasting time series and retrieve rather better forecasting results compared to others one.

In this paper, we combine the results from [12, 14] and [15] to build a new model for forecasting time series. Empirical analyses determine that our proposed method can get the better forecasting accuracy rate than the existing methods.

The remaining of this paper is organized as follows: Sect. 2 introduces some basic concepts of fuzzy time series and hedge algebras, Sect. 3 presents proposed method for forecasting time series, Sect. 4 presents experimental result when applying the proposed method, and Sect. 5 gives some conclusions.

2 Basic Concepts of Fuzzy Time Series and Hedge Algebras

2.1 Fuzzy Time Series [16]

Definition 1. Let $Y(t)$ $(t = ..., 0, 1, 2, ...)$, a subset of R^1, be the universe of discourse on which $f_i(t)$ $(i = 1, 2, ...)$ are defined and $F(t)$ is the collection of $f_i(t)$ $(i = 1, 2, ...)$. Then $F(t)$ is called FTS on $Y(t)$ $(t = ..., 0, 1, 2, ...)$.

Definition 2. The relationship between $F(t)$ and $F(t - 1)$ can be presented as $F(t - 1) \rightarrow F(t)$. If let $A_i = F(t)$ and $A_j = F(t - 1)$; the relationship between $F(t)$ and $F(t - 1)$ is represented by fuzzy logical relationship (FLR) $A_i \rightarrow A_j$, where A_i and A_j refer to the left - hand side and the right-hand side of the FLR.

Definition 3. Let $F(t)$ be a FTS. If $F(t)$ is caused by $F(t - 1)$; $F(t - 2)$; $\cdots$; $F(t - m + 1)$; $F(t - m)$ then this FR is represented by $F(t - m)$; $\cdots$; $F(t - 2)$; $F(t - 1) \rightarrow F(t)$ and is called an m - order FTS model.

Definition 4. The FLR having the same left- hand side can be grouped into a FRG. Assume there exists FLRs as follows: $A_i \rightarrow A_{k1}, A_i \rightarrow A_{k2}; \cdots; A_i \rightarrow A_{km}$; these FLRs can be put into the same FRG as $A_i \rightarrow A_{k1}, A_{k2}; \cdots; A_{km}$.

Definition 5. The FLR is determined by the relationship $F(t - 1) \rightarrow F(t)$. Let $F(t) = A_i(t)$ and $F(t - 1) = A_j(t - 1)$, the FLR between $F(t - 1)$ and $F(t)$ can be denoted as $A_j(t - 1) \rightarrow A_i(t)$. Also at time t, we have the following FLR $A_j(t - 1) \rightarrow A_i(t); A_j(t_{1-1}) \rightarrow A_{i1}(t_1); ...; A_j(t_{p-1}) \rightarrow A_{ip}(t_p)$ with $t_1; t_2; ..., t_p \le t$.

2.2 Hedge Algebras [17]

Definition 6. The HA is defined by $AX = (X, G, C, H, \leq)$, in which, X is set of terms, $G = \{c^+, c^-\}$ is the set of primary generators, where c^+ and c^- are, *respectively*, the negative primary and positive term belong to X, $C = \{0, 1, W\}$ is a collection of constants in X, H is the set of hedges, $H = H^+ \cup H^-$, where H^+, H^- is, respectively, the set of all positive and negative hedges of X; "$\leq$" is a semantically ordering relation on X.

Each *hedge* is considered as a unary operator. When applying $h \in H$ to x, we obtain term $hx \in X$. The positive hedges increase semantic tendency and vice versa with negative hedges. It can be assumed that $H^- = \{h_{-1} < h_{-2} < \ldots < h_{-q}\}$ and $H^+ = \{h_1 < h_2 < \ldots < h_p\}$.

If X and H are linearly ordered sets, then $AX = (X, G, C, H, \leq)$ is called linear hedge algebras, furthermore, if AX is equipped with additional operations $\sum$ and Φ that are, respectively, infimum and supremum of $H(x)$ ($H(x)$ is the set of terms $u \in X$, $u = h_n \ldots h_1 x$, with $h_n, \ldots, h_1 \in H$, generated from x by applying the hedges of H), then it is called complete linear hedge algebras (ClinHA).

Definition 7. Let $AX = (X, G, C, H, \leq)$ be a ClinHA. An *fm*: $X \rightarrow [0, 1]$ is said to be a fuzziness measure of terms in X if:

(1). $fm(c^-) + fm(c^+) = 1$ and $\sum_{h \in H} fm(hu) = fm(u)$, for $\forall u \in X$; in this case fm is called *complete*;

(2). For the constants 0, W and 1, $fm(0) = fm(W) = fm(1) = 0$;

(3). For $\forall x, y \in X$, $\forall h \in H$, $\frac{fm(hx)}{fm(x)} = \frac{fm(hy)}{fm(y)}$, that is this proportion does not depend on specific elements and, therefore, it is called the fuzziness measure of the hedge h and denoted by $\mu(h)$.

Proposition 1. For each fuzziness measure fm on X the following statements hold:

(1). $fm(hx) = \mu(h)fm(x)$, for every $x \in X$;

(2). $fm(c^-) + fm(c^+) = 1$;

(3). $\sum_{-q \leq i \leq p, i \neq 0} fm(h_i c) = fm(c)$, $c \in \{c^-, c^+\}$;

(4). $\sum_{-q \leq i \leq p, i \neq 0} fm(h_i x) = fm(x)$;

(5). $\sum_{-q \leq i \leq -1} \mu(h_i) = \alpha$ and $\sum_{1 \leq i \leq p} \mu(h_i) = \beta$, where $\alpha, \beta > 0$ and $\alpha + \beta = 1$.

Definition 8. The fuzziness interval of the linguistic terms $x \in X$, denoted by $\Im(x)$, is a subinterval of $[0,1]$, if $|\Im(x)| = fm(x)$ where $|\Im(x)|$ is the length of $fm(x)$, and recursively determined by the length of x as follows:

(1). If length of x is equal to 1 ($l(x) = 1$), that mean $x \in \{c^-, c^+\}$, then $|\Im(c^-)| = fm(c^-)$, $|\Im(c+)| = fm(c^+)$ and $\Im(c^-) \leq \Im(c^+)$;

(2). Suppose that n is the length of x ($l(x) = n$) and fuzziness interval $\Im(x)$ has been defined with $|\Im(x)| = fm(x)$. The set $\{\Im(h_j x)| j \in [-q\hat{\ }p]\}$, where $[-q\hat{\ }p] = \{j \mid -q \leq j \leq -1$ or $1 \leq j \leq p\}$, is a partition of $\Im(x)$ and we have: for $h_p x \leq x$, $\Im(h_p x) \leq \Im(h_{p-1} x) \leq \ldots \leq \Im(h_1 x) \leq \Im(h_{-1} x) \leq \ldots \leq \Im(h_{-q} x)$; for $h_p x = \geq x$, $\Im(h_{-q} x) \leq \Im(h_{-q+1} x) \leq \ldots \leq \Im(h_{-1} x) \leq \Im(h_1 x) \leq \ldots \leq \Im(h_p x)$.

3   Proposed Method

Suppose that $c(t)$ is a time series that we need to forecast. The following presents two phrases applied to forecasting $c(t)$.

Modeling Phrase
Step 1: Set k is the number of linguistic terms used to qualitatively describe the values of $c(t)$.

Step 2: Calculate the universe of discourse of $c(t)$, $U = [Dmin - D1, Dmax + D2]$ where $Dmin, Dmax, D1$ and $D2$ are, respectively, minimum, maximum historical values of $c(t)$ and proper value chosen so that all the values of $c(t)$, in the past or future ones, belong to U. Set $L = Dmin - D1$, and $R = Dmax + D2$.

Step 3: Denote $f(t)$ is the fuzzy time series generated after using the terms in Step 2 to qualitatively describe $c(t)$. At first, $f(t) = \emptyset$.

Use $AX = (X, G, C, H, \leq)$, where H includes only two hedges, h_{-1} and h_{+1} and $G = \{c^-, c^+\}$, to generate the terms.

Let p be FiFo list, Lo and Hi respectively be primary generators, and to be an integer number.

Add Lo and Hi to p;

$t=2$;

While $(t \leq k)\{$

      Let x be a linguistic term

      $x=$ first element of p;

      Use h_{-1} and h_{+1} operate to x in order to generate two new linguistic terms, $h_{-1}x$ and $h_{+1}x$;

      Add $h_{-1}x$ and $h_{+1}x$ to rear of p;

      $t=t+1$;

$\}$

      Sort p in ascending order of semantically ordering relation.

(3) Compute fuzziness intervals of the linguistic terms in p following Definition 8. Assign each fuzziness interval to a interval on U.
(4) Remove the intervals which do not contain any historical values. Suppose that the number of the intervals is m.
(5) The following tasks will be conducted:

(a) Firstly, find the interval which having the maximum number of distinct historical values and to be leftmost position, suppose that this interval is referred by a. Then, partition A_i's interval into two sub intervals corresponding two linguistic terms, $h_{-1}A_i$ and $h_{+1}A_i$.

(b) Add two new terms to p.

(c) Remove the terms that its fuzziness interval do not contain any historical values.

(d) Loop (a), (b) and (c) until get m terms (to get k terms). If all the terms's intervals have only one historical value or same historical values, then break loop.

(e) Replace each value of $c(t)$ by a appropriate term getting from p and add the term to $FTS(t)$.

Step 4: Building relationship groups

Relationship groups are set up following Definition 5:

– Build relationship for couple of consecutive values of the $f(t)$ at time point t_k where $t_k \leq t$:

$A_i \rightarrow A_j$ where A_i and A_j is, respectively, value of $f(t_k\text{-}1)$ and $f(t_k)$.

– Group relationships have same left side, for example:

If we have

$$A_p \rightarrow A_u,$$
$$A_p \rightarrow A_q,$$
$$A_p \rightarrow A_v,$$

then the relationships are grouped into $A_p \rightarrow A_u\, A_q\, A_v$.

Forecasting Phrase

Let $Mid(A_j)$, $Mid(A_k)$ respectively be mid point of fuzziness intervals of $A_j \dots A_k$.

If A_i is left side of the relationship $A_i \rightarrow A_j$ (1)$\dots A_k$ (m), where (1), $\dots$, (m) refer to order of occurrence of $A_i, \dots A_k$ in the relationship following time, then the forecasting value, denoted vf, at $t + 1$ of $c(t)$, is calculated by following formula:

$$vf = \frac{1 * Mid(A_j) + \dots + k * Mid(A_k)}{1 + \dots + k}$$

If A_i is left side of the relationship $A_i \rightarrow \emptyset$, then vf is $Mid(A_i)$.

4 Implementation

This section presents experimental results after applying the proposed method for forecasting time series of enrollments of Alabama University (from 1971 to 1992), Unemployment rates of Taiwan (from 1/1/2013 to 12/1/2013) and Bitcoin close price (from 15/7/2020 to 15/8/2020). These time series are abbreviated as ALA, UNE, BIT.

The first order of fuzzy time series based on HA is employed to forcast the time series. The HA, $AX = (X, G, C, H, \leq)$ is used to generate the terms which are used to describe ALA. Let $G = \{Low, Hight\}$, $C = \{0, 1, W\}$, $H = \{Very, Little\}$. *Low*, *Hight*, *Very* and *Little*, respectively, are denoted by *Lo*, *H*, *V* and *L* for short.

ALA time series

Similar to previous studies, this paper take $U = [13000, 20000]$, where $Dmin = 13055$, $Dmax = 19337$, $D1 = 55$, $D2 = 663$, $LU = 7000$.

With 7 intervals.

If we suppose that the number of enrollments is less than 16000 is low, then we can set up the following parameters:

$fm(low) = \frac{16000-13000}{20000-13000} = 0.428$, this means that $fm(high) = 0.572$. Mapping these values to U we have $covfm(low)$ and $covfm(high)$ that are determined respectively by $fm(low) \times LU = 0.428 \times 7000 = 2996$, $fm(hight) \times LU = 0.572 \times 7000 = 4004$.

We can choose $\mu(Little) = 0.4$, $\mu(Very) = 0.6$. From $\mu(Little)$ and $\mu(Very)$ we have $\alpha = 0.4$, $\beta = 0.6$.

Seven terms which are used to describe ALA are *very very low (A1)*, *little very low (A2)*, *very little low (A3)*, *little little low (A4)*, *little little hight (A5)*, *very little hight (A6)* and *very hight (A7)*.

The intervals of the terms and midpoint of the intervals are printed in the following table (Tables 1, 2, 3, 4 and 5):

Table 1. Terms, intervals and midpoints

Terms	Intervals	Midpoint
A1	[13000, 14079)	13539.5
A2	[14079, 14798)	14438.5
A3	[14798, 15517)	15157.5
A4	[15517, 15996)	15756.5
A5	[15996, 16637)	16316.5
A6	[16637, 17598)	17117.5
A7	[17598, 20000]	18799.0

Table 2. Fuzzifying ALA

Years	Enrollments	Linguistic terms	Relationship groups
1971	13055	*A1*	
1972	13563	*A1*	*A1 → A1*
1973	13867	*A1*	*A1 → A1A1*

(continued)

Table 2. (*continued*)

Years	Enrollments	Linguistic terms	Relationship groups
1974	14696	A2	A1 → A1A1A2
1975	15460	A3	A2→ A3
1976	15311	A3	A3 → A3
1977	15603	A4	A3 → A3A4
1978	15861	A4	A4 → A4
1979	16807	A6	A4 → A4A6
1980	16919	A6	A6 → A6
1981	16388	A5	A6 → A6A5
1982	15433	A3	A5 → A3
1983	15497	A3	A3 → A3, A4, A3
1984	15145	A3	A3 → A3, A4, A3, A3
1985	15163	A3	A3 → A3, A4, A3, A3, A3
1986	15984	A4	A3 → A3, A4, A3, A3, A3, A4
1987	16859	A6	A4→ A4, A6, A6
1988	18150	A7	A6 → A6, A5,A7
1989	18970	A7	A7 → A7
1990	19328	A7	A7 → A7A7
1991	19337	A7	A7 → A7A7A7

From the intervals, we have:

Applying the formula determining forecasting values of the proposed method, we have forecasting values.

For example, suppose that we need to forecast ALA value: At 1979, we use relationship group $A4 \rightarrow A4A6$ to compute forecasting result following the formula in Forecasting phrase: $= (1*\text{midpoint}(A4) + 2 * \text{midpoint}(A6)/(1 + 2) = (1 * 15756.5 + 2 * 17117.5)/(1 + 2) = 16663.83$. At 1990, we use relationship group $A7 \rightarrow A7A7$, so the forecasting value at this point is $(1*\text{midpoint}(A7) + 2 * \text{midpoint}(A7))/(1 + 2) = (1 * 18799 + 2 * 18799)/3 = 18799$.

Table 3. Forecasting results of ALA (7 intervals)

Year	Historical data	Chen 2013	Wang 2014	Lu 2015	HNV 2016	Bisht 2016	Tinh 2019	Proposed method
1972	13563	14347	13944	14279	13820	13595.67	13307	13539.5
1973	13867	14347	13944	14279	13820	13814.75	14066	13539.5
...	...	...	...	...	...	......	...	...
1990	19328	18907	18933	19257	19135	19357.30	19514	18799
1991	19337	18907	18933	19257	19135	19168.56	19831	18799
1992	18876	18907	18933	19257	19135	19168.56	19589	18799
1993	N/A	N/A	N/A	N/A	N/A	N/A	18932.2	N/A
RMSE		486.3	506.0	445.2	441.3	428.63	374.2	318.2

With 17 intervals

Table 4. Forecasting results of ALA (17 intervals)

Year	Historical data	Lu 2015	HNV 11/2016	HNV 8/2016	Proposed method
1972	13563	13678	13544	13563	13517.5
1973	13867	13678	13906	13867	13863
...	...	...	...	...	
1990	19328	19574	19167	19152	19567.5
1991	19337	19146	19167	19152	19567.5
1992	18876	19146	18878	18876	19567.5
RMSE		256.3	237.7	237.6	186.9

UNE Time series

Table 5. Forecasting results of UNE (with intervals and universe of discourse same as [10])

Date	Historical data	Wang 2013	Chen 2013	Wang 2014	Lu 2015	HNV 11/2016	Proposed method
02/01/2013	7.7	7.39	7.60	7.62	7.58	7.51	7.6
03/01/2013	7.5	7.39	7.60	7.62	7.58	7.51	7.5
...	...	...	...	...	...	...	...
10/01/2013	7.2	6.89	7.12	7.13	7.07	6.99	7.2
11/01/2013	7.0	6.89	7.12	7.13	7.07	6.99	7.1
12/01/2013	6.7	6.89	7.12	7.13	7.07	6.99	6.4
RMSE		0.20	0.18	0.19	0.17	0.16	0.12

BIT Time series

Bitcoin price is a time series that has strong fluctuations. So bigger U is applied when the Bitcoin time series has intensive fluctuations, and the smaller one is applied for the opposite case. In general, bigger U generates lower accuracy forecasting values compared to smaller one. With this time series we propose two U for comparing, the first one is [6334.6, 14695.5] and second one is [8900, 12100]. In the following we introduce the way to build U for BIT in both cases. The way can be applied for BIT at different time interval.

The first one is set up as follows: We have maximum of BIT value is 11908.5323 (Max), and minimum one is 9121.566153 (Min). $Max - Min = 2786.97$. So we settup $L = Min$ - 2786.97 = 6334.6, and $R = Max + 2786.97 = 14695.5$.

The second one is determined as follows:

- Calculating variations of BIT
- Compute average of the variations, denoted as A
- $L = Min - A, R = Max + A$

Applying rules for second one, we have $L = Min - A$ =9121.566153 - 211.2416382 = 8910.325, $R = Max + A = 11908.5323 + 211.2416382 = 12119.77$ and we then round these numbers, so U = [8900, 12100] (Table 6).

Table 6. Forecasting results of BIT

Date	Historical data	$U = [6334.6, 14695.5]$	$U = [8900, 12100]$
7/15/2020	9194.75252	9246.768001	9134
7/16/2020	9121.566153	9246.768001	9134
...	...	...	...
8/13/2020	11499.9903	11567.97464	11649.42857
8/14/2020	11845.17405	12090.93273	11710.77143
8/15/2020	11899.94978	12754.32168	11543.68
RMSE		645.7887	138.7998

5 Conclusion and Future Work

How to determine intervals on the universe of discourse, how to set up relations and how to build formulas for computing forecasting values are threes problems when using the fuzzy time series model to forecasting time series. This paper proposed a new method for resolving the problems. In order to evaluate the proposed method, this is used for forecasting enrollments of Alabama university, unemployment rates in Taiwan and Bitcoin prices. Experimental results show that, the proposed method made forecasting values that having accuracy rate is smaller than some existing methods.

This study can be improved when apply some techniques to optimize the parameters of HA to get more suitable intervals on the universe of discourses of time series that need forecasting, for purpose advancing quality of forecasting results. This work can be done in the our future study.

References

1. Wang, C.-C.: A comparison study between fuzzy time series model and ARIMA model for forecasting Taiwan export. Expert Syst. Appl. **38**, 9296–9304 (2011)
2. Arumugam, P., Anithakumari, V.: Fuzzy time series method for forecasting Taiwan export data. Int. J. Eng. Trends Technol. (IJETT) **4**, 3342–3347 (2013)
3. Senthamarai, K., Sakthivel, E.: Fuzzy time series model and ARIMA model – a comparative study. Indian J. Appl. Res. **4**, 624–636 (2014)
4. Huarng, K.: Efective lengths of intervals to improve forecasting in fuzzy time series. Fuzzy Sets Syst. **123**, 387–394 (2001)
5. Huarng, K.: Ratio-based lengths of intervals to improve fuzzy time series forecasting. IEEE Trans. Syst. Man Cybernet.—Part B: Cybernet. **36**, 328–340 (2006)
6. Gautam, S.S., Abhishekh, S.R.S.: A new high-order approach for forecasting fuzzy time series data. Int. J. Comput. Intell. Appl. **17**, 1–17 (2018)
7. Cheng, C.H., Chen, T.L., Teoh, H.J., Chiang, C.H.: Fuzzy time series based on adaptive expectation model for TAIEX forecasting. Expert Syst. Appl. **34**, 1126–1132 (2008)
8. Wang, L., Liu, X., Pedrycz, W.: Effective intervals determined by information granules to improve forecasting in FTS. Expert Syst. Appl. **40**, 5673–5679 (2013)
9. Wang, L., et al.: Determination of temporal information granules to improve forecasting in FTS. Expert Syst. Appl. **41**, 3134–3142 (2014)
10. Wei, L., et al.: Using interval information granules to improve forecasting in fuzzy time series. Int. J. Approximate Reasoning **57**, 1–18 (2015)
11. Bas, E., Uslu, V.R., Yolcu, U., Egrioglu, E.: A modified genetic algorithm for forecasting fuzzy time series. Appl. Intell. **41**(2), 453–463 (2014). https://doi.org/10.1007/s10489-014-0529-x
12. Van Tinh, N., Dieu, N.C.: Handling forecasting problems based on combining high-order time-variant fuzzy relationship groups and particle swam optimization. Technique Int. J. Comput. Intell. Appl. **17**, 1–19 (2018)
13. Chen, S.-M.: Forecasting enrollments based on fuzzy time series. Fuzzy Sets Syst. **81**, 311–319 (1996)
14. Tung, H., Thuan, N.D., Loc, V.M.: Partitioning method based on hedge algebras for FTS forecasting. J. Sci. Technol. **54**, 571–583 (2016)
15. Yu, H.K.: Weighted fuzzy time series models for TAIEX forecasting. Phys. A **349**, 609–624 (2005)
16. Van Tinh, N., Dieu, N.C.: A new hybrid fuzzy time series forecasting model based on combining fuzzy c-means clustering and particle swam optimization. J. Comput. Sci. Cybern. **35**, 267–292 (2019)
17. Ho, N.C., Long, N.V.: Fuzziness measure on complete hedge algebras and quantifying semantics of terms in linear hedge algebras. Fuzzy Sets Syst. **158**, 452–471 (2007)

Finding Maximum Stable Matchings for the Student-Project Allocation Problem with Preferences Over Projects

Hoang Huu Viet, Le Van Tan, and Son Thanh Cao[⊠]

School of Engineering and Technology, Vinh University, Vinh City, Vietnam
{viethh,tandhv,sonct}@vinhuni.edu.vn

Abstract. This paper proposes an efficient algorithm to find a maximum weakly stable matching for the Student-Project Allocation Problem with Preferences over Projects. We consider the problem as a constraint satisfaction problem and solve it using a local search approach based on the min-conflicts algorithm. By choosing a student generated by a fixed-increment rule and removing the undominated blocking pair formed by the student, we aim to remove all the blocking pairs formed by the student at each iteration of our algorithm. This allows our algorithm to obtain a solution of the problem as quickly as possible. Experimental results show that our algorithm is efficient in terms of both performance and solution quality for solving the problem.

Keywords: Student-Project Allocation Problem · Matching problem · Stable matching · Blocking pair · Local search

1 Introduction

In many undergraduate courses of universities, students have to undertake projects offered by lecturers. To do this, students firstly need to be assigned to projects such that both students and lecturers meet their preference and capacity constraints. This problem originally described by Abraham et al. [7] and known as the *Student-Project Allocation problem* (SPA). In the setting of SPA, each lecturer offers a set of projects and ranks a subset of students in strict order that he/she intends to supervise, whilst each student ranks a subset of the available projects that he/she finds acceptable in strict order. There exist capacity constraints on the maximum number of students that can be assigned to each project and lecturer. The aim of SPA is to allocate projects to students to satisfy the constraints on these preferences and capacities. Abraham et al. [7] proposed two linear-time algorithms to find a *stable matching* of students to projects in SPA. The first one returns a *student-optimal* stable matching in which each student gets the best project that he/she could get in any stable matching, while the second one returns a *lecturer-optimal* stable matching in which each lecturer gets the best set of students that he/she could get in any stable matching.

© Springer Nature Singapore Pte Ltd. 2020
T. K. Dang et al. (Eds.): FDSE 2020, CCIS 1306, pp. 411–422, 2020.
https://doi.org/10.1007/978-981-33-4370-2_29

In SPA requiring each lecturer to rank a subset of students in a strict order is unfair for both lecturers and students. For example, lecturers often strongly prefer to supervise students with good academic results rather than students with poor academic results. This sometimes leads to conflicts among lecturers and students. Manlove and Malley [2] proposed a variant of SPA, called SPA *with Preferences over Projects* (SPA-P), where lecturers rank a subset of projects they offer in strict order rather than a subset of students. Given an SPA-P instance, Manlove et al. showed that stable matchings can have different sizes and the problem of finding a maximum cardinality stable matching is NP-hard.

Both SPA and SPA-P have recently received a great deal of attention from the research community in building automated applications for allocating students to projects. Examples may include the School of Computing Science, University of Glasgow [10], the Faculty of Science, University of Southern Denmark [1], the Department of Computing Science, University of York [8].

In the last few years, there are several researchers focused on designing efficient approximation algorithms to consider the lower and upper bounds for SPA-P. An algorithm is called r-approximation algorithm for SPA-P if it always finds a stable matching M with $|M| \geq |M_{opt}|/r$, where M_{opt} is a stable matching of maximum size. Manlove and Malley [2] extended the well-known Gale-Shapley algorithm [3] to find an 2-approximation algorithm, namely SPA-P-approx. This algorithm consists of a sequence of apply operations, in which an unassigned student with a non-empty list applies to the first project on his/her list to form pairs of a matching such that the lecturers and projects satisfy their capacity constraints. The algorithm returns a stable matching in a finite number of iterations. Iwama et al. [6] modified SPA-P-approx using Király's idea [9] to find an $\frac{3}{2}$- approximation algorithm. Recently, Manlove et al. [11] investigated an integer programming approach to SPA-P and proposed an $\frac{3}{2}$-approximation algorithm to find stable matchings that are very close to having maximum cardinality.

In this paper, we propose an algorithm to find maximum weakly stable matchings of SPA-P instances of large sizes. Our approach is based on a local search strategy applied for constraint satisfaction problems [12,13]. The local search strategy uses very little memory and can quickly find solutions in large state spaces and therefore, it is used for solving SPA-P of large sizes. Our experimental results show that our algorithm is much efficient than the SPA-P-approx algorithm [2] in terms of performance and solution quality for SPA-P instances of large sizes.

The rest of this paper is organized as follows. Section 2 describes preliminaries of SPA-P. Section 3 presents our proposed algorithm. Section 4 discusses the experiments and evaluations, and Sect. 5 concludes our work.

2   Preliminaries

This section recalls the SPA-P problem given in [2,4,5]. The SPA-P is defined consisting of a set $S = \{s_1, s_2, \cdots, s_n\}$ of *students*, a set $P = \{p_1, p_2, \cdots, p_q\}$ of *projects* and a set $\mathcal{L} = \{l_1, l_2, \cdots, l_m\}$ of *lecturers*. Each lecturer l_k offers a set

P_k ($k = 1, 2, \cdots, m$) of projects ranked in strict order of preference. We assume that $P_1, P_2, \cdots, P_k$ partitions $\mathcal{P}$ and each project $p_j \in \mathcal{P}$ is offered by a unique lecturer $l_k \in \mathcal{L}$. Also, each student s_i ranks a set of projects $A_i \subseteq \mathcal{P}$ in strict order of preference. If project $p_j \in \mathcal{P}$ is ranked by student s_i, we say that s_i finds p_j *acceptable*. Finally, each lecturer l_k has a capacity d_k, indicating the maximum number of students that can be supervised by l_k, and each project p_j has a capacity c_j, indicating the maximum number of students that can be assigned to p_j.

Definition 1 (assignment). *An assignment M is a subset of $S \times P$ such that $(s_i, p_j) \in M$ implies that $p_j \in A_i$. If $(s_i, p_j) \in M$, we say that s_i is assigned to p_j, p_j is assigned to s_i and we also say that s_i is assigned to l_k, l_k is assigned to s_i, where l_k is the lecturer who offers p_j.*

For any student $s_i \in \mathcal{S}$, if s_i is assigned to p_j in M, we let $M(s_i)$ denote p_j, otherwise, we say that s_i is *unassigned* in M or $M(s_i) = \emptyset$. For any project $p_j \in \mathcal{P}$, we let $M(p_j)$ denote the set of students assigned to p_j in M. We say that project p_j is *under-subscribed*, *full* or *over-subscribed* if $|M(p_j)| < c_j$, $|M(p_j)| = c_j$ or $|M(p_j)| > c_j$, respectively. Similarly, for any lecturer $l_k \in \mathcal{L}$, we let $M(l_k)$ denote the set of students assigned to l_k in M. We also say that lecturer l_k is *under-subscribed*, *full* or *over-subscribed* if $|M(l_k)| < d_k$, $|M(l_k)| = d_k$ or $|M(l_k)| > d_k$, respectively.

Definition 2 (matching). *A matching M is an assignment such that $|M(s_i)| \leq 1$ for each $s_i \in \mathcal{S}$, $|M(p_j)| \leq c_j$ for each $p_j \in \mathcal{P}$, and $|M(l_k)| \leq d_k$ for each $l_k \in \mathcal{L}$.*

Definition 3 (blocking pair). *A pair $(s_i, p_j) \in (\mathcal{S} \times \mathcal{P}) \backslash M$ is a blocking pair of a matching M, or blocks M, if the following three conditions are met:*

1. *$p_j \in A_i$ (i.e. s_i finds p_j acceptable).*
2. *Either s_i is unassigned in M or s_i prefers p_j to $M(s_i)$.*
3. *p_j is under-subscribed and either*
   (a) *$s_i \in M(l_k)$ and l_k prefers p_j to $M(s_i)$, or*
   (b) *$s_i \notin M(l_k)$ and l_k is under-subscribed, or*
   (c) *$s_i \notin M(l_k)$, l_k is full, and l_k prefers p_j to l_k's worst non-empty project, where l_k is the lecturer who offers p_j.*

Definition 4 (dominated blocking pair). *A blocking pair (s_i, p_j) dominates a blocking pair (s_i, p_k) if s_i prefers p_j to p_k.*

Definition 5 (undominated blocking pair). *A blocking pair (s_i, p_j) is undominated if there is no other blocking pair that dominates (s_i, p_j).*

Definition 6 (stable matching). *A matching M is called weakly stable if it admits no blocking pair, otherwise it is called unstable. The size of a weakly stable matching M, denoted $|M|$, is the number of students assigned in M.*

Table 1. An instance of SPA-P

Student preferences	Lecturer preferences	Project capacities
s_1: p_1 p_2 p_6	l_1: p_3 p_1 p_2 p_4	$c_1 = 1$
s_2: p_1 p_4	l_2: p_5 p_6	$c_2 = 2$
s_3: p_1 p_2 p_5		$c_3 = 2$
s_4: p_3	Lecturer capacities	$c_4 = 1$
s_5: p_3 p_5	$d_1 = 3$	$c_5 = 1$
s_6: p_5 p_3 p_6	$d_2 = 3$	$c_6 = 2$

In this paper, we consider only weakly stable matchings and therefore, we simply call a weakly stable matching a stable matching. The aim of SPA-P is to find a stable matching of maximum size, i.e. the stable matching admits the smallest number of unassigned students.

Definition 7 (perfect matching). *A stable matching M is called perfect if all students are assigned in M (i.e. $|M| = n$), otherwise it is called non-perfect.*

An instance of SPA-P consists of $S = \{s_1, s_2, s_3, s_4, s_5, s_6\}$, $P = \{p_1, p_2, p_3, p_4, p_5, p_6\}$ and $L = \{l_1, l_2\}$ is shown in Table 1, where $P_1 = \{p_3, p_1, p_2, p_4\}$, $P_2 = \{p_5, p_6\}$, $A_1 = \{p_1, p_2, p_6\}$, $A_2 = \{p_1, p_4\}$, $A_3 = \{p_1, p_2, p_5\}$, $A_4 = \{p_3\}$, $A_5 = \{p_3, p_5\}$, $A_6 = \{p_5, p_3, p_6\}$. The matching $M = \{(s_1, p_6), (s_2, p_4), (s_3, p_2), (s_5, p_3), (s_6, p_6)\}$ is unstable since there exist blocking pairs $\{(s_1, p_1), (s_1, p_2), (s_2, p_1), (s_3, p_1), (s_6, p_5)\}$ of M. Moreover, blocking pair (s_1, p_1) dominates blocking pair (s_1, p_2) since s_1 prefers p_1 to p_2 and blocking pair (s_1, p_1) is undominated. The matchings $M = \{(s_1, p_1), (s_2, p_1), (s_3, p_5), (s_4, p_3), (s_6, p_6)\}$ and $M = \{(s_1, p_6), (s_2, p_1), (s_3, p_1), (s_4, p_3), (s_5, p_5), (s_6, p_6)\}$ are stable with sizes 5 and 6, respectively.

3   Algorithm for SPA-P

In this section, we propose an algorithm to find a maximum stable matching for SPA-P. We consider SPA-P as a constraint satisfaction problem (CSP), in which students are variables, projects ranked in each student's preference list is the domain of each variable and constraints are conditions of the blocking pair definition. Accordingly, a stable matching is an assignment of projects to students such that it does not violate constraints. Our key idea is that we adapt the min-conflicts heuristic for the CSP [12,13], in which at each iteration we select a project $p_j \in A_i$ to assign for a student s_i that results in the minimum number of conflicts with other students in terms of the number of blocking pairs. This means that we have to remove blocking pairs to improve stability of an unstable matching. However, some blocking pairs removed may be useless since the student remains involved in other blocking pairs. We thus focus on the

concept of undominated blocking pairs applied for the stable marriage problem
with ties and incomplete lists [4, 5].

Algorithm 1: SPA-P-MCH Algorithm

Input: - An instance I of SPA-P.
        - A maximum number of iterations max_iters.
Output: A matching M.

1. **function** Main(I)
2. $M :=$ a randomly generated matching;
3. $M_{best} := M$;
4. $s_i :=$ a random student;
5. $iter := 0$;
6.   **while** $(iter \leq max\_iters)$ **do**
7. $iter := iter + 1$;
8.   **for** $(r = 1 \cdots n)$ **do**
9. $s_i := mod(s_i, n) + 1$;
10. $p_j :=$ Find_Project(s_i, M);
11.   **if** $(p_j \neq \emptyset)$ **then**
12.   break;
13.   **end**
14.   **end**
15.   **if** $(p_j = \emptyset)$ **then**
16.   **if** $(|M_{best}| < |M|)$ **then**
17. $M_{best} := M$;
18.   **end**
19.   **if** $(|M_{best}| = n)$ **then**
20.   break;
21.   **else**
22. $M :=$ a randomly generated matching;
23.   continue;
24.   **end**
25.   **end**
26. $M := M \cup \{(s_i, p_j)\}$, where p_j is offered by l_k;
27.   **if** $(p_j$ *is over-subscribed*$)$ **then**
28. $s_w := p_j$'s worst non-empty student;
29. $M := M \backslash \{(s_w, p_j)\}$;
30.   **end**
31.   **if** $(l_k$ *is over-subscribed*$)$ **then**
32. $p_z := l_k$'s worst non-empty project;
33. $s_w := p_z$'s worst non-empty student;
34. $M := M \backslash \{(s_w, p_z)\}$;
35.   **end**
36.   **end**
37.   **return** M_{best};
38. **end function**

Our algorithm based on the min-conflicts heuristic for the SPA-P, so-called
SPA-P-MCH, is shown in Algorithm 1. Initially, the algorithm assigns the best
matching, M_{best}, to a randomly generated matching, M, and takes a random

student $s_i \in \mathcal{S}$. At each iteration, the algorithm finds a project $p_j \in A_i$ so that the pair (s_i, p_j) is an undominated blocking pair of the current matching, as shown in Algorithm 2. If there exists no such project p_j for every student, the algorithm has rearched a stable maching. If so, the algorithm checks if the current matching is better than M_{best} in terms of its size, it assigns the current matching to M_{best}. Moreover, if M_{best} is a perfect matching, the algorithm returns M_{best}, otherwise, it restarts at a randomly generated matching. However, if there exists a project p_j such that (s_i, p_j) is an undominated blocking pair, the algorithm removes (s_i, p_j) of M by assigning p_j to s_i, i.e. $M(s_i) = p_j$. Next, the algorithm checks if p_j is over-subscribed then it removes the pair $(s_w, p_j) \in M$ such that p_j is full, where s_w is the worst student assigned to p_j. Since p_j is assigned to s_i, this means l_k is assigned to s_i, where l_k is the lecturer who offers p_j. Therefore, the algorithm has to check the capacity d_k of l_k. Specifically, if l_k is over-subscribed, the pair $(s_w, p_z) \in M$ is removed such that l_k is full, where p_z is the worst project offered by l_k and s_w is the worst student assigned to project p_z. The algorithm repeats until either M_{best} is a perfect matching or a maximum number of iterations is reached. In the latter case, the algorithm returns either a maximum stable matching or an unstable matching.

Given a student $s_i \in \mathcal{S}$, the function to find a project $p_j \in A_i$ such that the pair (s_i, p_j) is an undominated blocking pair of a matching M is shown in Algorithm 2. The function performs an iteration for each project p_j in an ascending order of ranks in A_i and stops at the first blocking pair encountered, then (s_i, p_j) is an undominated blocking pair. If a blocking pair is found, the function returns p_j, otherwise, it returns an empty set.

Algorithm 2: Find pj such that (si, pj) is an undominated blocking pair

Input: A student $s_i \in \mathcal{S}$ and a matching M.
Output: A project $p_j \in A_i$ or empty.

1. **function** p_j = Find_Project(s_i, M)
2. $p_j := \emptyset$;
3.   sort s_i's rank list in ascending order;
4.   **for** (each $p_k \in A_i$ such that $rank(s_i, p_k) < rank(s_i, M(s_i))$) **do**
5.   **if** ((s_i, p_k) is a blocking pair) **then**
6. $p_j := p_k$;
7.   break;
8.   **end**
9.   **end**
10.   **return** p_j;
11. **end function**

An execution of the algorithm for the SPA-P instance shown in Table 1 is illustrated as in Table 2, where we initialize $M = \{(s_1, p_2), (s_2, p_4), (s_3, p_2), (s_5, p_5), (s_6, p_6)\}$ and the algorithm starts from s_1. After 5 iterations, the algorithm terminates and returns a stable matching $M = \{(s_1, p_6), (s_2, p_1), (s_3, p_1), (s_4, p_3), (s_5, p_5), (s_6, p_6)\}$, where every student is assigned to one project.

Table 2. An execution of the algorithm for the SPA-P instance shown in Table 1

Iter.	s_i	p_j	Matching M	Blocking pairs
0	s_1	-	$\{(s_1,p_2), (s_2,p_4), (s_3,p_2),$ $(s_5,p_5), (s_6,p_6)\}$	$\{(s_1,p_1), (s_2,p_1), (s_3,p_1),$ $(s_4,p_3), (s_5,p_3), (s_6,p_3)\}$
1	s_2	p_1	$\{(s_1,p_2), (s_2,p_1), (s_3,p_2),$ $(s_5,p_5), (s_6,p_6)\}$	$\{(s_1,p_1), (s_3,p_1), (s_4,p_3),$ $(s_5,p_3), (s_6,p_3)\}$
2	s_3	p_1	$\{(s_1,p_2), (s_2,p_1), (s_3,p_1),$ $(s_5,p_5), (s_6,p_6)\}$	$\{(s_4,p_3), (s_5,p_3), (s_6,p_3)\}$
3	s_4	p_3	$\{(s_2,p_1), (s_3,p_1), (s_4,p_3),$ $(s_5,p_5)\}, (s_6,p_6)\}$	$\{(s_1,p_6)\}$
4	s_1	p_6	$\{(s_1,p_6), (s_2,p_1), (s_3,p_1),$ $(s_4,p_3), (s_5,p_5), (s_6,p_6)\}$	$\{\}$
5	$\forall s_i$	$\emptyset$	$|M| = 6 \rightarrow$ return $M = \{(s_1,p_6), (s_2,p_1), (s_3,p_1), (s_4,p_3),$ $(s_5,p_5), (s_6,p_6)\}.$	

4   Experiments

In this section, we present experiments to evaluate the efficiency of our SPA-P-MCH algorithm. To do so, we compared the execution time and matching quality found by SPA-P-MCH with those found by SPA-P-approx [2]. We implemented both SPA-P-MCH and SPA-P-approx algorithms by Matlab R2017a software on a laptop computer with Core i7-8550U CPU 1.8 GHz and 16 GB RAM, running on Windows 10.

Datasets. To compare the efficiency of SPA-P-MCH and SPA-P-approx algorithms, we randomly generated SPA-P instances by varying parameters such as the number of students, lecturers and projects; the total capacities of the lecturers and projects; the number of projects ranked by each student in his/her preference list. Table 3 shows the number of students (n), lecturers (m) and projects (q) in our experiments. For each n varying from 500 to 5000 with steps 500, we randomly generated 100 instances of parameters (n, m, q) such that $0.02n \leq m \leq 0.1n$ (i.e., the student-to-lecturer ratio is from 10 to 50) and $0.1n \leq q \leq 0.5n$ (i.e., the student-to-project ratio is from 2 to 10 and each lecturer offers from 1 to 25 projects). In addition, we set a probability of incompleteness, $|A_i|/q$, indicating that, on average, each student s_i ranks $|A_i|$ projects in his/her preference list, where $|A_i| = 10, 20$ and 30.

Experiment 1. In this experiment, we set the total capacity, C, of projects offered by all the lecturers: $C = 1.1n$. Then, we distributed C to the capacity c_j of each project p_j such that $2 \leq c_j \leq 11$ (since the number of projects is $0.1n \leq q \leq 0.5n$). Next, we set the capacity of each lecturer l_k to be $d_k = \sum_{j=1}^{|P_k|} c_j$, where c_j is the capacity of project p_j offered by lecturer l_k. Figure 1(a) shows the average execution time of SPA-P-MCH and SPA-P-approx algorithms. The average execution time of both SPA-P-MCH and SPA-P-approx increases when n increases. When students increase the number of projects, $|A_i|(i = 1, 2, \cdots, n)$,

Table 3. Parameter values for experiments

ID	n	Number of lecturers $(0.02n \leq m \leq 0.1n)$		Number of projects $(0.1n \leq q \leq 0.5n)$		Number of projects offered by lecturer l_k (i.e. $|P_k|$)	
		Min	Max	Min	Max	Min	Max
1	500	10	50	50	250	1	25
2	1000	20	100	100	500	1	25
3	1500	30	150	150	750	1	25
4	2000	40	200	200	1000	1	25
5	2500	50	250	250	1250	1	25
6	3000	60	300	300	1500	1	25
7	3500	70	350	350	1750	1	25
8	4000	80	400	400	2000	1	25
9	4500	90	450	450	2250	1	25
10	5000	100	500	500	2500	1	25

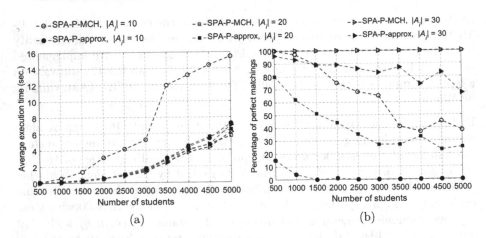

Fig. 1. Results for Experiment 1: (a) the average execution time and (b) the percentage of perfect matchings

in their preference lists, the average execution time of SPA-P-MCH is almost the same as that of SPA-P-approx. However, when $|A_i| = 10$, the average execution time of SPA-P-MCH is larger than that of SPA-P-approx. This is because when a found matching is non-perfect, SPA-P-MCH applies a restart strategy from a new random matching to find a better one in terms of matching size. Figure 1(b) shows the percentage of perfect matchings found by SPA-P-MCH and SPA-P-approx. When n increases, the percentage of perfect matchings found by both SPA-P-MCH and SPA-P-approx decreases. However, the percentage of perfect matchings found by SPA-P-MCH is always higher than that found by SPA-P-

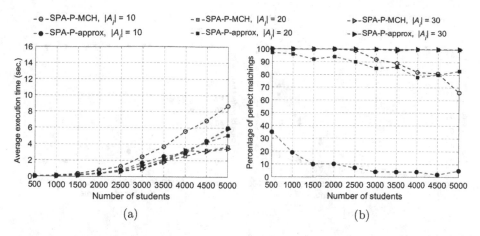

Fig. 2. Results for Experiment 2: (a) the average execution time and (b) the percentage of perfect matchings

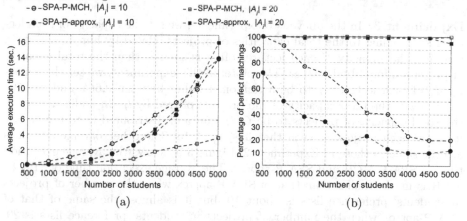

Fig. 3. Results for Experiment 3: (a) the average execution time and (b) the percentage of perfect matchings

approx. In particularly, when $|A_i| = 20$ or $|A_i| = 30$, SPA-P-MCH always finds 100% of perfect matchings.

Experiment 2. In this experiment, we increase the total capacity of projects offered by all the lecturers: $C = 1.2n$. Then, we distributed C to the capacity c_j of each project p_j such that $2 \leq c_j \leq 12$. The other parameters are set the same as those in Experiment 1. Figure 2 shows our experimental results. When the total capacity of projects is increased, i.e. the capacity of each project is increased, the average execution time of both SPA-P-MCH and SPA-P-approx decreases, while the percentage of perfect matchings found by both SPA-P-MCH and SPA-P-approx increases. This is because when the capacity of each project is increased, the opportunity to assign a project for students is increased.

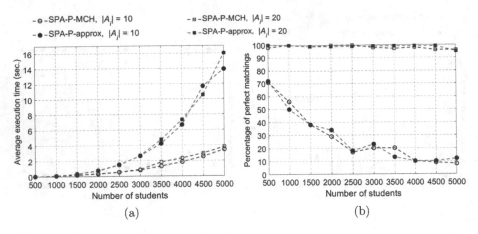

Fig. 4. Results for Experiment 4: (a) the average execution time and (b) the percentage of perfect matchings

Experiment 3. In the above two experiments, we set the capacity of each lecturer to be equal to the total capacities of projects offered by him/her. But, in practice, the capacity of each lecturer often is smaller than the total capacity of projects offered by him/her. Therefore, in this experiment, we set the capacity d_k of each lecturer l_k to be a random number between $0.6C_k$ and $0.85C_k$, where C_k is the total capacity of the projects offered by l_k. In addition, we set the total capacity of projects to be $C = 1.5n$ and distributed C to the capacity c_j of each project p_j such that $3 \leq c_j \leq 15$. The other parameter values are the same as those in Experiment 2. Figure 3(a) shows the average execution time of SPA-P-MCH and SPA-P-approx. The average execution time of SPA-P-MCH is much smaller than that of SPA-P-approx when the number of projects in students' preference lists is about 10, but it is almost the same of that of SPA-P-approx when the number of projects in students' preference lists is 20. Figure 3(b) shows the percentage of perfect matchings found by SPA-P-MCH and SPA-P-approx. SPA-P-MCH always finds 100% of perfect matchings when $|A_i| = 20$ and finds more than 65% of perfect matchings when $|A_i| = 10$. SPA-P-approx always finds the percentage of perfect matchings that is much lower than that found by SPA-P-MCH.

Experiment 4. In the above experiments, the maximum number of iterations in SPA-P-MCH is 20000. It should be noted that, when the umber of iterations in SPA-P-MCH is increased, the opportunity to find perfect matchings increases, but the execution time is also increased. In this experiment, we run SPA-P-MCH in which it returns the first stable matching found in iterations. Figure 4 shows the average execution time and matching quality found by SPA-P-MCH and SPA-P-approx, where the parameter values of SPA-P-MCH are the same as those in Experiment 3. It can be seen that the average execution time of SPA-P-MCH is much smaller than that of SPA-P-approx, while the percentage of perfect matchings found by SPA-P-MCH is almost the same as that found by

SPA-P-approx. In other words, SPA-P-MCH outperforms SPA-P-approx in terms of execution time in this case.

5   Conclusions

This paper proposed a SPA-P-MCH algorithm to find a maximum weakly stable matching for the SPA-P problem. Our algorithm starts to search a solution of the problem from a random matching. At each iteration, the algorithm finds a project for a student such that the pair (student, project) is an undominated blocking pair. If there exists such a project, the algorithm removes the pair (student, project). Otherwise, the algorithm checks if a perfect matching is found, it returns the found matching, otherwise, it continues searching a solution of the problem from a random matching. Our algorithm repeats until it finds a perfect matching or reaches a maximum number of search steps. In the latter case, the found matching is either a maximum stable matching or an approximate maximum matching. Experiments showed that our algorithm outperforms the SPA-P-approx in terms of execution time and matching quality for the SPA-P problem.

References

1. Chiarandini, M., Fagerberg, R., Gualandi, S.: Handling preferences in student-project allocation. Ann. Oper. Res. **275**(1), 39–78 (2017). https://doi.org/10.1007/s10479-017-2710-1
2. Manlove, D.F., O'Malley, G.: Student-project allocation with preferences over projects. J. Discrete Algorithms **6**(4), 553–560 (2008)
3. Gale, D., Shapley, L.S.: College admissions and the stability of marriage. Am. Math. Monthly **9**(1), 9–15 (1962)
4. Gelain, M., Pini, M.S., Rossi, F., Venable, K.B., Walsh, T.: Local search for stable marriage problems with ties and incomplete lists. In: Proceedings of 11th Pacific Rim International Conference on Artificial Intelligence. pp. 64–75. Daegu, Korea (August 2010)
5. Gelain, M., Pini, M.S., Rossi, F., Venable, K.B., Walsh, T.: Local search approaches in stable matching problems. Algorithms **6**(4), 591–617 (2013)
6. Iwama, K., Miyazaki, S., Yanagisawa, H.: Improved approximation bounds for the student-project allocation problem with preferences over projects. J. Discrete Algorithms **13**(1), 59–66 (2012)
7. Abraham, D.J., Irving, R.W., Manlove, D.F.: Two algorithms for the student-project allocation problem. J. Discrete Algorithms **5**(1), 73–90 (2007)
8. Kazakov, D.: Co-ordination of student-project allocation. Manuscript, University of York, Department of Computer Science http://www-users.cs.york.ac.uk/kazakov/papers/proj.pdf (2001)
9. Király, Z.: Better and simpler approximation algorithms for the stable marriage problem. Algorithmica **60**(1), 3–20 (2011). https://doi.org/10.1007/s00453-009-9371-710.1007/s00453-009-9371-7

10. Kwanashie, A., Irving, R.W., Manlove, D.F., Sng, C.T.S.: Profile-based optimal matchings in the student/project allocation problem. In: Proceedings of 25th International Workshop on Combinatorial Algorithms, pp. 213–225. Duluth, USA (15–17 October 2014)
11. Manlove, D., Milne, D., Olaosebikan, S.: An integer programming approach to the student-project allocation problem with preferences over projects. In: Proceedings of 5th International Symposium on Combinatorial Optimization, pp. 313–325. Morocco (April 2018)
12. Minton, S., Johnston, M.D., Philips, A.B., Laird, P.: Minimizing conflicts: a heuristic repair method for constraint satisfaction and scheduling problems. Artif. Intell. **58**(1–3), 161–205 (1992)
13. Russel, S., Norvig, P.: Artificial Intelligence: A Modern Approach, 3rd edn. Prentice Hall Press, Upper Saddle River (2009)

Short Papers: Security and Data Engineering

Data Privacy in Its Three Forms
– A Systematic Review

Amen Faridoon[✉] and Mohand Tahar Kechadi[✉]

University College Dublin, Dublin, Ireland
amenjadoon2@gmail.com, tahar.kechadi@ucd.ie

Abstract. The constant growth of large amounts of data have gifted many fields, such as healthcare, business, e-commerce, education, social sites, and others, to make timely decisions and improve their services for their users. However, the considerable amount of these applications' data is of personal nature. Thus, the sensitive information of each individual should be protected to gain the trust of users how their private information is shared with the organizations. The privacy and security of the data are the dominating challenges and attracted much attention in recent times. They explored privacy threats and also introduced many privacy-preserving techniques to deal with a variety of data threats. In this paper, we present a systematic review of the techniques that have been used to tackle these threats depending on the state of the data – whether it is at rest (in data stores), in transit (over the network), or in-use (during the analysis). This has shown very interesting conclusions about the data privacy and security with regard to big data characteristics.

Keywords: State-of-the-art privacy techniques · Data at rest · Data in transit · Data in use

1 Introduction

In recent years, big data has gained significant attention from researchers and industrial experts as the world has faced challenges related to big data storage, transmission, management, processing, analysis, visualization, integration, architecture, security, quality, and privacy. It has been noted that 90% of the world's data was collected in the last two years. Moreover, this newly emerging area, called data science faces a major challenge that is, the collected data is usually private. It contains sensitive information, such as person-specific private and sensitive data; age, gender, zip code, disease, caste, shopping cart, religion, etc., and data analytics is prone to privacy violations. The most common case is when this data is released to third party who can access it and analyze it, they may extract valuable knowledge, and lead to inference attacks and violation of individuals' privacy [7].

The privacy of individuals is on the stake in each category of data that is; at rest, in transit or in-use. The Data at rest category is governed by the inactive

© Springer Nature Singapore Pte Ltd. 2020
T. K. Dang et al. (Eds.): FDSE 2020, CCIS 1306, pp. 425–433, 2020.
https://doi.org/10.1007/978-981-33-4370-2_30

data that is physically stored in a device. Due to the large amount and valence dimension of big data, data holders utilize new platforms for storing their data such as cloud data centers [16]. The use of these platforms high alerts the data holders that they require some new privacy-protection methods to make sure the privacy and security of their data are not violated. Data in transit is governed by data sharing. The challenge here is how to share a large volume of data without violating the privacy of individuals. This is usually called privacy-preserving data sharing. On the other hand, velocity and variability dimensions of the big data cause greater hindrance to monitor the traffic in real-time, and inconsistencies in data types, speed, and formats lead to privacy and security risks [28]. Data in use category is governed by the analysis of the data to extract useful knowledge. The objective here is how to analyse (or mine) the data without revealing individuals identifiable and sensitive information. This is called privacy-preserving data analytics. The data scientists usually have direct access to the dataset during the process of big data mining. In this case, there are two types of possible privacy violations: 1) intentional or unintentional leakage of personal information to an unauthorized party. 2) results of the analytic algorithm can violate the privacy of individuals such as linkage, re-identification, and other attacks are possible.

1.1   Need for Privacy-Preserving Techniques

Some common privacy-preserving threats that an individual may face after sharing their private information with an organization are: **Surveillance:** Many organizations use surveillance tools to observe the behavior of their customers and make product suggestions. But this is a serious privacy threat because surveillance can lead to more serious matters [17]. **Disclosure:** After removing identity attributes, data holders publish it or hand it to third-party for analysis. However, with the help of quasi-attributes, data analysts can match this data to other available datasets and disclose the sensitive information of a person [8]. **Embarrassment and abuse:** Big data analytics models not only contribute positively but also have some negative implications in the life of a person. **Discrimination:** is a serious noticeable privacy threat. When sensitive information of an individual is disclosed, discrimination can happen. Statistical analysis of electoral results is an example of discrimination. These forms of attacks are extremely dangerous, and one needs to deal with them urgently [4].

1.2   Our Contribution

Many regulations were put in place to protect personal data in domains. However, most of these regulations do not enforce absolute confidentiality, which would cause more harm than good, but rather protect individually identifiable data that can be traced back to an individual with or without external knowledge. This gave rise to a wide range of studies primarily focusing on the privacy-preserving data sharing and analytics techniques at a larger scale with the objective of keeping the data private while extracting useful knowledge from it.

We have conducted a wide review of various data privacy-preserving techniques. After deeply analyzing each of them, we come up with the classification of the state of the art techniques that best ensure the privacy of data in its three forms. The main objectives of this systematic review are as follows:

- Classify of privacy-preserving techniques into three forms of data.
- Study the existing data privacy-preserving techniques in its three forms.
- Highlight the gaps or limitations and possible attacks faced by the data privacy techniques.
- Perform critical analysis of data privacy techniques in relation to big data characteristics.

2   Classification of Privacy-Preserving Techniques

In this section, we present categorisation of privacy-preserving data mining techniques along with a brief analysis of existing techniques for all the three forms (at rest, in transit and in use).

2.1   Data at Rest

De-identification. Replacing sensitive values with more general values is called de-identification [15]. Any recognisable information should be first anonymised with semantically consistent values of generalisation and suppression before the data is analysed. The reverse process of de-identification is called data re-identification. The key de-identification techniques are K–anonymity, L–diversity, and T–Closeness. There are some common terms used in these techniques.

- **Personal Identity Attributes:** Personal identifying attributes are type of attributes that uniquely or directly identify the identity of a person like name, national identity card number, phone number, etc.
- **Quasi Attributes:** Type of attributes whose values match with external data to re-identify a person like gender, zip code, age, etc.
- **Sensitive Attributes:** Sensitive attributes contain the sensitive information of an individual. A person does not want to share it with others like salary, disease, etc.
- **Insensitive Attributes:** General information of an individual.

K–Anonymity: Sweeney et al. introduced a technique called K–anonymity in 1998 [14] to tackle the problem of privacy violation. The records that are present in the dataset are anonymised if the values of the attributes of each record cannot be distinguish from (K-1) other data records. So, personal identification columns are omitted. Suppression and Generalisation are the two methods that are most commonly used for data distortion to reach anonymity. Many algorithms are employed for creating attribute hierarchy to achieve anonymity the algorithms proposed in [23,26]. Hence, K–anonymity provides the primary outline for privacy-preserving. However, this technique has limitations. It cannot protect the attribute disclosure, and background knowledge, temporal, homogeneity attacks are also possible [6].

L-Diversity: To overcome the flaws of the k–anonymity approach, the L–diversity approach was proposed [19]. Distance, entropy and recursive l-diversity models represent the extension of k-anonymity. In this technique, sensitive attributes present in each equivalence group must have L diverse number of values for their representation. Suppose that the values of a sensitive attribute are positive and negative and only 1% of them are positive. This may allow adversaries to gain significant knowledge about individuals of a particular class. However, l–diversity has some drawbacks. If the original dataset has more than one sensitive attribute then it would be difficult to achieve l–diversity. It is even more challenging if the sensitive attributes have not diverse values. Therefore, it is also not sufficient to prevent attribute disclosure. Due to the velocity and variety dimensions of big data sometimes L–diversity is not possible.

T-Closeness: approach was proposed to enhance the l–diversity technique [15]. The threshold is decided to reduce the gaps between the equivalence classes. The dataset is considered to be t–closeness if all the equivalence classes have t–closeness, while the distance among the distribution of sensitive attribute values in an equivalence class and the distribution of attributes in the whole dataset is less than the threshold. There are two common distance measures; earth mover's distance and kullback-leibler are used to maintain the distance among the values of the sensitive attribute within a class and in the middle of the equivalence groups. T–closeness technique removes the quasi identifier attributes by replacing them by the most general value present in the hierarchy tree. However, the appropriate data distribution of a sensitive attribute is not always possible. Separate protection of quasi-identifiers is also deficient in t–closeness [13].

Randomisation consists of adding random noise in an original data. The new distorted data values are usually generated by probability distribution [1]. Randomisation is simple than the other privacy protection techniques and it does not need to know the information of other data records. It is applicable at the time of data collection and pre-processing. However, it also has some weaknesses such as, the randomisation process is not scalable with the increasing sizes of the datasets. The accuracy of the results is also affected by the additional noise. Moreover, the adversary can gain access to sensitive information of individuals with the help of faraway points present in the dataset because randomization cannot have a significant impact on outliers.

Cryptographic Techniques. There are a number of cryptographic techniques that are employed to preserve the privacy in a distributed environment. It solves the problem of an untrusted environment. Cryptographic technique, such as homomorphic encryption can encrypt the data while it is sharing among different parties during processing in a collaborative environment [27]. This technique enables the data holder to process their encrypted data without privacy violation. Moreover, cryptographic approaches empower the parties to compute their results from aggregated input rather than sharing their original data [22,24].

However, the involvement of a large number of participants can slow down the computation process. The use of data encryption during data analytics is difficult and it can also reduce the accuracy of the analysis.

2.2   Data in Transit

Distributed Privacy. Distributed privacy is popularized along with the attractiveness of distributed data mining. The goal of this technique is to perform data analysis within a distributed environment without violating the privacy of the original data [12]. Many algorithms, such as Naïve Bayes, ID3 decision tree, K-nearest neighbours, Support vector machine have been implemented in a distributed environment. However, distributed privacy has some limitations. Some participants are fully or partially adversaries and they do not wish to share their local data records with others.

Secure Multi-party Computation (SMC). The concept of two-party computation for solving the problem of two millionaires introduced and extended to secure multi-party computation problems [20]. Secure multi-party computation is a sub-field of cryptography with the aim to allow a number of parties to jointly compute some known functions on private data in a distributed environment without revealing their individual data sites. Multi-party computation (MPC) system has three basic roles: 1) Set of input sites: provide input data to the trusted computation. 2) The result sites: received the results from the trusted computation. 3) The computing sites: mutually computing the trusted computation. Each member of the MPC computation may have more than one role. In real world, multi-party computation has many applications; Jana system that provides MPC-secure database developed by Galois Inc., Cybernetica also developed MPC-secure database, Partisia used MPC for their commercial activities since 2009, ... [2]. However, MPC protocols need each pair of parties to communicate with one another but in many cases it is not feasible for all pairs of parties to exchange messages like an application running between a web server and a number of clients, communication rounds between parties depend on the depth of the network. Moreover, the involvement of large number of parties makes the implementation of MPC more complex.

2.3   Data in Use

Differential Privacy. In 2006, differential privacy was introduced to protect the information of individuals [10]. The goal of this approach is to give roughly equal privacy to each entity of the dataset. The analyst does not have direct access to the dataset. Four-step process is completed without violating the privacy of entities: 1) analyst can create a query on database, 2) privacy mechanism accepts the query to calculate privacy risk, 3) and execute analyst's query on the database, 4) at the end, the privacy mechanisms adds noise component (according to the calculated privacy risk) to the original results and give it back to the analyst. Noise component depends upon the privacy risk, [9]. In recent years, many organisations have used the differential privacy during the analysis stage, to protect the private and sensitive information; U.S Census Bureau in 2008 [18], Google's RAPPOR in 2014 [11], Google in 2015, Apple in 2016, Microsoft in 2017 [5], Privitar Lens in 2019 and LinkedIn in 2020. **Limitations:** one major challenge encountered by them is related to auxiliary information. For instance, a person "A" height is a very delicate piece of information and the disclosure of "A's" height is considered as privacy violation. If anyone only has access to the auxiliary information that "the person "A" has a height three inches shorter than the average height, they can deduce the person "A's" height.

Privacy-Preserving Machine Learning. The involvement of machine learning in big data analytics introduces the need for privacy on four stages i.e.; training, input, output, and model privacy. Big data analytics (or data in use) category has further divided the privacy approaches into two categories: data-centered and model-centered approaches. Data-centered privacy-preserving techniques are directly used on big data with the goal to protect sensitive data of individuals, such as homomorphic encryption [3], differential privacy [25], federated learning, secure multi-party computation [21], etc. Conversely, the combination of technologies can by some means protect the model from black-box (adversaries gain access to the functions of the model without having the internal knowledge about the model) and white-box (adversaries gain access to the individual's contributing information by reaching the internal knowledge of the model) attacks like homomorphic encryption plus Differential privacy, Secure Multiparty Computation plus Differential privacy, etc. Techniques used in side-channel attacks using machine learning could be used as a starting point for building countermeasures for real hardware-software systems (e.g., AI-enabled Security Watchdog).

3   Critical Analysis

The existing privacy-preserving approaches did not consider explicitly big data dimensions. Table 1 summarises the investigation that whether the particular technique is capable to cover 3Vs (volume, velocity, and variety) or not.

K-anonymity can deal with the volume and velocity dimensions, because data size and speed do not affect its fundamental principle. It needs to make quasi-identifier (QID) classes with at least k members that are moderately simple for huge volume of data. However, it does not support the variety, because the attribute categorisation (PID, QID, sensitive and non-sensitive attributes) is difficult when the data is of unstructured or semi-structured nature. L-diversity is more suited for large amounts of data. However, it cannot deal with the data velocity, because it is hard to designate a new record and balance equivalency class. If the data has stream and heterogeneous nature then the use of t-closeness is not possible, because it is difficult to find the closeness using variational, earth mover's distance and kullback-leibler distance measures.

Randomisation technique cannot stand with any of the 3Vs dimensions of the big data because of time complexity. Like randomisation, distributed privacy also cannot deal with any of the 3Vs of the big data, because of time complexity. The key purpose of this technique is to mine shared data records. If multiple sides contain large amount and increasing speed of data generation then its time complexity. Cryptographic techniques are a suitable tool for the big data features like volume and velocity because the primary purpose of cryptographic algorithms is to encrypt the data.

Differential privacy is the only contender for the variety dimension. The reason for its suitability is that it is not based on attributes. The key role of differential privacy is to add random noise to the result of the query and this does not affect with large quantity and heterogeneity of the data.

Table 1. Comparison between data privacy-preserving techniques and the characteristics of big data

Techniques	Volume	Velocity	Variety
K–Anonymity	✓	✓	✗
L–Diversity	✓	✗	✗
T–Closeness	✗	✗	✗
Randomization	✗	✗	✗
Distributed privacy	✗	✗	✗
Cryptographic techniques	✓	✓	✗
Differential privacy	✓	✗	✓

4   Conclusion

Manipulating and analysing private data is a very critical issue. Various techniques have been proposed to overwhelm the problem of privacy violation of individuals. But the blemishes of the already existing methods enforce to continue the research efforts in this area. Whereas, homomorphic encryption, secure multiparty computation and differential privacy are performing well while data is at-rest, in-transit and in-use respectively. Moreover, using machine learning in improving the security of devices and systems should also be explored. Techniques used inside-channel attacks employing machine learning could be used as a starting point to build counter measures. However, involvement of machine learning in big data analytics has introduce more challenges for researchers. In addition, most of the existing privacy protection techniques are not able to cope with the dominating characteristics of the big data (volume, velocity and variety). The differential privacy is the only contender for the variety dimension. Privacy-preserving data mining still requires advancement.

References

1. Agrawal, R., Srikant, R.: Privacy-preserving data mining. In: Proceedings of the 2000 ACM SIGMOD International Conference on Management of Data, pp. 439–450 (2000)
2. Archer, D.W., et al.: From keys to databases-real-world applications of secure multi-party computation. Comput. J. **61**(12), 1749–1771 (2018)
3. Aslett, L.J., Esperança, P.M., Holmes, C.C.: Encrypted statistical machine learning: new privacy preserving methods. arXiv preprint arXiv:1508.06845 (2015)
4. Chabot, Y., Bertaux, A., Nicolle, C., Kechadi, T.: An ontology-based approach for the reconstruction and analysis of digital incidents timelines. Digit. Invest. **15**, 83–100 (2015)
5. Ding, B., Kulkarni, J., Yekhanin, S.: Collecting telemetry data privately. In: Advances in Neural Information Processing Systems, pp. 3571–3580 (2017)
6. Domingo-Ferrer, J., Torra, V.: A critique of k-anonymity and some of its enhancements. In: 2008 Third International Conference on Availability, Reliability and Security, pp. 990–993. IEEE (2008)
7. Ducange, P., Pecori, R., Mezzina, P.: A glimpse on big data analytics in the framework of marketing strategies. Soft Comput. **22**(1), 325–342 (2017). https://doi.org/10.1007/s00500-017-2536-4
8. Duncan, G.T., Lambert, D.: Disclosure-limited data dissemination. J. Am. Stat. Assoc. **81**(393), 10–18 (1986)
9. Dwork, C.: Ask a better question, get a better answer a new approach to private data analysis. In: Schwentick, T., Suciu, D. (eds.) ICDT 2007. LNCS, vol. 4353, pp. 18–27. Springer, Heidelberg (2006). https://doi.org/10.1007/11965893_2
10. Dwork, C., McSherry, F., Nissim, K., Smith, A.: Calibrating noise to sensitivity in private data analysis. In: Halevi, S., Rabin, T. (eds.) TCC 2006. LNCS, vol. 3876, pp. 265–284. Springer, Heidelberg (2006). https://doi.org/10.1007/11681878_14
11. Erlingsson, Ú., Pihur, V., Korolova, A.: RAPPOR: randomized aggregatable privacy-preserving ordinal response. In: Proceedings of the 2014 ACM SIGSAC Conference on Computer and Communications Security, pp. 1054–1067 (2014)
12. Fukasawa, T., Wang, J., Takata, T., Miyazaki, M.: An effective distributed privacy-preserving data mining algorithm. In: Yang, Z.R., Yin, H., Everson, R.M. (eds.) IDEAL 2004. LNCS, vol. 3177, pp. 320–325. Springer, Heidelberg (2004). https://doi.org/10.1007/978-3-540-28651-6_47
13. Helma, C., Gottmann, E., Kramer, S.: Knowledge discovery and data mining in toxicology. Stat. Methods Med. Res. **9**(4), 329–358 (2000)
14. Khanaa, V., Thooyamani, K.: Protecting privacy when disclosing information: k anonymity and its enforcement through suppression. Int. J. Comput. Algorithm **1**(1), 19–22 (2012)
15. Li, N., Li, T., Venkatasubramanian, S.: t-closeness: privacy beyond k-anonymity and l-diversity. In: 2007 IEEE 23rd International Conference on Data Engineering, pp. 106–115. IEEE (2007)
16. Liu, C., Yang, C., Zhang, X., Chen, J.: External integrity verification for outsourced big data in cloud and IoT: a big picture. Future Gener. Comput. Syst. **49**, 58–67 (2015)
17. Liu, Y., Guo, W., Fan, C.I., Chang, L., Cheng, C.: A practical privacy-preserving data aggregation (3PDA) scheme for smart grid. IEEE Trans. Ind. Inform. **15**(3), 1767–1774 (2018)

18. Machanavajjhala, A., Kifer, D., Abowd, J., Gehrke, J., Vilhuber, L.: Privacy: theory meets practice on the map. In: 2008 IEEE 24th International Conference on Data Engineering, pp. 277–286. IEEE (2008)
19. Machanavajjhala, A., Kifer, D., Gehrke, J., Venkitasubramaniam, M.: l-diversity: privacy beyond k-anonymity. ACM Trans. Knowl. Discov. Data (TKDD) 1(1), 3-es (2007)
20. Micali, S., Goldreich, O., Wigderson, A.: How to play any mental game. In: Proceedings of the Nineteenth ACM Symposium on Theory of Computing, STOC, pp. 218–229 (1987)
21. Mohassel, P., Zhang, Y.: SecureML: a system for scalable privacy-preserving machine learning. In: 2017 IEEE Symposium on Security and Privacy (SP), pp. 19–38. IEEE (2017)
22. Pinkas, B.: Cryptographic techniques for privacy-preserving data mining. ACM SIGKDD Explor. Newslett. 4(2), 12–19 (2002)
23. Samarati, P.: Protecting respondents identities in microdata release. IEEE Trans. Knowl. Data Eng. 13(6), 1010–1027 (2001)
24. Sgaras, C., Kechadi, M.T., Le-Khac, N.A.: Forensics acquisition and analysis of instant messaging and VoIP applications. In: Garain, U., Shafait, F. (eds.) IWCF 2012, IWCF 2014. LNCS, vol. 8915, pp. 188–199. Springer, Cham (2012). https://doi.org/10.1007/978-3-319-20125-2_16
25. Song, S., Chaudhuri, K., Sarwate, A.D.: Stochastic gradient descent with differentially private updates. In: 2013 IEEE Global Conference on Signal and Information Processing, pp. 245–248. IEEE (2013)
26. Sweeney, L.: Achieving k-anonymity privacy protection using generalization and suppression. Int. J. Uncertainty Fuzziness Knowl.-Based Syst. 10(05), 571–588 (2002)
27. Tran, N.H., Le-Khac, N.A., Kechadi, M.T.: Lightweight privacy-preserving data classification. Comput. Secur. 97, 101835 (2020)
28. Xu, L., Jiang, C., Wang, J., Yuan, J., Ren, Y.: Information security in big data: privacy and data mining. IEEE Access 2, 1149–1176 (2014)

Incremental Learning for Classifying Vietnamese Herbal Plant

Phan Duy Hung$^{(\boxtimes)}$ and Nguyen Tien Su

FPT University, Hanoi, Vietnam
hungpd2@fe.edu.vn, su18mse13007@fsb.edu.vn

Abstract. Herbal plant image identification application is expected to be able to help users without specialized knowledge about botany and plant systematics to figure out the useful information, thus it has become an interdisciplinary focus in both botanical taxonomy and computer vision. A computer vision aided herbal plan identification system has been developed to meet the demand of recognizing and identifying herbal plants rapidly. In this paper, the first herbal plant image dataset collected from 2 sources: take by mobile phone in natural scenes and craw from the Internet, which contains approximately 5,000 images of 4 herbal plant species in Vietnam. A pre-trained deep learning model called ResNet50 is used to extract features from the images. Since it was assumed that data was not sufficient before the learning process, the extracted features are separated into five same part. Then an incremental learning process took place using extracted features as input data. The accuracy results increase from 72,3% to 91,2% and also demonstrate that the system is likely to be improved and make practical sense when more data is added including future types.

Keywords: Vietnamese herbal classification · Convolutional Neural Network · Incremental learning · Transfer learning · Feature extraction

1 Introduction

It is a desire to have an automated plant identification system that helps users without specialized knowledge and in-depth training in botany and plant systematic to find out the information of some herbal plants by taking pictures of the plants to feed into an automated plant recognition system. Using the new advances in the computer vision field, plant identification systems have been developed to meet the demand of botanists to recognize and identify unknown herbal plants more rapidly.

Some positive results are achieved by many researchers who conducted studies on the classification of plants. In the early stages when the era of Artificial Intelligent (AI) has not really developed, the authors used low-level features such as shape, color, and texture of leaves to distinguish between species [1–5]. Kumar et al. [2] implemented the first mobile application to identify plant species using automated visual recognition tools. This system identifies plant species from photos of leaves that were taken by mobile camera. The main idea of this is to find out features that represent of leaf border

© Springer Nature Singapore Pte Ltd. 2020
T. K. Dang et al. (Eds.): FDSE 2020, CCIS 1306, pp. 434–442, 2020.
https://doi.org/10.1007/978-981-33-4370-2_31

on multiple scales. The system achieves significant performance on the actual image. In [3], Aakif et al. presented a method including three steps: preprocessing, extraction, and sorting. These extracted characteristics were the input of artificial neural network (ANN). A classifier was trained with the dataset including 817 leaf samples from 14 different fruit trees and gave an accuracy of over 96%.

It is no doubt to say that most of the studies mentioned above have focused on the recognition with hand-crafted image features which there are two limitations. Firstly, because most of these hand-crafted features are low-level image representation it is easily affected by noise and background. Secondly, the input images should be very clean without any background, almost ideal, which makes it difficult to use in practical environments. Therefore, to be used in practical applications, it requires to use a high-level image representation with less affecting by the environment and good for recognition and retrieval in real-world plant images. This trend recently attracts more attention in works of literature [6–10]. Lee et al. [6] developed a deep learning method to learn distinctive features from leaf images then use them to classify plant species. The result has demonstrated that learned features from a Convolutional Neural Network (CNN) can provide better resources for leaf images than the hand-crafted features. In [11], Sun et al. have used of CNN in the identification and query of herbal information. The authors used a CNN for Chinese herbal medicine images. For the recognition, the soft-max loss function was used to optimize the model accuracy; then for the retrieval problem, the recognition network was fine-tuned by adding a triplet loss to search for the most similar herbal medicine images.

Inspired by the recent progress of deep learning in computer vision, we realize that deep learning methods may provide robust herbal plant image representation. In this study, we propose to use the Convolutional Neural Network (CNN) for Vietnamese herbal plant images feature extraction together with the incremental learning process. The evaluation phase shows increasing accuracy after each of the training. Experiments on our collected dataset provide an effective solution to adapt in case of lack of data before the training process which is suitable for deep learned features in herbal plant image recognition systems.

The remainder of the paper is organized as follows. Section 2 describes the proposed method. Then, the results are analyzed in Sect. 3. Finally, brief conclusions are made in Sect. 4.

2 Methodology

2.1 Overview of the Proposed Method

The main idea of this paper is to apply the incremental learning technique for the Vietnamese herbal plant dataset. This technique is suitable since collecting a large dataset before the training process is quite difficult. The model will learn gradually whenever it has new data samples.

The proposed method for classifying the plant includes 4 stages (Fig. 1): (1) data collection and preparation, (2) feature extraction using a pre-trained model, (3) model training with the incremental learning approach and (4) evaluation. The whole process is repeated every time there is new data and the model is updated over time.

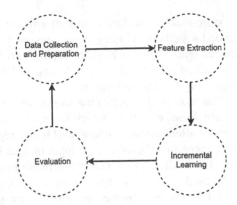

Fig. 1. Proposed method for herbal plant classification

2.2 Data Collection and Preparation

Introduce About Herbal Plants in the Dataset

The dataset has about 5000 images divided into 4 classes: culantro, heartleaf, rice paddy herb, and coriander.

Culantro grows in tropical and watery areas like paddy fields (Fig. 2.a). They often grow on the water surface and can be planted on the soil ground if they get watered regularly. When it is mature, it grows into bushes. The farmer can harvest culantro all year round. The recognizable feature of culantro is its saw-like leaves; long, thin and has serrated-edge. Its taste is a bit spicy, bitter, and often served with popular Vietnamese foods such as sour-soup, or put in a beef salad.

Heartleaf is a Vietnamese herb that has the leaves similar to heart shape in 4-8 cm in length (Fig. 2.b). It tastes a little sour and a bit fishy. It is used in remedy recipes for cooling off the body's temperature, fighting bacteria in the digestive system. It is often paired with peanut worm and spring rolls. Peanut worms are sea worms specialty dishes found in coastal areas like Halong Bay and Con Dao Island.

Rice paddy herb and sawtooth herb are an inseparable pair that is usually served with dishes like sour-soup, pho, hot pot and braised pig feet (Fig. 2.c). It has the taste and smell cross between that of lime and cumin leaves. Rice paddy herb grows well in warm weather and wet area like that in rice paddy fields and can be harvested all year round.

a) culantro   b) heartleaf   c) rice paddy   d) coriander

Fig. 2. Sample images

Its essential oil contains anti-oxidize and antibacterial substances, so it is an excellent choice of spice to add to your healthy diet.

Vietnamese coriander always grows in the water or wet areas (Fig. 2.d). Its leaf is long, thin, small and pointy at the top. Its smell is exceptionally fragrant. The taste is like mint, but a bit bitter and spicier. It is a common spice often used in many kinds of Vietnamese food such as rice noodles, sour soup, or spring rolls. The medicinal use of Vietnamese coriander is to help to digest foods better, so it is often paired with balut, seafood dishes, and a few Vietnamese street foods.

Dataset Collection and Preparation

The stage consists of 4 steps as shown in Fig. 3. Firstly, Vietnamese herbal plant images are collected from two sources: the Internet and camera. To download images from the Internet, the "Google Images Download" library is used with some different keywords such as "culantro", 'heartleaf', "rice paddy herb" and "coriander", etc. Two next steps are carried on manually by an expert who understands of botany deeply. Finally, all images are resized to (224,224) pixels before the features extraction process.

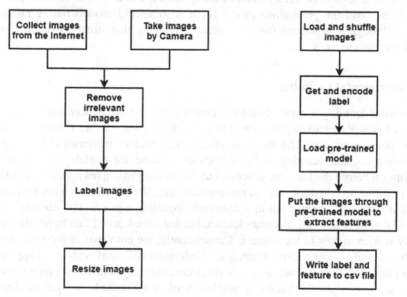

Fig. 3. Data collection and preparation flow   **Fig. 4.** Data extraction flow

2.3 Transfer-Learning Implementation for Feature Extraction

Before we can perform incremental learning, we first need to perform transfer learning and extract features from our dataset.

To accomplish this task, we'll be using the Keras [12] deep learning library and the ResNet50 network [13] (pre-trained on ImageNet). The ResNet50 model consists of 5 stages each with a convolution and Identity block (Fig. 5). The ResNet50 has over 23 million trainable parameters.

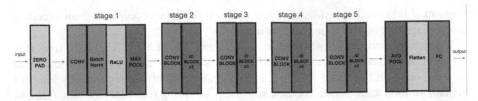

Fig. 5. ResNet50 model architecture

For extracting features, the fully connected layers are removed from the original ResNet50 model. Then we'll allow our images to forward propagate to a pre-specified layer. The final feature vector is obtained by concatenating from block 2 to block 5 into a single vector of 100352 dimensions, which is then fed into the incremental learning process stage. We separate extracted features into five same parts using for five different training times.

This stage includes five steps as shown in the Fig. 4. After loading and shuffling images, the label will be get and encode using LabelEncoder API of scikit-learn library [14]. Next, load the pre-trained model (here is ResNet50 model) before putting the images through it to extract features vector. Following that stream, extracted vectors will be written to a csv file.

2.4 Incremental Learning

Incremental learning is a machine learning paradigm where the learning process takes place whenever new example(s) emerge and adjusts what has been learned according to the new example(s). The most prominent difference of incremental learning from traditional machine learning is that it does not assume the availability of a sufficient training set before the learning process, but the training examples appear over time.

For a long time in the history of machine learning, there has been an implicit assumption that a "good" training set in a domain is available a priori. The training set is so "good" that it contains all necessary knowledge that once learned, can be reliably applied to any new examples in the domain. Consequently, the emphasis is put on learning as much as possible from a fixed training set. Unfortunately, many real-world applications cannot match this ideal case, such as in dynamic control systems, web mining, and time series analysis, where the training examples are often fed to the learning algorithms over time, i.e., the learning process is incremental.

The problem we solve in this study is one such case. We assume that there is only a small amount of data before starting model training, and the model will be updated incrementally each time a sufficient amount of new data is collected.

To implement incremental learning, there are some options such as scikit-learn, creme library [15], etc. Deep learning also trains the model based on the principles of incremental learning. In this study, the creme library was chosen because of its outstanding advantages. It implements a number of popular algorithms for classification, regression, feature selection, and feature preprocessing, has an API similar to scikit-learn, and makes it super easy to perform online/incremental learning.

3 Experiment and Evaluation

3.1 Environment Setup

This study uses a PC with the following configurations: Intel® Core™ i7-7700HQ CPU (4 cores, 8 threads) running at 2.80 GHz, 16 GB of RAM and a GeForce GTX 1050 GPU with 4 GB of VRAM.

3.2 Classification Evaluation

Precision, recall, and f-measure, accuracy is used to quantify the performance of the network as a whole (Fig. 6).

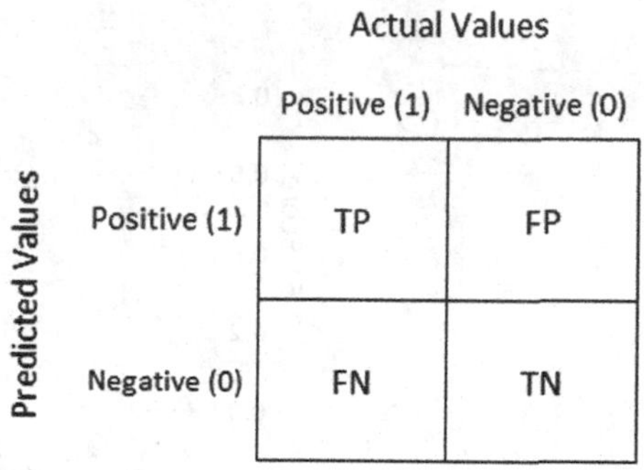

Actual Values

	Positive (1)	Negative (0)
Positive (1)	TP	FP
Negative (0)	FN	TN

Predicted Values

Fig. 6. Confusion matrix

Recall is the ratio of the Actual Positives the model managed to identify (True Positive).

$$Recall = TP/(TP + FN)$$

Precision is how precise/accurate the model is, i.e. out of the predicted positive, how many of them are actually positive.

$$Precision = TP/(TP + FP)$$

F1 Score is a balance between Precision and Recall.

$$F1\ Score = 2 * Precision * Recall/(Precision + Recall)$$

3.3 Results

The change of training accuracy, training precision, training recall, training F1 score and confusion matrix are shown in Figs. 7, 8, 9, 10, 11.

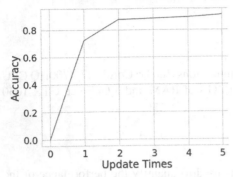

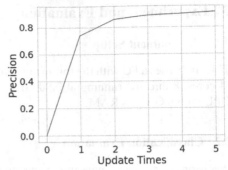

Fig. 7. Change of accuracy metric after five update times

Fig. 8. Change of precision metric after five update times

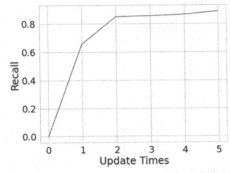

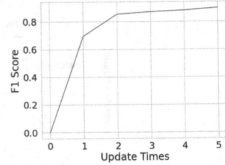

Fig. 9. Change of accuracy recall metric after five update times

Fig. 10. Change of F1 score metric after five update times

From the graphs, undergo five updates, it is observed that:

– The training accuracy increases from 72,3% to 91,2%.
– The precision increases from 73,93% to 91,05%.
– The recall increases from 65,63% to 88,61%.
– The F1 score increases from 69,51% to 89,8%.

The data has been added 5 times, the data here has been prepared after the feature vector extraction phase in Sect. 2.3. The classification accuracy obtained is increasing. The precision and recall also grows up leading to F1 score increases gradually through each update times. The overall uptrend has proved that the system has the potential to improve as the "incremental learning" progresses, and the system will have practical implications as more data including new herbal supplements is added in the future.

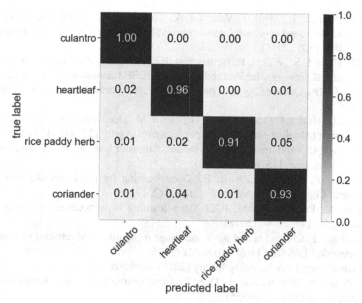

Fig. 11. Confusion matrix after five update times

4 Conclusion and Perspectives

This paper proposes an approach to classify Vietnamese herbal plants based on self-collected data. The use of incremental learning techniques has allowed to solve the real problem of building a system when the initial data is not much.

Experimental results have shown that after five update times, metrics such as accuracy, precision, recall, F1 score go up in value. Although the current result is not very high, it may come from the fact that the data is not large enough, this still proves that the strategy is suitable for our problem. Moreover, when new herbs are added, incremental learning is still effective.

This paper also can be given as a reference to many fields in Pattern Recognition [16, 17], Data Analytics [18], etc.

References

1. Zhao, C., Chan, S.S.F., Cham, W.-K., Chu, L.M.: Plant identification using leaf shapes - a pattern counting approach. Pattern Recogn. **48**(10), 3203–3215 (2015)
2. Kumar, N., et al.: Leafsnap: a computer vision system for automatic plant species identification. In: Fitzgibbon, A., Lazebnik, S., Perona, P., Sato, Y., Schmid, C. (eds.) ECCV 2012. LNCS, vol. 7573, pp. 502–516. Springer, Heidelberg (2012). https://doi.org/10.1007/978-3-642-33709-3_36
3. Aakif, A., Khan, M.F.: Automatic classification of plants based on their leaves. Biosyst. Eng. **139**, 66–75 (2015)
4. Barré, P., Stöver, B.C., Müller, K.F., Steinhage, V.: LeafNet: a computer vision system for automatic plant species identification. Ecol. Inform. **40**, 50–56 (2017)

5. Cerutti, G., Tougne, L., Mille, J., Vacavant, A., Coquin, D.: Understanding leaves in natural images – a model-based approach for tree species identification. Comput. Vis. Image Underst. **117**(10), 1482–1501 (2013)
6. Lee, S.H., Chan, C.S., Wilkin, P., Remagnino, P.: Deep-Plant: plant identification with convolutional neural networks. In: Proceedings of the IEEE International Conference on Image Processing (ICIP), Quebec City, QC, pp. 452–456 (2015). https://doi.org/10.1109/icip.2015.7350839
7. Grinblat, G.L., Uzal, L.C., Larese, M.G., Granitto, P.M.: Deep learning for plant identification using vein morphological patterns. Comput. Electron. Agric. **127**, 418–424 (2016)
8. Fu, Y., Aldrich, C.: Froth image analysis by use of transfer learning and convolutional neural networks. Miner. Eng. **115**, 68–78 (2018)
9. Sun, Y., Liu, Y., Wang, G., Zhang, H.: Deep learning for plant identification in natural environment. Comput. Intell. Neurosci. **2017**, 6 (2017)
10. Kamilaris, A., Prenafeta-Boldú, F.X.: Deep learning in agriculture: a survey. Comput. Electron. Agric. **147**, 70–90 (2018)
11. Sun, X., Qian, H.: Chinese herbal medicine image recognition and retrieval by convolutional neural network. PLoS One **11**(6), e0156327 (2016)
12. Keras: The Python Deep Learning library (2020). https://keras.io
13. He, K., Zhang, X., Ren, S., Sun, J.: Deep Residual Learning for Image Recognition (2015). (arXiv preprint arXiv:1512.03385)
14. scikit-learn: Machine Learning in Python (2020). https://scikit-learn.org
15. Creme: Incremental machine learning in Python (2020). https://creme-ml.github.io
16. Nam, N.T., Hung, P.D.: Padding methods in convolutional sequence model: an application in Japanese handwriting recognition. In: Proceedings of the 3rd International Conference on Machine Learning and Soft Computing, ICMLSC 2019, pp. 138–142. Association for Computing Machinery, New York (2019). https://doi.org/10.1145/3310986.3310998
17. Hung, P.D., Kien, N.N.: SSD-Mobilenet implementation for classifying fish species. In: Vasant, P., Zelinka, I., Weber, G.-W. (eds.) ICO 2019. AISC, vol. 1072, pp. 399–408. Springer, Cham (2020). https://doi.org/10.1007/978-3-030-33585-4_40
18. Hung, P.D., Hanh, T.D., Tung, T.D.: Term deposit subscription prediction using spark MLlib and ML packages. In: Proceedings of the 5th International Conference on E-Business and Applications, ICEBA 2019, pp. 88–93. Association for Computing Machinery, New York (2019). https://doi.org/10.1145/3317614.3317618

Using Topic Models to Label Documents
for Classification

Khang Nhut Lam[1]([✉]), Lam Thanh Truong[1], and Jugal Kalita[2]

[1] Can Tho University, Can Tho, Vietnam
lnkhang@ctu.edu.vn, truongthanhlam202@gmail.com
[2] University of Colorado, Colorado Springs, USA
jkalita@uccs.edu

Abstract. Document classifiers are supervised learning models in which documents are assigned categories based on models that are trained on annotated datasets. In this paper, we use topic models to automatically assign categories to documents, which later are fed to document classification models. We perform experiments on several datasets in Vietnamese, collected from free online resources. Our method is promising and applicable to many datasets that have not been labeled.

Keywords: Text classification · Topic modeling · LDA · LDA2Vec

1 Introduction

Text classification plays an important role in text mining. A text classifier classifies documents into predefined categories or classes. In general, a classification task starts with a training dataset consisting of documents such that each document is labeled with a class label from a set of discrete value indices. The training data is fed into a classification model for training. Given a new document whose class is unknown, the trained classifier predicts a class for this document.

Approaches used to solve the text classification problem include decision trees, Naïve Bayes, SVMs and neural networks. Hasnat et al. [1] experimented with several text classification approaches. These methods consisted of Mini-Batch K-means, Naïve Bayes, K-Nearest Neighbors (K-NN), decision trees, and Support Vector Machines (SVM). The authors classified into 4 categories, English documents extracted from a text classification corpus provided by Sklearn. They claimed that the Naïve Bayes classifier achieved the best result with a precision of 84.51%. Benkhelifa and Laallam [2] classified Facebook's textual posts using the SVM, Naïve Bayes and K-NN classifiers. About 20,000 posts collected from August to November 2015 were labeled manually into 6 categories. The K-NN classifier had the highest speed, but the lowest accuracy. The accuracies of the SVM, Naïve Bayes and K-NN classifiers were 80.3%; 79.4% and 61.3%, respectively. Dadgar et al. [3] classified news using the TF-IDF and SVM approaches. Their performance on the BBC classification dataset and the 20 newsgroups dataset achieved precisions of 97.84% and 94.93%, respectively.

© Springer Nature Singapore Pte Ltd. 2020
T. K. Dang et al. (Eds.): FDSE 2020, CCIS 1306, pp. 443–451, 2020.
https://doi.org/10.1007/978-981-33-4370-2_32

Document classifiers based on neural network models have achieved significant results. Kim [4] trained several CNN models using the word2vec vectors to classify sentences. Kim's performance on various datasets showed that CNN models perform better compared to other existing models such as SVMs with N-gram and other word features [5], Naïve Bayes SVM and Multinomial Naïve Bayes with bigrams [6], and semi-supervised recursive autoencoders using word embeddings [7]. Various deep neural models used for classification include document modeling with gated recurrent neural network [8], recursively regularized deep graph-CNN [9], LSTMs and word embeddings [10,11], and bi-directional LSTM with attention mechanism and convolutional layers [12]. Although these models perform very well with accuracy rates of about 90%, they require a large sized corpus for training.

In this paper, we focus on classification of documents in Vietnamese. Trần and Phạm [13] classified text documents in Vietnamese using SVMs along with feature selection using singular value decomposition (SVD). Their experiment on a dataset containing 7,842 documents in 10 categories achieved better results (91.0% precision) than using the decision tree approach (84.1% precision). Linh et al. [14] developed a method to classify Vietnamese text documents based on a topic model. From the documents, they extracted core nouns with the highest occurrence counts such that the conditional probabilities between them are greater than 0. After constructing the core topic terms, the Naïve Bayes classifier was used to classify documents. They performed experiments on 220 Vietnamese documents (6 topics) labeled manually. Their classifier had a precision of 94.07%.

A prerequisite for any supervised learning approach is a labeled dataset for training. It is time-consuming and expensive to annotate data. Besides, the size and quality of the training dataset may affect the results of the classification models. In this paper, Vietnamese documents are classified by supervised text classifiers, which use the training data labeled automatically by topic models.

2   Proposed Approach

Supervised text classification models require labeled data for training. Topic models are an unsupervised machine learning technique, which can generate term-topic and document-topic matrices without training. In this paper, we use topic models to construct these matrices, and train classifiers using information extracted from these matrices.

We have an unlabeled document dataset D consisting of M documents d, $D = \{d_1, d_2, ..., d_M\}$. Each word is denoted by w and each document is a collection of N words $\{w_1, w_2, ..., w_N\}$. Topic models are used to discover topics associated with individual documents in the collection. Based on the term-topic matrix extracted, we manually assign real topics to the documents in human language, called $topic_{name}$. The documents and the document-topic matrix are fed into the text classification models to train. Our proposed method is presented in Fig. 1.

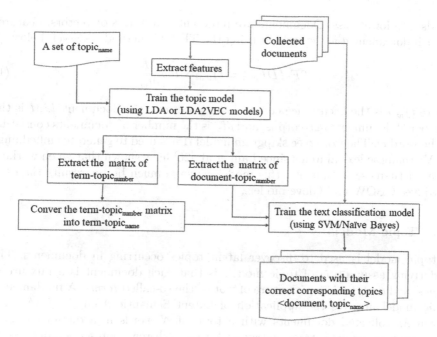

Fig. 1. Using topic models to label documents for classification

2.1 Collecting Documents

We collected data from two free online resources as follows. Although some collected documents are labeled, we disregard this information.

- Over 15,000 articles were extracted from a large-scale Vietnamese news text Classification Corpus[1].
- We built a Vietnamese corpus containing about 14,000 articles extracted from popular online magazines in Vietnam, from a website named vnexpress.net[2]. These articles belong to 8 common subject areas such as science, education, technology, travel and sports.

2.2 Processing Data and Extracting Features

The NLTK toolkit[3] is used to segment sentences in documents; then a Vietnamese toolkit named Underthesea[4] is used to tokenize words in Vietnamese. We remove stopwords in documents using a stopword list[5] and convert all remaining

---

[1] https://github.com/duyvuleo/VNTC.
[2] https://vnexpress.net/.
[3] https://www.nltk.org/.
[4] https://github.com/undertheseanlp/underthesea.
[5] https://github.com/stopwords/vietnamese-stopwords.

words into lower case. Documents are represented in terms of vectors. Features of each document d are extracted using the TF-IDF method, as given below:

$$TF\text{-}IDF_{w,d} = tf_{w,d} \times log\frac{M}{df_w} \tag{1}$$

where $tf_{w,d}$ is the occurrence count of the word w in the document d, M is the number of documents in a corpus, and df_w is the number of documents consisting of the word w. The word2vec skipgram model [15] is used to generate embeddings for Vietnamese lexical items since Lam et al. [20] have shown that when working with Vietnamese documents, this model achieves much better results than the word2vec CBOW and Glove models.

2.3   Topic Models

A topic model is used to discover latent topics occurring in documents. The underlying assumption of topic models is that each document is a mixture of topics, and each topic is a mixture of words, the so-called *terms*. A fundamental topic model involves the application of Latent Semantic Analysis (LSA) [16]. Given M collected documents with a total of N words in a dictionary, LSA constructs a document-term matrix such that each row represents a document, and each column represents a word. Each entry in the document-term matrix can be the raw count or the TF-IDF value of that specific word occurring in the corresponding document. LSA decomposes this document-term matrix into the term-topic matrix and document-topic matrix by using the SVD method. The LSA model needs a large dataset to get good results. pLSA [17] is a generative model developed from the LSA model by changing the SVD to a probabilistic model. A drawback of the pLSA model is that the model cannot assign probabilities to new documents. The Latent Dirichlet Allocation (LDA) model [18], which overcomes the issue with pLSA mentioned above, is the most popular topic model. In the LDA model, a document is represented as a mixture of latent topics using the Dirichlet distribution. Given the α and β parameters, the distribution of a topic mixture θ of k-dimensional Dirichlet, a set of N topics z, and a set of N words w are computed as below:

$$p(\theta, z, w|\alpha, \beta) = p(\theta|\alpha) \prod_{n=1}^{N} p(z_n|\theta)p(w_n|z_n, \beta). \tag{2}$$

To take into account the semantics of words, the LDA2Vec topic model [19] has been designed as a mix between the LDA and word embedding schemes. In the LDA2Vec model, a word vector is represented using the word2vec skipgram method, and each document vector is generated by adding a topic matrix and a document proportion vector. The sum of the document vector and the word vector is the context vector, which later is used to for predictions.

In our implementation, we use the LDA topic modeling functionality supported by Gensim[6] and the LDA2Vec modeling provided by the author, Christopher Moody[7].

2.4   Preparing Input for Text Classifiers

One of our goals is that the proposed model should be able to work with datasets whether the documents are annotated or not. As mentioned earlier, we do not take into account the categories of the collected documents. At this stage, we convert the $topic_{number}$ into the $topic_{name}$ which humans can understand. A $topic_{name}$ can be a word or a phrase. From the topic-term matrix produced by the topic models, we extract terms belonging to each $topic_{number}$ and manually label them with a $topic_{name}$. We argue that labeling documents using topic terms is significantly less time consuming than labeling all documents used for training with topics.

2.5   Classification Models

After using the LDA and LDA2Vec to assign categories to documents, we feed documents and the document-topic matrix into the SVM and Naïve Bayes text classification models. We use the library toolkit supported by Gensim.

3   Experiments

In this section, we first discuss our experiments for classification using a dataset with labeled documents. Then, we perform experiments with our proposed model using datasets whose documents have not been labeled.

3.1   Using Documents Labeled for Classification

We experiment with supervised classification models using a training dataset in which each document has been already assigned a category. This training dataset is also extracted from the vnexpress website. The supervised learning classifiers use the neural network classification models provided by Anubhav Gupta[8]. The CNN classifier and the sequence-to-sequence with attention classifier achieve precisions of 90% and 85%, respectively.

---

[6] https://radimrehurek.com/gensim/index.html.
[7] https://github.com/cemoody/lda2vec.
[8] https://github.com/AnubhavGupta3377.

3.2   Using Topic Models to Label Documents for Classification

We perform experiments on the 20 newsgroups text corpus on 20 topics in Scikit-learn [21] and evaluate results using the Palmetto online tool[9]. All of the experiments using the LDA2Vec model use a word vector of dimension 300 and β value of 0.75, as suggested by Christopher Moody.

Table 1 presents some topics and their corresponding terms discovered by the LDA and LDA2Vec models after labeling manually on the 20 newsgroups corpus. Table 2 and Table 3 show some topics and terms discovered by the LDA and LDA2Vec models on the VNTC corpus and vnexpress corpus, respectively, after labeling manually. Two people were requested to label topics for given terms. The agreement between them is over 75%.

We also experiment with the LDA and LDA2Vec topic models on a dataset consisting of 264 documents used as supporting evidence for the Self Assessment Reports (SAR) for the AUN-QA of the Bachelor Study Program in Information Technology and the Bachelor Study Program in International Business of Can Tho University in the Vietnamese language. Every SAR has 11 criteria, and each criterion is considered a topic in our work. Each of these documents can be used to support one or many criteria. However, the results are not as expected; many topics have similar terms, and terms in each topic are not related.

Table 1. Topics - terms discovered in the 20 newsgroup corpus

Topic models	Topics - terms			
	sci.crypt	rec.motorcycles	rec.sport.baseball	alt.atheism
LDA	key	car	team	sin
	encryption	bike	player	moral
	security	buy	game	atheism
	encrypt	cost	win	atheist
	government	ride	baseball	god
Topic coherence	0.4931	0.4951	0.5458	0.5873
LDA2Vec	key	bike	game	jesus
	encrypt	honda	win	god
	cryptosystem	ride	play	orthodox
	encryption	jeep	baseball	faith
	cryptography	tire	score	worship
Topic coherence	0.70859	0.5504	0.6067	0.6047

After labeling documents using the LDA or LDA2Vec topic models, we feed documents with their corresponding categories into the SVM and Naïve Bayes

---

[9] https://palmetto.demos.dice-research.org/.

Table 2. Topics - terms discovered in the VNTC corpus

Topic models	Topics-Terms			
	Giáo dục	Sức khỏe	Kinh doanh	Thể thao
LDA	giáo dục	thuốc	kinh doanh	huấn luyện viên
	học sinh	bệnh nhân	doanh nghiệp	thi đấu
	thí sinh	bác sĩ	thị trường	đội tuyển
	trung học phổ thông quốc gia	điều trị	đầu tư	bóng đá
	giáo viên	bệnh viện	dịch vụ	câu lạc bộ
LDA2Vec	học	sức khỏe	đầu tư	trận đấu
	giáo dục	bệnh	hợp tác	bóng đá
	trung học phổ thông quốc gia	điều trị	doanh nghiệp	giải
	giảng dạy	bác sĩ	công ty	huấn luyện viên
	chuyên môn	tính mạng	sản phẩm	đối thủ

Table 3. Topics - terms discovered in the vnexpress corpus

Topic models	Topics - Terms			
	Du lịch	Công nghệ	Kinh doanh	Thể thao
LDA	du lịch	màn hình	doanh nghiệp	huấn luyện viên
	máy bay	thiết bị	thị trường	thi đấu
	khách sạn	smartphone	đầu tư	đội tuyển
	chuyến	điện thoại	dịch vụ	bóng đá
	du khách	camera	kinh doanh	câu lạc bộ
LDA2Vec	khách du lịch	phần mềm	chi nhánh	cầu thủ
	máy bay	USB	trị giá	đội
	di chuyển	ổ đĩa	tổng giám đốc	giải đấu
	du lịch	đồ họa	phòng	huấn luyện viên
	dịch vụ	file	tập đoàn	câu lạc bộ

Table 4. The precisions of the classifiers

Corpus	Classification models	LDA model	LDA2Vec model
20 newsgroup	Naive Bayes	74%	35%
	SVM	75%	44%
VNTC	Naive Bayes	75%	65%
	SVM	77%	69%
vnexpress	Naive Bayes	73%	32%
	SVM	74%	30%

classifiers provided by Gensim. Our evaluation shows that the LDA model helps achieve the best results. Table 4 presents the precisions of the classifiers.

In our performance, the LDA model helps achieve better and more stable results than the LDA2Vec model. In contrast, the experiments of Jedrzejowicz and Zakrzewska [22] show that the LDA with word2vec algorithm (LDA-W2V) achieves better and more stable results than the traditional methods for searching topics including Gaussian LDA and LDA models. We notice the difference is that Jedrzejowicz and Zakrzewska use Wordnet to extract lemmas in the pre-processing step, and they use 0.1% or 0.5% of labeled documents for the initial step of the LDA model. In addition, these authors [22] use word embedding provided by Google while we use word embeddings created by training word2vec on the Wikipedia corpus. For future work, we will address which factors affect our models.

4   Conclusion

We describe a method to use topic models for annotating documents for classification. We believe that our proposed approach has a potential to remove the dependence of supervised learning classifiers on labeled datasets for training. We are investigating the factors which can affect the process of automatically assigning labels to documents. In addition, we plan to study a model which can produce labels for unseen data from a small labeled dataset.

References

1. Hasnat, F., Hasan, M., Khan, N.H., Ali, A.: Text classification using machine learning algorithms. Doctoral dissertation, Brac University, Bangladesh (2018)
2. Benkhelifa, R., Laallam, F.Z.: Facebook posts text classification to improve information filtering. In: International Conference on Web Information Systems and Technologies, pp. 202–207 (2016)
3. Dadgar, S.M.H., Araghi, M.S., Farahani, M.M.: A novel text mining approach based on TF-IDF and support vector machine for news classification. In: IEEE International Conference on Engineering and Technology, pp. 112–116 (2016)
4. Kim Y.: Convolutional neural networks for sentence classification. arXiv preprint arXiv:1408.5882 (2014)
5. Silva, J., Coheur, L., Mendes, A.C., Wichert, A.: From symbolic to sub-symbolic information in question classification. Artif. Intell. Rev. **35**(2), 137–54 (2011)
6. Wang, S.I., Manning, C.D.: Baselines and bigrams: simple, good sentiment and topic classification. In: the 50th Annual Meeting of the Association for Computational Linguistics (Volume 2: Short Papers), pp. 90–94 (2012)
7. Socher, R., Pennington, J., Huang, E.H., Ng, A.Y., Manning, C.D.: Semi-supervised recursive autoencoders for predicting sentiment distributions. In: The Conference on Empirical Methods in Natural Language Processing, pp. 151–161 (2011)
8. Tang, D., Qin, B., Liu, T.: Document modeling with gated recurrent neural network for sentiment classification. In: The Conference on Empirical Methods in Natural Language Processing, pp. 1422–1432 (2015)
9. Peng, H., et al.: Large-scale hierarchical text classification with recursively regularized deep graph-CNN. In: The 2018 World Wide Web Conference, pp. 1063–1072 (2018)

10. Rao, A., Spasojevic, N.: Actionable and political text classification using word embeddings and LSTM. arXiv preprint arXiv:1607.02501 (2016)
11. Xiao, L., Wang, G., Zuo, Y.: Research on patent text classification based on Word2Vec and LSTM. In: The 11th International Symposium on Computational Intelligence and Design (ISCID), vol. 1, pp. 71–74 (2018)
12. Liu, G., Guo, J.: Bidirectional LSTM with attention mechanism and convolutional layer for text classification. Neurocomputing **337**, 325–38 (2019)
13. Trần, C.D., Phạm N.K. Phân loại máy học với vector hỗ trợ và cây quyết định. Tạp chí khoa học Đại học Cần Thơ, Vietnam, pp. 52-63. (2012).
14. Linh, B.K., Hà, N.T.T., Tú, N.T.N., Tĩnh, Đ.T. Phân loại văn bản tiếng Việt dựa trên mô hình chủ đề. In: Proceeding of Publishing House for Science and Technology, Da Nang, Vietnam. (2017).
15. Mikolov, T., Chen, K., Corrado, G., Dean, J.: Efficient estimation of word representations in vector space. arXiv preprint arXiv:1301.3781 (2013)
16. Dumais, S.T.: Latent semantic analysis. Ann. Rev. Inf. Sci. Technol. **38**(1), 188–230 (2004)
17. Hofmann, T.: Unsupervised learning by probabilistic latent semantic analysis. Mach. Learn. **42**(1–2), 177–196 (2001)
18. Blei, D.M., Ng, A.Y., Jordan, M.I.: Latent Dirichlet allocation. J. Mach. Learn. Res. **3**(Jan), 993–1022 (2003)
19. Moody, C.E.: Mixing Dirichlet topic models and word embeddings to make LDA2Vec. arXiv preprint arXiv:1605.02019 (2016)
20. Lam, K.N., To, T.H., Tran, T.T., Kalita, J.: Improving Vietnamese WordNet using word embedding. In: The 3rd International Conference on Natural Language Processing and Information Retrieval, pp. 110–114 (2019)
21. Pedregosa, F., et al.: Scikit-learn: machine learning in Python. J. Mach. Learn. Res. **12**, 2825–2830 (2011)
22. Jedrzejowicz, J., Zakrzewska, M.: Text classification using LDA-W2V hybrid algorithm. In: Czarnowski, I., Howlett, R.J., Jain, L.C. (eds.) Intelligent Decision Technologies 2019. SIST, vol. 142, pp. 227–237. Springer, Singapore (2020). https://doi.org/10.1007/978-981-13-8311-3_20

Genome-Wide Association Analysis for Oat Genetics Using Support Vector Machines

Hiep Xuan Huynh[1(✉)], Toan Bao Tran[2,3], Quyen Ngoc Pham[1], and Hai Thanh Nguyen[1(✉)]

[1] College of Information and Communication Technology, Can Tho University, Can Tho 900100, Vietnam
{hxhiep,pnquyen,nthai}@cit.ctu.edu.vn
[2] Center of Software Engineering, Duy Tan University, Da Nang 550000, Vietnam
tranbaotoan@dtu.edu.vn
[3] Institute of Research and Development, Duy Tan University, Da Nang 550000, Vietnam

Abstract. An approach, namely genome-wide association study (GWAS), is usually deployed in genetics research to associate specific genetic variations with particular diseases. This method can be scanning the genomes from a vast of sources and looking for genetic markers that can be used to discriminate phenotypes. In recent years, advancements in computational resources have proposed and published to provide robust tools supporting studies on GWAS. This study aims to propose a method based on machine learning on Oat sequences to provide insights into the genetic architectures to discriminate phenotypes comparing to a statistical analysis on Genome-Wide Association Analysis provided in a R package.

Keywords: Genome-wide association · Genetic variations · Phenotypes

1 Introduction

Gene technology is a subdivision within biotechnology, the collection of all technological applications using biological systems, living organisms or their derivatives. Genetics uses DNA modification and an increasingly maturing range of technologies to enhance plant and animal qualities through selection and reproduction. There are many different directions in genetics, depending on the applications. GWAS stands for Genome-Wide Association Studies which means Correlated Research across the entire genome. In genetics, GWAS is the study of genetic changes throughout the genome in distinct individuals to look for and find genetic changes that are associated with a certain trait. The GWAS typically focuses on correlations between SNPs with traits as major genetic diseases

© Springer Nature Singapore Pte Ltd. 2020
T. K. Dang et al. (Eds.): FDSE 2020, CCIS 1306, pp. 452–460, 2020.
https://doi.org/10.1007/978-981-33-4370-2_33

in humans, but it is applicable to all other species. GWAS aims to detect Single-nucleotide polymorphisms (SNPs) and genetic variations in the genome are associated with a disease. GWAS studies also identify alleles of the genetic variation that appear to be multiple anomalies in individuals with inherited diseases or traits of interest.

Oat is one of the important food type which is also one of the most widely consumed grains worldwide. Genetics from oat contribute the most knowledge in the world genetic mechanisms involved in growth, development and tolerance to adverse conditions of the environment and plant morphology Asian rice which is of great significance in ensuring food security. The scientists suggest that discovering a gene in oat that is resistant to drought will help future crops resist some of the effects of climate change. Numerous potential phenotypes of oat should be investigated to increase productivity and improve the quality.

2 Related Work

Genome-Wide Association Analysis (GWAS) is used for the first time over 10 years ago in human genetics. There are numerous studies using GWAS in human, tissue organisms shaped and crops, especially with rice series of studies for many recent years. The basic principle of GWAS is to find the correlation between each genetic indicator with a trait of interest in a population the same species. GWAS also produces insight into Genetic characteristics of the above traits, for allows selection of the best parental pairs for stools QTL analysis, as well as potential genes attributed qualitative interest.

In recent years, the advancement of science and technology has created many advantages in genetic sequencing and single-nucleotide polymorphism. Furthermore, the Genome-Wide Association Study (GWAS) provides insights into agronomic traits correlating with genotypes. The work in [5] reviewed the primary types of genetic analyses performed for atrial fibrillation, including linkage studies, genome-wide association studies, and studies of rare coding variation. They also presented some highlights of the existing knowledge gaps and future directions for atrial fibrillation genetics research. In the study of [6], the authors also introduced an openly accessible repository of summary-level GWAS association information, providing over 70 million P-values for over 3800 studies investigating over 1400 unique phenotypes. The authors in [7] presented the principles, potential applications, and the challenges of GWAS in rice breeding. The study [8] presented the assignable of psychiatric PRSs to individuals with different familial and societal backgrounds. The authors recruited the PrOMIS cohort at the Instituto Nacional Materno Perinatal (INMP) in Lima, Peru. The PRSs and GWAS standard procedures also applied to carry out the noise ancestry. The results indicated the affection of genetic on depression, PTSD, suicidal tendencies, and self-harm.

The authors in [9] researched about 13 dietary habits including consumption of alcohol, foods, and beverages. The data is collected by the nationwide hospital-based genome cohort, namely BioBank Japan. The proposed approach revealed significant associations in nine genetic loci for 13 dietary characteristics. Furthermore, the authors exhibited eight characteristics and ten associations between five loci as new findings. Human diseases and clinical diagnosis are affected by five of the dietary trait-associated loci. The study [10] presented a systematic approach for identifying the lipid metabolism and regulators of cholesterol by integrating mouse liver with GWAS data from human lipid. The proposed approach detected 48 genes presenting the associated with plasma lipid traits in humans and the replication in mouses. 25 out of 54 of these genes have no impact on lipid metabolism. The authors indicated Sestrin1 is an associated gene with plasma cholesterol levels in humans based on several studies and the integration with additional human lipid GWAS datasets. The results presented the discovery of lipid genes is based on the combining between mouse and human datasets for the prioritization of human lipid GWAS loci. The authors in [11] used the GWAS Atlas which is a resource of genome-wide variant-trait associations from a high-quality of 75 467 variant-trait for 614 traits across two domesticated animals and 7 cultivated plants from 254 publications. The authors combined these associations with GWAS Atlas as terms of variants, genes, traits, studies, and publications. Furthermore, the authors used a suite of ontologies for annotating all the associations and traits. GWAS Atlas and integrates high-quality curated GWAS play a key role in genetic research of breeding applications and important traits. Another study in [12], the authors carried out and experimented a two-staged GWAS using 13,746 cases and 70,316 controls from the Japanese population, followed by a replication analysis using 3,483 cases and 4,795 controls to identify a significant loci, including a novel locus. The study [13] described an approach using machine learning techniques for analyzing the post-GWAS analysis phase. Several machine learning models can be applied for GWAS prioritization, for instance logistic regression, random forest or gradient boosting. The authors presented the selected models, features, and the performance based on the prioritizations of complex disease-associated loci.

3   Genome-Wide Association Analysis

3.1   Dataset and Preprocessing

We considered using the dataset from the study [3] which contains 932 phenotypic, 329 genotypic data with 3629 markers from the wheat dataset. Furthermore, the yield observations were measured in four dissimilar environments, namely ENV1, ENV2, ENV3, and ENV4. In each environment, the yield of oats is slightly different. Numerous oats were retrieved on four environments (e.g: *Oat*1, *Oat*2, *Oat*3...), the rest were retrieved on three, two, or one environments (e.g: *Oat*4, *Oat*8, *Oat*9...). We described further information of yield in Table 1.

In order to investigate the yield distribution and the possible outliers, the authors in [3] visualized the yield data in histogram and conducted the Shapiro–Wilk test. We followed the footprint of the authors in [3] for preprocessing dataset. The preprocessing progress includes: removing the possible outliers,

Table 1. The details of yield data on four environments ENV1, ENV2, ENV3, and ENV4.

Environment	Min yield value	Max yield value	Avg yield value
ENV1	4902.79	7741.22	6373.24
ENV2	5136.03	8108.11	6546.74
ENV3	4786.72	7326.44	6035.40
ENV4	5305.46	8024.12	6787.96

filtering the genotypes, predicting the missing data, studying the population structure, and matching the phenotypes and genotypes.

3.2   Machine Learning Approach

We presented an approach for genome-wide association analysis (GWAS) with machine learning. The purpose of GWAS is to detect the causal mutations on a phenotype. Based on the Oat with Markers features and yield data, we investigated the performance with the Random Forest model [4]. We implemented 500 "trees" in the "forest" and measured the tree quality with Mean Squared Error (MSE) which is equal to variance reduction as the feature selection criterion.

We conducted to train the regression model on 10-folds cross-validation and evaluated the error with Root Mean Squared Error (RMSE) and Mean Absolute Error (MAE) estimator. Both RMSE and MAE present the average model prediction error, the range value is from 0 to ∞. The MSE and MAE are negatively oriented scores, the lower scores are better. The RMSE abd MAE are computed by the Eq. 1 and Eq. 2 respectively.

$$RMSE = \sqrt{\frac{1}{n}\sum_{n}^{i=1}(y_i - \hat{y}_i)^2} \tag{1}$$

$$MAE = \frac{1}{n}\sum_{n}^{i=1}|y_i - \hat{y}_i| \tag{2}$$

Where y_i denotes the true values and $\hat{y}_i$ denotes the predicted values.

We used the preprocessed data as the input and the yield data as the output for the learning model. The input data is the same as for all environments whereas the yield data depends on each environment. We presented a sample of input and output data in Fig. 1. As we mentioned above, there are several Oat were not retrieved on four environments, in this sample, $Oat6$ only have yield information on ENV1 and ENV2.

Furthermore, we extracted the important features of the models in four environments and visualized the results to compare them with the statistical analysis method. In the Random Forest algorithm, the importance of a feature is computed the total reduction of the criterion brought by that feature. Furthermore, the important features assign scores to input features and indicate the relative importance of each feature. In other words, we computed the Gini importance.

INPUT								
	Oat1	Oat2	Oat3	Oat6	Oat7	...	Oat n	
Marker2297	-1	-1	-1	-1	-1			
Marker3125	1	-1	-1	-1	-1			
Marker2100	-1	1	1	0.22543	-1			
Marker1797	1	-0.42597	-1	-1	-1			
Marker3191	-1	1	1	1	1			
Marker1403	-1	1	1	-1	-1			
...								
Marker n								

OUTPUT				
	ENV1	ENV2	ENV3	ENV4
Oat1	6613.54	6855.85	6126.51	5984.45
Oat2	5711.48	5510.55	5707.59	6148.88
Oat3	6462.31	6745.48	6381.64	7418.95
Oat6	7227.83	6646.04	-	-
Oat7	6335.88	6506.14	6055.52	6969.59
...				
Oat n				

Fig. 1. The sample of input and output data.

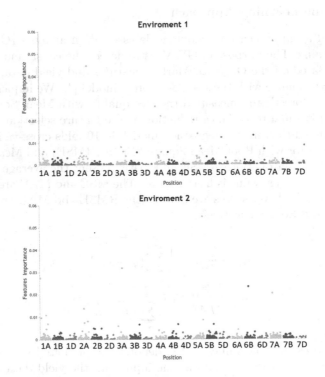

Fig. 2. The visualizations of important features on the environment 1 and 2.

3.3   Experimental Results

As mentioned above, we investigated the regression performance on 10-folds cross-validation. On the ENV1, the training and validation RMSE reached 31368.15 and 227887.33 respectively, whereas the training MAE of 137.92 and validation MAE of 373.75. The RMSE and MAE increased slightly on the ENV2, 32972.58 and 230498.89 of training and validation RMSE; 146.61 and 387.11 of training and validation MAE. The performance is quite better on the ENV3 compared with ENV1 and ENV2, the training and validation of RMSE and MAE of 27789.09, 191200.58, and 137.37, 361.11 respectively. In the last environment, the training and validation RMSE and MAE are not as good as the others.

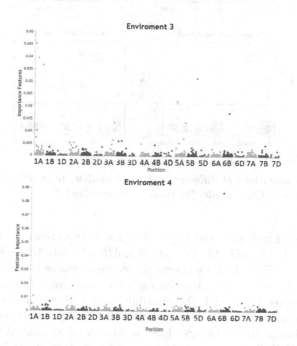

Fig. 3. The visualizations of important features on the environment 3 and 4.

Table 2. The comparison of performance on four environments ENV1, ENV2, ENV3, and ENV4.

Environment	Training RMSE	Val RMSE	Training MAE	Val MAE
ENV1	177.11	447.38	137.92	373.75
ENV2	181.58	480.1	146.61	387.11
ENV3	166.7	437.26	137.37	361.11
ENV4	191.96	499.26	150.92	399.29

In specific, the training and validation RMSE obtained 36846.98 and 249258.59 and MAE of 150.92 and 399.29. We presented the performance details in Table 2. We visualized the important features of the model on ENV1, ENV2,

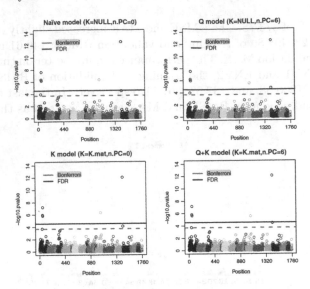

Fig. 4. The visualizations of different statistical models. In specific, Naive mode, Q model, K model, and Q+K model [3]. (Color figure online)

ENV3, and ENV4 in Fig. 2, and Fig. 3. The x-axis represents for the chromosomal location (1*A*, 1*B*, 1*D*, 2*A*, 2*B*, 2*D*, 3*A*, 3*B*, 3*D*, 4*A*, 4*B*, 4*D*, 5*A*, 5*B*, 5*D*, 6*A*, 6*B*, 6*D*, 7*A*, 7*B*, and 7*D*) whereas the y-axis contains the Gini importance. The difference between yield data on each environment influences the performance of the regression model, the distribution of features are slightly different on each environment. In general, the number of important features on each environment are similar to the others. The authors in [3] visualized the significant Manhattan of GWAS of SNP with the chromosomal location in Fig. 4 with four models, namely Naive, Q, K, and Q+K model. The authors also presented the Bonferroni correction and False Discovered Rate (FDR) by the blue line and red dashed line. The markers with p-value are greater than Bonferroni value and FDR are considered to be in linkage disequilibrium. Based on Fig. 4, the naive model is slight differences to the others. In comparison with the statistical model, the Random Forest model presents a similar performance on visualizing the discriminate features. The most important features are floated above the rest and those features have a propensity to inflate the importance of the high-cardinality categorical. Furthermore, they provide insights into the genome data.

4   Conclusion

We presented an approach to analyze Oat genetics using the Random Forest model which is among the most popular machine learning model. We computed the Gini importance which is represented for the important features of each dataset. We also visualized the distribution of features based on the chromosomal location. The visualizations of our method have a similarity close to the statistical model. The preprocessing data plays a key role in analyzing the phenotypic and genotypic from the dataset. The data from matching phenotypes and genotypes are used as the input of the learning model, whereas the yield is used as the output. Due to the yield value is in the range from 4700 to 8100, the RMSE and MAE values are relatively large. The smallest validation RMSE and MAE ware evaluated on ENV3, 437.26 of RMSE, and 361.11 of MAE.

Our study only leveraged the Random Forest model to estimate the yield data and extract important features. In the future, a further regression model can be considered to use for genome-wide association analysis.

References

1. Geschwinde, E., Schoening, H.-J.: PHP and PostgreSQL Advanced Web Programming. Sams Publishing, Indianapolis (2002)
2. Valentini, L.: P.mapper-based WebGIS, Politecnico di Milano - Polo Regionale di Como, Italia (2011)
3. Isidro-Sánchez, J., Akdemir, D., Montilla-Bascón, G.: Genome-wide association analysis using R. In: Gasparis, S. (ed.) Oat. MMB, vol. 1536, pp. 189–207. Springer, New York (2017). https://doi.org/10.1007/978-1-4939-6682-0_14
4. Breiman, L.: Random forests. Mach. Learn. **45**(1), 5–32 (2001). https://doi.org/10.1023/A:1010933404324
5. Roselli, C., Rienstra, M., Ellinor, P.T.: GWAS, genome sequencing, polygenic risk, and beyond. Genetics of atrial fibrillation in 2020 (2020). https://doi.org/10.1161/CIRCRESAHA.120.316575
6. Beck, T., Shorter, T., Brookes, A.J.: GWAS central: a comprehensive resource for the discovery and comparison of genotype and phenotype data from genome-wide association studies. Nucleic Acids Res. **48**(D1), D933–D940 (2020). https://doi.org/10.1093/nar/gkz895
7. Ta, K., Phung, L., Do, S.: Genome wide association study (GWAS): potential applications and challenges for rice (Oryza sativa L.) breeding programme. In: Vietnam National Conference on Plant Science (2016)
8. Hen, H., Gelaye, B., Huang, H., et al.: Polygenic prediction and GWAS of depression, PTSD, and suicidal ideation/self-harm in a Peruvian cohort. Neuropsychopharmacology **45**, 1595–1602 (2020). https://doi.org/10.1038/s41386-020-0603-5
9. Matoba, N., Akiyama, M., Ishigaki, K., et al.: GWAS of 165,084 Japanese individuals identified nine loci associated with dietary habits. Nat. Hum. Behav. **4**, 308–316 (2020). https://doi.org/10.1038/s41562-019-0805-1
10. Li, Z., et al.: Integrating mouse and human genetic data to move beyond GWAS and identify causal genes in cholesterol metabolism. Cell Metab. **31**(4), 741–754.e5 (2020). https://doi.org/10.1016/j.cmet.2020.02.015
11. Tian, D., et al.: GWAS Atlas: a curated resource of genome-wide variant-trait associations in plants and animals. Nucleic Acids Res. **48**(D1), D927–D932 (2020). https://doi.org/10.1093/nar/gkz828

12. Sakai, K., et al.: Identification of a novel uterine leiomyoma GWAS locus in a Japanese population. Sci. Rep. **10**, 1–18 (2020). Article number: 1197

13. Nicholls, H.L., et al.: Reaching the end-game for GWAS: machine learning approaches for the prioritization of complex disease loci. Front. Genet. **11**, 350 (2020). https://doi.org/10.3389/fgene.2020.00350

Develop High School Students Recommendation System Based on Ontology

Thanh Nguyen Vu[1]([⊠]), Thi Dieu Anh Nguyen[2]([⊠]), and Tuan Dinh Le[3]

[1] Ho Chi Minh City University of Food Industry, Ho Chi Minh City, Vietnam
nguyenvt@hufi.edu.vn
[2] Van Hien University, Ho Chi Minh City, Vietnam
anhntdgm@gmail.com
[3] Long an University of Economics and Industry, Tân an, Long an Province, Vietnam
le.tuan@daihoclongan.edu.vn

Abstract. The user model is one of the crucial components in the knowledge management system in general and the recommendation system in a specialty. Usually, the user model is created from simple profile information such as full name, date of birth, gender, etc. The data extracted from this information is limited, easily duplicated, and has not featured vector personal, so it is difficult to give exact recommendations. The decision to choose a university and majors is very important, but students at high school are not sure how to match their interests, their strengths with their working future or majors. Therefore, high school students need guidance and support. Moreover, students need to filter, prioritize, and efficiently get appropriate information from the web in order to solve the problem of information overload. This paper proposes an ontology-based approach to exploring information about hobbies, fingerprints, friend circles, social relationships, and reviews from parents, friends, and teachers in the recommendation system for high school students.

Keywords: Recommendation system · Collaborative filtering · Implicit effect rating · User modeling · Ontology-based · Semantic recommendation system · Machine learning

1 Introduction

The current recommendation systems are mainly in the service and business sectors. Learning-related, student-support systems are still under development. In particular, we can mention the recommendation system for online learning. The support for high school students has not been exploited optimally.

Currently, three methods, which have been widely used in a recommendation system, are content filtering, collaborative filtering, and hybrid methods.

Content filtering (CF) based on purchase history, view user information, thereby suggesting products with content similar to buyer's needs. Some popular techniques

© Springer Nature Singapore Pte Ltd. 2020
T. K. Dang et al. (Eds.): FDSE 2020, CCIS 1306, pp. 461–468, 2020.
https://doi.org/10.1007/978-981-33-4370-2_34

currently used for content filtering are Bag of the word, TF-IDF (term frequency-inverse document frequency), Graph, Grid, TF (term frequency) and VSM (Vector Space Model) [1, 2].

Collaborative filtering is a technique that determines a user's interest in a new product based on previous products they rate, recommending similar products with consumer appreciation. The recommended system in this approach identifies the similarity of the objects through adjacent measurements. Current techniques for collaborative filtering: Pearson correlation (CORR), Cosine (COS), Adjust Cosine (ACOS), Constrained Correlation (CCORR), Mean square Difference (MSD), Euclidean (EUC), SM SING (singularities) [2].

Hybrid methods are a combination of content filtering and collaborative filtering, relying on the advantages of one technique to overcome the disadvantages of the other. For example, collaborative filtering has a problem with a cold - start, which is challenging to suggest for items that do not have a rating. This is simple for the content-based approach when the prediction for new items based on user descriptions is available and quite easy.

In Ho Chi Minh City, the statistics of the Center for Human Resource Forecast and Labor Market Information in Ho Chi Minh City show that about 80% of graduates have jobs, and about 60% of them are in the wrong field [3]. Thus, the problem is that career orientation for high school students is extremely important. Currently, most career activities are conducted offline; there is no specific analysis system for personalizing users. Developing such a recommendation system will minimize time, effort, and make accurate predictions so that students can choose the right field of study and limit non-matched major after graduation.

Input data determines the accuracy of the recommendation system, so it is necessary to collect both explicit and implicit information into the analysis system. We care about user information through fingerprints, human personality, their relationships, reviews from family, friends, teachers, and make an essential contribution to career orientation, choosing the right school. The approach of this article is to use Ontology to semantic analysis of the above input data to extract useful information. The remainder of the paper is presented as follows: part 2 introduces related platforms such as Ontology-based recommender system, Semantic recommendation system, and E-learning recommendation system. Part 3 proposes an archive to develop a high school student Recommendation system based on Ontology. Part 4 is the conclusions of the paper.

2   Related Work

2.1   Ontology-Based and Semantic Recommender System

The Ontology-based recommendation system approach has been studied and proposed for many different models. Some recent featured studies as below [7]:

In 2012, Werner, D. et al. presented a recommender system based on the semantic description of articles and customer profiles [4, 8]. This system used the semantic web to improve e-learning through two layers, the information exploitation management on the first layer and the semantic Ontology-based layer, used to manage profiles and articles [8].

In 2013, Stuti Ajmani and Anupama Mallik presented a novel method for the content-based recommendation of media-rich commodities using probabilistic multimedia ontology [4]. The ontology encodes subjective knowledge of experts that enables interpretation of media-based and semantic product features in the context of domain concepts. This recommendation system analyzes semantics based on product compatibility and customer usage contexts. The approach has been validated with the fashion preferences of several individuals with a large collection of Sarees, an ethnic dress for women in the Indian subcontinent [4].

In 2019, Charbel Obeid et al. represents an approach for developing an ontology-based recommender system improved with machine learning techniques to orient students in higher education [8] (Fig. 1).

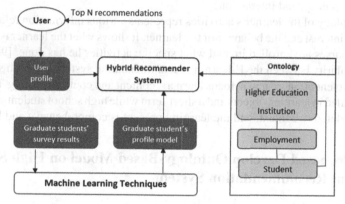

Fig. 1. Ontology-based recommender system (Charbel Obeid -2019)

This article provides a system of recommendations for high school students to choose schools and majors based on their profiles, including strengths, weaknesses, interests, and capabilities [8].

The limitation of the article is only exploiting the ontology of students, not yet exploiting information about personal recognition such as fingerprints, face recognition, and information from objects around students.

2.2 E-Learning Recommendation System

Many recommending systems were developed, from fields like the hotel, tourism to film, clothes, online shopping, but there is very few E-learning recommendation systems. The e-learning recommendation system allows users to choose a course that suitable their needs, with standard features with the recommendation system for choosing a major or school that is oriented towards the user model.

Most architecture e-learning platforms have three layers: the presentation layer, the application layer linked to the server, and the data layer related to the database server [9].

Tan et al. [9] used a person correlation to calculate the proximity between learners by neighborhood algorithm. Domain in this two-recommendation system is indeterminate. The adaptive e-learning system is ontology-based, where this research works on preference and neighbor interest. Applied ontology in this research consists of Java programming languages, which named JLOO (Java Object Learning Ontology) [9].

In 2019, Bouchra Bouihi and Mohamed Bahaj proposed a new e-learning recommendation system model, add an additional Ontology layer to improve recommendation efficiency. This Onlotoly layer consists of Learning Context Ontology and Learning Content Ontology [9].

The content of learning objects is often inconsistent. The learning content Ontology aims to standardize the content so that learners can easily access, share, interact in semantic terms and especially reuse. To improve learning content, standards are set for quality, consistency, and interaction.

The ontology of the learner's activities represents various information relating to the educational interest and the behavior of the learner. It shows what the learner is interested in, which courses are enrolled in, and what specific activities he has done. [9].

The similarity between the E-learning recommendation system and high school students recommendation system is focus learners, content and context learning. E-learning is more detailed in learning objects and a short-term while high school students need more input data related to context, and the learning process is comprehensive and long-term.

3   The Proposed Develop Ontology-Based Model on High School Student Recommendation System

3.1   Summary

This paper proposes to add some of the elements introduced into Ontology for potential exploitation, including fingerprints Ontology, human personality derivation using Ontology, and comment of relatives Ontology. Such as opinions in Sect. 2.1, information from the students themselves is not enough to make accurate predictions about career, major, and school orientation for high school students in Vietnam. This system also needs further analysis of the traditional income and occupation of the family or region. Others tend to be more interested in their friends' choices. The teacher's assessment factor also plays an essential part in giving suggestions to high school students.

Another way, if only collecting survey information is not enough, because the activeness of high school students in Vietnam is lower than the world, many students do not know their strengths, weaknesses, and desires by yourself.

These three factors exploit a lot of hidden information, and it plays a vital role in choosing a future career for the user (Fig. 2).

Many algorithms can be applied to filter and cluster collected data such as k-means, self-organizing maps, and hierarchical clustering algorithms.

The higher education institution ontology contains information such as name, code, ranking, tuition, address, and majors. Student ontology concerns the student profile information and personal preferences. The employment ontology contains information about the average salary and the employment rate per domain [4]. The ontology classes

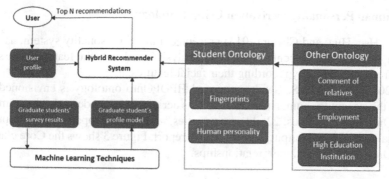

Fig. 2. High school students Recommendation System based on Ontology

in this paper are presented in the next section. Most of the ontologies are built using Protégé ontology editor.

3.2 Fingerprints Ontology

Fingerprints Ontology is closely related to the genome, so it is studied a lot in the fields of medicine, psychology, and genetics. The popular proposed method is supervised and unsupervised learning. It has many positive contributions to biomedical literature and its capacity discovery.

In 2018, Zalmiyah Zakaria et al. presented personality Ontology-based on the Methodology Approach [9]. Fingerprints Ontology described as class hierarchy and provided facilities for the description and definition of their properties, constraints, and their links with other concepts. This visualization function helps developers and users understand the structure of the ontology more easily than merely showing a text-based ontology structure [5].

According to previous studies on fingerprint research, there are nine kinds of intelligence in scientific talent analysis (STA), consist sound, picture, languages, logical thinking, activities, communication, in sign mind, natural feeling, and transmit.

Nevertheless, fingerprint biometric has only been applied in separated recommending systems. It hasn't combined with other inputs yet, so the recommending results are still relative. Putting fingerprint biometric results in a general recommending system contributes to improving recommending outcomes.

Currently, in the career programs of universities and colleges have a lot of software that interact with students to perform fingerprint biometrics. However, the information provided to students is still quite vague, general, with no specific and accurate results. Building a recommendation system add in fingerprints is advantageous because it already has an actual database set, but there are also many challenges about technical and data synchronization.

3.3 Human Personality Derivation Using Ontology

In 2013, Hsu, Hua, and Cheng (2013) presented a novel personality system, as 'Physiognomy Master' that present's personality analysis based on facial features. The system learns from volunteers by recording their facial features.

In 2017, Dr. Rebhi S. Baraka proposed HPDPOnto ontology is envisioned to be used in the system for human personality traits derivation by modern physiognomy. The HPDPOnto has 27 classes, 22 object properties, and 7 data properties [10]. Input data are facial features, and output is a personality report. Figure 3 shows the Core classes of HPDPOnto ontology and their relationships.

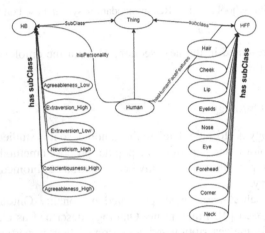

Fig. 3. Core classes of HPDPOnto ontology and their relationships (2017, Dr. Rebhi S. Baraka)

The individual exploiting the good elements will provide information about strengths, weaknesses, and career-appropriate personalities, so human personality helps develop recommendation systems for high school students. Thus, in addition to explicit information, we can use the technique of exploiting additional hidden factors. This method also aims to provide an optimal user model and is recommended by many other areas outside the system [6, 10].

The difficult problem is that face recognition does not have much information connected with suggestions related to careers, majors, and University. The challenge is building a knowledge platform for machine learning

3.4 Comment of Relatives Ontology

The idea to build Comment of relatives Ontology is that the effect of people, who have a relationship with high school students, is an integral part of the recommendation process. Many students need to consider additional financial factors when choosing a high school, and there are families with good conditions that want their children to attend a famous University.

The subjects interested are the opinions of parents, brother, and sister, teachers and friends. This model ontology considered as a social ontology but smaller in scale and focuses on ideas related to the purpose of choosing majors and schools for students. We build specific classes as follows:

STT	Parents	Brother and Sister	Teacher	Friends
1	Finance	Job	School reviews	Friends circle
2	Learning mode	Support	Rated capacity	School reviews
3	Distance	School reviews	Personality assessment	Environmental performance
4	Parent's job	Business connection	Paperwork process	

For exam: School reviews are considered as product reviews in other recommendations, so it is possible to apply collaborative filtering algorithms, extracting data to create an input database. Parent's comment is information directly related to tuition rates or family traditions. Especially, some regions in Vietnam have decisive career inheritance factors.

The comment of relatives data is aggregated into the standards of high school students' context classes. Based on input data, system use filtering and classification techniques, then we use machine learning to build recommends on the students' similar results. The system can suggest the same major but different schools if students have passion, strengths in one field but are different financially or differ in adaptation to the learning environment. The system may also recommend the same school but different majors for students with similar conditions, personalities, extracurricular interests, and student clubs activity.

4   Conclusion

In this paper, we present the overall model of the high school student recommendation system based on semantic analysis using Ontology. Each component of the system is a problem and requires large amounts of data to be collected.

Choosing a career for high school students now takes a lot of time and effort not only for the family but also with the participation of career guidance experts, high schools and colleges, University. Therefore, it is useful to provide a high school recommendation system, and the ontology is suitable for analyzing data of user modeling

In the future, we plan to split the above model into small parts and collect real data to complete them.

References

1. Maher, M.: Singular Value decomposition (SVD) in recommendation systems for Non-math-statistics-programming wizards (2016)

2. Koren, Y.: Factorization meets the neighborhood: multifaceted collaborative filtering model. In: Proceedings of the 14th ACM SIGKDD International Conference on Knowledge Discovery and Data Mining (KDD), pp. 426–434 (2008)
3. https://svvn.tienphong.vn/svvn-giao-duc/vi-sao-60-sinh-vien-ra-truong-lam-trai-nganh-1624467.tpo/
4. Obeid, C., Lahoud, I.: Hicham El Khoury. Ontology-based Recommender System in Higher Educationv, Pierre-Antoine Champin (2019)
5. Guocai, C., Alex, T., Hua, X.W., Jim, Z.: Predict effective drug combination by deep belief network and ontology fingerprints (2018)
6. Stuti, A., Hiranmay, G., Anupama, M., Santanu, C.: An Ontology Based Personalized Garment_R (2013)
7. Samreen, Z., et al.: Ontology-based Sentiment Analysis Model for Recommendation Systems (2015)
8. Werner, D. et al.: Ontology-based recommender system of economic articles. In: 8th International Conference on Web Information Systems and Technologies, pp. 725–728, April 2012
9. Bouchra, B., et al.: Ontology and Rule-Based Recommender System for E-learning Applications (2019)
10. Rebhi, S.: Baraka Human: Personality Derivation Using OntologyBased Modern Physiognomy (2017)

Digital Signatures Using Hardware Security Modules for Electronic Bills in Vietnam: Open Problems and Research Directions

Minh-Tuan Truong$^{(\boxtimes)}$ and Quang-Vinh Dang

Industrial University of Ho Chi Minh city, Ho Chi Minh City, Vietnam
18104761.tuan@student.iuh.edu.vn, dangquangvinh@iuh.edu.vn

Abstract. The usage of electronic bills in Vietnam become more popular in recent years. As required by law, the e-bills need to be signed digitally. Deploying the digital signature services in practice raised new issues in security and usability. In this paper we describe some open practical problems in deploying digital signature service in Vietnam. We discuss the research directions that address the issues. We draw the research plan to resolve the problems in the industry.

Keywords: Digital signature · Security · Load balancing

1 Introduction

Over two last decades, the electronic bills have became more popular in our daily life [18]. In Vietnam, as of this writing, many service providers have stopped issuing the paper receipts and only issuing the electronic receipts. Furthermore, the Vietnamese Government has stipulated in the decree *119/2018/ND-CP*[1] that all enterprises, economic organizations, other organizations, business households and individuals must register for electronic invoice application by 01 - November - 2018.

In the comparison to the paper receipts, the electronic receipts have a lot of advantages. It helps the organizations reduce the cost significantly. According to the General Statistics Office of Vietnam, each paper receipt will cost about 2,000–2,500 VND, around 0.1 US dollar [17]. Furthermore, the electronic receipts are easier to issued, distributed, stored and managed.

The government requires that an e-invoice must be accompanied by a digital signature to verify that e-invoice belongs to which issuer. This requirement provides a legal fundamental to apply digital signatures in Vietnam. It can be considered as a major step in the social digital transformation of the Vietnamese

---

M.- T. Truong and Q.- V. Dang—Authors contributed equally to this work.

[1] Named as the "decree prescribing electronic invoices for sale of goods and provision of services.", issued on 12-September-2018.

© Springer Nature Singapore Pte Ltd. 2020
T. K. Dang et al. (Eds.): FDSE 2020, CCIS 1306, pp. 469–475, 2020.
https://doi.org/10.1007/978-981-33-4370-2_35

government. Before the decree, there is only a small subset of enterprises can provide e-receipts, due to the lack of the legal background.

From the legal's point of view, a digital signature has the same effect as a wet signature. Both signatures are used to confirm the intention of the signee. When an individual or an organization sign to a document, either by a wet signature or a digital one, they state that they agree with the content of the document. From this moment they are binding to the document.

The idea of digital signatures as we know today are presented to the public by Diffie and Hellman in 1976 [5], then completed by the following research studies such as the work of Rivest, Shamir and Adleman (RSA) [14] or Lamport [11]. RSA is the most popular digital signature scheme today [1]. In the RSA scheme, the signee creates a pair of key: a public key and a private key. The signee signs by using the private key, and other organizations and people can verify the signature by using the public key.

There are two main approaches for signing digitally in practice: software-based and hardware-based signatures [15]. In the software-based approach, the signature is calculated by a software running on the typical CPU. In the hardware-based approach, the signature is calculated by a dedicated device, such as token [7].

In the past, the use of digital signatures with a token device caused many shortcomings such as speed, convenience, centralized signing in the process of signing many different consecutive invoices at the digital signature department at the same time, and easy to decentralize use for related departments. And from that, **HSM** - Hardware Security Module was introduced and replaced the token device to use in digital signing. HSM device is a device with many more advanced features to serve the operation of a whole enterprise application system such as generating and protecting PIN, protecting transactions in the internet environment, or even an automatic signature confirming the tax declaration with the General Department of Taxation. The most important feature of HSM is that it supports the signing process by an API call over the Internet.

With support for diverse operating systems, HSM becomes flexible in all current issues of enterprise systems such as API availability. The integration with web applications, application servers, databases becomes easy but still ensures safety, tight security in authentication. Currently on the market there are quite a few units providing HSM API services such as VNPT, Viettel, FPT and others. We choose HSM provided by VNPT to study in depth the problem and practical application in the verification of electricity bills.

Based on our own practical experience in building and deploying the digital signature service in Vietnam, in this paper we describe the current system flow and point out several open problems with the system.

2   Digital Signature Scheme

RSA (Ron Rivest, Adi Shamir, Leonard Adleman) introduced a cryptographic algorithm in 1978, replaced the less secure National Bureau of Standards (NBS) algorithm was previously available.

RSA is an algorithm used by modern computer to encrypt and decrypt message. RSA is an asymmetric cryptographic algorithm. This is called the public key cryptography, because one of the keys can be given to anyone, and the other kept private. RSA is the first algorithm that is suitable for creating digital signatures in parallel with encryption. The algorithm is a remarkable advance in cryptography.

Basically, the RSA algorithm requires two keys to operate: the public key and the private key. A public key is a key that is made public to everyone and is only used in the encryption process. However, all information encrypted with the public key can only be decrypted with the secret key corresponding to the public key. Therefore, everyone can use the public key to encrypt data, but only the person holding the secret key can decrypt. RSA is public and private keys can be performed as the following steps [10]:

Step 1: Create 2 large p and q and random prime numbers with $p \neq q$
Step 2: Calculate $n = pq$ and $\phi(n) = (p-1)(q-1)$
Step 3: Choose an integer e such that $1 < e < \phi(n)$ and $gcd(e, \phi(n)) = 1$
Step 4: Compute d to satisfy the congruence relation $de \equiv 1 mod(\phi(n))$
The public key is (e, n)
The private key is (d, p, q)

The integers e and d generated in the algorithm above are called the encryption exponent and the decryption exponent is also known as the modulus of RSA. Special and important because they are inputs of and allow for calculation when known. Once the key generation is completed, they are deleted.

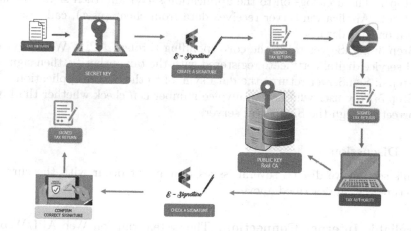

Fig. 1. RSA signing flow

In the digital signature scheme, the above process is reversed. A document will be signed by using the private key, hence only the authorized person can sign the document. On the other hand, everyone who have the public key can verify the signature. We visualized the signing process in Fig. 1.

3   Digital Signature in Practice

In this section we discuss the deployment of digital signature for e-receipts in Vietnam. The process is visualized in Fig. 2.

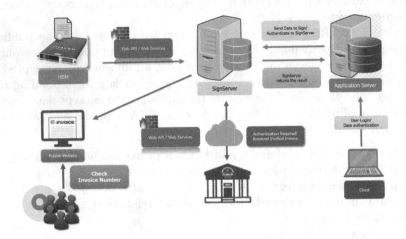

Fig. 2.   Model SignServer

The steps to sign an e-receipt is as follows:

Step 1: The user logs on to the application server and then signs the data.

Step 2: Application server receives data from client (user), calls SignServer to sign on that data.

Step 3: SignServer takes the corresponding through API / Web Services of HSM service digital certificate registered with the tax authority, then signs data

Step 4: SignServer returns the data symbol to the Server application

Step 5: Any user who has an invoice number can check whether the Invoice is correct through the SignServer server.

3.1   Discussion

In this section we discuss several issues that might occur with the current e-signature system described above.

Unreliable Internet Connection. The system runs on Web API/Web Services from the provider, so the connection must be stable during the digital signing process. During the experimental implementation in a few enterprises, we realized that this is a defect of the system, when the connection has problems, the process must stop then restart from the scratch. If the connection is not stable enough, the process might be never ended. We might apply some techniques borrowed the security community for IoT devices [16] to enhance the integration level of our system.

Long Computational Time. The digital signing should be executed in real-time basis [19]. According to the current industrial requirement, the SignServer should be able to cope with up to 500 invoices in five seconds. Furthermore, an individual sign should not take more than 30 s. Several real-time digital signature schemes have been proposed in the last two decades [9,19], but indeed there is a room for improvement to equip HSM with real-time feature.

Single Point of Failure. Figure 2 shows a clear disadvantage of the current model: if the SignServer failed, the entire process will collapse. In business transactions, the issue of smooth connection is the most important. With the limited nature of service providers like in Vietnam, users should be able to switch to another service provider if necessary. However, as of this writing, this functionality is not possible in practice because the end-users will have to declare the entire system specification again.

We suggest that a standard for digital signature service, that is similar to the HL7 standard in healthcare service [6], is required. If so, we can provide a unified access point by combining multiple service providers rather than depend on a single unit.

In Vietnam, this digital signature model is deployed by different service providers. However they must comply with the government regulations. Each provider can choose services from various international suppliers to develop their own digital signature products. In the future research we will study and compare the pros and cons of different systems.

DDoS. DDos, stands for distributed denial-of-service attack, is one threat should be considered in designing the e-signature service. DDoS has many types of attacks and requires specific types such as SYN Flood, HTTP Flood, Ping of Death, Fraggle Attack, Slowloris, Application Level Attack, NTP Amplification, Advanced Persistent Dos (APDos), Zero-day DDos Attack and many others.

In fact, when a system is deployed, it cannot completely avoid DDoS attack on the host system and obstructs the digital signature authentication. However, so far we have not observe this type of attack happening in Vietnam, because service providers and businesses and user agencies have deployed other independent services including firewall and anti-virus software. Nevertheless we should consider this type of attack in the future research study. We note that recently the research in DDos prevention has gained a lot of improvement due to the application of machine learning [3,4].

Congestion. Similar to other countries [2], there are a few special period of time over the course of a year in Vietnam when most of enterprises, organizations and individuals will need to issue and sign their invoices. We might expect the congestion during these periods of time.

In order to reduce the workload and congestion, we suggest to use some forecasting techniques [8] to predict the congestion and automatically optimize the time to sign the documents without the human intervention [12,13].

4   Conclusions

In this paper, we describe the current industrial practice of deploying the digital signature service in Vietnam, based on our own experience in building the service. We discuss several open problems and draw the potential research directions. We hope that this work might increase the awareness of the community in the problems of the practical digital signature system.

References

1. Aufa, F.J., Affandi, A., et al.: Security system analysis in combination method: RSA encryption and digital signature algorithm. In: 2018 4th International Conference on Science and Technology (ICST), pp. 1–5. IEEE (2018)
2. Chittenden, F., Kauser, S., Poutziouris, P.: Tax regulation and small business in the USA, UK, Australia and New Zealand. Int. Small Bus. J. 21(1), 93–115 (2003)
3. Dang, Q.-V.: Studying machine learning techniques for intrusion detection systems. In: Dang, T.K., Küng, J., Takizawa, M., Bui, S.H. (eds.) FDSE 2019. LNCS, vol. 11814, pp. 411–426. Springer, Cham (2019). https://doi.org/10.1007/978-3-030-35653-8_28
4. Dang, Q., Ignat, C.: Link-sign prediction in dynamic signed directed networks. In: CIC, pp. 36–45. IEEE Computer Society (2018)
5. Diffie, W., Hellman, M.: New directions in cryptography. IEEE Trans. Inf. Theory 22(6), 644–654 (1976)
6. Dolin, R.H., et al.: The HL7 clinical document architecture. J. Am. Med. Inform. Assoc. 8(6), 552–569 (2001)
7. Feng, D.: Trusted Computing: Principles and Applications, vol. 2. Walter de Gruyter GmbH & Co KG (2017)
8. Hyndman, R.J., Athanasopoulos, G.: Forecasting: Principles and Practice. OTexts (2018)
9. Kang, N., Ruland, C.: DiffSig: differentiated digital signature for real-time multicast packet flows. In: Katsikas, S., Lopez, J., Pernul, G. (eds.) TrustBus 2004. LNCS, vol. 3184, pp. 251–260. Springer, Heidelberg (2004). https://doi.org/10.1007/978-3-540-30079-3_26
10. Katz, J., Lindell, Y.: Introduction to Modern Cryptography. CRC Press, Cambridge (2014)
11. Lamport, L.: Constructing digital signatures from a one-way function. Technical Report CSL-98, SRI International (1979)
12. Nesterov, Y.: Lectures on Convex Optimization. SOIA, vol. 137. Springer, Cham (2018). https://doi.org/10.1007/978-3-319-91578-4
13. Pinedo, M., Hadavi, K.: Scheduling: Theory, Algorithms and Systems Development, 4 edn. Springer, Berlin (2012). https://doi.org/10.1007/978-3-642-46773-8_5
14. Rivest, R.L., Shamir, A., Adleman, L.: A method for obtaining digital signatures and public-key cryptosystems. Commun. ACM 21(2), 120–126 (1978)
15. Sghaier, A., Medien, Z., Machhout, M.: Fast hardware implementation of ECDSA signature scheme. In: ISIVC, pp. 343–348. IEEE (2016)
16. Shamsoshoara, A., Korenda, A., Afghah, F., Zeadally, S.: A survey on hardware-based security mechanisms for internet of things. arXiv:1907.12525 (2019)

17. Times, F.: Electronic receipts help reducing the cost for enterprises (in vietnamese) (2018).   http://thoibaotaichinhvietnam.vn/pages/thue-voi-cuoc-song/2018-10-08/ap-dung-hoa-don-dien-tu-giam-chi-phi-tuan-thu-nghia-vu-thue-cho-doanh-nghiep-62863.aspx

18. Wadsworth, K.T., Guido, M.T., Griffin, J.F., Mandil, A.: An innovation in paper receipts: the electronic receipt management system. In: 2010 IEEE Systems and Information Engineering Design Symposium, pp. 88–93. IEEE (2010)

19. Yavuz, A.A., Mudgerikar, A., Singla, A., Papapanagiotou, I., Bertino, E.: Real-time digital signatures for time-critical networks. IEEE Trans. Inf. Forensics Secur. **12**(11), 2627–2639 (2017)

Automatic Vietnamese Passport Recognition on Android Phones

Phan Duy Hung[✉] and Bui Thi Loan

FPT University, Hanoi, Vietnam
hungpd2@fe.edu.vn, loanbtmse0102@fpt.edu.vn

Abstract. This paper presents an intelligent application that runs on Android phones to extract important information from Vietnamese passports. Instead of processing information from the passport by manually entering important information into the computer, this application can scan and analyze to get the information fields on the passport automatically. The main algorithm flow includes five parts: 1) capture the passport by the camera, 2) preprocess the image, 3) recognize optical characters 4) extract important information, 5) linguistic processing. After all processing steps, the application will return to a screen with full information extracted. Information fields in cases that are extracted with low confidence will be highlighted for users to easily see and modify. The result has proved that our application has a definite advantage in recognizing the Vietnamese passport (being presented in bilingual English and Vietnamese) when compared to the existing commercial application on the Google Play store.

Keywords: Vietnamese passport recognition · Image processing · OCR system · Android application

1 Introduction

A passport is a travel document, usually issued by a country's government to its citizens, that certifies the identity and nationality of its holder primarily for the purpose of international travel. Standard passports may contain information such as the holder's name, place and date of birth, photograph, signature, and other relevant identifying information. This type of document is used as much as a mandatory identification document in airlines, labor export and import companies, international test and certification organizations, etc. The problem is that organizations or companies want to save the information of each person to the computer, they have to enter manually or record it in books and of course this is time-consuming. The application to scan and extract important information on Android devices provides a good and convenient solution because the number of Android smartphone users is huge. On the Google Play Store, there is a highly rated Passport Scanner app to read English passport information. However, when testing with many Vietnamese passports, this application did not get a very important information that is ID card number - people's identity card document. Some other information in the passport is not extracted such as: Place of birth, Date of issue. The full name received

© Springer Nature Singapore Pte Ltd. 2020
T. K. Dang et al. (Eds.): FDSE 2020, CCIS 1306, pp. 476–485, 2020.
https://doi.org/10.1007/978-981-33-4370-2_36

is Vietnamese without accents. Another requirement in Passport Scanner is that when scanning an image, the user must set the coordinates and angles exactly in the predefined frame. The application in this paper will allow taking photos more easily, more flexibly, and get complete, more accurate information for Vietnamese passport. Figure 1 show an example with obtained and not obtained information from Passport Scanner.

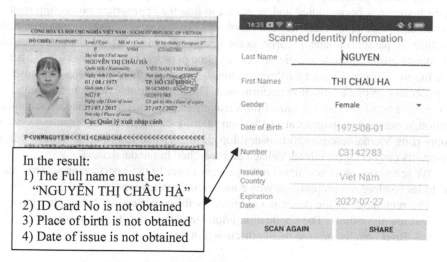

Fig. 1. Example of using "Passport Scanner" application.

The results of some researches have been found such as: In [1], the author presented an OCR solution step by step, applying for Spanish identity cards and Spanish Passport. Scanned images from webcams, computer applications will perform OCR and return results. The OCR combines approaches based on the statistical distribution of points and structural techniques. In the first family of techniques, characters are classified following a zoning technique. Zoning divides the frame containing the character into zones and uses as features the densities of points in the different regions. The paper also performs a statistical background analysis of characters. Particularly, characteristic- loci techniques are used to take as features the number of times the vertical and horizontal vectors intersect line segments for every white point in the background of the character. Finally, a third technique is used to analyze the structural features of characters represented by a set of characteristic points distributed along its skeleton. Authors in [2] integrate text detection and structured data extraction into a unified deep learning-based Image Text Extraction (ITE) scheme. Their ITE is an end-to-end trainable model and able to handle multi-scale and multi-lingual text in a single process. Experiments on large-scale real-world passport and medical receipt datasets have demonstrated the superiority of the proposed method in terms of both effectiveness and efficiency.

During the research process, it was found that the problem of identifying passport is quite complex. It requires breaking down the problem, designing the steps carefully, and dealing with many technical aspects. The problem involves image, text and linguistic processing. Initial studies provide some insights as follows. Image processing is influenced by lighting conditions [3, 4], shooting angles [5, 6] and the complexity of the background image [7, 8]. Text processing results depend on the optical character recognition [9, 10], the separate text groups on the card, ones with different fonts and of different sizes [11, 12]. In addition, this problem requires linguistic post-processing for ID card numbers, date, names [13, 14].

The main contribution of this paper is to develop a complete algorithmic process that, at each step, has been studied and evaluated to find the appropriate processing method for automatic passport identification problems. This process is divided into five parts: capture the passport image, preprocess the image, recognize optical characters, extract important information, linguistic processing. Image processing, information extracting and linguistic processing are the three sections whose algorithms this research focuses on in order to improve application performance. The information extracting and linguistic processing is, of course, optimized for Vietnamese passports. As an additional contribution, a passport management application running on the Android operating system, supporting Vietnamese passports is developed. Images and information extracted from passports can be added, edited, deleted and searched in the database.

We tested our proposed algorithmic process to verify their performance. This study includes results and comparisons with commercial applications.

The remainder of the paper is organized as follows. Section 2 describes passport recognition algorithms. The application implementation and its results are analysed in Sect. 3. Brief conclusions are finally discussed in Sect. 4.

2   The Algorithmic Process

2.1   Passport Capturing

This application receives input images taken from the camera. The main screen of the application is in a vertical layout. The requirements of the capture to ensure the process of identifying the text is correct: all the texts on the passport are in the red rectangle frame. You can increase the sharpness of the image by rotating the passport horizontally, then pressing the "Hoz" button, the red rectangle frame will be rotated accordingly (Fig. 2). The resulting image is the cropped image portion of the red rectangle.

2.2   Image Processing

Illumination change is one of the factors that affect card recognition accuracy. Therefore, in order to limit the negative effect of lighting conditions, the white balance method "grey-world" is utilized. This technique assumes average values of red (R), green (G) and blue (B) channels to be equal [4].

In many cases, the background of an RGB image may contain multiple shapes with different colors or RGB images are of low quality, blurry and noisy. Such images are not a good input for OCR processing [15, 16], causing long processing time and low output accuracy. So next stage aims to make a razor-sharp image from the RGB input image. The output is a binary image in which most of the unwanted shapes, colors and noise will be removed from the background, but all text is kept in the foreground. The algorithm for text binarization is based on a study by Kasar et al. [15]. The resulting binary image will be the input for the next OCR step.

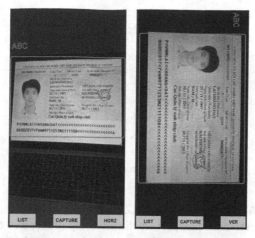

Fig. 2. Take picture from camera. (Color figure online)

2.3 OCR Processing

There are a number of libraries that support OCR implementation such as: ML Kit [16], Tesseract [17], Mobile vision [18], etc. At the present time, ML Kit gets some better reviews [19]. In this work, an offline ML Kit is used on the images containing text with the background cleaned up. ML Kit is a mobile SDK that brings Google's machine learning expertise to Android and iOS apps in a powerful yet easy-to-use package. ML Kit is highly suitable for text printed in passports. The text recognition result is a text segment consisting of blocks → lines → elements (FirebaseVisionText object), where: an element is a set of characters or word, a line is a sequence of words in a single axis or line, a block is a set of lines like a paragraph.

2.4 Extracting Important Information

The result of the OCR step will be the input for extracting important information. From the blocks, we list all the lines and classify them into groups with similar properties. Then from these groups, the work continues to use regular expressions (RegEx) to select information, or based on the relative distance of the lines to determine which line, or which phrase in the line belongs to which information field. Group 1 includes machine-readable lines, consisting of 2 lines containing many of the characters '<'. The algorithm to detect these two lines is counting number of '<' character. Group 2 contains the date format "dd/mm/yyyy", detect them by regular expressions. Group 3 contains uppercase lines, they are recognized by characters uppercase counting and rate of uppercase character calculating. Group 4 contains many numeric characters, count number of numeric character and calculate the rate of numeric characters. An example of the result of grouping lines is described in Fig. 3.

Group	Content
1	P<VNMNGUYEN<<THI<CHAU<HA<<<<<<<<<<<<<<<<<<<<<<<< C3142783<0VNM7508011 F2707277022951585<<<<<12
2	01/08/1975 27/07/2017 27/07/2027
3	P VNM NGUYEN THI CHAU HA NU/F VIET NAM/VIETNAMESE TP. HO CHI MINHSL
4	C3142783 022951585

Fig. 3. An example of result after grouping lines.

Information from the Machine-Readable Zone

Machine-readable texts in the passport are the most important piece of passport information. This section contains the most basic personal information. It is standardized according to "Document 9303" of the International Civil Aviation Organization (ICAO), and certified by the International Organization for Standardization (ISO) and the International Electrotechnical Commission (IEC) as ISO/IEC 7501-1 standard.

All information will be written according to the specified location convention (Fig. 4). When scanning all characters, the software can rely on the index of the characters to parse and determine the information of each specific field.

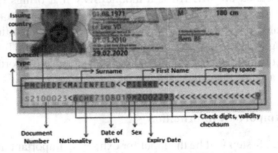

Fig. 4. The general structure of machine-readable zone in passport.

Full Name

In the group of uppercase text lines, find the first line of text that is longer than 1 (i.e. ignore the two lines "P" and "VNM"). The found line is the Full name information, in the form of accented Vietnamese. When the necessary information is found (Full name), remove this line from the list of uppercase lines.

Dates

Date information can be extracted from the machine-readable zone, but it is also in the group of date lines. The extraction of exact dates in this group compares and corrects errors with information found from the machine-readable zone. There are three types of dates in Vietnamese passports: date of birth, date of issue, date of expiry. To identify these date lines, the coordinates of the lines are used to calculate the distance and thereby allow quick identification of each date. The distance of each line is calculated by the formula:

$$\text{Distance of date line} = \text{line.x} + \text{line.y}$$

Thus, with the above distance calculation, after sorting in ascending order, the list of dates received in the correct order: date of birth, date of issue, date of expiry.

Passport Number and ID Card Number
Passport number and ID Card number can be extracted from the machine-readable zone. However, they can also be retrieved from a group of lines that contain multiple numeric characters (group 4), which include lines with numeric characters that account for 65% or more. Check the condition that if the line has the number of characters equal to 8, it is the passport number, the line with the number of characters equal to 9 is the ID card number.

Sex
In group 3, lines with uppercase letters, for each line, remove all space characters, verifying the line to see if it is similar to "NỮ/F" or "NU/F", then Sex is female; 2) is similar to "NAM/M" the Sex is male.

Nationality and Place of Birth
In the list of group 3 remaining 2 lines of information including Nationality and Place of birth. Remove spaces, if the lines are similar to "ViệtNam/Vietnameses" or "Viet-Nam/Vietnamese" then get the Nationality field as "Vietnam/Vietnamese". The remaining line is the Place of birth information. This is the end of the extraction of the important information fields needed for a Vietnamese passport. All of these fields are stored in PassportModel object as input for the next step of standardizing information according to Vietnamese vocabulary standards.

2.5 Linguistic Processing

From the information extracted above, this step corrects the characters that may be mistaken during OCR on similar characters in geometric structure. Mistaken recognition can recognize letters as numbers or vice versa. Especially in Vietnamese, many characters with accent marks that cause confusion between the marks or not receiving the accent are very likely to occur. For example, the vowel word A has the additional vowels Ă, Â; the word vowel O has: ÔƠ; U: Ư; E: Ê; D: Đ. There are 11 single vowels: a, ă, â, e, ê, i/y, o, ô, ơ, u, ư. Besides, the vowels are pronounced with different tones, a total of 6 tones for each sound, each of which is indicated by the corresponding marks: level, hanging, sharp, asking, tumbling, heavy. For example: AÀÁẢÃẠ, ƠỜỚỞỠỢ. Through the test, the result obtained after OCR of the accented vowels is easily confused with other accented letters in Latin (German, French,..).

Some characters after OCR may be mistakenly identified as one of the same characters. To decide whether to replace it with a correct character, the test uses a list of pairs

o-0	5-S	1-I	1-L	I-Ị	Ŭ-Ủ
9-g	7-T	1-i	2-z	Ä-Â	Ã-Ả
6-G	4-A	6-b	J-Ị	ŏ-ô	ỈA-ỈA
8-B	0-D	1-l	°-O	6-ố	Ẹ-Ệ

Fig. 5. Some of the most common cases of character confusion.

of characters that have a high probability of confusion. Figure 5 lists some of the most common pairs.

The replacement of characters can be decided in some cases, for example, with fixed-format fields such as Passport numbers always starting with 1 letter, followed by 7 digits. If the first character is wrongly identified as a number, it is converted into a character, the next 7 characters if the character is a letter, convert back to the corresponding number. The same goes for fields with the date format, ID card number. Full name and Place of birth fields usually contain alphabetic characters. If these texts contain alphanumeric characters, convert them back into alphabetic characters. In the case of a single-digit that can be deduced into multiple letters (1-I, i, l or 6-G, b), it is only possible to prioritize by 1 character of the letters.

Information including Full name (first name, middle name, and surname) and Place of birth are further checked with the Vietnamese provincial dictionary [20] and the Vietnamese name dictionary [21].

3 Evaluate Results

The processing time of the application is about 3–5 s (the tested device with camera 8.0 and 2 GB Ram). The example for final result is as shown in Fig. 6.

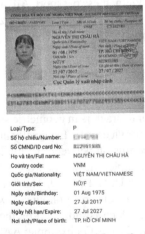

Loại/Type:	P
Số hộ chiếu/Number:	
Số CMND/ID card No:	
Họ và tên/Full name:	NGUYỄN THI CHÂU HÀ
Country code:	VNM
Quốc gia/Nationality:	VIỆT NAM/VIETNAMESE
Giới tính/Sex:	NỮ/F
Ngày sinh/Birthday:	01 Aug 1975
Ngày cấp/Issue:	27 Jul 2017
Ngày hết hạn/Expire:	27 Jul 2027
Nơi sinh/Place of birth:	TP. HỒ CHÍ MINH

Fig. 6. Information results obtained from the passport in Fig. 1.

For the results, the accuracy of the different components are evaluated (%) on each image: Full name, Passport number, Sex, ID Card number, Date of birth, Date of issue,

Date of expiry, Place of birth. Statistics on the recognition accuracy of 50 Vietnamese passports are obtained. The average recognition results as shown in Table 1 are quite accurate with the majority of results are over 92%. (The accuracy is calculated by rate of correct characters number over total character of string.) The result is obtained in good bright condition and the quality of passport is not too blur or lack information.

Table 1. Recognition result.

ID		Rate								
		Full name	Full name (%)	Passport No (%)	Sex (%)	ID Card No (%)	Date of birth (%)	Date of issue (%)	Date of expiry (%)	Place of birth (%)
1	Cxxxxxx	NGUYỄN THỊ CHÂU HÀ	94	100	100	100	100	97	97	95
2	Cxxxxxx	LÊ THỊ HỒNG GIÁ	93	100	100	100	100	98	98	94
3	Cxxxxxx	NGUYỄN VĂN HUÂN	97	99	100	100	95	95	100	100
4	Cxxxxxx	PHẠM THỊ KIM LÀI	96	100	100	100	98	98	100	100
5	Cxxxxxx	PHẠM THUÝ HẰNG	97	100	100	100	96	94	96	100
6	Cxxxxxx	PHẠM HỮU SƠN	80	90	100	90	97	97	97	92
...										
		Average	92.24	97.3	99.8	98.12	96.32	96.25	98.1	96.41

4 Conclusions and Perspectives

This study implements an application for automatic Vietnamese passport recognition. The algorithm is based on the analysis of studies related to image processing, OCR and linguistic processing. The proposed algorithmic process, at each step, has been studied and evaluated to find the appropriate processing method for automatic passport recognition problems. The information is extracted as "Full Name", "Passport No", "Nationality", "Date of birth", "Date of issue", "Place of issue", "ID Card", "Date of expiry", etc. in the application. Our application has a definite advantage in recognizing Vietnamese passports when compared to the existing commercial application available on the Google Play store.

In the future, the Vietnamese linguistic processing for passports needs to be further improved due to the complexity of the Vietnamese language. The work is also a good reference for image pattern recognition problems [22, 23].

References

1. Liados, J., Lumbreras, F., Chapaprieta, V., et al.: ICAR-identity-card-automatic-reader. In: Proceedings of the Sixth International Conference on Document Analysis a Recognition, Spain, pp. 470–474 (2001)
2. Kim, T.J., Kwon, Y.B.: Crosscheck of passport information for personal identification. In: Liu, W., Lladós, J. (eds.) GREC 2005. LNCS, vol. 3926, pp. 162–172. Springer, Heidelberg (2006). https://doi.org/10.1007/11767978_15
3. Gu, Z., Ju, M., Zhang, D.: A novel retinex image enhancement approach via brightness channel prior and change of detail prior. Pattern Recognit. Image Anal. 27(2), 234–242 (2017)
4. Nikitenko, D., Wirth, M.: Applicability of white-balancing algorithms to restoring faded colour slides: an empirical evaluation. J. Multimedia 3(5), 9–18 (2008)
5. Winkler, J.R.: Singular projective transformation matrices. Appl. Math. Model. 20(10), 771–778 (1996)
6. Jirasuwankul, N.: Effect of text orientation to OCR error and anti-skew of text using projective transform technique. In: Proceedings of the IEEE/ASME International Conference on Advanced Intelligent Mechatronics (AIM), Budapest, Hungary, September, pp. 856–861 (2011)
7. Anaraki, A.T., Sheikh, U.U., Rahman, A.A.A., et al.: An alphabetic contour-based descriptor for shape-based image retrieval. In: Proceedings of the IEEE International Conference on Signal and Image Processing Applications (ICSIPA), Kuching, Malaisia, pp. 145–148 (2017)
8. Lee, H., Kwak, N.: Character recognition for the machine reader zone of electronic identity cards. In: Proceedings of the IEEE International Conference on Image Processing (ICIP), Quebec City, QC, Canada, pp. 387–391 (2015)
9. Brisinello, M., Grbić, R., Pul, M., et al.: Improving optical character recognition performance for low quality images. In: Proceedings of the 60th International Symposium ELMAR, Zadar, Croatia, pp. 167–171 (2017)
10. Mantoro, T., Sobri, A.M., Usino, W.: Optical Character Recognition (OCR) performance in server-based mobile environment. In: Proceedings of the International Conference on Advanced Computer Science Applications and Technologies (ACSAT), Kuching, Malaysia, pp. 423–428 (2013)
11. Vo, Q.N., Kim, S.H., Yang, S.H., et al.: Text line segmentation using a fully convolutional network in handwritten document images. IET Image Process. 12(3), 438–446 (2018)
12. Vil'kin, A.M., Safonov, I.V., Egorova, M.A.: Algorithm for segmentation of documents based on texture features. Pattern Recogn. Image Anal. 23(1), 153–159 (2013). https://doi.org/10.1134/S1054661813010136
13. Ertopçu, B., Kanburoğlu, A.B., Topsakal, O., et al.: A new approach for named entity recognition. In: Proceedings of the 2nd International Conference on Computer Science and Engineering (UBMK). Antalya, Turkey, pp. 474–479 (2017)
14. Li, Z., Chng, E.S., Li, H.: Named entity transliteration with sequence-to-sequence neural network. In: Proceedings of the International Conference on Asian Language Processing (IALP), Singapore, pp. 374–378 (2017)
15. Kasar, T., Kumar, J., Ramakrishnan, A.G.: Font and background color independent text binarization. In: Proceedings of the 2nd International Workshop Camera-Based Document Analysis and Recognition, pp. 3–9 (2007)
16. Ahmad, M., Ray, S.: Theoretical foundation of relevance frequency for text categorization. In: Proceedings of the International Conference on Intelligent Computing, Instrumentation and Control Technologies, India, pp. 112–125 (2017)
17. Urolagin, S., Nayak, J., Satish, L.: A method to generate text summary by accounting pronoun frequency for keywords weightage computation. In: Proceedings of the International Conference on Engineering and Technology (ICET), Antalya, pp. 1–4 (2017)

18. Majumder, A., Changder, S.: A Generalized model of text steganography by summary generation using frequency analysis. In: Proceedings of the 7th International Conference on Reliability, Infocom Technologies and Optimization (Trends and Future Directions), Noida, India, pp. 599–605 (2018)

19. Zain, S.: Choose the Right On-Device Text Recognition (OCR) SDK on Android Using DeltaML (2018). https://heartbeat.fritz.ai/choose-the-right-on-device-text-recognition-sdk-on-android-using-deltaml-9b4b3e409b6e

20. Vietnam Cities Database (2019). https://simplemaps.com/data/vn-cities

21. Vietnamese Name DB (2019). https://github.com/duyetdev/vietnamese-namedb

22. Hung, P.D., Linh, D.Q.: Implementing an android application for automatic vietnamese business card recognition. Pattern Recognit. Image Anal. **29**(1), 156–166 (2019). https://doi.org/10.1134/S1054661819010188

23. Nam, N.T., Hung, P.D.: Padding methods in convolutional sequence model: an application in japanese handwriting recognition. In: Proceedings of the 3rd International Conference on Machine Learning and Soft Computing. Association for Computing Machinery, New York, NY, USA, 138–142 (2019). https://doi.org/10.1145/3310986.3310998

A Third-Party Intelligent System for Preventing Call Phishing and Message Scams

Manh-Hung Tran[1,2,3]([✉]), Trung Ha Le Hoai[1,2], and Hyunseung Choo[3]

[1] University of Information Technology, Ho Chi Minh City, Vietnam
{hungtm,trunghlh}@uit.edu.vn
[2] Vietnam National University, Ho Chi Minh City, Vietnam
[3] Sungkyungkwan University, Seoul, South Korea
{hungtm,choo}@skku.edu

Abstract. The damage from voice phishing reaches one trillion won (around 0,84 billion USD) in the past five years, following a report of Business Korea on August 28, 2018. Voice phishing and mobile phone scams are recognized as a top concern in Korea and the world in recent years. In this paper, we propose an efficient system to identify the caller and alert or prevent dangerous to users. Our system includes a mobile application and web server using client and server architecture. It aims to automatically display the information of unidentified callers and warnings to the user when they receive a call or message. A mobile application installs on a mobile phone to automatically get the caller's phone number and send it to the server through web services to verify it. The web server applies machine learning to data on a global phone book with Blacklist and Whitelist to validate its phone number.

Keywords: Anti call phishing · Intelligent system · Machine learning

1 Introduction

Nowadays, using a telephone is indispensable for every person to communicate with others. Every day, people often receive plenty of phone calls and text messages. Along with that, the problem of receiving impersonation calls and unwanted calls or spam messages is increasing, such as voice phishing and messages scam. Besides, phishing attacks have spread to cover vast areas of services, as shown in Fig. 1. The most target of phishing attack is payment and related to financial. For example, in Korea, 48,743 voice phishing victims were reported [1,2] in 2018, and total economic damage from voice phishing scams up to 444 billion won. According to the numbers and figures are shown here, we conclude that phishing attacks on mobile devices are increasing dramatically with the enormous financial damage to the economy. Because of these warning numbers, it is necessary to have a solution to prevent people from phishing attack on mobile phone.

© Springer Nature Singapore Pte Ltd. 2020
T. K. Dang et al. (Eds.): FDSE 2020, CCIS 1306, pp. 486–492, 2020.
https://doi.org/10.1007/978-981-33-4370-2_37

Phishing is pronounced fishing. It is just a scam where a criminal uses text messages, phone calls, and other contact methods to pretend to be someone they are not, to get access to critical information of a victim. Two common ways of phishing attacks on mobile are voice phishing and message, or email scam is shown in Fig. 2. With voice phishing, the victim receives directly fraudulent calls and request to provide financial-related information or transfer money to a phisher. With the second way, a victim receives a message/email with a malicious link. By clicking on this link, users may lose information or pay for a new item. Besides, this link can also be a fake website to ask users to submit their essential data.

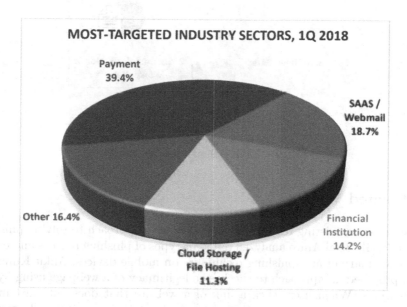

Fig. 1. Distribution of phishing attacks [3]

In this paper, we propose an intelligent system - iCaMs - to identify the caller and prevent the mobile phishing attack by using a proactive approach. iCaMs uses a global phone book with Whitelist and Blacklist. It is an automatic system using AI to learn and analyze the phone number based on their data in a global phone book and the internet. An international phone book is collected by using the data in contact list of each user. Moreover, this system is a full solution with various functions against the mobile phishing attack.

The remainder of the paper is organized as follows: In Sect. 2, the related work is presented. The proposed architecture is discussed in Sect. 3. Finally, Sect. 4 concludes the paper with final remarks and perspectives for future work.

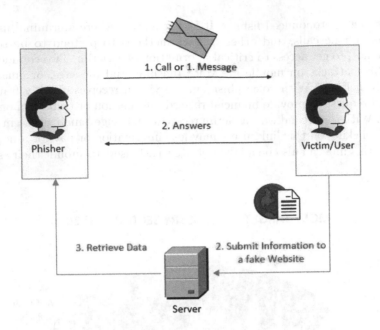

Fig. 2. Mobile phone phishing attack

2   Related Work

There are some existing researches with a reactive approach to solving phishing attach. In [4], Belal Amro analyzed different types of phishing attacks and examined a summary of anti-phishing techniques on mobile devices. Ankit Kumar et al. [5] proposed an approach to checks the legitimacy of a webpage using hyperlink features. When users click a link of a website that does not exist in the white list, the browser warns users not to submit their sensitive information. Madhuresh Mishra et al. [6] proposed a preventive anti-phishing technique to avoid being victims of phishing attacks. This technique helps people identify the correct website compared with a fake link received from a phisher. However, these research only deals with preventing users from providing information to the phisher through a phony web page like email/message phishing. It cannot solve the voice phishing problem.

Many mobile applications with a proactive approach aim for blocking calls from unwanted numbers and spam numbers such as Should I Answer, Blacklist Plus, Call Blocker Free. These applications protect a user from unknown calls related to telemarketing, advertisement, etc. It allows users to access Blacklist, Whitelist, and block spam calls with call reminders and notifications. It also provides various blocking options like blocking calls from hidden numbers, foreign countries, premium-rate numbers, and numbers that are not in users' contact list. Additionally, it displays notifications like phone number rating, information, and user reviews once the phone starts ringing. However, these applications only

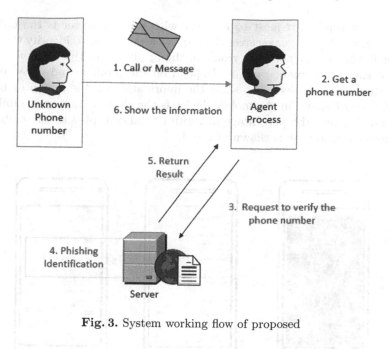

Fig. 3. System working flow of proposed

have a local phone book. Moreover, users must manually add phone numbers to Whitelist and Blacklist. It cannot help with an unknown number from phishers that do not have in their phonebook.

T-Mobile provides a Mobile security application [7] to help users against unwanted calls and scams by using users' information on their own and their partner database. This application only works with the customer of T-Mobile in the USA. In Korea [1], an AI mobile application that auto-detect "voice phishing" scam was introduced in March 2019. It uses machine learning base on voice recognition to detect some words that scammer usually uses when the victim/user receives a call. If a scammer is caught, it will notify an alert to the user on their mobile screen. However, it only helps users against voice phishing. And in my opinion, this application only works with a small number of users because the number of phone calls every day is tremendous.

3   Proposed Solution

We proposed an intelligent system using a mobile application and machine learning-based to prevent the mobile phishing attack. The operational flow of the system is shown in Fig. 3. Firstly, a mobile application is installed on the mobile phone of users registered as a regular user in the iCAMs system after a verification process. An agent works as a background process on the smartphone. It occupies a phone number when a user receives a message or phone call. Firstly, the agent will check the phone number with the local contact list of the users. If the phone number is in the contact list, then it will do nothing.

Otherwise, it sends a request to a server with the parameter is the unknown phone number. The server receives the request and process to identify the phone number is phishing or not. The result of the phishing identification will return to the agent on the mobile phone. Depend on the product and users' privacy policy, the agent will decide to show the information on the screen or block a call. The report shows in the mobile device is the classification of the unknown phone number and the percentage of legitimate also display to the mobile UI. The client UI prototype is shown in Fig. 4.

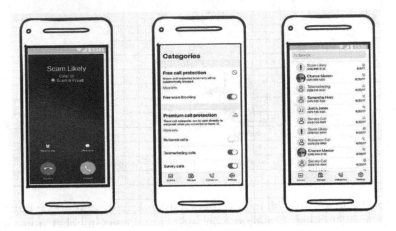

Fig. 4. Client UI prototype

The architecture of phishing identification of the proposed idea is depicted in Fig. 5. Our Architecture is divided into three main modules. The first module is the Global Phone Book, including three data sets e.g., White-list, Blacklist, and Users Contact. The White-list indicates the legitimate phone number, and the Blacklist identifies the phishing number. The phishing number is classified into four categories: Telemarketing, Survey Call, Nuisance Call, and Scam Likely. The User Contact dataset is the local contact of all registered users. All of these datasets are encoded to guarantee information security. It could be manually updated with the verified information and user-report or automatically updated by the machine learning module. The second module is Working Flow module. This module matches the requested phone number with Whitelist and Blacklist datasets to indicate the request is phishing or legitimate. If the requested phone number does not exist in both datasets, it will send a request to a Machine Learning module. The third module is the Machine Learning module. This module will responsible for the classification and analysis of the phone number combine with other information e.g., the number of references in the Users Contact dataset, calling time, and some useful information from searching on the internet. The output of the classification process is the percentage of prediction for each category. The output data is compared with the threshold to determine which type it belongs to. After that, it updates the Whitelist or Blacklist dataset and resends the request to the Working Flow. The system working is a continuous process of training and classification. The accuracy rate of machine learning will increase when the number of registered user increase.

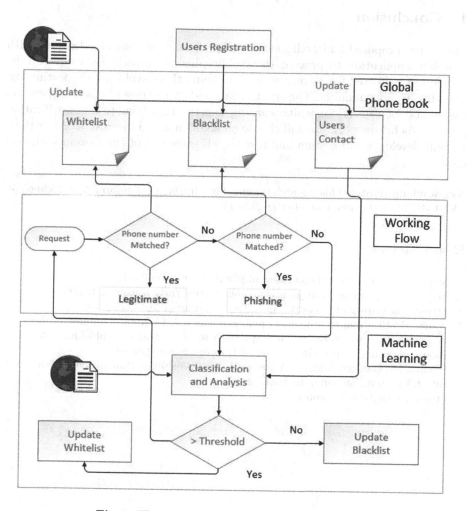

Fig. 5. The architecture of phishing identification

The client in our system is a mobile application developed for both android and IOS systems. It provides many functions for a user, such as a user verifies and registration, phishing report, private policy setting, etc. The server side providing a web service is implemented by PHP language programming. The storage of the Global Phone Book is the MySQL database. JSON is a protocol of communication between client and server in iCaMs. The server-side also provides a web page for the management of the phonebook dataset. It gives some essential functions like authors and authentication, edits and updates the global phone-book. To implement the classification and analysis process by machine learning, we use TensorFlow developed by Python 3.6 under platform Anaconda3.

4   Conclusion

This paper proposed an intelligent system that combines machine learning with a mobile application to prevent the mobile phishing attack. By using iCaMs, people are protected from voice scams and help others avoid it by reporting the scam likely phone number. The effectiveness and correctness of iCaMs depend on the number of users and machine learning algorithm applying to the classification process. As future work, we will choose an algorithm and improve it. After that, we will develop a full system and test the effectiveness of the system with real data.

Acknowledgments. This research is funded by University of Information Technology - VNU-HCM, under grant number D-2020-12.

References

1. http://www.koreaherald.com/view.php?ud=20190317000115
2. http://koreajoongangdaily.joins.com/news/article/article.aspx?aid=3059014
3. https://docs.apwg.org/reports/apwg_trends_reportq1_2018.pdf
4. Amro, B.: Phishing techniques in mobile devices. J. Comput. Commun. (2018)
5. Jain, A.K., Gupta, B.B.: A novel approach to protect against phishing attacks at client side using auto-updated white-list. J. Inf. Secur. (2016)
6. Mishra, M., Gaurav, Jain, A.: A preventive anti-phishing technique using-code word. Int. J. Comput. Sci. Info. Technol. (2012)
7. https://www.t-mobile.com/

Author Index

Printed in the United States
By Bookmasters